Management Information Systems: A Strategic Leadership Approach

Management Information Systems: A Strategic Leadership Approach

Paul S. Licker

The University of Calgary

THE DRYDEN PRESS
HARCOURT BRACE COLLEGE PUBLISHERS

Fort Worth   Philadelphia   San Diego   New York   Austin   Orlando   San Antonio
Toronto   Montreal   London   Sydney   Tokyo

Acquisitions Editor	Robb Linsky
Developmental Editor	Rebecca Johnson
Project Editor	Amy Schmidt
Art Director	Bill Brammer
Production Manager	Carlyn Hauser
Product Manager	Scott Timian
Marketing Coordinator	Becky Bertino
Copy Editor	Teresa Chartos
Proofreader	Teddy Diggs
Compositor	Weimer Graphics, Inc.
Text Type	10/12 Goudy
Cover Image	© Mark Lewis

Address for Orders
The Dryden Press
6277 Sea Harbor Drive
Orlando, FL 32887-6777
1-800-782-4479 or 1-800-433-0001 (in Florida)

Address for Editorial Correspondence
The Dryden Press
301 Commerce Street, Suite 3700
Fort Worth, TX 76102

ISBN: 0-15-500244-9

Library of Congress Catalog Card Number: 95-71897

Printed in the United States of America

6 7 8 9 0 1 2 3 4 5 039 9 8 7 6 5 4 3 2 1

The Dryden Press
Harcourt Brace College Publishers

To Lily

WHY THIS BOOK? WHY NOW? WHY SO MANY QUESTIONS?

- What is an information system?
- Why are information systems so difficult to create and use?
- How do managers make their computer requirements heard?
- Who are the real gainers and losers when an information system is installed?
- When is the best time to buy or build a new system?
- How can a manager evaluate an information system?
- How do information systems provide support for managers?

Students of management often ask these questions. The first question they are likely to raise, however, is simply this: "My field of study is marketing, finance, accounting, production, and so forth, so why do I have to study information systems?" Sometimes the question is phrased thus: "I already have a microcomputer and know how to use it, so why should I have to learn anything else?"

Primarily students are worried about having to learn to program a computer or to understand complexities such as networking and operating systems. And, until recently, students *did* have to study arcane topics and learn programming in order to appreciate management concepts of information systems. Primarily because the field of information systems is relatively new and because there are no all-embracing theories of information in management, the most practical way of relating management to information systems was through exposure to the technology—in other words, by induction. While this might be a good way to learn geometry, it's not a very effective learning method for students who don't already have an intuitive feel for information technology. Additionally, the technology that students are exposed to in school is guaranteed to be obsolete by the time they attempt to use it in the workplace.

The better way is to begin from basic principles. Practical experience then can be easily related to it. This makes it easier for students to realize how what they are learning relates to other topics and how generalities can be appreciated rather than merely accepted. In addition, students can test their own experiences against these general principles to counter false first impressions and to prevent the development of bias and prejudice.

That's why this book is different from others. Rather than focusing on the technology that you see around you, we look at the general principles that the technology of any particular era must obey. The emphasis is on the management of technology, of which information technology is merely one example. To make this more relevant to general management, we explore the management of technology as a means of improving management practice. You will not become a technological expert after reading this book and carrying out its exercises. You could, however, become a technological leader. As a manager, you can always hire technical expertise, but if you hire technical leadership, you're going to be out of a job!

Why is this? As we pass from one century to the next, we see the demise of management as we knew it, a very personal, charismatic, idiosyncratic, and interpersonal kind of activity. This demise is being hastened by the unprecedented, multitrack development of technology on many fronts: telecommunication, transportation, manufacturing, information processing, warehousing, and marketing are all becoming technology intensive. To be a manager today almost inevitably means mastering one or more new technologies, not just once, but perhaps every few years. In addition, the technology revolution is, to a great extent, driven by information systems; most of the aforementioned technologies rely on intelligent devices, instant access to information, and the processing of huge amounts of data. Finally, the telecommunication revolution involves distributing intelligence throughout time, space, and organizations to such an extent that managers are beginning to manage through an information "window" as much as they managed in the past through an interpersonal window. The readers of this book are likely to be the first generation of managers to manage exclusively from information "outlets" on their desks (or in their pockets, which is more likely). Interpersonal skills will remain important, but the really important work that managers will do in the future—coordinating work, informing others, and assembling and delivering arguments—not only will be done using computer assists but will likely occur entirely through a computer.

This brings us back to what this book is about. It's about becoming a better, more effective manager through the technology of information systems. It's about coping with the modern management imperatives known in shorthand as reach, reaction, responsiveness, refinement, reconfiguration, redeployment, and reputation. It's about the essential role that information systems plays in supporting management. And it's about becoming a technological leader—a manager who harnesses information technology and successfully employs it in a strategic manner for professional and corporate gain. Ultimately, it's about profit in the face of risk.

LEARNING/TEACHING APPROACH

While this text employs a traditional format of words, paragraphs, pages, and chapters, its approach to learning and teaching is somewhat different. With two exceptions, each chapter presents a theory, discusses the terms of the theory and justifies it, and discusses the implications of the theory for management practice. So, the teaching is theory-based. What is a theory? A theory is a collection of statements that describe in abstract terms some aspect of the real world. We create and use theories in an attempt to understand the world and to package it for better communication. Sometimes theories attempt to explain why something occurs. Sometimes theories succeed only in showing how sets of events go together. Even simpler theories merely describe natural phenomena in more general terms. There are two alternatives to theory-based teaching. The first is to teach by example and to build up patterns or habits or masses of facts and impressions in the hope that students will "get it." A second alternative is simply to say what is or should be, providing a kind of guidebook or cookbook. Law, for instance, is taught generally by the first method; cooking, often by the second.

Another component of the teaching/learning methods of this text is to use a case example throughout the book. We use a story-telling approach to the case, with 18 episodes involving the same cast of characters. And, indeed, they are characters. Many texts contain cases, some even a single case threaded through the textbook. But our case here is seen almost exclusively through the eyes of managers and the problems they face. Connie, Sid, Lily, and Shawna face management challenges that include dealing with angry employees, poor quality control, and the aging of their company's executives.

We also take the approach that information systems are the means to the ends of solving these management problems. Every theory has a practical management source and practical implications for managers. Information systems are not studied in this book merely for their own beauty (there is beauty here, but this is not an art text), or as closed logical systems (they can be, but they are better seen in a management context), or as a series of isolated facts or historical events (there is a fascinating history, but you'll never know what comes next). Instead, we will come to understand information systems as cooperative ventures involving technology, management, and people.

Another aspect of the approach of the text is to take a critical, sometimes skeptical, view of the wonders of technology. Technology isn't wonderful, it's merely exciting: it's not wonderful because it arises from the laws of nature and from the application of scientific principles to the necessities of business and management. It is not a panacea; it creates as many problems as it solves. It is part of the whole fabric of human existence, not mystic, transcendent, or a gift of the gods. It's a human creation, albeit a complex and sometimes difficult-to-understand creation, but it is surmountable. Consequently, this textbook continually tries to demystify, humanize, and debunk information systems. It's a field like many others, with fads, bandwagons, flavors of the month, gross generalizations, vested interests, evil-doers (and do-gooders, it should be pointed out), and outright lies passed off as eternal truths. It has a history as well as a future (not everything arrived yesterday), and there is often a clear evolutionary path from a simple idea to a commercial product to an accepted "principle" that many are unaware of. And, yes, there is an excitement that can sometimes overwhelm users and managers and drag them through a wonderland that they really should not be visiting.

Finally, the orientation of the book is leadership rather than mastery. Becoming a technological leader is far more important than learning how to program a computer. Understanding *why* is the first step in controlling, and understanding *when* to program is the first step in leadership. Although the text also stresses becoming a critical and intelligent consumer of information systems goods and services, this is only a means to an end: becoming a more effective manager through and with a specific technology. This theory- and case-based, critical book is aimed at a practical goal—nurturing management leaders.

FEATURES OF THIS BOOK

The book offers readers a number of attractive features to enhance learning. Every chapter begins with one or two mini-cases that raise the key management question the chapter is concerned with. Answering this question means meeting the learning objectives that appear with each of the mini-cases. At the end of the chapter a table summarizes how the chapter material enables managers to meet seven modern management imperatives that shape the fabric of management at the end of this century. The chapter opening mini-case is revisited, and several questions prompt a review and test of primary chapter objectives.

Each chapter has a summary of the main points. Key terms and references round out the passive features of the chapter. Students become involved through several discussion questions. These questions are generally very challenging and prompt readers to take a hard look at the assumptions made in the chapter in order to keep the learning atmosphere critical. In keeping with a more practical approach, each chapter has an episode of the continuing case, with questions that exercise the theories and concepts introduced in the chapter.

STRUCTURE OF THE BOOK

The book contains four modules organized around a short story about technology. Organizations vie with one another to achieve their goals, and, in the struggle, they seek to gain advantage over each other. Managers are the ones who direct the struggle over resources. However, this struggle is complex, and managers need assistance and support from technology. Such support isn't cheap, however, and there are many attendant risks that have to be managed. Those who successfully cope with these risks do so because they take leadership roles in using technology.

- Module 1 discusses the strategic advantages derived from employing information systems in competing organizations. Managers are key in this, and their use of information is a central aspect. Module 1 ends by examining the two major aspects of information systems that provide competitive advantage: linking business processes through shared databases and linking business sites through telecommunications.

- Module 2 begins by noting that managers need support in using information. It develops a theory of management support in which advising is the core concept. Managers are supported through the advice they receive from various sources. The general theory is discussed more specifically by examining two classes of management support systems: those that support individual managers in information exploration and decision making and those that support groups or communities of managers for the same ends.

- But there are risks involved in building management support systems. Module 3 examines these risks in detail and provides some advice on coping with them.

- Finally, Module 4 introduces you to technological leadership. Leaders take command of the means at their disposal, and information technology is the driving means available today to managers. The chapters in this module treat information technology as a business and pursue the answers to various marketing, accounting, business management, and human resource questions. Clearly, being a technological leader means much more than just using technology.

SUPPLEMENTARY MATERIALS

Supplementary materials available with this title include an instructor's manual, test bank (in both printed and computerized versions), and case analysis software. The case analysis software is fully integrated with the Evergreen case running throughout the textbook. The Dryden Press may provide complimentary instructional aids and supplements or supplement packages to those adopters qualified under its adoption policy. Please contact your sales representative for more information. If, as an adopter or potential user, you receive supplements you do not need, please return them to your sales representative or send them to: Attn.—Returns Department, Troy Warehouse, 465 South Lincoln Drive, Troy, MO 63379.

ACKNOWLEDGMENTS

In the late 1980s, I first taught the course for which this textbook is intended, thereby discovering that there were no textbooks that stressed the "management" in "management information systems." Over the years that I have taught the course, I have accumulated a great debt to students who first complained about not having a book, then complained about the ones they had, and then had to put up with my notes on the subject. A great deal of thanks goes to Richard Bonacci, who first heard my ideas for the text and then, as an editor at The Dryden Press, encouraged me to write the first drafts of the text. Almost as patient was Frank Thirkettle, who cotaught the course with me for several years and who has endured earlier versions of the text; Frank is my favorite student and one of my most vocal fans. To Barry Shane go my thanks for helping me understand competitive advantage and encouraging me to pursue my ideas about consulting systems. I would also like to thank Ron Thompson, of the University of Vermont, who worked with me on my original ideas concerning management support systems and who also served as an early reviewer of one of the final versions of this text. My thanks go to the many other professors who also reviewed early versions. They include: Fred Niederman, University of Baltimore; Beverly Amer, Northern Arizona University; Ruth King, University of Pittsburgh; James B. Shannon, New Mexico State University; Murali Venkatesh, Syracuse University; Gary R. Armstrong, Shippensburg University; Donna Mitchell, Louisiana State University; and William Cats-Baril, University of Vermont.

There were several editors at Dryden who worked with me to make the text as readable and error-free as they could; I would like to thank Robb Linsky, Joni Harlan, Becky Johnson, Elizabeth Hayes, and Amy Schmidt for their help in this regard. Thanks, too, go to Emily Hamer and Zaria Hamer for their help. My kids have heard too much about this book, so thanking them for being quiet about it is critical. Most of all, I would like to thank Susannah Cameron Crichton, who was my inspiration for the case that goes along with the text and is my inspiration for the life that I lead that goes along with her as my wife. She put up with hours, days, and weeks without my company but had the grace to say, "I understand."

Paul S. Licker

BRIEF CONTENTS

Preface   vii

Module 1   INFORMATION SYSTEMS FOR STRATEGIC ADVANTAGE   3

Chapter 1   Introduction   4
Chapter 2   Management and Information   23
Chapter 3   Organizations as Systems of Business Processes   46
Chapter 4   Strategic Advantage   76
Chapter 5   Bridging Disciplines: IS Architectures for Strategic Advantage   98
Chapter 6   Bridging Distances: Telecommunications Architectures for Strategic Advantage   123

Module 2   SUPPORTING MANAGERS THROUGH INFORMATION SYSTEMS   155

Chapter 7   Management Support Systems   156
Chapter 8   Supporting Individuals through DSS, ESS, Hypermedia, and Multimedia   200
Chapter 9   Supporting Groups through Groupware, Electronic Mail, and Bulletin Boards   223
Chapter 10   Evaluating Management Support Systems and Usability   251
Chapter 11   The Changing Role of Information Systems   279

Module 3   MANAGING RISK IN THE APPLICATION LIFE CYCLE   305

Chapter 12   Application Life Cycle   306
Chapter 13   Application Management   335
Chapter 14   Project Management   374
Chapter 15   Human Issues in Management Support Systems   398

Module 4 INFORMATION SYSTEMS AND TECHNOLOGICAL
LEADERSHIP 433

Chapter 16 The Software Marketplace and Outsourcing 434
Chapter 17 Managing Technological Innovation 460
Chapter 18 Technological Leadership 486

GLOSSARY 511
INDEX 529

CONTENTS

PREFACE   VII

Module 1   INFORMATION SYSTEMS FOR STRATEGIC ADVANTAGE   3

Chapter 1   INTRODUCTION   4

What This Book Is About   5
Competition, Risk, Knowledge, and Action   6
Basic Problem-Solving Paradigm   6
Applying Models in Cases   8
An Information Systems Model   10
Advice and Modern Management Imperatives   10
Summary   15
Discussion Questions   15
Key Terms   15
References   16
**Case—Introducing Evergreen Landscaping and
    Maintenance   16**

Chapter 2   MANAGEMENT AND INFORMATION   23

Introduction   24
Competition and Cooperation   24
The Role of Managers in Organizations   25
Seven Models of Management   27
Supporting Management Activities   33
The Information Payoff   35
Information Styles   37
Summary   42
Discussion Questions   42
Key Terms   43
References   43
**Case—Evergreen Landscaping and Maintenance: Connie
    Somerset, Sales Manager   44**

Chapter 3   ORGANIZATIONS AS SYSTEMS OF BUSINESS PROCESSES   46

Introduction   47
Why Systems Are Systems   48
System Architectures   51
Organizations as Systems and Business Processes   56
Modeling Business Processes   57
Modeling Information Processes   60
Business Process Reengineering   66
Summary   71
Discussion Questions   72
Key Terms   72
References   72
**Case—Evergreen Landscaping and Maintenance: Business
    Processes   73**

Chapter 4   STRATEGIC ADVANTAGE   76

Introduction   77
Strategic Means Competitive   78
The Customer Product Life Cycle   82
Porter's Competitive Forces Model   84
Sustaining Technologically Derived Competitive Advantage   88
Strategic Advantages Provided by IS   89
How IS Strategies Are Employed   91
Conclusion   92
Summary   93
Discussion Questions   94
Key Terms   94
References   94
**Case—Evergreen Landscaping and Maintenance: Assisting
    Strategic Advantage   96**

Chapter 5   BRIDGING DISCIPLINES: IS ARCHITECTURES FOR STRATEGIC
    ADVANTAGE   98

Introduction   99
An Information Architecture   100
A Dynamic Architecture   103
Shared Information Architecture   104
Relational Databases   107
Object-Oriented Architectures   114
Conclusion   117
Summary   119

Discussion Questions 119

Key Terms 120

References 120

Case—Evergreen Landscaping and Maintenance: An Integrated Database for Connie 120

Chapter 6   BRIDGING DISTANCES: TELECOMMUNICATIONS ARCHITECTURES FOR STRATEGIC ADVANTAGE 123

Introduction 124

Telecommunication Challenges 124

Client-Server Architectures 139

Interorganizational Systems 142

Strategic Advantage through Architecture 143

Summary 146

Discussion Questions 147

Key Terms 147

References 148

Case—Evergreen Landscaping and Maintenance: Distributing Processing 149

Module 2   SUPPORTING MANAGERS THROUGH INFORMATION SYSTEMS 155

Chapter 7   MANAGEMENT SUPPORT SYSTEMS 156

Introduction 157

Management and the Value Chain 158

Management Values and Action Areas 160

Management Activities and Informational Support 161

Seven Management Support Levels 162

A General Model of Management Advising 165

Information as the Mediator in Providing Value 174

The Manager's Information Workbench (MIW) 180

The User's View of Information 189

Dimensions of the Information-Centered Enterprise/Environment 191

Summary 196

Discussion Questions 197

Key Terms 197

References 197

Case—Evergreen Landscaping and Maintenance: Supporting Connie 198

Chapter 8   SUPPORTING INDIVIDUALS THROUGH DSS, ESS, HYPERMEDIA, AND
MULTIMEDIA   200

Introduction   201
Decision Support Systems   201
Executive Information Systems and Executive Support
Systems   209
Hypermedia and Multimedia   214
Summary   220
Discussion Questions   220
Key Terms   221
References   221
**Case—Evergreen Landscaping and Maintenance: A Crisis
Management System for Lily   221**

Chapter 9   SUPPORTING GROUPS THROUGH GROUPWARE, ELECTRONIC MAIL, AND
BULLETIN BOARDS   223

Introduction   224
Rationale: Groups Are Important   224
Technology to Support Meetings   226
How GSS Works   231
GSS Tools   233
Electronic Mail and Bulletin Boards   236
The Internet   240
Work Group–Oriented Groupware   244
Research in Group Systems: Management Opportunities   245
Summary   247
Discussion Questions   247
Key Terms   248
References   248
**Case—Evergreen Landscaping and Maintenance: Producing the
Crisis Management Plan   249**

Chapter 10   EVALUATING MANAGEMENT SUPPORT SYSTEMS AND USABILITY   251

Introduction   252
Quality Evaluation   253
Usability   266
Standards   271
Working with Technical Professionals   274
Summary   276
Discussion Questions   276
Key Terms   277

References 277
**Case—Evergreen Landscaping and Maintenance: Crisis
Management System Evaluation and Standards 277**

Chapter 11   THE CHANGING ROLE OF INFORMATION SYSTEMS 279

Introduction: The Future of IS 280
Changes in Management 280
Changes in Competition 283
Changes in Organizations 285
The Changing Meaning of Intelligence 288
Preparing Organizations for Change: Technological
   Leadership 294
The Geodesic Organization 296
Summary of Module 2 299
Summary 300
Discussion Questions 301
Key Terms 301
References 301
**Case—Evergreen Landscaping and Maintenance:
Organizational Realignment 302**

Module 3   MANAGING RISK IN THE APPLICATION LIFE CYCLE 305

Chapter 12   APPLICATION LIFE CYCLE 306

Introduction 307
What Is an Application? 307
The Problem-Solving Life Cycle 308
The Application Life Cycle (ALC) 312
ALC Challenges for Managers 320
Alternatives to Application Life Cycle 322
Summary 332
Discussion Questions 332
Key Terms 333
References 333
**Case—Evergreen Landscaping and Maintenance: Developing
Applications 334**

Chapter 13   APPLICATION MANAGEMENT 335

Introduction 336
Information Requirements Analysis 336

Feasibility   345

Implementation Strategies   350

Managerial Responsibilities   356

Interviewing, Joint Application Design, and User
Participation   362

Conclusion   367

Summary   368

Discussion Questions   369

Key Terms   369

References   369

**Case—Evergreen Landscaping and Maintenance: Developing a
Skills Management Application   370**

Chapter 13 Appendix   372

Chapter 14   PROJECT MANAGEMENT   374

Introduction   375

Why Systems Projects Are Different   375

Dysfunctional Coping Strategies   377

Analyzing Project Risk   381

Managing Project Risk   383

Computer-Aided Software Engineering   388

Summary   394

Discussion Questions   394

Key Terms   394

References   394

**Case—Evergreen Landscaping and Maintenance: Managing the
Skills Management System Project   395**

Chapter 15   HUMAN ISSUES IN MANAGEMENT SUPPORT SYSTEMS   398

Introduction: The Human Sphere   399

Roles People Play in an Information Environment   400

Managing People in an Information Environment   416

Ethical Concerns   420

Summary   428

Discussion Questions   428

Key Terms   428

References   428

**Case—Evergreen Landscaping and Maintenance: Personnel
Shake-Ups   429**

Module 4 INFORMATION SYSTEMS AND TECHNOLOGICAL LEADERSHIP   433

Chapter 16 THE SOFTWARE MARKETPLACE AND OUTSOURCING   434

Introduction   437
Essential Characteristics of Software   437
Building versus Buying   444
Outsourcing   446
Selling Your Own Software   452
Summary   455
Discussion Questions   456
Key Terms   456
References   456
Case—Evergreen Landscaping and Maintenance: Evaluating an Inventory System   457

Chapter 17 MANAGING TECHNOLOGICAL INNOVATION   460

Introduction   461
Basic Terminology   461
A Model of Adoption   463
A Model of Contagion   467
Influences on Adoption   471
Influences on Subjective Norm   478
The Completed Model: Behavioral Intention   479
Summary   483
Discussion Questions   483
Key Terms   483
References   484
Case—Evergreen Landscaping and Maintenance: Diffusing the Inventory System   484

Chapter 18 TECHNOLOGICAL LEADERSHIP   486

Introduction   487
Technology Transfer   489
Technology Assessment   491
Technology Forecasting   494
Technology Management   496
The Technology Life Cycle   497
Managing Innovation   499
Commercialization and Marketing of Technology and Ideas   500
Linking Corporate and Technology Strategies   501
Technological Revolution   503

New Technologies to Know, Watch, and Respect 505

Summary 508

Discussion Questions 509

Key Terms 509

References 509

Case—Evergreen Landscaping and Maintenance: Connie Somerset, Technological Leader 510

Glossary 511

Index 529

About the Author

Dr. Paul Licker   Dr. Paul Licker is Professor of Information Systems at the Faculty of Management of the University of Calgary. His career represents his interests in communication, information, and management. All of his academic qualifications—his BA in mathematics, MSEE in computer and information sciences, and Ph.D. in communication—are from the University of Pennsylvania. He has worked as a computer programmer, systems analyst, communication researcher and consultant, meeting facilitator, trainer, and management consultant in Canada, the United States, Britain, and South Africa. Research by Dr. Licker has always focused on the human side of computing, including ergonomics, user perceptions, and managerial responsibilities. Because the built environment has become increasingly computerized, Dr. Licker has concentrated his efforts on enhancing the technology management process for organizations and individuals. At the same time, he has become increasingly critical of whole-cloth acceptance of technology as the solution for existing problems or as a culturally and ethically neutral actor in our civilization. Most recently, his research is concerned with cultural factors in the acceptance, use, and evaluation of information systems technology in the developing world. His own personal developing world includes his wife, Susannah, and a constantly moving entourage of children and a cat in Calgary, Canada. His hobbies include cycling, woodworking, tennis, and his motor scooter, Bluebell.

Management Information Systems: A Strategic Leadership Approach

Module 1

INFORMATION SYSTEMS FOR STRATEGIC ADVANTAGE

CHAPTER ONE

INTRODUCTION

OBJECTIVES

After you have read and studied this chapter, you should be able to:

■ Define what a management information system is.

■ Discuss the need for management support in the face of competition and risk.

■ Apply the basic problem-solving paradigm to management problems and cases.

■ Identify the seven modern management imperatives.

Question: What is this book about? Why is it important? What good will it do me? When?

Adam Chen is a business student, and in his first year in a business program, he took some courses that interested him as preparation for the program. Now he is taking a series of required courses, and only one or two of them are in his field of interest. One of the requirements is a management information systems class. Of course, everybody must learn how to use computers, but what is important about them beyond word processing, spreadsheets, or database searches? Adam is concerned that this course will be either about fancy technology ("bit twiddling," as his computer science buddies call it) or how important computers are in business. Adam thinks that computers are just machines that cost a lot of money and don't produce any income. He wonders what computers have to do with business or management and whether the course will do him any good.

Answer: While reading this book, Adam will learn how an information system (IS) can advance corporate strategy; how people who use, create, and promote such systems think; how ISs support managers in their daily activities; and how the risks involved in having (and not having) information systems can be determined and managed. Modern management imperatives make it increasingly important that future managers such as Adam also become informed consumers and users who are not left in the competitive dust after graduation.

WHAT THIS BOOK IS ABOUT

This text discusses how managers who work in an organization use management information systems to meet their organization's goals. A **management information system (MIS)** is an integrated user+machine system that provides information to support operations, management analysis, and decision-making functions in an organization. An MIS contains hardware, software, procedures, data, and people; each component is as important as the others and, to an extent, equally influences the others. The MIS should relate to the goals of the organization. However, this book is *not* about the technological intricacies of programming, circuits, or diskettes. Although technology helps managers, this book will focus on information systems as a means to an end—managerial productivity. While focusing on managerial productivity, we will reflect on how managers work, what they do for an organization, and how they are evaluated. We will also look at the role information plays in helping managers meet goals by examining the characteristics of information systems that make managers' jobs easier or harder to perform.

Structure of the Book

This book is divided into four modules that focus on four main themes: strategic advantage, management support, risk, and technological leadership.

In more detail, the modules cover

1. Acquiring strategic advantage through information systems

2. Supporting managers and executives through IS applications

3. Managing the risk inherent in developing and using IS applications

4. Attaining and practicing technological leadership

We begin with a discussion of the imperatives of modern management and how these imperatives differ from more traditional views of management. We end with a discussion of how managers can become technical leaders in a technological age. In between, we attempt to tie these ideas together by describing how managers use information to support themselves and others to attain strategic advantage over competitors.

Because this text focuses on managers, our examples tend to be managerial in nature. It may appear that we think IS applications play little or no role in operations, but this is far from the truth. In fact, we will use operational activities in many of our examples. However, the emphasis is on management activity, and operational IS is a part of the managerial environment in an organization. As a source of much of the data managers need, operational ISs are important to all managers.

This book is also about using information in *competitive circumstances*. Does this mean a student who intends to work in a nonprofit or public-sector organization need not understand the concepts in this book? Decidedly not. Nonprofit organizations compete among themselves for sponsors, donors, volunteers, air time, and newspaper space, and public-sector firms compete with themselves to improve their services.

Managers face many ethical dilemmas, and information sometimes increases those dilemmas. This text will not duck these challenges, so ethical information practices are discussed as the most effective and efficient way to produce and use information.

Finally, one of the most exciting trends in information systems is the internationalization of technology and the globalization of business. Students should be aware not only of the international sources of technology but also of the opportunities available for acquiring and employing information technology almost anywhere. We will explore many of these challenges in this text.

COMPETITION, RISK, KNOWLEDGE, AND ACTION

The relationships among the four themes, in simplified form, is that **competitive motivation** is a real part of our culture, that is, people naturally compete. They compete not necessarily from an inherent feistiness but because resources (money, time, effort) are scarce. Resources tend to go to those who perform better; however, resources are *required* for better performance, so there is a strong correlation between the two. Some societies are more competitive than others and some are more cooperative than others. Competition creates a certain dynamic that cooperation does not because it forces individuals to distrust others and it tends to limit the lifetime of specific, cooperative relationships. Competition is relatively riskier than cooperation. It maximizes individual benefit, so it minimizes shared responsibility, hence increasing the risk of failure. Those who compete have to accept those risks.

Accepting risk, however, is not simply a matter of throwing oneself to the mercy of the fates. Only a fool accepts potentially life-threatening risks unless the potential payoff outweighs the risk. Unfortunately, we do not always know what the risks are. Once we do, however, we are less likely to gamble with our own futures.

Managing **risk** entails support of various kinds, but the support we are concerned with in this course is called **data-based knowledge.** The type of knowledge that is germane here is knowledge derived from empirical data. This **knowledge** can be obtained from laboratory experiments, surveys, or other systematic research, or, more commonly in business, from a relatively systematic evaluation of one's own experience. Having this knowledge of experience lowers the risk because we can assume that the future will be similar to the past and we can extrapolate from one person's experience to determine another's. This kind of support is valuable because we can move from accepting risk to evaluating alternatives; we then act on that evaluation, perhaps by selecting and executing the best one.

Competition, risk, knowledge, and action require problem solving, which is a basic aspect of how we compete successfully.

BASIC PROBLEM-SOLVING PARADIGM

The simple model presented in Figure 1–1 is called a *box-and-line* or *box-and-arrow* model. It illustrates an activity by depicting it as a series of discrete stages or steps. One step follows from the previous step, from some known start to some known conclusion. Although there may be many reasons to dispute every step and stage in the model, it is useful for illustrating where information-based support becomes important in meeting challenges posed by a competitive society. Many such box-and-line models will be used in this text to simplify the discussion, but often these models make assumptions that are arguable. For example, sometimes the processes do not have specific beginning and end points or it is not clear when we have moved from one stage to another. In these cases, we will support the model with a discussion that justifies the assumption the model makes.

Figure 1–1   FOCUS OF THIS TEXT

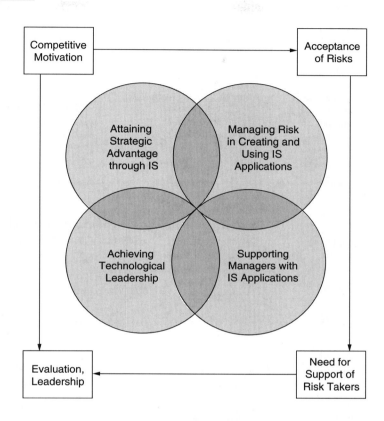

Figure 1–2 illustrates a basic **problem-solving paradigm.** A paradigm is a pattern of thoughts or words that can be used as a guide or template for other thoughts or words. The preliminary step, which is not illustrated in the figure, is to define or state a problem. This step is difficult and may constitute all or most of the solution. In many cases, the problem may not be stated at all, or may be determined in later stages or when the situation is better understood.

Beyond problem definition, three stages are labeled descriptively as "see, think, and say." We *see* and collect data on what is happening. We ask, "What are the facts? What are my goals? What am I trying to do? What do I know about this problem? Have I seen it before? Do I know how to solve it?" These questions form a kind of investigative stage.

Next, we *think* about what we discovered. We look for patterns by drawing pictures and making lists or charts. We ask, "What is this problem like? What models or images do I know about that can be applied to this problem?" Finally, having gathered data and diagramed the problem, we proceed to *say* what we are going to do. We ask, "What conclusions can I draw about potential or future actions based on what I know about the situation and models at my disposal? Do these conclusions stand up under scrutiny or reality checking? What will actually happen if I attempt to carry out the solution?" In this

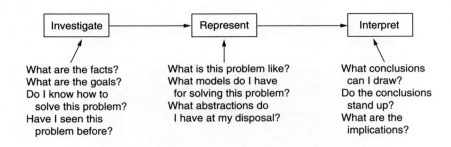

Figure 1–2   BASIC PROBLEM-SOLVING PARADIGM

final step, we interpret the situation in light of theories or models we know or have been taught. Note that the basic problem-solving paradigm brings together three aspects: data gathered about the problem, theories that have been created out of other situations, and conclusions drawn from data and theories. Throughout this course, we will rely heavily on this interaction: Data + Theory = Conclusion.

APPLYING MODELS IN CASES

One challenge you will face in this text is using **models** in cases. A certain kind of reasoning must be applied to case analysis. The reasoning we will employ is the basic problem-solving paradigm (see Figure 1–3). Facts about the case (data) are "run through" the model (**theory**) to derive conclusions that, if implemented, lead to certain conclusions in the face of reality. Case data may be stated in the cases or they may be reasonably assumed.

Consider the problem of a graduating finance major such as Adam Chen, who has always wanted to get into banking. He is offered several jobs and must decide which one to accept. Adam wants to stay close to home for a few years, keep expenses under control, and network locally. He is also concerned about future career plans and making successful placements that lead to a permanent position. Adam must choose one of these three jobs:

- Junior trainee financial analyst at a lending institution a day's drive from home
- Team supervisor in an oil company's financial analysis department in a large city far from home
- Controller at his uncle's local plastics-pressing business

Each job pays about the same for the first few years, but the job at the lending institution offers a chance to get into the banking industry in a major, if somewhat low-ranking, way. Working for the oil company would give Adam a chance to diversify and add to his experience, although a future career in the energy sector is risky and not his ultimate career goal. Still, he is wondering if being flexible might not be more important than the career goals he worked out in high school. Working for his uncle is secure and local, but

| Figure 1–3 | USING MODELS IN CASES |

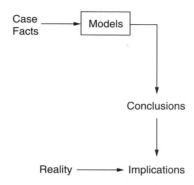

the responsibilities are not really connected with his career goals. Although the job is relatively important, there isn't much chance for advancement, and it's basically account-ing. This information is represented in Columns 1 through 3 of Table 1–1.

Adam has gathered these facts (he *sees* the problem) and then constructs a model or theory about what is important to him. He decides that working locally is twice as important to him as making a long-term career move right now, and the relative rank of the position is only one-third as important as a long-term career prospect. This analysis results in Columns 4 through 6 of Table 1–1.

Now Adam uses the model and the data to draw a conclusion. He multiplies the evaluation of each job characteristic by the corresponding characteristic weight and adds these products for each job. Similar calculations are done for the other two jobs.

For Adam, the choice is fairly clear: Working for his uncle (74) is more highly valued than working as a financial analyst (55). The team supervisor job is a poor third choice (26).

The model has additional value because Adam notes that no matter what the job or rank is with his uncle, that job's total will be higher than the other two jobs'. Even being janitor is better than working in his chosen field (60 points, or $10 \times 6 + 0 + 0$). Because his model is highly skewed toward selecting any local position, Adam thinks some more about his model and his values. Perhaps career and rank have the correct relationship, but career is actually more important than working locally.

This new thinking results in a change in the table (see Table 1–2). Now the financial analyst position (78) looks more promising than working as the uncle's factory controller (68), although they are close. In fact, all three selections' ranks are closer (a range of 34 versus a former range of 48), and this reflects Adam's initial indecisiveness. For the moment, Adam will pursue the out-of-town financial analyst position but keep an eye open for additional factors that are important to him in making this selection.

We apply the model to the case by noting the implications of using the model. The first model resulted in a solution that just did not seem right; there was a weakness in the model. After the model was improved, the results made more sense. More important, Adam's thinking about job selection became more sophisticated because he became more aware of the interplay of various factors in job selection.

Table 1–1	JOB DECISION MODEL: FIRST VERSION						
Job	**Characteristic**			**Weight**			**Total**
	Local	*Career*	*Rank*	*Local*	*Career*	*Rank*	
Financial analyst	4	10	1	6	3	1	55
Team supervisor	1	5	5	6	3	1	26
Uncle's controller	10	2	8	6	3	1	74

Table 1–2	IMPROVED JOB DECISION MODEL						
Job	**Characteristic**			**Weight**			**Total**
	Local	*Career*	*Rank*	*Local*	*Career*	*Rank*	
Financial analyst	4	10	1	4	6	2	78
Team supervisor	1	5	5	4	6	2	44
Uncle's controller	10	2	8	4	6	2	68

AN INFORMATION SYSTEMS MODEL

The basic **IS model** will be used frequently in this course (see Figure 1–4). Input received from a business source is called **data.** The data are processed through a program to create output (**information**) that is routed to an end user, who may share this information with other users. Information is routed back to the source through a communication channel, and this information is called **feedback.** The program is created by IS professionals such as programmers, programmer analysts, and analysts who operate under the direction of management and users. This model is called a **process model** because it depicts a process, while the model discussed previously is a **decision model** because it helps us make a decision. The basic IS model differentiates between input and output, data and information, IS professionals and end users, and shows the relative influences users and management have on the process of creating information in an organization.

ADVICE AND MODERN MANAGEMENT IMPERATIVES

One goal of this text is to educate students about the art of **consulting**—the task of talking things over with others who have a problem. Derived from the Latin word *consulare* meaning "to deliberate," consulting has evolved into a business title that refers to the giving of advice. We use it here to mean the use of models in business (see

Figure 1–4   BASIC IS MODEL

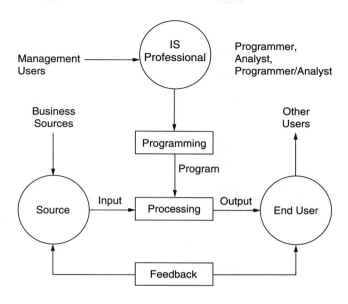

Figure 1–5). A consultant uncovers facts (investigates), refers the facts to principles (represents), and draws conclusions (interprets) for a client. Then the client or the consultant determines the implications of the consultant's advice.

Consulting in itself is easy but *effective* consulting is hard to do. For example, no matter how much data are gathered, not all variables can be known. Not every principle works in all cases, and there are often conflicting principles or theories. Sometimes *all* the principles are suspect. Not all conclusions can be drawn from models as easily as we did using Tables 1–1 and 1–2. Sometimes gut feelings and intuition are more important. Even when clear recommendations are generated, they cannot always be implemented, and even if they can be implemented, almost anything can happen in the real world. Sometimes clients won't believe a consultant's advice—they have to be sold on it. Nevertheless, managers need advice to make decisions, and both models and consulting combine data and theory to help managers draw conclusions.

Why do managers need advice? The most important reason is that the world is becoming increasingly complex and managers cannot be expected to keep track of everything. In the past, firms employed people to "remember" the important facts of the business, but today they hire consultants to limit continuing costs. The business world has changed greatly over the past generation, and management is facing a very different set of imperatives. Figure 1–6 identifies seven imperatives by short names, all beginning with the prefix "Re." We will return to each of these imperatives in each chapter.

Back in management prehistory, it was probably sufficient to be big, fast, and ugly to succeed, but in this century, the primary key to success has been to have a good product and the skills to sell it. Global competition is changing that. Competitors are no longer limited to the shop across the street or across town and the people who share the same culture and

---

Figure 1–5 PRINCIPLES OF CONSULTING

■ Find Out the Facts
Gather data, state assumptions.
But: Not everything is or can be known.

■ Refer Facts to Principles
Concepts are the links to principles.
But: Not every principle works in all cases.

■ Draw Conclusions
Conclusions are generated from models.
But: Not every conclusion can be
mechanically drawn.

■ Implement Conclusions
Conclusions must be sold (i.e.,
understood and accepted by all parties).
But: Not every recommendation can be
carried out.

---

the same experiences. Your business is threatened by competitors that not only can undersell you but that you don't even know exist. The development of inexpensive and reliable road and air distribution, along with very large and reliable shipping facilities, has made it unnecessary for your competitors to live in your city or country. The key to increased global competition is information. Competitors use high-speed telecommunications to learn about the possibility of a sale, make the sale, finalize the deal, arrange the delivery, and receive payment. They can generate a profit from a product that may have a useful sales life of six months or less by using labor brought together for the sole purpose of assembling the product this week without the continuing costs of a physical plant and site, taxes, and training. It is likely that global competitors will not respect your trademarks, copyright, and patents (at least this is currently the case in the software and entertainment industries, especially in the Far East). They can also gather information on your customers as quickly as you can, producing exactly what customers want instantly. If you wait, you're out of business. So you don't wait and instead you open a branch of your business in *their* backyards, because the same information and technology empower you, too.

Customers expect to provide quick feedback and they expect you to listen to it. Because worldwide educational levels are rising, customers are developing far more sophisticated needs and abilities to specify what they want and don't want. This trend, coupled with the certainty that if you don't respond with the required product or service somebody in the world will, means that suppliers are forced into shorter **concept-to-customer cycle times,** which may be as short as a few weeks. This sort of response time is now considered standard—people don't want to wait to satisfy their needs.

Quick adaptation to changing conditions is the hallmark of modern competition. This may mean shorter concept-to-customer life cycles, but it may also mean rapid response to employee needs, societal trends, legislative change, and technological advancement. Quick adaptation means that organizations have to reconfigure their skills and factories almost continuously, resulting in continuous reorganization of the firm,

Figure 1–6	MODERN MANAGEMENT IMPERATIVES

Reach: Global Competition	The ability that everyone has to compete with everyone else, regardless of geographic constraints.
Reaction: Quick Customer Feedback on Products and Services	The power that customers have to make their views known and the desire to have them respected.
Responsiveness: Shortened Concept-to-Customer Cycle Time	The process of turning an idea into a product or service that can be marketed; sometimes called *commercialization*.
Refinement: Greater Customer Sophistication and Specificity	The ability of customers to distinguish fine differences among products and compare them with their own needs or desires.
Reconfiguration: Reengineering of Work Patterns and Structures	The structure of work and work flow from idea to product or service.
Redeployment: Reorganization and Redesign of Resources	The financial, physical, human, and information resources required to create and market a product or service.
Reputation: Quality and Reliability of Product and Process	The satisfaction that a customer experiences when the product or service meets or exceeds expectations and requirements.

continuous redesign of products, and continuous improvements. This last concept is called *total quality management (TQM)* and literally means the improvement of products on a daily, not yearly, basis.

How are these shortened cycle times met? Through information. Customer feedback (data) has to be quickly processed and understood, before competitors can develop a better product. Shortened concept-to-customer cycle times require exact information about a firm's existing products and production processes as well as excellent resource management, and all this depends on information availability and accessibility. Specific customer requirements may lead to individualized products and narrow niche markets of only a few customers. To manage a lot of products requires information. **Reconfiguration** and resource **redeployment** requires knowing where the resources are, what they are doing, how they can be reconfigured and redeployed, and what the fallout is likely to be. Quality management is based on knowledge of where we are and where we want to go.

In the business world of modern management imperatives, strategic advantage means having good ideas that match what the customer wants and quickly getting those ideas to the customer in the form of available and sellable products and services. Strategic advantage may not last long, but while it is attained, it is information-intensive. To attain (or reattain) this advantage, managers need support in handling data, making decisions, and operating the firm. In doing that, managers take risks that also have to be managed. Managing risks helps managers become leaders, and these leaders must master and use technology to meet their organizations' goals.

The Modern Management Imperatives

Reach: Global Competition	The extent or reach of individual businesses, on the one hand, has been enhanced by technology and, on the other, is a result of technology. Information technology both allows global competition and requires that businesses take information-based countermeasures to survive. Managers must become globally knowledgeable and seek information everywhere.
Reaction: Quick Customer Feedback on Products and Services	Customers are now more selective than ever; they know how to ask for what they want and use the bargaining power of their selective purchases to demand that businesses and managers listen to them. Access to and the ability to interpret this feedback are critical to business success.
Responsiveness: Shortened Concept-to-Customer Cycle Time	Because everyone has access to the technology needed to respond rapidly, someone somewhere has a product ready for your customer. Businesses cannot afford to wait for customers to wander by. It's important to move product ideas to the marketplace quickly and manage this increasingly complex, interdependent process well.
Refinement: Greater Customer Sophistication and Specificity	Customers are better educated. They not only know more about the services and products you want to sell, they know more about how to communicate their desires to you. Niche markets appear, grow, and disappear quickly. A single marketing strategy is no longer appropriate.
Reconfiguration: Reengineering of Work Patterns and Structures	A single work style, production method, or marketing technique is no longer adequate. Worldwide niche markets for selective customers who make their needs known require a flexible approach to production, marketing, and distribution. Business processes can no longer be designed and used forever. Managing multiple processes requires enormous information resources.
Redeployment: Reorganization and Redesign of Resources	Similarly, resources can no longer remain dedicated to specific processes or products. Managers are faced with instant redeployment of financial, human, physical, and informational resources to meet targeted customer needs. Maintaining information on resource utilization is critical.
Reputation: Quality and Reliability of Product and Process	Coupled with these imperatives, which tend to speed up an organization's metabolism, is a trend toward increasing quality and reliability of the product.

■ ADAM RESPONDS TO THE IMPERATIVES

Adam Chen is not immune to the imperatives of management—after all, he is a kind of manager, too. He manages his time and limited economic and personal resources, schedule and classes, social life, studies, and so forth. Because he is certain he doesn't know everything, he sometimes asks for help, both in his academic pursuits and in his personal life. He realizes that he is competing with other students for his instructors' attention and ultimately for jobs. On the other hand, he knows that cooperation with others in group projects and friendships is important, so he spends time on teams, does volunteer work, and participates in student clubs. Finally, he recognizes that doing things right as well as doing the right things will enable him to achieve the rewards he values—good grades, friends, contentment, jobs—so he considers it important to make the right decisions based on the right information. One important decision Adam has to make soon is about his major. He's leaning toward finance, but tourism and marketing also appeal to him. He knows information is important and has learned that making decisions is often an exercise in self-consulting and planning. So now he must plan for his decision. ■

1. Adam asks you to help him solve this problem (selecting a major) in a systematic way. With a partner, role play this consulting situation and talk your partner through the basic problem-solving paradigm.

2. Adam is experiencing all seven modern management imperatives as he selects a major and ultimately competes for a job. Discuss how these imperatives affect Adam and how he might plan to cope with them.

Summary

Achieving competitive advantage poses risks for managers. Many of these risks can be effectively lessened through the use of information systems technology. Being able to lead with and through technology is an important managerial skill. The primary use of technological tools is to solve problems. Problem-solving is a three-step process of gathering information, looking for patterns and solutions, and selecting the best solutions. Carrying out the processes implied by the selected solutions may entail further problem-solving. Problem-solving with information systems involves like processes: gathering input from sources, processing the input based on programs, and creating output for end users. Output is necessary for managers to implement the conclusions of their problem-solving activities. The need for information-based support for managers is increasing as the modern management imperatives of reach, reaction, responsiveness, refinement, reconfiguration, redeployment, and reputation become more important.

Discussion Questions

1.1 To what extent do you think that computers are necessary for an information system? Can you think of examples of information systems that do not involve computers or any high technology at all? What do these systems have in common with computerized systems? Do you think the kind of support that managers need requires expensive high technology? Can you think of examples?

1.2 Think about your relationship with technology. What is your attitude about technology, especially information technology? Where did this attitude come from? What are the implications of your current attitude? Do you see yourself as a leader, as a follower, or as someone who stands off to the side?

1.3 Consider the model of problem-solving presented in this chapter (see-think-say-do). Imagine that you are trying to solve the problem of whether to change your course registration roster (that is, whether to drop one course and add another). What corresponds to "see," "think," "say," and "do" in this case? Can you think of situations in which one or more of these steps are bypassed or repeated in solving a problem?

1.4 The modern management imperatives are pressing because of global competition and increasing customer sophistication and buying power. Information technology may be seen as a way of coping with these imperatives, but it may also be the cause of some of them. Sketch out the ways in which faster and more powerful access to information can increase the pace and scope of competition and customer demands.

Key Terms

competitive motivation
concept-to-customer cycle time
consulting
data
data-based knowledge
decision model
feedback

information
IS model
knowledge
management information
    system (MIS)
model

problem-solving paradigm
process model
reconfiguration
redeployment
risk
theory

References

Beck, Nuala. *Shifting Gears: Thriving in the New Economy.* Toronto: HarperCollins, 1992.

Bell, D. *The Coming of Post-Industrial Society.* New York: Basic Books, 1973.

Branham Consulting Group. *Things Change, Economies Evolve, Are You Prepared?* Mississauga, Ontario: Information Technology Association of Canada, December 1992.

Drucker, P. F. "The Coming of the New Organization." *Harvard Business Review* (January–February 1988): 45–53.

———. *The Practice of Management.* New York: Harper & Row, 1954.

Gory, G. A., and M. S. Scott Morton. "A Framework for Management Information Systems." *Sloan Management Review* 13, 1 (Fall 1971).

Henderson, J., and N. Venkatraman. "Strategic Alignment: A Model for Organizational Transformation via Information Technology," in T. Allen and M. S. Scott Morton, eds., *Information Technology and the Corporation of the 1990s.* New York: Oxford University Press, 1994.

Huber, G. "The Nature and Design of Post-Industrial Organizations." *Management Science* 30, 8 (August 1984).

Licker, P., ed. *The Management of Technology and Innovation.* Calgary, Alberta: University of Calgary, 1989.

McFarlan, F. W., J. McKenney, and P. Pyburn. "The Information Archipelago—Plotting a Course." *Harvard Business Review* (January–February 1983).

Niederman, F., J. Brancheau, and J. Weatherbe. "Information Systems Management Issues for the 1990s." *Management Information Systems Quarterly* 15, 4 (December 1991).

O'Brien, James. *Management Information Systems: A Managerial End User Perspective.* Homewood, IL: Irwin, 1993.

Scott Morton, Michael S. *The Corporation of the 1990s.* New York: Oxford University Press, 1990.

Toffler, Alvin. *Future Shock.* New York: Random House, 1970.

CASE

INTRODUCING EVERGREEN LANDSCAPING AND MAINTENANCE

Evergreen Landscaping and Maintenance Co. Inc. (see Figure 1–7 for Evergreen's history) is a full-service residential landscaping firm offering lawn, garden, and patio landscaping services and supplies to homeowners in the suburbs of a large city. In addition, Evergreen runs a retail nursery and gardening center that sells trees, shrubs, seeds, seedlings, and flowers to customers on a cash-and-carry basis. As a special service to customers, the company takes orders for rare plants and trees from homeowners and professional landscapers. During the winter, Evergreen works with local and national landscapers to create sample plans for residential gardens and patios, order supplies, and keep Evergreen's greenhouses stocked. In the spring, Evergreen is busy with home gardening customers, with business increasing throughout the summer until early autumn.

Evergreen's annual sales are about $22 million. It employs 60 people year-round, mostly on the retail side (Christmas is a big season) and in planning, but the number increases to 200 during the summer months. Evergreen's planning cycle begins in December when it places orders for plants for the coming year. Ironically, while everyone knows how quickly or slowly most trees or shrubs grow, it is almost impossible to place orders more than three months in advance. Given the recent unusual weather all over North America, maybe that's good. On the other hand, the California growers who supply most of Evergreen's junipers, for instance, play their cards very close to their vests. Meanwhile, Evergreen has to accurately predict what it wants to or can sell each season. One

| Figure 1–7 | EVERGREEN'S CORPORATE GENEALOGY |

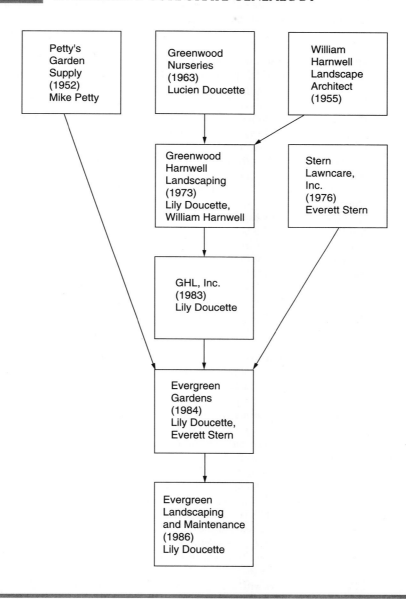

year a freak storm destroyed all its poinsettias three weeks before Christmas, and nobody within 1,000 miles had any to spare.

Evergreen's History and Structure

A relatively young company with old roots, Evergreen's current management structure was the result of the amalgamation of two firms. One, Greenwood Nurseries, was established in 1963 as a commercial tree farming operation by Lucien Doucette, a Canadian lumberjack. Nearing retirement, Doucette decided that growing trees, rather than hacking them down, would be a relatively painless way to spend his retirement years. After his death in 1973, control of the business passed to his daughter Lily. At about the same time, William Harnwell, a landscape architect, was looking for a partner for his practice. Having worked extensively with Greenwood, Harnwell entered into a partnership with Lily Doucette to form Greenwood Harnwell Landscaping (GHL). Under this agreement, GHL would act as a vertically integrated landscape architectural firm, providing all the services from design through installation and project management.

For ten years, GHL prospered and built a solid reputation in the commercial landscaping community for quality products and services. GHL expanded into residential landscaping and began carrying a number of nonnursery products such as fertilizer and pesticides. In addition, it began providing grounds care services, but this service was discontinued because of high labor costs and a shake-up in management precipitated by Bill Harnwell's retirement in January of 1983, when Lily bought him out. At that time, GHL employed several contract landscape architects, but none was willing to take over the landscaping side. Meanwhile, Lily was finding it burdensome to handle the increasingly heavy paperwork. She then hired Shawna Eggert as sales director and Tom David-off to run the tree farm. But it clearly was time for GHL to grow or to evolve into something different.

The opportunity came in the summer of 1984, with the chance to buy Petty's Garden Supply. Mike Petty had run the family business for three decades and had built up a trusting, loyal clientele of mostly weekend gardeners. Petty's was locally well known as the place to find everything and anything for gardens. While Lily had little experience in the retail side, she was convinced that she wasn't seeing the forest for the trees and bought the controlling interest in Petty's. Her partner in this acquisition was Everett Stern, a farmer who operated a lawn care and maintenance service from his rural home. Everett and his brother held several important patents in liquid fertilizer and herbicide distribution. For years the Stern family had produced liquid fertilizers for area farmers. A brief joint venture with the local agricultural college produced plans for a revolutionary method to get the fertilizers into the ground quickly and more safely than traditional methods and to farm more efficiently with less expensive materials. Additionally, Everett had been making good money since 1982 by selling fertilizing services for homeowners through a company called Stern Lawncare. As a lucrative sideline, Stern Lawncare continued to sell liquid fertilizer to agribusiness. Everett felt the deal with GHL was good because retail garden customers would also be good lawncare customers. The new joint venture was called Evergreen Gardens, Inc.

By 1986, it was clear that the organizational umbrella (Stern Lawncare, GHL, and Evergreen Gardens) was really one big concern; Everett felt it was more like a big headache. He approached Lily with the idea of retiring from active participation in Stern Lawncare, allowing the business to merge with GHL into Evergreen Gardens, and becoming a silent partner. Lily thought that bringing together the legacies of four firms into a single lawn, garden, and landscaping services company with 130 employees and $12 million in annual sales was a good idea.

In 1986, Lily sold the nursery business to a young entrepreneur and moved Evergreen away from its roots and into retail and service. In addition, there was the agribusiness, with its important nonfinancial benefit of close relations with agricultural researchers, including biotechnology specialists and the nearby university. By the spring of 1987, Evergreen Landscaping and Maintenance opened its doors, and since then business has been growing. Projections for next year are around $24.3 million in sales with a net profit of $2.8 million, $1 million of which is intended for expansion to a second retail site.

Structure and Competition

Evergreen enjoys the legacy of four different businesses (see Figure 1–8) and in a way competes in four different, though related, markets: gardening, lawns, trees, and landscaping. The employees come from four different cultures. First, there is the legacy of Petty's Garden Supply—a purely retail operation based on Mike Petty's love of gardens. Then there is the lawn maintenance operation, which is still very much the inheritance of Stern Lawncare and Everett Stern's no-nonsense

Figure 1–8   EVERGREEN LANDSCAPING AND MAINTENANCE CO.
ORGANIZATIONAL STRUCTURE

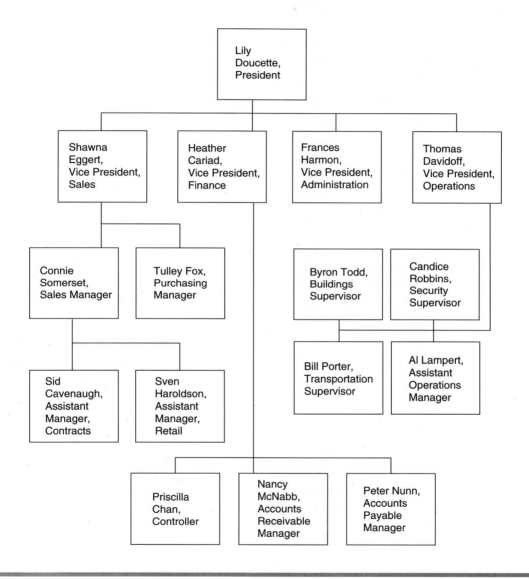

approach to farming as a business. The landscaping heritage from William Harnwell Landscape Architecture is artistic, quirky, idiosyncratic, and very hands-on. While landscaping and lawn care have been folded together into contract services under Sid Cavenaugh, they still don't work closely together. Finally, there are Lily, Shawna, and Tom, who have been together for a long time, running Evergreen with the memory of Lucien Doucette's tree farm never far from their minds.

In the garden supply business, Evergreen has at least a dozen local strong competitors that offer general gardening supplies: seeds, tools, fertilizer, basic landscaping materials, pesticides, and so forth. Most of the local hardware stores, major department stores, and major grocery stores also sell at least some of the products that Evergreen handles. However, none of them offer the range and quality of products that Evergreen has. These nongardening stores rarely have staff available to answer questions, even during prime growing season in the spring and summer. Lately, however, the major discount stores have been selling gardening tools, seeds, hoses, and other high-volume items at very low prices. Lily is certain that customers shop at Evergreen for information and then buy the products at lower prices at discount stores.

From Lily's point of view the landscaping business is a "prestige" service, although culturally the practitioners of ground art are worlds apart from the meat and potatoes of Evergreen. While there are almost two dozen firms in town that offer at least some landscaping services, Lily and Shawna agree that there are only three competitors that provide quality service, and even then they have only limited relationships with local suppliers to ensure availability and range of reasonably priced supplies. Rocks, pebbles, railroad ties, and liners for ponds are not available at all times everywhere, and landscape architects try to form strategic alliances with suppliers so that they aren't fouled up by delays that make customers angry. Evergreen, of course, has that sort of relationship built in.

The lawn care business competes with only one major alternative in town, although there are dozens of "student" lawn services that spring up with the passage of each vernal equinox, only to wither and die with the second frost, never to bloom again. Lawn maintenance is a tricky business because, like dentistry, it thrives on the threat of rot and decay and regular recall. Customers are loyal, although they don't understand the chemicals and application requirements. If they did, they could maintain their lawns themselves. Evergreen entered this business through the Stern brothers and has operated it successfully by being reliable. As noted, healthy lawns make for increased retail business, and lawn contacts create landscaping business.

Finally, there is the tree business. Although Evergreen no longer operates a nursery, it does a brisk business in trees and shrubs. They are temperamental, take up a lot of real estate, and have to be kept alive all year round if they aren't sold. While the live material business has been neatly folded into the garden supply activity, both Lily and Shawna realize that this is really the heart of Evergreen. Growing things—not lawns, hoses, or even landscaping—is the core business of Evergreen. Evergreen's logo is a tree. Marketing trees and shrubs is still the main way that Evergreen makes sales.

Budgets

In the most recent completed fiscal year, Evergreen had sales of $22 million, distributed as follows (in thousands of dollars):

Division	Sales	Expenses	Profit
Retail	$20,000	$17,450	$2,550
Landscaping	1,400	1,250	150
Lawn care	500	300	200
Other	150	50	100
R&D		75	(75)
Administration		275	(275)
Total	$22,050	$19,400	$2,650

Notes: R&D includes research grants to the agricultural college; administration includes undistributed expenses for management. Warehousing costs are charged to retail. Computer costs are distributed according to expenses.

Estimated budget summary for the current year:

Division	Sales	Expenses	Profit
Retail	$22,000	$19,500	$2,500
Landscaping	1,750	1,250	500
Lawn care	450	250	200
Other	175	50	125
R&D		125	(125)
Administration		250	(250)
Total	$24,375	$21,425	$2,950

Notes: Evergreen foresees a small loss of business in lawn care owing to problems with one of its annual promotions. It will be taking on an additional R&D contract, which accounts for the increased costs. Retail income is expected to rise 10 percent, but profit margins won't change much. Because of increased attention to overhead costs, the charge to administration should decrease by about 20 percent this year.

Projections for the following year:

Division	Sales	Expenses	Profit
Retail	$30,000	$26,000	$4,000
Landscaping	1,900	1,500	400
Lawn care	500	350	150
Other	50	0	50
R&D		300	(300)
Administration		450	(450)
Total	$32,450	$28,600	$3,850

Notes: Additional R&D contracts will double costs. Opening the second retail store mid-year will dramatically increase sales.

Questions

1. Let's explore the four themes of this course (competitive advantage, risk, management support, and technological leadership) introduced in this chapter in relation to this case. Does Lily seem concerned with each of these? What seems to be her major concern(s) and which are considered less? Why do you think this is the case?

2. Lily and her management team will be doing a lot of problem solving in the cases following the end of each chapter in this book. Consider the problem-solving paradigm presented in the text. If Lily follows this model, which aspects of problem solving will be easiest for her? Hardest or riskiest? Why?

3. We have not yet mentioned information systems in this case. Lily's major interest seems to be to increase her business strategically by expanding to a second site. Suppose you were called in to brief Lily and Shawna on the influence and role of information systems in business. What would you tell them? What roles does information play in a hands-on business such as Evergreen?

4. After the briefing, Lily says to you, "Very impressive. Now I want you to go look around and let me know what kind of computer I need." How would you respond to this challenge? *Should* you respond to it? How should you act as a consultant in this situation?

5. Lily is aware that the business world has changed a lot in the past quarter century. Acting as a consultant, write her a memo detailing the modern management imperatives and how information systems play a role in meeting those imperatives specifically in a business like hers.

CHAPTER TWO

MANAGEMENT AND INFORMATION

After you have read and studied this chapter, you should be able to:

■ Discuss the role and function of information at strategic, tactical, and operational levels of management.

■ Identify seven management models.

■ Describe how information supports a manager's activities and goals.

■ Describe ten dimensions of information style and discuss how each style affects how managers use information.

Question: What role does information play in management and how is it beneficial to managers?

Bonnie Long is the store manager of a suburban women's clothing store. She is responsible for all aspects of the store's day-to-day operations, including sales, accounting, order processing, and store maintenance. Lately she feels that the job may be getting the better of her because, despite five years' experience at this store and an undergraduate commerce degree, she is losing confidence in her ability to make quick and effective decisions, especially in the area of stocking. She thinks that perhaps fashion trends are getting out of hand or she's just getting stale in her job; for whatever reason, she doesn't feel confident about the clothing selections she's making. In addition, Bonnie wonders if she should better *anticipate* what's coming in fashion and be proactive in handling her staff. She knows the competition in women's clothing is fierce and feels isolated in her store. The owners maintain a hands-off attitude, and the workers, although motivated, are not well trained and don't tell Bonnie much. Bonnie wonders if her problem is caused by something she doesn't know or is unable to use rather than by some skill she doesn't have.

Answer: In management activity, information provides improvements in work quality, decision making, organizational culture and climate, influence, teamwork, creativity, and learning. At whatever level a manager works, his or her job is information-intensive. Supporting managers' activities means increasing their powers to work, breadth of contact, confidence, and freedom of action. Information style and tasks also determine how managers use information and to what extent the information is beneficial.

INTRODUCTION

This chapter answers the question, "What role does information play in management?" More specifically, it addresses the issue of how information gives managers an advantage. To answer this question, we will examine a manager's job in general and information needs that arise from that description. Then we will look at seven different views, or models, of management, focusing on the outcomes and measures of management support. Certain management activities are supported by information; hence, we'll look at the concept of information and see how it works in general. Our foremost concern is with the advantages information brings. Finally, we will focus on information style as it varies from manager to manager. We'll also look at the tasks managers perform with information to get an idea of the ways information can support them. However, because this chapter is preparation for both Modules 1 and 2 in this book, we will begin with a discussion of the advantages of information, especially those we will later term *strategic* or *competitive*.

COMPETITION AND COOPERATION

People and organizations interact in two distinct ways: competitively and cooperatively. Our society is, for the most part, a blend of these two ways of interacting because every person is simultaneously an individual as well as a member of many groups of cooperating individuals. However, each mode of interaction is driven by a different set of motivations. **Competitive interaction** is aimed at increasing or maximizing individual gain regardless of the potential for loss among other individuals or groups. **Cooperative interaction** is aimed at increasing or maximizing a group's gain regardless of the effects on individuals. One distinction that *cannot* be made between the competitive and cooperative views is based on a disagreement over whether the world is resource scarce (i.e., we either share resources or some group takes over all of them). Both views can see the world either as a limited set of resources or as a relatively infinite set.

The critical difference between competition and cooperation is based on the role of the individual and the individual's role in producing the goods and services a society requires. In a competitive view, individuals alone are responsible for their own incomes and outputs; in the cooperative view, the group is the source of rewards. Competitors value information because it enables them to make decisions and take actions with some confidence. Thus, they jealously hoard (or at least attempt to control) information about themselves or information they discover about others. In a cooperative situation, individuals are keen to share information because otherwise their cooperative efforts may be for naught or perhaps inefficient. Regardless of motivation, individuals will see information as a valuable commodity.

A situation is far more complex when both competition and cooperation are needed. Consider a manager who is seeking a promotion (competing with others) by shepherding a project to completion (cooperating with others). There is a need to share information, but only so much of it. The decisions of how much and what information to share, how much to demand, and when to barter become strategic issues for managers when both competition and cooperation are needed.

Does this mean that in a cooperative society more information is shared than in a competitive one? No. Competitors obtain information from sources for a fee, or it may be obtained by compiling it from secondary sources, surveys, government or industry databases, and so forth. Also consider that in a competitive situation information on *all* competitors is needed by *each* competitor, while in a cooperative situation the only really valuable information is on group performance. Because performance is presumed to be at least mildly coordinated, far less additional information may be needed by participants in a cooperative situation. Hence, information processing is more critical to individuals in a competitive situation in which both data and refined information become far more valuable. Information systems (information plus processing) are key players in competition and may become, at least partially, the basis for competition.

While information plays an important role in both competitive and cooperative situations, it is clear that in competitive situations information systems are *strategic* in nature. Although cooperation may also be strategic (e.g., making and executing plans for future operations), competition greatly enhances the strategic value of information systems because of the large number of closely guarded and expensive sources needed and the volume of information to be processed. It should be clear that individual managers, who may play cooperative roles in organizations, are going to experience the strategic value of information systems firsthand. It is on this note that we turn to the role of managers in organizations.

THE ROLE OF MANAGERS IN ORGANIZATIONS

Management work is characterized by Anthony as having a specific level of influence (see Figure 2–1). **Operational management** (supervisors and overseers) handles the day-to-day activities of producing services or products and works directly with customers and suppliers. It is at this level that profits are made or losses are incurred. Compared to other management levels, operational management tends to be measurable (there are fixed, well-defined tasks to be performed), concrete (focused on products and other deliverables), and relatively simple (involving only a few connected tasks). Operational management activities are directed at

---

Figure 2–1   ANTHONY'S TRIANGLE: JOB DESCRIPTIONS

| Figure 2–2 | ANTHONY'S TRIANGLE: INFORMATION CHARACTERISTICS |

controlling people, assembly lines, products, and machinery. Decisions are implemented quickly and remain in effect for relatively short periods of time before they are overridden or corrected.

Efficiency is the important criterion on which operational managers are judged. Decisions are made infrequently and demands are in the form of commands or orders. Operations are relatively well ordered and managers are expected to analyze problems and fix them quickly. At this level, there is not as much freedom of action as at higher levels, and behavior and decisions are constricted.

Tactical management involves creating coping mechanisms that ensure operations will continue no matter what happens in the firm's environment. Tactical management responsibilities include some of those of operational management and some of those of strategic management. The strategic management level includes executives, boards of directors, and high-level consultants. Their tasks are less measurable than those of tactical management because their work is more abstract and complex and difficult to evaluate.

Strategic management focuses on the future—the present is taken care of by operational management—so decisions made by strategic managers are long term. Work at the strategic level is far more creative than at the lower levels because it concentrates on planning rather than controlling. At this level, executives are expected to work in an integrative fashion, bringing ideas together and spanning boundaries in the organization. Multiple, and often conflicting, demands are placed on strategic managers by customers, employees, regulators, and suppliers. These demands and the complexity of the job itself dictate that work is relatively scattered, so the major challenge is holding all the pieces together while planning for a turbulent future.

Managers at all levels use information (see Figure 2–2). At the lowest levels, information concerns immediate past performance and instructions on current performance as well as information about the goods and services produced. At this level, information is usually derived from the organization itself, is narrowly focused on production or performance, and is prespecified (managers know what kinds of data they should be collecting and what information is important). Basically geared to shifts, production cycles, or seasons, information is historical in nature and collected frequently in great detail.

At the tactical level, information concerns schedules, revenues, profits, costs, and other economic indicators. Although the organization's performance is of interest at the tactical level, it is how that performance translates into profits or other resources that affects the manager.

At the strategic levels of the organization, executives are concerned with hypothetical policies, plans, budgets, and objectives. Even budgets, for all their seeming concreteness, are actually only guesses or promises of performance—they may or may not be met. Information that is important to executives often comes from sources outside the organization such as suppliers, competitors, regulators, industrial spies, hired consultants, information services, and the media. The information they examine also covers a wide scope typically including all functions or divisions within the firm. Because this information is of an ad-hoc, unprespecified nature, strategic managers often decide on the spur of the moment to collect some information they feel is important to reach a certain conclusion. The spontaneity and unpredictability of their jobs results, in part, because the information they receive arrives randomly and may not strictly conform to the company's timetable. In most cases, too, executives' information is oriented toward the future, collected infrequently, and generally summarized. Because executive decisions affect the organization for a long time, precision is less of a concern than having a general picture of trends.

You see then that how information is requested, used, and disposed of varies as we move from level to level. What looks like information to strategic managers might resemble chaos to managers at the operational level, while managers at the strategic level may find the information that their line managers and supervisors use to be narrow and restricted. Why managers at different levels do different tasks and have different information needs depends on the view we have of management as an activity. There are many different approaches to management activity, but seven major models have evolved in the past 5,000 years.

SEVEN MODELS OF MANAGEMENT

Since the time of the earliest preserved writings, human beings have been fascinated by the managerial role. This might be so because people are basically hierarchical in their social structures, and they tend to preserve this structure in their family, social, and business lives. The earliest business structures we know about are family and government. These structures generally tend to be hierarchical in nature, but the hierarchical approach is not the only one we use.

We will review seven theoretical models of management (see Figure 2–3), each of which stresses a different aspect of management work. The hierarchical management model emphasizes responsibility and authority. The task-oriented model focuses on five common management activities associated with projects. The allocational model views managers as responsible for handling organizational resources. Transactional models see management activity as stemming from and dependent on the transactions an organization conducts with its environment. The team effort model views managers as members of a team and concentrates on cooperation, leadership, coordination, and commonalities.

Figure 2–3 SEVEN MODELS OF MANAGEMENT

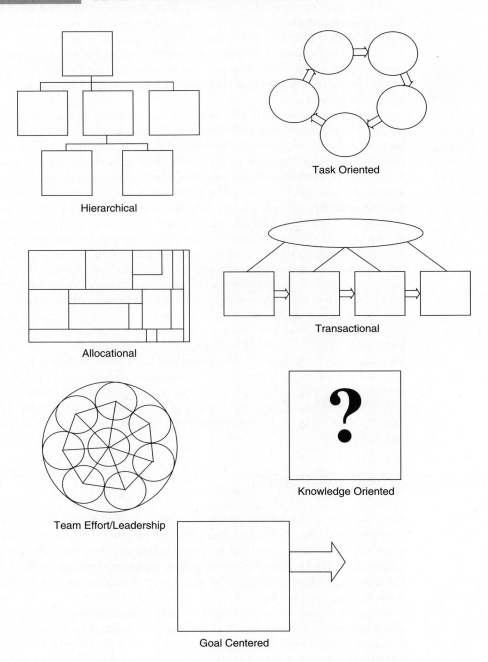

Hierarchical

Task Oriented

Allocational

Transactional

Team Effort/Leadership

Knowledge Oriented

Goal Centered

The knowledge-oriented model concentrates on the development and use of management knowledge. Finally, the goal-centered model focuses on the role management plays in translating organizational goals into action. Each has pros and cons as a single model of management, and when used as the basis for specifying management support, each dictates a different kind of support.

As the oldest view of management, the **hierarchical management model** stresses responsibility and authority. In this model, managers receive authority from superiors to control the work of subordinates in return for responsibility. That is, managers have the legitimate right to command resources and order others into action while at the same time responding to superiors' requests. Management support helps managers delegate responsibilities, coordinate incoming information, and handle political problems when delegation fails. Conflict is handled at the highest common level.

In our chapter-opening example, Bonnie is given responsibilities by the owners, who have adopted a hands-off attitude. Bonnie hires employees and trains them, but she doesn't get a lot of feedback from them. Because Bonnie has all the responsibility of running the store, she has to delegate some responsibilities to her employees, who put a lot of pressure on her because of the high turnover rate. Bonnie depends on her employees, but she has control over their activities.

The hierarchical view simplifies organizational life, explains why people follow others, provides a simple algorithm for work analysis, gives workers the rationale for why they do what they do, is relatively stable, and allocates blame if things go wrong. To that extent this model is quite useful. Because hierarchies tend to be stable, we know a lot about them and work well within them. However, this view generally oversimplifies because it cannot explain leadership or the role of charisma and it does not account for information connections and communication.

Hierarchies are relatively unresponsive and difficult to change. Hence, we tend to take their characteristics as static when in fact they may be changing, however slowly. Thinking about management as a hierarchy tends to create a heavy management overhead; that is, channels of communication generally run only along formal lines, which increases the probability of duplication or crossed wires. The implications of adopting this view of management include bureaucracy, fragmentation of work, duplication, and unresponsiveness. Another implication is slow information processing that does not promote information sharing. This is brought about by the necessity to move information along only specified channels, causing delays.

The **task-oriented management model** is also a classical model. In this view, managers perform five major tasks: planning, staffing, organizing, directing, and controlling. These tasks are almost always chronologically ordered: (1) behavior is planned and contingencies are noted, (2) individuals are located to engage in the behavior, (3) work is organized to fit the plan, (4) individuals are directed to do the work planned, and (5) individuals' behavior is controlled based on the contingencies and management skills needed to meet the goals implicit or explicit in the plan. Management support is seen as functional, supporting these five basic activities. While these activities are most evident in projects, they may appear in any management situation in which work has to be planned, structured, and executed.

Bonnie Long uses this management cycle every season to plan for the new fashions that arrive. Depending on the season and the time of year, she may have to hire more staff and organize the store's displays, advertisements, and stock. Newly hired staff as well as longer-term employees have to be shown or told how to sell the stock, especially if it's innovative. Far too frequently, Bonnie thinks "green" staff are improperly trained because she doesn't have the time to do it. When these employees make mistakes with customers and the store loses sales, Bonnie has to step in and tell the sales staff what to do. Just as the season is under way, she has to plan the orders for the next two seasons.

An advantage of the task-oriented view is that it focuses attention on actual managerial activities by neatly categorizing all kinds of management work and responsibility. It also stresses the process nature of managerial work—that different kinds of support will be necessary at different stages. On the other hand, not all activities fit into one, or even any, of these categories because managers may be doing all these things at once. The process is not linear—it can have cycles and create arbitrary and perhaps artificial lines between managers and workers. Support systems may *have* to function across activities. Use of the task-oriented model implies that management has a set of well-defined tools that can be used in sequence or in parallel, perhaps designed by noncommunicating segments of the organization and characterized by duplicated expertise and redundant support systems.

In the **allocational management model,** managers control or own resources within the organization. Historically, these resources have been money, people, and physical objects. A resource manager obtains, allocates, shares, monitors consumption of, and returns resources, keeping the "cup topped up" as necessary. Management support is required in these five phases of resource management.

Bonnie Long sees her job as managing two kinds of resources. The first are those related to the business itself—people and money. She feels increasingly confident about this part of her job. The other resource is the stock and, more specifically, fashion. Her biggest problem is anticipating fashion trends and placing orders up to half a year in advance. Once the stock is on the racks, Bonnie can handle the customer problems with her relatively inexperienced sales staff. However, obtaining the resource (fashions) that the store is all about is vexing her.

An advantage of adopting the allocational model is that it distinguishes among types of resources and stages of resource use. It also recognizes the political nature of an organization and the economies that arise when resources are scarce and must be shared or negotiated. The allocational model takes a systems viewpoint wherein multiple systems compete for resources. It also recognizes multiple classes of resources and the need for support in allocating these resources. Because it focuses only on the phases of resource allocation, the model does not provide a true process view of management. It also fails to distinguish multiple reasons for requiring resources and their ultimate disposition or transformation into products. The allocational view ignores nonresource-based interactions while remaining focused on competition to the exclusion of cooperation. Management support in this view is based on the need to locate, track, and manage resources.

The **transactional management model** is another common and more modern model that views management as a stage in the **value-added chain** of organizational effort. Transactional management models stress the role management has in adding value to the raw resources an organization uses to produce its products or services.

For example, Bonnie acquires products that she sells to the public. Bonnie feels she adds value to the business by making the highest-quality, attractive fashions available to her customers. She also adds value by training the sales staff to be helpful so that customers buy what they like. Bonnie likes to think she is very valuable not only because she "keeps order," but also because she makes the shopping experience better for her customers.

There are a number of value-added models, but they focus on the actual process of manufacturing and delivering products. Management support is needed at each stage of the process. The transactional model, on the other hand, closely examines the process through which management adds value. It sees management as integral to an organization rather than just a control or overhead. It also views management as transaction driven and related to the business of the firm, pointing out the need for management support at various stages of value addition. The value-added viewpoint creates a key link to the data derived from the transactions. However, it's a limited view because it ignores management activity that does not relate to transactions, may be specific to certain kinds of products and services and not others, fails to note that individual managers may be involved with several products or at several points in the value-added chain, and ignores factors outside the firm that influence management action. With this model, supporting managers means providing tools for handling information coming from transactions only, which is not easily translated into higher management needs. Systems based on the transactional viewpoint cannot support nontransactional activities involving knowledge, power, and communication.

Some theorists define the **team effort management model** as a complex set of interlocking teams in which some players are coordinators and the primary goal of the team is cooperation. Managers are effective when they cooperate with other managers and instill a cooperative spirit among their fellow team members. This view is closely aligned with the self-directed work group view of production. In this view, it is the team rather than the individual that produces and directly contributes added value in production, thereby enhancing the functioning of the team. In theory, the team reaps the rewards for productivity. Individual contribution (positive and negative) is regulated through social channels and by feelings of affiliation with a productive group. In this team model, managers are concerned with group development and functioning. Groups are seen as having a definite life cycle, moving from forming to storming (conflict), to norming (conflict resolution and the establishment of norms of interaction), to performing.

As team leaders, managers are expected to embody the typical characteristics of the group in order to motivate the group. The group's performance depends on the manager's leadership powers and style. Over the years, several leadership studies have shown that no single style is best in all circumstances. In order to apply themselves properly to leadership, managers require information about the needs, abilities, and expectations of other team members.

Bonnie definitely doesn't see herself as part of a team, but she does think about the team model because she feels so isolated. The owners' hands-off attitude bothers her a lot, especially because she used to work so closely with them as a team. And because her staff is not particularly communicative, she wonders if something is wrong with her leadership style. Bonnie wants to buy into the business, and she knows that the closer the owners feel to her, the better her chances of becoming a partner are.

The team-oriented view is becoming more and more appropriate as actual work teams become increasingly charged with responsibilities and individual contributions are diminished. Although diminished, individual contributions and, more important, individuals' perceptions of their own contributions remain high. Regardless of the attractiveness of this cooperative view of work and management, the competitive spirit is alive and well in most organizations, many of which adopt several of the theoretical models discussed here. Individuals still vie for rewards regardless of team incentives, and, clearly, individuals differ in their abilities, motivations, backgrounds, and personalities. Adopting the team-oriented model implies that managers have the means to gather and evaluate information on team performance as well as individual contribution to these teams. Also, individuals in teams not only need information on their own work, they need to coordinate with other team members. Because teams require complex interactions both internally and with other teams, a great deal of data are available. However, it's not clear how to process this information, especially given the human tendency to become emotional in a group. Supporting team leaders means providing the entire team with management tools (see Chapter 9 for a discussion of group support systems).

The **knowledge-oriented management model** emphasizes the role development and diffusion of knowledge play in today's management. Management develops knowledge through experience, and this knowledge is diffused to employees through mentoring relationships, teaching, coaching, and active training. The advantage of this model is that organizations must learn to adapt and win in changing environments. Managers accumulate knowledge over time and direct the learning of others. The accumulated wisdom of an organization is evidenced in the expertise of individuals in the organization. On the other hand, there is obviously a hierarchy of knowledge, because not all knowledge is valuable in all situations. Also, much of what goes on in organizations is based on a lack of knowledge or on hunches.

Bonnie Long uses this model of management in her role as trainer and mentor. Because employee turnover is so high, she continuously teaches and coaches her sales staff. Since fashions change constantly and she has to stay abreast of trends, Bonnie appreciates any knowledge she can tap in to. Without advice from the owners, Bonnie has had a difficult year and her confidence has suffered.

Using the knowledge-oriented view to improve or support management requires easy-to-build systems that support individuals. Support needed for groups is much more difficult to obtain. Knowledge-based support is still in its infancy and is closely tied to the concept of the "learning organization." Such organizations accumulate knowledge over time by saving and analyzing their experiences as well as by acquiring information outside the organization.

Finally, the **goal-centered management model** concentrates on management's role in moving organizations toward goals, explicit or otherwise. This model resembles the other models in that it is extremely general and views management as a control function. Managers receive information from internal and external environments and order adjustments so that an original plan can be adhered to. Goal-centered models incorporate resource management, a feedback loop, hierarchies, and a number of specialized management tasks. Management support consists of tools that keep the organization on an established path toward one or more goals.

Bonnie uses the goal-centered method by setting inventory and hiring objectives each season. Budgeting, for example, is an important aspect of her business. Keeping fiscal goals in mind for the business and career goals in mind for herself, Bonnie seldom loses sight of the need to set and meet objectives.

This view correctly notes that all the other models exist to translate organizational goals into action. It also notes that management plays a translational role, has the sophistication necessary to explain the multiple roles and activities in which managers engage, and accounts for fragmentation and occasional conflicts managers experience. On the other hand, goals might not be met because support for goal-oriented views requires enormous amounts of external data that are unreliable and difficult to collect. Goals themselves are complex and often nebulous, and measurements of progress toward goals are not necessarily available, valid, or reliable. Adopting the goal-oriented view implies management support based on analysis of goals and necessary tools to translate these goals at various organizational levels.

These seven management models are not mutually exclusive. Most organizations integrate these views depending on the circumstances, the work, and the manager. There are clear differences among the models (for example, some focus on individuals and others on teams), but there are also striking similarities:

- In each model, managers have certain kinds of *information* to locate and process.
- *Information flows*, as well as the information itself, determine how managers carry out their responsibilities.
- Most models postulate a number of *stages* or *phases* during which different kinds of information become important.
- In each model, a great deal of information is required in a variety of formats to perform *specific tasks* and to make critical decisions or take critical actions.
- Finally, each model explicitly or implicitly shows that information is unequally distributed. This implies that certain information is valuable to individuals in certain *positions* only at certain times, and often this information is not available.

The concepts of information, information flow, phase-specific information, task-specific information, and position-specific information are crucial to understanding the role of information in management. In order to support management activities, information must be made available in the appropriate amounts, time, formats, and degree of refinement.

SUPPORTING MANAGEMENT ACTIVITIES

Major activities of managers include measuring and gathering information, making decisions, changing the environment, motivating change, and distributing resources. Measuring implies the need to gather information about the environment. Gathering, in turn, implies locating reliable sources, assessing the reliability of those sources, matching sources to environments, paying for information, and relating it to others. Information used to do this may include indicators, trends, current data, historical data, and rumors. Common business activities relating to the environment include selecting appropriate environments and assessing the need for information.

Making decisions is a complex process of convincing oneself that a specific course of action is the best one. Hence, decision making relates to one's comfort with one of many alternatives. Managers need to know what the alternatives are and the value of their implications. A manager is more ready to accept alternatives that are (1) likely, (2) communicable, (3) familiar, (4) understood, (5) simply related to outcomes, and (6) independent of other alternatives. Unlikely alternatives are often threatening.

Consider Bonnie's decisions about new fashion orders. Suppose she has to make her selections from many new fashions she's seen in trade magazines. Some of these fashions are simply outrageous, while others are unexciting. Bonnie is likely to ignore fashions that probably won't make it to market, are difficult to describe, too outrageous to be stocked in her store, or unlikely to sell. On the other hand, she is likely to consider outrageous fashions if she thinks they have a good possibility of coming to market, are being talked about in the industry, have been seen on models, are created by designers who have effectively communicated why these fashions are important, stand some chance of bringing customers into the store, or complement other selections she might make.

Management's ultimate purpose is to change the environment—make things happen. While this is closely related to management powers (i.e., strength or position), it also depends on opportunity and confidence in those powers. To a great extent, the business environment is capricious and ornery—it does what it pleases. Global competition, for example, means that competitors can appear anywhere, work in any language, and offer any terms. Being able to counter these kinds of competitors calls for a new basis of competition: high-quality products, excellent service, and niche markets, for example. Successful managers not only have the strength and courage to compete on different bases in different markets, they have knowledge that builds the required confidence.

Having power doesn't mean that management decisions always result in action. Motivating change means convincing others to act with conviction in the face of apparent risk. Other people are convinced through a process similar to self-persuasion, but the interpersonal dimension is extremely important. Individuals are more likely to be convinced by those they see as similar to themselves, nonthreatening, informed, neutral, unemotional, committed to the group, and charismatic. Convincing others goes beyond mere persuasion, because those who are convinced must also be convinced to act and continue acting on the alternative selected until the goals are met. This implies that people see a manager as a credible source of decisions, that they are committed to carrying out the decision, and that their commitment can be maintained over the life of the decision. Continued commitment requires periodic review of the decision in light of new information that others may have received. Commitment maintenance is every bit as challenging as initial conversion.

Finally, resources are needed to change the environment. Meting (rationing) resources to reconfigure the environment (resource allocation) requires knowledge of the status of existing resources, the availability of other resources, and confidence in the selected distribution pattern and schedule.

Management requires support to carry out all of these activities. Supporting management means increasing management's ability to act so that it can overcome obstacles, which enables management to achieve greater commitment, increase breadth of contact with others, and enlarge the freedom to act. A **management support system (MSS)** is a system designed to support managers in the pursuit of their goals. The specific MSS used may depend on the model of management employed. Management support systems provide physical, emotional, interpersonal, and informational support. Such systems may be computerized; however, the most common form of support is a hierarchy of employees who are ready and able to provide information as part of their responsibilities.

An MSS may take a number of forms, one of which might be a network of people. For example, individuals who work for a manager often support the manager by performing delegated tasks and reporting on their own effectiveness. Even supervisors may support their subordinates by helping them define and monitor goal pursuit, by evaluating their own performance, or by providing counseling.

Another MSS may be a collection of machines or equipment. Machines may physically do the work for the manager or maintain records of the work. Technology such as telephones or other communication systems may enable managers to contact individuals whose services are needed.

A collection of procedures may also support managers by providing continuity and regularization. "Going by the book" may not always be bad, especially when the book procedures are effective and usable.

Managers may also be supported by one or more sets of data. Data support managers by providing them with evidence of what has happened, is happening, or will happen.

Finally, management support may be achieved from a computerized information system that combines features of all the forms listed above. Regardless of the form, an MSS gives physical, emotional, interpersonal, and informational support to managers in carrying out their tasks. Physical support is provided when tasks are actually performed. Emotional support is provided by raising managers' confidence, clarifying their risks, and helping them seek additional support. An MSS gives interpersonal support by assisting managers in forming alliances and coalitions among peers. Finally, informational support can help managers locate and use information. We now turn our attention to this last kind of support to discuss how information supports management in meeting its major modern challenges.

THE INFORMATION PAYOFF

When an individual judges a situation to be more accurately and precisely described after receiving a message (information), he or she has become "informed." Information informs in several ways, each of which contributes in one or more ways to management support.

Information informs by increasing the range of possible alternatives, increasing the precision of these known alternatives (having a more accurate description of them, for example), and by increasing the manager's confidence in these alternatives and their implications.

Alternatives

Alternatives may be unknown for a variety of reasons, and information lets managers know that other alternatives actually or potentially exist. Some of the various types of alternatives include:

1. *Hidden alternative:* The alternative is hidden in another known alternative.

2. *Overruled alternative:* The alternative has been ruled out because of conventional wisdom, although some of the assumptions of conventional wisdom might be wrong.

3. *Partly described alternative:* The alternative is not completely known; enough aspects are left undescribed to make it risky.

4. *Impossible alternative:* The alternative is considered a logical, moral, social, or physical impossibility according to assumed, perhaps unspoken, rules.

5. *Potential alternative:* The alternative may not currently exist, but could exist if certain events happen or certain actions are taken.

Information thus uncovers alternatives, counters conventional wisdom, completes descriptions, exposes hidden assumptions, and describes how alternatives could be manufactured.

Information also increases the precision of known alternatives. Known alternatives may be "fuzzy" when information is lacking (partly described alternatives), and obtaining further information may make the alternatives more precise and, therefore, easier to evaluate. Imprecision can stem from several sources:

1. *Incompleteness:* Alternatives may be incompletely described.

2. *Linguistic problems:* Alternatives may be described in terms that are irrelevant, imprecise, unclear, or ambiguous.

3. *Inconsistencies:* Alternatives may have internal elements that are mutually inconsistent or it may not be clear where or how to apply the alternative.

4. *Evaluation difficulties:* Alternatives may be described in terms that are difficult to evaluate or assign numbers to.

Because being informed means having increased confidence in alternatives, alternatives are valuable only when the risks and benefits can be evaluated in terms of the current situation (i.e., gains or losses). Confidence increases when knowledge of potential outcomes increases. Several reasons for lack of confidence include:

1. The alternative is rejected because it is hard to evaluate.

2. The set of related alternatives is difficult to distinguish.

3. The expected outcomes of several closely related alternatives are in conflict.

Support

Information plays a strong role in supporting management functions and activities. Information supports managers by increasing the strength, breadth, and depth of management knowledge, increasing the confidence in what is (and is not) known, enhancing the quality of contact with others, and increasing freedom of action.

Strength of knowledge is the degree to which individual facts (data, events, etc.) are easy to relate to one another. When Bonnie reads about fashions in trade magazines and sees trends in sales data, she strengthens her knowledge. **Breadth of knowledge** is the range of subject matter that is understood and available. Bonnie understands how to manage the store's employees and money, but she wants to increase the breadth of her knowledge in terms of fashions. **Depth of knowledge** is the amount of knowledge (the number of facts) available that relates to problems to be solved. The more Bonnie hears from her staff about how they are doing, the better she feels she understands them. Together, increased strength, breadth, and depth of knowledge mean that more facts, on more topics, and in a more related fashion, can be brought to bear more quickly on a problem or opportunity.

Information also increases managers' confidence in what is known, thus making it more useful. Information influences knowledge and thereby supports managers because it helps remove doubt about outcomes. Increased confidence arises because, although the future is not known, it is possible to rule out certain outcomes.

Information enhances the quality of contact with other people who are important in obtaining, verifying, filtering, and evaluating information. People are also needed to test hypotheses about outcomes, thus directly influencing confidence. In interpersonal contact, information exchange is important for building trust. This is especially true with regard to source credibility, source reliability, relevance, and validity. If a manager asks about an employee, "Does Joe know what he's talking about?" he is testing source credibility. The question, "Is Mary generally correct?" challenges Mary's reliability. The statement, "Look through this report and tell me what it says about sales targets" requests relevance judgments. The request, "Run these numbers by Sarah and see if they're right" asks for Sarah's assessment of validity. Managers also "try out" decisions on others to see if there are objections and to determine the degree of buy-in prior to implementing the decision. Buy-in by others also increases confidence.

Information therefore provides four major supports to management: (1) increases the specificity of individual alternatives for action, (2) decreases the risks involved in implementing selected alternatives with potential undesired outcomes, (3) increases confidence in the selected alternative, and (4) increases the quality of support from others. All of this is accomplished through (1) information acquisition, (2) information processing, and (3) information presentation.

Information acquisition involves locating sources of information, obtaining the information, formatting the information, and building an information supply by amassing information into databases, files, and spreadsheets. **Information processing** includes manipulating information according to the manager's needs. Finally, **information presentation** is the display of information in tables, graphs, text, sound, presentations, simulations, or visualizations.

Information has a number of qualities that affect how management is supported and to what degree. These **characteristics of information** include (1) precision, (2) specificity, (3) timeliness, (4) accuracy, and (5) usefulness.

1. *Precision:* Information should provide enough detail so that what the manager is concerned with is described by the information.

2. *Specificity:* Information should be specific, not general (or vice versa). The level of detail is important because managers either need information on specific events or just have to understand trends or overall characteristics.

3. *Timeliness:* Information should be timely because managers often must act within a limited time. Late or out-of-date information is useless.

4. *Accuracy:* Information must reference the exact state of the events it describes. Information cannot be in error.

5. *Usefulness:* Information must be in a form that makes it easy to apply to the situation at hand. This can include attributes such as understandability, readability, conciseness, and various formatting concerns.

Management support systems are basically information-driven. They provide support in the ways mentioned by implementing a number of models managers can use to find and evaluate solutions to problems or approaches to opportunities. Information-based support systems meet managers' needs by making management more informed, flexible, proactive, and powerful.

INFORMATION STYLES

People who use information have different styles. An **information style** is a way of working with information, how information is perceived and used, cut up, and put back together again. Each information style has a different implication for management support.

Individuals work with information in different ways depending on personality traits, job stress, the nature of the work itself, and the tools provided. Individual traits influence

Figure 2–4	DIMENSIONS OF INFORMATION STYLE

Dimension	Anchor 1	Anchor 2
Processing style	Analytic	Synthetic
Processing mode	Systematic	Intuitive
Input mode	Receptive	Perceptive
Orientation	Exploratory	Conservative
Information storage mode	Piling	Filing
View	Broad	Narrow
Capacity	Large	Small
Chunking	Holistic	Specific
Format/Code	Lexical	Pictorial
Channel width	Single	Multiple

how managers work with information, which we term **information workbenching.** The traits determine how individuals actually see information fitting into their work and how they respond to information-laden aspects of work.

Ten important information style dimensions are illustrated in Figure 2–4. One should be careful about reading the chart as though all "Anchor 1" traits go together and all "Anchor 2" traits go together. In fact, the traits are mostly independent. Managers can learn new styles just as they learn new clothing styles or manners, so at any moment during a particular task a manager could be characterized by any of these dimensions. Understanding how these characterizations affect a manager's work style and ability is important in determining the kinds of support that are needed.

Analytic versus Synthetic Processing Style

Information can be examined either as pieces of a puzzle or as the whole puzzle. Management information style favors either taking information apart or using it to construct other forms. The analytic style implies that information has a "grammar" or a preferred way of deconstructing it into parts that more or less tell the same story as a whole whereas the synthetic style accepts an approach that is more personal and creative. This approach stresses that bits of information can go together in various ways, each of which "says" something different. To distinguish between the two styles, consider the manager who approaches the question, "What does this information mean?" by breaking the information into factors or items of data. The manager with a synthetic processing style will try to find out what the bits of information mean when they are merged with other information. Choosing the correct tools for analysis and synthesis is important in all facets of management support, but choosing ones that are consistent with processing style is also important. Most information systems professionals are highly analytic, as they are trained to delve into systems, but most successful and charismatic managers are highly synthetic—they see the whole business picture and can make their followers see it, too. Hence, the tools systems analysts might prefer may not be the tools managers may prefer.

Systematic versus Intuitive Processing Mode

Managers may process information systematically (by rules) or intuitively (without stated rules). Systematic managers may lean toward numerical support because numbers lend themselves to formulas. Intuitive managers may shun numbers and seek support in a variety of other ways, including communication with others, to try to get a big picture or to put an idea into a proper context. Systematic managers may need support from others in the form of a consensus (after all, they've got the numerical bases covered), and intuitive managers may need support that will translate their hunches into a tangible format that convinces others and galvanizes them into action. Therefore, consensual and contextual support systems may be useful to systematic and intuitive managers who seek the support of others or need to convince themselves that a decision is right in context.

Receptive versus Perceptive Input Mode

Individuals acquire information in a variety of ways. Receptive managers seek information without first filtering or evaluating it while perceptive managers filter and evaluate information before acquiring it. Managers may be primarily one or the other or a mix. Inevitably, the kind of support required is dictated by the problem to be solved and the needs of the manager. If the information environment is relatively rich, a receptive style may result in information overload. In a sparse information environment, a perceptive style may make it impossible to obtain enough information.

Exploratory versus Conservative Orientation

Individuals can either play with information or conserve it. Playfulness implies that information can be explored, deconstructed, and reconstructed in multiple and valuable ways, even at the risk of losing it or being unable to put it back together. The conservationist saves all information, knowing that its parts do not say the same thing as its whole. The exploratory manager will ask "what if" questions whereas the conservative manager will ask "why this way" questions. An MSS that provides continuous backup is more useful to a conservationist, while a system that allows easy movement from database to database and from procedure to procedure will suit an explorer.

Piling versus Filing Storage Mode

Some people prefer lists or piles of information while others prefer information filed by keywords or indices in file folders. Pilers access information by location or content relationships; filers access information by keywords or indices. A piler will answer the question, "What do we know about X?" with "I left it here," while the filer will respond with "How do you spell 'X'?" Pilers tend to be visually oriented—they know where they have left something but not the name of the place. Because filers tend to be text oriented, graphic user interfaces (GUIs) manipulated through mouse devices may not be effective for filers, although most GUIs also have a strong textual component. Because many GUIs are built atop a file-oriented operating system (such as DOS for microcomputers), regulating this combination of the visual and textual may prove important to both pilers and filers.

Broad versus Narrow View

Information has a breadth (span of topics) as well as a depth (amount of information). Managers may prefer broad information that contains all details and all topics, or they may prefer narrowly confined and limited information such as abstracts or summaries. Their preference is also affected by time pressures and the need to make decisions as well as the amount of available information. A manager interested in broad information will answer the question, "What else do you want to know?" with "Everything," while the manager interested in narrow information will respond with "Specifically, X, Y, and Z."

Large versus Small Information Capacity

Many people are information-averse because they want to counter information overload, they mistrust information sources, or they have an innate small capacity for information. These people may actively filter or avoid information. Others bask in information either because they know how to handle it or because they are able to process it quickly. Because managers' information environments are active and unpredictable, managers who are information-averse are rarely successful, but even within the large-capacity range there are variations among managers. Systems that complement managers' information capacity and can respond to varying needs provide better support.

Holistic versus Specific Chunking

This dimension distinguishes individuals who want the whole picture from those who want to focus on specifics. Some managers work best at high levels of abstraction—averages, trends, overviews, and summaries are their meat and potatoes. Given managers' time and resource pressures, many are forced to learn to work this way. Others, however, don't feel comfortable with the whole picture and want specific data. They tend to want to "drill down" from generalities to specifics, literally trying to get to the bottom of the situation. Many managers find that the level of abstraction they work at depends on how much time they have and to whom they are responding. Executive support systems and information systems have this kind of flexibility built into them, which enables managers to move from summaries to details with ease. For example, hypertext and hyperspace systems provide this flexibility along with exploration capabilities.

Lexical versus Pictorial Mode

These modes are often presented as a verbal versus imagery distinction. Some managers who are concerned with language and words may spend most of their time wordsmithing, arguing, and reporting. Others may prefer images, sounds, and emotions—things not so easily expressed in words. The lexical manager will ask for a report; the pictorial manager will ask for a chart.

Single Channel versus Multiple Channels

Some information channels are inherently richer than others in terms of both the amount of information carried and their range of expressiveness. Managers seem to prefer channels that match their individual needs. Informally, the term *channel* means medium; *multichannel* means multimedia. Multimedia presentations can be informative for some, confusing to others. Information that can be expressed in a variety of ways is sometimes best expressed in only one or two ways at a given time. Some managers are able to process many "chunks" of information simultaneously, while others may want to spend time pondering each chunk.

Responding to managers' varying information styles is an important concern when designing systems to support managers. Because a specific system may be used by many managers, flexibility is the major concern. When flexibility cannot be designed into the system, managers should at least watch out for problems when they attempt to use systems that are contrary to their preferred styles of working with information. Many managers do not recognize their information styles, and some actually develop styles to match the systems they have been forced to use over a number of years.

The Modern Management Imperatives

Reach: Global Competition	Global competition has increased pressure on managers to respond intelligently. Because the range of competitors has increased, there is a greater need for, and expense of, information about competition. Managers are increasingly asked to look outside their organizations and think globally.
Reaction: Quick Customer Feedback on Products and Services	Management decision makers are asked to be responsive to customers in nontraditional ways. Operational managers are the first line of responsibility in channeling customer feedback to the organization.
Responsiveness: Shortened Concept-to-Customer Cycle Time	A manager's job is made more complex by a need for efficiency and speed as well as accuracy and reliability. These complex demands increase the need for relevant information in a form and format that managers can use quickly.
Refinement: Greater Customer Sophistication and Specificity	More sophisticated and demanding customers increase the breadth of information required to create and market products. Managers require this information quickly and accurately and in nontraditional formats for data processing. Managers need to be more creative and flexible, enabled by information.
Reconfiguration: Reengineering of Work Patterns and Structures	Modern managers serve a number of roles as work managers. They must be prepared to work organizationally as well as in their own disciplines to respond to customer needs quickly and intelligently. Organizational learning is a critical aspect of managerial work and depends on accurate information gathering and dissemination as well as knowledgeable interpretation of data.
Redeployment: Reorganization and Redesign of Resources	Resource management is now a critical aspect of managerial work. Managers must have detailed, relevant information on resources at all times and be able to redeploy human, financial, material, and information resources almost instantaneously.
Reputation: Quality and Reliability of Product and Process	Managers are now responsible for control and consistency of processes under their authority. Information systems are a critical element of this in supporting the movement to high quality. Benchmarks of quality, quality measurements, and group-based control techniques rely greatly on information.

■ INFORMATION HELPS BONNIE

Bonnie has worked closely with the store's owners since she was promoted to manager last year. She feels she knows the store, but the business itself is still very much a mystery to her. Part of the reason is the owners' hands-off attitude. While they don't interfere with the day-to-day operations, they also don't give Bonnie much direction. They are, however, very encouraging to her personally and have rewarded her well in terms of salary. In fact, Bonnie thinks that she has the owners' confidence to the point that she might be able to buy into the business if she can improve the store's competitiveness. One hurdle, however, is the way employees are hired and trained. Because style and fashion are important to the store's "twenty-something" customers, Bonnie hires young people, but they leave as soon as they are trained in sales. They go to competitors who can pay better or have more locations in the city. Excitement and movement are also part of the business. Fashion changes quickly and it's more difficult to anticipate fashion trends. Bonnie increasingly relies on her staff, but they seem to lack loyalty. These two aspects of managing the business (people and money) and managing the product (fashion) seem separate but somehow related. As Bonnie gets better at the first, she is losing control of the second. ▪

1. Bonnie has responsibilities at all levels of Anthony's triangle. Using this model, discuss her job and the information she requires.

2. Examine the seven models of management and discuss how Bonnie might see her management role in seven different ways.

3. What tasks does Bonnie have to perform now? Would more or better information help her? How?

Summary

Information plays different roles and has different values for managers at different levels. Operational managers are concerned with detailed, prespecified, and scheduled internal information with a narrow, historical focus. Strategic managers look for summarized, ad hoc, and unscheduled information, which often comes from external sources, is broad in scope, and is oriented toward the future. Obtaining the right information in the right format at the right time is important for managers. Viewing management as goal centered and knowledge oriented helps us understand why managerial work is very information intensive. Information is valuable to managers in increasing the number of possible alternatives for action, decreasing the risks involved in implementing the selection of the course of action, increasing confidence in the selected alternative, and increasing the availability of support from others. The quality of information is expressed in terms of precision, specificity, timeliness, accuracy, and usefulness. Each manager uses information in a unique style.

Discussion Questions

2.1 Competitive motivation implies taking risks, as does cooperation. Consider the kind of cooperation required in student clubs (such as a students' union). What kinds of risks become important in creating and maintaining cooperation among groups that might normally compete for money and members? What kind of information supports would the executive of a students' union need to maintain the required level of cooperation?

2.2 Consider the careers of managers as they move up in organizations. At each level, managers have different information concerns and preferences. What training or experience do managers have that prepare them at each level to work with information at the next level? How will your education in business and management prepare you to handle business and management information?

2.3 Think about a group or team effort you've participated in recently and how you might express the management and coordination of that effort in terms of the seven theoretical models presented in this chapter: hierarchical, task-oriented, allocational, transactional, team-effort, knowledge-oriented, and goal-centered. Which, if any, is the most appropriate way of describing this particular effort? What role did information play in contributing to the success (or failure) of the effort?

2.4 The chapter asserts that becoming informed empowers managers, increasing their confidence and enriching their interaction with others. Does this hold true for all kinds of information? Can you think of situations in which obtaining more information can have a negative effect? Why do you think this is so?

2.5 Using Figure 2–4, describe your personal information style and that of an individual you interact with on a daily basis. Are there differences in these styles? How important are these differences? How does your personal information style influence your management or leadership style?

Key Terms

allocational management model
alternatives
breadth of knowledge
characteristics of information:
  timeliness, precision,
  accuracy, usefulness,
  specificity
competitive interaction
cooperative interaction
depth of knowledge
goal-centered management
  model

hierarchical management model
information acquisition
information presentation
information processing
information style
information workbenching
knowledge-oriented
  management model
management support system
  (MSS)

operational management
strategic management
strength of knowledge
tactical management
task-oriented management
  model
team effort management model
transactional management
  model
value-added chain

References

Anthony, R. *Planning and Control Systems: A Framework for Analysis*. Cambridge, MA: Harvard University Press, 1965.

Barnard, Chester. *The Functions of an Executive*. Cambridge, MA: Harvard University Press, 1968.

Daft, R., and R. Steers. *Organizations: A Micro/Macro Approach*. Glenview, IL: Scott Foresman, 1986.

Gorry, G. A., and M. S. Scott Morton. "A Framework for Management Information Systems." *Sloan Management Review* 13, 1 (Fall 1971).

Huber, G. "Cognitive Style as a Basis for MIS and DSS Designs: Much Ado about Nothing?" *Management Science* 29 (May 1983).

Jaques, Elliot. "In Praise of Hierarchy." *Harvard Business Review* (January–February 1990).

Keen, P. G. W. "MIS Research: Reference Disciplines and a Cumulative Tradition." Proceedings, First Annual International Conference on Information Systems, Philadelphia, PA, 1980.

Kotter, J. "What Effective General Managers Really Do." *Harvard Business Review* (November–December 1982).

Laudon, K., and J. P. Laudon. *Management Information Systems: Organizations and Technology*. 3d ed. New York: Macmillan, 1984.

McKenney, J., and P. G. W. Keen. "How Managers' Minds Work." *Harvard Business Review* (May–June 1974).

Minzberg, H. *The Nature of Managerial Work*. New York: Harper & Row, 1973.

Zwass, V. *Management Information Systems*. Dubuque, IA: William Brown, 1992.

EVERGREEN LANDSCAPING AND MAINTENANCE: CONNIE SOMERSET, SALES MANAGER

As the sales manager for Evergreen Landscaping and Maintenance Co., Connie Somerset manages retail sales and contract services. She is helped by two assistant managers, one for the retail side and the other for handling the professional landscape and lawn maintenance trade. Each department presents unique challenges both to staff and to Connie. Retail customers range from weekend seed-stuffers to prize-winning rose raisers. The contract services side is the most challenging, because it deals with services rather than products. Connie has noticed that customer relations differ between the two sides like night and day. Retail customers are in and out—they may make repeat visits during the growing season, but they are primarily faceless. Good customer service therefore means making them feel like valued patrons. Contract services customers are instantly identified and think of themselves as unique. Their patronage is by subscription or contract and they immediately notice any decrease in attention.

Connie is facing a difficult problem with contract services. Sid Cavenaugh is the assistant manager of contract services. Two seasons ago, after considerable market research, Sid introduced additional lawn-care services, including a guaranteed lawn green-up (raking, aerating, tilling, fertilizing, and seeding). The service proved to be popular among many suburban homeowners intent on outgreening their neighbors. Unfortunately, in order to make good on the guarantees, Sid had to hire extra workers in the spring, and many of them were college students who knew little about lawns other than how to operate a lawnmower. The guarantee was expensive, but the work was difficult, too, requiring several extra visits to each customer during the spring. Many properties proved especially difficult because of dew worms, fairy ring, roaming neighborhood dogs, and a very dry early summer. Although the guaranteed green-up program lost almost $30,000 last year, a program that popular isn't easily dismissed—customers had been phoning all winter requesting it for this year.

Connie is not sure that Evergreen can afford to offer this service again, but she *is* sure that they cannot afford not to offer something similar. She's certain, too, that the same service would cost a customer almost 50 percent more elsewhere. Although fewer customers would mean less chance of a loss, more customers would mean higher retail sales.

Part of the problem with the green-up program was the weather, but another aspect was managerial. Connie and Sid were busy with other programs and products and didn't have time to plan the guaranteed green-up well. Connie has noted that there are problems with marketing and operating this program, especially with regard to labor and avoiding selling the program to people with problem lawns. Her boss, Shawna Eggert, vice president of sales, is concerned about Evergreen's image should it fail to offer a similar service again. Shawna also recognizes that a properly priced and executed service would provide a boost to retail sales. Not surprisingly, healthy lawns generate more sales than unhealthy ones, and it is not inconceivable that satisfied customers may want to get some more professional landscaping done, too. Because she sees a lot of promise in Sid's ideas, Shawna is prepared to put some resources behind building a better service and integrating it better with Evergreen's product and service line.

Redesigning and reoffering the guaranteed green-up service will require spending a lot of time with last year's data, this year's cost projections and staffing availability forecasts, and income and expense targets developed by the management executive committee. Connie isn't sure she has the time and energy to put into this, but she doesn't want to miss a good thing when competition in lawn care is so intense. Much of the information is available from the company's small data-processing staff, but other data will be gathered with great care and at great expense before any decisions can be made.

Questions

1. Analyze Connie's management challenges with each of the seven management models mentioned in this chapter (hierarchical, task-oriented, allocational, transactional, team effort/leadership, knowledge-oriented, and goal-centered).

2. How are the imperatives of feedback, speed, specificity, reconfiguration, and quality affecting decision making at Evergreen with regard to products like the guaranteed green-up?

3. How can information assist Connie and Sid in this case? How would this information help in terms of increasing the strength of their power to do their jobs? The breadth of their contacts with others? Their freedom to act?

4. How does information function like other resources (funds, people, and materiel)? In what ways does it function differently?

5. What roles do various people play in the information system regarding the guaranteed green-up service?

6. What would you advise Connie and Sid to do before planning for next year's lawn-care services with regard to information?

CHAPTER THREE

ORGANIZATIONS AS SYSTEMS OF BUSINESS PROCESSES

OBJECTIVES

After you have read and studied this chapter, you should be able to:

■ Define the components of a business system and describe how business systems interact with one another and with their environments.

■ Identify three important system architectures that enable systems to cope with particular environments.

■ Identify three classes of business processes and describe how they interact.

■ Explain the role information plays in relating business processes.

■ Illustrate how data flow diagrams reflect relationships among data processes.

■ Describe the role information systems play in business process reengineering and discuss its challenges for management.

Question: How can a manager understand a business system so that it can be improved to meet the competitive challenges that have to be faced?

"It's infuriating that everyone continues along their merry ways, ignoring the fact that no one actually understands anything that happens around here." This feeling isn't new, but this is the first time that Donna Dougherty has put it into words. "If we really knew what happens around here, we'd be able to improve things, maybe create products faster or better instead of always responding to crises." Donna, a shift supervisor, is reacting to yet another problem, this one involving one of the four machine operators who works for her at TieTanium Garments (TTG), a manufacturer of ties and other specialty clothing items. Because TTG is using an old manufacturing system that was set up almost 40 years ago, it's difficult to get information about production, difficult to respond to sales agents' requests, and hard to plan ahead. Donna, trained in the far more competitive outerwear industry, is used to systems that respond to people, not vice versa. And more important, she really doesn't understand TTG's system, set up by its founder. Instead, she spends her days tracking down information that everyone swears to her is either unavailable, inaccurate, or isn't used anyway. What is Donna to do?

Answer: Donna needs to model her business environment, composed of basic, support, and administrative processes. To do this, she must understand the value of models and certain information-based models, foremost among them the data flow diagram. Knowing where inputs come from, where outputs go, and what processes are involved in transforming data into information will empower Donna to make procedural changes that will rationalize TTG's production.

INTRODUCTION

In order to lay the groundwork for examining the role and function of information in organizations, this chapter explores organizations as systems. The **system view** enables us to pinpoint where and how information and information systems support managers in competitive and cooperative situations. Systems operate to maximize benefits in an environment in which benefits aren't easily maximized. That is, in the competition for resources, systems often experience negative consequences of competition such as termination or extinction. Even when they are prospering, systems competing for scarce resources must remain alert to threats and opportunities. Consequently, business systems, like all systems, engage in a variety of strategies to overcome obstacles that may prevent them from meeting goals. This chapter discusses these obstacles and shows how information has an important, even key, role to play in goal attainment.

In this chapter, we adopt a more generic view of systems, championed by von Bertallanfy, Ashby, Bateson, and others, called *general systems theory*. **General systems theory (GST)** is not so much a theory as a unified and orderly way of thinking about complexity. Some of the many benefits of GST include the following:

- It is a framework for discussing common and important business concepts such as organization, authority, responsibility, reporting, production, productivity, planning, organizing, and controlling.
- It is consistent with our existing terminology concerning information systems, models, and consulting.
- It is a method of referring to management plans, action, and support that is constant across any kind of business or management situation or activity.

In this chapter, we first explain what a system is. This internal view of systems is important for our examination of business processes and their reengineering. A discussion of internal systems leads to an examination of the external interaction of competing systems (critical for Chapter 4). This in turn motivates a discussion of generic system architectures (important in Chapters 5 and 6) of which two, cybernetic and learning, are significant for businesses and managers who have responsibilities in business organizations.

This chapter focuses on models and their role in remaking or reengineering an organization or firm. According to Webster, a model is "a small representation of a planned or existing object . . . a person or thing regarded as a standard of excellence to be imitated." Models, whether for planned or existing objects, are appreciated because they are small and easy to comprehend, change, discuss, and use. Furthermore, as representations they are likenesses or images of what they represent, which makes them useful because it's not always possible to have the existing object and it is, of course, impossible to have the planned object. Finally, models represent ideals—the way things ought to be rather than the way they actually are. Sometimes problems get in the way or make real objects useless or difficult to use; models do not have these limitations. So long as we don't confuse a model with the real or planned object, we can appreciate the model for its usefulness in helping us understand the real world.

Business models help managers make decisions, convince others, make sales, and are used when it is necessary to understand complex business phenomena in a limited amount of time. Business modeling has recently taken on another important role—business

| Figure 3–1 | WHY SYSTEMS ARE SYSTEMS |

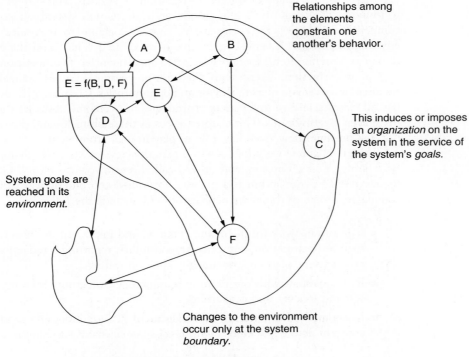

Relationships among the elements constrain one another's behavior.

$E = f(B, D, F)$

This induces or imposes an *organization* on the system in the service of the system's *goals.*

System goals are reached in its *environment.*

Changes to the environment occur only at the system *boundary.*

We learn about a system's organization by observing the effects of the organization on the behavior of the system's elements.

process reengineering (BPR). Responding to competitive pressures from abroad, North American industry has turned inward and begun examining the assumptions on which businesses operate. One important outcome of this self-examination has been to focus on the efficiency and effectiveness of business processes. High labor costs and relatively low investment in modern processing technology have led to a push to reengineer business.

WHY SYSTEMS ARE SYSTEMS

A **system** is a collection of elements (things, procedures, people) that interact in order to meet a goal. Systems are defined in terms of their elements and the relationships that bind them together. These relationships may change over time, however, as depicted in Figure 3–1. A system is distinct from its **environment,** a set of systems within which a given system interacts. At any time, elements are either within a system or in its environment, and elements pass between the system and its environment. Systems' goals may be set for them by other systems or by themselves. How goals are established is an important subject that will be discussed later in this chapter.

The goals a system attempts to reach may be observed in the environment. For example, suppose a business called Newprod has a goal of achieving a 20 percent market share. It attains this goal by motivating customers (who are not in the system but in its environment) to alter their behavior and buy Newprod's products. Elements of the business system are employees, machinery, and processes. The relationships include those connected with authority (reporting relationships), production (an assembly line, for example, or parts of the value chain), or communication within the company.

Much of a system's activity is based on mutual interaction of its elements. For example, an element (E in Figure 3–1) may interact with many other elements within the system (B, D, and F, for example). If E's actions are determined entirely by what these other elements are doing, we say that E = f(B, D, F) or that E's behavior is a function of the behaviors of B, D, and F. These relationships tend to constrain the behavior of individual elements. For instance, in the opening case, workers in the garment factory read various gauges and dials and base their decisions on what to do next on these readings. Their behavior is a matter of reading dials and gauges and making adjustments. Hence, someone observing might draw the (justified) conclusion that workers' behavior is constrained by these dials and gauges. The dials and gauges are in turn influenced by conditions of the product and the machinery. This chain of effects determines the relationships among the elements.

Some of a system's elements deal both with other elements within that system as well as those in its environment. After all, how is a system to meet its goals if it cannot influence its environment? Elements of a system that have this dual nature are said to lie along the **system boundary.** It is at the system boundary that a system causes changes in the environment. We can watch a system achieving its goals by observing what happens to its environment. Similarly, we can understand the network of relationships by observing the effects of mutual constraint on the elements. When people refer to the **organization** of a system, they are referring to a set of mutual constraints. Observing a system from the outside, we can see it is achieving its goals because it is making noticeable changes in its environment. However, we also have to infer what's happening inside the system by observing the elements over the long term. In doing this, we resemble scientists who take measurements over a period of time to establish patterns.

Of course, we may be tempted to ask people in a business to define their interrelationships. Actors within a system may be familiar with their own relationships but, except for boundary elements, they may not understand the system's (business's) goals from which they may be well insulated. This may alter impressions of their interrelationships because people naturally attempt to bring order to their observed universe. Actors within a system will attempt to explain whatever happens in terms of activities they observe at the time, but understanding relationships requires observation over a long period of time. In a later chapter, when we discuss information requirements analysis, we will return to this problem, restated as one of asking people what information they need.

Systems also interact with each other in systems of systems. We can think of all the interactions that take place at a system's boundary as falling into two classes: input and output. Input means bringing resources such as materials, food, money, or information into the system, and output means sending resources out. Systems that exchange resources in this fashion are said to be in equilibrium (see Figure 3–2). **Equilibrium** is a condition of a set of systems in which long-term exchange of resources is balanced. From moment to moment, some systems may take in more resources than they put out; they are growing. Others may be losing more resources than they take in; they are shrinking. If systems shrink too much, they fail to maintain their relationships with others, die, and

Figure 3–2	SYSTEMS IN EQUILIBRIUM

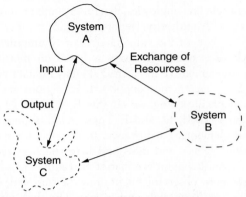

Equilibrium is a condition of a set of systems
in which the long-term exchange of resources
(on average) is balanced. This condition may
not be apparent during any short-term observation.
There may be cycles or periods that do not seem
to follow any pattern.

disappear. When this happens, we say that the equilibrium is disturbed. Then a new equilibrium position is established, probably with some systems now permanently larger and some smaller or destroyed. New resource exchange relationships almost always imply new equilibria. Consider a set of businesses competing with each other for customers. Over time, each business may have a certain percentage of customers. One business may sell more in the summer and another may sell more in the winter. But while these percentages may change or even be cyclical, they remain relatively stable, on average, over the long run.

Suppose one of several competing businesses experiences complete failure of its manufacturing line and is unable to produce products for three months. It may not be able to reestablish its market share and will slip to a lower share while the competing businesses pick up the slack. The equilibrium is disturbed and a new equilibrium is established. Consider what happens if another one of these businesses develops an entirely new product. This, too, will disturb the equilibrium. If a new competitor enters the marketplace, relationships among the existing competitors will change and yet again equilibrium will be disturbed. For example, when the airline industry was deregulated, the preexisting equilibrium was disturbed and cutthroat competition resulted. At first, many new competitors entered the market, but after a while the number of competitors decreased and market shares were redistributed. Some old, familiar businesses disappeared and new powerhouses appeared.

In this book, we are concerned only with systems in equilibrium. Systems that are not in equilibrium are interesting but difficult to manage because we don't have the intellectual hardware to analyze and anticipate changes. The study of nonequilibrium business systems lies in the realm of business policy. Historically, information systems such as sales management and accounting have been tailored for equilibrium conditions.

Figure 3–3 SIMPLE SYSTEM ARCHITECTURE PRIMARY (ACTION) LOOP

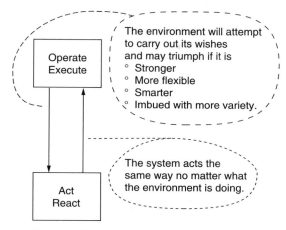

Operate Execute

The environment will attempt to carry out its wishes and may triumph if it is
° Stronger
° More flexible
° Smarter
° Imbued with more variety.

The system acts the same way no matter what the environment is doing.

Act React

Simple systems can survive only in placid environments or benign circumstances where the situation changes slowly and the environment is less powerful than the system.

SYSTEM ARCHITECTURES

Despite the relative calm of equilibrium, most systems, including businesses, live in dangerous and unpredictable environments. Systems evolve and develop architectures that enable them to cope with environments of varying peril. **System architecture** refers to the design and construction of the system. Architectural style emphasizes appearances. Some styles of architecture are more complex than others because they must cope with or take advantage of more competitive environmental conditions. Three architectures are of interest to us here—simple, cybernetic, and learning—which differ in several ways. As we shall see, each architecture is dedicated to surviving in environments of differing degrees of competitiveness.

Simple Architecture

A **simple system** (shown in Figure 3–3) does not change no matter what the environment is doing. The interaction between a simple system and its environment is cyclical. The simple system acts, its environment reacts, the system reacts to its environment's reaction, and so on. This interactive loop is called the primary or **action loop.** Simple systems are relatively powerless because they are "dumb"; that is, they will always be swamped by environments that are stronger, more flexible, smarter, or more creative. They can thrive only in benign and placid environments in which not much is changing or threatening because they cannot adapt. In reality, simple systems rarely survive for long but instead act as resources for more complex systems.

Figure 3–4	CYBERNETIC SYSTEM ARCHITECTURE SECONDARY (CONTROL) LOOP

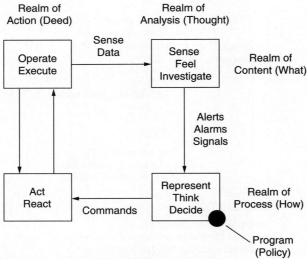

Cybernetic systems adjust their behaviors to environmental tactics by referring sensed changes to programs that relate change data to preferred counteractions. These programs are *predetermined.* Cybernetic systems can deal with moderate disturbances; however, they may fail in the presence of strong turbulence.

Cybernetic Architecture

Simple systems react blindly to their environments. A more complex architecture, called a **cybernetic system** (see Figure 3–4), is needed to react appropriately. Systems must counteract what the environment is doing in order to achieve system goals. So long as the environment is behaving itself, there is no need for any action, but if some event threatens the system's ability to meet its goal, the cybernetic system is able to take corrective action and thus advance toward its goals.

To take corrective action, a cybernetic system adds two functions to those of a simple system: sensing and deciding. It adds a second loop, called the secondary or **control loop,** and through this loop senses what the environment is doing in order to choose an appropriate reaction. While the primary loop is an exchange of physical resources and energy, the secondary loop also involves information (plus the energy needed to pass messages and the media through which messages are recorded or sent). Cybernetic systems adjust their behaviors to environmental tactics by referring sensed changes in the environment to programs (or policies) that relate data and changes in the environment to preferred counteractions.

The term for this process in general systems theory is **feedback.** The results of system actions are "fed back" to a mechanism that programmatically compares the results to the desired outcomes. If the results fall within a desired range, nothing happens, but if not, an alarm goes off. For example, suppose Newprod wants to achieve a 20 percent market

Figure 3–5	CYBERNETIC SYSTEMS: THE NATURE OF THE PROGRAM

State of the Environment

Recommended Actions	A	B	C	D	E	F	G	Outcomes	Cost
p	.8				.7		.5		
q	.4	.3		.6					
r	.1					.6			
s		.6	.2				.7		
t				.5					
u			.1		.8		.2		
v		.9		.4		.4			
w				.2			.3		
x			.3		.1	.3			
y					.9		.1		

The program indicates which actions are recommended to correct environmental states to the desired outcomes at which cost. The value of the program depends on the completeness of the state list, the validity of the outcomes and cost data, and the effectiveness of the actions. Creating the program is a dynamic activity.

share, and to do this it has to know whether or not it is anywhere near that value. Assume that Newprod's managers realize that a 25 percent market share is unattainable and that they would be happy with anything between 18 and 23 percent. The sensory function of the cybernetic system then measures, through market research, Newprod's market share. So long as the market share is between 18 and 23 percent, nothing happens. However, if the share falls below 18 percent or rises above 23 percent, alarms go off that inform sales management that something has to be done. These alarms may take the form of memos, telephone conversations, or similar signals meant to alert decision makers to a problem.

Decision makers heed these warnings and consult their predetermined program (see Figure 3–5). This program relates environmental conditions to recommended actions. In our example, assume there are five states of the environment: market share less than 15 percent, between 15 and 18 percent, between 18 and 23 percent, between 23 and 28 percent, and greater than 28 percent. In real life, there may be dozens or hundreds of different conditions observed. We can imagine the program will give the following advice:

> (1) If the market share (MS) is less than 15 percent, we need to do sales training and look carefully at who is doing the selling; this will probably change the staff a lot and cost us a lot, but we need drastic action. (2) If the MS is between 15 and 18 percent, we should introduce a sales award system to motivate salespeople. There is some cost to this, about 10 percent of margin on each item sold. (3) If the MS is between 18 and 23 percent, don't do anything. (4) If the MS is between 23 and 28 percent, we can lower sales commissions by 1 percent; this may cause an immediate drop in sales, but we can't supply much more than we do now and we don't want to promise things we can't deliver to our customers. (5) If we are capturing more than 28 percent of the market, we must immediately spin off some of that business to our strategic partners. We can't produce enough product anyway, and we've got a great opportunity here. The benefit is a strong partnership, and the cost is the risk that they will steal *all* the business.

Often, the program is expressed not in absolute terms (if you see this, then do that), but in probabilistic terms (most of the time, if you see this, then do that, but sometimes do something else), and sometimes there are several "best" ways of doing things. Perhaps the rules would be expressed in these terms:

> (1) If the MS is less than 15 percent, the most likely (66 percent) thing we should do is to offer some sales training, but another course of action (about 34 percent) is that we should look carefully at who is doing the selling and shift assignments. (2) If the MS is between 15 and 18 percent, the best bet (about 90 percent of the time) for success is to introduce a sales award system to motivate salespeople, but there is a slim chance (10 percent) that we should bring in key salespeople for training. . . .

As you can see, for one condition there are two choices and one is a 2 to 1 favorite. For the other condition, there are also two choices and one is a 9 to 1 better choice (i.e., it works better 9 times out of 10). This is not the kind of policy found in policy manuals, but it does characterize the kind of procedures that people really do follow. Sometimes some policies work and other times other policies work. The value of the program depends on the completeness of the state-of-the-environment list and the effectiveness of the actions recommended for these conditions. If the state of the environment is hard to know, if the actions are useless, or if the probabilities are incorrect, then the program is bound to fail.

Learning Architecture

Any program will eventually fail because the world is just too complex; however, in many cases a system may be able to reprogram itself. Such a system is called a **learning system** (see Figure 3–6). A learning system is more complex than a cybernetic system because it contains a third loop, called the tertiary or **policy loop.** This loop examines the effectiveness of the current program (and architecture) and creates a new program (or a new architecture) that will work better. People who perform this type of work are called *policy analysts*. All business systems are learning systems, because if businesspeople who work within the systems don't learn from their mistakes, they generally don't last long. Policy

| **Figure 3–6** | LEARNING SYSTEM ARCHITECTURE TERTIARY (POLICY) LOOP |

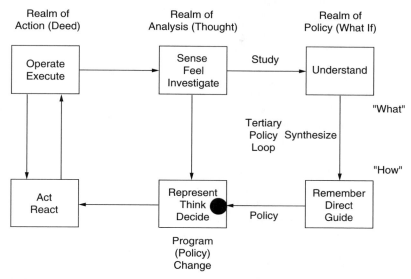

Policy analysis attempts to understand how well existing policies operate to produce desired outcomes. The policy loop operates far more slowly than the action or control loops and deals with much more aggregated, long-term data. Organizational learning is the goal of this loop rather than error correction. Learning systems are made to deal with great turbulence.

changing is important but time consuming and expensive to do, so learning systems are inherently more expensive than cybernetic systems. If you rotate Figure 3–6 90 degrees, you will see a not-accidental resemblance to Anthony's triangle, with higher levels of the architecture corresponding to higher management levels.

Learning systems are also inherently slower and more complex than cybernetic systems. Learning systems can adjust to complex environmental situations, but because they are slower, they may fail to adjust in time. This is exactly the problem most organizations face when they try to adjust their policies to changing environmental conditions.

Consider Newprod's sales targets and incentive plan. The plan might prove effective at one time, but suppose the marketplace is under stress from overseas competition that can produce a slightly superior product at a far lower cost. It may be true that if Newprod can capture more than 28 percent of the market it can afford to share some of the excess business with strategic partners. But what if the strategic partners make off with the best segment of the market and repeat customers who want superior products? The result of this policy is that Newprod will be seen as a low-end producer (or at least not high-end), which severely erodes its brand image. A cybernetic system would be incapable of making any changes that would prevent this erosion. A learning system, however, examines the effects of existing policy on important variables that go beyond market share (such as brand image). When these other variables become affected or are threatened, the learning system will change its program by modifying the sales and incentive policy. The program to change the program will, implicitly or explicitly, contain statements like this:

> If brand image is impacted negatively, then create a policy that spins off low-cost production to a generic brand with incentives to sell to mass marketers while some funds are put into bringing a high-end product to market in direct competition with other producers.

We can see that the program that changes the program is more complex than the program itself. This is because analysts who plan the higher-level program must anticipate all the "ailments" that could affect the cybernetic system, including failure to measure important values correctly or at all. The more experience a learning system has with its environment, the more it can perfect the program or policies. However, if the environment becomes unruly and changes rapidly or capriciously, a learning system may not be able to cope. Such environments are called *turbulent*, and if they are sufficiently nasty, even the most complex, expensive learning system will succumb.

In this sense, "coping" means "learning about the environment." Most business systems are learning systems that try to accumulate information about their environments. As discussed in Chapter 2, a competitive environment is information-intensive, but information is jealously guarded and thus expensive to obtain. Expense may be in terms of real money or it may be in terms of effort, time, or actual danger to the organization. Consider three ways a learning system can acquire information:

- *Indirectly:* It can buy information from other learning systems (in effect paying them for their effort or danger in gathering the information).
- *Covertly:* It can obtain information indirectly from others through observation or espionage (this latter course of action is not recommended).
- *Directly:* It can experience the environment directly (including negative consequences), and accumulate information from the experience.

For example, Newprod may develop its sales incentive policies by hiring consultants who have knowledge of its competitors (indirect), by trying to find out what competitors are doing (covert), or by trying several different tactics and observing what happens (direct). Because direct experience is risky, a trial-and-error technique is affordable only when an organization has resources to spare and can withstand strong environmental pressure. Organizations tend to use indirect methods and milder forms of espionage, which do not directly threaten the organization. However, indirect methods are relatively slow and sometimes expensive (they are, after all, a form of insurance). Upcoming chapters discuss in some detail the indirect advice-seeking techniques and technologies that form the basis for management support.

ORGANIZATIONS AS SYSTEMS AND BUSINESS PROCESSES

From our discussion of learning systems, we now can see businesses as learning systems. Businesses are collections of mutually interacting elements working together toward a goal. The goal may be creation of a product (using raw resources to create finished materials) or a service (assisting another system in its production). Success is measured in terms of how well goals are being met and how well critical values are maintained. A business is programmed with policies and procedures that determine how the organization will interact both internally (among employees) and externally (with suppliers and markets). These policies and procedures are the result of a planning process that attempts to foresee as many contingencies as possible, and they control activities of the firm's productive forces that conduct transactions with the environment (i.e., with other systems).

When the productive forces aren't working properly, feedback-driven elements within the system work to inform decision makers of needed changes. This negative feedback is then used to generate information to select a corrective action from the program. Because businesses are learning systems, the programs themselves are subject to changes by policy analysts and higher-level managers. The hierarchy that is created through these levels of control determines the authority structure of an organization, just as the differentiation of jobs within the business determines the day-to-day interaction of employees. We refer to this mass of interactions (hierarchically and differentially) as the *organization*. The business grows and changes in response to its environment to the extent that it learns about its environment, alters its own program, and gathers resources (capital) to counter the environment in order to meet its goals. This systems analysis of businesses forms the basis for the subject of the business process reengineering, discussed later in the chapter.

Our focus in the rest of this chapter is on improving business processes through understanding. Business processes are linked in two ways: physically and informatorily. Physical linkages, like the movement of goods from one station on an assembly line to another or the stages a hamburger goes through from grill to gullet, are a visible part of a manufacturing or service organization. Plants and processes are designed around the needs and opportunities posed by these linkages. Information linkages, on the other hand, are created by business needs, not by production or customer needs. Business needs are reflected in the kinds of information gathered, which in turn influence the way we design our processes.

MODELING BUSINESS PROCESSES

An organization has three kinds of processes: basic, support, and administrative (see Figure 3–7). **Basic processes** convert inputs into its products and services. This is sometimes called the *value chain* (to be discussed in Chapter 7). Basic processes are why a company exists—to build a product or provide a service for a customer. Sometimes the basic process is quite simple; for example, a broker matches suppliers with customers. Factories have far more complex basic processes, including warehousing, fabrication, quality control, billing, and so forth. Basic processes are generally physical in nature, taking raw materials and organizing them into products or services; information processing (such as a computer service bureau or a newspaper) is an exception.

Basic processes are supported by other processes. **Support processes** do not directly affect the company's products or services. They do, however, contribute to or make possible the basic processes. Many support processes are concerned with managing or studying basic processes in order to keep them working correctly. Support processes have a heavy information component because they deal with managing, scheduling, or controlling basic processes.

Administrative processes manage or account for resources that the basic processes require: capital, human resources, physical plant, information, and organization itself. Administrative processes are heavily information oriented because a lot of information is required to manage resources or account for them to others (such as regulatory agencies).

Figure 3–7 BUSINESS PROCESSES

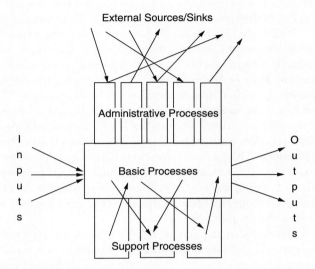

In this text, we will employ a number of different models, many of which are process models—representations of the stages something goes through. **Process models** are box-and-arrow models that resemble those of a cybernetic system. Boxes indicate processes and arrows indicate influence, change, or the movement of goods or data. These diagrams are generally read as follows (see Figure 3–8):

- In communication, messages flow from the sender to the receiver through a channel.
- Manufacturing uses raw materials to create finished products and services through a process that requires labor and capital as catalysts.
- An information system uses data as input and produces information as output through a process that transforms the data systematically.

Process models have starts and finishes so that the flow of goods or data can be traced. Each process has one or more inputs and creates one or more outputs. The usefulness of such a model is to locate bottlenecks, dead ends, redundancies, and slowdowns without having to observe the real system. Process models are also the first step in understanding strategic information systems opportunities.

Consider the basic processes of a hypothetical manufacturer that makes Usewunce disposable cameras. The manufacturer takes an order from a dealer by phone and gives the customer an order number, which the order department sends to accounts receivable. However, the order is not assembled or shipped until it is paid for. When the customer payment is received, accounts receivable releases the order and notifies the dealer that the order is being filled, giving an estimated shipping date. The factory produces a camera and an order for film is sent to a supplier. When both film and camera are in the warehouse,

Figure 3–8	PROCESS MODELS

Communication

Manufacturing

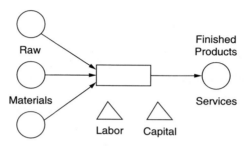

Information System

they are assembled, packaged, and shipped to the customer. In this process model, shown in Figure 3–9, we depict both basic processes (the chain from customer order to shipping) and the administrative processes (accounts receivable). The figure does not show support processes such as sales and advertising.

The process model is useful in answering the following questions:

- Where is the critical path in relations with customers?
- What kinds of delays could outside suppliers impose?
- Which process(es) would be a bottleneck in the overall process?
- How do the individual processes communicate with each other?
- What resources (data, raw materials, semifinished products, final products) flow between individual processes?
- Where could errors occur and in which processes further down the line could errors occur?
- What does this set of processes cost?
- Are there any redundant (duplicated) or extraneous (useless) processes?
- If a customer is dissatisfied or doesn't like the product, how does this affect the individual processes in the business?

| Figure 3–9 | USEWUNCE: BASIC AND ADMINISTRATIVE PROCESSES |

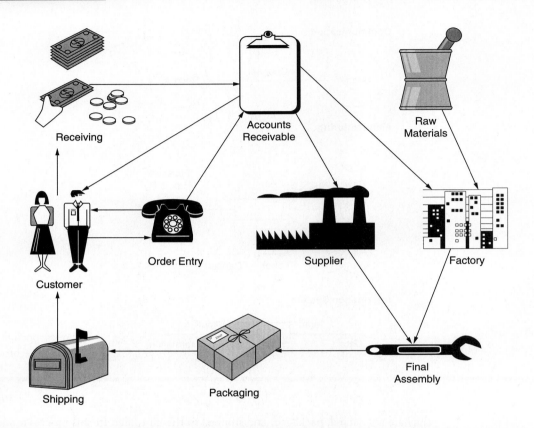

- To what extent do individual processes contribute to the overall sales and customer service goals?

Our example is focused on operations rather than management; we will add management extensions to the example later. Different businesses have different business process models. For example, an insurance company model will certainly look different from a factory model, and both of these will differ in important ways from a social services agency model. Models help us understand differences, too.

MODELING INFORMATION PROCESSES

Some interactions among processes involve information, others do not. In general, basic processes may produce information as a byproduct. For example, Usewunce's manufacturing and packaging process creates plenty of information (about orders, how the factory is working, how responsive the film supplier is, about costs, etc.), but the basic process is still producing disposable cameras for dealers. Support processes, however,

---

Figure 3—10   DATA RELATIONSHIPS AMONG USEWUNCE'S PROCESSES

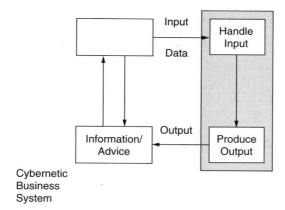

Cybernetic
Business
System

---

require information in order to gauge how much and what kinds of support or resources are needed. These support processes are cybernetic systems attempting to respond to their environment (i.e., the basic processes) and thus depend on continuous monitoring (i.e., information) to make decisions. On the other hand, administrative processes are almost totally information-driven. Because administrative processes are mostly for controlling or reporting, information is the input and output. The accounts receivable (A/R) process controls creation of the final product because the manufacturing, film ordering, and assembly processes must wait for payment.

There is an essential **data relationship** among most of Usewunce's processes (see Figure 3–10). Any system that interacts with another using data as the primary vehicle is said to have this sort of relationship. One of the characteristics of information-driven processes or systems that have essential data relationships with other systems is that they have memory. Memory is a device that stores information for later use (see Figure 3–11). A characteristic of systems that control others is that they accept input from outside. For example, Usewunce's accounts receivable process controls the processing of an order because no camera is assembled and shipped until it's paid for. Notice that A/R accepts two inputs, one from the dealer and one from the ordering process. The A/R process remembers between the time of the original order and receipt of the customer payment that an order payment is outstanding.

Information systems contain subprocesses that have specialized functions (see Figure 3–12) including:

- Handling input (sensing information from the environment or neighboring systems or processes)
- Producing output (information that controls elements in the environment)
- Memory
- Intermediate processes that change input into output

Figure 3–11   ADDITIONAL DATA SOURCES

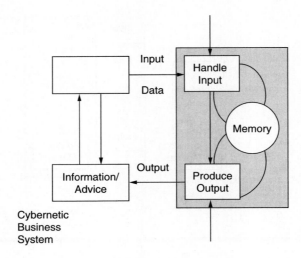

Connecting all these subprocesses are **data flows**—input-output relationships between processes. It is useful to think of a subprocess as a subsystem. By doing this, we identify the input-output relationships as subsystem interactions.

We will call a system analyzed into subprocesses this way an *information system*. We depict an information system using a **data flow diagram (DFD),** which is shown in Figure 3–13. The shapes used in a data flow diagram correspond to the specialized functions previously mentioned:

- Depicted as rounded boxes, *processes* handle data and transform it into information.
- Depicted as open rectangles, *data stores* temporarily provide memory of data from previous activities.
- Depicted as labeled arrows, *data flows* show essential data relationships among processes.

In addition, a DFD may show environmental or external sources of information (sometimes appearing as requests) and external sinks for information (sometimes in the form of responses). In the Usewunce example, the customer is both a source and a sink during the ordering process. Note that the business process model mixes information-driven systems with physical, resource-driven systems. The package going back to the dealer is *not* information, it is a camera with film. Money coming from the customer indicates payment, part of which is information about the order and part of which is money. A check is a request from the customer to a bank to honor payment, so a check is also information. When the money ultimately arrives, it is *not* information, it is a resource.

The "language" of data flow diagrams is spare. Labeled arrows depict the flow of data from process to process, each of which is depicted by a box with rounded corners.

Figure 3–12   SPECIALIZATION

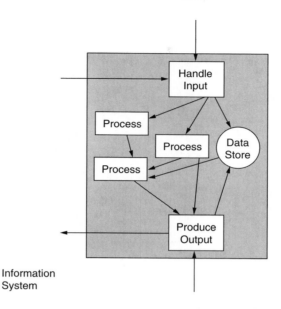

Processes are identified by names, and it is recommended that processes be named descriptively by using verb plus noun sequences such as "Post bill," "Check order number," "Release order," "Notify factory," and "Notify supplier." Data stores are drawn as indicated in Figure 3–14 and are usually named with titles reminding us of files (such as "Pending order file" or "Inventory").

A number of guidelines relating to data flows can help managers understand and analyze these systems. First, in a properly designed information system, all information leaving a system can be traced backwards through data flows and processes to information that has come to the system from outside. In other words, information systems don't create information, they merely process it. Information is created outside information systems by noting or describing events in the real world. It is, of course, these events we want to control by noting the information. If information came from inside the information system, we would be controlling the system itself, but this is not the nature of a cybernetic design. Similarly, in a properly designed information system, any information brought from outside should be traced forward through data flows and processes to useful information heading for an external sink. In other words, efficient systems don't waste information. For each item of information brought in, some useful output should be generated.

Information systems processes can be analyzed by looking inside them (see Figure 3–15). The term we use for this is *exploding*. For instance, the process of creating a month-end report may require two inputs, sales data and cost data (for simplicity, the other processes that send and receive information have been left out of the figure). We can look inside, or explode, the process called "Create Month-End Report" (note the verb plus noun construction of the name) and see that there are four subprocesses (accumulate revenue

Figure 3–13 DATA FLOW DIAGRAM

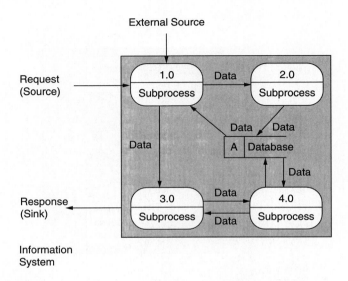

data, accumulate cost data, determine exceptions, and create report) connected internally by a set of data flows. There are also two data stores for accumulating information for the month, one for cost and the other for sales. Finally, note that even when we explode the process, there are still two inputs and one output, exactly the same as in the unexploded process. Exploding neither creates nor destroys data flows; all it does is provide us with a look inside.

In general, business information processes do more than change one input into one output. Most accept a set of inputs and produce a set of outputs. The following examples are common forms of processes found in information systems:

- One input, two outputs—splitting one set of data into two by sorting through accounts receivable and sifting out orders that are at least 30 days overdue from orders not overdue; each is processed differently
- One input, many outputs—splitting one set of data into a series of categories by sorting through a mailing list and generating a series of form letters for different customer classes
- Two inputs, one output—merging two sets of data into one by merging a set of new members into a membership list
- Two inputs, two outputs—updating a master file where the inputs are the transactions and the old master file, and the output is a new master file and a list of bad transactions
- Multiple inputs, multiple outputs (see Figure 3–16)—a complex general query in which input consists of an old master, a request from a user, a prestored set of parameters that describe the user (for example, bill

| Figure | 3–14 | DATA FLOW DIAGRAM SYMBOLS AND TITLES |

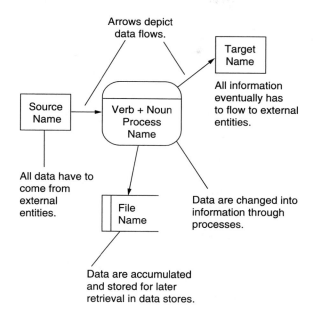

payment history), and system parameters (for example, inventory levels). Output consists of a new master, new information on the user (if supplied in the request from the user), a log of errors that may have occurred while processing the user's request, an audit or transaction log that merely copies the user's request (useful if the user turns out to be someone who is trying to sabotage the master file), and responses to the user's request as well as error messages, prompts, and help messages to the user. There are at least four inputs and six outputs in this complex situation. Note that two of the outputs are directed back to the same place (the user) and that we have indicated files (data stores) as sources and sinks of information rather than indicating other processes. These are considered valid patterns in DFDs.

The previous list of examples focused only on operational processes in a DFD, but informational roles for higher-level managers may also be depicted. In Figure 3–17, Manager A informs shift supervisors that extra care needs to be taken with packaging—a change in policy requiring a new procedure. Manager B, attempting to understand why sales have dropped off, asks for production figures and delivery schedules. Manager C has received sales projections from marketing and is revising productivity requirements that factory supervisors will be asked to comment on. Manager D compiles production exception reports (such as equipment failures) and is trying to determine a maintenance pattern to formulate new equipment procurement policies. Finally, Manager E is an executive who receives summary production reports on a regular basis. Only some of this

Figure 3–15 EXPLODING DFDs

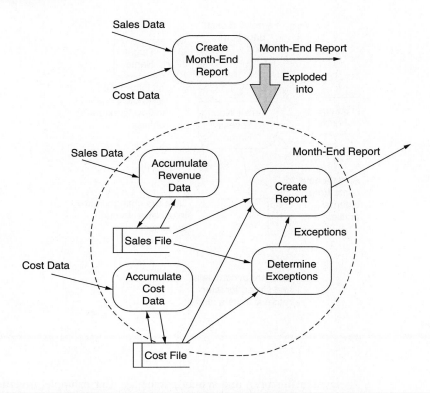

interaction with management concerns day-to-day production; the rest is focused on organizational learning to better cope with a capricious environment.

By using DFDs, we can understand both information-intensive business processes as well as information-driven processes that we call information systems. Certainly, these diagrams can become rather complex. Even the complex general query described previously is simple in comparison with large information systems such as those we will refer to later in this text. However complex or simple, DFDs clearly model the important functions of information systems: accepting and handling input, transforming and memorizing data, and producing output used to control other systems in the environment.

BUSINESS PROCESS REENGINEERING

Knowledge of business processes and associated information processes can lead to improved organizations and, more specifically, to competitive advantage. This is known as **business process reengineering (BPR).** The term is associated with an article by Michael Hammer called "Reengineering Work: Don't Automate, Obliterate" and the resulting best-seller, written with James Champy, entitled *Reengineering the Corporation: A Manifesto for Business Revolution.* Hammer and Champy see information systems as central to

Figure 3–16 COMPLEX GENERAL QUERY

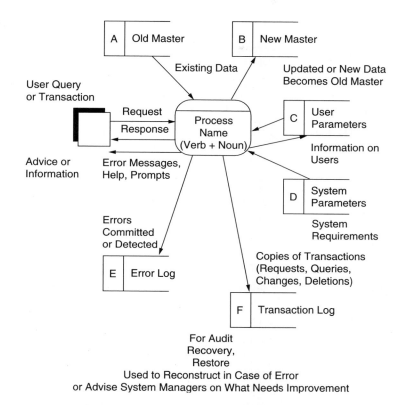

the process of reinventing the organization by using information power to eliminate unwanted or redundant processes rather than merely automating them.

Central to BPR is understanding business processes and the key role information plays. For example, Hammer and Champy examine rules such as "Managers make all the decisions" or "Personal contact is the best contact." At one time these rules may have been the best or only way to work, but today systems, and processes that grow up around them, are often dysfunctional. When only one person makes all the decisions or all paperwork is channeled through only one person, bottlenecks occur. Today, highly trained people can take responsibility for their own performance, and decision support systems, databases, and modeling software diffuse this responsibility in appropriate ways. Personal contact may be best in some cases, but it's always expensive to have downtime caused by travel. Interactive systems (e-mail, group systems, videoconferencing, Internet) are good substitutes for personal contact and have some added benefits in terms of recording and paperwork.

The goals of BPR include not only improvement but also rebuilding the organization based on processes that reflect organizational goals. BPR challenges the assumptions upon which business processes and the resulting organization and information systems are built. BPR asks: Are these processes central to our mission? Are the processes effective? Are the

---

| Figure 3–17 | MANAGEMENT ROLES IN THE BUSINESS PROCESS |

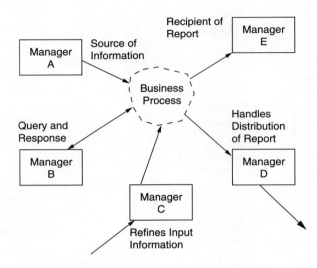

---

processes efficient? These are not simple questions. For example, to determine whether a process is central to the organizational mission means that the mission must be clear. A core process is one that is critical to, or part of, delivering a service or product to a customer. Core processes can be valued in economic terms. We called them *basic processes* earlier in this chapter, but many organizations are confused about what their basic processes are because their mission is ambiguous, confused, diffused, or intangible.

For a process to be effective it is necessary first to know how to measure the effectiveness of the process. Consider a process by which customer orders are taken. This process is effective when customer orders are taken accurately and rapidly. Do we have measures of accuracy and speed for this sort of process? Developing a set of measures may be a complex task. The same difficulties arise when efficiency is analyzed. Many existing processes were efficient at one time, but some of the original purpose of the process may have been lost. For example, it may have been necessary at one time to ask for complete customer information. Now, however, we can use a customer database that supplies partial customer data, which makes the order-taking process more efficient. The old need for redundancy to ensure accuracy is no longer present so the process is inefficient.

BPR is heavily dependent on understanding organizations as systems of interlocking processes. It is one of a set of methods of organizational redesign or renewal. These methods include organizational development (OD), total quality management (TQM), business system planning (BSP), and systems analysis and design (SAD). The methods come from different fields including human resources, organizational behavior, information systems, and industrial engineering, but what they have in common is a philosophy of analyzing organizational effectiveness either on a personal or interpersonal basis or as a system with inputs and outputs. In Module 3, we will look much more closely at organizational renewal techniques from an information systems vantage point. Business process reengineering combines information systems techniques with approaches from strategic business planning. Its goal is to achieve major improvements (revolutionary, not merely incremental) in these areas:

- New systems, including new information systems for new business functions
- Improved job designs and appraisal and monitoring systems
- New or improved work flows for new and complex interactions both internally and with customers

The creation of business models can be challenged, redrawn, and improved. Most organizational renewal activities rely on diagrams and models to some extent. BPR is especially closely tied to models because of the key role information plays in redesign activities.

Measurements are essential when using models in BPR because they enable analysts to compare proposed models with existing situations from economic and performance standpoints. More important is that models used in BPR must be understandable to managers, who have the responsibility for executing the business processes. Unless the models give managers a strong feeling for what is right, the managers cannot be faulted for failing to understand the advantage of one design over another.

Thomas Davenport has proposed a detailed framework for implementing BPR. His advice is to seek out and destroy processes that Hammer and Champy call *dysfunctional*. Dysfunctional symptoms include:

- Redundancy, rekeying (high processing costs that don't add value)
- Inventory and buffers for information (high storage costs are indicated)
- Lots of checking and control relative to value adding (high overhead)
- Rework, iteration
- Complexity, exceptions, special cases

Davenport's advice is to enumerate the business's major processes and determine where processes interact—the system boundaries. Next he advises assessing the strategic relevance of each process, judging the value or health of each process, and examining political issues and the corporate culture surrounding each process. Managers will be able to recognize these characteristics far more quickly than IS professionals. A high-cost process will be accompanied by frustration, error, anger, conflict, boredom, and a feeling of lack of accomplishment. These symptoms show up in employees' work habits, productivity, and attitudes. Most managers should be able to locate dysfunctional processes within minutes if they have access to appropriate business models.

According to Jenny McClune, companies are reengineering in six ways that directly involve information systems:

- By standardizing the kind of software used across the entire firm
- By purchasing and tailoring standard packages rather than building their own
- By switching from large mainframe systems to more flexible ones based on networked microcomputers
- By integrating applications, systems, and machines across departmental boundaries

■ By eliminating redundancy in hardware

■ By building "once and done" processes to eliminate repetition and data redundancy

These goals are also consistent with the trend toward quality management in which customer needs and service come first; processes are designed with customer needs in mind rather than hardware limitations or programmer demands. Simple, nonredundant integrated systems are easier to build and maintain and, more important, are easier for managers to understand and use. A recent survey of reengineering projects points out that while more than half of such efforts are aimed at cost reduction and productivity improvement, customer satisfaction is an expressed goal in about one-third of the projects.

There is by no means universal agreement that BPR is a panacea for business revitalization, but there is a lot of hype around BPR as a movement, which Davenport acknowledges in a mid-1994 article. Because BPR is in its infancy, we should be questioning its assumptions, especially its uniqueness and the need to obliterate. Furthermore, whatever the short-term effectiveness of BPR (and the long-term effectiveness has yet to be established scientifically), the reality is that there is no such thing as a permanent, effective change. Systems and businesses that have been reengineered will have to be reengineered again as systems and businesses change the equilibria they have established.

The Modern Management Imperatives

Reach: Global Competition	Business process modeling is essential in moving from organizational goals to strategic competitive processes. Only if we understand what is core to our business can we counter global competition. To compete globally, we have to rationalize, simplify, and organize core processes.
Reaction: Quick Customer Feedback on Products and Services	Customer feedback is an essential element of a core, or primary, business process. Designing these processes into the process rather than reverse engineering them in later is a key element in BPR.
Responsiveness: Shortened Concept-to-Customer Cycle Time	The business process model, along with key measurements of efficiency and effectiveness, can expose bottlenecks in the product/service delivery process. Design processes support and renew primary, core business processes. Integrating these can introduce new efficiencies to shorten the concept-to-customer cycle time.
Refinement: Greater Customer Sophistication and Specificity	Customer sophistication drives the quality movement and is fragmenting markets. Support processes focus on customers and keep customer information up-to-date.
Reconfiguration: Reengineering of Work Patterns and Structures	A business process model is the key element in BPR. Understanding data flows and information relationships is crucial to rebuilding the organization's processes in response to rapidly changing customer needs.
Redeployment: Reorganization and Redesign of Resources	Redeployment of resources requires special attention to systems for controlling and maintaining the resources, a key aspect of support processes and essential in BPR. Administrative processes maintain information about resources.
Reputation: Quality and Reliability of Product and Process	A focus on customers implies key informational roles for customers (for example, feedback or design) in business processes. Performance analysis is key to maintaining quality as part of the core business activities.

■ TIE TANIUM GARMENTS' PRODUCTION SYSTEM PROCESSES

Each shift begins with work orders detailing the materials to be used, the number, type, and style of garments to be produced, and the lot number to which a work order belongs. Types and styles are found in the garment catalog. Lot numbers are used to decrease the need for storage and to produce only as many garments of a specific type and style as are needed when it takes more than one shift to produce a lot for a specific customer. Machine operators produce the garments and then fill out additional information on the work order, indicating the number of garments produced of each type and style, amount and type of materials used, problems encountered (such as material shortages, inability to fill the order, damage done to the lot), and the initials of the operator. The work orders, provided by the Order Processing department (using information from sales agents in the marketplace), are then examined by the shift supervisor for reasonableness, initialed, and returned along with the lot to Order Processing.

The Material Control department is concerned with raw materials (fabric, accessories, thread) and one copy of the work order is sent there. Material Control uses the information on type of materials used to keep a rough inventory of fabric and accessories and to place orders through buyers, if necessary. It prepares a weekly report on materials used that is sent to the general manager. Shift supervisors prepare a shift report (a summary of each lot handled including number of garments of each type and style made) based on the work orders and file them away to be used later to prepare a weekly report that is sent to the general manager. In the general manager's office, the two reports are reconciled, and weekly and monthly efficiency reports are prepared, summarizing productivity by operator, by type of garment and style, and by shift, and sent to the vice president of production. ■

1. Draw a diagram illustrating the ongoing business processes at TTG.

2. Prepare a data flow diagram modeling the information flow for production at TTG.

3. Identify processes at TTG that potentially may be reengineered. How does the information system analysis in Question 2 help with this identification?

Summary   Businesses are systems. They adapt to their environments of other business systems while at the same time attempt to accomplish their goals. Their interaction consists of an exchange of resources, energy, and information. Components of a business system facilitate adaptation by sensing environmental conditions, alerting to crucial changes in these conditions, and making decisions about how to counter the conditions. Systems that can perform this adaptation are cybernetic systems. Business systems are even more complex; they adapt to capricious and dangerous business environments by changing their decision-making patterns and their business processes based on information from the environment.

Three classes of business processes are basic (creating the firm's products or making the firm's services available), support (assisting the basic processes), and administrative (controlling or accounting for the other processes in a cybernetic sense). Administrative and support processes are information-driven in that they require and produce information. Information systems such as these business processes incorporate information in essential ways. An information system can be modeled with the use of a data flow diagram that reflects the ways information relates processes to one another. Because information is essential to business processes, improving or reengineering business processes relies heavily on information systems for effectiveness.

Discussion Questions

3.1 The definition of a system seems to leave open the question of how to determine whether a particular element is in a system or not. What challenge does the looseness of this definition present to analysts who are trying to improve a business system? To illustrate this challenge, write a paragraph that defines and describes the registration system of your university or college, and discuss the challenges of specifying what should be in the system and what shouldn't be.

3.2 One of the disadvantages of increased cybernetic complexity and learning systems is the additional assemblies of elements needed to sense the environment and make decisions and the cost of interconnecting these assemblies. What are the costs and how are they evidenced? There are also increased risks. What are they and how are they evidenced?

3.3 An element need not reside within a single system. People, in particular, may play roles in many systems simultaneously. Consider yourself and the many systems within which you act. Describe your interaction within several of these systems. Are there conflicts? How do you resolve these conflicts? Do managers also experience these kinds of conflicts? How do they cope?

3.4 A data flow diagram (DFD) can be used to describe any system in which information flows play a key role. What do you think the advantages and disadvantages would be of using a DFD to describe how managers make decisions? Explain, for example, why it takes a long time to process loan applications and the improvements that could be made in processing student-union election votes.

Key Terms

action loop	data flow diagram (DFD)	policy loop
administrative process	data relationship	process model
basic process	environment	simple system
business process reengineering (BPR)	equilibrium	support process
	feedback	system
control loop	general systems theory (GST)	system architecture
cybernetic system	learning system	system boundary
data flow	organization	system view

References

Ashby, W. R. *An Introduction to Cybernetics*. London: University Paperbacks, 1965.

Bateson, G. *Steps to an Ecology of Mind*. San Francisco: Chandler, 1972.

Brousell, David, J. Moad, and C. Staiti. "CIOs Put the 'T' back in IT." *Datamation* 39, 23 (December 1, 1993): 28–33.

Davenport, Thomas. *Process Innovation: Reengineering Work through Information Technology*. Boston: Harvard Business School Press, 1993.

Davenport, T., and D. Stoddard. "Reengineering: Business Change of Mythic Proportions?" *MIS Quarterly* 18, 2 (June 1994): 121–128.

DeMarco, Tom. *Structured Analysis and System Specification*. Englewood Cliffs, NJ: Prentice-Hall, 1979.

Douglas, D., ed. "The Role of IT in Business Reengineering." *I/S Analyzer* 31, 8 (August 1993): 1–16.

Gane, C., and T. Sarson. *Structured Systems Analysis: Tools and Techniques*. Englewood Cliffs, NJ: Prentice-Hall, 1979.

Hammer, Michael. "Reengineering Work: Don't Automate, Obliterate." *Harvard Business Review* (July–August 1990): 104–112.

Hammer, Michael, and James Champy. *Reengineering the Corporation: A Manifesto for Business Revolution*. New York: Harper, 1993.

Housel, T. J., C. J. Morris, and C. Westland. "Business Process Reengineering at Pacific Bell." *Planning Review* (May–June 1993): 28–33.

Licker, P. *Fundamentals of Systems Analysis with Application Design*. Boston: Boyd & Fraser, 1987.

McClune, Jenny. "Information Systems Get Back to Basics." *Management Review* (January 1994): 54–60.

Rupp, C. G. "Integrated Process Capture and Process Analysis Tools in Support of Business Reengineering Applications." Proceedings, CE&CALS, Washington, DC, 1993.

Wiener, Norbert. *Cybernetics*. Cambridge, MA: MIT Press, 1948.

Yourdon, E. *Techniques of Program Structure and Design*. Englewood Cliffs, NJ: Prentice-Hall, 1979.

CASE

EVERGREEN LANDSCAPING AND MAINTENANCE: BUSINESS PROCESSES

Connie Somerset, sales manager, worked for Shawna Eggert, vice president of sales, for five years and in that time made Evergreen's marketing systems hum. Tulley Fox is the purchasing manager who handles the paperwork and does some buying. Tulley's been in the business for more than 20 years and really knows growing things. His contacts in the industry have kept costs and delivery times down. Tulley runs his own shop and considers Connie to be a good customer. Sid Cavenaugh, assistant manager of contract services, and Sven Haroldson, assistant manager of retail, are both recent university graduates with little experience in the lawn, landscaping, or gardening business, but they are competent organizers and face challenges head-on. Sometimes they have good ideas, but as the guaranteed green-up program demonstrated, good ideas aren't always enough. Connie has had to keep close tabs on their innovations.

Evergreen works very much like a hybrid retail/consulting organization. On the retail side, Connie makes projections of what will sell and Tulley looks around the world to find these items. Connie runs promotions and sets prices, both of which she frequently adjusts as inventory levels and the need to meet sales and profit targets become more important at different times of the year. Sven's staff works to attractively and efficiently fill the retail space with the products. Most products are ordered through wholesale dealers and growers are contacted by Tulley. Sometimes an opportunity arises when a vendor is promoting a new product, and Connie makes additional shelf space available if she thinks the product will boost sales of related items or bring in new customers. Customers generally look at the shelves or wander through the greenhouses to find items they want. But often customers request items that are misplaced, out of stock, or just invisible in all that greenery. Clerks consult printed inventory lists that are updated weekly during the year and every other day, in theory, during the busy seasons. In fact, however, these updates are performed far less frequently. This is a problem Connie is aware of but is not handling right now. She knows that keeping inventory up-to-date will require an online system integrated with the cash registers. But Evergreen has only just installed point-of-sale (POS) terminals to handle sales. Whenever a retail sale is made, sales information is generated about the item, date, volume, and price. Priscilla Chan, the controller, handles the money accounting, and Al Lampert makes sure the live plants inventory is kept alive and available.

In Sid's operation, things are less volatile, although a lot of paperwork must be done. Customers are found through advertisements in local newspapers, newspaper supplements, magazines, the yellow pages, or through word of mouth. Sid usually negotiates the contracts himself, although when business increases he gets help from one of the architects he employs. Part of each bid is an estimate of materials. When Evergreen wins a bid, a copy of this estimate is passed to Tulley, who verifies availability, prepares the necessary order forms, and alerts the operations manager to prepare for stocking items. Al doesn't have space to store large items such as fountains, big trees, and boulders, so he wants to make sure these items are delivered to the site instead of to Evergreen's warehouses and greenhouses. However, delivery dates are always approximate, and weather can pose problems. Smaller items are less of a problem, but finding space and, more important, putting items where they can be retrieved are concerns Al has. His assistants move all the stock using trucks that Bill Porter, transportation supervisor, controls, so there is a potential for friction when there is a rush or a delay because of weather or customer wavering. Bill needs his trucks to move stock to customers, not to move trees around the greenhouse. Operational difficulties with stock, transportation, and disposal are constant challenges that Thomas Davidoff, vice president of operations, has faced since his days with the tree farm. Juggling the simultaneous demands of contract customers with the more steady "background" needs of retailing requires the tact of Solomon and the speed of an olympic hurdler.

While all this is going on in retail, Lily Doucette, president, does medium- and long-term planning with the management executive committee (MEC). The MEC handles policy matters and is comprised of a core of vice presidents and their assistants. Heather Cariad handles money and Frances Harmon handles everything else. Heather's operation is a traditional accounting function involving accounts receivable (mostly from contracts and credit card buyers), accounts payable, and cash flow and investment management. Evergreen has a lot of money tied up in inventory at crucial times of the year, and its plan to upgrade and expand the retail store, including opening a second store this year, has given Heather and Priscilla a lot to think about.

Frances Harmon, on the other hand, is concerned with the employees. There is a high turnover among the seasonal staff, and she must handle employee benefits and a great deal of internal communication. During the spring and early summer, life is frantic at Evergreen, and Frances has responsibility for keeping employees on track, motivated, and feeling rewarded. She also works closely with Priscilla and Connie on public and community relations. Because Evergreen is really three businesses (landscaping, lawns, and retail gardening), there is a need to integrate the employees, the work, and the products, and responsibility for this falls to Frances. Finally, Frances is concerned with employee development, so she conducts an annual performance appraisal exercise aimed at updating skill profiles (she stresses the importance of maintaining this data) and recommending training. Frances puts on a number of in-house training sessions, especially for seasonal workers, and she sends a number of managers and supervisors to management training courses each year as appropriate to their job descriptions. Performance in these courses is noted in employee files along with job performance appraisal data.

The final member of the MEC is Thomas Davidoff. Tom has been with Lily since the early days of the company and handles anything to do with operations and the physical plant. Byron Todd is the supervisor of all buildings, all of which require constant maintenance and planning. High humidity required for the plants makes maintenance a nightmare, and the glass greenhouses are fragile and targets for vandalism. Candice Robbins handles security. She has four security guards who patrol the buildings 24 hours a day; they also prevent pilferage and try to keep plants from being crushed. Carts used by customers are sometimes stolen, and hardly a week goes by without a child getting lost among the annuals or a customer getting scratched by a cactus.

Evergreen is a complex operation simultaneously engaged in many processes. Connie knows she can't sell without knowing what's happening with inventory, in the greenhouses, in the parking lots, in the bank accounts. Everything seems tightly interconnected to her and a lot more challenging than the hardware store she was used to.

Questions

1. Describe Evergreen as a system. What is its boundary? What elements lie in its environment? What are the internal elements and some of their relationships?

2. Evergreen has basic, support, and administrative processes. Provide three examples from the case for each category.

3. Draw a diagram similar to Figure 3–14 depicting the interaction of various processes found at Evergreen. A "driving process" (or "business driver") is a process that originates or motivates all or most of the activity. Locate the driving process(es) in this diagram and tell how they function. What sort of influence (indicated by arrows) comes from the driving process(es), and what power does Connie have to affect the amount and kind of influence (that is, what power does Connie have at Evergreen to make things happen)?

4. Answer the following questions (restated from this chapter) for Evergreen.

   ■ Where is the critical path in relations with customers?

   ■ What kinds of delays could outside suppliers impose?

   ■ Which process(es) would be a bottleneck in the overall process?

   ■ How do the individual processes communicate with each other?

   ■ What resources (data, raw materials, semifinished products, final products) flow between individual processes?

   ■ Where could errors occur and in which processes further down the line could errors occur?

   ■ What does each process cost Evergreen? What is the nature of these costs?

   ■ Are there any redundant (duplicated) or extraneous (useless) processes?

   ■ If a customer is dissatisfied or doesn't like the product, how does this affect the individual processes in the business?

   ■ To what extent do individual processes contribute to the overall sales and customer service goals?

5. What role does information play in the processes that are of concern to Connie? Working with another person, discuss the information processes that are important to Connie. Then draw a data flow diagram detailing the information flows in the marketing function. What role does Connie play in sourcing, processing, and/or receiving this information? Remember the principles of cybernetic systems when you answer this question. (Do not worry about technical accuracy at this time.) Creating DFDs of this sort is the first step in classical application development (see Chapters 12–15) as well as in BPR.

CHAPTER FOUR

Strategic Advantage

OBJECTIVES

After you have read and studied this chapter, you should be able to:

■ Define the word *strategic.*

■ Identify five generic strategic advantages that a business might employ.

■ Apply three models of competition: Porter's competitive forces model, the customer product life cycle, and the strategic IS cycle model.

■ Describe the type and degree of strategic advantage specific activities engender.

■ Discuss how to implement information system-initiated strategic advantage.

Q u e s t i o n : What competitive advantages can an information system provide to an organization? What does it mean to "compete with information"?

As sole proprietor of Vacuums-R-Us, Ed Angelica knows that the competition is stiff in his business. Not only are margins dreadfully low, but his marketplace is becoming increasingly demanding and cautious; too many people have been stung with central vacuum systems that don't work correctly, are expensive to repair, or have been installed poorly by amateurs. Ed runs his business from a strip mall near the old core of town, not exactly the most advantageous place to be but all he can afford. Besides, a lot of traffic passes his door. A trained mechanical engineer, Ed moved into retail and service when he was laid off from his previous job a year ago. After a lot of soul-searching, he took his termination payout and used it to buy an existing vacuum business, figuring his technical knowledge would be enough. It's been tough and he's barely making it, but he wants to achieve some advantage over his competitors. He suspects that using information systems to maintain a better relationship with customers and suppliers would help, but he doesn't know where to start. How can he use computers to bring in a few more customers?

A n s w e r : Ed will learn that being competitive means offering more, new, unique, attractive, or cheaper services. He can choose to offer his products at lower cost, provide different products or services, aim at a niche market, form a new business, or form an alliance with existing businesses. IS can help in each area. Understanding the customer product life cycle will also show Ed some places where increased or better information can help combat the five competitive forces.

INTRODUCTION

Information systems have always provided advantages to organizations; however, these advantages are also easy for competitors to gain or negate. This chapter explores the idea of using information systems technology to gain **competitive advantage.** At first glance it may not seem apparent how information systems technology can provide competitive advantage. Aren't they really just used to crunch numbers and produce reports? The answer is complex and fascinating. While computers do indeed crunch numbers and produce reports (in great numbers, at high speeds, and with remarkable accuracy), our focus is on the use of information in business and management. Consider the difference between coin tossing and market intelligence. In the former case, there cannot be any competitive advantage in marketing products because the outcomes are randomly distributed. Unless all competitors are pathologically poor decision makers, one business's decisions cannot be any better than others' over a significant period of time. From time to time, a coin toss will direct a business to make a good decision, but the more complex the market, the less likely that the coin's instructions will be appropriate.

However, if a business is engaging in rational and effective market intelligence, it is gathering information. To the extent that the information is appropriate in the first place, a business cannot be put at a disadvantage having it. Assume, however, that the same information is available to other businesses in some form and the major tasks are (1) assembling the information, (2) making sense of it, and (3) not being overwhelmed by the volume. Wouldn't a business have considerable advantage if it were able to perform these tasks efficiently and effectively? These are precisely the tasks information systems perform.

Furthermore, value that is added by this information is enhanced through human creativity, communication, and personal power. Because an effective information system can be directed in flexible ways, advantage is increased by facilitating rapid assembly, recombination, and display of information for more creativity. Because an effective information system links people with databases and with each other, communication can be added to strengthen the advantage. In many cases, increasing the number of people is a drag on performance because of the overhead involved in information sharing and consensus. Clearly, being able to manage interaction allows the group's power to be channeled profitably. Finally, because an effective and efficient information system assists rather than impedes individual information handling, an individual's advantage in exercising personal power can only be increased. Thus, information systems support and empower corporate and individual decision making in ways that directly provide advantages.

In this chapter, we will examine the meaning of strategic advantage and introduce two important models that clarify strategic advantage: the customer product life cycle model and Porter's five competitive forces model. These models will help us locate where and when information systems can be used for strategic advantage and how that advantage can be achieved. The chapter ends by looking at specific ways in which information systems provide strategic advantage to individuals and firms during a life cycle of strategic employment of technology using Cash, McKenney, and McFarlan's strategic grid model.

This chapter is the first of three that examine strategic advantage of information systems, both to individual managers as well as to firms within an industry. The models introduced in this chapter help us locate where strategic advantage might be achieved through the use of technology or information or both. Chapter 4 focuses mostly on technology and how increases in efficiency can lead to cost reduction or lowered risks in introducing new products or services while building barriers to competition. However, technology is not all there is to strategic advantage in information systems.

Venkatraman's critical article, "IT-Enabled Business Transformation: From Automation to Business Scope Redefinition," introduces a hierarchy of information-technology assisted changes to business, of which technological advantage is only the first, and often the least, effective. As noted later in this chapter, technologically based advantages are often transitory and difficult to maintain. Venkatraman points out that the experience an organization gains—its knowledge—is the sustainable advantage. Organizing that knowledge into an integrated database is the focus of Chapter 5. Integration, according to Venkatraman, affords a higher level of strategic advantage because it makes an organization more flexible and able to provide better service to customers.

The next level of strategic advantage is achieved through business process redesign with information (the subject of Chapter 3). At a higher level, Venkatraman sees strategic advantage institutionalized through interorganizational links, a network of knowledge that a firm can build not only within the firm but with strategic partners (Chapter 6). Finally, Venkatraman sees a business's ability to use and diffuse knowledge as a key component in redefining its scope by selling information-based products and services that it controls. In the past, these services and products have been created almost accidentally in many cases, because information technologists don't necessarily have the corporate vision or power to sell them and corporate leaders don't have the necessary technological savvy. Bridging this gap is the subject of later chapters.

STRATEGIC MEANS COMPETITIVE

We use the word *strategic* somewhat narrowly to mean *competitive*. *Strategic* often is used to mean looking into the future or predicting what others will do. Here we mean it in its original sense: developing tricks or plans for deceiving or outwitting an enemy (*strategy* is derived from two Greek roots meaning "to lead an army"). Because the word *strategic* is often used to mean what businesses do to be competitive, it is important to examine that word and ask, What makes something, anything, strategic? (See Figure 4–1.)

- Strategic means having a specific advantage over a competitor. This usually means that a firm's products are cheaper or better than those of a competitor or that a firm is in a better position to compete (for example, by having a longer-term lease in a tightening real estate market or having more well-trained staff).

- Strategic means being new, novel, or innovative. A company's products or services might never have been seen before or never used in a particular way. For example, a company may invent a new process for making photocopies or be especially innovative in how it handles customer complaints.

- Strategic often means being unique. No other firm can create or deliver a particular product or service. This product or service may not necessarily be new (the only shoe store in town has a strategic advantage, but it's probably not the case that no one in town has heard of shoes before).

- Strategic can also mean attractiveness to customers. Customers want a product or service and willingly pay for it.

| Figure 4-1 | STRATEGIC MEANS COMPETITIVE |

What Makes Something "Strategic"?

□ Advantage over Competitors
  • Competitors' Offerings Are Less

□ Newness, Novelty, Innovation
  • Never Seen Before, Never Used This Way

□ Uniqueness
  • No One Else Has This or Can Make or Deliver It

□ Attractiveness to Customers
  • Customers Want It, Will Pay for It

□ Profitable
  • Not Too Expensive to Make or Offer

- Strategic must mean profitable (in the for-profit sector, of course; supportable at a specific funding level in the not-for-profit sector). Without profit, advantage is not worth having. Anybody can make a unique, new, attractive product to be given away, but this kind of advantage is nonsustainable.

A company can attempt to achieve **strategic advantage** in a variety of ways. Five generic competitive strategies appear in the business literature, illustrated in Figure 4–2.

1. **Low cost.** This strategy makes the product or service available at a cost that is lower than that of all or most of a firm's competitors. Naturally, customers see this as an advantage. Cutting prices doesn't require a lot of effort, but there are obviously limits to this strategy when profitability disappears. Also, as profits shrink, the ability to innovate and differentiate other products and services disappears.

2. **Differentiation.** Using differentiation as a strategy means making a firm's products or services noticeably different. Consider household appliances. Manufacturers and retailers continually attempt to make them different by applying different finishing touches or adding different features. One minor league baseball team differentiated its product (live athletic entertainment) by starting its games at 7:05 just to make it different from other sports teams that usually start on the hour or half hour. Differentiation works by making a product more memorable and easy to compare favorably to other products. Differentiation's advantage is that it doesn't have to involve price haggling and can, in fact, be done completely with advertising and positioning. A disadvantage is that it is easy to differentiate so much that the base market is lost.

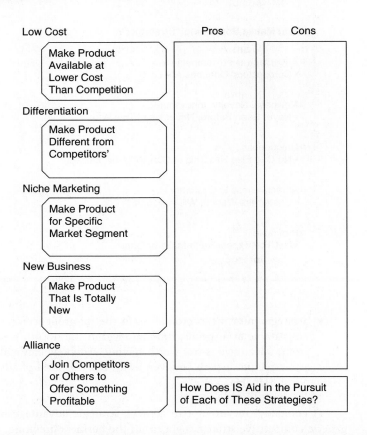

Figure 4—2 GENERIC COMPETITIVE STRATEGIES

3. **Niche marketing.** Pursuing a niche market entails selling a product or service into a small, relatively homogeneous market that is interested in one type of product. For example, many magazines sell to specialty markets that are very small compared to the larger markets of general news magazines, and pet cemeteries and premium pet foods are a niche market. Niche markets are relatively easy to service because the homogeneity in the marketplace makes selling easier. However, niche markets are relatively small and subject to fads and whims that may make them disappear overnight. Microcomputers began as a niche market for hobbyists, but today there are many niche markets for microcomputer software. Publishers can create magazines for any market including sports that are pursued by only a few hundred people, collectors, and fans of the British royal family.

4. **New business.** Sometimes a firm creates a product that is so different that it radically changes how the firm does business, so much so that the firm is really in a new kind of business. A computer consulting firm that makes its living contracting out its own labor to competitors (sometimes called a body shop) might discover that it has achieved enough experience to offer specialty courses. It thus

reorganizes itself as a training/consulting firm with an entirely different structure, payroll, vision statement, and corporate goals. IBM began as a firm that sold paper-tape, programmable clocks, but when it took over a failing computer business, it drastically changed into a marketing firm, then later became a high-tech manufacturer, and now seems to be a cross between a marketing firm and a service bureau. American Airlines hinted recently that its profit is made mostly from its Sabre reservations system. Its president has stated publicly that AA could sell its fleet, subcontract passenger transportation, and retain the highly profitable computerized Sabre system, thereby becoming a service bureau rather than an integrated, full-service airline. Generally, pursuing this strategy is risky, and many firms fall into new businesses by accident rather than actively pursue this strategy.

5. **Alliance.** Firms may join with their competitors, suppliers, or buyers to form an alliance. There are several kinds of alliance. A strategic alliance is built around supplier-buyer relations in order to create efficiencies and guarantee supplies. The **vertical integration** thus achieved makes a firm secure, although the exclusiveness implied by the relationship also means that not much redundancy is built in; if the marketing arm fails to sell correctly, even the best product will not be bought. Firms often buy suppliers to guarantee supplies. Systems that support strategic alliances are often called **interorganizational systems**—systems that span organizational boundaries. One of the best examples of such a system is called **electronic data interchange (EDI),** which uses electronic equivalents of paperwork or forms. Because the computer at the heart of the system reads and stores information, forms are simplified and shortened; there is never any need for multiple copies. EDI is great as a link between buyer and supplier companies or for work teams. Other firms may enter into **precompetitive consortia,** associations of competitors who agree that some aspect of their business should not be the basis of competition. They may develop systems or processes that raise the whole industry's quality or cost effectiveness, and so long as they deal honestly and are correct in their assumptions about the basis of competition, governments encourage this sort of activity. Numerous precompetitive consortia exist in various industries to create technology or to develop new business processes. For example, the oil industry may support an initiative to make available all core drilling data that make the geological aspect of oil searching less risky. Alliances are valuable because they create and help disseminate knowledge and lower the original ante for competition. A problem with alliances is that if a firm locks in a supplier, it may be at the mercy of that supplier. Automobile companies learn this every time their suppliers experience labor problems.

A key factor is determining how information systems can assist firms that choose to pursue each of these competitive (or precompetitive) strategies. For example, computers have historically been used to lower costs by supplanting human labor, and we are probably seeing some of the negative effects of this in a displacement of clerical labor in the work force. After 40 years of routinizing and computerizing clerical work, few purely clerical jobs are left that individuals with only a high school degree can obtain. Now information systems are changing factory work through automation and robotics. Whether the move toward executive information systems (Chapter 8) will ultimately displace executive labor is a matter for speculation, but, clearly, automation and computerization require new skill requirements at every level if they don't actually displace labor. There is probably some limit to how far businesses can go with computer-driven cost cutting.

Differentiation is aided through information systems in a variety of ways. Market research can establish customer preferences and determine complaints. Advertising, positioning, and packaging can affect how a product is perceived, and these activities are largely based on data that have to be manipulated for understanding. Management support systems (Module 2) can assist organizations in discovering what is unique about their product or others' products.

Niche marketing depends entirely on discovering and entering a niche market, also data-sensitive activities. Maintaining a niche market requires staying alert to an entire marketplace that may exist due to a fad, a momentary change in tastes, or demographics. Mailing lists, advertising, and test marketing generate and require a lot of data and many decisions. Some decision support systems aid in bringing order to what may otherwise seem a chaotic situation.

New businesses, however they are created, are especially susceptible to information storms, a flood of information that inundates a new venture when it starts up. Red tape can strangle almost any business, but new ones, struggling under debt and high expectations, are especially vulnerable. Even established businesses that switch to new markets or new ways of doing business may find that changed regulations, policies, customers, and distribution channels generate a lot of information that has to be handled accurately and quickly.

Alliances, whether informal or by acquisition, require communication among existing information systems. Whether these systems are working well or are cranky, creaky, and incompatible, the job of making them work together is overwhelming. In this case, information systems may be seen by the faint of heart as an impediment to alliances rather than a motivator.

Communication among existing information systems is the trickiest part of managing information technology. Systems specialists are fairly good at automating existing processes in a *single* organization, but many of them have yet to learn about merging or linking *multiple* organizations, for several reasons. First, ever-present technical challenges are made even more difficult by changing standards over the years. Also, severe and difficult human resource problems attend any merger or acquisition that interacts in complex ways with information systems. Consider what happens when modern information systems based on relational databases (Chapter 5) and client-server architectures (Chapter 6) allow linking without actually physically connecting databases. The integration problem becomes more of an opportunity and opens up a profusion of potential cooperative applications beyond the initial reasons for strategic alliance. The experience of Baxter-Travenol, a pharmaceutical supply company, shows how such advantage can be played out. Baxter-Travenol created an ordering system that was based on installed equipment that was expensive for customers to purchase. It made little economic sense for customers to fail to use the computer equipment for which they had paid a high price. Baxter-Travenol's decision to install terminals in its hospital customers' sites assisted in locking in these customers and later provided Baxter-Travenol with the opportunity to list competitors' products for a fee and make money even on sales to competitors. This is the ultimate strategic alliance: a secure customer base and competitors paying you money for every sale they make.

THE CUSTOMER PRODUCT LIFE CYCLE

Another way to look at strategic advantage is to examine a business process model and come to some conclusions about where in the process advantage could be gained. This is called the **customer product life cycle model** (see Figure 4–3). For example, in a given industry, most competitors do business the same way. Suppose we look at a retailer from

| Figure 4–3 | CUSTOMER PRODUCT LIFE CYCLE |

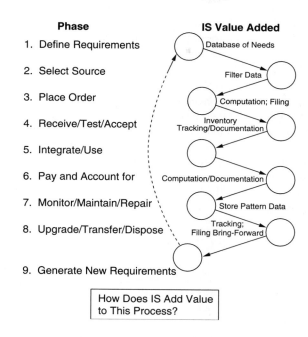

Phase

1. Define Requirements
2. Select Source
3. Place Order
4. Receive/Test/Accept
5. Integrate/Use
6. Pay and Account for
7. Monitor/Maintain/Repair
8. Upgrade/Transfer/Dispose
9. Generate New Requirements

IS Value Added

Database of Needs
Filter Data
Computation; Filing
Inventory Tracking/Documentation
Computation/Documentation
Store Pattern Data
Tracking; Filing Bring-Forward

How Does IS Add Value to This Process?

the customer's viewpoint. In general, a retailer works the same as any other retailer. Customers define the product or service requirements from their viewpoint (Phase 1). Customers select the source(s) (Phase 2) and place the order (Phase 3). In Phase 4, customers receive or test and accept the product. Phase 5 is the customers' use of the product or integration (enjoyment) of the service. In Phase 6, customers pay for the product (Phase 6 could come earlier, too). Customers then have to monitor, maintain, and repair the product in Phase 7, and there will come a time (Phase 8) when the product will have to be significantly upgraded, transferred (sold or lent to someone else), or disposed of (especially if it is a hazardous product such as a used propane tank). There is also another way of looking at this customer product life cycle—from the vendor's point of view.

For each of these phases, we can ask a question about the strategic advantage of any process, business tool, or technology. In particular, we are interested in information systems technology, so we can ask whether or not IS (sometimes called *information technology* or IT) gains value or achieves strategic advantage in each phase. For example, a customer could use a database to define product requirements; in fact, a catalog is a printed database. An information system may also go through a supplier database and select the most likely sources, providing a filter for a customer. Placing an order is a tedious task for which it may be advantageous to use information technology to handle computation and filing—a misfiled customer order is a product unsold. Customers who receive products or test them can use assistance in logging the product in. For example, think of a commercial customer who receives a shipment of purchased parts, all of which have to be logged into inventory. Documentation is also part of receiving products. Druggists who maintain prescription information by keeping a log of all customers' prescriptions perform this service.

In general, there is little strategic advantage to employing information systems tools to use other products, but there could be for specific products, particularly those that run on or with computers. Payroll and accounting are the oldest commercial information systems applications, but they no longer offer strategic advantage because almost everyone uses computers to perform these tasks. Many firms keep maintenance records of customers' purchases, especially when they purchase service agreements, and registration cards guarantee a steady flow of promotional and advertising literature and chances for customers to receive upgrades and new models at the best prices. Auto companies keep records of customers to manage recalls. Some firms that manufacture hazardous goods are finding it advantageous to call consumers if the firms anticipate that their product needs to be checked in the future based on estimates of mean time failure or disaster. And don't forget dentists—they make their money on recalls for examinations. At the end of the customer product life cycle, customers generate new requirements (Phase 9), so the cycle begins again.

PORTER'S COMPETITIVE FORCES MODEL

Porter's **competitive forces model,** illustrated in Figure 4–4, is useful because it expands on the notion of what competition is by requiring businesses to attend not only to existing industry rivals and competitors but to other forces in the competitive environment that influence how they compete. It also helps businesses understand what the advantages of high technologies such as information systems may provide in this competitive environment. In the following discussion "the firm" refers to one of the existing competitors and analysis is done from that firm's point of view.

Porter notes that rivalries among existing competitors exist in conjunction with four other forces. Along the supplier-firm-buyer chain is the **bargaining power of buyers,** who attempt to force prices down and quality up while they pick and choose among existing competitors. Buyers do this by creating buying cartels or agencies or simply by refusing to purchase at the existing price or quality. The firm, on the other hand, wants to lock buyers in by making it expensive to switch to other competitors. This is called building in a **switching cost,** and can be accomplished in the following ways:

- Charging customers to switch because they have a legally binding contract
- Changing the way customers do business so that it is expensive to change to another way of doing business
- Changing customers' physical plant so that it becomes expensive to replace buildings or equipment
- Getting customers so comfortable or used to a particular product or service that there is a high psychological cost to be paid by switching

Information systems technology can help build in a switching cost. Customers may be attracted to a particular way of doing business that is computerized and sign a contract for services. If equipment is sold or leased to customers in order to facilitate buying, it may be expensive to remove this equipment and install a competitor's. Of course, movement toward compatibility and standards may make this switching cost much lower than

| Figure 4–4 | PORTER'S FIVE COMPETITIVE FORCES |

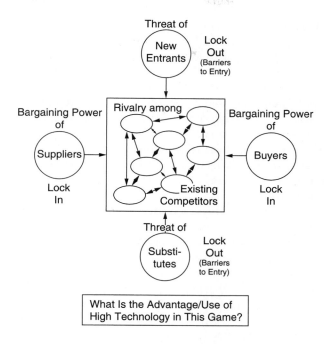

What Is the Advantage/Use of
High Technology in This Game?

expected. With standards, hardware could probably be reused, and software or databases built around commercial platforms compatible with a standard language such as SQL might be inexpensive to convert. Because learning curves for information systems are rather shallow, customers may not want to change how they work because they know they will have to learn a new system. As an example, American Airlines' Sabre system locks in travel agents with exclusive contracts that seriously limit their access to other airlines' reservation systems.

The **bargaining power of suppliers** is similar to that of customers, but in reverse. Suppliers want to secure the firm's business, giving it no option to go elsewhere for supplies. At the same time, suppliers want to deliver lower-quality supplies because they are easier and cheaper to make. The firm, in response, wants to lock the supplier in to an exclusive contract (assuming, of course, that the price and quality are satisfactory) that the firm can violate at will but the supplier must honor. Companies want assured supply lines at a given price and quality, and suppliers like to pick and choose among their customers to get the best terms. A firm that seals a nonexclusive contract for technology that makes ordering easy and error-free may lock in the supplier simply because of the advantages such technology brings. This makes life easier and more predictable for the supplier, even without an exclusive contract. Suppliers that can tap into a customer's inventory and receive notice of impending stockouts will find business a lot more predictable than those suppliers that receive urgent phone calls in the night (even if they can ask a higher price); this predictability may be most important, especially if rush orders are hard to fill.

Porter points out that besides the supplier-firm-buyer chain there are two other sources of competition, new entrants and substitutes. The threat of **new entrants** is looked upon with dismay by existing competitors. In most situations, this threat increases competition by increasing the number of competitors, thereby giving buyers more sources and suppliers more customers, driving up the cost of doing business, and forcing existing competitors to scramble to keep their existing customers.

The firm wants to lock out new entrants by raising **barriers to entry.** These barriers can be legal, physical, cultural, economic, or anything fair and allowed. Technology can assist here in many ways. As mentioned previously, there are high costs to beginning any new venture. Potential new entrants do not have industrywide information (except what is available publicly) or the experience of existing competitors. In particular, they lack information on customers, products in research and development, and detailed knowledge of supplier-buyer relationships that have already been established. They may be unfamiliar with all the details of the regulatory environment. For example, consider what a new entrant to long-distance trucking must find out about national and international road regulations.

If the firm wants a sophisticated information system in all these areas, there is an initial high cost to obtain the technology and learn how to use it. If the technology supplies real strategic advantage to a small group of competitors, then the technology cannot be purchased (i.e., it will be proprietary like American Airlines' Sabre system), so it will have to be developed at high cost. When the technology grows old, the firm may be willing to share it on a precompetitive basis with other competitors or new entrants, thus earning additional money while losing no strategic advantage (because the technology is old, it probably isn't doing much for competition at this point). Examples include customer information systems, accounting systems, point-of-sale technology, inventory systems, and production control software.

Many industries now use computers as an integral part of their competitive strategies. Consider pizza parlors that use sophisticated technology to schedule and deliver pizzas within a guaranteed time period. Airlines rely entirely on their reservations systems, and courier companies like Federal Express depend on information systems to keep their payloads in motion and know where they are. New entrants *must* have this technology or some simulation of it even to enter the business. Of course, continuing innovation means that the new entrant may already have such technology or even better. In general, information systems raise barriers to entry that are temporary but expensive; however, these barriers have to be renewed quickly or they erode.

Finally, Porter points out that we are an innovative society, always developing **substitutes** for existing products or services. Consider that most of what we buy or receive in the way of services is a replacement for something that self-sufficient families used to do for themselves. Restaurants are substitutes for cooking at home; automobiles are substitutes for walking; radios are substitutes for singing and chatting; TVs are substitutes for everything else. Likewise, computers are substitutes for calculating, filing, and writing.

As new substitutes come along, existing competitors attempt to raise barriers to their entry. Unfortunately, technology cannot really help here. The primary use of technology is to substitute for some human activity that is limited by speed, power, attention, and so forth. The only way the firm can use information systems technology to raise barriers to entry is to become its own substitute through technology. The pizza parlors mentioned previously have transformed the nature of the pizza business (at least from a customer's point of view) to a demand feeding situation. ATMs extend banking hours, becoming for many a substitute for the bank. It is now possible to arrange simple loans or insurance

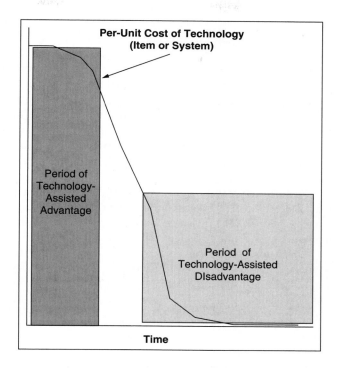

Figure 4–5   TECHNOLOGY-ASSISTED ADVANTAGE

policies through modem-connected microcomputers and bank-supplied software; the bank is becoming a home-based financial consultant.

Through this type of innovation, firms can continuously reinvent themselves, thus staying a step ahead of existing competitors and out-substituting the substitutes. Northern Telecom, a major high-technology producer of telecommunications equipment and systems headquartered in Mississaugua, Ontario, has generally given up legal pursuit of offshore chip imitators. Nortel feels that in the six months or a year it takes pirates to copy proprietary designs, it will have received more than its share of profit (see Figure 4–5). By then, cloners can fight over whatever market share scraps remain. Meanwhile, Nortel will build a new chip that substitutes for the current chip and continue to skim the top 80 percent of the marketplace without expensive legal costs. Pareto's Law tells us that getting the last 20 percent of the market will take 80 percent of the sales effort, so this strategy has solid theoretical foundations.

In Porter's view of the competitive world, the advantages of an information system are that it builds in switching costs, creates expensive barriers to entry, and allows competitors to become their own substitutes. People become accustomed to working in certain ways and resist change, especially if monetary costs are involved. Information systems present high start-up costs for potential new entrants, and software makes it easy to produce upgrades quickly without retooling factories. Whatever else it does, technology surely increases the metabolism of business, speeding up business processes and making them more information-intensive and targeted to customers.

SUSTAINING TECHNOLOGICALLY DERIVED COMPETITIVE ADVANTAGE

Whether or not information technology can create **sustainable competitive advantage** is debatable. In this section, we explore a number of ideas about the sustainability of such advantages.

In a recent article, Vitale pointed out that because technology has a limited life span, advantages from it tend to be time-limited. Vitale uses the example of a manufacturer that computerized the process of generating product and instruction lists from a customer's specifications. This provided immediate advantage in terms of cost and product innovation, but a competitor used the same technology to create an identical system on a personal computer that was given to the customer. As a bonus, the microcomputer transmitted the results via modem. The initial good idea was taken one step further and used by the first innovator.

As technology costs decrease, initial advantage is lost quickly. In fact, those who stick with innovations too long find that competitors can adopt the innovation more cheaply later on, and that the initial advantage is turned into a disadvantage in terms of cost and flexibility (see Figure 4–5).

Cragg and Finlay have expanded Porter's simple five forces model by adding a strategic dimension they call PEST (political, economic, social, and technological). They emphasize that for most industries the technological environment is wholly outside the industry using the technology, hence it is very much distinct, uncontrollable, and to an extent incomprehensible. The IT industry has several interesting attributes from a competitive standpoint:

- It exists in a global marketplace—it is a knowledge industry that has no particular geographical bias or advantage (except perhaps linguistic).
- There are many suppliers, especially of software and microcomputers.
- Product information is readily available.
- Many powerful products are available at affordable prices.
- The products work, are relatively easy to use, and help is available.

These characteristics have become true only in the past decade. In the first 30 years of modern computing, the marketplace was dominated by specific U.S. concerns. Product information was difficult to obtain and understand, products were expensive, and they often didn't work or were difficult to use. In those early days, advantage came at high risk but appeared sustainable. As Cragg and Finlay point out, however, much of today's information technology is easily transferable. Particularly when technological advantage comes at a low price, and if that advantage is not accompanied by special circumstances such as a unique or especially reliable source of information, it will not be sustainable.

Not only is hardware an easily purchased commodity, but software and the intellectual techniques behind the software are also widely available. Vendors of information technology are developing business savvy, too. They recognize that one system for a small group can easily be turned into a niche offering to a much larger market. Even high initial costs, normally a barrier to entry for other firms, may not be sustainable as cheaper technological substitutes become available. High initial costs may also bring high capacity that has to be filled to justify the costs. Keeping information systems "busy" brings with it the high costs of either (1) generating sufficient transaction volume—sufficient transactions, which implies potential price cutting, or (2) adding more applications, which implies writing new software and training new users—an additional cost that lowers profit and hence advantage. However, Cragg and Finlay point out that this analysis is specific to what they call *structured activities*—activities generated by routine transactions. When ill-structured activities inherent in nonroutine business processes such as strategic planning, market research, and production design form the basis for the use of technology, Cragg and Finlay claim that advantage may be maintained so long as the activity is information-intensive rather than technology-intensive. As discussed in Chapters 8 and 9, these sorts of applications involve poorly understood problems. An organization's knowledge can be advanced or enhanced with management support systems in ways other firms' knowledge cannot because they don't have the initial idea or the will to continue to support the activity.

Additional advantage may be achieved through use of information systems to support coordination of complex or interrelated activities. This means supporting managers' ability to visualize and solve coordination and management problems rather than process transactions. Because coordination is in the class of ill-structured problems, the general principle, articulated by Cragg and Finlay is this:

> Advantage achieved through the application of information systems to ill-structured problems is much more likely to be sustainable than such application to well-structured problems. Thus, (1) if the problem is ill-structured and the organization has the will, be a pioneer. (2) Otherwise, if the organization lacks the will, be second. (3) Otherwise, when the problems are well structured and involve routine technology, follow the crowd. (4) Finally, if the problem is really out of control, avoid automation.

STRATEGIC ADVANTAGES PROVIDED BY IS

What kinds of strategic advantage does IS provide? We can examine our initial list in Figure 4–1 of what makes something strategic and note the characteristics of IS-provided advantage in Figure 4–6. First, IS offers values and leverage by being relatively error-free, able to process large amounts of data, and being flexible. More to the point, software is easy to innovate with because of its flexibility. Initially, computers computed lots of numbers but now they draw pictures, process text, control devices and machinery, entertain, and communicate. Few other tools in our culture provide this broad range of talent in a small box.

Sisodia did an extensive analysis of the strategic advantages of various information systems in the marketing of services. Several trends are relatively predictable and benefit services marketing as they benefit most areas. Among these benefits are increased storage and graphics capabilities, online databases, and improved user interfaces using natural language and expert systems. Greatly enhanced network capabilities, however, promise to change by magnitudes the capabilities of services marketing.

Competitive boundaries are likely to change as telecommunications make it possible to merge or sidestep traditional product and market boundaries. The linkage of previously unrelated areas, such as banking and shopping, will create new opportunities, and electronic data interchange (EDI) will facilitate strengthened relations between marketers and suppliers. For example, Sisodia cites savings of $200 per vehicle

| Figure 4–6 | STRATEGIC IS APPLICATIONS FOR COMPETITIVE ADVANTAGE |

Why Are IS Applications Strategic?

□ Advantage over Competitors
 + IS Offers Value Added, Leverage

□ Newness, Novelty, Innovation
 + IS Applications Are Easy to Innovate

□ Uniqueness
 + Can Copyright Software
 − Easy to Imitate

□ Attractiveness to Customers
 + Customers See Immediate Productivity Advantage
 − These Benefits Are Hard to Measure and Are Often
  Oversold with Too High Expectations

□ Profitable
 + Applications Are Relatively Cheap to Build
 − Controlling Costs/Risks Is Hard

Summary
 + Strategic Advantage Is Easily Obtained
 − Hard to Keep for Long
 + Innovation Choice Is Broad
 − Managing Technology Is Difficult

achieved by the U.S. Big Three automakers by using EDI to automate inventory control and reordering. Some of the many ways marketing information systems provide competitive advantage include:

- *Sales management:* Maintain long-term relationships, expert training systems
- *Customer contact:* Expert systems for prompting
- *Complaint resolution:* Identify competitor's weak points
- *New-service development:* Technology-led innovations
- *Pricing:* Reducing price sensitivity
- *Advertising:* Monitor changes in perception over time
- *Sales promotion:* Expert systems to measure long-term impact and potentially reduce promotions
- *Distribution:* Create electronic distribution channels

Some examples of advantages Sisodia includes are computerized scheduling systems to enhance customer retention; computer-generated financial statements that may themselves be a product that can be sold separately; computer-aided service design to decrease the risks of being the first mover; and EDI links with customers that will put up barriers to competitors.

| Figure 4–7 | STRATEGIC IS CYCLE |

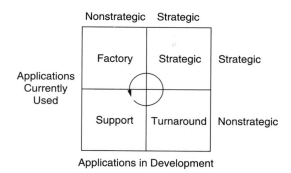

	Nonstrategic	Strategic	
Applications Currently Used	Factory	Strategic	Strategic
	Support	Turnaround	Nonstrategic

Applications in Development

HOW IS STRATEGIES ARE EMPLOYED

We end this chapter by examining the **strategic IS cycle,** illustrated in Figure 4–7. This cycle is derived from the **strategic grid** of Cash, McFarlan, McKenney, and Applegate, who note that firms that employ information systems for competitive ends may be characterized in terms of these two dimensions:

- How strategic the existing applications are (i.e., how necessary they are to achieving competitive advantage over any of Porter's five forces)
- How strategic the portfolio of applications under development is (Chapters 12 and 13)

Firms that do not use IS for competitive advantage and don't contemplate doing so are in the **support quadrant;** IS serves a support function in their organizations. However, some firms have recognized the strategic advantage of IS and are developing new applications. They are in the **turnaround quadrant;** they are "turning around" in their assessment of IS. Firms that have existing strategic IS applications and are developing new ones are fully committed to using IS in their strategic efforts and are in the **strategic quadrant.** These firms recognize the value of IS across the firm and thus are organized to create and use these applications without hassle. They generally have a chief information officer (CIO) who reports directly to top management (or may be a member of top management) and employ steering committees of high-ranking executives to oversee information systems operations and make quick corporatewide decisions. Some firms no longer develop new strategic applications but continue to use those they have; they are in the **factory quadrant.** An example is a pizza company that has just installed a sophisticated phone-ordering and delivery system. The expense of this system and the company's judgment of the limitations of the pizza business may have led it to consider this application as all it needs. The business uses IS like a factory—essential to its business but not in need of innovation at this time. These quadrants have a natural cycle. Firms that have no strategic insight into the use of IS may be "converted" and have one or more applications developed to help them become competitive. As these applications are developed and brought online, they are used extensively, and perhaps some new ones are developed. Eventually, firms stop developing new strategic applications but continue to use the existing ones. However, as time goes by, these applications lose their strategic advantage—remember, such advantage is time-limited—and the firms slip back into using IS merely as a support mechanism. The two principles at work here (IS advantage is time-limited and it takes time to create new applications) create this dynamic that causes the cycling.

CONCLUSION

This chapter examined the question of whether information systems can and do confer strategic competitive advantage on companies and individuals who obtain and use them. We have concluded that there are some specific advantages that such systems bring, but these advantages are difficult to maintain except when the application of information is

The Modern Management Imperatives

Reach: Global Competition	Information technology enables global competition and thus puts pressure on managers to respond to global, rather than merely local or regional, pressures. Global competition implies information networks, interorganizational systems (such as EDI), and systems that can work anywhere.
Reaction: Quick Customer Feedback on Products and Services	Competition today means pleasing the consumer, responding quickly to customer needs and desires. An IS helps by providing customer information rapidly and accurately and by providing customers with ways to provide feedback to a company. Managers can use IS to keep track of customers, products, and projects.
Responsiveness: Shortened Concept-to-Customer Cycle Time	Competitive advantage using technology is, in general, short-lived. Technology investment is capital-intensive but the costs of technology fall over time, limiting the value of innovation. However, software is extremely flexible and new software-based products are quickly developed and marketed.
Refinement: Greater Customer Sophistication and Specificity	Customers can no longer be locked in with technology because they are becoming increasingly sophisticated in their use of computers. However, they respond well to systems that respond to them. Knowledgeable customers are good customers; they recognize efforts to tailor systems to respond to them as opposed to having to change what they do to suit a computerized system. However, customer or client expectations have to be managed well.
Reconfiguration: Reengineering of Work Patterns and Structures	Many firms have discovered that architectures such as client-server allow them to decentralize to respond much more quickly to customer and competitor challenges. Because niche markets are very specific and sometimes short-lived, the ability to reengineer work quickly using computers is a great competitive advantage.
Redeployment: Reorganization and Redesign of Resources	Controlling inventory and labor is a major challenge in any competitive strategy involving cost. While information systems have traditionally offered advantages here, the new paradigm sees information itself as a major competitive resource. Many firms find that selling information or information systems is a profitable business. Sharing resources via interorganizational systems is also a good competitive strategy.
Reputation: Quality and Reliability of Product and Process	Customers base buying decisions on quality as well as price. Information systems assist innovation and product development in terms of speed, but they also assist quality management and quality control efforts in ways that manual systems cannot. Computers and information systems are integral to product development, testing, and marketing as well as customer service after the sale.

used to solve difficult and complex business problems, there is a life cycle to the use of information systems to meet strategic goals, and the advantages of information systems can appear at any point in the customer product life cycle.

The next two chapters examine the concept of architecture and relate it specifically to firms that require information for strategic advantage to bridge the gaps between disciplines or subject matter areas or to shorten distances through telecommunications approaches. Chapter 5 looks closely at database architectures that integrate data sources and increase managers' ability to span departmental and divisional boundaries to solve complex business problems. Chapter 6 takes a different view of integration and looks specifically at client-server architectures that distribute information across a number of sites.

■ VACUUMS-R-US'S STRATEGIC ADVANTAGE

Ed has decided to purchase a used two-station microcomputer network from a doctor who is renovating his office. While there is no business software available with the system that has immediate use in the retailing and servicing of vacuums, Ed is intrigued by the ideas of "diagnosis" and "prescription" and wonders if some lateral thinking on the idea of "curing the dust problem" might help him come up with some competitive advantage. Ed has also contacted the MIS department at a nearby university and has obtained the name of a hotshot database programmer who is a student there and does contract programming in commercial database packages. A database package was bundled in with the computer system picked up for a song. Also, a supplies-ordering package in the system probably can be tailored to vacuums and parts instead of medical supplies. Ed is looking for an angle, something that will make Vacuums-R-Us novel, unique, more valuable. He recognizes that this advantage will probably not last long, but he's willing to use the power of computers to innovate. Maybe it will help him cut his costs, too. As an engineer, he knows that understanding the numbers is always the first step toward wisdom; as a businessperson, he feels that being confident of where you are makes it less scary to take a step in some direction. ■

1. Suggest one or more applications Ed might try and describe the type and degree of strategic advantage each might gain him.

2. Why are these advantages short-lived? What is inherent in technology that makes advantages short-lived in general and even shorter for Ed's business?

3. Using the strategic IS cycle model illustrated in Figure 4–7, predict how things might go in the future for Ed's use of IS to gain competitive advantage. What skills, attitudes, and resources will he need to retain this advantage?

Summary   Strategic advantage means developing plans for overcoming or outwitting the competition. It involves specific advantages, innovativeness, uniqueness, attractiveness, profitability, and a view to the future. Five generic ways to achieve strategic advantage include selling at the lowest cost, differentiating one's products from those of competitors, appealing to a niche market, developing a new kind of business, and forming alliances with suppliers, customers, or competitors. Information plays an important role in each of these generic strategies. In the eight-step customer product life cycle, information is critical in every stage to provide advantages over competitors. Porter's five forces model points out where competition comes from and also shows where information can be used to lock in buyers and suppliers and lock out substitutes and new entrants.

Competitive advantage derived from the use of technology has a definite life cycle and provides specific kinds of advantages, especially when coupled with knowledge or coordination of activities. Information systems applications are strategic in that they lower costs, are easy to innovate, can be copyrighted, and are relatively inexpensive to build. Such advantages are difficult to maintain because applications are easy to imitate, technology tends to be oversold, expectations of information systems tend to be high, and technology is difficult to manage. Organizations that employ information technology for strategic advantage tend to go through a cycle in which strategic applications are developed and used and then become nonstrategic as the competition catches up or the technology matures and becomes generally available.

Discussion Questions

4.1 Because we have used the term *strategic* to refer to competition, the term might be thought to apply only to the for-profit, private sector. In what ways might the term be applied to the not-for-profit and public sectors? How would the generic "competitive" strategies (low cost, differentiation, etc.) apply in these sectors? Can you think of examples within these sectors where organizations are competing?

4.2 In which phase(s) of the customer product life cycle would information play the greatest role? The weakest role? Provide additional examples of the value that information and information systems add in each phase of the CPLC.

4.3 Porter's five forces model isn't specific to information systems. Provide examples of how information systems create switching costs, build barriers to entry, and allow firms to create and offer their own substitutes. Doesn't this type of easily created technology merely "up the ante" for competition without increasing product variety, quality, or reliability?

4.4 Compare and contrast the kinds and degrees of advantages provided by each of the following types of technology (with the specific examples listed):
- Information systems applications (microcomputers)
- Transportation improvements (highway networks)
- Communications (television)
- Manufacturing (assembly lines)

Key Terms

alliance
bargaining power of buyers
bargaining power of suppliers
barriers to entry
competitive advantage
competitive forces model
customer product life cycle model
differentiation
electronic data interchange (EDI)

factory quadrant
interorganizational system
low-cost strategy
new-business strategy
new entrant
niche marketing
precompetitive consortium
strategic advantage
strategic grid

strategic IS cycle
strategic quadrant
substitute
support quadrant
sustainable competitive advantage
switching costs
turnaround quadrant
vertical integration

References

Cash, J., F. W. McFarlan, J. McKenney, and L. Applegate. *Corporate Information Systems Management: Text and Cases*. 3d ed. Homewood, IL: Irwin, 1992.

Clemmons, E. "Evaluation of Strategic Investments in Information Technology." *Communications of the ACM* 34, 1 (January 1991): 22–36.

Clemmons, E., and M. Row. "Sustaining Information Technology Advantage: The Role of Structural Differences." *Management Information Systems Quarterly* 15, 3 (September 1991): 275–292.

Cragg, Paul, and Paul Finlay. "IT: Running Fast and Standing Still?" *Information and Management* 21 (November 1991): 193–200.

"For Our Next Trick . . . " *The Economist* 331, 7861, Special Survey of International Banking (April 30, 1994): S-28.

Freedman, David. "The Myth of Strategic I.S." *CIO* (July 1991): 42–45, 48.

Ives, Blake, and G. Learmouth. "The Information Systems As a Competitive Weapon." *Communications of the ACM* 27, 12 (December 1984): 1193–1201.

Ives, Blake, and R. Mason. "Can Information Technology Revitalize Your Customer Service?" *Academy of Management Executive* 4, 4 (November 1990): 52–69.

Keen, P. G. W. *Competing in Time: Using Telecommunications for Competitive Advantage.* Cambridge, MA: Ballinger, 1988.

Malone, T. W., J. Yates, and R. Benjamin. "Electronic Markets and Electronic Hierarchies." In T. Allen and M. S. Scott Morton, eds. *Information Technology and the Corporation of the 1990s.* New York: Oxford University Press, 1994, 61–83.

McFarlan, F. W. "Information Technology Changes the Way You Compete." *Harvard Business Review* (May–June 1984): 98–103.

Meechling, J. "Barriers to Customer Service in Government." In *Customer Service Excellence: Using Information Technology to Improve Service Delivery in Government.* Cambridge, MA: The Program on Strategic Computing and Telecommunications in the Public Sector, June 1993, 1–4.

Mills, Dale. "Marketing Information Systems' Potential to Senior Management." *Journal of Information Systems Management* (Winter 1990): 76.

Porter, M. E. *Competitive Advantage.* New York: Free Press, 1985.

————. *The Competitive Advantage of Nations.* New York: Free Press, 1990.

————. "How Competitive Forces Shape Strategy." *Harvard Business Review* 57, 2 (March–April 1979): 137–145.

Porter, M. E., and V. E. Millar. "How Information Gives You Competitive Advantage." *Harvard Business Review* (July–August 1985): 149–160.

Sisodia, Rajendra. "Marketing Information and Decision Support Systems for Services." *The Journal of Services Marketing* 6, 1 (Winter 1992): 51–64.

Venkatraman, N. "IT-Enabled Business Transformation: From Automation to Business Scope Redefinition." *Sloan Management Review* (Winter 1994): 73–77.

Vitale, M. "The Growing Risks of Information Systems Success." *MIS Quarterly* 10, 4 (December 1986): 327–334.

Von Huppel, E. "Determining User Needs for Novel Information-Based Products and Services." In T. Allen and M. S. Scott Morton, eds., *Information Technology and the Corporation of the 1990s.* New York: Oxford University Press, 1994, 111–124.

CASE

EVERGREEN LANDSCAPING AND MAINTENANCE: ASSISTING STRATEGIC ADVANTAGE

Because of Connie's experience as sales manager with the guaranteed green-up program, she has become concerned about the way Evergreen develops and markets new contract services. In the past, Evergreen could rely on its customers' needs for lawns, trees, shrubs, walls, gardens, and so forth, to drive the company's offerings. And because it was fairly obvious what constituted a lawn or a tree, Evergreen could afford to be fairly lazy in this area. Besides, the retail side of the business, a cash cow, generated the overwhelming bulk of income and profit; services were seen mainly as necessary to maintain an image. No one really took services very seriously until the guaranteed green-up program lost $30,000 last year servicing its most affluent customers.

Now everyone is taking these services seriously and many are asking Connie to discontinue *all* services, not just the guaranteed green-up program, and get back to "our bread and butter," the retail side and what Sid (assistant contract manager) irreverently calls "the home farming business." Connie has this to say in private to her boss, Shawna Eggert:

> Shawna, I'm not sure I have the courage to say this in front of the other members of MEC, some of whom have been working for Evergreen since I was able to spell the word, but I don't see why they are so service-shy. It's not as if we were betting the store on our services, and even losing $30,000 in one year won't break us. I can understand their desire not to stray far from our real business in retail sales, but what really gets my goat is that they don't see that the new values, like environmentalism, require us to be innovative and, what's more important, stay closer to our customers. Maybe we—and they—will learn what sells from cash register tapes* and questions they ask our salespeople in the store, but as I see it, we—and our customers—get much more out of a service relationship. We find out what they need, what their lawns or gardens are really like, how they think when they're not in the store. Customers, on the other hand, can learn how to control weeds without damaging the environment, the best way to compost, exactly what can be recycled from their gardens, how to use water, and so forth. Without these services, Shawna, we're flying blind, or at least in fog.

Shawna's reply startled Connie:

> Connie, it's too bad that you don't see things the way the others in MEC do. They're *not* service-shy at all. They just don't see the value in putting effort into risky ventures when there is a perfectly good retail business going on. After all, not everyone has your background in operations and accounting. And while they say *environmentalism* with their mouths, they are really saying *not our business* with their hearts. For the most part, they don't understand it and they fear it, especially the political side. They've seen toxic waste regulations decrease our sales of pest control products for years. They worry about finding people willing to work with fertilizers and take the risk of applying some chemical to a mother's lawn that will make her kids sick and we'll get sued. No, they're not service-shy, just risk averse. To them, a blade of grass is a blade of grass, not a chance to teach someone something. They want Evergreen to continue to be known as the reliable place to go for gardening and lawn needs, where the customer counts, and prices are reasonable. Maybe you should invest a little in seeing things their way, Connie.

Connie wasn't satisfied with this response. It seems to her that business opportunities exist, if only Evergreen were ready for them. But Evergreen isn't ready for her message—yet.

---

*Three years ago, Evergreen got rid of its old cash registers and installed a computerized point-of-sale (POS) system. Connie is just being dramatic here. She knows that having this system has made her job much, much easier because now she knows exactly which stock is moving how fast and can even relate sales to ads, the weather, and newspaper features.

Connie's big fear is that retail gardening centers are under assault from at least two sides, and the edge that Evergreen acquired from its corporate history, the goodwill of Harnwell and Petty, is a pretty thin insulator against the cold competitive winds coming from mass marketers and discounters. Connie still thinks of the MEC as being anti-innovative, smug, and not really forward-looking. Connie has been looking at the possibilities posed by the point-of-sale terminals and wonders if there are new products there, even new ways of doing business by direct marketing or working *with* discounters. Evergreen, she knows, has its roots in the nursery business. She wonders if it can create new products as well as new services based on the enormous amount of retail data it gets from customers as well as some good projections of trends from its contract clients. If Evergreen doesn't become more competitive, it might just find its corporate branches pruned significantly by the competition.

Questions

1. What does it mean for a firm such as Evergreen to think strategically? Give examples of the kinds of strategic thought Evergreen might have.

2. Evergreen is pursuing only one of the five possible generic competitive strategies. Which one is this? Why do you think this is Evergreen's conscious choice? What would it take for Evergreen to employ the other strategies? What are the risks and advantages of these other strategies to Evergreen? What information from what sources would be necessary in these other strategies?

3. Using the customer product life cycle, point out the role information plays in delivering a quality product to Evergreen's retail and contract customers. How does Evergreen's information system (including the POS terminals, clerks, stockers, and managers) assist in creating additional value for the customers and clients?

4. Use the five competitive forces model to list the five sources of competition for Evergreen. Which forces do you think are farthest from being locked in or out? Why is this so? Are there any advantages to using information technology to counter these forces? Against which one(s) would information technology be most effective?

5. In small groups, brainstorm and determine a short list of potential new products or services with an information or information systems content that can convey competitive advantage to Evergreen. What generic competitive strategies would these products or services abet? What is the nature of the strategic advantage of each of your suggestions? How strong would the advantage be and how would it fare over time? Now, rank order the short list based on the relative strengths and staying power of the advantages.

6. How would you characterize Evergreen's position now in the strategic IS cycle? What would have to happen to change that position? Why would Evergreen ever move from its current position anyway? What forces within the MEC should Connie attempt to sway or take advantage of in order to move Evergreen's position?

CHAPTER FIVE

BRIDGING DISCIPLINES: IS ARCHITECTURES FOR STRATEGIC ADVANTAGE

OBJECTIVES

After you have read and studied this chapter, you should be able to:

■ Define an information architecture and explain why it is important to managers.

■ Define a shared information architecture and describe its strategic advantages from a manager's perspective.

■ Describe how the relational database models facilitate integration of information across disciplines.

■ Discuss the object-oriented view of information and explain what its advantages are to managers and developers.

Question: How can information components of an information system be brought together to gain strategic advantage?

Consider the problem facing Farrice Gulamhusein, president and CEO of Forged Tools, Inc. This business manufactures and sells drop-forged hammers and other tools in the commercial and consumer markets, primarily through retailers. Normally, the factory can produce 2,000 high-quality hammers per month and sell them for about $20 each. However, Gary Scott, a salesperson on holiday overseas, just had lunch with a government minister who has access to World Bank money that gives thousands of citizens the means to construct their own homes. This could mean a lot of sales for Forged Tools if it can produce 50,000 hammers in 2 months, with the possibility of a sale of another 50,000 in 6 months. Gary phones Farrice and asks, "Can we submit a bid? We are the only people being spoken with right now and if we can get a bid in by tomorrow, we'll almost surely get the contract. And, by the way, they will certainly want saws, levels, screwdrivers, the works. And don't forget the nails." Forged Tools, which normally produces about 25,000 hammers a year, may be asked to produce twice that in two months. What are the risks? What are the opportunities? Farrice wonders if she, or anyone, at Forged Tools has the information she needs to answer Gary's question. Where should she find needed data? And how can she get her hands on it? Can Farrice answer Gary's question in a few hours?

Answer: An IS architecture that brings together all levels of the organization and all functions will make it easier for Farrice and others to tap into the information basis of the firm. Business processes, organizations, databases, and information systems play roles brought together by the very nature of information.

INTRODUCTION

In this chapter, we will view a system in terms of information a user needs and references, and how this information is broken into manageable pieces and distributed across disciplines such as marketing, accounting, finance, and production. This is called the **information architecture.** We'll see an application as a set of interlocking information relationships that have to be "solved" to meet a management goal.

These applications depend on data to create advantages for the firm. For example, if a tactical manager designs an incentive plan to increase positive perceptions of customer service in a differentiation strategy, the manager may have the problem of deciding whether an incentive plan will actually increase positive perceptions. The solution may be to compare customer comments about all employees who received bonuses last year with the same employees' customer comments this year. A strategic manager may have developed a training program to increase productivity in an attempt to keep costs down and might be interested in using production, sales, and employee performance data to project profits for the coming year based on estimates of the capabilities of new, state-of-the-art automated equipment and the costs and effectiveness of training programs. The company may be pursuing several niche markets, repackaging a set of products into a variety of formats, one for each market. At the operational level, a supervisor may be examining quality data to make sure that packages are kept separate and that invoicing reflects no errors in shipping.

In each of these cases, the manager has to "navigate," or move among data or databases, to locate, retrieve, array, process, and report on the data. The results inform the manager in ways that the original mass of data does not. The exercise makes sense of the data by putting aside irrelevant data (Chapter 2), calculating values that indicate problems or opportunities (Chapter 3), processing the information into formats that are useful to those who have to take action in a business context, and producing reports that are of value to those charged with keeping the firm profitable or productive (Chapter 4). **Navigation** is done by moving from database to database, picking up relevant information along the way, and building sets of data that will be further processed later. Each step in the navigation adds value to the previous step. The journey is aided by software that keeps track of what has been retrieved and the structure of the data thus accessed. Imagine how difficult it would be to keep track of the activities mentioned above using Post-it notes and legal pads. The voyage is facilitated because the software knows the architecture of the database—without this knowledge, the manager will be guided into oblivion.

The information architecture of a firm is seldom written down the way a building's blueprints are. On the other hand, there is a structure to the information, even if it's a mess of separate databases, filing cabinets, and lists kept in clerks' heads. Sometimes the architecture is planned, but more commonly it simply grows out of a succession of user needs, technology acquisitions, and data collection efforts.

Derived from two Greek words (*archos*, meaning chief, and *tekton*, meaning carpenter), the word *architecture* means designing and constructing as well as a style of designing and constructing; the word is used in both of these senses in IS. In this chapter, we use the word to mean how various parts of a system interconnect or communicate with each other on a systematic basis. For example, in a typical bureaucracy (recall Anthony's triangle), the higher a manager is in the organization, the less likely it is that he or she will use detailed information to make decisions. Part of the information architecture of most bureaucracies is the relationship that upper management has with lower management. Upper management

---

Figure 5-1 ANTHONY'S TRIANGLE

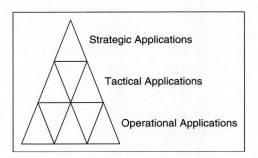

---

deals with summaries and trends, not with details; their communication is in these terms, not in terms of reams of paper or screens of data. Another feature of a traditional bureaucracy is that different divisions rarely communicate directly. Information flows up, over, and down. A building's architecture refers to how rooms are arranged along hallways, how stairways go between floors, whether the front door opens into a living room or an entranceway, and so forth. Architecture is both a static and a dynamic aspect of the thing designed.

It is important to distinguish the words *architecture* and *design*. The design of a building is purely static—it does not change—and it does not refer to how the building will be used. We use the word *architecture* to mean design + use or design-in-use. An information architecture is much more than the design of a specific piece of software; it refers to the general flow of information and the style of that flow.

This chapter is about information architecture. Because the focus of the text is information support for managers pursuing strategic advantage, the emphasis is on the tools managers use. Databases and applications are the most likely tools managers will see and use. Other architectures refer to hardware and telecommunications; the next chapter will explore telecommunications architectures in some detail. However, this chapter emphasizes how databases interrelate and how applications make accessing information easier and more effective for managers.

AN INFORMATION ARCHITECTURE

In Anthony's Triangle, shown in Figure 5–1, a typical organization assumes that different kinds of work go on at different levels of the firm. We refer to the totality of what an employee does as a *job*, and various parts of the job may be called *tasks*, *projects*, and so on. There is also a view of work that describes it in terms of goals that have to be achieved. The tasks and tools that achieve these goals define the kind of work an employee performs. Shift supervisors at factories handle safety, schedule shift work, review daily logs, and inspect work. How they perform these tasks may vary from day to day, site to site, or project to project, but when workers are evaluated, it is on whether or not they get these tasks done. In Chapter 3, we referred to the actions involved in achieving these goals as *business processes*, which are carried out in some fashion using a

| Figure 5–2 | ANTHONY'S TRIANGLE REVISITED |

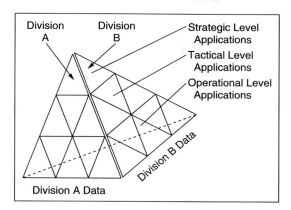

variety of tools. When an information system is applied to accomplish a predefined goal, we call the tool an *application*. If we restrict ourselves to managerial work, we could perhaps call all these tasks applications whether or not a computer is used. After all, information is an important component of most managerial work. Therefore, we can, without much loss of generality, relabel Anthony's Triangle as in Figure 5–2. Here we see a section of the organization characterized not by workers or tasks but by the nature and structure of the applications found at the three levels. Of course, not all tactical level managers do the same thing, and the triangles indicate different applications. Most firms are divided by different types of work. Suppose a firm has two divisions, A and B. A could be production and B could be marketing. We now have a two-dimensional structure (levels and divisions), and each division deals with at least some unique data. For instance, Division A could keep data on products while Division B could store data on customers. The applications in each division may also be different, but they may also have some tasks in common. We could multiply the number of divisions and, by flattening the diagram, examine the two-dimensional chart (see Figure 5–3) that results.

In the chapter-opening vignette, Forged Tools' marketing has its sales information files and the factory has its production information. The director of human resources, who is also the controller, has accounting information and human resource data. Each division has a set of applications, mostly procedures that are followed using pen, paper, and calculator, but some run on computers using spreadsheets and database managers. The applications are as follows (by management discipline):

- Marketing: sales analysis, market research, customer data and prospect marketing, order processing
- Factory: production scheduling, bill of materials, quality control, inventory
- Human Resources: performance appraisal, employment history
- Accounting: accounts receivable, accounts payable, general ledger, bank statements, payroll

| Figure 5-3 | IS ARCHITECTURE |

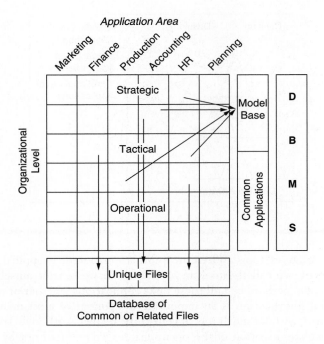

Each division has unique files that refer to unique events that each division handles or experiences. But there are also **common events,** such as sales, which affect both marketing and factory, and these events generate common data. There are also **related events** that are not common. For example, accounting has to be informed of each sale because even though the event doesn't directly affect accounting operations, it does generate an accounting event. The set of files of common and related events forms a **shared database** for the organization. Note that the shared database is *not* just the sum total of the unique databases. Unique databases refer to records of events unique to a division or operation. Nonunique databases are also found in the shared database. For example, information on the performance of sales staff "belongs" to the marketing department as well as the human resources department. While quality control data is important to operations, it's also vital to marketing, which has to plan for returns and customer dissatisfaction. Employment history may seem most relevant for human resources, but production managers may also want to look at this information to find out if employees should be promoted or retrained.

Thus, when applications deal with common or related events, they tend to interact or interrelate. While many applications are unique to a division, the phenomenon of data sharing tends to create a set of shared or common applications. A sales information system may also be used by production managers and accountants because it may serve to notify them of how much product will be needed.

A set of common applications may require a set of models (Chapter 3). For instance, a finance department may be creating a series of projections based on different sets of assumptions about production, market growth, and regulation. Each of these sets of assumptions plus the formulas that relate input (parameters) and output (forecasts) forms a model. Sometimes these models look just like spreadsheets. At other times the formulas are embedded in software, even in programming language statements such as EOQ = 0.5*X**2-2*PDQ. A set of models is called a **corporate model base.** Models are distinct from applications, and many information architectures have a separate model base management system to handle them. We will use the term *database management system* here to refer to all three components. While this term is also often narrowly applied to refer to a software package for manipulating data in a general sense, we'll use it to mean the way that a set of tools is made available to corporate information users. Thus, the database management system manages:

- Data and its structures (relationships)
- Applications (and structures of them) that work with the data
- Models that tell how to work with the data

A DYNAMIC ARCHITECTURE

Thus far, we have shown a static view of architecture. A **dynamic architecture,** illustrated in Figure 5–4, enables us to see where structures come from and how they influence managers' behavior. To construct this dynamic view, we must first understand that a useful architecture arises from the interaction of business processes and the organization, not from the keyboards of computer programmers who create the software. Business processes such as order entry, inventory control, and shipping are performed to meet organizational, divisional, departmental, or personal goals. For example, order entry may be a business process within the sales department; shipping within the transportation department; and strategic planning within a planning department. When these processes are heavily information-driven, an information system is involved and we refer to the processes as **applications.** The data (or information) involved in these applications is called a **database.** It is unfortunate that all four components are sometimes called by the same name. For example, there may be an A/R department, an A/R application, an A/R database, and an A/R information system. Often the *accounts receivable* term is applied to all four, but they are different.

Organizations require, create, and use business processes to meet business goals, and these business processes generate and require data and information. Data in turn are processed by a variety of information systems as the information flows among the business processes. Consider a single sale. The sale will generate an order (information) to be picked (application) by the warehouse (organization). The transaction may be processed through a variety of systems including a computer system; the mind of the product picker; a pencil, used to check off the list as each item is picked; and a paper-based system of forms that are returned to the warehouse for restocking purposes and to the customer as a packing slip. Managers may tap this information to spot check the quality of the process or solve a problem relating to customers or high costs. The architecture shows and uses a structure of applications, data, and processes.

Figure 5-4 A DYNAMIC ARCHITECTURE

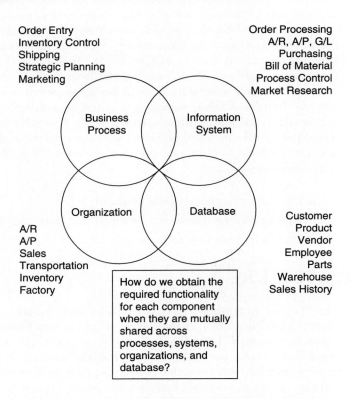

Order Entry
Inventory Control
Shipping
Strategic Planning
Marketing

Order Processing
A/R, A/P, G/L
Purchasing
Bill of Material
Process Control
Market Research

Business Process

Information System

Organization

Database

A/R
A/P
Sales
Transportation
Inventory
Factory

Customer
Product
Vendor
Employee
Parts
Warehouse
Sales History

How do we obtain the required functionality for each component when they are mutually shared across processes, systems, organizations, and database?

SHARED INFORMATION ARCHITECTURE

The architecture of an information system influences, limits, motivates, and dictates the processes to a great extent. If we don't have the tools to accomplish a task, we probably will not try to do it.

Let's return to the Forged Tools example (see Figure 5–5). Its hammers are manufactured in stages, three of which require specific machine tools. One of these machine tools is a polisher, which polishes the hammer heads to remove burrs resulting from the forging process. The polisher has many parts, one of which is a drill assembly. The drill assembly is important to Forged Tools because it's highly mechanical, breaks frequently, and must be serviced regularly. After manufacturing, the hammers go into inventory where they are identified by an item number (a number customers use) as well as by an order number that is used to maintain inventory. When Forged Tools sells a hammer, it keeps track of the number left in stock. If that number falls below a specified number (which can be adjusted by management), more are reordered from the factory. Forged Tools sells most hammers in lots of five for $21.75 each.

We would not normally link the price of hammers and the sizes of lots sold to a drill assembly for a polisher, but because the polisher is a weak link in the manufacturing

| Figure 5-5 | ONE SHARED INFORMATION SYSTEM |

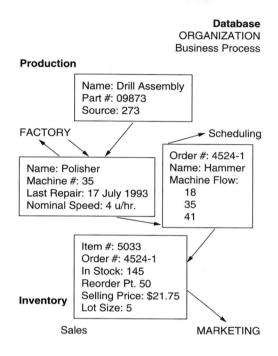

Database
ORGANIZATION
Business Process

Production

Name: Drill Assembly
Part #: 09873
Source: 273

FACTORY

Scheduling

Name: Polisher
Machine #: 35
Last Repair: 17 July 1993
Nominal Speed: 4 u/hr.

Order #: 4524-1
Name: Hammer
Machine Flow:
 18
 35
 41

Item #: 5033
Order #: 4524-1
In Stock: 145
Reorder Pt. 50
Selling Price: $21.75
Lot Size: 5

Inventory

Sales

MARKETING

chain, it's important to know about the drill assembly when orders are being taken. Recall the order for 50,000 hammers from the opening vignette. Forged Tools normally makes about 100 per working day, so 50,000 would require 500 days' production just for this order alone. Forged Tools' managers must ask themselves: Can we accept this order? Should we charge more? Less? When can the order be filled? What will be the effect of meeting this specific production goal on routine production? On regular customers? Is the firm forgoing long-term customer relationships for short-term profit?

With one kind of information architecture (partitioned, with no communication between sales and production databases and applications), sales managers would have to make guesses based on past performance statistics. They would not know whether production was elastic (i.e., can we make 500 hammers per day and, if so, at what cost?) or insensitive to loads (i.e., can we operate at full capacity all day for 500 days? No, we have only 60 days). Another information architecture might allow marketing managers to access production data directly to see just how weak the link is (i.e., can we push through this many hammers over a long period of time?). *A third kind of architecture links the databases and the applications,* facilitating the sharing of information. A sales manager wanting to know what the cost would be of selling (i.e., producing) 50,000 hammers in 50 days (1,000 per day) could link sales spreadsheets with profit and loss outcomes to production models of the drill assembly's reliability in order to predict capacity. Furthermore, in exploring the question of cost, marketing and production could approach senior management with a proposal to buy additional drill assemblies to have on hand in case of a series of failures. Or, for a larger order (say, 100,000), Forged Tools may want to buy the company that makes the assemblies, a decision that also requires linking with the financial data.

This kind of architecture, called **shared architecture,** is linked to the structure of the processes themselves as well as to the structure of the business. You can see that information architecture decrees just how effective information-driven business processes can be (telecommunications architectures refer to wires and connections, a much more physical construction than we're speaking of here) and how important this relatively simple architectural concept is to businesses. Of course, if there is no information, there is no need to think about information architecture.

Because it limits or provides opportunities, information architecture also influences an organization's ability to respond to its environment strategically. Strategic applications generally affect the entire firm; they cut across divisional boundaries and almost always cut across levels of management. Because they affect competition, strategic applications almost always include marketing, and because they affect cash flow, they almost always include some elements of finance. Because marketing dictates a need for product, they almost always affect production or procurement. Finally, because strategic applications affect many operations, they require a well-integrated shared architecture.

There are some obvious advantages and some not so obvious disadvantages to such tight integration. Tight integration is a quick and easy way to build cross-divisional applications. Executives can use executive information systems (Chapter 8) to get broad views of the situation quickly, and different divisions can access the same data without error, redundancy, or conflict. But there are many drawbacks to tight integration, the first of which is cost—it is expensive to create and maintain an integrated system. First, conflicting goals and needs have to be handled (Chapter 13). Second, errors that appear in data are passed on to all users and may be copied and integrated with other data very quickly, just as rumors spread quickly in crowds. Third, security is a real problem because many people have access to the data. Any tool that you can use can be used by someone else as smart as you but perhaps not as ethical. Backup, disaster recovery, and security are three difficult problems that must be solved. Also, such tightly integrated systems tend to be brittle and break easily.

There are compensations, however. While such systems are expensive, so are the alternatives. Without common access, people hide data from others, which in turn causes others to hoard data. Or, alternatively, people seek out data, make (undated) copies, and pass them around. Soon there are four or five versions of the same data floating around divisions of the organization, all different and all undated. Some or all of these redundant copies are inaccurate (assuming there were no mistakes in the copying) merely because they are out-of-date. No one actually knows who has the correct data, and since decisions will be made based on the data, it's difficult to know who should be trusted.

If a shared architecture has good security and backup, then recovery from disasters will be quicker and more accurate because data only have to go to one place and copies do not have to be made. When errors are found, correcting them is easier because there are no redundancies. If errors are not found, however, they will be around for a while, but it may be easier to find the errors because more people are looking at the same data. While integration is expensive, modern technologies such as relational databases, object-oriented databases, and client-server architectures are helping to bring that cost down.

Hardware considerations must be taken into account in a shared architecture. Data has to be stored in some place, on some medium. There is a cost to this in terms of both physical machinery that has to be purchased or rented and maintained and the users' time and effort in finding and processing the data. The simple problem of where to store information on a single floppy disk illustrates why data storage can be a concern. Data can be found on disks in records, and each record contains information on a single event or a single object. A given record may not, however, have *all* the data on an event. Imagine a file containing information on 10,000 customers is stored on a single 1.4MByte floppy disk used in a microcomputer. Suppose three related pieces of information—customer address, account balance, and account status (paid up, 30 days overdue, 60 days overdue, in collection, over limit)—are stored in three distinct physical locations on the disk. Every time a purchase is made, the customer address, account balance, and account status must be accessed and the balance and status updated based on recent purchase information. If the data are physically stored together in a single record, all data can be retrieved in one access and updated in another. But if the information is spread around the disk as in our example, it may be necessary to make five separate accesses. If each access takes 200 milliseconds, it would take one second (5 x 200 milliseconds = 1,000 milliseconds = 1.0 second) just to update the data on the disk, regardless of how long it might take to process the information. If there are 500 transactions per hour, then over 8 minutes of every hour is spent accessing the information.

When data can be stored close to other data needed in an application, data access costs are minimized. Otherwise, accessing data can become onerous. Even when data are designed to be in the same record, accessing costs can increase significantly. Files in which updates and rewrites have spread data apart are called *fragmented*. The cost of using fragmented files is a noticeable increase in response time for simple applications and potentially lethal delays in complex ones.

Other physical design problems can also become crucial, especially in large databases. The number of characters stored dictates physical storage medium costs even for nonfragmented files. Sometimes information needed for a certain application may be found in several different databases, significantly increasing response times to queries and updates. Also, these databases may be spread physically across different, perhaps incompatible, computer systems. In these cases, information architecture also requires a look at the physical architecture of an information system. We will examine in a later chapter the problem of bringing data together across distances.

RELATIONAL DATABASES

The **relational database model** is one we have been tacitly using in our discussion. In this model, data represent an event or an object, and each event or object exists in a class of such events or objects. Each can be described in terms of characteristics, or **attributes,** that distinguish events from one another within a class of events or objects. For example, in Figure 5–6, each event involving a retail sale (i.e., a sale to a customer) involves a date, a customer, one or more items and the number bought, and a disposition (cash or credit). We can further describe the customer by name, address, phone number, and customer account number. The customer account number is a unique identifier because it distinguishes this customer from all the others. We call this unique identifier a **key.** An item can be characterized by its name, retail price, cost, and supplier. This simple, intuitive model is depicted in Figure 5–6.

Note several things about this model. First, there is little **redundancy.** While each item has a retail price, it is not stored twice, once with the sales event and once with the description of the item. Of course, if the price is expected to change, it will have to be

Figure 5–6 THE SALES-EVENT RELATION

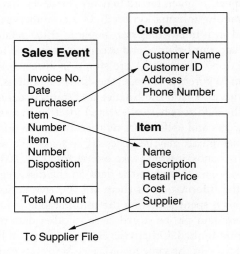

To Supplier File

stored twice, once with the price at the time of purchase and once with the item. In this example, we assume the price doesn't change. One major advantage of the relational model is that information that is created only once need be stored only once. One of the most attractive aspects of the relational data model is that all data pertaining to a class of objects or events are stored in a file dedicated to that class, which eliminates redundancy. With a large number of classes, there will be a large number of files, which makes navigation and processing more complex. Fortunately, today's user-friendly technology makes most of this transparent to the user. A user's view of the data need not correspond to the technicalities of where or how data are stored and retrieved.

Second, the model in Figure 5–6 contains an item description in addition to the item name, which gives the user a better idea of what the item is or what it does. Finally, the model assumes that each item is supplied by only one supplier. This architecture is expandable, of course, and the model could contain a file that stores information about suppliers (such as address, phone and fax numbers, name, and so forth).

The model in Figure 5–6 now can be made more elaborate or simple. First, because there may be several sales involving the same purchaser and the same item, a unique identifier (key) for each sales event, an invoice number, can be added. Second, the total amount of the sale is important, but note that the total amount could always be computed by multiplying the price of each item by the number of items bought and adding these numbers together across all items bought. This sum of extended amounts (Total amount) doesn't have to be stored with the data—it can be computed whenever this number is needed. In the early days of computing when calculations took a long time, it was a time-saver to store calculated numbers, but this is actually a drawback today as heavily populated files with thousands or millions of records become cumbersome to process and individual records become fat with unnecessary data.

Now Figure 5–6 looks relatively spare, with little redundancy, but suppose the customer buys more than two items. Suppose the customer buys 50 items. Does the sales

Figure 5–7 THE ITEM–INVOICE RELATION

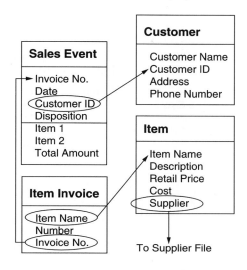

record have to be made large enough to hold 50 items on the rare chance that someone will buy that much? The answer is no. Just as numbers can be computed when they are needed, relations between items can also be computed when needed. In this case, another file is created called "Item Invoice" (see Figure 5–7). This file will simply hold records, each of which indicates that a certain quantity of a specific item was purchased during a specific sales event. This file is created so that each record contains only this information: Item, Number purchased, and Invoice number. In order to give each record a unique identifier, a sequence number is affixed to the invoice number and called the II number ("II" refers to "Item" and "Invoice" together). This allows us to take all references to items purchased out of the sales event record, which greatly simplifies saving and retrieving information and makes it possible to have a small, fixed-size record for each sales event.

Will the model now be able to show what was bought? Not directly. As mentioned earlier, that relationship would be computed by scanning the entire "Item Invoice" file for references to the particular invoice number, compiling that list as it goes. This is a lot of work, but so long as these kinds of requests don't occur frequently, the saving in storage costs (which are compounded on a second-by-second basis, forever) greatly outweighs any infrequent computational cost. An advantage of the relational database model is that managers can take advantage of efficiencies and tradeoffs in terms of storage and computation. In Figure 5–7, the references needed to rebuild that relationship are indicated by ovals and arrows. Also, "Purchaser" has been changed to "Customer ID" to be consistent. Most organizations would also have an "Item ID," a unique number for each item, especially if it sold two or more brands of items that have the same name.

This relational model now has a number of desirable characteristics. First, there is no redundancy, so valuable disk space isn't lost by storing the same data many times, and database searches are faster because the files are more compact. Second, data that do not

Figure 5–8 USING A RELATIONAL DATABASE TO LOCATE SPECIFIC RECORDS

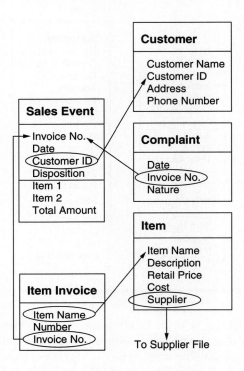

have to be stored, but could be computed, are not actually stored in the files. Third, it is relatively easy to change the design. Suppose, for instance, we wanted a file to contain all invoices for sales events that resulted in a customer complaint. How would such a file be built? Rather than copy all the records of sales events that resulted in customer complaints, another relation called "Complaints" would be added that has the following information: Date, Invoice no., and Nature, where "Date" is the date of the complaint and "Nature" is a textual description of the nature of the problem. This is indicated in Figure 5–8.

Consider the example in Figure 5–8 as an illustration of how the relational model works. Suppose we want to contact all customers who had complaints on invoices totaling more than $50 and offer them a coupon for 50 percent off their next purchase up to $50. Normally, a lot of time would be spent going through all the invoices, looking up the complaints and computing the amounts, and then sending out letters. A relational architecture would allow integrated, relatively compact databases and standardized ways of linking data to locate the desired records. A relational architecture would also make it easy to send the list of located records to a word processor that would perform a mail merge with a form letter that makes the coupon offer.

Figure 5–9 shows one of the complaint records. Billy Adams (customer number A708) paid for five items relating to a compost heap he is building, three of which were

| **Figure 5–9** | COMPLAINT RECORD |

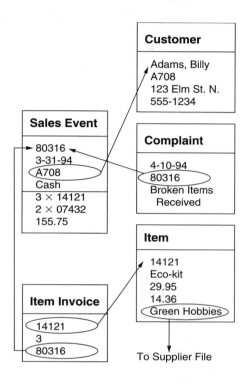

"Eco-kits" (item number 14121) retailing for $29.95 each (the cost to the retail shop was $14.36 each). The items arrived damaged and he complained about this on April 10th, almost two weeks after the purchase date (invoice number 80316). The price of the five items purchased totaled $155.75, $89.85 of which was for three Eco-kits and $65.90 of which was for two bags of chemicals (item number 07432) to go with the kits, costing $32.95 each (cost of $15.10 each—the record for the chemicals doesn't appear in the figure). The Eco-kits are available through Green Hobbies. More important than these prices is the customer information record, which can be used to merge with the form letter to make the coupon offer.

It is possible to use the relational model to determine a lot of important relationships and information in this example. For instance, Billy's payment of $155.75 included a cost of goods sold of $73.28 and a margin of $82.47. It should be relatively easy to calculate the total margin at risk from complaints, and if a coding scheme for complaints is adopted, the effect of complaints, damage, loss, and poor-quality items on profits can be determined. Various decision support and executive information systems (Chapter 8) have "drill-down" capabilities that enable managers to locate and process this kind of data. The relational model is extremely flexible and economical, as well as easy to learn, and thus facilitates management support of a strategic nature.

Figure 5–10 COMPLEX INTERDEPARTMENTAL RELATIONAL DATA ARCHITECTURE

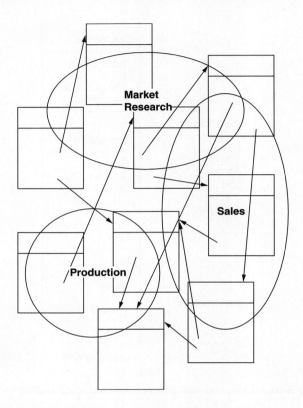

Applying the Relational Model to Shared Information

Now we will apply the relational model not simply to a small set of relations representing files for a single application but instead to a manager struggling to sail through a flood of corporate data. Imagine that the shared information architecture in Figure 5–10 focuses on a higher level and ignores the linkages among the relationships. In this corner of the corporate database, Sales, Production, and Market Research information is interlinked. Market research files reference sales data which in turn reference production data. There are no direct links from production information to sales, but there are links in the other direction. Managers who are concerned with sales, for example, will find it very easy to move from sales data to production data, but production managers will not find it easy, without the assistance of some software, to get from production data to sales data relating to production.

This model may be as it should be—salespeople need to know when items will be available for sales, but production people do not necessarily need details on who is buying. Market research analysts and their managers can access sales information easily, and they should be able to do so because their jobs require sales details. However, production information is not necessarily important. Suppose, however, that upper management is

| Figure 5–11 | SOFTWARE ARCHITECTURE LEVELS |

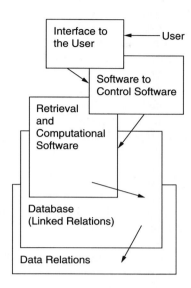

considering farming out all production and becoming a purely marketing-oriented firm. Decisions about finding suppliers depend on current and projected marketing, production, and market research data as well as financial and accounting information and human resource records. The integrated database we have looked at from a distance will not be sufficiently flexible for this sort of decision making. Instead, relatively complex software will have to be written, and information systems professionals probably will gather the required data together into reports on costs, benefits, and timetables.

In order to discuss the required system, we need to speak in architectural terms at five levels of:

- Data itself, in relations or tables
- Databases of mutually linked relations
- Software to manipulate the data
- Software to create, save, and edit parameters for manipulation
- User interface

The required software will have the architecture depicted in Figure 5–11. At the lowest level, there are relations or tables already depicted. These relations are organized into a set of databases and interlocked through references by keys to each other. The software provides capabilities to query, retrieve, array, process, and report. This particular software may not be available to users, although it is this software that eventually manages the data.

Another level of software manages activities as sets of commands for query or action. For example, producing a profitability report requires a set of queries on a subset of retrieved and arrayed data, various calculations, and the production of a report. It is possible for the managers involved to use the "language" of the database manager itself to retrieve the data and perform the calculations. DBMSs such as *dBase* or *Paradox* have this capability. If the report is needed only for a one-time use, there is probably a good reason for using the database manager. However, if the report has to be redone (perhaps data have changed, an inconsistency was found, or an additional production value has to be taken into account), it should not be necessary to create an entirely different program.

Hence, a fourth layer of software is often made available to users so that they can specify, save, retrieve, and edit commands. This higher level of interaction is often called a *system*. For example, a production planning system (PPS), which is really a set of programs, asks managers to describe which data they want, what reports they want, and how they want the reports distributed. The PPS then performs the required retrieval and computations and produces the report.

The fifth level of the architecture is the user interface. In many cases, this is a set of menus, mouse buttons, or forms that users work with. In general, users don't do real programming, not because they can't or don't want to, but because the data are too precious to be manipulated by many users. In addition, the DBMS will want to keep the data reliable and nonredundant. Also, user interfaces can be tailored to individual user desires.

The relational approach to database modeling examines data from the point of view of an intellectual problem solver who asks: what do I need to know? An alternative approach is to think of a problem as a construction of a set of alternatives by asking, what do I need to have done? This approach is facilitated by a model of data called the *object-oriented* approach, which includes in data characterization a description of what can be done with the data and how to do it. We turn our attention now to this alternative approach.

OBJECT-ORIENTED ARCHITECTURES

The impact of object orientation on managers is that services, files, programs, screen icons, and windows—the essence of the manager's information workbench—can be created and used as objects. These objects can be collected in a library and reused whenever appropriate, thereby speeding system construction. Far more important is the fact that managers can dispense with the necessity of *understanding* systems as links, data, keys, and so forth. Often these concepts, like components of any language, build artificial barriers around systems. Think about the first time you visited a foreign country, arrived at a college campus, attended a formal event such as a graduation, or started a new job. While the activities you performed (walking, looking, sitting, standing, smiling, etc.) weren't particularly foreign to you, the words others used to describe these activities were foreign. When and why these activities were performed wasn't familiar either (Why stand now? Why are we sitting here? Why are we not allowed to smile now?). Understanding the structure and language around an activity in large part determines how well we will perform the activity, especially if we have to do it again unaided by a guide. An **object-oriented approach** allows us to think about what we're doing in our own terms, which is inherently more attractive than one that compels us to understand others' microconcepts and their structure. Unfortunately, this approach has its *own* jargon.

Think for a moment about the objects you deal with on a daily basis, even mundane objects such as pencils, books, tables, and chairs, or more complex objects such as cars and rooms, or very complex ones such as libraries, courses, classes, assignments, and friends. What is there about these objects that gives them this status? Why, for example, don't we think of a chair as a collection of parts? What gives a room coherence besides its four walls, floor, and ceiling? Why is it that we can talk with other students about STAT 331 and they understand what we mean?

The answer is that objects have a built-in coherence that we have learned because we've interacted with them for some period of time. There are certain things we can do with specific objects. They appear to us in consistent ways and we do consistent things with them, or they do things to us. This principle is called **encapsulation.** Each object's appearance can be described in terms of a limited set of dimensions or attributes. (Not surprisingly, we use the term *attribute,* which was used in discussing the relational model.) Along with the attribute, we include a description of what the object can do or what can be done with the object, called a **method.** A menu, for example, has among its attributes a length (number of choices). Among its methods is a way of selecting the desired choice. If all the attributes and methods are known, this object (menu) can be referred to within an application without worrying about how the attributes may change depending on where the screen menu is displayed or how a menu choice is to be handled; all this is contained within the menu-object. Such objects can be moved from program to program or application to application without worry. Such movement is called **reuse,** and object reuse contributes significantly to a reduction in application development time.

Seen this way, an application is a collection of interlocking objects that interact with one another. Objects interact by sending each other **messages,** much as we do with our body language and formal communication. Consider a typical organization. Its objects include, among others, employees and tasks, defined for the firm along with procedures of work and other rules that limit or define behaviors. Employees' behaviors and defined tasks mesh because they are coordinated through messages, which are most critical in response to a changing environment. This object-oriented view of an organization differs dramatically from the bureaucratic view of individuals programmed to work based on inputs and outputs.

In management applications, objects may include customers, products, equipment, material, inventory, salespeople, accounts, and so forth. Customers make purchases by sending messages to salespeople about products. Salespeople send messages to inventory (which may send more messages to production) and back to customers. The way these messages are communicated depends on the methods the objects know and can execute. Designing systems in these terms requires only that managers understand how they themselves work and what their rules are. This design is independent of computers, programming languages, and specific programming or systems analysis techniques.

Because objects fall into classes and members of the same class have similar attributes and methods, systems are simplified. Classes may be **subclasses** of other classes called **superclasses.** For example "manager" and "shipping clerk" are classes of people that fall into the superclass of "employee." For a given class, all objects in its subclass have the same attributes, with perhaps additional attributes. For instance, a manager will have subordinates while a shipping clerk will not. The relationships between classes and subclasses are important in object-oriented approaches because they determine how subclasses will be designed and how methods and attributes can be **inherited** from one class to another, simplifying design and construction of management applications.

Consider the example in Figure 5–12. The object-oriented view seeks to describe the complex sales/return/complaint situation involving salesclerks, customers, and managers in terms that all the players will understand. Three classes are represented in

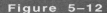

Figure 5–12 INHERITANCE IN OBJECT-ORIENTED DATABASES

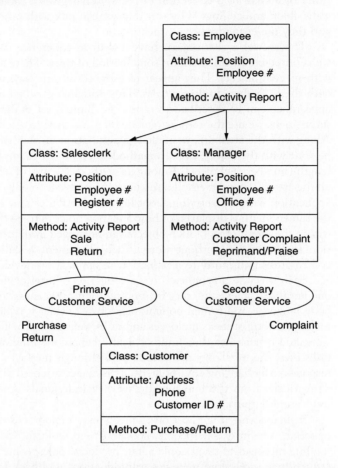

the figure: salesclerks, customers, and managers. Salesclerks and managers are subclasses of the superclass of employees. Both inherit some attributes from the superordinate class, such as position and employee number, but each has one or more unique attributes. Clerks, for example, work at numbered cash register stations, while managers have offices with telephone numbers. Clerks and managers use common methods—they both file weekly activity reports—and unique methods—clerks make sales and handle returns and managers handle customer complaints and have the power to reprimand or praise salesclerks. Customers, too, have attributes and methods that define them. The primary sales situation is a salesclerk making a sale to a customer or handling a return. The customer can complain, however, about the salesclerk to the manager by phoning the telephone number that is one of the manager's attributes. If the customer complains about the salesclerk by name, all the attributes of the clerk are available to the manager. Not included in the figure is the object, which is the sale itself. A complaint probably concerns the sale, too, which would be identified by a unique sales slip number.

The object-oriented approach illustrates both the inheritance of attributes and the relationships between classes that result from the interactions businesses generate. The primary sales situation in Figure 5–12 ("Purchase/Return") shows one relationship between objects (the item purchased is the third object involved, but it is not pictured in this figure). The secondary sales situation ("Complaint") shows another relationship (again, leaving out for simplicity the sale itself). Because this model speaks only about relationships, activities, and attributes, it is a model of *any* system that involves salesclerks, managers, and customers and can therefore be referred to and reused anywhere this set of interactions occurs with these objects. It doesn't matter what the products are, where they are sold, how they are produced or procured, or what happens to them after the sale. So long as these objects accurately model the behavior of salesclerks, managers, and customers, the design can be transferred to any system and referred to by a single name. Managers can continue referring to the system by names they are familiar with as can clerks or even customers.

An advantage of the object-oriented approach is that applications can be created more quickly and consistently by technical specialists, thereby allowing a broader range of management support. Fast response means that strategic advantage, short-lived at the best of times, can be obtained more quickly. Applications that refer to common objects are easier to link together, making cross-functional applications easier to develop.

At Forged Tools, an application that forecasts the need for maintenance of production machinery would be helpful to the CEO, as would an application that forecasts leasing versus purchase costs for equipment such as drill assemblies. A third application that estimates the effect of specific sales levels on firm profitability would also be helpful. The CEO would certainly like an application that evaluates the effects of sales on production schedules. These applications can easily refer to all the data in the integrated database, but putting the applications together, even on a temporary basis, would require an enormous amount of programming effort. The CEO would probably choose to do the data navigation personally with a little tutoring from the IS technical staff.

Rather than this ad hoc approach, however, the object-oriented approach looks more promising. Objects such as drill assemblies, sales, schedules, profits, and lease costs are easier to pull together than the software that manipulates these objects. The CEO, who actually understands the relationships among these objects, is the likely person to be the source of this information. An adept programmer, working with objects rather than other programmers' code, can design the new application very quickly without having to touch anyone else's programs. This means that Forged Tools can respond even more quickly with the appropriate answer. Database integration is one help; object orientation is another.

CONCLUSION

This chapter discussed three approaches to data architecture. The information architecture approach attempts to model data in terms of relationships among the data while the object-oriented approach models both data and procedures in terms of business activities that the modeled objects engage in. An older approach, the relational database model, is in widespread use and is intuitive for managers who think of their world as data and their tasks as data processing. The object-oriented approach is far newer and managers may not yet be comfortable with its concepts, but it promises to revolutionize how managers think of the systems that support them.

The Modern Management Imperatives

Reach: Global Competition	An information architecture must be flexible enough to anticipate information from a worldwide environment. Global competition means global data; what you don't know or can't access your competition already has. If you can obtain data more quickly and effectively, you have an advantage. Because managers can't always anticipate their information needs, they must be able to sail into uncharted waters fearlessly to find what they need.
Reaction: Quick Customer Feedback on Products and Services	Integrated databases mean that customer relationship information is easily collected and available. This implies that all customer contacts, customer surveys, employee suggestions, market surveys, and product research can be interlinked. In this way, customer needs can be identified systematically rather than guessed.
Responsiveness: Shortened Concept-to-Customer Cycle Time	The complexities of product and service development mean that the former "over-the-wall" mentality cannot continue to be supported. Individuals working on some aspect of product/service development need access to each other's data, thoughts, and ideas on a continuous basis. Without this access, false starts, needless iterations, delays, and lost opportunities occur.
Refinement: Greater Customer Sophistication and Specificity	Customers can also access product and service information. Online information services, shop-at-home services, home banking, and a variety of prerecorded and computed response dial-in phone information services are available now for consumers. Integrated information architectures make the hunt for information far less painful for consumers without sophisticated information search skills.
Reconfiguration: Reengineering of Work Patterns and Structures	Online and on-the-spot redefinition of a company, its work styles, and its resources require incredible coordination skills and effort. An integrated data architecture encourages this coordination because it facilitates comparisons and data sharing.
Redeployment: Reorganization and Redesign of Resources	A well-developed information architecture can track resources and schedules without difficult programming or data searching. This supports managers by easing the transition from one business format to another.
Reputation: Quality and Reliability of Product and Process	The complexities of an organization mean putting together internal and external data, production/marketing, and customer experience. The quality effort involves coordinating the internal and external view to see if customer expectations are matched. Integrated data architectures expedite these efforts.

■ AN IS ARCHITECTURE FOR FORGED TOOLS, INC.

At Forged Tools, four applications have been proposed to help decision makers handle rapid-response situations. One could be used to forecast the need for maintenance of production machinery. Another would help forecast leasing versus purchase costs for equipment such as drill assemblies. A third application could predict the effect of specific sales levels on firm profitability. Farrice would certainly like an application that evaluates the effects of sales on production schedules. The benefits of these applications are clear. Knowing when maintenance is necessary would help scheduling of preventative maintenance and thus decrease equipment downtime. The lease versus purchase decision is critical because the wrong decision could lock Forged Tools into a costly long-term contract or cause loss of opportunity. High sales levels don't always mean profit, especially if Forged

Tools can't meet contract commitments, which creates unhappy customers or, in the case of production loads, unhappy workers.

Currently no data is shared between the firm's divisions (marketing, finance, and production). Factory information is stored in one database, sales in another, contracts in a third, and administration (accounting and so forth) in a fourth. This makes it very difficult to get timely, up-to-date, accurate information for anything other than what is currently being produced on the factory floor. Farrice relies on phone calls to obtain information. ■

1. Describe the current IS architecture at Forged Tools. Identify business processes, organizations, and databases. From a manager's point of view, what is good about this IS architecture? What is bad?

2. What should be done with Forged Tools' information architecture to make it easier to have applications such as those proposed? Are there any positive side effects? What would be the drawbacks? From the point of view of users such as Farrice, does the type of information architecture used make a difference? Why or why not?

Summary

An IS architecture arranges information across functions and at levels within an organization so that it can be located, retrieved, processed, and distributed efficiently. An IS architecture should reflect the levels of management as well as the disciplines and functions. It should include shared and nonshared databases. Corporate databases consist of data, applications, and models created to meet organizational goals in a dynamic fashion. Architectures should take into account business processes, departments that carry out the processes, databases storing critical information, and the information systems that make data available and useful. A shared, dynamic information architecture makes it possible to navigate across databases, access the most up-to-date and accurate information, and link business functions without duplicating information. The tight linkages implicit in such an architecture make security, integrity, and backup paramount.

Two approaches to information architectures are important for managers. The relational approach to database design simplifies the creation, use, and maintenance of shared, dynamic databases. Five levels of software facilitate the storage of data, the linking of data into databases, the processing of the data, the creation of data-manipulation applications, and the use of user-friendly interfaces to other levels. The object-oriented approach does not focus on data per se but on the objects that the data describe, allowing managers to deal with the objects directly (through software) rather than through databases. This creates information systems that more closely resemble the business systems that the information systems are intended to support, thus facilitating managerial action.

Discussion Questions

5.1 Think about how managers at different levels act and about their information needs. What does an integrated, shared information architecture have to have in order to satisfy different managers' needs? What conflicts could arise? How could they be resolved?

5.2 Consider the way you make complex decisions involving many sources of information. How do you access the various sources? What obstacles do you encounter in trying to bring the information from diverse sources together? What tools do you use to do this?

5.3 The Forged Tools example may seem extreme, but what is there about strategic opportunities or threats that make shared, dynamic information architectures so necessary? What characterizes these high-risk situations? What kinds of support do managers receive through dynamic, shared information architectures?

5.4 You are probably familiar with information systems that advertise and stress access to data in files and records. On the other hand, the object-oriented system approach avoids references to files, records, and fields. What kinds of interaction would you design for yourself to handle your world as objects? What tools would you want to have to retrieve, display, process, report on, and distribute objects? What advantages would you have if you could handle objects directly without handling data? Are there disadvantages to this approach?

Key Terms

application	inheritance	related events
attribute	key	relational database model
common events	message	reuse
corporate model base	method	shared architecture
database	navigation	shared database
dynamic architecture	object-oriented approach	subclass
encapsulation	redundancy	superclass
information architecture		

References

Allen, B., and A. Boynton. "Information Architecture: In Search of Efficient Flexibility." *Management Information Systems Quarterly* 15, 4 (December 1991).

Anthony, R. *Planning and Control Systems: A Framework for Analysis.* Cambridge, MA: Harvard University Press, 1965.

Codd, E. F. "The Relational Model of Data for Large Shared Data Bases." *Communications of the ACM* 13, 6 (June 1970): 377–387.

Date, C. *An Introduction to Database Systems.* 5th ed. Reading, MA: Addison-Wesley, 1990.

Everest, G. *Database Management: Objectives, System Functions and Administration.* New York: McGraw Hill, 1985.

Harrington, J. *Relational Database Management for Microcomputers: Design and Implementation.* New York: Holt, Rinehart and Winston, 1987.

Kronke, D. *Database Processing.* 4th ed. New York: Macmillan, 1992.

Martin, J. *Managing the Data Base Environment.* Englewood Cliffs, NJ: Prentice-Hall, 1983.

CASE

EVERGREEN LANDSCAPING AND MAINTENANCE: AN INTEGRATED DATABASE FOR CONNIE

While Connie's work is focused on marketing and sales, she finds that human resource management is a challenging aspect. A great deal of what goes on at Evergreen is labor-intensive, and closing a sale or getting a contract doesn't depend exclusively on the products but may hinge on how salespeople and contract workers relate to their customers. Connie and Shawna, vice president of sales, have spoken in general terms about building a human resource information system to help them with hiring and tracking staff, especially temporary staff. One of the more rewarding but tricky aspects of Connie's job is hiring students for temporary summer work. Generally, she relies on her two assistant managers to handle this job by using intuition, fairness, and good judgment. Both Sid (assistant contract sales manager) and Sven (assistant retail sales manager) have hired temporary

Figure 5–13   EVERGREEN'S APPLICATION FORM

```
Return to:
HR Department
Evergreen Landscaping
and Maintenance, Inc.
2010 Forest Road
                              EVERGREEN
EMPLOYMENT
APPLICATION                 Landscaping and Maintenance, Inc.
- - - - - - - - - - - - - - - - - - - - - - - - - - - - - - - - - -
Name: _____
Address: _____
       _____

Phone: _____
Position Desired: _____
(Check one) Full Time _____ Part Time _____
If part time, indicate days, times:



Prior landscaping experience/training



Prior retail experience/training



How did you hear about this position?



Signature _____ Date _____
```

help for the store as well as contract services (primarily lawn maintenance). Sven usually hires a dozen students for stocking, pruning, watering, and cashier work during the busiest months. Lawn maintenance starts a month earlier and lasts almost six weeks longer, so Sid and Sven share staff from time to time. Sid likes using staff that Sven has trained because they know what's in stock and generally are better team players. Sven finds, too, that students who have worked for a summer tending lawns often are better with customers than those who don't have experience.

However, because of the popularity of the guaranteed green-up service, Sid's need for additional staff has increased and he must hire more temporary employees than last year. This staff must be willing to work long into the fall and start as soon as frost has left the ground. Of course, it's not always possible to find students who have the right kind of experience and the right attitude, and Sven doesn't want his pool of experienced workers raided either.

To get the job done, Sid and Sven are producing a piece of software that helps them identify individuals who have exactly the right kinds of experience for specific jobs. Eight jobs are available: stocker, cashier, inside maintenance, outside maintenance, yard maintenance, driver, mechanic, and foreman. Each job requires a certain kind of experience. Applicants are asked to fill out forms (see Figure 5–13), and these data go into the computer's database. This software will be useful for keeping track of applicants as well as tracking who is employed in what capacity. The data can be recalled next year so that the best temporary help can be called back. Sven also knows that some good temporary employees might be interested in working permanently for Evergreen, so he can make sure they are called first.

Connie realizes that this is only one isolated application and has been working with Frances (vice president of administration) to build an integrated human resources information system (HRIS) that will keep track of full-time and part-time employees and make additional information available to Frances, Sid, and Sven. This HRIS would store information on employees, how to locate them, positions held, salaries, evaluations, periods of time employed, and skill profiles as agreed upon with their supervisors. Beyond the HRIS, Connie also sees a tie-in with sales and marketing. She has noticed that some of the sales staff sell well; there are rarely any returns from dissatisfied customers. Other salespeople, especially new employees, make some mistakes and customers come back with complaints. The good salespeople should be a good source of information about their customers because they intuitively know what works, what to sell, and how to sell it. Of course, Connie can't count on the novices to tell her what *doesn't* work. However, it is clear that analysis of the returns can at least point out training needs and at best show problems with the sales system. Furthermore, the HRIS may show some patterns in the returns such as which products are hard to sell. Connie would like to analyze these data; Sid would like to know which contracts his workers have worked on so that when a client asks for the same crew as last year he can deliver; and Sven wants to tie the human resource database into the product database to find out who is familiar with which products.

Questions

1. In Figure 5–3, locate where the various applications described above fit in. Which application areas and organizational levels are affected? What are the unique files? The common files? What applications are common across several areas?

2. Consider each of the following applications: applicant information system, HRIS, returns analysis program, and crew composition database. How do these applications fit together? What commonalities do they have? What relationships do these applications have to the business subsystems for marketing, sales, production (servicing the greenhouses or providing landscaping services, for example), and human resources? Create a diagram in the style of Figure 5–10 that reflects these relationships.

3. Using relational database concepts, design a set of tables or files that reflect the content described above for the applicant information system.

4. Figures 5–6 through 5–9 refer to sales transactions at Evergreen. How would you modify these relations and/or add additional relations to reflect Connie's needs to analyze returns based on who the salesperson is? What assumptions are you making as you do this? Notice that we are linking the sales, customer, and inventory (item) databases with the HRIS. What additional support does this linking give to Connie, Sid, Sven, and Frances?

5. List the objects that are important in the HRIS. How do these objects fit together? Consider the applications in Question 2. How would an object-oriented approach to data make it easier to create these applications? To create new applications?

CHAPTER SIX

BRIDGING DISTANCES: TELECOMMUNICATIONS ARCHITECTURES FOR STRATEGIC ADVANTAGE

OBJECTIVES

After you have read and studied this chapter, you should be able to:

■ Identify the nine telecommunications challenges and discuss how they affect managers.

■ Discuss how client-server architectures can provide firms with strategic advantages.

■ Describe the challenges of interorganizational systems and the strategic advantages they can provide.

Question: What advantages come from distributing information processing across several sites via telecommunications?

Zero ("No Problem") Sanchez knows he should be worried. As customer service manager of Continental Transfer's subsidiary, Shakers' Movers, Zero has to make certain that moves go without a hitch. Shakers' Movers has a program of guaranteed executive relocation, and Zero runs the operation from headquarters. Customers are guaranteed trouble-free moves from home to home. Shakers' has a network of agents in major cities who handle the paperwork, direct the furniture unloading, stock the fridge, and arrange housecleaning so that customers can move right in. Because Continental has few trucks of its own, Zero works with nine major national franchised movers and can call on more than 40 others in emergencies, usually in January or June. Zero mostly uses the telephone and facsimile and he has had few problems so far, but the volume is increasing and businesses are moving executives around so rapidly, and expectations are rising so quickly, that Zero wonders if he should consider some options involving more advanced information systems than his microcomputer, his phone, and a notepad.

Answer: Zero should understand that despite the challenges of distance, volume, cost, noise, error, coordination, configuration, mobility, and the need for standards, moving information processing to multiple sites has significant advantages. Interorganizational systems promote cooperation and strength, assuring strong links with suppliers and customers. Client-server strategies can cut costs, increase reliability, and guarantee the flexibility needed to compete in today's business environment.

INTRODUCTION

This chapter expands on the ideas discussed in the previous chapter and looks at architecture from a slightly different viewpoint. In Chapter 5, we focused on simplifying access to information about multiple events or multiple descriptions of the same event by a single user. Now we will concentrate on architectures that allow many users access to shared resources. These users are spread out geographically, perhaps in different buildings, cities, countries, or continents. Some users attempt to access information that may be found in a single database while others may try to integrate information across databases belonging to other users. In some cases, individuals work independently; in others, they strive to collaborate.

The common experience that all these users have is that they are removed by distance from the data and, in fact, do not wish to know how or even where the data are stored and they are not generally concerned about the hardware or software that maintains the data. Their concern is for the problem they are working on or the opportunity they perceive to be hidden in the data. Because they are distant from the data, it becomes even more important that they not have to know how (through what path) they need to "address" the data.

This chapter is about telecommunication or data communication or telematics. While there are some differences in these terms, each refers to the fact that users are so far removed physically from the data and each other that having to "address" the data is a daunting task. Telecommunications is not a new field and these problems aren't new, either. We have always had communications from a distance—mail, for example—but we have never had the problems brought on by huge volumes. Large networks mean that additional growth increases the costs of coordinating new nodes with existing ones, and both data and opportunity age ungraciously. With increasing time pressures in business, the need for up-to-the-moment data also rises, and the telecommunication problems we have always had are even more pressing now. The modern management imperatives listed at the end of the chapter are for the most part time-based and require efficient communication to meet. How we overcome the inherent problems through a telecommunications architecture is the focus of this chapter.

We will explore three architectural dimensions of telecommunications. First we discuss telecommunication basics from a user's viewpoint. Next we look at one particular architecture—client-server architecture. This architecture is revolutionizing computer use by motivating replacement of single, large mainframes with networks of microcomputers (called servers, although not all servers are microcomputers), each of which provides a service to other machines, often microcomputers, called clients. A client-server architecture is not necessarily a single kind of hardware design. Clients and servers engage in transactions using digital "conversations" that make hardware compatibility less of a problem.

Finally, we examine an architecture of systems that serves or represents multiple organizations, called interorganizational systems. Our focus is on users in diverse organizations who, in most cases, are attempting to reach cooperative strategic goals. Such systems may join firms with their suppliers, firms with groups of their customers, or groups of firms.

TELECOMMUNICATION CHALLENGES

The focus of this chapter is on **telecommunication.** *Tele* is from a Greek root meaning "far off," *communication* comes from a Latin root meaning "common," and *com* means "with." After the parts are joined together, we have a wonderful neologism that implies a contradiction—being together at a distance. How very much like our modern world that we

| Figure 6–1 | NINE TELECOMMUNICATION CHALLENGES |

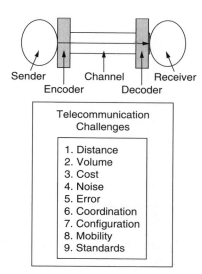

Sender   Channel   Receiver
Encoder   Decoder

Telecommunication
Challenges

1. Distance
2. Volume
3. Cost
4. Noise
5. Error
6. Coordination
7. Configuration
8. Mobility
9. Standards

create technology that makes something that is logically impossible not only possible but mundane.

Telecommunications systems face a number of challenges (see Figure 6–1). The first challenge is distance. Long distances increase the difficulty of communicating because the signals sent tend to attenuate or lessen with distance. Regardless of the medium used, signal strength decreases proportionately to the square of the distance unless it is extremely well confined (say, down a wire, pipe, or optical fiber). Signals have to be encoded by a sender and decoded by a receiver, hence, there is a question of senders' and receivers' capacity to code and decode quickly enough. There is also concern with a channel's capacity to transport messages. Volume considerations often override other concerns because higher volumes almost always mean higher costs.

In traversing distance, there are transportation costs, and these costs increase proportionately with each increase in volume per unit time required. These costs are also closely tied to quality, because as the volume of signals increases, noise increases, too, and as a signal weakens over distance, noise makes a larger intrusion. Noise may be in the form of competing signals that make it hard to distinguish the wanted from the unwanted signal. Alternatively, static noise masks the signal and makes it hard to discern.

Weakened signals are even more difficult to understand among noise, which creates the very real, almost unavoidable situation of error. So, because signals tend to be weak, contaminated, and subject to fallible interpretation, it is important for communicating stations to coordinate their activities. For example, it may not be easy to discern when a signal is starting when there is also background noise.

Because there are always at least two communicators, it is also important to understand when the sender is done and when the receiver can respond. Turn-taking procedures may require special signals or messages that themselves are subject to error. Add to this the problem that not only are the sender and receiver at a distance, but they may be

Figure 6–2   THE FATE OF A SIGNAL OVER DISTANCE

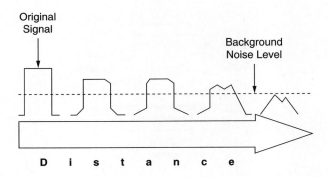

mobile and hence difficult to locate among a welter of potential receivers and senders. This problem is exacerbated because many telecommunications situations involve multiple senders and receivers configured in a network. Creating and maintaining a valuable configuration is one of the major communication challenges.

Finally, telecommunication, more than any other human activity, must have standards established in advance. Imagine how hard it would be to decide over a noisy telephone line what language you would speak with another person. Because telecommunication is encoded (more on this later), and coordination relies on codes to succeed, establishing standard codes is crucial. Without standards, communication is very difficult, and *tele*communication merely compounds these problems.

The nine problems of distance, volume, cost, noise, error, coordination, configuration, mobility, and standards make telecommunication the challenge that it is. Every telecommunications system has faced these challenges in a unique way. For example, microwave systems were developed to increase bandwidth, but at a relatively high cost and, until recently, requiring stationary receivers and transmitters. The nine problems are reviewed in some detail next along with the basic concepts of telecommunication.

Distance

The problem of **distance** and the corresponding problem of signal **attenuation** have spurred the greatest efforts in the area of physical technology (see Figure 6–2). Early electrical technologies included telegraphy and telephony, both of which use wires; these wires are, to a great extent, the mainstay of most local communication today. Wire-based transmission media are referred to as **twisted pairs** because the pair of wires required for the circuit are twisted around each other to reduce static. They are quite limited, relative to today's volume requirements, in their capacity to move digital data. **Coaxial cable** is another form of wire with greater capacity and other positive characteristics, but it requires real estate from which to string it from point to point. Microwave technology circumvents the problem of taking up physical space along the route and, in conjunction with satellites, can significantly change the geography of distances by avoiding land altogether.

| Figure 6–3 | BASIC COMMUNICATION SYSTEM COMPONENTS |

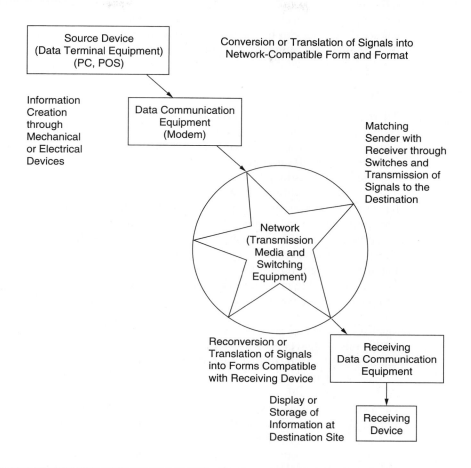

Some technologies are less subject to attenuation problems than others, but most forms of transmission lose energy over distance and must be amplified repeatedly. Amplifiers cost money, take time and energy, introduce noise and error, and must be serviced. In general, the greater the distance, the greater will be the chance for error, the higher the maintenance cost, the less flexible the entire system, and the more time and expense incurred with coordination and overhead.

Figure 6–3 illustrates a basic, generic network that spans distances. A **source device** (such as a keyboard, scanner, or mouse) accepts input from a user and converts these actions into electrical signals. These signals are then converted into standardized formats (often tones representing ones and zeros) by a **data communication device** (commonly a modem, which stands for *mo*dulator *dem*odulator) for transmission over a distance. Transmission uses many different media, including ordinary copper wires, coaxial cables, and land- and space-based microwaves. These formatted signals may be dispatched to a variety of destinations through a **switching system.** Many of the transmission and switching systems used were designed to handle voice telephony; hence, they are appropriate for audio signals (tones) to carry information. More modern networks are intended for digital (on-off) signals. Regardless of what kinds of signals are present, switched signals are subsequently received by another data communication device and formatted for receiving or destination devices (such as screens, audio output, or disk storage). At each stage, a variety of services can be provided to make the movement of data more efficient, effective, or usable for managers.

Volume

There are many ways to measure the **volume,** or rate of information or messages, in communication. The primary unit used by technicians is a **baud,** or signal per second. Commonly, digital signaling is measured in terms of bits, and each signal can contain one or more bits of information.

Modems have the job of converting signals from analog to digital formats and back. They do this in a variety of ways, but their purpose is to handle digital signals that may have to be sent over an analog network. One common technique is to transmit a certain tone for a brief period of time when signaling a binary "0" and to use another tone when signaling a binary "1." This sequence of rapid tones, called **frequency shift keying (FSK),** allows digitally coded data to be sent over a network that is designed to carry electrical impulses representing sounds.

The capability of a network to move signals is measured in two ways. If a network component (say, a modem or a transmission line) can handle 1,800 signals per second, it is said to operate at 1,800 baud. If each signal can represent eight bits (2^8 or 256 different values), then the component will be rated at 14,400 (i.e., $8 \times 1,800$) **bits per second (BPS)** (also abbreviated as 14.4KBPS). This latter figure is also referred to as **bandwidth.** For a network, bandwidth as a whole is limited by the slowest component.

Clearly, bandwidth is a key economic concept. Higher bandwidth costs more money. Although bandwidth costs are always dropping, at any moment in time the very highest bandwidths are always expensive, while the smallest bandwidths tend to be too slow for today's applications. Transmitting a 14.4MB file at 3,600 BPS will take four times as long as transmission at 14.4KBPS; hence, network fees may be four times as high. For this reason, most networks have the capability of providing **data compression** either in the network itself, in the data communication devices, or in the software in the data terminal equipment. Data compression entails removing redundant data prior to transmission and its replacement after reception. For example, a string of 1,000 zeros can be replaced by special codes that the receiving equipment can interpret to mean 1,000 zeros. These codes are generally far shorter than the original material, and compression ratios of 2 to 1 or even 10 to 1 are possible, thus further cutting transmission costs.

Modems were originally designed to convert digital signals into audio tones suitable for low-quality audio telephone lines. These lines are very noisy and are not suitable for carrying digital signals directly. The equipment found in telephone networks (such as switches) treats digital pulses as noise and tries to eliminate them. Modems are generally low-cost devices with limited bandwidth, operating at speeds of up to 28,800 baud (generally with two levels of signaling—one tone indicating a 1 and another a 0—giving an effective information rate of 28,800 bits per second). Today, 4,800 and 9,600 BPS are common speeds across public dialed networks, along with 14,400 and 28,800 BPS. Higher speeds are possible with special hardware and compression. Digital modems work on an entirely different principle to match electrical characteristics between terminal devices (such as key-based equipment or personal computers) and digital networks.

Figure 6–4

EFFECT OF NOISE

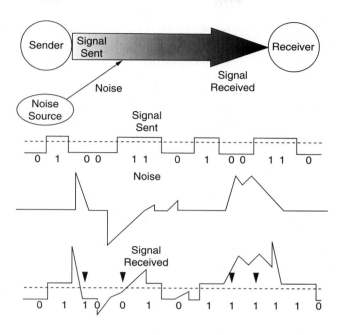

Cost

Details on cost are difficult to state because they change rapidly. **Costs** tend to increase with distance, rate, volume, lack of noise, and reliability. Consider that a very thin connector joins geographic regions and that all communication has to travel across that thin connector. Ultimately, cost is the major construction and operation criterion in telecommunications. Getting that thin line there in the first place and keeping it operating correctly cost money.

While costs increase with the factors mentioned, they have tended to fall over time. Also, costs may not always be proportional to distance. Users of common carriers may note that within a geographical region (state, province, or nation), costs are relatively distance-insensitive. Instead, costs respond both to the amount of time of network access (called *connect time*) and the volume of information passed. In many cases, these costs are interrelated (high volumes require more time). However, faster network access (higher-speed transmission), while decreasing network access time, is inherently more expensive. The interrelationship of these factors makes pricing telecommunication services complex, and the marketplace has lively competition that keeps prices and packages of services constantly changing.

Noise

Noise is an unwanted message (see Figure 6–4). Noise wouldn't be a problem if we had unlimited resources and could build machinery to separate our wanted message from all the other messages and nonmessages that pollute the electronic world. Unfortunately, neither is likely. Funds and time are limited, and it is often difficult to discern our bits from the welter of electronic fuzz caused by lightning, industrial sparks, radio, TV, gamma rays, and dry nylon carpets in the winter. But we can use what we know about noise to design systems that are less susceptible.

Noise can be countered in two ways, each of which costs money. Hardware and systems can be built as noise-insensitive as possible, and the transmission medium selected may be less susceptible to noise. Telephone wiring is likely to pick up industrial and commercial noise; microwave transmission is less likely to do so. The encoding scheme used to transmit information may also work to eliminate certain kinds of noise. Such fault-avoiding systems are, of course, expensive to build and economically risky.

Alternatively, systems can be built that adjust to noise and correct for problems that occur when noise affects transmission. In other words, the ill effects of noise can be undone, generally with software. Error detection and correction recognize that noise will always occur and attempt to reduce its effects. The major disadvantage of such fault-tolerant systems is a decrease in speed.

Error

The topic of fault-tolerant systems is highly technical, but the effects of **error** are clear. Speech is normally quite fault-tolerant. Consider how sloppily most people speak their native languages, making grammatical errors, creatively using words in ways Webster never imagined, and leaving sentences unfinished or even unconstructed. But the redundancy of language makes it possible to get along with these errors most of the time. If a message is unclear, we simply ask for a clarification. In speaking with others, people use three different techniques to make speech fault-tolerant:

- People agree in advance on the meanings of words; they learn their native language; they adopt conventions of speech including intonation, pauses, and so forth.
- People adjust their speech to the situation, speaking more loudly when there is a lot of background noise, enunciating more clearly when others are also speaking, simplifying their speech when talking with those who may not understand technical terms; people even spell out words they think others may not understand, such as their names.
- People agree that certain phrases indicate a message needs to be clarified or repeated.

Telecommunication systems employ three analogous techniques. First are conventional codes and rules of turn taking that have been developed to govern how telecommunication interchanges take place. These are called **protocols** and they cover error-correction techniques and signaling for the start and stop of conversations, called **sessions.** These protocols are most noticeable when they are used with facsimile or dialing into a computer network. The exchange of beeping and humming is the coordination of two systems agreeing on the protocol by which messages are sent and received.

The second class of techniques is mathematical, enabling receivers to determine whether an error has occurred in transmission (it is possible that senders may also know this, but in telecommunications it is far more likely that receivers will make this determination). Such **error-detection** and **error-correction techniques** consist of adding additional information to each message that automatically signals that the message is wrong if certain conditions are met. This **redundancy** is also useful sometimes in correcting the received message. The simplest techniques are called **parity techniques.** Among the simplest is a parity bit, which is commonly associated with character encoding. For example, suppose a particular coding scheme produces an "A" as seven bits thus: "1100001." A possible parity scheme is to append a bit at one or the other end that makes the total number of bits either even or odd, depending on the scheme selected. Using *odd* parity and postfixing will result in an "A" normally being "11000010" with the boldfaced "0" postfixed. Notice that the number of one bits is three, an odd number. Suppose the transmitted "11000010" is received as "11000110," which would be thought of as a "C." Notice that the number of one bits is now even. This is an indication that the character is incorrect, because a true "C" would be received as "11000111."

Unfortunately, because noise tends to come in bursts, such simple parity schemes can catch only half of all possible noise-originated errors. If all noise were spikes of infinitesimally short duration and if they occurred very infrequently, only one bit would ever be changed in any single character, and the parity scheme would let us know this. But if two, four, six, or eight bits were changed, we would not know. Imagine the first six bits of "11000010" were switched to "00111110." The parity is still odd. Because half of all numbers are odd and half are even, simple parity schemes tend to catch only 50 percent of errors, and they do not tell us what the original character was supposed to be.

There are other, more complex character- and message-level schemes, but they are not of interest to managers. The net effect of such schemes is to create longer messages and to slow down message transmission a bit and to build in either hardware costs, to catch errors in the receiving equipment, or software costs and speed reduction, to calculate error-detection and error-correction parameters.

A third level of error handling is also available. Having detected an error and determined that the error cannot be corrected or adjusted to, a receiving system may ask the sending system for clarification. As noise increases, the volume of clarifications and repeated messages builds up. Each wrong message can cost up to two additional messages. Furthermore, as anyone who has interacted with other people knows, having *said* something is not the same as having *been heard*. People want confirmation that their messages are getting through, and telecommunication systems are no different. Each sender needs to know that the previous message got through before continuing with the next message. This, too, increases traffic overhead, although confirmation and disconfirmation messages tend to be very short. Beyond the cost of traffic, additional housekeeping costs are involved in keeping track of which messages have been received correctly and are waiting for responses. Hence, a lot of effort goes into designing schemes to link communicators with a minimum of such interruptions. Again, there is no such thing as something for nothing, and there is a cost or risk involved in each scheme.

The net result of error recognition as a certainty is that most networks operate at less than their rated speeds and with less than perfect accuracy. This can be a problem in real-time systems (such as air traffic control or banking transaction systems) when error-related traffic increases and overwhelms the actual target information traffic. This can occur when a bursty noise intrusion occurs, when one or more lines or nodes in a network are impaired, or simply when traffic increases during certain times of the day and everything slows down so much that the required "acknowledge" messages indicating that the previous message did indeed get through are so delayed that the sender imagines (incorrectly) that the message was lost and retransmits it. This only serves to increase the load on the network, spelling disaster. Network managers look out for these sorts of situations and, with skill and some luck, can avoid these gridlocks.

Coordination

Two aspects of **coordination** that affect managers receiving services through networks are the kinds of network messaging being used and the way network managers do their jobs. Most of the networks we are familiar with are called **point-to-point networks** that involve only two individuals, as in a telephone call. In such simple situations, simple protocols are in effect, and as long as the exchange is simple, there are no problems. Using a simple protocol, people know when it is their turn to talk, they know when an error has occurred, and they know when the conversation is over. This simple protocol breaks down when others refuse to follow the rules or when the number of people gets so large that simply following the rules becomes too difficult—for example, a two-person discussion may become a conference, a formal meeting, or a symposium, each with a different set of rules. Each medium or method of communication has a range of available configurations and associated protocols. Managers selecting a technique (such as e-mail, a real-time computer conference, or a client-server architecture via a desktop computer) will either directly participate in the protocol by consciously following the rules or will have software to handle at least some of the rules, and they will experience delays or limitations because of this. Examples of limitations include the following:

- E-mail messages may sometimes get through immediately, especially if traffic is low, and sometimes may be delayed for hours; communicators may have their messages cross in the mail.

- When communicating with a group, individuals may see messages already composed but may not be able to retrieve messages once they have sent them.

- In a data retrieval situation, users may find themselves locked out of all or a portion of the data because others are updating it.

- In a telephone conversation, both communicators may speak and interrupt each other at the same time—messages flow both ways simultaneously (called **full duplex**), but other systems may operate in a me-then-you mode (**half duplex**). In telephony, the two communicators own the line between them for the duration of the conversation, but if one of them is "engaged," the other cannot communicate. However, using e-mail, each can carry on half of the conversation at any time without actually connecting with the other. Another aspect of coordination is the units used during communication. A unit may be a circuit connecting communicators, individual messages that pass among communicators, or parts of messages. Telephony is basically **circuit switching** (the whole electrical circuit is switched to the connected pair) while e-mail is **message switching** (in which the connection between the two occurs only for the brief period of time in which the message is actually sent from one to the other's mailbox). In Figure 6–5, A and D are communicating, as are B and E, C and F. With circuit switching, A and D own the line between them and can use it any way they like, typically taking turns talking. There may be long, silent periods during which the line is available—and typically is

Figure 6—5   TYPES OF SWITCHING

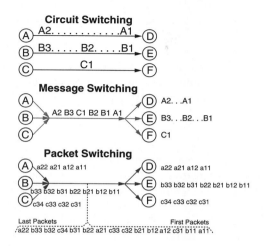

being paid for. In message switching, a smaller number of lines, here depicted as just one, is shared among pairs of communicators. As each message is completed, it is sent through the line to the receiver. This is a more efficient use of the line because silences aren't paid for. In many cases, however, even this scheme is inefficient. A third type of switching is called **packet switching** in which a network breaks up messages into smaller units called packets (often only 100 bytes or so in length) and transmits the message in pieces, reassembling it at the receiver's end. For point-to-point communication involving two communicators, this is not remarkably different from circuit or message switching, but in a network, this can make for complicated problems and potential delays. The value of alternatives to circuit switching is to utilize the quiet time on connecting lines for other communicators' messages. The smaller the unit, the better "packing" there is, and the higher the utilization, especially if the messages are being sent by people hunting and pecking on their keyboards. However, because each unit has to be handled from point to point, the small overhead costs for each packet can add up to large delays or hardware or software costs, and, of course, packets have to be acknowledged.

Network management is generally transparent to users, but management decisions, such as how traffic is routed, what is charged, and various design parameters, will determine the functionality of the network. In public, switched, or nonswitched networks, rates tend to be lower during off-peak hours. Two networks are generally available to the public. **Common carriers,** such as local, regional, or national telephone companies, operate equipment that is available to everyone on a fee-for-service or contract basis. Common carrier services are generally shared by users, and the services available tend to be nonspecialized, although some specialized common carriers are slowly appearing, many of which operate satellite networks for their users. Another type of network is called a **value-added network (VAN),** which offers basic telecommunication or services with additional value-added features, such as electronic mail, remote sensing, packet switching, access to specialized databases, or information services (including shopping) or specialized processing (such as the SWIFT network that connects banks worldwide, EDI services, ATM networks, 800 and 900 number services, among others). The nature, price, and availability of these services are determined by network operators and the marketplace. With the continuing convergence of telecommunications, entertainment, and information technology and business interests, the availability of specialized services on a legion of VANs is a certainty in the near future.

Configuration

As discussed, telecommunication between a sender and a receiver is difficult enough, but when there are many communicators, the challenges are more than multiplied. The number of possible connections increases as the square of the number of communicators; in a packet-switched network, the number of possible paths increases geometrically, and the potential for error and noise increases dramatically. Network **configurations** per se have two major reasons for existing:

- It is uneconomical to build a line between each pair of communicators; most of the time, most of these links will not be used.
- Sometimes it's important to reach multiple communicators. Not only is there point-to-point communication, but there is **point-to-multipoint** (broadcasting), **multipoint-to-point** (incasting, as in electronic polling, voting, or purchasing), and **multipoint-to-multipoint** (conferencing) **transmission.** As well, there may be a real or implied hierarchy among communicators such that messages intended for C from A should or must go through B; thus, a direct line from A to C is not required.

In other words, the "no network" situation depicted in Figure 6–6 is certainly not economical and may in fact be counterproductive. There are many alternatives to no networking, of which four are shown in the figure. These are referred to as **topologies.** A **star network** is very old and mimics the centralized authority of a leader. All message communication is initiated by the center, or hub. This hub controls all information flow and thus indirectly or directly controls all the equipment attached to it. Hubs are efficient and easy to manage, but if the hub itself is damaged, no communication is possible. Also, a hub design is inflexible. If the two terminals labeled A and B need to communicate often and are located close together, there is a great cost associated with shipping messages the long distance from A to the central node X and back to B. In addition, there is constant **contention** for attention from the central node to send messages, creating a potential bottleneck.

A **hierarchy** mimics a bureaucracy. All communication from R to P goes through Q, and vice versa. Hierarchies are important when the bulk of traffic is within specific areas (say, departments) and secondary traffic for control or statistical analysis is required from these areas. Each area may have its own structure. Secondary traffic is generated occasionally and sent through the hierarchy, perhaps by electronic mail, through a mainframe system. Generally, hierarchical networks are not composed of peers (i.e., machines, stations, or nodes with equal powers or responsibilities). P, for example, may be a mainframe

| **Figure 6–6** | NETWORK CONFIGURATIONS |

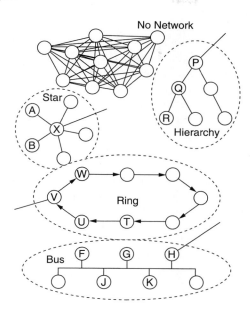

or host computer that contains most of the corporate data. Q may be a minicomputer that controls a subnetwork of workstations of which R may be one. R may request data from P via Q in a client-server configuration (more on this later). All of this, of course, is generally transparent to users (who might be using client machines like R). Large networks with many diverse machines and nodes performing a variety of tasks may be constructed as hierarchies. Subnetworks may have other structures such as stars, rings, or buses. Because the hierarchy is actually a hierarchy of specialized star networks, it can suffer from the same problems star configurations do.

A **ring** is a popular configuration that consists of peers (some of which are actually servers that provide data or access to other networks, among other services) connected in a one-way fashion (sometimes bidirectional, but this is seldom necessary or effective). In Figure 6–6, messages are passed clockwise so that a message from T to W passes through U and V and a message from U to T must pass through V, W, and several other nodes before it reaches T. While the ring may at first seem to be highly inefficient, in fact it is relatively spare in terms of the number of links required (the same number as nodes, which makes it no less efficient than a hierarchy and only marginally less so than a star), but a unidirectional route can make high-speed communication less expensive. Because there is no central node as in a star, there is no real bottleneck; thus, traffic volumes can be quite high, with every station having a good chance to send and receive. Contention is less of a problem, but because each message must pass through, on average, half of the nodes, traffic is very high.

Finally, and probably most simple, a **bus** configuration connects every node or station to a common link, called a bus, and everyone contends for the right to send a message.

There are a number of complex and interesting schemes for sharing a bus, but it comes down to software overhead for turn taking. However, a bus is very robust because the failure of any, or even most, of the nodes does not impair the overall operation of the network.

Each topology has advantages and drawbacks. Because of economics, stars and hierarchies are used generally for **wide area networks (WANs).** Rings and buses are found mostly in **local area networks (LANS).** WANs rely on the speed and power of mainframes and specialized minicomputers to keep traffic flowing reliably. A WAN is a network that may extend across a city, state, or nation while a LAN is often found within a single building or a campus of buildings. WANs face different challenges from LANs partly because of the problems of long distance transmission and partly because many firms rely on the services of other firms to create, install, and operate their WANs. LANs rely on short distances and high network speeds to keep messages flowing rapidly. WANs deal with batches of information, generally reports or screens of data or files that have to be moved, such as daily transaction files or e-mail messages. LANs are focused on shorter bursts, often a line or a character.

The high rate of information transfer in the shared-link topologies of LANs makes them inappropriate for massive data transfer. The expensive processors in WANs are not meant for handling information a character at a time. Many networks are **hybrids,** involving a WAN of LANs to handle information at appropriate rates for appropriate purposes. Links between the LANs or between the WAN and a larger world are handled by **gateways,** indicated in Figure 6–6 by lines extending beyond the networks. Gateways do more than provide an electrical connection, though. Different networks more than likely have different protocols requiring special software to do the translation. Sometimes they use different codes (ASCII, EBCDIC), different error-handling procedures, and different transmission rates.

A hybrid network is most likely found in large corporations. For example, there may be a central mainframe at the apex of a hierarchy. This mainframe does routine, massive information processing, such as keeping a firm's books, generating regular financial reports, or providing computing services for difficult simulations. A series of minicomputers may process divisional data before sending it on to the mainframe. Each minicomputer may gather information on a daily or hourly basis from remote locations or regional headquarters to compile reports, link divisions, or access data. One of the minicomputers may act as a gateway into the Internet and another may access specialized data services for a research department. Another minicomputer may act as a gateway to a client-server ring network of microcomputers that actually gathers divisional data and processes its transactions through **point-of-sale (POS)** terminals. Some of the micros act as servers (maintaining divisional data, for example, or performing specialized arithmetic functions). POS terminals themselves may be on a bus in each location, with one of the terminals acting as a communication server to the divisional client-server ring. This hybrid is depicted in Figure 6–7.

One important managerial consideration that affects corporate and divisional competitiveness is the flexibility of a configuration. In general, star networks are inflexible, concentrating all command and most power in a single central computer, and upgrades to processing are expensive. However, if nonhub nodes go down, other nodes in the network are rarely affected. Hierarchical networks are inflexible in terms of their wiring, and as functions change it may be difficult and expensive to rewire and reprogram the intermediate nodes. Buses, on the other hand, are limited in the load they can carry and may prove inflexible in terms of upscalability when traffic increases. Rings offer a good compromise

| Figure 6–7 | A COMPLEX CORPORATE NETWORK |

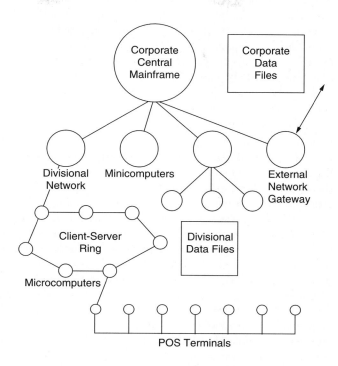

in that functionality is easy to increase by adding additional nodes with specialized services (such as file servers or print servers), but rings are also geographically limited and may be impossible to use outside a building or a campus. Hybrid networks generally grow this way because changing needs create the need to reconfigure, redesign, and patch formerly separate networks together.

This scalability problem, and the expense of purchasing and operating often incompatible mainframe and minicomputer systems and hierarchies as well as the growth of LAN software, have fostered a client-server approach, a revolutionary way of building networks. We turn our attention to this approach in a later section.

Mobility

To date, there are two major reasons to be concerned with mobility. **Mobility** is an increasingly important capability for today's flexible, rapidly changing organization. Many firms are experimenting with mobile employees who work from home or out of clients' offices. Salespeople have been traveling since Biblical times, sending in their sales information periodically by messenger, pony express, or modem. While these people might not move as they communicate, they do change their locations regularly. Organizations may be forming alliances, leasing facilities for short terms, and making brief investments in other firms. A manager may take a portable notebook computer to a construction site to gather performance data, make new completion date projections, and then send the data back to headquarters for archiving. With managers' empowerment to make increasingly higher-level decisions in the field comes the responsibility of the organization to collect the necessary data and provide feedback to these managers as quickly as possible.

Flexibility, mobility, speed, feedback, and responsiveness are the hallmarks of a modern manager, and these are enhanced by providing managers with network connections that help them achieve their goals. Global competition has made most forms of paper mail obsolete. The time zone–spanning nature of today's competition has put a premium on instant access.

Standards

Finally, **standards** are both the challenge and the answer to the challenge. Remembering that telecommunications implies the coordination of people and systems at a distance, we have to ask how the *original* coordination or agreement came about. The answer is that these standards exist because of two forces: competition and cooperation. As each organization or technology provider discovers a technological principle (the modem, for example, or the ring network), it creates an internal de facto standard for its own use and that of its customers. With many competing systems, concepts, and organizations, many competing standards arise. Sometimes these standards exist for a long time (for example, Morse code for telegraphy lasted almost 150 years), and sometimes they fail to catch on. Sometimes competing standards coexist for a long time—ASCII and EBCDIC character coding, for example, are available on competing equipment.

From an economic point of view, standards reflect the competitive struggle between users and suppliers of information technology. Suppliers generally want to keep systems proprietary because proprietary technologies lock users in and keep prices high. Users, on the other hand, want standards to make technology more of a commodity, and hence keep prices down. Because "a better way" normally means a competitive advantage, firms are loathe to give up their standards for others. This is so because a firm's customers incur costs in making a shift and, understandably, a firm's products might not work well under another standard. Standardization tends to stifle creativity in the early stages of a product's development, but it increases communication among developers and thus promotes idea sharing. It seems that when an idea is new and its basic technological principle is relatively simple, internal competing standards are the best option.

However, products and systems evolve. When they become very popular, as the telephone did in the early part of the twentieth century, interfirm standards arise, often goaded by survival. More often, however, the motivation is to enhance business by creating and satisfying customer expectations. In some cases, the customer is a government that has stepped in and by fiat appointed a standard (or set up a board to establish one) to bring order to a chaotic market. Almost everything we take for granted in the area of communications has been established over a period of time by government, in collaboration with the industry, to create standard products that customers can understand and purchase. In extreme cases, governments may act to create and commercialize the technology, thereby creating the standard at the same time.

The news for managers is relatively good. Managers are conservative by nature and exploratory by vocation. In an area such as telecommunications, where the technology is relatively opaque and hard to understand, managers are guided by standards. The **International Standards Organization (ISO)** created a series of standards for telecommunication, some of which (such as the ways modems are connected or what codes mean to terminal equipment) work at the electrical level and are of no interest at all to managers except to

| Figure 6–8 | CLIENT-SERVER PRINCIPLES |

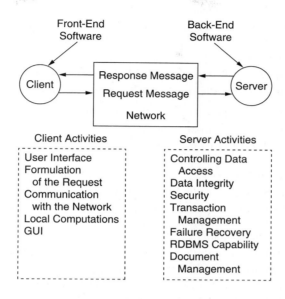

worry that all equipment purchased adheres to these standards. In the case of remote areas or third-world countries, it's important to assure that electrical supplies and local conditions can actually support the equipment that meets the standards. Others, such as standards for packet switching or for the design of the **Integrated Services Digital Network (ISDN),** affect the kinds of services available and ultimately their availability and cost. Staying on top of standards is usually a technical function, but managers need to be aware of how the development of standards will affect their future use of networks to get their jobs done.

CLIENT-SERVER ARCHITECTURES

A **client-server architecture** is a natural spin-off of the decentralizing force of networked PCs. A great deal of computing power resides in these relatively small and isolated machines. Unlike mainframe computers, PCs aren't individually capable of voluminous computation or managing very large databases. However, these machines, when net-worked, can combine their powers. The parallelism that individual microcomputers provides can accomplish a great deal, and the force that keeps them together is a client-server architecture that facilitates the interworking of separate machines.

Figure 6–8 illustrates how a client-server scheme works. Individual machines (called servers) are specialized to respond to particular requests in certain formats from other machines within a network. Just as society is organized around individuals with specializations, so a client-server architecture assumes that specific machines are outfitted with hardware and software to accomplish certain tasks. For example, print servers are capable of handling one or more printers (hence one or more print jobs) efficiently. File servers manage relatively large and/or complex databases while network servers handle e-mail and access to remote networks. Even compute servers are specialized to perform calculations lightning fast. Other terms that are used include *application server* (programs that perform part of a business function, but not the front-end GUI or the back-end file serving) and *resource server* (which includes files, tapes, communications, and security). All of these servers respond to messages in particular formats from other machines, called clients, for service. These messages will have meanings such as these:

- Find a file called "SHARE.RPT" (file server).
- Print the file on a printer capable of handling certain forms (print server).
- Send a priority message to the chairperson of the board (network server).
- Perform standard statistical analyses on specified data (compute server, directed to a file server).

Client-server architectures neatly solve the problem of common storage of software (such as spreadsheet applications) on a network because a copy of the software does not have to be stored on every machine. Of course, if a network goes down, everyone suffers without access to any software.

File servers are the central player in most client-server systems. Access to information means bringing information together from diverse, often incompatible, sources. These servers have to supply information to applications that are also mutually incompatible. To get these various components to work together requires standard communication techniques and languages. Thus, an important component of most client-server systems is a **relational database management system (RDBMS)** that uses a standardized language to make requests. This language is often some form of **structured query language (SQL).** For example, suppose two managers are responding to a request by the firm's attorneys for information on promotion patterns among staff. One manager (A) uses a mainframe HRIS; the other (B) uses a microcomputer database manager. For security reasons, employee information is stored on a remote minicomputer acting as a file server. The file server "speaks" SQL, but neither manager has to be knowledgeable in SQL. Instead, manager A uses a menu system to set up a query by responding as follows (menu selections are in italics):

1. File: *Employee*
2. Action: *Pick by*
3. Field: *Salaries*
4. Range: *Below 20,000*; back up to 2.
5. Action: *Report Format*
6. Format: *Sort*
7. Sort Field: *Last Name*
8. Sort Order: *Ascending*; back up to 7, then to 6.
9. Action: *Select Fields*
10. Fields: *Include*
11. Fields Selected: *Employee number, First name, Last name, Salary*; then back to 9.
12. Action: *Retrieve*

Manager B uses a visual query package involving a mouse. Selections are made by moving the mouse to an image on the screen denoting the employee file. When a map of the file comes up, the manager uses the mouse to select the salary field as the way of picking out the records desired. Next, the manager chooses from among a set of prepackaged report formats. A check-off form allows the manager to click on those fields desired in the report. Many of these selections are made by using a mouse to click on an icon from an action bar at the top of the screen. Eventually, the manager selects the icon that indicates the report is to be printed.

Neither manager knows anything about SQL, but in both cases the client application generates a set of SQL statements like the following:

- *Query to retrieve a list of employees earning less than $20,000 p.a., sorted by last name*
- SELECT Empl-no,Firstname,Lastname,Salary
- FROM Staff-data
- WHERE Salary < 20000
- AND Department= xxxx
- ORDERBY Lastname

Here the server is being asked to examine the file called Staff-data (and the client doesn't care where this data is), extracting the employee number, the full name of the employee, and the monthly salary in the case that the annual salary is less than $20,000, and then sorting it by last name before returning the information. Each client automatically inserts the filter "Department= xxxx" with the appropriate department ID.

Many microcomputer-based RDBMSs have the capability of operating with SQL-like commands, interspersing commands and using functions in the specifications. Used along with a client-server architecture and, of course, a file server, this relieves programmers and users of the necessity of knowing where and how data are stored, so long as the field names (e.g., empl-no, lastname) are known to both client and server.

The beauty of client-server architecture is that it allows structures of programs, files, and machines according to services provided to evolve rather than having the strict, predetermined relationships of older architectures. As new services evolve, they can be assigned to servers, and all existing clients can request them. This contrasts strongly with the older model in which programs were written for certain machines and would run only on those machines. Only predetermined other machines and applications could access them (if at all). In effect, managers can now request services in what is called a "transparent" fashion, without knowing which machines these services will appear on or even caring how the services will be provided. A service is treated as a black box or object, from which benefit can be derived.

This characteristic also contributes to the **scalability** of systems. Older systems have functionality added by increasing the software available on a central, usually mainframe, computer. But the more functions that are available, the heavier the load on the mainframe and the worse the service. This is like a Mexican restaurant suddenly deciding to serve French cuisine. With the enlarged menu comes an increase in clientele, but this increase in volume is at the expense of prompt service. A mainframe isn't necessarily suited to providing dozens of different services to clients. A client-server approach is scalable simply by adding an additional, usually low-cost, specialized server. Costs are lower for two reasons:

- Microcomputers provide more computing power for the dollar than mainframes, and
- Retrofitting mainframes to accommodate newly introduced software and hardware functionality is far more expensive than building new functionality in the first place and offering it on a flexible network.

In addition, as business increases and the pressure to scale up (or down) comes from the volume of business rather than the number of functions needed, it is far easier to add or remove microcomputers from a network than to add or remove pieces of a mainframe.

One final word on the client-server approach. It's relatively new, there is a lot of hype, and theory is more advanced than practice in many cases. Someone still has to determine where databases go and make them accessible. Software that cuts across database and system boundaries still has to be developed. While there are a few automated tools making their way to the marketplace to simplify the development of client-server applications, this industry is still in its infancy. Managers should remain alert to the relatively experimental nature of client-server approaches. It's important to note that mainframe vendors, such as IBM, have responded to the client-server movement with a mainframe-based client-server approach, where both client and server reside within a single system. Where a lot of number-crunching is required and where data can be effectively concentrated, the mainframe approach is still effective and far less experimental.

INTERORGANIZATIONAL SYSTEMS

Some networks extend beyond a single organization. While perhaps not technologically different from WANs or LANs, **interorganizational systems (IOSs)** do differ in how they are conceived and run and in their effects on a firm's competitive position. Interorganizational systems are of four major types:

- Some treat organizations as peers so that they can share information. These networks generally provide shared services and access to industrywide, public data through consortia. The purpose of these systems is to enhance the profitability of an industry as a whole. A premier example is the oil industry, which shares information that is already publicly available, thus saving the industry as a whole the cost of arraying and formatting this data.
- Others cut across industries and offer services through value-added networks (VANs) to anyone who is willing to pay the price. Stock prices, economic data, and news are commonly accessed in this way through Dow-Jones, government data brokers, and *The New York Times, The Globe and Mail,* and *The Wall Street Journal.* These are commonly commercial interests, unconcerned with competition or cooperation.
- Some systems are built to create more controllable ties between a firm and its suppliers or its customers. These are more likely developed and operated by large firms that can afford the resource costs of building these networks. As mentioned in Chapter 4, there is some cost associated with locking in customers and suppliers and, as N. Venkatraman insists—and we'll explore this at the end of this chapter—the real sustainable competitive advantage may come from what a firm does with the data rather than merely locking in suppliers or customers through a prior hardware or software investment or contract.

■ Some systems that are developed for one purpose are extended to serve others. Two examples are American Healthcare's ASAP ordering system and American Airlines' SABRE reservation system. Each was opened up to competitors and each has proven to be profitable in its own right—the leasing of reservations systems to competitors was American's only profit-maker during the 1990–1992 recession.

Interorganizational systems are tricky for some obvious and some nonobvious reasons. Obviously, a firm doesn't want to share strategic advantage with others. Cooperation carries a price, and even a system such as SABRE, while making a profit for its owner, in effect shares the wealth by providing services to others at a price they find advantageous. Who should own and operate the system, how much control should be shared, who should have access to the databases, and what does fair access mean are difficult questions for cooperating firms and harder for competitors. When does cooperation mean connivance? When does a system work against competition and set up a de facto cartel? These are questions that regulators like to ask and managers find hard to answer.

One force in making interorganizational systems more important has been the growth of **electronic data interchange (EDI).** By one estimate, there were 25,000 firms using EDI by the end of 1992, and the number will certainly double every couple of years. EDI refers to the standardization of documentation, the ubiquitous paperwork that seems to accompany every order. Think of EDI as a set of standard forms that companies can fill out and send electronically. Hwang et al. surveyed EDI users in 1993 and discovered that a significant number of the responding firms actually named someone as a supervisor of EDI, indicating that this trend is important organizationally. Most EDIs were built to link with customers while the bulk of the rest linked with suppliers. Consistent with other studies of EDI, most firms (70 percent) adopted EDI because their customers demanded it. Thus, it seems that customers either experience the pain of paperwork more than suppliers or they are more aware of the advantages EDI supplies. Most firms have spent very little on these systems, often in the $40,000 range. The reason for the low expenditure is that 75 percent of the respondents are using third-party WANs; only 22 percent have built their own. Most systems are less than five years old, indicating rapid growth. Consistent with the supplier-customer relationship, most systems are used for purchase orders, invoicing, and shipping, with far smaller major uses including status inquiries, quotations and payment, and product availability. The lack of EDI use in inventory and particularly with just-in-time schemes is an artifact of the survey, which focused on the service industry. Clearly, automated, standardized requesting of and reporting on inventory movement should be an advantage.

STRATEGIC ADVANTAGE THROUGH ARCHITECTURE

Chapters 5 and 6 have explored ways of bridging disciplines and distances to provide strategic advantage. To conclude this discussion, we turn to Venkatraman's hierarchical model of business transformation (see Figure 6–9). Venkatraman's idea is that advantages gained through IT appear at five levels, of which only the lowest, with the least and least sustainable advantage, is really based on technology as opposed to information. The other levels are based more on what technology supplies (i.e., information) than on the peculiarities of information technology itself. Venkatraman stresses the role of organizational learning and knowledge acquisition and the deployment of this knowledge to improve services and products. The levels are described as follows:

Figure 6-9 FIVE LEVELS OF IT-ENABLED BUSINESS TRANSFORMATION

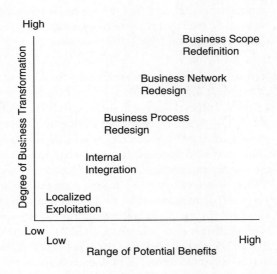

Source: N. Venkatraman, "IT-Enabled Business Transformations: From Automation to Business Scope Redefinition," *Sloan Management Review* (Winter 1994): 74.

- *Level One: Localized Exploitation*—Characterized by little change to basic business processes; easily imitated standard technological applications; little learning about IT; reactive to operational problems; unintegrated; not well evaluated; most gains are from efficiency; isolated applications or small systems

- *Level Two: Internal Integration*—Characterized by technical interconnectivity of systems and interdependence of business processes; integrated databases; use of information and information analysis rather than technology to provide advantage; appearance and management of business knowledge; development of standardized protocols and applications; blurring of organizational boundaries

- *Level Three: Business Process Redesign*—Characterized by operations and processes redesigned with information functionality (what information can do for managers and the business) in mind

- *Level Four: Business Network Redesign*—Characterized by redesign across a set of companies; business process distribution is changed; interorganizational systems develop and capitalize on interdependencies across organizations; information-based partnerships based on sharing of knowledge and mutual learning; proactivity

- *Level Five: Business Scope Redefinition*—Characterized by redefining what the firm does and what it does through relationships with other firms; creation of a more flexible business; interfirm relationships substitute for vertical integration; development of knowledge-intensive measures of performance.

Clearly, the view here is that as business transformation proceeds from nonsustainable efficiency to sustainable gains in knowledge, information and information links become increasingly important. Information brings enhanced coordination and control and the ability to bring knowledge together in unique packages. The key is that individual managers need to feel supported by their information systems, which merely underscores the commonplace opinion that an organization is only as good as its members. When they learn, the organization learns, and what they learn is their advantage.

Information systems that link knowledge sources, either across disciplines or across distances, provide the vehicle for smarter organizations and enhance learning. Understanding why something occurs is, after all, the first step in controlling the phenomenon. Because control (over markets, customers, competitors) is the advantage desired, it is clear that

The Modern Management Imperatives

Reach: Global Competition	The globe has shrunk because of transportation and communication technologies. Networking means that your neighbor is competing against you thousands of miles away, where there is another competitor. Networking also enables single organizations to act either in a unified manner, to experience economies of scale, or as a set of coordinated teams, to maximize creativity and freedom of action. Interorganizational systems build competitive alliances through EDI and proprietary and special-purpose systems.
Reaction: Quick Customer Feedback on Products and Services	Customers can be networked into critical aspects of a business as suppliers of ideas (i.e., feedback on existing products or their own needs), suppliers of labor (working on some aspect of the product, usually evaluation, as it is being designed), or online users of an information product.
Responsiveness: Shortened Concept-to-Customer Cycle Time	Client-server technologies make it possible for work to be distributed in space as well as time, to make simultaneous, concurrent processing happen through coordinated information. This can only speed up development times for new products and services, some of which can be delivered through networks (such as LANs or WANs) or the Internet. Prototyping (Chapter 14) is enhanced by netware that delivers early versions of products or services to prospective consumers.
Refinement: Greater Customer Sophistication and Specificity	Customers network among themselves. User and interest groups form continually on the Internet and private networks. Because information is more available in more formats, users are becoming not only more informed but more technically sophisticated in their demands for information.
Reconfiguration: Reengineering of Work Patterns and Structures	Business process reengineering is more often than not pointing toward client-server solutions, revitalizing bureaucratic and linear organizations with concurrent processing and efficiency. Because these techniques are easily replicated, continuous reengineering is more of a likelihood than at any time in the past.
Redeployment: Reorganization and Redesign of Resources	Client-server architectures make redeployment at will almost a reality because they enable the construction of "virtual organizations" without regard for where data are stored. Integrated databases relieve managers of the responsibility for knowing how data are stored or structured. Together, they make resource modeling relatively easy, because resource information is more accessible in common formats.
Reputation: Quality and Reliability of Product and Process	All the above trends underscore an increased emphasis on quality and reliability. Customers are more aware; organizations are more vigilant. A firm is far more likely now to approach very small niches with quality products that can be made or services that can be offered at a profit.

integrating databases, distributing processing, and making analysis tools available to those who have to do the learning form the fundamental principle and benefit of modern information systems. Merely automating, as Michael Hammer points out, is not enough. A modern organization requires intelligence for sustainable competitive advantage.

■ MAKING "ACROSS THE CONTINENT" LIKE "NEXT DOOR"

Zero books moves he knows customers will be satisfied with from cities with guaranteed pickup capability to areas where he has listed move-in agents. He arranges most of the moves over the telephone, but he has thought about using the Internet with executive clients who have Internet accounts on networks like CompuServe and America On Line. His 200 franchised agents across the country visit clients after the initial contact to get particulars on the move and give instant quotations using proprietary software on the portable microcomputers his agents use. After the quote has been accepted, agents mail or fax the particulars, including layouts indicating what furniture goes where and even the culinary preferences of the clients being moved. Then Zero contacts the national or regional movers involved, requests bids for the move, and also faxes the move particulars to his agents in the destination city. This work comes together as a sheaf of faxed papers and contracts, and the move is on. After each move, paperwork journeys through the phone network again to produce bills; checks are then printed and mailed. Zero also insists that each destination city agent file a move-in report detailing problems or creative solutions to problems. The reports are made available to other destination agents if they are needed. Zero's paper storm is about to overwhelm him. If business grows any, he knows he's going to be in trouble. ■

1. What problems involving distance, volume, cost, noise, error, coordination, configuration, mobility, and the need for standards is Zero facing? What would help him overcome them?

2. Interorganizational systems offer Zero some advantage in his business. What are they? What might the costs be? How should he go about creating these systems? With whom?

3. Continental has offices in 100 cities. Zero has read about client-server strategies. How would these strategies work for Shakers' Movers?

Summary

Telecommunications (communicating at a distance) is of particular importance because today's systems consist of many parts dispersed geographically. There are several challenges that must be met for a telecommunications architecture to be of value to an organization. These challenges include overcoming distance, capacity, volume, cost, noise, error, configuration, mobility, and standards limitations. Architectures have been developed according to various standards to meet these challenges. Networking (LANs and WANs) and communications among networks present further challenges. The client-server architecture is a simple approach to sharing work among components in a network. Interorganizational systems usually involve a number of architectures, as well as independent value-added networks (VANs) that further complicate the picture. Interorganizational systems develop and capitalize on interdependencies across organizations to create information-based partnerships that share knowledge and mutual learning. Strategic advantages from telecommunications are based more on sharing of knowledge than more short-lived advantages that come from the technology itself.

Discussion Questions

6.1 Communication systems and information systems are obviously different, but they have a lot in common. What needs to be added to each to enable the systems to simulate the other? From what you know about your local telephone service provider, what does it lack, if anything, to provide a full-service, information systems facility? From your knowledge of data communications, what needs to be done to achieve full telephone services?

6.2 The turn-taking problem in telecommunications is solved through protocols, a set of standards for who goes first and how stations respond. Why is turn taking so important? Provide some examples from human communication to illustrate how and where problems come up in telecommunications turn taking. How are these problems solved?

6.3 The client-server approach partitions information tasks into two parts, some handled by the server and some by the client. Is this the *only* alternative to having a central computer attached to a set of "dumb" terminals? What other forms of cooperative computing are conceivable? Use your experience in human networks to think of these alternatives.

6.4 The modern organization requires intelligence for sustainable competitive advantage. This implies interorganizational systems, among other approaches. But there are great risks involved in cooperating in a climate of competition. What risks does technology (information systems and computers) pose? How can organizations cope with these risks? What are the costs?

Key Terms

attenuation
bandwidth
baud
bits per second (BPS)
bus configuration
circuit switching
client-server architecture
coaxial cable
common carrier
configuration
contention
coordination
cost
data communication device
data compression
distance
electronic data interchange (EDI)
error
error-correction technique
error-detection technique
frequency shift keying (FSK)
full duplex

gateway
half duplex
hierarchy configuration
hybrid
Integrated Services Digital Network (ISDN)
International Standards Organization (ISO)
interorganizational system (IOS)
local area network (LAN)
message switching
mobility
modem
multipoint-to-multipoint transmission
multipoint-to-point transmission
noise
packet switching
parity technique
point-of-sale (POS)

point-to-multipoint transmission
point-to-point network
protocol
redundancy
relational database management system (RDBMS)
ring configuration
scalability
session
source device
standards
star network
structured query language (SQL)
switching system
telecommunication
topology
twisted pair
value-added network (VAN)
volume
wide area network (WAN)

References

Beck, Nuala. *The Third Circle: Shifting Gears in the New Economy*. Toronto: Macmillan, 1993.

Bourne, Michael. "Data Communications and Networks." In R. Drummond, ed., *Data Communication for the Office*. New York: Bantam, 1993, 5–56.

Cash, J., F. McFarlan, J. McKenney, and L. Applegate. *Corporate Information Systems Management*. 3d. ed. Homewood, IL: Irwin, 1992.

Drummond, Richard. "Electronic Data Interchange." In R. Drummond, ed., *Data Communication for the Office*. New York: Bantam, 1993, 157–198.

Fischer, David. "Electronic Mail." In R. Drummond, ed., *Data Communication for the Office*. New York: Bantam, 1993, 57–104.

FitzGerald, Jerry. *Business Data Communication: Basic Concepts, Security, and Design*. 3d ed. New York: John Wiley & Sons, 1990.

Hwang, K. T., C. C. Pegels, R. F. Rao, and V. Sethi. "Electronic Data Interchange Systems—State of the Art." *Journal of Systems Management* 44, 12 (December 1993): 12–15.

Keen, Peter, and J. Michael Cummins. *Networks in Action*. Belmont, CA: Wadsworth, 1994.

LaBarre, J., W. M. Korn, and S. Hale. "Client/Server Computing: The Current Computing Revolution." *Journal of Computer Information Systems* (Winter 1993–1994): 12–15.

Lane, Malcolm. *Data Communications Software Design*. Boston: Boyd & Fraser, 1985.

Lile, E. "Client Server Architecture: A Brief Overview." *Journal of Systems Management* 44, 12 (December 1993): 26–29.

Martin, James, and Joe Leben. *Data Communication Technology*. Englewood Cliffs, NJ: Prentice-Hall, 1988.

Martin, R. J. "Clients (vs. Servers)." *Journal of Systems Management* 45, 3 (March 1994): 26–27.

———. "Scalability." *Journal of Systems Management* 45, 5 (May 1994): 26–27.

———. "Servers (vs. Clients)." *Journal of Systems Management* 45, 4 (April 1994): 26–27.

Moshos, George. *Data Communications: Principles and Problems*. St. Paul: West Publishing Co., 1989.

"Plans and Policies for Client/Server Technology." *I/S Analyzer* 30, 4 (April 1992): 1–12.

Price Waterhouse Technology Center. *Technology Forecast, Version 3.5*. Menlo-Park, CA, September 1992.

Silver, Gerald, and Myrna Silver. *Communications for Business*. Boston: Boyd & Fraser, 1987.

Sinba, Alok. "Client-Server Computing." *Communications of the ACM* 35, 7 (July 1992).

Sprague, R., and B. C. McNurlin. *Information Systems Management in Practice*. 3d ed. Englewood Cliffs, NJ: Prentice-Hall, 1993.

Stallings, William. *Data and Computer Communications*. 2d ed. New York: Macmillan, 1988.

Venkatraman, N. "IT-Enabled Business Transformation: From Automation to Business Scope Redefinition." *Sloan Management Review* (Winter 1994): 73–77.

| CASE | EVERGREEN LANDSCAPING AND MAINTENANCE: DISTRIBUTING PROCESSING |

Evergreen is physically distributed across several sites (Figure 6–10). The major retail location was opened in 1987 and contains the sales area (the "store"), the headquarters offices of the vice presidents, and the administrative functions. As sales manager, Connie's office is located close to the store on the ground floor; Sven's office is next to Connie's. Located immediately adjacent to the store is the greenhouse, which is open to customers during the spring and summer. Plants to be sold live at the back of the greenhouse and are called the "live material inventory." Greenhouse workers tend these plants, giving them loving care and playing new age music over the PA system (for sensitive, new-age plants).

About a five-minute walk away is the warehouse, where retail items other than plants are stored. It's essentially a Quonset hut, purposely unattractive and removed from the retail area because many of the items kept there are corrosive or poisonous. This building is carefully guarded by security supervisor Candice Robbins and her "police" force. Located on the second floor of the warehouse, for political as well as practical reasons, are the landscaping offices. They are kept near the landscaping materials for the benefit of the clients. Because the landscape architects employed or contracted by Evergreen think of themselves as above the commercial fray, they like being apart from the business office and the store. Sid Cavenaugh has his office there.

Transportation vehicles are housed in the lot beyond the warehouse and Bill Porter (transportation supervisor) parks himself there. Two fork-lift trucks, two pickup trucks, three vans, a large

| Figure 6–10 | DISTRIBUTION OF EVERGREEN FUNCTIONS |

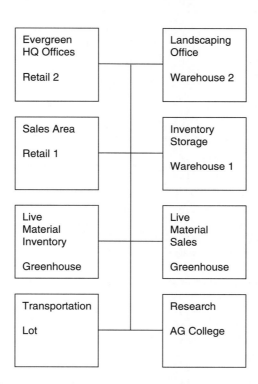

Figure 6–11   PLANNED DISTRIBUTION OF EVERGREEN FUNCTIONS

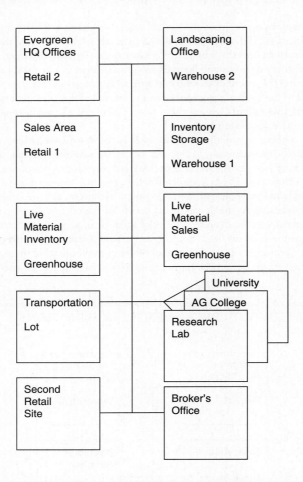

tree transporter, and seven specially outfitted lawn maintenance vehicles are parked there. All except the lawn maintenance vehicles (which are converted pickups) are used to move stock to and from the warehouse and greenhouse and to and from contract customer sites.

One other office is four miles away at the Agricultural College. Here, Evergreen sponsors a research project on ways to increase the over-winter survival rate of common garden materials such as trees and shrubs to cut losses.

Lily has plans for three important changes at Evergreen (Figure 6–11). First, she wants to increase her research activity by starting two more projects. One will be financing a project in the botany department at the local university. Evergreen sponsors a graduate student to examine the commercialization possibilities of a number of weed control techniques that will significantly reduce the quantities of herbicides now used. Evergreen is also interested in setting up a strategic alliance with a biotech firm to develop disease-resistant strains of shrubs and trees. Some members of MEC think this is a waste of good money, but Lily knows that the Evergreen stamp will mean exclusive ownership of procedures and genes. If the student and the lab are successful, these rights will make Evergreen money in license fees even during the slow business months.

Second, Tulley Fox (purchasing manager) is nearing retirement, and Lily has been exploring strategic alliances with a botanical broker, Pindar Gopal of Portland, Oregon. Pindar has promised his customers that he can get the best possible prices and more certain delivery times through his Internet-based information tools. Tulley has relied on wit and contacts. Pindar has compiled an up-to-date listing of more than 3,000 growers of live material and 8,000 suppliers of gardening, landscaping, and horticultural materials and tools across the world. He is directly connected with many of them via the Internet. Pindar charges a fixed monthly fee plus a percentage of the order and guarantees the delivery time and conditions and the lowest prices.

Finally, after 30 years and several incarnations, Evergreen is ready to open up a second store. Lily has found a suitable building site on the other side of town, where a lot of new housing is going in and there will obviously be a good market for existing products and services. Evergreen will be the only such store in that part of town, but Lily knows that won't last for long. The second retail store will be constructed during the autumn and winter at a cost of close to $1 million, but Lily has looked at the figures and is confident that the expansion will pay off within two years.

Although Lily hasn't considered this yet in great detail, a critical component of the expansion plans will be the modernization of Evergreen's information systems. Currently, there are four major systems with little connection between them. On the retail side, six POS terminals act as cash registers and are connected through a LAN to a minicomputer. The retail system keeps track of the hard goods inventory and produces daily reports for Connie on sales by category. The accounting system, separate from the retail system, is used by Priscilla Chan to keep the books. Priscilla has a microcomputer system for accounting work and to do forecasts. This system is tied into the mini so that she can get access to the retail data, but she finds this clumsy. Special orders are handled through the retail system. Both of these systems run on the IBM RISC 6000 computer housed in the HQ offices on the second floor and are run by a staff of four (see Figure 6–12).

The bulk of the rest of the administrative data processing is handled on a microcomputer in Frances Harmon's office by her administrative assistant, Kim Backer. Frances uses several off-the-shelf packages to keep personnel information, to create and file memos, and to do some graphics. Most of the executives and their assistants also have microcomputers, almost exclusively devoted to word processing. The executives do not access operating data directly but have their assistants track down the facts manually when needed. The vice president of finance, Heather Cariad, who sometimes thinks she should be more plugged into the financial data, uses her computer mostly to do spreadsheet projections using data copied by Priscilla onto a diskette. Among the managers, Connie is the most adventurous. She has been investigating a variety of packages, especially expert systems for product development and sales management.

The fourth system is a landscaping CAD system used by the "artists" on the second floor of the warehouse. They use a small network of three SPARC stations connected into a powerful minicomputer that maintains electronic drawings for clients. This architectural database has proven useful in the past. It's a lot faster than sketching drawings by hand for proposals and major bids and the designs can be reviewed and reused if similarities are discovered between projects. One of the major advantages of this sort of system, built around a commercially available package, is that it can produce a bill of materials that can be printed out and included with a proposal. A weakness in the current architecture is that this bill cannot be automatically forwarded to the warehouse or the greenhouse to get availability and pricing information. The CAD system also cannot be used to draw up contracts, so a stand-alone microcomputer is used to boilerplate proposals and contracts and print them out on special forms.

The focus of the rationalization is to integrate the data better, to provide a broader range of applications to more managers, to support planning more thoroughly and further down the management chain, to give everyone who needs it access to all the operating data, and to integrate the contract and retail sides but still provide flexibility and freedom to the operating divisions.

Questions

1. List the advantages and disadvantages of information processing the way Evergreen is doing it now. How would you characterize information systems planning so far at Evergreen?

Figure 6–12	SYSTEMS ARCHITECTURE AT EVERGREEN

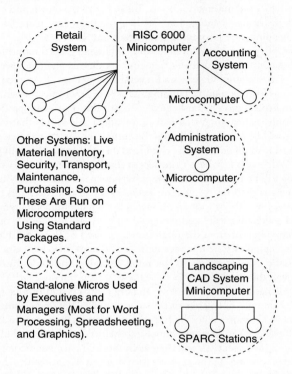

2. Examine the list you have created. Compare the list to the nine telecommunications challenges outlined in Chapter 6. Which challenges are being met well? Which are causing the most problems?

3. Look at Figure 6–11. What kind of network topology does this figure represent? Based on the description above, redraw this figure to include more detail on the major systems used at Evergreen. Which systems involve computers of what type? Which systems do not involve computers at all?

4. Now redesign the communication architecture based on your judgment of how these systems should actually fit together to meet Evergreen's business goals. (Hint: Consider the major subsystems: retail sales, administration, contract design, contract sales, inventory, security, maintenance, and transportation.)

5. Consider how a client-server approach to the architecture you have laid out in Question 4 would work. What advantages would be gained by this approach? What do you think the disadvantages would be? What impact would the opening of a second retail store have on the desirability of the client-server approach?

6. What interorganizational systems currently exist (none using computers, by the way)? In Lily's plans for the future, there are roles for four such systems. What are they?

7. At which level of Venkatraman's hierarchical model of business transformation (see Figure 6–9) would you place Evergreen *at this time*? Where will Lily's plans take

Evergreen? If you were a consultant hired to assist Evergreen in moving up this hierarchy, what advice would you give to Lily?

8. Overall, how would you evaluate Lily's plans for changes at Evergreen in terms of their competitiveness? What role would information systems play in achieving these competitive goals? Are there additional benefits? Is Evergreen's information system in this case merely a follower of planned change or will it bring changes of its own?

Module 2

SUPPORTING MANAGERS THROUGH INFORMATION SYSTEMS

CHAPTER SEVEN

MANAGEMENT SUPPORT SYSTEMS

OBJECTIVES

After you have read and studied this chapter, you should be able to:

■ Discuss the four major values managers bring to the value chain.

■ Identify the important activities managers perform that enable them to bring value to their jobs.

■ List the seven kinds of advising systems and describe how each one supports managers in their work.

■ Describe how information can act as a mediator in providing value.

■ Discuss the four ways in which managers cope with information overload.

■ Describe each tool that exists in a manager's information workbench.

■ Discuss the advantages and disadvantages of an information-centered enterprise/environment.

Question: How does information support managers in their jobs? What do managers do that information can enhance?

Geoffrey Wainwright is the western district sales manager for Holbein Holdings, a commercial space leasing agency. Holbein leases building space as well as land, and Geoff is in charge of a group of people including four clerks, nine salespeople, and a sales analyst, who acts as his assistant. Geoff works hard to make sure that operations are uniform, consistent, and regular. He knows that his work is information-intensive, managing space in more than 200 buildings, handling special events, and continuously seeking new business from both owners and tenants. He also feels he doesn't have enough of the right kind of information on a predictable basis. Instead, he has too much of the wrong information. For instance, customers today want specific kinds of space, even specific decors, and they want to know traffic patterns, demographic profiles, and even noise levels. Meanwhile, much of the space Holbein leases is in older buildings with horrible architectural, structural, and environmental problems that need a lot of attention. Geoff is worried that missing information is really impacting his capabilities as a manager, decision maker, and leader.

Answer: Managers are effective when they can add uniformity, certainty, authority, and regularity to their work. These attributes enhance quality, decision making, organizational culture and climate, creativity, organizational learning, and interpersonal influence in an environment of conflict, dynamism, and irresolution. Information counteracts turbulence, uncertainty, risk, and stress. The manager's information workbench (a component of the information-centered enterprise) is a conceptual "workplace" that supports managers in acquiring, processing, and profiting from information.

INTRODUCTION

This chapter introduces Module II, "Supporting Managers through Information Systems." We have already introduced the idea that information supports managers and explored in some detail how such systems can provide strategic advantage to a firm. We have not looked very closely at how information systems support managers in their everyday work. With the exception of a brief discussion of executive support systems and executive information systems in Chapter 8, our focus in this module is on the practicing manager and management at the operating and tactical levels of an organization.

As we move into the next century, the enterprise you will work for will be increasingly information-centered, and skills in information tasks, augmented by the systems now becoming available, will be the hallmark of successful management. The evolution of these systems is hard to predict. However, if current trends are any indication, they will grow out of existing transaction processing systems, extended area by area from sales to production to human resource management and then to design and administration. Currently, many factories are run by what might be called "remote control." Managers tap into information as products pass through various stages or stations in manufacturing. Merging production with marketing provides an almost complete value chain automation.

Two other technical trends also provide evidence of this evolution. First, the client-server movement has made it possible to connect independent production and marketing systems with even more unruly design and administration systems. The object-oriented approach will then make it easy for marketing to refer to production objects and pass these objects to accounting. It will be easier to create and manage work teams when such teams, along with their inputs and outputs, can be referred to as objects. New objects can be created in human resource management as work design changes how work is done and as new regulations, customs, and labor-management agreements dictate. Thus, we are left with the happy marriage of increased connectivity (client-server) with paradoxically increased flexibility (object orientation). Developing new management support systems may become an everyday occurrence rather than a rare event.

This chapter begins with two models of management activity. The value chain model illustrates where managers add value to a firm by examining the processes through which a firm creates its products and services. The management activity area model that follows focuses on six areas of management work and, again, helps us pinpoint places where management activity adds value. Next we discuss the role information plays in increasing or maintaining these values. Management works in an environment that is information-sensitive, sometimes information-poor and sometimes information-rich, but never devoid of the influence of or need for information. We finish this chapter with a discussion of the information-centered enterprise/environment in which managers work. This is a concept developed in anticipation of a future in which managers view their work almost entirely through an information window on one or more computers.

This chapter also introduces the concept of the management information work-bench. This concept involves a set of information-based tools that managers can use to add value to a firm's products or services. The values managers add are almost all related to information or interpersonal interaction, which are enhanced by appropriate tools.

The goal of this chapter is to show how systems provide information to managers and support them in achieving strategic goals as they carry out the processes of the firm. We define a **management support system** as an information system that assists managers in carrying out their responsibilities. Such systems need not involve computers; assistants and aides, for example, are management support systems. However, the systems primarily

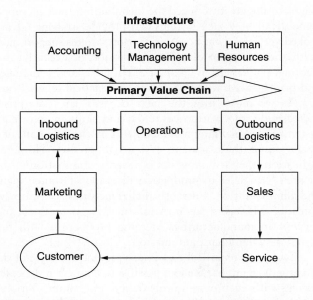

Figure 7–1   THE VALUE CHAIN

intended to gather, store, process, and disseminate information today are computer-based. The systems may also require communication networks. The convergence of these technologies is rapidly driving business down a busy, and somewhat chaotic, information highway in a variety of conveyances.

MANAGEMENT AND THE VALUE CHAIN

Porter and Millar's **value chain** is a concept that relates the idea of organizational processes to the notion of an organization as an open system that adds value to raw materials by creating finished products or providing services. Chains of processes add value in sequence (see Figure 7–1). In a typical organization, value chains can be thought of in three ways. A **firm value chain** is a linked series of processes within a company or organization that provides the added values buyers are willing to pay for. **Buyer** and **supplier value chains** are corresponding chains from buyers' point of view (they buy something because its value increases their wealth, power, comfort, etc.) and suppliers' point of view (who have similar ideas).

The value chain model in Figure 7–2 is broken down into two parts, basic and support activities. Among the support activities are infrastructure, including administration. Basic activities are broken down into five categories that generally follow raw, semifinished, and finished materials and products through a series of activities including inbound logistics, operations, outbound logistics (these activities generally mimic a manufacturing process but can also apply to services), marketing, and service.

Managers add four major additional values to these chains:

| Figure 7–2 | VALUES MANAGEMENT ADDS IN THE VALUE CHAIN |

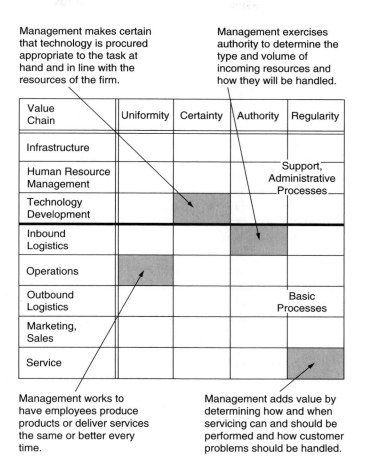

Management makes certain that technology is procured appropriate to the task at hand and in line with the resources of the firm.

Management exercises authority to determine the type and volume of incoming resources and how they will be handled.

Value Chain	Uniformity	Certainty	Authority	Regularity
Infrastructure				
Human Resource Management				Support, Administrative Processes
Technology Development		▓		
Inbound Logistics			▓	
Operations	▓			
Outbound Logistics				Basic Processes
Marketing, Sales				
Service				▓

Management works to have employees produce products or deliver services the same or better every time.

Management adds value by determining how and when servicing can and should be performed and how customer problems should be handled.

- **Uniformity:** The basic and support activities work the same way all the time to produce the same product or deliver the same service. Managers, for instance, supervise others and provide guidance to keep production stable. Uniformity can also be thought of as a kind of quality control. For example, Geoff Wainwright sees to it that a standard of quality for space that Holbein Holdings leases is adhered to.

- **Certainty:** One of the main reasons managers are employed is to be certain that the product gets out or the service is provided. When a crisis occurs, management is expected to handle the situation. Geoff makes sure that space is available when it is leased. When this fails to occur, Geoff handles this crisis.

- **Authority:** Consider what happens during a crisis when managers are called in to help. Such crises are situations that are unpredictable, require rapid response, have high costs both for action and inaction, and are generally underinformed (i.e., information is incomplete). Managers have the authority to circumvent standard procedures and bring in new information. They actually "create" information in these circumstances or seek other sources that might not normally be available. Finally, managers have the right to ask others to act in these new, nonstandard ways or to prevent others from acting in these ways. Geoff has the authority to renegotiate leases when required, to spend money to bring space up to standards, and to hire and fire where needed.

■ **Regularity:** Managers are expected to bring a measure of regularity to a situation. Managers' responses to crises are relatively standard (typical managers do not exceed the authority granted to them, for example) and understandable (employees discern what they are supposed to do because the commands are issued in clear language and relate to the situation at hand). However, managers are also expected to manage this regularity by continually expanding their repertoire of responses to crises. That is, managers need to learn new responses to the environment even while remaining relatively predictable to their employees and internal management.

Given this framework, it is reasonable to ask what these values contribute to the value chain. Managers add uniformity to the product, for example, by making certain that the same raw materials are made available through the inbound logistics every time they are required. They add certainty to operations by correcting flaws in production methods. They add authority to outbound logistics by having at their disposal a number of techniques for handling distribution crises and the authority to "clear the tracks" when needed. They provide regularity to sales by redirecting sales efforts where required in standard and clear language. Finally, they add uniformity to a firm's services by making sure that all customers get the service they require in the same way.

MANAGEMENT VALUES AND ACTION AREAS

Another way to look at management values is to examine the areas in which managers are expected to act and bring value to a firm (see Figure 7–3). How are values and activities related? Managers bring values to their jobs by performing activities; six important ones are the following:

■ *Improving quality:* Value is added through control and consistency to create uniformity. Geoff assures quality standards are maintained.

■ *Making decisions:* Value is increased when managers are able to make choices among effective alternatives. Geoff makes decisions to keep Holbein space available and to handle crises.

■ *Fostering organizational climate and culture:* Managers are expected to provide confirmation to others and increase confidence in their actions. Geoff directly influences how confident others are in performing their work activities by confirming their performance.

■ *Influencing others:* Value is enhanced through management powers and the ability to lead others. Geoff is a leader in his organization.

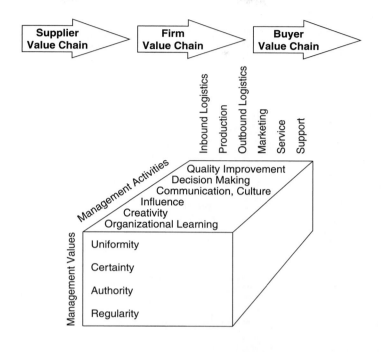

Figure 7–3   MANAGEMENT ACTIVITIES AND VALUES

- *Creating ideas and innovating:* Managers provide the organization with new ways of doing things and flexibility for change. Geoff is constantly challenged to think up new approaches to the business not only to please customers and counter competitors but to feel rewarded when they work.

- *Helping the organization learn:* Firms that learn are more effective at meeting later challenges. Information gained from managers' experiences is organized by them into valuable organizational learning and wisdom. Geoff is a repository of knowledge—he learns from his employees and teaches them.

As with the value chain, we can question where specifically the values of uniformity, certainty, authority, and regularity are added in these six areas. Different jobs and different managers make these contributions differently. In this and the next chapters, the activities in the list will become important in describing the kind of support information and information systems provide to managers.

MANAGEMENT ACTIVITIES AND INFORMATIONAL SUPPORT

Now let us put together several models introduced in this text so far. Chapter 2 discussed several views of management including hierarchical, allocational, task-oriented, transactional, team-oriented, knowledge-oriented, and goal-centered models. Chapter 3

Figure 7–4   CYCLE OF MANAGEMENT WORK

discussed cybernetic and learning systems and how they cope with turbulent environments. Chapter 4 examined those competitive environments and contemplated the role that information-based systems play in achieving competitive advantage. Finally, this chapter details values that management adds to a firm's products and where management action provides benefits.

The result of combining these models is a depiction of a management work cycle that adds values to a firm's products or services through specific management activities that depend on or use information and information systems (see Figure 7–4). The task-oriented view provides the basic structure of the model: plan, organize, staff, direct, and control. We have amended this structure by showing that (1) organizations learn from their own experience, (2) managers have a major responsibility to innovate, (3) organizing and staffing are two of several resource allocation responsibilities, (4) communication and decision making are major components of all management activity, and (5) influence and leadership are key to all management-directed teamwork.

SEVEN MANAGEMENT SUPPORT LEVELS

The seven levels of management support systems (see Figure 7–5) are:

- *Consensual:* To create ideas, to broaden experience (example: face-to-face meeting or electronic mail)
- *Contextual:* To define or visualize problems and opportunities (example: graphics processor or presentation manager)

Figure 7–5	LEVELS OF MANAGEMENT SUPPORT

Example	Theory Level	Driven by	User Role
Consensual			
OIS, TP, e-mail, Netware	None: the Case Exists	Need for Ideas	Experience
Contextual			
Text and Document Management, Hypertext, Graphics	Depictional: the Case Is Related to This or Seen This Way	Need for Comparing Concepts on Some Basis; Need to Define	Presenter
MIS Oriented			
DBMS, Q&A	Descriptive: the Case Was This	Need for Data	Explorer
Consultative			
None	Classificational: the Case Is Like These Others	Need to Tap Past Experience and Guide Behavior	Judge or Guide
Implicative			
AI, NLPS, Expert Systems, Neural Nets	Logical: the Case Implies These Conditions	Need to Predict Implications of Actions	Implementor, Builder, Motivator
Computational			
DSS, GDSS, ESS, EIS, Simulation, Programs	Causal: the Case Causes These Conditions	Need to Predict Results	Implementor, Builder, Cause
Operational			
Process Control	Physical: the Case Becomes This	Need to Control	Operator

- *MIS:* To explore a collection of data (example: database manager or public library)
- *Consultative:* To tap past experiences of a guide (example: management consultant)
- *Implicative:* To predict the implications or outcomes of specific actions in order to determine the best possible actions as a builder or implementor (example: expert system or diagnostic flowchart)

- *Computational:* To predict the value of outcomes of specific actions as a builder or implementor (example: spreadsheet)
- *Operational:* To control or operate a system, department, project, or task (example: computer operating system or manufacturing control system)

For each of these seven levels of management support systems is a corresponding theory that is tapped at that level. Consensual systems, embodied in e-mail or office information systems, do not embody any theory; all ideas belong to the participants and the system itself knows nothing at all, only how to connect people. Contextual systems such as word processors, graphics, or presentation managers manipulate images or texts but don't understand what they mean. We call the theories underlying contextual systems **depictional theories** because they are based on what things look like.

At the next level, an MIS describes events so that a data "explorer" can examine the data in a coherent way. The MIS doesn't understand the meaning of individual records but embodies a **descriptive theory** that basically states what you need to know to describe an event in this database. Consultative systems (there are really no computerized examples, but think of a human consultant) require **classificatory theories** about what makes cases similar. In other words, they say that certain events go together and other events form other classes.

An implicative system runs on a **logical** or **relational theory** that says under certain conditions, one description implies another. This is not causality but association; the theory says that situations go together but it doesn't say that one causes the other. The next level, computational, actually states that two events are related by causality—one event makes another occur. For example, a spreadsheet containing formulas is a computational system. **Causal** or **computational theories** say that so much of one situation brings about so much of another, giving managers the ability to precisely predict outcomes. Why an event occurs is embodied in these theories—it occurs because of causes mentioned in the theories.

Finally, operational systems contain theories that actually make events happen that, when put into operation, control the world and make it change. These are **physical theories.** A computer's operating system (from which the name of this level is derived) contains a series of interpreters of commands; a user simply enters these commands (or points to them if a GUI is used) and what is desired is done. This remote control is possible because the operating system "knows" what controls what, how things are linked together, and what various machinery responds to.

An example of a depictional theory is a photograph of an event. We don't know why this event occurred or even what kind of event it was; it just *is*, as presented in the picture. A descriptive theory would provide information about the event; for example, two people are seated at desks. This event is described in terms of the number of individuals, what they are doing, and where they are (three dimensions or variables). All other related events are also described through three variables. Photos of 8 people walking in a park, 14 people running through puddles, or 1 person standing in a market all can be described in the same three ways.

A classificatory theory might say that locale is most important. Such a theory groups together all photos of people in the park even though they may be doing diverse things. It would also group all photos of people in puddles regardless of how many there are or what they are doing. Such classifications are useful in determining how the event under discussion relates to other events and what advice is best for events in that class.

A logical theory is exemplified by a decision table that relates descriptions of situations to recommended courses of action. A computational theory is backed up by a

Figure 7–6 A GENERAL MODEL OF ADVISING

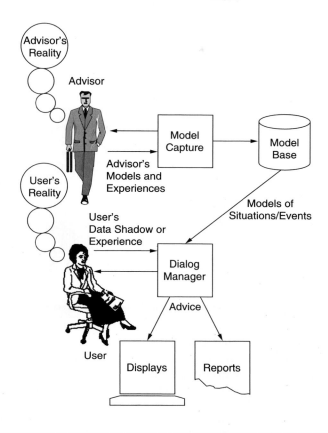

program or an algorithm for turning inputs into outputs, relating one set of values to an outcome value such as in the formula Area = 3.14159 × RADIUS^2. Physical theories are either actual wires or electronic pathways that control devices or procedures for communicating with these devices (or *protocols*) to find out what they are doing in order to control them.

A GENERAL MODEL OF MANAGEMENT ADVISING

A general model of advising (see Figure 7–6) shows that users get advice in display form and reports from a dialog manager that accepts a description of the current situation from users and examines a model base of theories and past experience to determine the advice. The model base is "captured" from advisors prior to or during the session with users.

Each of the seven support systems is described in terms of this model. A consensual system (Figure 7–7) is intended to find out what other people know about a situation a user is experiencing. All the system does is connect a user with others. The knowledge base of this system is really in the minds of other users. The system has no knowledge of

Figure 7–7   A CONSENSUAL SYSTEM

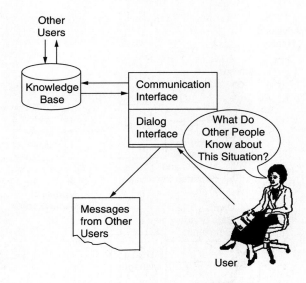

what is going on, but its goal is to link people. Other users possess data, information, and knowledge that can be useful if they communicate. A group has more knowledge than an individual, so connecting people is an advantage.

A contextual system (Figure 7–8) enables a user to explore experience with others by making presentations in text, graphics, sound, and so forth. A user's interface is called a **presentation manager** (such as Harvard Graphics, DrawPerfect, etc.) and two kinds of bases are used. A **view base** contains prestored images, charts, sounds, texts, and so forth, while the **model base** contains a set of rules for combining views (such as superimposition, sequencing, adjusting for the viewing situation, and conversion from one form to another. A contextual system does not really understand what the data mean. Most spreadsheets contain ways of creating graphs, but the graph display function does not understand what the data in the graph mean; only users can make the leap from presentation to meaning.

To see this, examine Figure 7–9. Here, the same data can be viewed in three ways depending on the focus of the viewing lens. The data can be seen as (A) short-term improvement if viewed with a zoom lens, as (B) cyclical, long-term recovery if viewed with a wide-angle lens, or as (C) medium-term decline if viewed from halfway between. Viewpoint matters in trying to determine the nature of the phenomenon or what is happening. Contextual systems are valuable when there isn't much agreement on how to describe events (i.e., which data should be collected). The reasoning in contextual systems is that various ways of viewing data can give insight primarily by separating signals from noise and foreground from background, or by seeing data in different ways. In Figure 7–10, what appears to be randomly scattered points in a graph are actually grouped along one axis when the axes are rotated, thereby simplifying the appearance of the data. Such visualization techniques are commonly used in the sciences, and with the development of less expensive and more reliable hardware and software to display virtual reality,

| Figure 7–8 | A CONTEXTUAL SYSTEM |

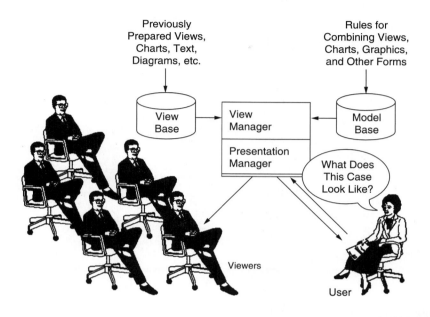

these techniques are making their way into the business world, especially in finance. Highlighting important facts, statements, or images is a useful way to bring a figure out of a noisy background that helps managers understand their experiences better.

Management information systems (Figure 7–11) answer the question, "What do we know about this case?" through regular and ad hoc reports initiated by managers who pose questions (queries) and make requests as they navigate through a database. A manager may, for example, suspect that there is subtle discrimination in her company against older employees. To check her suspicions, she needs to look for patterns in promotion, so she requests that the MIS display all the records of employees over 50 years of age. Since she's only interested in promotions, she asks the system to display only the years and titles of each position held. Then she can cull this set of records by removing those who have plateaued for a variety of reasons (such as illness or lack of desire to relocate), examining related human resource records to do this. The list that remains may show a pattern of discrimination. The database is the personnel records; the model base is the **data dictionary,** which is the words that describe each field in the personnel record [age, for example, might be a certain field, having values from 15 to 99; another field might be management position, ranging from 0 (nonmanagement) to 9 (senior executive)].

A user interacts with a dialog or report manager which in turn requests data through a database manager. Most microcomputer systems that are called *database managers* have all these facilities, especially a query language (often based on SQL, an industry standard language), to allow users to pose questions of enormous complexity. The reasoning is that amassing and exploring data will lead to insights into why things are happening the way they are.

Figure 7–9   THREE VIEWPOINTS OF THE SAME INFORMATION

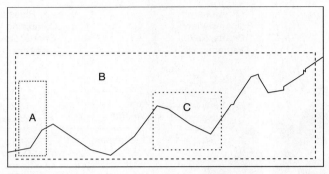

- A Short-term Improvement
- B Cyclical, Long-term Improvement
- C Medium-term Decline

Figure 7–10   REASONING IN CONTEXTUAL SYSTEMS

We have an intuitive idea how things should look— an implicit theory. Various ways of viewing data can help us achieve the insight needed to separate signal from noise, foreground from background.

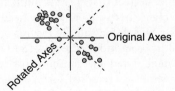

A consultative system (see Figure 7–12) is intended to provide advice on the form of what works in similar cases. The output of a consultative system is a list of similar cases, perhaps sorted by actions taken, with a rating of outcomes. The dialog manager gets a description of the case at hand and asks the data/model manager to look up similar cases, find out what was done in those cases, and how good the outcomes were. Consider asking a consultant for advice about how to handle a project for a client organization that has changed its mind about massive staff retraining. We ask the consultant what has been

| Figure 7–11 | A MANAGEMENT INFORMATION SYSTEM |

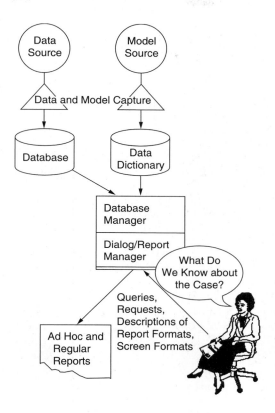

done in the past and how effective the outcomes were for projects similar to this one. Table 7–1 shows the results.

The consultant may say, "I can't tell you precisely why this works, but of the 125 projects I've worked on, 24 are similar to yours and of those 24, 15 just went ahead and retrained the staff, whatever the cost, and on a relative scale, they did very well. Hiring outside workers was almost as good, but dropping the project or delaying really did not work out very well." Note that the hiring outside workers option cannot be trusted as advice because the consultant has had very limited experience with projects like this one that hired outside workers. The database is the consultant's experience; the model base is the consultant's (implicit) rules for how to judge projects as similar. If the consultant says, "All I'm really concerned with are size and time to deadline," this is an indication that only two dimensions are counted in judging cases to be similar. The reasoning consultants employ (Figure 7–13) is that the best judge of the future is the past; that is, actions taken in similar circumstances in the past should have similar results in the future.

An implicative system (see Figure 7–14) answers two separate but related questions: "What happens if I do X?" and "What do I have to do to make Y happen?" Because the implicative system is based only on associational theories, causality is not a consideration.

Figure 7–12	A CONSULTATIVE SYSTEM

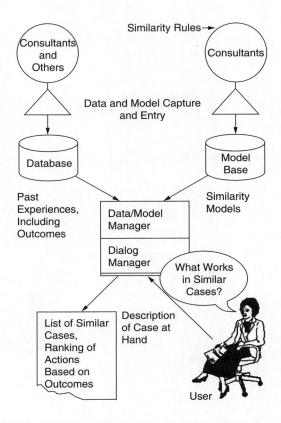

The questions should be phrased more precisely as "What seems to happen whenever X is seen to happen?" and "What things seem to happen when Y happens?" (i.e., the same question). A dialog manager examines a database of facts and then it looks into a model base of rules (If-Then statements or classifications) that show what goes with what (see Figure 7–15). The dialog manager then collects statements about the case at hand (e.g., data) and proposed actions and derives implications (outcomes) from the data and model bases based on these theories. This process may also work backwards from a description of a desired outcome to determine what *has* to happen in order for the desired outcome to appear.

In implicative systems, the reasoning is that a web of relationships can be linked forward and backward either to outcomes or associated events. The model base contains relationships that reflect understood wisdom or scientifically determined relationships. Clearly, such wisdom is dependent on the advisor or the knowledge about an area. For example, Evergreen Landscaping might install an expert system to give advice about reordering stock. A rule of thumb may be that a product should be reordered when its stock is low, but company policy discourages ordering too much of a high-cost product. Purchasing agents may also know that purchasing small lot sizes is expensive. These

Table 7–1	RESULTS OF CONSULTATIVE ADVICE		
Action Taken		**Number of Cases**	**Rating of Outcomes**
Retrain staff to new standards		15	7.5
Hire outside workers		5	7.2
Drop the project		3	4.0
Delay until client changes specifications		1	2.0

Figure 7–13	REASONING IN CONSULTATIVE SYSTEMS

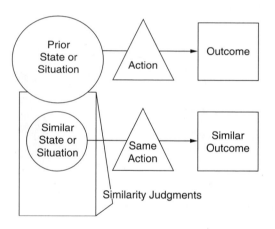

considerations form part of the model base. Another recent fact is that stock levels of a product called Flexout is low. The expert system will then analyze the relationships just mentioned to provide advice about whether to order more Flexout. On the other hand, it is possible to ask "What level of Flexout would we have to have to cause a reorder?" As you can see, these questions are related but not identical.

Several kinds of "truth" must be encoded in expert systems. They include business facts or data that form part of a firm's information shadow, rules of thumb that derive from expectations or perceptions built up over a period of time, company policies, and basic business practices that all businesses recognize. Of these four truths, only the perceptions of relationships constitute proprietary knowledge (i.e., knowledge that "belongs" to a firm because of its unique experiences). These perceptions form the basis of the informal *expertise system* that provides the foundation for any expert system supporting managers.

An implicative system does not address causality; the computational system (see Figure 7–16) does. The user poses a question: "What is the effect of doing X?" and the system computes the outcomes numerically. The database is the same as those already

Figure 7–14   AN IMPLICATIVE SYSTEM

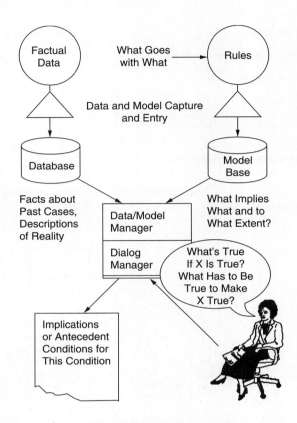

discussed, and the model base consists of a set of mathematical relationships (e.g., formulas in a spreadsheet) and provides the rules of computing (such as recomputing a spreadsheet in row-major order—these rules can be changed sometimes depending on the processor). The dialog manager takes a description of the current case in the form of parameters and runs the numbers through the formulas to determine output values that are the results of the computation.

Reasoning in computational systems is based on causality: so much of a certain variable *causes* so much of another (see Figure 7–17). If the system has a complete description of one event, it should be able to compute the outcomes of a change in that event by the simple logic: If so much of X gives so much of Y, then so much of a *change* in X gives so much of a *change* in Y. Given the formulas, representing received wisdom, scientific fact, and textbook relationships, the system should be able to create outputs easily with the inputs (a description of the current event and the desired action). A what-if scenario in a spreadsheet is precisely this action.

The final level of support is an operational system (see Figure 7–18) that is intended to make things happen given a few parameters. The dialog manager solicits a user's desires in some form (commands for DOS, mouse selections in *Windows* and OS/2, and so forth),

| **Figure 7–15** | REASONING IN IMPLICATIVE SYSTEMS |

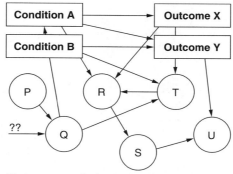

Various events in the world have implications
(outcomes) and are related to others in
necessary ways. If we could construct a model
of those relationships, we could determine
what the (complex) effects of various actions
would be. In addition, we could reason back to
possible causes of events we want to occur.

uses various bases to compute what has to be done, and then makes things happen by
controlling equipment. The data and model managers act as controllers of external
devices. Facts about the systems being controlled, ways in which parameters change other
parameters (models), and rules by which objects have to interact (rules unknown to the
user; for example, users don't care where on a diskette their data are stored, but this is
crucial to the operating system) are used to determine the appropriate commands to issue
to the equipment to accomplish a user's request. For example, suppose a user is controlling
machinery to assemble a car. The system has stored in it facts about particular subassem-
blies and how they go together (database), a model base of algorithms relating parameters
to activities that the equipment can perform, and a set of rules that govern the equipment
itself. The operator presses a few buttons and the operational system then translates the
operator's input into commands to the equipment to assemble the parts.

Selecting the Appropriate Level of Support

Given the wide range of support available for a wide range of management activities, how
can a manager select the appropriate tool, application, or system? The key to this selection is knowing the proper level of support needed to solve the problem at hand. A
spreadsheet can be used only if the appropriate formulas are known, that is, if there is a
causal theory available. Expert systems do not require numerical values based on causal
theories. MIS and more complex systems require a database and a data dictionary because
manipulation of data in fields is important. For systems less complex than MIS, no theory
of the data itself exists and the systems don't "understand" the data they are carrying; that
is the responsibility of the users. With systems of higher complexity, users need to
understand less because the system has knowledge.

Figure 7-16 A COMPUTATIONAL SYSTEM

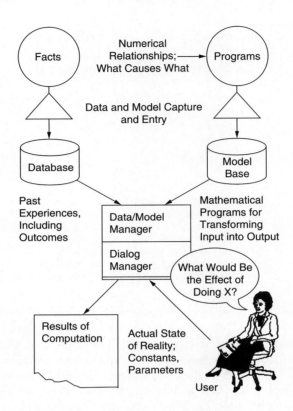

The trend toward **end user application development** complicates this picture somewhat. Users who want to build their own spreadsheets or logical models need to understand a lot, of course. They are supplying their own theories and are the "experts," and here lies both the bane and the benefit of end user application development. The user who feels confident with his or her knowledge of a domain can safely build spreadsheets, but the user who only *feels* competent and is actually ignorant will build a spreadsheet full of errors and subsequently act on the basis of the spreadsheet application's advice. This is a formula for disaster. Applications created by computer professionals are often full of bugs, so it follows that those created by nonprofessionals will have errors too. Many of these errors will be mechanical (typos, misspellings, use of wrong function names in spreadsheets, and so forth); however, many of them will result from lack of knowledge of the domain or idiosyncratic theories that may work in a limited area but fail in new areas.

INFORMATION AS THE MEDIATOR IN PROVIDING VALUE

It is easy to see the role information plays, but why does information play any role whatsoever? The reason is that in most organizations managers do not work directly in the primary production or secondary support activities. They don't actually assemble, take

Figure 7–17	REASONING IN COMPUTATIONAL SYSTEMS

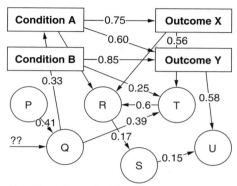

Conditions (states) of the world actually bring about changes. So much of one thing causes something else to happen to a certain degree. If we could build an arithmetic model of these relationships, we could predict (and thus control) the outcomes of our actions. We could even prescribe actions for certain desired outcomes and thus be in a better position to take advantage of what we know by changing the world to our benefit.

orders, help customers, or do acceptance testing. Instead, they deal with what is called the **information shadow** (see Figure 7–19), sometimes also called the **data shadow,** generated by these real-world events. The real work is full of conflict, irresolution, and dynamism. Resources are limited, and firms compete with each other or struggle against natural forces (organic material rots, machinery rusts, and people resist), so there is a more or less constant atmosphere of conflict among various players. This conflict is an important motivator for growth, learning, and progress.

However, **conflict** initially creates situations of struggle that are unresolved. Individuals and firms are in a perpetual state of "becoming" rather than "being." By this we mean that goals are not met, opportunities are passed by, and problems are perceived of as hard rather than easily solved by standard operating procedure. **Irresolution** means that conflicting parties constantly vie for position, which can be thought of as a dance for advantage accompanied by strategies and planning in which managers play a key role. This dance fosters a **dynamism** that is characteristic of business environments: change, change, and more change. These environmental changes are the motivation behind the need for management action.

Managers do not deal directly with these environmental events; they tend to deal with information about the events. In this view, real-world events generate information shadows on the plane of management action, and managers must deal with these shadows as well as with the events themselves. Consider the scenarios Geoff Wainwright faces. While he may occasionally visit buildings, he doesn't actually lease space himself and the bulk of his work is examining data about buildings and tenants from his office. Geoff does

Figure 7–18	AN OPERATIONAL SYSTEM

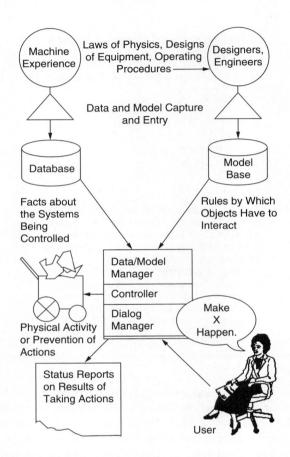

not cause leasing or renovations but describes to, instructs, and commands others what to do in certain situations. In other words, Geoff deals with the information shadow generated by activities in the business environment. He collects information, ponders it, and decides what has to be done. Then he convinces others to take the actions he describes or develops.

Information shadows reflect events in the business environment. Each time an event occurs, a record of it is created. For example, a sale generates sales information such as a receipt. Hiring someone creates an employment record put into an employee file. Every machine breakdown generates a service call. These examples show two things. First, data are about events, and if we fail to notice things during an event, we fail to record information about it. Second, if an event occurs but no one records data about it, then no event exists at the information shadow level. The information shadow is, of course, constantly changing, just as real shadows do, depending on both what is happening in the real world and the availability and accuracy of the recording. In Figure 7–19, the clouds drifting by are events and the sun is the recording instrument. When there are no clouds

| Figure 7-19 | THE INFORMATION SHADOW |

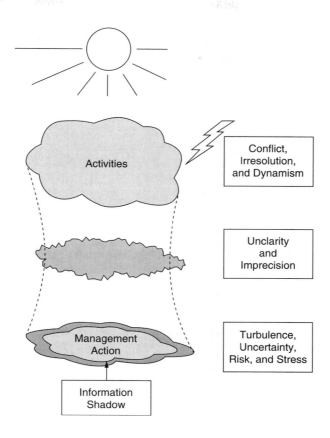

or the sun isn't shining, there are no shadows; when no events occur or no one records them, there are no data (shadows). Where the air is filled with dust, shadows are indistinct; when events are poorly observed or recorded, data are unreliable or inaccurate. Of course, if someone steals stock from a warehouse without anyone seeing or recording it, the event still takes place. In this case, the information shadow fails to reflect reality and decisions based on it will be invalid. Relying on information alone may not be sufficient in many cases, especially where awareness and recording are ineffective or inefficient. Recall that when sensory components in a cybernetic system either fail to notice threatening events or inadequately notify decision makers, the system as a whole is in danger.

Managers can be thought of as inhabiting a flat land of data. Events in the real world are created by conflict, irresolution, and dynamism, but what can be said of events in "data land"? Life in a manager's data world (i.e., in the information environment) is characterized by turbulence, uncertainty, risk, and stress (see Figure 7–20). **Turbulence** means that data are highly unpredictable, causing managers to ignore data they are unprepared to handle. This unpredictability brings uncertainty. In this context, **uncertainty** is a mental state rather than an objective quality of the environment. Uncertainty

Figure 7–20 | THE INFORMATION ENVIRONMENT

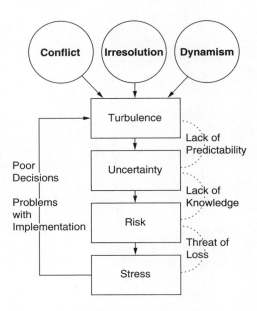

in the environment means knowledge is lacking. It is difficult to learn in a turbulent, uncertain environment because causes and effects are not known.

Lack of knowledge is the intellectual equivalent of **risk.** When causes are known, there is no risk at all. Risk is not inherently dangerous unless the outcome is threatening, such as an actual loss or an opportunity cost. The threat of a loss induces stress and psychological conditions that may cause managers to make rash or bad decisions or just flip a coin. This behavior has repercussions in the real world because bad decisions increase conflict, irresolution, and dynamism, thus creating more turbulence.

Because events in the real world refuse to become less conflicting, unresolved, and dynamic just because managers want them to, turbulence and uncertainty are not under their direct control. However, gaining information lowers risk and makes managers feel more confident that the actions they take will ultimately (not necessarily immediately) decrease turbulence, uncertainty, and stress. Overall, today's business environment is becoming more turbulent. Substitute products and services, an increasing number of new entrants, new configurations of suppliers, and the need to move products more rapidly through the value chain (in fact, all the modern management imperatives) imply more unpredictability and a greater need for information.

Information Overload

Managers sometimes can have too much information. **Information overload** occurs when managers have too much information to use profitably in a particular situation. For instance, Geoff Wainwright is inundated with information, which may make it more difficult for him to seek out and use the information he actually requires. Most people cope with information overload in any of these five ways:

- **Avoidance:** Managers simply avoid information they judge as useless or difficult to process. For example, Geoff may stop asking for regular reports from his staff because he can't find the time to process and respond to their reports.

- **Filtering:** Filtering means avoiding information from specific sources at specific times or avoiding information on specific topics. Geoff may filter information by tossing management memos into his trashcan. By his reckoning, if something is important, someone will phone him. He doesn't have to handle or respond to information he hasn't seen.

- **Lumping:** Managers at all levels use this tactic by creating summaries and averages, examining trends, creating graphs, and so forth. Lumping, or aggregating, is a way to reduce or remove information in a systematic way. Geoff hopes averages are going to be valuable, but when he gets a report on the average retail rental rate per square foot for the whole country, it doesn't do him much good in his six western cities.

- **Delay:** Managers can put information aside and deal with it later. (Who among us doesn't regularly put bills aside to be read at the end of the month or when we can face them?) Geoff has a few problem clients who regularly complain by mail and fax. He has started putting them aside to read when he has time. This habit is not particularly nice or valuable, but it does delay the problem for a while.

- **Redirecting:** Managers send information to other people to handle. Redirecting inevitably causes delays. Sometimes not *enough* information is passed to others, which can cause confusion and stress. Geoff regularly gives his assistants information that he doesn't have time to file or handle. Some might call this "delegating"; others think of it is "fobbing off."

These coping mechanisms are not in themselves irrational or counterproductive. Without effective ways to manage information overload, however, managers are likely to lose both time and valuable information. Information overload is actually the result of having to make a decision within a time frame that is too short to process all the necessary information effectively in the face of an undifferentiated stream of information. A danger is that one of the coping tactics will remove or hamper the discovery of important, pertinent information. A good management support system will avoid these problems by providing indexing, summarizing, abstraction, and routing tools.

Examples of **indexing** include key words or a search facility that allows for filtering after the information has been collected. **Summarizing** can be achieved with paragraphs, tables, diagrams, and images. **Abstracting** occurs when many information items are merged in a way that shows the underlying unifying concepts or ideas, as with article abstracts, survey articles, and analyses. Both summarizing and abstraction are forms of lumping that are useful because truly valuable information isn't lost. **Routing** occurs when information not handled by the decision maker is sent to appropriate people for indexing, summarizing, or abstraction to remove irrelevant or confusing information. Routing is a form of avoidance or redirecting that generally pays off.

Is information overload a common problem? Yes. The microcomputer revolution—and the accompanying explosion in networked communication such as the Internet—have exacerbated this problem for managers. What is needed for managers to handle too much information are corresponding information-based tools that are well integrated with managers' work patterns and capabilities. To be effective, these techniques have to be coupled with appropriate information-handling tools in what is called the *manager's information workbench*.

THE MANAGER'S INFORMATION WORKBENCH (MIW)

While strategies abound, they do not solve the problem of information overload, and if handled poorly, they merely cause additional problems. Information overload is really more a symptom than an actual problem. The real problem is an inability to function well in an information environment, which can happen in any of the following ways:

- Lack of understanding of what an information environment is
- Lack of tools to work in an information environment
- Inability to use the available tools
- Poor tools to work in an information environment

Recall that the cybernetic system introduced in Chapter 3 tries to accomplish its goals by building a "shadow" environment that reflects critical aspects of the real environment. Alarms and warnings are signaled when the environment is not behaving itself. Managers act as the sensing and deciding elements of organizational systems and they work through an information environment to create commands, directions, and instructions for others to carry out in the real business environment. Historically, managers were limited in their ability to function in this sort of environment. Hampered by a lack of tools appropriate to working with information, managers were left to perform simple computations and compile massive paper files that were difficult to access and even harder to sort, maintain, and report on.

Unlike the information deluge, this situation has improved with the microcomputer revolution. First, computers allow managers to process vast amounts of data and receive regular, accurate reports. Second, microcomputers, networks, and servers deliver information to managers' desks. Finally, modern user-sensitive software gives managers a set of tools that empower them in the information environment. Much of the bad information-handling habits managers engage in today are derived, unknown to them, from what was once a valuable practice in the past. Information hoarding was useful then because information was hard to find, expensive to copy, and bound in heavy volumes. Information filtering developed because information overload was reached quickly without tools to process or save anything other than a small amount of data. Quick rules of thumb developed and became enshrined in work practices in preference to detailed computations because computation was expensive, slow, and error-ridden.

Consider how a carpenter works. Tools are on a workbench, a different one for each task. Each tool is finely tuned to perform best when it is matched to a specific carpentry operation. All important preassembly tasks are done at the workbench, where the carpenter is familiar with each tool and keeps each one in the best working condition. The carpenter passes tools over the work rather than moving the work around from tool to

| Figure 7–21 | THE MANAGER'S INFORMATION WORKBENCH |

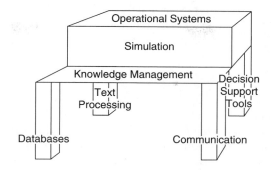

tool or place to place. At the workbench, a crafted item takes form as tools accomplish the goals they are uniquely designed for.

The piece that finishes the puzzle and enables managers to work like a carpenter in the information environment is the **manager's information workbench (MIW)** (see Figure 7–21). Be aware that the MIW is a concept; there is no such product available (yet) on the market. We use this concept to sensitize readers to expect a change in the way management work is done. In the future, more and more "crafting" of a manager's work will be done in an information environment using a select set of tools. Each tool will be suited to a particular task and yet finely machined to work either in conjunction with other tools or one after the other. Many of the parts already exist. Some environments such as *Windows* already use many of the concepts, allowing, for example, cutting and pasting of graphs or spreadsheets directly into documents, or vice versa. Some integrated packages such as *Guru* add in an expert system shell that makes it possible to move rather freely from one format to another.

Managers will not be expected to create their own workbenches. Information systems specialists will have to be available to help select and configure the appropriate tools. In many cases, they will build or alter tools for individual managers as they need them.

If such integrated workbenches existed today (more sophisticated ones will exist in the future), they would contain tools such as these:

- Databases accompanied by a data description, access, and manipulation language (abbreviated as DDL, DAL, and DML); the capabilities of these languages are best accessed through menus and GUIs rather than through typing commands
- Communications packages that simplify contact with other people or remote databases
- Text and graphics processing tools along with appropriate displays and presentation managers (examples include word processors and drawing programs)
- Decision support systems, often built around spreadsheet capabilities

■ Knowledge creation, capture, and management tools through expert system shells and artificial intelligence–based tools

■ Simulation and statistics packages (such as SPSS, SAS, SIMSCRIPT, or GPSS) or firm-specific simulation programs

■ Operational systems, real-time peepholes into and controls of online processing, which include process control software

Databases

This discussion complements Chapter 5 in relation to information architectures. Here we look more closely at how databases themselves are constructed and what support they provide. A **database** is a collection of information with an internal structure. This is the *minimum* requirement for creating an information workbench. There are two related species of databases. First, a personal database contains information collected, processed, and managed by an individual. Among a manager's personal databases would be contacts, correspondence, timetables, to-do lists, project notes, reports-in-progress, and personal information. In contrast, the corporate database is a large, complex structure whose integrity is critical to a firm's success—even to its survival. A personal database can have errors that an individual might easily find. Errors in a corporate database, however, may persist because everyone assumes someone else is responsible for it. Understanding the complexities of corporate databases is important for managers who want to use that data.

Databases are multifaceted and the word often refers to a set of components such as the following:

1. A description of the data (the technical term is a *data dictionary*)

2. A set of relations that link parts of the database; this is the architecture or structure of the database; the structure can be hierarchical, object-oriented, a tree or network, or a set of relations that characterize a relational database

3. A set of objects or events that can be described by the data (called the *domain*)

4. A set of rules determining how objects described by the database can be manipulated

Implemented in software, this complex set of components is called a *database manager*, and the rules are the commands and access language of the database manager or a commonly accepted code such as SQL. The database package generally has these components: a set of data in a standard format (DDL model); an interface language (DAL) that provides access to data; a data manipulation language (DML) that makes it easy to express relationships and thereby retrieve information; and a reporting component that facilitates presentation of information relating to objects in an appropriate, understandable, and usable format.

Holbein Holdings has a paper database that Geoff can access. This database contains information on all of Holbein's customers and can best be described as follows:

■ *Data:* About Holbein's customers

■ *Relations:* The database links customers to space and contracts for space. The database also contains information about services performed including dates, who did the work, and notes about the results.

- *Object:* Each record refers to one contract involving one paying customer.
- *Rules:* Each record is identified by customer name and filed in alphabetical order by customer name. There are also paper carbon copies that cannot be changed.

Geoff and his assistant are considering boosting profits and getting rid of some excess capacity by dramatically altering some space to appeal to upscale, premium customers. Significant costs to modernization, refurbishing, and advertising would be incurred, but it seems to Geoff that this strategy would signal a vibrant entrance of Holbein into a new marketplace and position it very well against its competitors. Geoff wonders if premium space should be a separate subsidiary, so he examines the data to try to find "premium" customers and what they have wanted done to their space. He finds he needs additional help.

Communication Support

Communication systems allow individuals to tap each others' expertise and opinions. The basis of this interaction is not necessarily data but rather comments about data and data-related "conversation." The power of the MIW with regard to communication is its ability to access appropriate individuals with regard to a topic and retain and reaccess their comments on these topics. Because opinions and issues may be complex, the information workbench will help by keeping track of these ideas and personal dispositions in a structure, making them more available.

Among the most common computerized communication components of the MIW is electronic mail, which can substitute not only for mail but also for telephone calls. Group communication techniques, such as computer conferencing, form an additional component of tools such as *Lotus Notes*. This product, like others in its class, enables individuals to share mail, comments, and files with others both in their own work groups and across functional lines and levels of authority.

Geoff meets an analyst weekly in her office to review ongoing projects. In one of these meetings, they toss around some ideas about how to improve occupancy ratios. The meetings begin with statements such as "How about if we . . . " and end in arguments about whether the department will make money. Geoff trusts the analyst to come up with solid, profitable ideas and to evaluate his, too; they both have many years' experience in the leasing business as well as with Holbein. While much of their conversation is data-based (e.g., "We lost $30,000 last year fixing up space for Murphy Paint"), a great deal concerns feelings and intuition (e.g., "We shouldn't be in that business; we can't ever make guarantees, in my opinion"). Sometimes Geoff has to ask his boss to come in and help them evaluate an idea about marketing. He values his boss's opinions—even if she doesn't know the answer, she can usually find someone who does. No computer is used in any of these conversations, but Geoff feels supported by the communication abilities of the analyst and access to his boss.

Information Creation and Contextualization

Information creation requires that the workbench be able to translate facts, numbers, impressions, feelings, and so on, into data recorded and maintained in a database in a variety of forms. These forms include words and documents, whole texts (perhaps with abstracts), and a variety of analog formats including graphics (tables, graphs, pictorials), sounds, or moving or changing images. The goals of information creation are to record events and to come to an understanding of what those events mean in context. It is the latter concept that gives rise to the word for the tools—*contextualizing*.

Contextualizing consists of information capture, formatting, and display. A contextualizing tool works as follows: Information is captured in some mechanical way, formatted so that it is displayable, and displayed to the author and others. These people may make changes to it; more than one version of the formatted data may exist at any one time. Eventually, a single version is adopted for use.

There are limits to contextualization. They include:

1. *Display compatibility*—different displays may not be compatible.

2. *Information capture*—managers may not like inputting large amounts of information.

3. *Vocabulary control*—various viewers must share at least the basic meanings of the items displayed across contexts.

4. *Reformatting*—words can be changed to pictorials or various modalities (sounds, images, text) can be combined.

5. *Aesthetic considerations*—displays can be made more pleasant to read, view, or hear with attention to layout, color, design, clutter, timing, sequence, and proportions.

6. *Version management*—events may be recorded at different times; each recording makes obsolete previous ones; keeping track of which is the current version is an important consideration.

The MIW can help managers control these six limitations primarily by providing (1) basic compatibility among displays and across modalities, (2) a database facility to manage versions, and (3) tools to handle aesthetics and vocabulary.

One important problem with contextualizing systems is the ease with which it is possible to create information. Why is ease a problem? First, there is a false security in having created a document or an image so quickly. Speed does not imply usefulness or validity. Second, there is a feeling of authority in having created something that formerly only highly skilled artists or technicians could do. However, these are only tools and tools don't have judgment, only capability. They can produce beautifully crafted trash just as easily as works of art. A third problem is version management. With many versions of essentially the same document or image available, it's important to know which one has been viewed by whom and which version is most official. Even in a computerized setting, electronic messages may cross in the mail, and readers may not know that another version of the report they are reading or working on has already been approved and acted on. Finally, having the capability doesn't mean knowing when to use it. Spending a day producing a slide for a colleague's presentation usually isn't time well spent. A conversation might do the job more quickly and effectively.

Geoff uses a spreadsheet and a word/image processor to create and present arguments to his managers concerning his ideas for the upcoming leasing year. In the spreadsheet, Geoff generates tables showing where losses were incurred, what the threat is of incurring these losses again, and what Holbein must spend to guard against similar problems in the future. He uses a related product to compose a series of graphs showing projected sales, costs, and profits for various alternatives. The spreadsheets and the graphs are imported into a document he is building with a word processor to create dummies of transparencies he intends to use in the meeting. Finally, he uses a color laser printer to print out the transparencies for his presentation. He doesn't worry about display compatibility, and since he doesn't like entering a lot of data, he asks his secretary to fill in the tables for him. Because he is using numbers and charts, Geoff seldom has to explain the meaning of his presentations. However, he knows he is not a wonderful graphic artist, and sometimes the diagrams do not look very professional, particularly when he strays from using only graphs. At these times, he wonders if he should use a professional artist. Also, one persistent worry stems from how easy it is to prepare these materials: Unless he's careful to label and date everything, he can easily confuse himself and others with which version he's using.

Decision Support

Support of decision making requires a number of tools built around a set of components. These components allow the creation, manipulation, and display of information in a variety of ways for comparison and judgment. **Decision support** generally has these components: problem formulation and description, modeling, evaluation, and execution. Decision support works in the following fashion. First, managers require assistance in formulating the decision problem, in understanding what decisions have to be made, and the terms of the decisions required. Then they model the decision problem. Principles guiding action form rules for decision making. These rules are translated into statements, sometimes of an arithmetic nature (e.g., Profit = Selling Price minus Cost of Goods Sold minus Selling Costs), but often merely expressed as relationships (e.g., Profit increases with sales beyond a certain point). Having these rules enables evaluation of scenarios. For example, if Evergreen Landscaping increases the price of its guaranteed green-up service, what will be the effect on sales? On profit? What about decreasing the price? Will that increase sales? What will be the labor requirements?

There are limits to decision support. In order to support decision making, the assumptions behind the decision making must be understood. For example, Geoff is primarily concerned with profit but also with the company's image and reputation. He's unsure that this decision should really be a data-based decision. He may have to go with the analyst's gut feeling rather than just numbers. Besides, Holbein can afford to lose a few thousand dollars to improve its image and protect its reputation—but how many thousands? Another decision maker might make a different decision based on the same data; Geoff's decision is not programmed and involves qualitative data. Also, Geoff is not really sure of the relationship between cost and profit, given the tight labor market for skilled workers. Perhaps raising the leasing price and targeting more upscale clients might help to reposition Holbein in customers' minds. No fast rule guides this decision.

Decision making is only part of the story. Managers need support to implement decisions and that support may range from emotional to financial. Much of what is decided is qualitative in nature. Implementation means managing image and expectation and communication of rationale and projected results—in short, leadership of a team. Classical computerized decision support speaks only to the numbers; managers speak to the people.

Geoff is using a spreadsheet program to make projections of profit versus price for two situations: occupancy rates and profit for space as it currently exists and rates and profit for premium, upscale, improved space. Geoff has asked Sandy Galinka, the analyst, to gather data on current and projected costs and some formulas relating costs to sales for each case. For example, premium space will rent for 40 percent more. Geoff feels that in a particular part of town, occupancy is price-sensitive, and only specific, premium clients will be interested. So Holbein will lease out less space to fewer clients in that area. His costs are directly proportional to sales plus improvements plus a constant for overhead paperwork, but this paperwork is already handled in the regular leasing. On the other hand, if premium leasing is offered as a standalone subsidiary, demand would not decrease rapidly as price increases. However, space leasing directly depends on the dollars regular customers have, so the price of the premium space program would strongly dictate how those customers respond. These formulas are built into the spreadsheet and enable Geoff to begin to understand the premium space leasing program in a variety of ways.

Knowledge Management

Managers deal with knowledge in the form of facts, rules, and descriptions. This knowledge is seldom well organized, so information about knowledge enables managers to organize knowledge into groups related to the work being done. Knowledge-related information is different from other forms of information because it is almost always incomplete and tentative. Rules are known to be breakable, facts may change, and descriptions may vary from observer to observer. Managers require tools to compare knowledge and extract the valuable kernels therein.

Components of **knowledge management** are accumulated data, rules, modeling, evaluation, and execution. Knowledge management tools accumulate data in the form of facts or statements of truth, which state what is true now based on available data. A statement such as "Cameron Towers is our most consistently occupied property" is only true now; next year this may be a false statement. Truth in an information system depends on what data are collected and how the data are manipulated.

Rules are guidelines for reasoning and are thus statements about data. They are generally of the form, "If A is true, then B is true." A would be a statement that may be true or false (in some knowledge management tools, "true" and "false" may not be the only values allowed; we might be able to talk about "sort of true" or "possibly true"; in this case, the truth of B depends on just how true A is). B could be a statement, command, or suggestion. Here are some examples of possible rules:

- If net profit on a product exceeds 40 percent, then this product is highly profitable; if the net profit exceeds 20 percent, then this product is very profitable; if the net profit exceeds 5 percent, then this product is profitable; otherwise, the product is not profitable.

- If sales of a product increase over one year, order 15 percent more next year.

- If a customer complains about product quality, send the customer to the sales manager.

- If an employee is late three days in a month, seek an informal meeting to discuss the problem.

- If a product arrives damaged and the shipment value exceeds $100, then fill out a Receipt of Damaged Goods form and send it to accounts payable; otherwise, phone the shipper and ask to return the goods.

The collection of rules and data is referred to here as a *logical model*. This model can then be processed, much like a spreadsheet, to determine new values. For example, the first rule indicates how a product can be classified according to net profit. On the other hand, the other rules provide simple advice about product ordering, what to do with a complaining customer, how to handle an employee with a possible pattern of lateness, and what paperwork to do when damaged goods are received. Processing evaluates the model in terms of the current situation and provides advice to be followed.

The limits of knowledge management are clear from the structure of the knowledge management tool. First, the data determine how "true" the resulting advice is. Unreliable or incomplete data make it difficult to trust the results. Second, in order to be useful, a great many rules need to be available, but it's not always clear what the rules are, and many rules are really only systematized ignorance or hunch (sometimes called *rules of thumb*). Third, for such a tool to be useful, both data and rules need to be in a common format or at least a format that makes them compatible. Finally, keeping a large set of rules up-to-date and maintaining current data are daunting tasks.

Lynelle Spring, Geoff's boss, has asked Frank Harnwell, vice president of administration, to set up a flexible benefits system for Holbein staff. Recent changes to labor law and Lynelle's feeling that employees should be smart enough to set up their own benefits packages from a cafeteria of choices have prompted Lynelle to reform how Holbein handles benefits. Frank has looked at a number of such systems and has spoken with more than a dozen employees. He has concluded that the cost to change the system will be very high and that despite Lynelle's optimism, many employees are confused about benefits and would not trust their own judgment. In a recent conversation, Frank learned about an expert system for employee benefit packaging specially tailored for medium-sized retail firms like Holbein. The initial cost of the system is $2,500. Frank would have to input about 20 rules pertaining to Holbein's insurance carriers and taxation position as well as a lot of data about current and possible benefits. Then each employee would enter pertinent personal information. Finally, the employee would answer a number of questions about financial planning, retirement, health, and family to get a personal profile detailing benefit choices. The system would make it easy to create profiles, but Frank wonders if employees would feel confident getting this sort of advice from a computer.

Simulation

Information can be used to make decisions, but often not all the data are available; they have to be generated. In these cases, it is necessary to create a model of the situation at hand and work on the model, a process called **simulation.** To an extent, all computation is a simulation, but simulations more precisely mimic a situation.

A simulation works very much like a knowledge management system, but in place of rules are either arithmetic formulas or complex data manipulation routines. One can think of a simulation tool as a spreadsheet or a computer program, although many simulation tools are very sophisticated. Languages such as SIMSCRIPT or GPSS allow managers to set up complex simulations of, for example, manufacturing or marketing systems. It is possible to simulate at a very high level (say, a national economy and behavior of its industries) or at a very low level (such as a chemical manufacturing plant's flow of materials through pipes controlled by valves).

Most managers are familiar with spreadsheet simulations that set up an arithmetic model. A good example is a budgeting exercise in which the final total is known (for example, last year's budget minus 5 percent in a cutback situation). The goal of this sort of simulation often is to determine the optimal value of specific line items within a given range. This is called *solving*. In simulations, the goal is not specific advice but a set of numbers or readings; often these are predictions that result from making different assumptions (e.g., What if our factory has a major glitch and we can only produce 85 percent of quota? What will be the effect on sales and profit?). Spreadsheets used for decision support are at the low end of simulations. Far more complex are real-time simulations of dynamic systems. The value of these simulations is that we don't actually have to build the chemical manufacturing plant to observe its behavior or we don't have to make changes to the national economy to see the effects of crippling strikes (or taxes) in one or more sectors. In effect, simulations construct a virtual reality that is far more controllable and, of course, less likely to be harmed in case a wrong number is plugged in.

The limitations of simulation tools are also similar to those of knowledge management tools. Unreliable data lead to unreliable solutions, and errors in formulas lead to similarly untrustworthy or incomprehensible results. Because formulas work on the data, it is important that they be in compatible formats. There is also the problem of updating the simulation when new data arrive or new formulas are determined. A last problem is that of interpreting the results. Simulations tend to be very complex and, in fact, substitute for our own ability to process huge amounts of information. So the results must be trusted implicitly if each formula or relationship cannot be tested. Test conditions for simple database processing are relatively easy to derive. For complex situations, however, we may not actually know what to expect and hence cannot easily tell if something is wrong with the simulation.

Another of Lynelle Spring's concerns at Holbein Holdings is disaster planning and crisis management. She is worried that the spaces Holbein rents could be vulnerable to disasters and has spent a lot of time talking with the company's insurers about the high cost of insurance. One of the things the insurers keep stressing is that Lynelle doesn't actually know what the effects of certain disasters would be. She only has hunches, and insuring hunches is expensive. The insurers referred Lynelle to Southwestern Software, which has some experience with disaster simulation software. A number of sessions with Lynelle, the vice president of operations, and the vice president of finance were held. Southwestern finally produced a simulation of Holbein's space and its vulnerabilities to fire, earthquake, and water and power outages—a complicated set of relationships. Southwestern had to hit the books to learn about buildings, utilities, soil composition, fire hazards, and city supplies. The simulation accepts assumptions and descriptions of buildings, contents, and characteristics. Then it simulates a series of disasters (such as a power failure, an earthquake, or a fire), producing a report detailing financial losses, time to recover, and implications for staff and suppliers. The simulation will have to be updated as Holbein's physical space, clientele, and suppliers change. So far, it's pinpointed exactly what Lynelle needs to insure, thereby saving tens of thousands of dollars in insurance premiums and assisting in setting up a disaster plan that would have been only guesswork in the past.

Operational Systems

Unlike simulations, **operational systems'** activities generate data needed to change things in the real world. In order to operate systems, managers need real-world information and the ability to act and react at real-world speeds. Knowledge may not be enough without the skills to apply it immediately, effectively, and accurately. The related term, *operating system,* is of course familiar to computer users as the system that operates a computer. An operating system is an operational system. Through a set of commands or a graphic user interface (GUI), the user instructs the operating system to manipulate files, process data, turn equipment on or off, and to report on the results. The operating system handles the nitty-gritty of the electronics and mechanics, allowing the user to ignore the "insides" of the computer. Other operational systems, such as automated production lines or point-of-sale terminals, act in a similar fashion.

An operational system contains the components of a simulation system except a simulation is not "live" and shows results that must be interpreted by managers while an operational system itself takes action. Thus, an automated production line will treat its operator as another, perhaps more interesting, input device, some of whose data refer to production parameters such as speed, product type, volume, and quality. But the operator need not understand the relationship between the data (e.g., produce 500 widgets) and electrical signals that make the equipment work or the data stored that describe the products and machines. This work is left to analysts who typically examine these signals and data only when something goes wrong or when changes are made in product design.

Because operational systems take all or most decision making and control away from operators, limitations are obviously either in the design or in the expectations of users. Most of us who use microcomputer operating systems, shells, or GUIs (such as DOS, *Windows*, or *Unix*) think after a while that we are controlling something real. Then, when an error message appears to tell us that a piece of equipment has failed, a disk has gone bad, or some software is missing, we are at a loss about what to do because the facade of simple commands has been shattered. In reality, we use the actual computer through layers of simulation, and our reality bears no relationship to that of the real computer. As soon as our reality becomes untenable (we might say things like "The computer is dead," "My keyboard is locked up," or "What happened to my diskette?"), we are totally lost. Whereas some of us can debug our simulations and most of us can proofread our contextualized documents for errors, the kinds of errors operational systems make are beyond our grasp. Perhaps this is why operators of complex equipment have to be trained to recognize the signs of incipient problems before the virtual reality becomes an actual calamity.

John Iverson has just finished installing a greenhouse environmental system that completely controls temperature, humidity, light, ventilation, and security in one of Holbein's potential premium buildings. Through a complex arrangement of electrical, hydraulic, and pneumatic equipment, John can program a day's or a week's settings in much the same way one might program a home thermostat to regulate temperature daily. The system prompts John through a menu soliciting requirements for the various parameters. It then makes a decision about the best way to achieve and maintain those values for the period of time John has selected. In addition, the buildings are sectored, and the first-floor lobby is treated differently from the penthouse on the top floor. While the system can be overridden if necessary (as was the case when several panes of glass were being replaced, necessitating additional heating for two days), it tends to "do its own thing," in John's words. John has taken the trouble to speak with the system's manufacturer and now understands exactly how it works from his point of view. John trusts that the mechanics of the system work correctly. He sent Cal Stone, his building engineer, on a three-day course conducted by the manufacturer, and now Cal can do immediate repairs if something goes wrong. And, of course, John has let Geoff know how the system works in general, so that the disaster management software could be updated.

THE USER'S VIEW OF INFORMATION

Information can be presented to and manipulated by users in a variety of formats. Several formats are related to specific products or the particular way in which computer technology has developed. Others are styled on existing ways of presenting information (e.g., spreadsheets are a well-recognized feature of accounting). Some applications embody several of these models. For example, a simple multimedia encyclopedia incorporates hyperspace navigation through pictorial images to databases.

Spreadsheets, databases, hyperspaces, procedures, and images/objects are the five most common and well-understood views of information today. A description of each follows.

- *Spreadsheets:* Information workbenching is done exactly as it would be done on a paper worksheet, in rows and columns or even three or more dimensions, facilitating processing of rows and columns that refer to the same attributes of the data.

- *Databases:* Various items of information are naturally related to one another because they are attributes of the same event. Database models treat data as inert objects that programs or people collect and operate on.

- *Hyperspaces:* Each individual data element is related to others through reference, specifying, generalizing, or sequence. For example, while reading about pesticides, one may come across a reference to a specific chemical. Users move through hyperspace, directly accessing information about that chemical.

- *Procedures:* Information relationships reflect an input-process-output paradigm. The focus is on transformations rather than the data itself. Procedures are relatively blind to the data being processed; a given procedure could conceivably be asked to work on any data of the appropriate format. Applications that work on a question-and-answer basis are procedural, as are most programs that require the user to fill out a form.

- *Icons, objects, or images:* Carrying out some information tasks is naturally pictorial and tools used to do this should manipulate images. The object-oriented view sees the world as a set of classes of objects. Emphasis is on individual objects, and the goal is to build up a model of reality based on these objects and their associated individual and group behaviors and relationships.

There is no single best information format; each is valuable in a specific context. However, it is clear that spreadsheets are better suited to calculations than are hyperspaces, if only because we are taught to use formulas step-by-step rather than as a geographic configuration. On the other hand, some problems are explored more easily, if not solved, using a set of hyperspace-navigated experiences (such as those that may be found in a game or on the World Wide Web) rather than a structured set of formulas.

For some situations, then, the adopted format may be crucial because it determines what sorts of processing, hence what sorts of information, tasks will be appropriate. Users are moving toward information tasks that more closely reflect the actual objects they are concerned with. Emphasis has moved from a high level of abstraction (information, reflecting the data) to the object itself, with the computer taking care of the details. It is as if the metaphors users have created with computers (spreadsheets, for example) can now be treated as if they are the reality. To do this requires no computer skills, but it puts a great burden on software builders to create realistic and versatile objects and icons that behave somewhat as real objects do.

| Figure 7–22 | THE INFORMATION-CENTERED ENTERPRISE (ICE) |

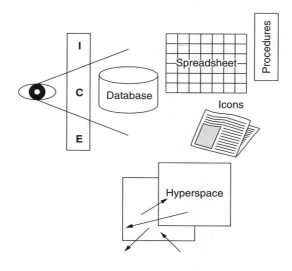

Support for managers in information tasks implies the right level of management support system and presenting information in ways managers are comfortable with. Information environments that are rich and easily handled and shared with others are characteristic of the information-centered environment (ICE). An ICE presents as much of a manager's business environment as possible in terms of information views and supplies the appropriate tools to managers. Hence, managers can carry out information-intensive tasks through an integrated set of tools and information views, called the information-centered enterprise, also identified by the acronym ICE.

DIMENSIONS OF THE INFORMATION-CENTERED ENTERPRISE/ENVIRONMENT

Few firms have implemented a computer-based **information-centered enterprise/ environment (ICE)** that covers the entire business. The ICE concept doesn't require computers; any environment that is information-rich can be considered information-centered. Many firms, however, have built ICE-like environments around existing automated systems, especially in production facilities. Still, a computer-based ICE remains a vision or speculation for the future of business, so the discussion that follows is somewhat hypothetical. In many places, we say, "The ICE is . . . " when we might better say, "The ICE should be . . . " The fact that few firms have moved to workbench all their activities doesn't prevent speculation about how the ICE concept might benefit managers today.

As shown in Figure 7–22, the ICE is a generalization of the management information workbench that also encompasses information on the firm itself. There are similarities between the MIW and the ICE. The major difference is that the ICE, rather than being a workbench that managers come *to*, is an environment managers work *within*. So the acronym *ICE* refers to both the enterprise and the environment. The easiest way to imagine an ICE is to think of a firm that operates entirely through an information interface. In this firm, every business event that occurs is recorded and made available (through computers) to managers. Managers then use the information to make decisions, effect communication, carry out organizational tasks, and make changes. To a great extent, most financial institutions function this way. Other than handling cash and obtaining signatures, almost every event that occurs in a bank or a brokerage firm is handled as a data shadow and accessed through computers.

Four dimensions characterize the ICE: breadth, depth, power, and usability. Breadth is the proportion of a firm's functions the ICE can handle or express and manipulate. Depth is the degree to which individuals can carry out these individual functions with the ICE. When an organization's business is reflected completely and accurately in the ICE, the ICE becomes a rich medium that influences the enterprise. When the model is incomplete or inaccurate, the ICE is a poor medium, and users will naturally seek other ways of obtaining information and carrying out their responsibilities.

For example, Geoff's information environment is relatively complex. He is showered with data on sales, marketing, and products, but few functions can be handled through the relatively weak MIW he has at his disposal. Some of these functions, such as sales analyses and reporting, are highly automated and are based on well-understood marketing and sales models. This part of his environment is rich, but in general the ICE he works within is a poor medium despite a plethora of information.

The power of an ICE is reflected in the effectiveness of its users. Power is influenced by a number of technical characteristics including:

1. **Transparency versus opaqueness:** The ICE doesn't get in the way of the user's visualization of what the data represent, that is, organizational events. Transparency implies that the user has access to appropriate data formats, too.

2. Tools to view the organization

3. Tools to influence the organization

4. Tools to communicate about the organization

5. Tools to check on and redirect influence

These characteristics determine usability. For example, Geoff receives a lot of information about maintenance and sales, but it is hard for him to communicate this information upward without laboriously making summaries. Because his clerks deal with different sides of the business but often require similar information, Geoff has to work hard to coordinate their efforts. For example, all are concerned with leasing space, but they work with different clients and services in different buildings. They all report building maintenance activities on different forms, in different ways, at different times, and in different terms. In every case, Geoff writes reports and provides suggestions without much of an idea of where his reports and suggestions go. He's unsure about his influence. An ICE takes as a given that information shared is influence and does not ignore this aspect. In an ICE, Geoff would know exactly who reads his reports, what parts they extract and redistribute, and how to coordinate the clerks' information work.

When the ICE is broad, deep, and powerful, it is more useful. When the views of the organization presented through the windows are intuitive and reflect established or (organizational) culturally mandated ways of thinking or working, the information environment is

Table 7–2	ADVANTAGES AND DISADVANTAGES OF THE ICE

Advantages	Disadvantages
Better quality of information	Diffusion of responsibility
Higher leverage (use) of information	Diffusion of influence
Better organizational buy-in	False security
More individuals involved	Dependence on technology
Clearer vision of organization	Masking of reality through technology
Faster reconfiguration of views	Lack of fixed vision for organization
Tool for managing change	Rapid change

certain to be more usable. The ICE enables managers to set up views of the organization for themselves or to share with others. These views can be created by a manager or imported from others, including analysts and experts. The ICE has facilities for acquiring, blending, separating, and manipulating sets of views in standard ways so that managers can work individually or cooperatively.

Components of the ICE

An effective ICE provides business models, data descriptions of each aspect of the firm, a variety of appropriate information views, and some knowledge about its users' preferences. All of these components are accessible to users through an interface language appropriate to each user. This language may use specific technology (such as mice, drawn windows on the screen, soft buttons, etc.). Alternatively, users should be able to design their own languages.

Evaluating the Concept of the ICE

The ICE concept has a number of advantages and disadvantages (see Table 7–2) when compared to enterprises that are not information-centered. The advantages are as follows:

1. *Better information quality:* Information used by a lot of people means that more people check the value and validity of the information.

2. *Higher leverage of information:* Items of information are not used in isolation, but affect many parts of the organization.

3. *Better organizational buy-in:* Better-quality information means more trust. The more people who use information know they are sharing it with others, the greater is their confidence that decisions based on this information will be good and for the good of others. Hence, there is more trust and buy-in.

4. *More individuals involved:* The ICE makes sharing easier and more natural; information hiding becomes abnormal.

5. *Clearer vision of the organization:* As more people share information, it becomes easier to work as a team and to derive clearer vision statements.

6. *Faster reconfiguration of the views:* Disparate views and conflict can be noted and handled more easily.

7. *Ability to manage change better:* Conflict is lowered and change becomes more manageable.

However, each advantage has an associated possible disadvantage:

1. *Diffusion of responsibility:* "The computer made me do it" syndrome may take over. Alternatively, users may not act solely on the basis of human authority but may require computer corroboration.

2. *Diffusion of influence:* Information without source identification is suspect; it is possible that not knowing where information comes from can undermine trust and influence.

3. *False security:* If the ICE works well, people may not question irregularities and may be shielded from reality, especially if the ICE has some inaccuracies or errors built in.

4. *Dependence on technology:* If the ICE ceases to function well, can workers and managers function at all?

5. *Masking of reality through technology:* Each technology presents a modified, mediated view of reality and not a pure, objective view. These views can be manipulated, too.

6. *Lack of fixed vision for organization:* More views means less chance of a single, fixed, and dominant one important for leadership.

7. *Rapid change:* Change can take place too fast, without some of the checks and balances humans use.

Comparing ICE and Non-ICE Roles

In an ICE, a manager takes on more information roles and fewer authority roles. Hierarchical and task-oriented views of management (see Chapter 2) depend strongly on information hiding and persuasion by coercion rather than information sharing and persuasion by data-based reasoning. Neither view promotes communication except in specific, limited ways. Allocational views are consistent with the ICE because in modern firms, resource allocation must be highly flexible and responsive. However, resource allocation concepts, while stressing the negotiation aspects of resource conflict resolution, do not go beyond enabling organizational work. They do not take into account the work itself and the motivation to do work. Transactional views are consistent with the ICE and stress communication, negotiation, and collaboration, but they focus almost exclusively on a predetermined set of transactions. In fact, most computer-based management systems for organizations are extensions of transaction processing and production-management systems. Thus, they do not take into account nontransactional aspects of the firm such as design, creativity, organization, and leadership. Knowledge-oriented and goal-centered views of the firm are very consistent with the idea of the ICE. In fact, they require a pervasively information-centered view of the firm as an originator, consumer, processor, and appreciator of information.

Thus, implicit managerial models determine the roles managers play. In the ICE, a manager is a custodian of information (data and knowledge) with the rights and responsibilities that go with it. In a non-ICE, managers control resources, time, keys, authority, and so forth. With few exceptions, these are physical objects that must be guarded and rationed according to some schedule or through personal influence. In the non-ICE, managers are tempted, and sometimes forced, to forgo sharing. After all, they derive their power from specific knowledge or resources they possess or control, and those they might share with have limited abilities to process information reliably.

Managerial roles in the ICE include those of facilitator and coach because managers make information flow. In the non-ICE, the managerial role is conservative because resources and influence have to be guarded. In the ICE, managers are natural sources of information and knowledge first because others need it and, second, because they have the ability to view it according to their task requirements.

The Modern Management Imperatives

Reach: Global Competition	Management support systems provide access to other people, other units' data, and other systems to bridge space conveniently and accurately with lowered cost. This makes it possible for every business to be a global competitor. Having information and the tools to process it at hand means quick, accurate response, anywhere, at any time.
Reaction: Quick Customer Feedback on Products and Services	Having access to large amounts of data is only the first step. Bringing order to that data, locating patterns, and getting advice means much faster and more accurate response to customer needs. Managers ultimately anticipate customer needs because they understand (can build a model of) the customer.
Responsiveness: Shortened Concept-to-Customer Cycle Time	The ICE, facilitated by connectivity of machines and people and integration of databases with management support tools, means that interdisciplinary, multifunction teams can work on products and services much more quickly. Managing such teams is eased by having management support systems available to obtain advice and bring information from many sources together in a single report.
Refinement: Greater Customer Sophistication and Specificity	Customer sophistication is increasing the turbulence of the business environment, necessitating the collection of far more information. Having information available is only half the story; having access to appropriate tools for obtaining advice is the other half. The ICE provides consensus, contexture, data management, and other higher-level tools for this purpose.
Reconfiguration: Reengineering of Work Patterns and Structures	Complex work structures generate complex data that must be discussed and visualized when complex problems arise. Management support systems enhance managers' ability to respond and control complex networks of job functions.
Redeployment: Reorganization and Redesign of Resources	As organizations grow and meet obstacles, they reorganize their resources. The need to do this rapidly with little loss means understanding the organization of these resources. A management support system enables managers to visualize these complex arrangements and manage them through models.
Reputation: Quality and Reliability of Product and Process	Quality means customer satisfaction, which is part of understanding customers. Management support systems link managers with others who have the appropriate experience, either directly (consensus systems, MISs, consulting systems) or indirectly (through implicative or computational models).

◼ ICE STORM AT HOLBEIN HOLDINGS

Holbein Holdings is creating a type of ICE that it calls HolSpace. This system is intended to give managers like Geoff the ability to process information effortlessly. Hol-Space is conceived of as a series of rooms interconnected by hallways. Within each room, information can be processed in relatively fixed ways (such as text processing, database queries and reporting, decision support spreadsheets, electronic mail, a variety of simulation scenarios, and so forth). Data are moved from room to room by "mousing" it down a hall; conversions from one format to another are handled automatically. One room has a printer; "mousing" the results of a decision tool to this room will print the output. One room contains a series of "conversations" or "interviews" that gathers data. Another room guides the user through one or more decision tables to make knowledgeable decisions about pricing, space availability, and client desirability. No other systems will be required of managers or clerks (clerks will be given keys only to rooms they need to access). ◼

1. What are the advantages and disadvantages for managers like Geoff of using this system? What should this system do or appear as in order to help Geoff meet major management challenges?

2. How will having this kind of information available affect Geoff in terms of meeting goals, leadership, creativity, decision making, communication, knowledge acquisition, and organizational learning?

Summary

A business adds value to raw materials by creating finished products or providing services. The value chain is a model of the organization that depicts stages in the value-adding process, including marketing, in-bound logistics, production, outbound logistics, sales, and service. Managers contribute four qualities to that chain: uniformity, certainty, authority, and regularity. They do this in several ways: by improving quality, making decisions, fostering organizational climate and culture, influencing others, innovating, and helping the organization to learn. Seven information-based kinds of systems support managers in these activities. These systems help create ideas (consensus), visualize problems (contextualization), provide access to date (management information), tap past experiences (consulting), indicate logical conclusions of the courses of actions (implicational), compute specific outcomes (computational), and control other systems (operational). The support that these systems provide is generally in the form of advice based on stored models, accumulated data, a description of the current situation, and devices to display the advice.

The seven systems provide increasingly sophisticated and precise advice based on increasingly well-researched models. Matching the level of advice required with the state of knowledge in the problem domain is critical for managers. Supporting advice is necessary because a manager's information environment is characterized by turbulence, uncertainty, risk and stress. This is due to the unclarity and imprecision in data collection and recorded experiences of a working environment that demonstrate conflict, irresolution, and dynamism. Management support systems aid managers in bringing sense to this world of data. In addition, managers may find themselves overloaded with information; management support systems make coping with the flood of information easier. A set of tools that provide such support is called the *manager's information workbench* and includes communications packages, text and graphics, processing tools, decision support systems, knowledge management applications, simulation and statistics packages, and operational systems such as process control software. Where a manager's interaction with work is completely mediated by such tools, this environment is called an *information-centered enterprise/environment* (ICE). While such environments do not yet exist, most of the pieces are available through networks to provide advantages such as increased quality of information, more effective use of information, and more effective tools for managing change.

Discussion Questions

7.1 Most managerial work involves meeting and talking with other workers. How do managers develop and put into effect the four qualities that they bring to the value chain in a communication situation? What role does effective information play?

7.2 The most common way of coping with information overload in any situation is to ignore new information. Why is this an especially poor strategy for managers? Which of the four ways of coping is most effective for managers, in general?

7.3 Think about a way in which you have received advice recently. What models and what bases of experience have been tapped for that advice? What level of advising systems have you used in obtaining the advice? Who possessed what knowledge? Who gave you the advice and interpreted it?

7.4 The MIW and the ICE are concepts rather than actual systems or packages. However, all the pieces are available. What commercial packages and suites of software are available to support students in their "workbench" needs?

7.5 Imagine what it would be like working in an ICE. In a typical day, what kinds of interactions would managers have with other members of the organization? Do you see the ICE as a positive or as a negative idea? What kind of organization climate and culture might arise if the ICE concept is carried to its logical conclusion?

Key Terms

abstracting
authority
avoidance
buyer value chain
certainty
classificatory theory
communication systems
computational (causal) theory
conflict
contextualizing
data dictionary
database
decision support
delay
depictional theory
descriptive theory
dynamism

end user application
    development
filtering
firm value chain
indexing
information-centered enterprise/
    environment (ICE)
information (data) shadow
information overload
irresolution
knowledge management
logical (relational) theory
lumping
management support system
manager's information
    workbench (MIW)
model base

operational systems
physical theory
presentation manager
redirecting
regularity
risk
routing
simulation
summarizing
supplier value chain
transparency versus opaqueness
turbulence
uncertainty
uniformity
value chain
view base

References

Cyert, R., and March. *A Behavior Theory of the Firm.* Englewood Cliffs, NJ: Prentice-Hall, 1967.

Licker, P. "Management Advice: Six Models and a Simulator." *Database* 21 (March 1990).

Licker, P., and R. Thompson. "Consulting Systems: Bridging the AI/DSS Gap." Proceedings, International Conference on Systems Science, Honolulu, Hawaii, January 1986, Vol IA, 471–478.

Porter, R., and M. Millar. "How Information Gives You Competitive Advantage." *Harvard Business Review* (July–August 1985): 149–160.

Simon, H. *The New Science of Management Decision*. New York: Harper & Row, 1960.

Sprague, R. "A Framework for the Development of Decision Support Systems." *Management Information Systems Quarterly* 4, 3 (June 1980): 10–26.

Sprague, R., and E. Carlson. *Building Effective Decision Support Systems*. Englewood Cliffs, NJ: Prentice-Hall, 1982.

Sprague, R., E. Carlson, and H. Watson, eds. *Decision Support Systems—Putting Theory into Practice*. Englewood Cliffs, NJ: Prentice-Hall, 1990.

Turban, E. *Decision Support and Expert Systems*. New York: Macmillan, 1990.

CASE   EVERGREEN LANDSCAPING AND MAINTENANCE: SUPPORTING CONNIE

Connie Somerset, sales manager, her manager Shawna Eggert, vice president of sales, and Sid Cavenaugh and Sven Haroldson, assistant managers of contract and retail services, respectively, are playing out a drama at Evergreen. Connie has noticed a pattern and has been drawing Shawna's attention to it for a while, but Shawna isn't convinced a pattern exists or there is much to be excited about. The pattern shows up in how Evergreen plans and, more specifically, how it reaches conclusions about how it should implement plans. Connie has also talked this out with Frances Harmon, vice president of administration, who seems less convinced than Shawna.

    The pattern is that new ideas workers and supervisors originate tend to be ignored, but ideas that come from the vice presidents or other members of the management executive committee (MEC) (see Figure 7–23) tend to be seriously considered and well supported. Neither source of ideas has an impressive track record. Connie is aware of only one grassroots idea that caught the attention of the MEC in the past three years, the guaranteed green-up service. This service lost a bundle last year. The executive committee started a quality management program that seemed promising, but their suggestion for a unified reporting scheme hit a snag when the consulting firm hired to implement it discovered that the paperwork burden would kill contract services and

Figure 7–23   EVERGREEN'S MANAGEMENT EXECUTIVE COMMITTEE

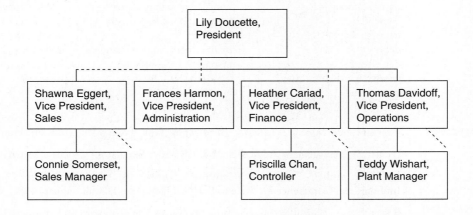

hamper customer relations. Evergreen's reputation for rapid response to customers while maintaining a focus on the environment was endangered by this move to systematize reporting patterns.

Connie's observations extend to how the MEC works in general. As the most junior member of the MEC, Connie finds it difficult to translate ideas from above into actions for her workers; at the same time, she doesn't have a way to convince MEC to take action on what her staff sees as threats from competitors, the environment, and social trends. Connie thinks this is because MEC focuses on long-range planning (two years or more) and reasons based on finances. Connie has noticed that data are scarce in most MEC discussions and that several people, particularly Frances Harmon and Shawna Eggert, shy away from data-based discussions. On the other hand, Heather Cariad revels in numbers. Because of these various personalities, the MEC is not effective and tends to retrace steps repeatedly, coming back to things long after Connie is sure they have been handled. Thus, while important (to Connie) problems are ignored, pet projects and peeves are revisited over and over. The MEC, which meets weekly, doesn't seem to be an effective voice, ear, or arm of Evergreen. Although it specifically handles business proposals that arise within MEC or from employees or customers, it doesn't seem to be able to create an effective plan to respond to what Connie sees as imperatives for relatively small and vulnerable retail firms such as Evergreen. It seems especially incapable of handling crises like the guaranteed green-up service deficit; it seems more able to respond to planned problems such as budgeting or seasonal hiring policies than to real crises that threaten the company's image or ability to stay in business. While everyone seems committed to certain ideals (for example, everyone is keen to advance environmental causes without the usual corporate bottom-line argument, primarily, of course, because Evergreen is in the environment business), the process doesn't seem to be professional, systematic, or reliable.

In the face of these problems, Connie finds that going to the MEC meetings is increasingly frustrating. Her relative youth (she's 29) that worked for her when she was an energetic, environmentally conscious MBA, seems to be impelling more impatience than wisdom at these meetings. Connie is wondering what kind of support she's going to need to meet the challenges she faces working with upper management and especially what she should be doing about the guaranteed green-up problem to handle it now and prevent problems like this from happening in the future.

Questions

1. What values does a group like the MEC add to a firm such as Evergreen, assuming that the MEC actually functions the way it is supposed to?

2. The MEC doesn't seem to like information very much, does it? How would information assist the MEC in terms of control and consistency, confirmation and confidence, choice and effectiveness, power and leadership, alternatives and creativity, and learning and knowledge?

3. Consider ways in which Connie could bring information to the table in MEC meetings to increase or improve the quality of Evergreen's products and services; how MEC makes and effects decisions; the organizational climate and culture; the influence of MEC on employees and customers; the possibility for true innovation and creativity; and how Evergreen learns from its experiences.

4. From what you know about the case, how would you characterize Evergreen's information environment in terms of turbulence, uncertainty, risk, stress, and information overload?

5. Given the components of the manager's information workbench, how and what would you advise Connie to introduce to the MEC meetings and in what order? What technologies would you recommend and what benefits would accrue to Evergreen?

6. What is the potential value to Evergreen of better decision making at the MEC level?

7. Imagine that Connie actually proposes an ICE for Evergreen. What might be the immediate effects on the group? What are the advantages? The disadvantages?

CHAPTER EIGHT

SUPPORTING INDIVIDUALS THROUGH DSS, ESS, HYPERMEDIA, AND MULTIMEDIA

OBJECTIVES

After you have read and studied this chapter, you should be able to:

■ Describe the architecture of decision support systems and how such systems support managers.

■ Differentiate decision support systems and executive support systems and describe how they support managers and executives in their work.

■ Describe the emerging roles and capabilities of hypermedia and multimedia systems and their contributions to management.

Question: What are some examples of commercially available systems that provide management support to individual managers?

Tanya Billet is the owner/operator of Casino Cleaners, a unique drive-through dry cleaning service. Tanya started this business just two years ago with some borrowed money and a lot of courage. Her idea was simple but innovative. People don't like carrying dry cleaning around, so Tanya built her store in a shopping mall to allow customers to drive up and deposit their dry cleaning without getting out of their cars. Tanya doesn't actually have any dry cleaning equipment. Instead, she contracts with local cleaners to use their excess capacity to handle her customers' clothes. She promises one-week service with home delivery. Because she is using others' excess capacity, her costs are very low and she can afford to offer home delivery. Tanya is discovering that keeping track of her customers and suppliers is a full-time job and she often has to make quick decisions about where to send the dry cleaning and garment repair work. She is really worried about losing customers' clothing and spends a lot of time planning and negotiating the purchase of blocks of dry cleaning services. What kinds of support can information systems give Tanya?

Answer: Many specific kinds of systems are useful to managers. Decision support systems assist managers in making difficult, relatively unstructured decisions. Executive information systems enable higher-level managers to examine data from across the firm at any level of detail. Executive support systems add in features of DSS and communication. They support managers at the consensual, contextual, MIS, and computational levels. Hypermedia and multimedia systems provide additional visualization and data navigation features.

INTRODUCTION

Chapters 8 and 9 discuss specific systems, mostly hybrids of various types covered in Chapter 7, that managers commonly use in their work. This chapter examines systems that support individual managers while Chapter 9 looks at work group, task force, and corporatewide systems that support groups of managers or managers working with other people.

This chapter examines a number of different forms of computational and **hybrid systems,** such as decision support systems (DSS), executive support systems (ESS), and hypermedia, that span a variety of management support formats. These hybrid forms are not specifically a single kind of management support system. Instead, they provide support to managers at different levels, sometimes simultaneously, because the problems managers work on are multifaceted and require a variety of support forms. The term *decision support system* covers a variety of computational systems (but not all). Executive support systems (ESS) and the related executive information systems (EIS) are intended for executives and provide support at all levels.

DECISION SUPPORT SYSTEMS

There are a variety of definitions of **decision support systems (DSS)** and each stresses a different aspect (see Figure 8–1). Because there are a lot of ways to make a decision, there are a lot of DSS models, but most of them are activated to produce results that assist rather than take over decision making in an unstructured problem-solving environment.

DSS models are generally mathematical in nature rather than logical and rely on theory that is based on an idea of what causes what. Using these theories, we can predict that so much of this will cause or produce so much of that. The most common form of DSS is a simple spreadsheet in which the spreadsheet's formulas [for example, @sum (B4 . . . B15) or + B33 − B34 + B35] embody the model.

The type of decision making supported by DSS tends to be of a semistructured nature (see Figure 8–2). **Semistructured decisions** lie between those that are fully structured (or programmed) and those that are unstructured. Making a **structured decision** resembles pushing a button—the decision is implicit in the facts and no discretion is required. Making an **unstructured decision** is like bowing to intuition—it is not really based on

---

| Figure 8–1 | DEFINITIONS OF DECISION SUPPORT SYSTEMS |

- A model-based set of procedures for processing data and judgments to assist a manager in decision making.

- An interactive computer-based system intended to help decision makers utilize data and models to solve unstructured problems.

- A system coupling intellectual resources of individuals with the capabilities of computers to improve the quality of decisions; a computer-based support system for management decision makers who deal with semistructured problems.

Figure 8–2   DECISION SUPPORT SYSTEMS DECISION TYPES

Structured	Semistructured	Unstructured
Routine and Repetitive Problems		"Fuzzy," Complex Problems
Standardized Procedures		No Cut-and-Dried Procedures
Can Be Totally Turned over to the Computer		Human Intuition Is an Important Component
Example: Accounts Receivable		Examples: New-Product Planning, Hiring

A DSS Combines the
Strengths of Computers
with the Strengths of
Human Decision Makers

What Are the Appropriate
Problems? How Best to Provide
This Blend of Strengths? Where
Does Human Responsibility Lie?

data. Structured decision making is found in a decision table or procedures manuals and it is the kind of decision making discussed native to the cybernetic system. Structured decisions are highly routine and so well practiced that we hardly pay attention to them. Of course, even the most highly structured decisions, ones that come straight out of a manual, need to be watched and checked. Totally unstructured decisions, on the other hand, are very difficult to handle and generally are not undertaken reliably because each time such a decision is made, it is made on the basis of intuition, not data.

The bulk of interesting decisions are called *semistructured*. Such decisions are not easily derived mechanically, but they are not so difficult and ill defined ("ill behaved" is another term applied to them) that they require formulas that are unreliable or even partially guesswork. Semistructured decisions tend to be nonroutine; the problem and its parameters are recognized but the outcome cannot be decided mechanically. Procedures for making semistructured decisions are not found in procedures manuals nor are they wholly automatic or intuitive. Rather, they are some blend of the two. Figure 8–2 illustrates the differences between these two extremes and cites accounts receivable as a structured problem and new-product planning and hiring as unstructured. Now consider these three additional decision problems:

Decision 1. I want to refinance my corporate loan at the lowest current competitive rate. I have researched all the current rates and listed them in order by rate from the lowest to the highest. I will select the lowest rate and refinance my loan with that institution.

Decision 2. I would like to refinance my corporate loan at the lowest current competitive rate consistent with my personal philosophy regarding the lending institution's solidity and social responsibility. I have all the information from Decision 1 and in addition have gathered some data on most of the institutions about to whom they make loans and on what basis. I rank them all according to an informal formula that takes rate, solidity, and social responsibility into account and then order them with the highest ranking at the top of the list. I will then refinance my loan with the agency at the top.

Decision 3. I want to refinance my corporate loan at the lowest current competitive rate consistent with my personal philosophy regarding solidity of the lending institution and its social responsibility. Also, I will use the institution among those that score the highest that will be the most supportive of my firm in 20 years' time. I gather all the information in Decision 2 and then order them. I will guess which one among the top five will be the best friend of my firm well into the next century.

As you can see, Decision 1 is a routine, repetitive problem involving selecting a financing source. Decision 2 is not routine and repetitive, but it can be clarified when a list of criteria for social responsibility is created, a concept that is rather more well developed in the 1990s than it was in the 1970s. Decision 3, on the other hand, is a complex, fuzzy problem. What does "friend of my firm" mean—or what will it mean in 20 years? "Current competitive rate" is certainly very specific, but "supportive" can mean almost anything depending on the day of the week. Similarly, I can use standardized procedures to gather and evaluate data for Decision 1 and most of Decision 2, but there are aspects of Decision 3 that simply defy use of standardized procedures, mostly because the problem refers to the distant future.

Decision 1 can be turned over to a computer. The rules are simple and known, and so long as the program used has a sort function or a subroutine to pick out minimum values, it can find the lowest current competitive rate. Decision 2 is harder to make with a computer alone and is much more appropriate for a DSS. It's easy to gather and array data, but assigning figures for social responsibility and then interpreting the sorted results requires some heavy human intervention. We would certainly want to see how Fidelity Mutual, for example, came to the top given its relatively high current loan rate and why First National Trust came in 16th despite its ridiculously low rate. Decision 3 is altogether a different kettle of fish, because predicting the future is not something computers do any better than any other mechanism. To the extent that human intuition is the key component here, it is difficult to imagine what a computer might add beyond simple data entry and arithmetic computations. Of course, in many cases a combination of high data volume, involved computations, difficult data access, and complex data navigation is so daunting that even a structured decision problem may appear to be unstructured. In these cases, the computer is a boon. Part of why DSS has become so smoothly interwoven into the fabric of business decision making is that it neatly converts daunting semistructured problems into two parts: a structured computational part that the computer handles and an unstructured, intuitional part that the manager handles.

Key concerns for managers with respect to DSS use are the following:

Table 8–1	DISTINGUISHING DSS AND TPS	

Dimension	Decision Support System	Transaction Processing System
Mode of use	Active, making decisions	Passive, entering data
User	Line-and-staff managers	Clerical staff, operations
Goal	Effectiveness	Efficiency
Time horizon	Present, future	Past, present operations
Objective criterion	Flexibility	Consistency

- What problems are appropriate for a DSS to handle?
- How can the strengths of computers (speed, reliability, tirelessness) and those of people (judgment, intuition, heuristic abilities) be combined?
- What is a manager's responsibility when using a DSS to make a decision; that is, who is responsible for what?

Part of the answer to the first question is found in Table 8–1. A transaction processing system (TPS) involves using computers to produce output mechanically according to formulas. The user of a TPS merely provides data and the computer produces an answer. These systems are intended for clerical staff whose performance is judged not on the basis of effectiveness or creativity but on efficient use of time. A TPS is concerned with historical data and is judged on consistency. Such systems affect programmed or structured decisions and are focused on the lowest levels of management where little discretion or responsibility is found. An example of a TPS is a point-of-sale (POS) system that notes items being purchased, looks up their prices, totals the prices, and prints an itemized receipt. There is no decision making in this system; human interaction is limited to supplying data on the sale and monitoring the computed results.

DSS, on the other hand, is aimed at users who actively participate in finding a solution, such as line-and-staff managers who are judged on their effectiveness and/or creativity in discovering solutions or putting them into effect rather than executing commands. These decisions focus on the near-term future and, because they are focused on this future in a dynamic world, the primary criterion for evaluation is flexibility. Such systems are heavily used to perform analysis and scenario testing ("what if" computing) to anticipate potential outcomes and derive potential actions based on optimizing the near-term future. Often this means performing sensitivity analyses to determine whether a proposed solution will be effective for its cost.

The key to a DSS is its ability to segregate the purely mathematical and mechanical from the creative. As illustrated in Figure 8–3, the computer serves three functions in a DSS:

- First, it performs mathematical transformations according to the arithmetic, causal model that lies at the heart of the transformation.

| Figure 8-3 | STRUCTURE OF A DSS |

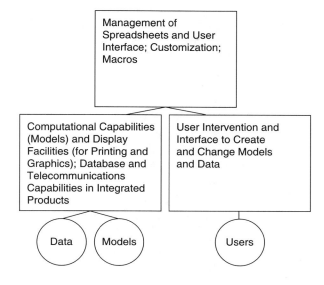

- Management of Spreadsheets and User Interface; Customization; Macros
- Computational Capabilities (Models) and Display Facilities (for Printing and Graphics); Database and Telecommunications Capabilities in Integrated Products
- User Intervention and Interface to Create and Change Models and Data
- Data
- Models
- Users

- Second, it presents the results of these transformations in ways that are conducive to creative and informed use by managers who interpret the results.
- Finally, it manages the transitions between mechanical computer performance based on the causal model and user intervention to change data, formats, or the model.

DSSs come in two major varieties. **Specific DSSs** support managers making decisions in specific areas. Such DSSs might include programs that assist managers in deciding on staff work loads during busy seasons; software to select the best acquisition from a set of candidates based on a flexible set of criteria and procedures and perhaps not involving only computers; or a program to select the best course of action following a disaster.

Generic DSSs or **DSS shells** or **generators** include all of the popular microcomputer **spreadsheet packages/processors** such as *Lotus 1-2-3, Excel,* and *QuattroPro.* Using these programs, managers can create both the data and model bases required to make arithmetic computations. In addition, the programs generally have a stunning array of tools to display and print data and associated graphics, often in association with word processors, presentation managers, and database managers. Finally, these shells generally contain a **spreadsheet macro language** that makes it easy to create spreadsheets that perform. These performances can include **menu-managed data entry and display,** easy navigation around the spreadsheet, automatic generation of output, and interfaces with other programs. Because most of these products include hooks for data communication and advanced word processing and text and document management, the world *integrated* has sometimes been applied to these products. For a manager, it is not important what these tools are called. Of critical importance is that such products' flexibility to link databases and word processors (perhaps through GUIs such as *Windows*) makes them ideal tools for managers

Table 8-2	DSS CHARACTERISTICS, ADVANTAGES, AND DISADVANTAGES	
DSS Characteristic	**DSS Disadvantage/Cost**	**DSS Advantage/Benefit**
Supports managerial decision makers	Requires assistance of technical personnel to build models	Interface with operational data
Supports semistructured decision situations	Not useful for unstructured problems	Helps simplify and regularize difficult decision making
Extends managers' capabilities	May lull managers into thinking that everything about the decision is easy	Frees managers for more critical aspects of decision making, such as judgment
Evolves over time	May evolve in the wrong direction. If documentation is not high quality, users may not know what they have.	Improvements to decision model
Easy-to-use interfaces	May be too attractive and divert attention from the problem to flashy interfaces and graphics	Overcomes computer "shyness"
Graphical capabilities	May be too attractive and divert attention from the problem to flashy interfaces and graphics	Makes it easy to visualize trends and not get lost in details of data
Interactive	Some interactions could be better done as regular, "canned" reports.	Easy to check on validity or reasonableness and provide information to correct or improve model or data
Supports a wide variety of decision and information styles, processes, situations, and personalities	Cost of flexibility	Both processes and results can be shared and use can be tailored to individual needs and capabilities.

to use to do data exploration, experimental data tweaking (such as "what if" computation), and graphing. For managers, an **integrated spreadsheet program** can be seen as the central tool or agent in viewing the world as data because it contains ways of seeing the data as spreadsheets, databases, graphics, and icons (and to some extent as hypertext). As these products mature, they will become more seamlessly integrated with other products. *QuattroPro,* for example, has built-in tools to paste up beautiful graphs for display, and *Excel* promises seamless movement of spreadsheets to and from *Microsoft Word* documents through *Windows OLE* (object linking and embedding; see Chapter 14).

DSS characteristics are as follows (see Table 8-2):

- Support and extend the managers' capabilities rather than displace them as decision makers
- Involve semistructured decisions
- Evolve over time
- Depend on an easy-to-use interactive interface with some graphics capabilities

- Support a wide variety of decision styles, processes, and situations as well as personalities that range from closed-minded to open-minded

Because DSSs are model-based systems, they evolve over time. Consider employees working at well-defined tasks, such as assembly of parts at a workbench. As the decision maker becomes familiar with the subject matter and makes more decisions, the models (formulas) become more exact, and data collection becomes more well performed and directed to assemble the right data in the right way. As the models get better and sensitivity analyses become more exact, decision making becomes increasingly structured (because the underlying model is more accurate) until the decision maker finds that there is little need for discretion. On the other hand, the problem might not lie within the realm of problems that a computational system can handle. For example, it is almost impossible to make performance evaluations of professionals by formula, a problem that will continue to remain difficult. In this case, the formulas remain only as general guidelines, and managerial discretion remains the most important aspect. In the extreme, such rules of thumb may merely produce a figure of merit that can indicate trends or the need for action. Specifically which trend or which action is up to the manager to determine.

Because the model management aspect of DSS is often exacting and requires excellent mathematical skills, managers often use toolsmiths to create these models for them. **DSS toolsmiths** are people skilled at creating models and well versed in mathematics. Creating such systems is often called *developmental* because initial models are generally inexact and poor in their ability to predict or control. But they get better with each change to the model (unless, of course, the problem is too hard to solve). The topic of DSS development will be discussed in more detail in later chapters.

One other aspect of DSS is graphical interfaces, used primarily to create graphical output. These visualization tools are really elements of built-in contextualization to help managers see trends (and thus label phenomena that they otherwise might miss) in the data. It is important to note that managers using such tools begin with the assumption that they know more than they actually do (i.e., that the formulas they have at their disposal provide the knowledge that they need). The use of contextual system tools enables them to use lower levels of theory to spot trends and other relationships to create or re-create theories that they didn't know before or that they knew incorrectly. Then, armed with this theory (in the form of relationships), they can perform sensitivity analyses to find out what the actual relationships are and then create new formulas with correct numbers in them. For example, consider a manager who merely types in sales figures for the past 48 months (using the DSS simply as a contextual tool) and displays the graph. This manager would note the periodicity (sales rise every summer, drop every winter), thus enabling the creation of corrections to make the data seasonally adjusted. Now, more exact comparisons can be made of current performance against historical trends in order to determine just how well sales actually are doing. The corrections create a new causal theory (that sales depend on the season).

On the other hand, Cale and Eriksen, writing about their experiences developing a DSS for a bank, noted some drawbacks to visualization. They found that the use of graphics impressed everyone using the system. However, when graphs contained both historical and projected data—for example, in deposits for specific interest rates—those who viewed the output were quick to note that historical information was quite jagged (i.e., detailed) while the projected rate was a smooth curve. The latter, of course, was far less credible because it appeared to have far less detail. The proper level of detail is important to screen out noise (which may appear from time to time as information-laden detail) in order to see trends without oversimplifying the display.

In this way, a DSS provides a hybrid level of support. The DSS is a system driven by an approximate computational model a manager uses to solve a difficult problem by first simplifying it in order to visualize it in some way. Later refinements can add details back in as a manager better understands the problem. As with lower levels of management support, DSS models, especially spreadsheets and graphs, can be shared with others to achieve consensus about what needs to be taken into account before the model is further refined. Generally, however, a DSS is used by, thus is tailored to the needs of, a single managerial decision maker.

Imagine a manager has the difficult problem of determining how to apportion monetary rewards across a team of five workers about to engage in a project. The manager has an arbitrary amount of reward, say, $R, that can be given to the team. The difficulty is determining how much each member should get given a certain level of performance *on important criterion variables*. Because there is a set reward amount, the manager may think this way:

> OK, there is $R available for reward. I think a quarter of the reward should depend on delivery time for each component each team member is designing. Also, a quarter of the reward should depend on the quality of the component and the rest of the reward on how easily the component fits into the overall design when assembled.

The manager then creates a formula for individual rewards:

$$X(i) = k \times [0.25 \times T(i) + 0.25 \times Q(i) + 0.5 \times C(i)]$$

where T is the time to delivery in weeks, Q is a quality index that the manager creates before the project begins and publicizes to the team, and C is a compatibility index, handled similarly to Q. The coefficient k is used to adjust the values of X, because the manager knows that the sum of all the Xs must be $R.

The simple spreadsheet in Figure 8–4 displays numbers and evaluations for each team member. Imagine that $4,000 is available (R = $4,000) to be distributed to the team. This value is divided by the total to find the value of dollars per point and this number is then multiplied by the value of X(i) to give the reward for each member. However, working with estimated data based on hunches about how the team will perform, the manager notices that the formula punishes those who make their components incompatible with badly designed components. In fact, it doesn't do a good job of motivating people to work together. This can be at least partly corrected by adding a component that judges how well the component would function given that *all* the components functioned correctly. However, the manager doesn't know a formula that would make this correction, so the correction will have to be made in the evaluations of compatibility (see Figure 8–5).

The manager then guesses about evaluation to develop a theory of how the elements of quality go together, first independently of each other and then in conjunction with each other. Because there isn't enough knowledge about how these components *should* go together, the manager is left with a two-part support system: first, a series of formulas that manipulate the guessed numbers along with a set of challenges that appear with these index numbers and, second, how to adjust them so that they reflect the reality the manager only has a hunch about. The DSS that the spreadsheet represents is a hybrid of a computational system and a contextual system.

Figure 8–4   SPREADSHEET THAT COMBINES TWO TYPES OF DECISION
SUPPORT SYSTEMS

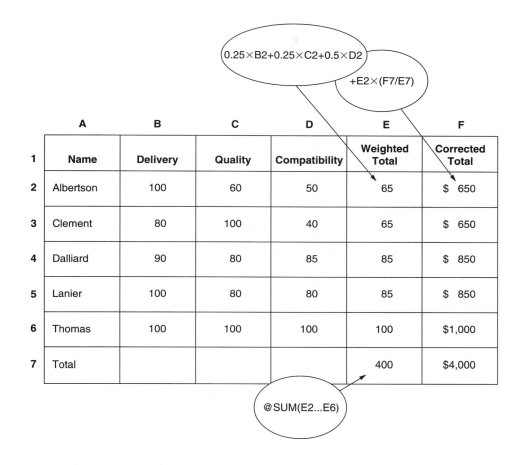

	A	B	C	D	E	F
					$0.25 \times B2 + 0.25 \times C2 + 0.5 \times D2$	$+E2 \times (F7/E7)$
1	**Name**	**Delivery**	**Quality**	**Compatibility**	**Weighted Total**	**Corrected Total**
2	Albertson	100	60	50	65	$ 650
3	Clement	80	100	40	65	$ 650
4	Dalliard	90	80	85	85	$ 850
5	Lanier	100	80	80	85	$ 850
6	Thomas	100	100	100	100	$1,000
7	Total				400	$4,000

@SUM(E2...E6)

EXECUTIVE INFORMATION SYSTEMS AND EXECUTIVE SUPPORT SYSTEMS

DSSs are aimed mostly at middle managers, but can be used by managers at any level. At the executive level, two types of systems are useful: **executive information systems (EIS)** and **executive support systems (ESS)**. They differ in several ways. An EIS is an information exploration system that counteracts some of the more serious drawbacks of information overload, adjusting to individual information styles. This is important for executives because their time is valuable and, given that there are far fewer executives, individualized style is far more feasible. An EIS focuses on information important to executives while an ESS includes capabilities, especially communication, that make executives more effective with the information they receive.

Figure 8–5 SPREADSHEET THAT USES CONTEXTUAL SUPPORT

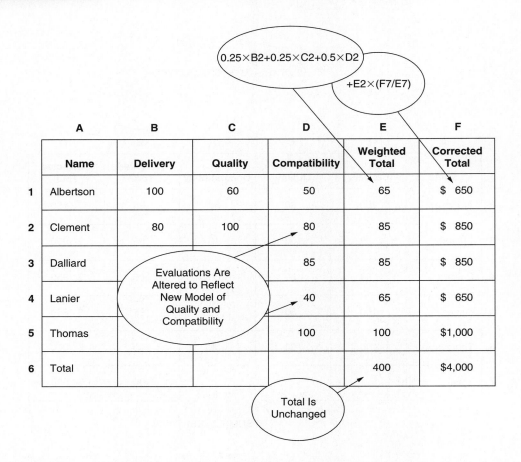

An EIS provides some simple, predetermined information processing functions (filtering, compressing, tracking), but its primary advantage is that it provides seamless **drill-down** capabilities to go from summary information that may indicate a problem in a particular area, down to the area, across functions, then down again, perhaps into products, then across salespeople, then perhaps to an individual salesperson, then across to personnel records, perhaps comparing monthly records to look for trends. This capability serves to find out "Why?"

Vella distinguishes MIS, DSS, and EIS for accountants as follows:

- MIS: What was: Control reporting emphasis such as variances
- DSS: What if: Forward planning, proposals
- EIS: What is: Integration and presentation of information

Vella sees an EIS as composed of two components—the *briefing book* and the *ad hoc query facility*. The briefing book is essentially a hierarchically ordered series of reports linked in

Figure 8–6	EIS DRILL-DOWN: STEP 1

Product Sales Target Analysis, 1994 Summary Figures Only

Product	SKU Number	Projected Sales	Actual Sales	Variance Percent	Sales (in thousands of dollars)
Hammer, #12	152352	2,000	2,400	250	$12
Hammer, #14	152353	1,200	1,200	0	16
Centerpunch	252166	400	300	(25)	1
Screwdriver #24	367554	2,000	1,800	(10)	5
Screwdriver #25	367555	2,500	3,000	20	9
Screwdriver #26	**367556**	**4,000**	**2,000**	**(50)**	**6**
Screwdriver set	389991	2,000	2,000	0	20

increasing degree of detail from summary to micro-level performance data. The important criteria for an effective briefing book are ease of drilling down, highlighting of important information (especially for exceptions), consistency of views across a set of users, and timeliness (or immediacy). By its very nature, however, a briefing book is precomposed; it may not be able to meet all needs that managers have for ad hoc information search. Thus, the ad hoc query facility gives managers an easy interface to compose queries built around a database manager. The briefing book can be compared to traditional MIS in its predefined nature of linked reports. The ad hoc query facility is very much the kind of MIS described in the previous chapter.

However, there is movement between the briefing book and the ad hoc query facility. Consider a manager who must determine what went wrong in a production situation with a sudden decrease in productivity and large amounts of waste. The manager is likely to collect standard reports; however, because these reports may prove to be uninformative, the manager is then led to make increasingly ad hoc investigations. The manager will try to find connections among variables such as production and machinery installation or errors and operator training. The most valuable nuggets of information may be obscure or hidden—they will not be found in standard reports. After all, this is not a standard problem. Eventually, the manager makes the connection: new equipment has been installed but the operators haven't been well trained in new procedures. The manager will remember the steps taken to find out what parts of the shop produced the problems, who works there, what the machinery is, and who manufactured and installed the machinery. Perhaps these ad hoc queries will point out the need to have a regular report on machinery installation and training to shorten the search time in the event the problem or a problem like it reoccurs. The ad hoc query may then become a standard report, part of several drill-down paths (material-usage/waste-to-machinery-to-installation/training information and employee-to-training information).

Recall the tool factory example introduced in Chapter 5. Summary sales figures for a variety of tools are made available to a sales manager through an EIS (Figure 8–6). Only

| Figure 8–7 | EIS DRILL-DOWN: STEP 2, MONTHLY SALES FIGURES |

Monthly Production Sales Figures by Product SKU Number, 1994

SKU Number	Jan.	Feb.	March	April	May	June	July	Aug.	Sept.	Oct.	Nov.	Dec.	Year
152352	200	210	250	220	160	150	210	220	180	205	210	185	2,400
152353	80	80	140	200	90	80	70	100	85	75	105	95	1,200
252166	40	15	15	5	25	30	35	25	30	40	12	27	300
367554	120	180	200	200	120	30	0	0	250	300	200	250	1,800
367555	260	280	310	350	100	50	0	300	350	260	350	240	3,000
367556	**200**	**186**	**250**	**175**	**100**	**0**	**0**	**100**	**300**	**321**	**180**	**179**	**2,000**
389991	100	150	180	170	200	150	140	110	250	150	220	180	2,000

summary information for the year is available: item name, SKU number, projected sales from the previous year, actual sales, a computed variance, and a rounded sales amount for the items sold expressed in thousands of dollars. An executive notices that some items sold as projected, others over, and a few quite a bit under and asks "Why?" In order to find out, the executive now selects an item (SKU number 367556) and explores details on monthly sales and production figures for the poorly performing item, drilling down to the monthly figures (Figure 8–7). Here it is discovered that sales figures are closely tied to previous months' production figures. There is also a serious dip in production for many months for the affected item. The executive now rolls across to production information for this item and discovers that a machinery malfunction took four months to repair. The executive finds out how the item under scrutiny is produced by moving from the SKU number to a manufacturing description and looks at the equipment involved. One piece of equipment is a polisher, so the executive brings up the polisher's maintenance log (Figure 8–8). It's now possible that the information that was hidden before and not obvious on routine production reports, shows up. The executive can see that a malfunction in the polisher took four months to repair, who did the repair, who manufactured and installed the equipment, and so forth. What appeared to be a sales problem turns out to be an equipment installation problem that needs to be handled on a permanent basis.

An EIS exists primarily to give executives hands-on access to data about their organizations. In the past, managers and executives have been fond of delegating the navigational aspects of "data surfing" to their staff assistants. However, doing this leaves these managers without any intuitive feel for the data and can contribute to executives' falling back on habit or intuition. While reacting this way may be highly valued if decisions are correct, it may also mean that decision makers are isolated from reality.

Now we turn our attention to executive support systems. An ESS provides much the same kinds of analysis tools that DSS provides, plus has the drill-down capability. Because executives have legitimate access to a broad range of data, it is thus much more important that an ESS be based on an EIS rather than a simple MIS. It should be able to move

Figure 8–8	EIS DRILL-DOWN: STEP 3, PRODUCTION REPAIR RECORD

Machinery Maintenance Log, 1994

Item: Polisher	March. Down 3/3–3/5. Called R&D. Reinstalled after adjustment.
Supplier: R&D Tools	April. Down 4/6–4/10. R&D replaced subbrush and switch. Readjusted.
Initial Install: 2/18/94	May. Burned 5/8. Withdrawn and sent back to R&D. Part on order 5/16.
	June. Still on order. Called R&D 6/3, 6/10, 6/17, 6/24.
	July. Still on order. Phoned R&D 7/1, 7/8, 7/15. Reinstalled on 7/20. Test run. Withdrawn on 7/22.
	August. New unit installed under warranty by R&D 8/3. Tested OK. Retrained operator in new technology.

horizontally—across databases—as well as vertically—drill-down—as executives seek answers to "why" questions. An additional feature of most ESSs is communication capabilities (i.e., access to consensual systems) because many of the problems executives work on are fuzzy and have little or no theory behind them. Executives work to uncover "why" and thus create new theories. So, an ESS really provides the entire gamut of management support, from consensual system to operational system. An ESS built around the EIS in Figures 8–6 through 8–8 incorporates the capabilities to graph, project, and move the data into and out of documents as well as an easy method to transmit all or parts of documents to other managers and executives. In the extreme case, an ESS has most of the capabilities of an ICE.

EIS and ESS depend on several critical factors for successful implementation (see Figure 8–9). Executives who use them have to be committed to computerization (i.e., rational and expensive information systems) and must know something about what they're doing. Their sponsors (people who collect the data and run the systems) must also be committed and informed. Another important factor is that these systems be somehow linked to business objectives. This is important because these systems contain data that can help solve problems in areas that are critical to the organization's success. Generally, these systems are of a strategic nature rather than a purely operational nature. An ESS is of little use if it merely enables executives to examine data that are used only for routine decision making and are unconnected to the company's strategic mission; it must focus on strategic or critical incidents that determine turning points in the company's fortunes. These incidents might occur during crisis management or at key product design meetings. EISs and ESSs must have a strategic focus or they are turned over to lower management and become only DSSs.

Another factor is that an ESS should have a lot of backup IS resources. Such systems are expensive to run and maintain and waste executives' time when they fail. IS resources are not limited to hardware and software; they also include time IS people need to repair

Figure 8-9 IMPLEMENTING AN ESS

Successful Implementation of an ESS

Committed and Informed Executive and Operating Sponsors

Linked to Business Objectives
- Critical business success factors
- Critical incidents
- Strategic focus

Backup IS Resources

Appropriate (Transparent) Technology
- Across time (trend analysis)
- Across space (broad views)
- Across levels (drill-down)
- Across situations (keyboard alternatives)

Successful Data Management

the system, train executives, and hold their hands in case something goes wrong. The technology must be transparent, that is, it must not require a lot of special training to learn or operate it. ESSs should enable managers to navigate seamlessly across time to spot trends; across divisions, departments, disciplines, or product lines to provide broad views; and across or through levels to provide drill-down to details or zoom in on summaries. Finally, executives may not want to be limited to keyboards but may want to use mouses, audio, touchscreens, paper, graphics, video, and so forth, and so may need to access multimedia.

Ironically, one drawback to ESS is its drill-down capability. As the examples show, a great deal of mental **visualization** is necessary to remember where one is in the drill-down, especially if three dimensions of movement are allowed (up and down through detail and summary, across linked databases, and through various versions or snapshots in time). Frolick and Ramarapu point out that executives often delegate data navigation to their subordinates. Doing this negates the most valuable features of an ESS and the major reason for having an ESS—to introduce information systems power and technology to executives. An ESS is an executive's window to the information shadow of the firm. Allowing an executive to see the "shape" of that information is crucial to successful implementation of ESS.

Another problem with EISs and ESSs is the basically hierarchical nature of most database systems. Frolick and Ramarapu propose that an EIS (and thus an ESS) be augmented with hypermedia capabilities, discussed in the next section.

HYPERMEDIA AND MULTIMEDIA

Text on a page is relatively linear—we have to read it in one order from start to finish. A **hypermedium** (see Figure 8–10) is a nonlinear medium that provides different ways of reading. The word *navigation* comes to mean something other than "skipping around"; it

| Figure 8–10 | DEFINITION AND EXAMPLE OF HYPERTEXT |

Definition (Ted Nelson)
A combination of natural language text and the computer's capacity for interactive branching or dynamic display . . . of nonlinear text . . . which cannot be conveniently printed on a conventional page.

Hypermedia
An extension of hypertext using
■ graphics or images
■ digitized speech
■ audio recordings
■ film, animation, video

Features and Components
■ Database
■ Windowing
■ Authoring (node creation and links)
■ Browser/online navigation

Value
■ Great for nonlinear materials
■ Multisensory, rich experience
■ Provides an "experience" rather than a "show"; more hands-on
■ Can match medium/mode with user needs

means a user can move throughout text or graphics in a particular manner, movements the system can learn and reproduce, if required. Hypermedia are extensions of **hypertext** because they are not limited to text but can utilize graphics, still and moving images, digitized speech, audio recordings, and so forth. These data are expensive to store and for the most part are not amenable to higher levels of management support. For example, most systems will not know the meaning of a stored image. Systems that can scan an image and make sense of it use expensive artificial intelligence techniques that are often imperfect. Speech recognition software can, however, be up to 95 percent correct with training in a relatively quiet environment—this is an area in which rapid advancement is being made.

Hypermedia systems require databases (or at least what we call *view bases* in Chapter 7) of frames. A **frame** is a view of data that users can read or use. Each frame may be an image, text, an audio clip, a program, or an animation, among others. Hypermedia systems also should have the ability to create frames that are linked to one another and some way of browsing or navigating among the frames. Such systems are great for nonlinear materials (which include almost all educational situations and databases that are not well structured or understood) and provide a rich, multisensory experience. A **multimedia system** is capable of displaying this wide variety of frames. Not all hypermedia systems have multimedia capabilities. Lynx, a common World Wide Web browser, is limited to text-only displays.

Figure 8–11 shows a static example of hypertext taken from existing software that uses a multimedia CD-based encyclopedia. In this example, the user is examining a map

Figure 8–11 HYPERTEXT EXAMPLE

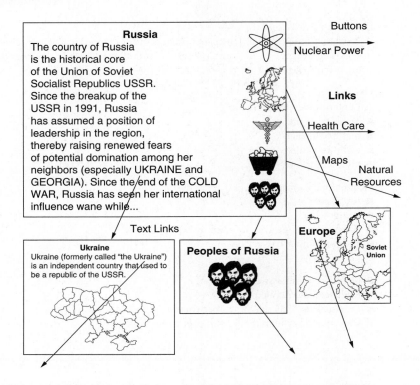

of Europe and is reading pages of information about Russia. At the right-hand side are graphical "buttons" that link to other information that may be standard categories for countries (such as nuclear power, health care, maps, people, and natural resources). Clicking the mouse over any of these buttons will bring up one or more screens on the topic (as the figure shows, the "peoples" button, when clicked, will bring up a sequence of screens on ethnic groups of Russia). Another way to navigate is to move the mouse symbol over any word in the text. Clicking will bring up a screen on that word (if such information is available). In this case, any term that appears in the encyclopedia appears in uppercase (such as USSR, UKRAINE, GEORGIA, and COLD WAR). In this example, clicking on UKRAINE brings up the first of a series of images and text on Ukraine. In this manner, nonpredetermined links can be explored.

Such hypermedia prove a rich, if potentially confusing, experience for executives who are exploring data to go from topic to topic (across databases that are particular to certain functions) and in-depth (drill-down from summaries to particulars), eventually ending up with numerical data, pictures, videos, or sounds. While such systems have only recently become widely used, they will be the typical systems of the future.

For the user interface, many multimedia systems are now available, particularly through workstations or PCs. The most ubiquitous is sound. High-quality sound boards are within the budgets of most PC purchasers, while the addition of a CD player may tax the purse a bit more. The possibilities for sound to support a variety of management activities are almost endless:

- Sound "gestures" to accompany technical activities such as opening a window or file, more pleasant sounds than beeps and buzzers to indicate an error or attention, musical alarms, and the seemingly limitless variety of sounds we have all become familiar with on video arcade games
- Talking calendars and clocks, speaking datebooks, and audio-verbal context-sensitive help and advice
- Voice e-mail, audio annotation of messages, and voice and data computer conferencing
- Music accompaniment of messages, memos, and files
- Sound files of spoken voice, audio clips, testimony and evidence, verbal annotation and commands, voice instructions, interactive activities initiated through voice input
- Voice-controlled computer

Recent releases of popular hardware and software feature most of the above and while the cost of storage is relatively high (approximately a megabyte of disk memory per minute of speech), a standard audio CD can store about 80 minutes. On the same medium it is possible to store about 540 megabytes. Continuing advances in compression and sound processing will eventually improve this ratio tenfold, making it highly likely that computers will soon feature sound as standard hardware and audio as standard components of popular software. Of particular interest to managers will be voice control of computers, voice annotation of messages, data, and spreadsheets, and the ability to create high-quality, voice-annotated and music-enhanced presentations distributable through networks or e-mail.

Other multimedia products feature moving images. For years, Apple Corporation has offered *Quicktime* and *Quickstep*, software for creating and managing movies. While a great deal of effort can be put into creating Hollywood-style productions, the *receipt* of moving images greatly enhances managers' ability to share information, make judgments based on trends, and visualize and derive creative solutions to problems seen in real time. Inexpensive CD-based software already features a variety of multimedia presentations that deliver moving, color images, animated cartoons, the spoken voice, and music to the desktop in ways that were barely imaginable in the 1980s (and extremely cumbersome and expensive). Packaged with desktop flat-bed or handheld scanners and CD photo cameras (now available as consumer items), such software will enable managers to capture and control more information than ever.

Of course, *control* is the noteworthy word here, because such huge volumes of information pose difficult management problems. Emerging technologies that combine desktop publishing, scanners, interactive design, audio, and video will not only open up new worlds of expression for managers seeking support for positions or ideas, they will also have to simplify the management task of handling large volumes of multimedia data. The emergence of standards (see Chapter 11) is always essential in establishing markets populated by capable and discerning users. As new technologies appear, old standards fall by the way as new generations of users master, then demand, specific appearances to the interface and discard older ways of working.

Kay makes the business case for multimedia primarily in the areas of marketing and training. Both sales presentations and training are heavily influenced by images and multiple views of products and processes. Appearance and the ability to visualize what a product will do for a customer weigh heavily in the buying decision. And learners need to be able to see or experience their materials from a variety of angles. Simulations are all the more realistic if the appropriate images and sounds come from the learner's desktop computer. Firms such as Chevron, Bell Atlantic, and Target Stores have found that corporate students learn more quickly and spend less time and money in travel by practicing at their own desks.

The Modern Management Imperatives

Reach: Global Competition	The complexity of global competition necessitates gathering data worldwide and processing it according to a flexible set of models. DSS and ESS allow model building and maintenance in a far more flexible and responsive way than traditional pencil-and-paper systems supporting human analysts.
Reaction: Quick Customer Feedback on Products and Services	Customer service systems are based on (1) accurate and timely customer data, (2) access to historical data, (3) access to a variety of models for trend analysis and forecasting, (4) integrated access across disciplines (particularly sales, marketing, production, and finance), and (5) quick data input from portable, in-the-field equipment. EDI lubricates the supplier-buyer relationship through standard interfaces. Because customer feedback can't always be captured in a single form, multimedia assist in understanding customer needs.
Responsiveness: Shortened Concept-to-Customer Cycle Time	Again, accurate customer information is key. Integrating sales, market research, production, and finance makes it easier to build and research prototypes, and building and maintaining multiple models help identify customer preferences more quickly. Multimedia and hypermedia make it easier to store and access data in more formats without losing information in the translation.
Refinement: Greater Customer Sophistication and Specificity	Consider customers as an environment that is changeable and unpredictable. Organizations must learn about customers' needs and, more important, what fashions those needs so that they can be anticipated. As customers gain more buying sophistication, their tastes and needs respond to more complex environmental conditions and not merely to simple ones such as price or variety. The gap between customer expectation and service/product quality has to be managed. EISs and ESSs assist in this understanding, and multimedia and hypermedia make it easier to convey appropriate information to customers.
Reconfiguration: Reengineering of Work Patterns and Structures	Hard decisions about products, processes, customers, and configurations require sophisticated models that go beyond simple one- or two-factor cause-and-effect models. DSSs and ESSs enable these models to be crafted and used with a wide variety of data, and multimedia systems allow the use of "softer" data. EIS plus multimedia coupled with LANs makes human resource deployment and job management different and far more data-based than previously.
Redeployment: Reorganization and Redesign of Resources	Development of new production or service delivery processes must become more flexible in the new world of rapid change. Decision models enable "what if" computation and simulation that reduce the risk of a redeployment effort. More flexible scheduling and dispatching also offer opportunities for more economical use of existing resources and, as the examples show, can even point out new business opportunities, especially in the area of customer service.
Reputation: Quality and Reliability of Product and Process	Quality is reduced by the gap between expectation and performance. The narrower the gap, the higher the quality. ESSs, EISs, and DSSs make it easier to explore that gap because of the navigational and modeling capabilities that these systems typically provide.

Another trend of great importance to managers is the movement to client-server architectures brought about not so much by user demand but by an enormous unleashing of creativity spurred by microcomputer technology in the 1980s. The multimedia world view just discussed would probably not have emerged in the mainframe universe owing to high costs and the relatively limited capabilities of mainframe-centered architectures. But the burgeoning of PC power has put a great deal of computing power onto the desks of creative users' desktops, who have discovered how to tailor their working environments in a kind of ICE to their own specifications. New architectures are built around powerful PCs that almost demand to talk to one another, share information, and work cooperatively. These two vigorous forces (the multiplication of creativity and the urge to merge) have naturally led to the client-server architecture that makes it possible to cross not only aisles to share the capabilities of desktop computers but to cross organizational boundaries relatively smoothly and transparently. It is easy to predict that with the development of appropriate standards, multimedia client-server capabilities will be next.

■ CASINO CLEANERS PLACES A BET

Casino Cleaners' niche is really a lucky break. Tanya got her start making deliveries for Checkmate Cleaners. Although Checkmate did not deliver to customers, it had supplies to pick up and occasionally did odd jobs for other cleaners when they had problems. Tanya started to think, "How is this business any different from pizza?" She knew that once she was in a car picking up chemicals or cleaned garments, she may as well deliver to customers. So she developed the idea of being a "cleaning broker." Now she accepts almost any garment either for cleaning or repair and farms out the work to other cleaners. Everybody wins. But Tanya has a complicated information management problem. Her business requires a lot of information linking customers, competitors, various suppliers, and basic accounting information. For example, any given customer's order may require sending out garments to several cleaners, and coordinating delivery dates on these orders is a difficult problem, one that Tanya's employees have to worry about when accepting garments for cleaning or repair. Tanya might have an agreement with one firm for 20 hours of excess capacity during a month, but only for garments of a particular type or fabric, while another firm may have two hours daily for ten days. Predicting when time will be available is a difficult enough problem, but promising customers is even more difficult. The task is made even more complicated because, acting as a broker, Tanya has to have absolutely correct information available at all times and, just as important, she needs to make crucial and complex projections of supply and demand. And while she often needs only to look at summary data of volume or cash flow, occasionally garments go astray or contracts are not honored. At these times, Tanya has to look through all of her paper files to match item, customer, supplier, and driver. What kind of information system will help her with this problem? ■

1. In what ways will a decision support system assist Tanya in her job? What are the benefits of such a system to her? What level(s) of support will a DSS provide her?

2. In what ways will an executive information system help Tanya? Of what benefit would the characteristics of an executive support system be to her? What level(s) of support will an EIS and ESS provide her?

3. Use this case as a platform for your imagination. What would a hypertext system look like to Tanya? What kinds of navigation would she perform? How would multimedia assist her in the kinds of activities that are important to Casino?

Summary

A variety of classes of information systems applications provide a hybrid of management support formats. Decision support systems (DSSs) are intended to assist managers (and others) in making semistructured decisions that are nonroutine and involve human judgment while requiring the processing and display of a considerable amount of information. These sorts of systems are appropriate when the user is expected to derive solutions creatively through analysis and scenario testing. DSSs provide support through mathematical or arithmetic models, data visualization (commonly in the form of graphs), and interaction to change models allowing them to view results until the best decision model is created. Executive information systems and executive support systems are intended for strategic managers who must be able to assemble, process, and visualize a wide variety of data in various formats (involving text, numbers, images) from diverse internal and external sources.

Major features of EIS and ESS include cross-database navigation, drill down (from summaries to specifics), data filtering, compressing and tracking, and ad hoc queries. ESS models tend to be far less sophisticated mathematically than those found in DSSs, reflecting the less structured problems that executives work on. Because ESSs tend to be idiosyncratic, implementing one means staying aware of specific business objectives and critical success factors and developing transparent technologies for executives to use trend analyses, broad summarization, navigation to specific data, nonkeyboard alternatives, and powerful visualization facilities.

Hypermedia provide alternative ways of structuring and exploring data useful to managers, for whom information structuring may prove a limitation as well as an advantage. Hypermedia features include windowing, authoring, and browsing. Hypermedia are suited for nonlinear materials that are not well structured. Multimedia extend the idea of a database to include graphics, pictorial images, speech, sound, animation, and full-motion video. Multimedia applications allow enhanced visualization capabilities, increased information-storage capacity, and more effective communication of results.

Discussion Questions

8.1 This chapter seems to indicate that DSSs are intended for middle managers and ESSs for executives. Do you think this is true? Can't executives also use mathematical models and graphs? Don't tactical and operational managers also want to drill down? What do you know about managerial activities that fall on one side or other of this issue?

8.2 Chapter 5 presented arguments that unified, tightly linked databases are "brittle" and hence more risky and expensive. But the notion of an EIS (or ESS) seems to require this sort of arrangement. Is there a basic conflict here? If so, what is it, and how can it be handled?

8.3 The highly structured nature of the relational approach to databases limits managers to specific kinds of searches (for example, it makes drill down both possible and necessary). How does hypermedia counteract this limitation and expand the powers of managers? At what cost, and to whom?

8.4 The attractiveness of multimedia and falling hardware and software costs have made multimedia almost standard outside the business arena. What kinds of management support beyond the few applications mentioned in this chapter might seem likely "to go multimedia" in the near future? What are the specific strategic advantages of multimedia? What are the risks?

Key Terms

decision support system (DSS)
drill-down
DSS shell/generator
DSS toolsmith
executive information system
  (EIS)
executive support system (ESS)
frame

hybrid system
hypermedium
hypertext
integrated spreadsheet program
menu-managed data entry and
  display
multimedia system
semistructured decision

specific DSS
spreadsheet macro language
spreadsheet package/processor
structured decision
summary information
unstructured decision
visualization

References

Alter, S. *Decision Support Systems: Current Practice and Continuing Challenges*. Reading, MA: Addison-Wesley, 1980.

Augustine, F., T. Surynt, F. Dezoort, and D. Rosetti. "Organizational Impact of Decision Support Technology: What's Ahead for the '90s?" *Journal of End User Computing* 5, 2 (Spring 1993): 26–30.

Cale, E. G., and S. E. Eriksen. "Design and Implementation Issues for a Banking Decision Support System." *Journal of Systems Management* (April 1994): 18–21.

Davis, M. "Anatomy of Decision Support." *Datamation* (June 15, 1984): 201–202, 206, 208.

Frolick, M., and N. Ramarapu. "Hypermedia: The Future of EIS." *Journal of Systems Management* (July 1993): 32–36.

Hackathorn, R., and G. W. Keen. "Organizational Strategies for Personal Computing in Decision Support Systems." *MIS Quarterly* 5, 3 (September 1981): 21–26.

Kay, Alan. "The Business Case for Multimedia." *Datamation* 41, 11 (June 15, 1995): 55–56.

Keen, P. G. W., and M. S. Scott Morton. *Decision Support Systems: An Organizational Perspective*. Reading, MA: Addison-Wesley, 1978.

McCall, M., and R. Kaplan. *Whatever It Takes*. Englewood Cliffs, NJ: Prentice-Hall, 1990.

Sprague, R. "A Framework for the Development of Decision Support Systems." *MIS Quarterly* 4, 4 (1980): 1–26.

Sprague, R., and E. Carlson. *Building Effective Decision Support Systems*. Englewood Cliffs, NJ: Prentice-Hall, 1982.

Stambaugh, C., and F. Carpenter. "The Roles of Accounting and Accountants in Executive Information Systems." *Accounting Horizons* (September 1992): 52–63.

Tran, H. "Successful DSS Development with Traditional Tools and Techniques." *Journal of Information Systems Management* (Summer 1990): 46–55.

Vella, Peter. "EIS: The Theory." *Australian Accountant* (October 1990): 49–50.

CASE

EVERGREEN LANDSCAPING AND MAINTENANCE: A CRISIS MANAGEMENT SYSTEM FOR LILY

Lily Doucette, president of Evergreen, Heather Cariad, vice president of finance, Frances Harmon, vice president of administration, and Thomas Davidoff, vice president of operations, have been meeting as a subcommittee of MEC to focus on crisis management. This committee is primarily concerned with three kinds of crises:

1. Financial crises that would affect Evergreen's ability to meet its financial obligations, especially bank debts

2. Supplier crises that would affect Evergreen's ability to obtain the products it needs to sell (and given the seasonal nature of the business, this is a very real potential problem)

3. Physical crises including natural and human-caused disasters such as fire, severe weather, or explosions

Four years ago, several of the firm's greenhouses were damaged by a severe, unexpected early-season hailstorm, causing $85,000 damage to physical property and $24,000 loss of plants. The buildings were rebuilt quickly but not very well. The plants were harder to replace on short notice. Ultimately, losses exceeded $200,000, only part of which was covered by insurance. While Evergreen hasn't experienced financial crises in recent years, it certainly is at the whim of suppliers, some of whom are start-up concerns severely underfunded and not very reliable. Working with Pindar Gopal seems a likely way to counter some potential disaster.

Lily has spent a great deal of time with Evergreen's insurers, George&Son, to create a crisis management plan. Part of the plan is a series of "how-to" steps to understand and react to crises far more rapidly than Evergreen does to normal retail, wholesale, or service situations. With hundreds of thousands of dollars riding on decisions that have to be made very quickly, Lily doesn't want to make any mistakes.

The how-tos consist of a series of description, evaluation, diagnosis, and action steps stemming from George&Son's experiences. For instance, they have determined that in the event of very large fires damaging retail space, it's best to shut down. On the other hand, fires in inventory areas may only damage some plants, creating the need to reprice slightly damaged goods quickly. This set of steps requires that the crisis management subcommittee meet quickly to assess various crisis scenarios by describing them with a small set of variables and then comparing them to a larger set to find similar cases (i.e., stereotypical situations) that have suggested solutions. In a way, this process is merely a more complex version of the diagnostic charts one finds on the last page of VCR instructions. But the cost of a mistake and the very short time for reaction make figuring out what's wrong with a VCR look as easy as watching TV.

Questions

1. How would you characterize a crisis management system in terms of level of management support? What kinds of models would be necessary for such a system to function effectively? Which people would use the crisis management system and at what times?

2. Is crisis management an appropriate problem for a decision support system? How would such a system blend computer and human strengths? If a DSS were built for crisis management support, what would be appropriate responsibilities for staff at Evergreen, both before and during a crisis?

3. What characteristics of an executive information system would a crisis management system have to exhibit? Why? Which executives would be involved in crisis management and use the facilities of the crisis management system?

4. What aspects of multimedia and hypermedia would prove valuable in a crisis management system setup? Role play the roles of Lily, Heather, Frances, and Thomas in small groups and determine what sorts of information would be best presented in formats other than text. What information would be best presented as text? How would the two go together?

CHAPTER NINE

Supporting Groups through Groupware, Electronic Mail, and Bulletin Boards

Question: What kinds of support are available to groups of people at work? What is valuable about this support? In what situations do the benefits outweigh the costs?

"And sales agent of the year is Paul Ajuwon!" rang out the voice of Trish Carmone. Trish is the owner of The Carmart, one of the biggest and historically one of the most successful car dealers in town. Paul is certainly a large part of why The Carmart is so successful, and it's not just because he has sold the most cars. Sales agent of the year is bestowed on the agent who has done the most for the company, its 22 sales agents, 16 office staff, and 11 technicians. Paul is a sparkplug, an inexhaustible fund of good humor and a tireless engine of ideas for the firm. His most recent idea for a sales campaign for computerized matching of customers to cars was a success not only because it was a good idea but also because Paul was able to sell it to everyone. Now Trish needs Paul's creativity even more, because it looks like The Carmart is simultaneously driving through financing potholes and being challenged by buying clubs. Trish wonders if other salespeople might also have good ideas. She has heard of quality circles but finds the idea pretty foreign. Information systems were part of the last good idea; she wonders if they can help now.

Answer: Yes, they can. Group support systems (GSSs) support work teams even in highly individualized businesses such as car sales. Companies need to tap individuals' creativity that the group process may stifle. GSSs allow businesses to tap this creativity at all organizational levels through anonymity, parallelism, rapid feedback, and structure. Technology can assist communication through decision aids or modeling at the same or different times and places and with a variety of hardware and software.

INTRODUCTION

In this chapter, we move the spotlight off the individual manager and explore the mushrooming garden of group support systems, which are systems intended to support work teams in coming to conclusions. Group support systems provide support at several levels of the model introduced in Chapter 8, but primarily assist in consensus formation and computational modeling.

In this chapter, we explore three classes of systems that involve human communication, loosely called **groupware.** One system type supports cohesive, managed groups or teams through meetings or sessions. The second type supports loosely coupled and relatively unmanaged individuals who may, from time to time, wish to share information as an information-based community. The third class of systems facilitates interaction of working groups by integrating the capabilities of the other two classes.

The first class of system supports teams of individuals working either in a face-to-face mode or dispersed geographically among two or more sites. This system is commonly called *group support systems (GSSs)* because their focus is on the "groupness" or interaction that occurs when people work together. GSSs are best thought of as meeting managers because they focus on managing meeting processes. Several commercial vendors supply GSSs in a variety of forms.

The second class of system we look at supports person-to-person communication. The most common computerized form of this is electronic mail. There are many variations of electronic mail, including computer conferences and list servers that are also becoming important to managers. In this discussion, we also look at some information-searching tools that are often associated with electronic communication. These tools support user communities, especially those that come together to discuss or share information on relatively narrow topics. The focus of these systems is the information itself. Most VANs and network-level operating systems offer at least electronic mail.

The third class of systems focuses on facilitating the interaction of individuals in working groups through information exchange, combining features and applications from the first two classes. These systems offer electronic mail, bulletin boards, computer conferencing, calendaring and scheduling, some database capabilities, and work flow (form-based processing of information) applications. By far, the most well known member of this class is *Lotus Notes*.

RATIONALE: GROUPS ARE IMPORTANT

Management support is moving toward the support of groups such as work teams, ad hoc groups (such as task forces), multiorganizational groups, and widely dispersed interest groups without a limited geographical locale. The impetus for this support comes from the modern management imperatives:

- Global competition increases the geographic spread of organizations and the likelihood that a competitor can be anywhere.

- The shortened concept-to-customer cycle increases the need for speed of interpersonal communication and teamwork. There simply isn't enough time for one person to do all jobs anymore.

- Volatility in resource deployment and redeployment implies the use of multidisciplinary teams and precompetitive and strategic alliances.

For a long time, these needs have gone unmet, but now the technology is available. Relatively inexpensive, reliable networks, good software, and powerful microcomputers make systems to support groups feasible today.

As tasks become increasingly complex and rich in information that is difficult to handle manually, teams are important for business. Flatter organizations shift responsibility to groups at lower levels. Collaborative strategies are seen more and more as being able to provide a competitive edge, especially through strategic alliances that in the past were thought of as incompatible. Information technology enables these alliances in ways that allow companies to keep their identities and operations separate while they cooperate on specific, information-intensive projects. Finally, given time pressures and a lack of meeting skills, many companies are becoming discontented with "normal" business meetings.

Although social scientists know some things about group processes and interaction, our knowledge is incomplete and people are always surprising, especially in groups. The quality and quantity of complicated communication channels are increasing with the use of computers, satellites, electronic whiteboards, microcomputers with all sorts of software in living color, slow-scan video, fax, and so on. However, most of us aren't very good at controlling equipment more complicated than telephones, and even they are becoming more complex. Most managers are not trained in running meetings, and most employees lack the discipline to sit through meeting after meeting while amateurs run them. People are continually overwhelmed by data and are too busy to attend meetings they should be attending, so the wrong people attend at the wrong time with the wrong (or no) preparation and the wrong motivation.

Consider Trish Carmone at The Carmart. She is interested in meeting competitive challenges as well as solving financial problems posed by her lenders. She thinks that her sales staff probably has good ideas about how to counter increased competition but has difficulty capturing those ideas informally, and the salespeople don't like to take a lot of time out from selling to attend meetings. Besides, there is a bit of prima donna in all of them, which makes meetings more like musical comedy than serious business. How can Trish get these creative people to come up with good ideas without trying to outshine one another?

One solution might be to use groupware. First, having been promised that the meeting will last two hours, not two days, the sales staff gathers one evening at a decision lab. There, using a network of microcomputers, groupware guides the sales staff into entering their good ideas anonymously. A facilitator, who is familiar with the technology and how to manage groups, keeps the meeting flowing without the spoken banter and posturing that is the trademark of this sales staff. The facilitator helps them get over their initial discomfort with typing rather than selling. Then, not knowing which ideas are whose, the sales staff uses an electronic vote process to rank the ideas and add their own comments to what they judge to be the best five. It's a salesperson's dream come true—he or she gets to "talk" all the time without interruption. Of course it's true that everyone else is also talking all the time, but because they are just typing, all anyone hears is the sound of keys clacking. Initially and privately, some don't like knowing that their best ideas won't be rewarded, but after a while they realize that no one else will be rewarded either. Two hours later, Trish has five solid ideas about how to counter the buying clubs, fleshed out with pertinent comments by sales staff—something that would have taken days in traditional meetings.

Recent research into meetings illustrates this group's problems. A large portion of a manager's day is spent in meetings, from 25 percent to about 80 percent or more. A third of this time is seen as unproductive (at a cost of more than $50 billion annually), and this time is increasing. Executives have almost no training in running meetings and they report that less than two-thirds of all meetings achieve their stated objectives. The typical meeting lasts one and one-half hours and includes about nine participants who have been given about two hours' notice. A written agenda is used about half of the time and only about half of that agenda is covered. The major problems with these kinds of meetings are that there are no or limited goals or agendas, the meetings are disorganized, people come poorly prepared and bring or focus on irrelevant information, and participants frequently drift off the subject. Often poorly led and poorly controlled, meetings sometimes last too long and are generally inconclusive. Managers need help.

Help can come from applications that support groups, either in meetings or other forms of communication. We look first at group support systems (GSSs), which support meetings, then we turn our attention to communication-based groupware, applications that support user communities.

TECHNOLOGY TO SUPPORT MEETINGS

A **group support system (GSS)** is a set of hardware, software, and procedures that supports a group of people engaged in activities intended to produce a conclusion. Another definition focuses on the problem to be solved: A GSS is an interactive, computer-based system that facilitates the solution of relatively unstructured problems by a set of problem solvers working together in a group. These definitions stress a number of common elements. First is the work; a GSS helps people obtain results. Second, computer assistance is critical, which does not mean simply adding information. In many cases, it is desirable to reduce information (as happens in a vote, for example, where we throw out information about who voted which way and settle for a total). Finally, the definitions stress "togetherness"; a GSS is intended to enhance group cohesion—people working together. Several assumptions about groups must be made:

- The group already possesses the necessary knowledge to solve the problem. Participants either already know enough or they can bring the information with them.
- The gap between problem and solution exists and is maintained because participants are blocked and their creativity is stifled, either because of their own limitations in expressing themselves or because other participants or the meeting format prevents them from being creative.
- A network technology can bridge this gap.

The benefits of computer-based meeting support are (1) shortened problem-solving time, (2) increased group buy-in and commitment to the outcome of the decision, and (3) better-quality solutions. Some research shows that groups waste significantly less time overall in coming to conclusions when they use a GSS, although in many cases the time needed to make decisions was actually increased. Often, there is a payoff in time when individuals play fewer games in taking turns and diverting discussion. In addition, a computer-controlled agenda is far easier to administer effectively. Often, GSS meetings are tightly controlled because many of the real-time tools in use (such as *GroupSystems*™ and *OptionFinder*™) require a highly trained person, called a **facilitator,** to run the meeting.

People who participate in a GSS, even if they don't ultimately sway opinion, feel more inclined to go along with the group's decision because they feel they have expressed

| Figure 9–1 | GROUP SUPPORT SYSTEMS: WHERE THEY WORK |

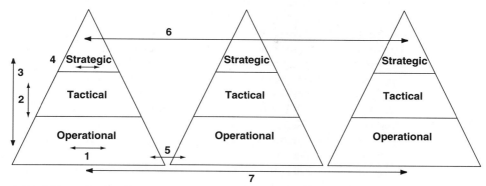

1. Work Team, Design Group
2. Departmental Planning
3. Organizational Budgeting
4. Strategic Planning
5. Joint Ventures
6. Precompetitive Activities
7. Professional Associations

themselves. Evidence shows that groups are more creative when they use tools that allow them to express themselves anonymously and if they don't have to wait their turns, getting frustrated and forgetful as they wait. There is also some evidence that groups using a GSS do not make as good decisions as their most competent members would, but in traditional meetings the most forceful generally have the floor the most and can push through their "best" decision more effectively. However, this traditional approach severely restricts creativity, and it is unlikely that the most forceful group members alone will have the solution to very difficult problems; they will have to develop it with others. This implies that letting others "speak" is extremely important with hard problems. Effective consensual systems rely on getting others' opinions when knowledge level is low and the possibility for creative decisions is high. "Creative" in this sense means a decision that no one could have predicted before the meeting. Synergy, rather than dominance, is the key characteristic of a GSS.

GSSs can work in a number of organizational contexts (see Figure 9–1). Work teams such as design groups are a common use. Another term for this kind of support is **computer-supported cooperative work (CSCW).** Such teams can take advantage of shared graphics and work spaces. CSCW applications tend to focus on design and implementation groups, particularly dispersed groups that have to decide on a design for a part or product. Departmental planning may cut across management levels, bringing together managers and workers. Each has a valid, but different, viewpoint on work. In traditional meetings, workers are wary of disagreeing with their bosses, but the anonymity of a GSS gives them confidence to speak their minds. Organizational budgeting is an example of a GSS context in which all levels of management work together to build a product. Reducing dominance is even more important here. While executives might make the final decision, it helps that all participants feel, rightly or wrongly, that what they have said has actually been heard.

At the executive level, a GSS can play a role both inside the firm as well as across firms. Executives deal with highly abstract and relatively untrustworthy information, and a consensual system of the sort a GSS provides is just the type of support they need. Joint ventures, on the other hand, cut across organizations at various levels. Trust-building is an important component here, and knowing that no one partner controls the agenda or the process is a prime contributor to an atmosphere of trust. A GSS has a strong role to play in putting together strategic alliances and building relations between firms and their suppliers and customers. Finally, GSS has been used to facilitate precompetitive cooperation, either between organizations or in professional associations.

A major concern about the use of computer-supported meeting tools involves group decision making. Two major concerns are what the nature of a decision is and how groups actually make decisions. The first issue is, of course, not confined to GSSs, but it is highlighted by a situation in which different individuals have different views of what a decision is and when it is made. While the traditional focus of a decision has been a change in a course of action, this text takes a view similar to that of Clyde Holsapple. He says managers don't necessarily "make" decisions but instead acquire knowledge. A decision "is a piece of knowledge indicating the nature of an action commitment."

The second issue, the nature of group decision making, is far more complex. Clearly, there are situations in which a group makes decisions like an individual. This can occur when a group is dominated by a single individual or when a group is a manager plus one or more DSSs. Holsapple calls these sorts of groups, either dominated by or composed of a single individual, a *team decision maker*. Where there are more autonomy and more equal authority, Holsapple labels these decision makers as *groups*. Such groups are the meat and potatoes of a GSS because the features most prevalent in the technology reduce the influence of specific individuals and promote information sharing. When the group itself is structured around a problem (i.e., is organized in some tangible way), Holsapple uses the term *organization decision maker*. Such decision makers decentralize knowledge generation, thereby creating three distinct additional problems: delegation, cooperation, and integration. Managers are very familiar with decentralized decision making and the problems of coordination. Because of the work involved in coordination, such structures are difficult to maintain and easily change into either group decision making (reduced structure) or team decision making (increased structure and decreased autonomy).

Thus, the second issue revolves around the nature of a group and how it reaches the kind of consensus that it desires. This academic question has a practical impact on any kind of group support envisaged for managerial applications. Groups that are charged with coming to a conclusion need to know when that conclusion has been reached. Whatever type of group is making a decision, it must structure tasks appropriately so that it knows when it is approaching the desired conclusion. Most researchers and facilitators agree that it is less important what conclusion has been reached than that the group understands that a conclusion has been reached.

Pros and Cons of a GSS

GSSs have five structural characteristics that provide the bulk of benefits (see Figure 9–2):

- **Anonymity** allows individuals to make entries without fear of punishment, and this freedom of expression opens the creative tap. Some researchers say this is because individuals feel immersed in the group and lose their individual identities. Others say that anonymity lets people take on many

Figure 9–2 GSS BENEFITS

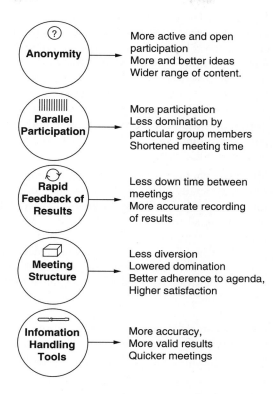

different persona and try out the problem from a number of perspectives. Whatever the reason, anonymous participation brings dividends in creativity. Anonymity also makes it less likely that existing leaders will lead or dominate the group or that new leaders will emerge. This lack of domination has been observed frequently in group meetings. It may, on the one hand, mean that groups become less effective in carrying out their conclusions—in making things happen—because committed leaders don't exist. On the other hand, the democratization of the group contributes to individual buy-in to the conclusion, making it more likely that strong leadership will not be necessary. Individuals may make things happen by themselves.

- **Participation parallelism** guarantees that no one needs to wait to participate. Everyone participates simultaneously, which restricts the ability of dominant persons to run the meeting, derail it, or change the topic. The larger the group, the greater the flow of ideas in a given period of time. Most real-time electronic meetings are limited by seating space. Groups of 10 to 20 participants are most common, although this writer has facilitated groups as large as 55 individuals. Regardless of the group size, parallelism means that everyone has a say. However, in very large groups, most participants actually see only a very small fraction of all the comments because each participant has a limited reading speed.

- **Participant feedback** is relatively quick with rapid printed output of results for participants. A set of *WordPerfect* macros, for example, can quickly convert the relatively bland output of *GroupSystems™* into a nicely formatted, structured report. Because all data are captured exactly as typed, the lengthy period of time needed to transcribe minutes or flip-charts into typed output is reduced to a matter of a few hours. A one-day meeting's output can be formatted, printed, and bound overnight, ready for distribution the next morning. Because enthusiasm and buy-in are perishable commodities, it's important to get results back to the participants quickly in order to keep the momentum.

- **Meeting structure** is enhanced with a computer-controlled agenda. The process generally allows a variety of structures so that meetings remain interesting, but the number is limited. Newer GSS products, especially those designed to run in a GUI environment such as *Windows*, allow for computer-controlled agendas with facilitator intervention if needed. Until recently, however, the standard was a predetermined agenda controlled in real time by the facilitator as the meeting progressed. From a managerial point of view, standardized structures make the meeting more understandable, especially for a manager who has to approve the agenda. However, when creativity is important or when the questions to be pondered aren't known until meeting time (or during the meeting), flexibility is more important.

- **Information-handling tools** simplify keeping track of meeting process and enhance output. Multicriteria evaluation, voting, and comment-organizing tools allow participants and facilitators to process information supplied by participants into more valuable formats. For example, a modeling tool that shows a correlation between two rankings immediately after the rankings are done by the group assists in clarifying whether or not there are really two issues (i.e., uncorrelated rankings) as opposed to one (i.e., highly correlated rankings).

Other advantages of GSSs are pooled knowledge of individuals in the group and emotional support, stimulation, and inspiration within the group that results in more creativity. The desire for social approval spurs greater efforts, and Holsapple, along with most observers of GSS, contends that GSS decisions are of higher quality than decisions made in the traditional way. One important research finding on group process in general is that groups, regardless of whether or not they use computers, tend to judge their conclusions, or those of people like themselves, as being better than conclusions of people who are not like them. This bias may be enhanced by users of what is perceived to be "high" technology.

There are also disadvantages to using GSSs. There is a distinct possibility of confusion or complex emotional interrelationships, the possibility of groupthink (in which a group narrows its field of vision, disallowing views not consistent with existing group ideas), the potential for hostility, the likelihood that the group dynamic will make it easier to achieve and support extreme decisions (that are either too cautious or too risky), and the often observed increase in time it takes to reach a decision. Another problem is entering ideas, which takes a lot of typing time. Many facilitators find that groups like to alternate periods of keyboarding with face-to-face discussion. The personal styles and preferences of facilitators have a strong influence on outcomes in GSS meetings, too. A poor facilitator can produce a meeting just as disastrous as any conducted by defensive company presidents.

There are also a number of challenges in GSSs that haven't been adequately addressed to date. The most outstanding challenge is information overload. How can participants and facilitators handle the great flood of ideas that come from brainstorming sessions? Systems that provide the kinds of capabilities found in MIS, DSS, and expert systems can provide support at the classification level, but consensual systems like those GSS tools that support brainstorming have no way of automatically combining ideas to create summaries, averages, or graphs. Consolidating 200 ideas generated in 1 hour into 20 useful ones may take 3 or 4 hours of frustrating work. A related problem is interpreting voting results when tools for creating averages and graphs are used. Unless a clear favorite emerges from among a small number of choices, groups may have to spend a great deal of time discussing which four of seven almost-tied preferences should be further examined.

There are other, more tangible problems. The software to run group sessions is still expensive, with commercial prices running more than $10,000. Many firms have a heavy investment in the kind of microcomputer technology that a GSS relies on, but others will find it too expensive to put together a dozen or more machines. A room has to be dedicated to meetings unless portable equipment is purchased at an even higher cost. Facilitators are needed, and every meeting has to be set up, at some cost in time. One university, which has been running meetings since 1990, has found that every four-hour meeting requires about four hours of setup, takedown, and report writing. Longer meetings or sequences of meetings may have much larger overheads.

From an individual manager's perspective, there are time and effort costs of working with facilitators. When dealing with confidential meeting matters, facilitators may prove to be a weak link if they are not scrupulously honest. Because computer-based meetings haven't been used very long, it is not likely that any meeting facilitator will have ten years' experience running hundreds of meetings. It is usually facilitators' experience that the first meeting is exciting because it is new but the second meeting is something of a letdown to participants, who expect a gain similar to that of the first meeting. Nonetheless, a sequence of meetings is preferable to a single, long one, because it takes some calendar time for participants to become familiar enough with the new technology to feel comfortable and productive. Still, as an emerging technology, GSSs appear to have a lot of advantages that are easy to capitalize on. We turn our attention now to how GSS works to produce results.

HOW GSS WORKS

Group support systems meetings can be categorized in three ways (Figure 9–3). First, they can be ranked in terms of the **level of group support** they offer. Level 1 support provides communication aids only. Electronic versions of brainstorming, or nominal group technique (NGT), and group writing tools fall into this category. We call a Level 1 GSS a consensual system. Level 2 support provides a number of group decision-making aids, such as voting. Most commercial tools support a wide variety of voting formats, including rank-ordering, proportional point assignment, absolute rating, multicriteria rating, true-false,

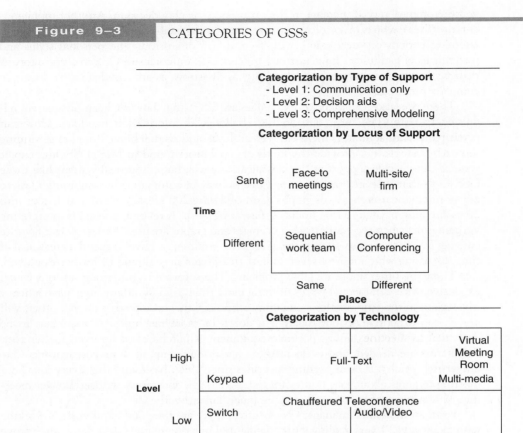

Figure 9–3 CATEGORIES OF GSSs

Categorization by Type of Support
- Level 1: Communication only
- Level 2: Decision aids
- Level 3: Comprehensive Modeling

Categorization by Locus of Support

Time		Place	
		Same	Different
Same		Face-to meetings	Multi-site/ firm
Different		Sequential work team	Computer Conferencing

Categorization by Technology

and scale judgment. These techniques provide a quick way to measure group consensus. These tools lie between consensual systems and contextual systems. Finally, a Level 3 GSS makes available a host of comprehensive modeling and simulation tools of the implicational and computational forms. Few of these Level 3 systems are available commercially. A shared spreadsheet is one example as is a live simulation of a business process that individuals can control from their terminals or microcomputers.

A second way to categorize a GSS is to look at the flexibility it provides in terms of meeting times and locales. An **electronic meeting** can take place at one time or at different times and at one location or more than one location. Same-time/same-place (STSP) meetings are face-to-face. Same-time/different-place (STDP) meetings are multisite meetings, where people meet as subgroups, coordinated by the information technology. A video teleconference or audio conference is an example of this. Different-time/same-place (DTSP) meetings are rare but may involve sequential work teams, say, shift workers, who drop into a meeting, work for a while, and then drop out as the shift changes. Finally, different-time/different-place (DTDP) meetings are known as computer conferences. Participants log into a meeting, say what they want, vote and make decisions, and then exit. DTDP meetings generally take place over a long period of time. Our experience with most of these formats other than face-to-face is confined to the past four decades. Running these other formats has always proven difficult without computers and advanced communications technology.

A third classification scheme for a GSS is to focus on the technology used in the meeting. Computer technology has been characterized in the popular press as "high" technology, while pencil and paper is thought of as "low" technology. While there may be some arguments about what characterizes technology as being high or low, we can make judgments about the relative sophistication of equipment. In addition, technology can be described in terms of how broad the communication spectrum is. Since most GSSs operate at Level 1 or 2, it's important to distinguish those systems that provide broad communication in a number of rich modes (such as face-to-face communication) with those that allow only limited interaction (such as use of a ten-key keypad). This gives rise to a two-dimensional classification scheme: level versus mode.

In this scheme, paper notes rate as low technology and narrow mode of communication. Higher technology with a broader communication spectrum is a system such as *OptionFinder*™. A **keypad system** utilizes keypads connected to a microcomputer by wires or infrared signals. Various questions are posed (for example, "Which of the following is the most advantageous project start date?"), and participants press one of ten keys that correspond to a menu of up to ten choices displayed by the computer. Votes are collected and an analysis of the distribution of responses is displayed. The keypad is able to provide only a few bits of information at a time (one of ten choices equals approximately 3.16 bits), far fewer than paper notes.

A **chauffeured system** is one in which a computer is used by a group through a facilitator who operates the computer and enters information that participants provide in a face-to-face setting. A full-text system such as *GroupSystems*™ or *SAMM*™ allows two-way or multipath communication among participants using any textual capability of a keyboard. Audio and video teleconferencing provides somewhat lower "tech" but fuller mode communication. When the two are combined, a multimedia conference involving computers, video, still images, and sound provides an even richer communication environment, leading to a virtual meeting room in which participants experience images of other participants who are not actually in the same room or experience visual and auditory scenes that are computer constructed.

GSS TOOLS

While various commercial systems exhibit a lot of variety in terms of the tools and functions they provide, a brief review of some *GroupSystems*™ tools will illustrate the kinds of sessions that can be run. *GroupSystems*™ is neither the oldest nor the best of the GSSs, but it is widely available and the tools found in *GroupSystems*™ are represented in most of the other major competitive products such as *SAMM*™, *VisionQuest*™, and *MeetingWare*™. The tools are divided into two classes: divergent and convergent. A **divergent tool** allows users to generate new ideas, to "diverge" from the general discussion and go off on tangents, to differ, and to avoid consensus. **Convergent tools** foster consensus, show similarities, reduce information, and lessen variety. A meeting of people is a blend of divergence and convergence (Figure 9–4). Ideas are generated and then consensus is reached on order, priority, or content. Then new ideas, generated based on the first

---

Figure 9–4   STYLES OF GSS MEETINGS

D=Divergent, generating; C=Convergent, eliminating

(D) ELECTRONIC BRAINSTORMING
Individuals enter ideas and comment on others'.
No one can restrict anyone else's comments.
Variations on Nominal Group Technique (NGT),
brainstorming, synectics and other creativity styles.

(C) IDEA CONSOLIDATION
Similar ideas are brought together and "useless"
ideas are eliminated or filed away for later.
May be done individually (and then pooled), as a
group with or without the computer, or the computer
may do this by itself using AI or other techniques.

(C,D) IDEA ORGANIZATION
Ideas are put into an order or matrix or some kind of
outline.

(C) VOTING
Ideas are rank ordered, evaluated on one or more
criteria in absolute terms. Yes/no, True/false,
questionnaires may also be used, Voting may be
partial or sequential.

(D,C) GROUP WRITING
Groups compose documents working individually on
paragraphs or ideas. They may (or may not) edit
each others' ideas.

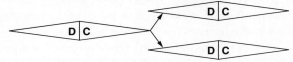

---

round, are culled, reduced, prioritized, and pigeonholed. This process continues until enough detail and agreement are reached.

Electronic Brainstorming (also called *brainwriting*) is a tool that mimics brainstorming to promote creativity. Individual participants comment on a specific topic, and when each finishes creating a comment, it is sent to a random participant. This second participant (who has just finished creating a first comment that is sent to someone else) adds a second comment, a comment on the initial comment, and these two comments are sent to a random third person. This third person comments on the comment on the comment, and the three comments are sent to a random fourth person, and so on. In this way, a simulated sequential "conversation" on a topic takes place, building up chains or threads of commentary. People are encouraged to go off the topic, to follow whims and leads triggered by the words others use. A related tool called Topic Commenter fixes a certain number of topics on which participants address their comments, creating only that many threads of ideas. Topic Commenter is meant to be more focused and less tangential than Electronic Brainstorming.

Idea consolidation is provided by a tool called Categorizer that is useful in culling many ideas created through a divergent tool to create a shorter list that lumps like items together. What is meant by "like" is a difficult question and, for many, consolidation is the weakest link. It is difficult to get a large group to agree that two phrases mean exactly the same thing, and it is difficult to know when to stop lumping categories together. Some experimental techniques simplify this process by using the power of computers. One tool known as Folders provides every participant with the ability to use a mouse to physically move items from a long list into a shorter set of piles or folders. Use of factor analytic and other statistical techniques enables the facilitator to determine a group "average" short list of categories and even derive coalitions of participants who agree with each other that certain items go together and others don't. A number of researchers are working to use artificial intelligence techniques to do lexical mapping of terms through the meanings of the words to automatically create categories. For example, this technique would lump "Increase profits," "Increase sales while keeping costs fixed," and "Decrease costs for the same sales" because they mean the same thing. It is also possible to organize ideas into a matrix or some sort of order. The tool called Idea Organizer does this. It can also be used to solicit one idea at a time from participants; hence, it is both convergent and divergent.

GroupSystems™ has a number of tools that enable participants to vote or pool their evaluations. The Vote tool allows yes/no, true/false, multiple choice, rank ordering, assignment of points from a pool, and scale ratings as well as the facility to send the votes back to the participants so that each participant can privately compare his or her vote with the group average. A questionnaire tool as well as a multicriteria evaluation tool called Alternative Evaluator enables participants to evaluate a large number of alternatives simultaneously on a set of criteria. A matrix form of this tool is called Group Matrix. Both provide for massive data collection as groups converge toward a small set of potential solutions from the large set generated by the divergent tools.

Finally, a group documentation tool called Group Writer permits participants to create a document in a group. Each person in the group works on one section at a time (an outline has to be created in advance) and when the participant has finished with the section, another participant may edit it or add additional comments. Participants can footnote, too. The resulting document is then available at all times to be read by participants. Depending on the group mood and task, this tool can be either divergent or convergent.

New tools for groups are created constantly. Many tools that are valuable to individuals—for example, graphical tools that create idea webs—have been difficult to translate to a group environment, but variations on these themes are now appearing in the groupware arena.

A "Typical" Meeting

Combining these tools gives a meeting facilitator enormous flexibility. Consider a meeting that is supposed to result in a manufacturing plan for the next decade. It may begin with brainstorming about "What will this firm be producing in the year 2005?" A group of 12 participants might produce 100 ideas in half an hour, some of them ridiculous, some hilarious, some very intriguing, some great but too expensive. But all ideas are captured and retained in a computer's memory. Then the group consolidates this list for half an hour and produces a smaller list of perhaps 20 items. "Bowling balls" may be lumped with "golf clubs" by the group because they are both sporting goods. Next, this short list of 20 items is rank-ordered in terms of feasibility, profitability, risk, and so forth, using one of the voting tools. This takes 10 to 20 minutes.

From this list, the top two valued suggestions are selected. Recall that nothing is ever lost because all the data are available on disk. For each of the top two suggestions, comments on feasibility and implementation are solicited from the group using Topic Commenter. This may last 40 minutes or so. Because two hours have gone by, the group takes a break while the facilitator prints out the comments and makes copies for everyone to read. Then, after the break, the group consolidates each of the two lists to create a short list of action items for each of the two top evaluated products. This could easily take half an hour or more. Then each short list is evaluated using Alternative Evaluator for another half hour, rating the two short lists in terms of cost, risk, and speed of implementation. Finally, the group spends an hour and a half writing a plan that details a migration path (getting to the new product from today's product) and preferences. The whole exercise has taken six hours. Everyone is tired but several days' work have been done, everyone has had a say, the group agreement is quite high, and buy-in is high.

Meetings are not the only form of group interaction. Many applications support more loosely joined and less intensive groups than real-time meetings. Electronic mail and various Internet services support communities of like-minded or cooperating individuals, either within the same firm or across organizations. Now we turn our attention to these applications, beginning with electronic mail.

ELECTRONIC MAIL AND BULLETIN BOARDS

One of the most surprising developments in computer-supported work has been the enormous but belated growth in **electronic mail (e-mail).** Prior to 1980, electronic mail was a curiosity of the computer community. Despite e-mail's obvious advantages, it took the PC explosion in the 1980s to improve the attractiveness of electronic mail. Lack of intelligence in most computer terminals and lack of privacy in public terminal rooms negated many of the advantages of electronic mail. With today's powerful microcomputers, however, managers appreciate the flexibility, speed, and convenience of electronic mail. Some drawbacks remain, however, that make e-mail problematic for a few users.

The concept of e-mail is neither new nor exciting. Electronic mail in its simplest forms merely substitutes an electronic analog for a printed page. Addresses and routing information (the "envelope") are maintained electronically. Nor is the method of sending and accessing mail much more sophisticated than typing and reading—and reading from a computer screen is not always easier than reading printing. It is the *additional* capabilities provided by computer processing that make e-mail flexible, fast, and convenient (see Figure 9–5).

First, e-mail has the capability to store and retrieve messages based on sender, content, and date. Messages can be precomposed and various edited versions sent to a variety of people either individually or with a mailing list. Closely related is its ability to reply using exact quotes from, or the entire text of, the original letter, which breeds the ubiquitous and sometimes annoying "chain letter" phenomenon in which A quotes B quoting C quoting D quoting E until it's not at all clear what is being said or commented on. Nonetheless, this archiving capability means that nothing ever really gets lost—only buried.

Next, e-mail offers a variety of envelope services, some of which are analogs of mail. Priorities can be assigned, especially through compatible mail systems. Reply requests are not uncommon—a message may arrive with the notation that a reply is requested—and mail can easily be forwarded without even being read. On some systems it is possible to check if the mail has indeed been read. Mail can be marked as "urgent" (but, curiously, never "nonurgent").

More interesting are e-mail's processing facilities that are hard to achieve in physical mail. They include the following:

Figure 9–5   ELECTRONIC MAIL FEATURES

Basic Features
Addressing
Date-time stamp
Subject header
cc:
Status information (read, unread, new)

Advanced Features
Indexed storage and retrieval of received mail based on sender, content, date
Mailing lists
Backups of sent mail
Envelope services
   Reply request
   Urgency marking
   Forwarding
Prescreening of received mail based on sender, subject, date
Automatic forwarding from host to foreign node
Mail merge
Automatic processing
File transfer
Inclusion of sound, graphics, nontextual material
Folders
Backup of sent/received/processed mail
Delivery time stamp; notification of delivery
Notification of error in delivery
Address translation across networks
Signature inclusion

Intelligent Features
Prescreening of received mail based on content
Search and destroy of sent mail across network(s)
Signature recognition
Style recognition for verification

- Prescreening of messages based on envelope characteristics (for example, sender or subject). This helps managers presift their mail and cope with a barrage of messages.
- Automatic forwarding between machines. Managers who work on multiple machines or systems like this facility, especially if they travel and use different kinds of workstations.
- Prescreening of messages based on content (key words, for example). Again, managers can use this feature to look at the most pressing issues first.
- Automatic processing of incoming messages.

- **List servers.** Messages coming in to the list server are automatically forwarded to all members of the list; members can request services such as "Subscribe" or "Unsubscribe" with special messages. A disadvantage to a list server is that every message is sent to every subscriber. A manager may subscribe to many lists that are periodically plagued by errors that occur when an individual, wishing to reply to the message originator, uses the e-mail command "Reply" and replies to the entire mailing list. Some very personal information has been broadcast in this way, to everyone's embarrassment. Heavily subscribed lists can overwhelm subscribers with mail. If only 10 percent of a 1,000-member list originate one message a day, this means there are 100 e-mail messages to be handled by every one of the 1,000 subscribers from this list alone.

- Mail-merge facilities make it possible for managers to direct one message to a list of receivers in a more personalized way than using list servers.

- **File transfer** in a variety of modes. Whole files, in a variety of formats, can be appended to messages or included as parts of messages.

- Inclusion of sound, graphics, and other nontextual material. For the most part, e-mail doesn't care what the content of a message is, although some codes may be a problem for the systems that transport the message because they will be confused with codes that are used to time, route, decompose, and compose the strings of bits that are transmitted between nodes.

- Maintenance of specialized folders of messages, such as project reports, human resource-related messages, and so forth. This helps managers keep track of separate aspects of work.

- Creation of backup copies of sent messages. Backup copies of deleted messages can be maintained for later recall.

Challenges and problems with electronic mail parallel those of group support systems. They include the following:

- Junk mail. Few mail systems provide general automatic screening of electronic junk mail—after all, one person's junk may be another's treasure.

- Once a message has been sent, it may be difficult to intercept it. In this way, e-mail is just like the post office, although some LAN-based systems allow reclaiming of messages before they are picked up by the sender.

- "Flaming" and rudeness. E-mail "manners" haven't been established and rude behavior is common enough to have a special name—**flaming.** Unlike face-to-face communication, it is far too easy to be crude and outrageous over e-mail.

- On the other hand, some researchers have commented on the relative blandness of the typed medium and that is more difficult to craft messages that convey precisely the intended emotional tone. Others have replied that this isn't much of a problem in correspondence; the greater letter writers of the seventeenth, eighteenth, and nineteenth centuries certainly could get their feelings across. Some call e-mail a "cold" medium and have proposed using special symbols such as :) and :((if they confuse you, look at them rotated 90 degrees) to indicate the supposedly missing emotions. The most likely explanations of the alleged coldness and blandness are that we are either (1) no longer used to communicating by printed word thanks to the near ubiquity of the telephone or (2) still unused to the "answering machine" qualities of store-and-forward messages. Meanwhile, as users get used to the medium, those who learn how to be warm and personable on e-mail will be as successful as any good communicator and those who insist on being boors and bullies will probably be rewarded in like measure.

■ E-mail may look a bit like phoning, but it actually creates a time-and-date-stamped, semiofficial record of what was said to whom, thereby raising questions of privacy. Often, messages are forwarded to others without the writer's permission. It is easy to send blind carbon copies (in which the announced receivers of the message are not informed about who else will see copies), and what might have been thought of at one time as private communication ends up being public.

■ As a corollary, senders often forget that the very permanence of e-mail messages and the fact that once a message has been received it comes under the control of the receiver put senders in jeopardy with respect to liability and responsibility. You may feel like telling your boss to go fly a kite and find it easy to say so in an e-mail message, but remember that this message may come back to haunt you when you are accused of insubordination. There are some issues of intellectual property with all forms of mail, but the practical fact is that once mailed, electronic messages are no longer under the sender's control.

■ In this regard, most corporations that have issued policy statements about e-mail claim that all e-mail messages are company property. Managers should check this policy before assuming that messages they send or receive belong to them—the legalities are indeed hazy.

■ Like physical mail, messages sometimes get lost or garbled, although they are rarely delivered to the wrong address (however, managers using e-mail should be very careful in addressing mail because the punishment for this error comes quickly, especially if the incorrect address is actually a mailing list).

■ The profusion of features found in many e-mail systems makes them difficult to learn to use and somewhat error-prone in early learning stages.

Despite these drawbacks, e-mail is a growing phenomenon because it is inexpensive, rapid, flexible, and increasingly sophisticated. Once a manager learns how to use e-mail, a great leap in communication effectiveness should occur. Like all media, however, it's what managers do with it that really counts. In the final analysis, the power of the computer can be used to increase productivity or increase confusion and damage that result from poor use.

E-mail systems are available from most mainframe and minicomputer vendors as bundled-in office software, including IBM's *Profs* system and DEC's *All-in-One*. Lotus Corporation has been highly successful at marketing *Lotus Notes,* which is intended for microcomputers and has a GUI that makes electronic mail far easier for novice users. Novell, the network software giant, has its own network mail program, as do Microsoft and many others. Regardless of the specific e-mail system considered, managers should remember that e-mail is basically intended to link two individuals together to communicate. Simplicity, ease of use, and ability to understand the messages should be the most important criteria.

One groupware mode is called **computer conferencing.** In this form of communication, groups communicate across time (and generally across space) by sending messages to a central clearinghouse, where each message is sorted according to topic and perhaps according to work group. Members of work groups can access messages by topic name and read them at their leisure. Topics may either be set up in advance by a meeting manager or they may arise naturally because individual participants desire to create new topics. Messages are maintained generally in order of their receipt, so participants can read transcripts that simulate conversations among participants in a group. In some ways, meetings of this sort resemble large file folders into which correspondence is placed according to the folder title (topic, for example) and then kept in chronological order. Group members can read any message, find out whether there are new messages, review messages already seen, and create and add their own messages.

Computer conferencing may also be seen as a kind of **electronic bulletin board** ranging from the very private (e.g., a bulletin board for all municipal and regional tourism directors in a country) to the very public (e.g., entertainment, cultural, or academic bulletin boards for anyone who has access to the Internet). Availability of these bulletin boards presents a challenge to legal and administrative authorities because they are unregulated. Individuals may access them anonymously or identified, giving rise to the usual questions of privacy and responsibility that human communication engenders. The merging of computer, voice, and video technology provides enhanced environments for this sort of messaging and thus enhanced challenges to technology providers (software mostly) and regulators.

Thousands of computer bulletin boards are in use and the number grows daily. *Lotus Notes,* discussed in more detail later, also has a built-in bulletin board feature. Many firms are discovering the major benefits of electronic mail can be multiplied through bulletin boards, which means the problems are also multiplied. Because of the abundance of bulletin boards and the existence of many different threads on each board, it is possible to spend many hours each day just devouring the previous day's production. For managers with an information hunger, the banquet of fact and fancy available on these bulletin boards can be a productivity enhancer or a productivity defeater.

THE INTERNET

The **Internet** is the name given to an amorphous collection of networks, nodes, participants, list servers, mailing lists, vendors, VANs, files, and programs with 25,000,000 users and 100,000 nodes worldwide according to some estimates. Run loosely by a nonprofit corporation, the Internet grew on the foundation of *Arpanet* and has, in recent years, been growing at a fantastic rate. While the two greatest uses of the Internet have been e-mail and electronic bulletin boards, in recent years the Internet has become a massive database with software links in the form of such programs as file transfer protocol (ftp), telnet, gopher, World Wide Web (WWW), and Archie. These links allow users to access remote computers through their own operating systems (generally unix or unix-compatible systems such as IBM's *AIX*) or through GUIs found on micros. Most recent has been a commercial push both from VANs (including those operated by common carriers in most countries as well as private networks such as America On Line and CompuServe) to handle electronic mail and vendors wanting to sell everything from flowers to games to legal advice. Analogous to 900 phone numbers, the Internet has become the digital way to receive telephone services, only the variety is much larger because the Internet can carry images, sounds, and full-motion videos (although these videos generally cannot be viewed in real time because of the relative slowness of transmission lines connecting computers). The ethics of selling through a nonprofit network are strained, and most Internet discussion groups in which advertisements are placed seem to reject commercialization of the Internet. But there is no doubt that some portion of the Internet soon will be reserved for commercial enterprises ranging from infomercials to gopher-like service directories, remote billing, and computer-related data handling.

Internet services fall into these classes:

- Basic communication (e-mail, discussion groups)
- Value-added communication (mailing lists, list servers)
- Information retrieval (gopher, archie, World Wide Web)
- Technical services (Telnet and ftp)
- Commercial services, databases
- Software for surfing (web browsers, for example)
- EDI

Communication services create communities of interest by making it easy to contact other people either directly (through e-mail, mailing lists, and list servers) or indirectly (through headers in discussion groups). Information retrieval services facilitate locating and browsing information offered more or less publicly through file servers attached to nodes. Gopher is a menu-based program that lets users browse through trees of menus to look for the tender shoots of information embedded within. Archie and World Wide Web (WWW) are unix programs that help information seekers find the sources of information they desire. Having found the information, Internet surfers can use programs like ftp to transfer it from the file server on the located node to their own nodes or PCs, perhaps using a GUI such as *Mosaic* or *Netscape*. If one of the information sources is a commercial site, users have to register or provide billing information before they can retrieve the information, play the game, view the video, or analyze the data. The information superhighway is only just now in the process of being paved and it is still not very easy for nontechnically-minded managers and others to use. But with the development of GUIs, access to and through the Internet is becoming more transparent, and capable managers will be rewarded by the wealth of information and services becoming available.

Clearly, the Internet presents great opportunities for entrepreneurs to reach a large number of potential customers. The Internet could also facilitate a variety of new business interactions among groups that are not yet considered effective players in business: multifirm work groups, international task forces, multilingual consortia, anonymous work groups, and even groups that include automated processes such as production facilities as "equal" participants. Indeed, business on the 'Net is the hot topic of the 1990s.

Doing Business on the Internet

The most exciting development in Internet services is the World Wide Web (WWW). The Web, essentially a network of databases, is like gopher in this regard (which is a menu of menus). However, the Web is a **hyperdatabase,** which allows relatively free movement from database to database through hyperlinks. In addition, the Web is more attractive because it contains not only text, but also sound, graphics, and video as well as programming such as guest books to be signed or e-mail interfaces. Software for navigating the Web (called a *web client*) such as *Mosaic, Web Explorer,* or *Netscape* provides easy GUI access for users. As with most other Internet clients, the major jobs of Web clients are twofold: (1) locate information in the Web and (2) display it in the appropriate format. Web servers are identified by addresses (known also as Universal Record Locators or URLs) such as http://www.whitehouse.gov, for example. These servers store hypermedia pages and Web clients navigate the Web to request the pages users want and display them. Most organizations create home pages that identify the organization to visitors (for example, http://*www.ucalgary.ca*/UofC/faculties/Mgmt). The server is denoted in italics and links to the home page are separated by slashes. Most netware allows access either through the server's address or directly by naming the home page. Thus, to get to the home page in the example, a visitor might "travel" to the server (where the University of Calgary's home page, /UofC, is displayed) and make the rest of the trip via hyperlinks first to "faculties" and then to "Mgmt"; alternatively, the visitor can use the full address and go directly to the home page.

Either way, users have the ability (as they do with gopher, veronica, and archie) to travel where they desire. In this sort of network, prospective customers call up a businesses home page and receive information on what the business has to offer. Growth of business on the Web has been spectacular, with many Fortune 1,000 corporations and many more small businesses (not all limited to information technology products and services) now available. Some businesses merely present information, often for free, as advertising. Others, however, offer more sophisticated, interactive services, which can range from simple logbook signing (useful for knowing who has visited) to requests for printed or faxed information, to purchasing of products or services charged with credit cards, to joining mailing lists, to requesting job applications.

As with any computer- and network-based business, there are pros and cons. Writing in an issue of *Datamation,* William Semich describes them this way:

Pros	Cons
Ease to create materials through HyperText Markup Language (HTML)	Technology is not mature
	Incompatibilities among competing technologies
Easy to navigate around the Web	Little experience in the commercial arena
Small economic barriers to entry	Clients and servers do not offer security
Software is inexpensive and available to clients and servers	Not necessarily compatible with corporate IS
Operating system independent	Speed may be a problem
Can replace phone and fax	
Multimedia is an obvious advantage in marketing	

The major advantage of computer business seems to be low entry costs. Because the Web grew out of an academic effort in 1989 rather than a commercial venture, client and server applications generally have been free of cost. Semich estimates that entry to the Web can be had for as little as $1,000 upfront and $600 per year up to more than $15,000 upfront and $30,000 per year for a sophisticated offering. However, the Web was not designed with commerce in mind (neither was the Internet) and there is little infrastructure to support business. Several free Web clients are available, but prospective Web vendors have had to supply their own software to support applications such as transaction processing. Security on the Internet is lax, discouraging customers from using credit card numbers and PINs. Market research is limited because, while there are perhaps as many as 25 million Internet users, general market research data are not applicable to such a small segment. Compared to services offered through telecommunication providers (such as EDI), the Web seems undeveloped and insecure. Larry Marion points out these five security threats, still generally unaddressed on the Web:

- Authentication: proof of ID
- Certification: proof that the ID is correct
- Confirmation: receipts for services or goods
- Nonrepudiation: holding buyers and sellers to their agreements
- Encryption: keeping transactions secret from others

Smart cards seem a likely route to correct many of these problems, but the Internet will never be a secure network (such as those used by airlines and governments). EDI and value-added network (VAN) offerings are more secure, but they are slower and not available to the general public. While there may be 40,000 companies using EDI, there are 500 times as many users of the Internet, few of which have EDI capabilities or are willing to pay for them. Also, EDI requires specialized client software; the Web does not.

Companies that intend to do business on the Internet, either through WWW, e-mail, discussion groups, or mailing lists, should consider the following:

- Ethical considerations that guide purveyors of junk mail may apply on the Internet, as electronic junk mail clogs up network arteries with unsolicited information and consumes already limited user time.
- Pressure to create complex and impressive displays of text, graphics, sound, and moving images drives up costs considerably both for vendors and users; user band width is quite limited, and many users will not want to wait a long time to see what the vendor has to offer.
- Interaction gives the *appearance* of attention to the customer, but businesses must follow through with actual attention, including accuracy, reliability, promptness, and services tailored to customers' needs.
- Web users travel to a business, so publicity is key; if users don't know where the business is, they can't find it. Web directories are in their infancy, however, and word of mouth has an entirely different meaning on the Internet.
- Web technology is sure to change. Any technological advantage a business has quickly passes and the business will be forced to spend money to catch up once it uses the Internet to sell or service.

- Alternate forms of commerce (stores, buying clubs, direct mail) will adopt and adapt Internet technologies to compete and their basic mode of doing business is far more well known, reliable, and widespread.

WORK GROUP–ORIENTED GROUPWARE

Work group–oriented groupware occupies the middle ground between GSS (formal meetings) and e-mail and its relatives' (loose, message, and data oriented) communities. Work groups focus on work tasks and their management and depend on integrated communication functions to share information, schedule interactions, and structure meetings about critical data. Work group applications also tend to integrate a variety of communications media, including telephone and facsimile, into a user group's workspace. Because of this architectural integration, work group systems are easily compared to a manager's information workbench (Chapter 7).

Several varieties of groupware are available commercially. *Lotus Notes* works on a foundation of enterprisewide electronic mail and data-sharing capability. Microsoft is approaching work group software by adding network capability to its latest product, *Windows '95*. Novell offers *GroupWise* as an adjunct to its network operating system called *NetWare*. DEC markets *LinkWorks* based on its strong application development tools. Other vendors are integrating through their strong database packages (e.g., *Oracle Office*) and fault-tolerance capabilities (e.g., IBM *WorkGroup*). What these groupware products have in common is group support at several levels and the promise of easy extension of support to higher levels such as computational or even operational. Work group support is based on the idea that workers in groups interact over task-critical data that they share, critique, and revise. Managers of work groups are concerned with tracking work progress and controlling resources without stifling creativity or artificially limiting production. Hence, work group applications tend to perform the following functions:

- Enterprisewide electronic mail, external gateways, and discussion groups
- Integration of phone and fax with desktop information processing, offering relatively seamless movement of data through a variety of forms and modes among members of a work group
- Easy, intuitive sharing of task-critical documents such as reports, definitions, memos, and working papers
- Management of task and project information creation, updating, version management, cataloging, distribution, and disposal
- Task and project management, including scheduling and commitments and work flow management on standardized forms
- A structure for protection of critical information and shielding of critical interactions
- Desktop video, still in rudimentary form
- Group documents (a feature of GSS)

These functions are often made available through vendor-supplied products that are coordinated by communication-based groupware. Few commercial products offer more than a subset of these functions directly at a price of $70 to $750 per user. An interesting aspect of some work group products is the capability for users to create their own applications by using a scripting language; however, this is an expensive feature that most users will not want to take advantage of.

How might an organization use work group products? Burger King Corporation developed nine scenarios that it has used to evaluate competing groupware. Here are a few of them:

- *Job change:* Scan the appropriate bulletin board, retrieve the correct application form, fill in as much information automatically as possible, send the form to the correct person
- *Discussion document:* Create a document, distribute it to everyone concerned, receive and collate returning comments
- *Information update:* Receive information from franchisee about store, update store information folder, distribute information to regional management

To perform these and the other six scenarios, one groupware product required seven components, five of which were not integral to the system and two of which were not available commercially at the time of the evaluation. The other product required ad hoc integration of 17 components, 4 of which weren't commercially available. In spite of these products' complexity, the trend is clearly toward this sort of integration.

RESEARCH IN GROUP SYSTEMS: MANAGEMENT OPPORTUNITIES

The use of groupware is quite new. While computer conferencing has been around since the 1960s pioneering work by Murray Turoff, face-to-face electronic meeting facilitation is very recent. There are still a lot of questions being asked about all forms of groupware including designs, implementation, and value. Some of the major questions that have been posed and are being reviewed in the research literature include these:

- In what situations are what forms of groupware most useful? Which tools are best for which tasks (such as generating solutions or determining the best solution)?
- What effects do the nature, competence, participants' attitudes, the type of task being performed, and the size of the group have on the quality and quantity of the results?
- What are the significant problems with the various commercial products?
- What functions or features would be useful in these products and in which business situations? How can groupware be evaluated in general?
- In what circumstances is the value of anonymity, parallelism, rapid feedback, and structure lessened or enhanced?

These questions are being answered in an attempt to improve the quality of groupware and to maximize use of these systems to support groups of managers. Research questions lead us directly into the next chapter, "Evaluating Management Support Systems and Usability." Jonathan Grudin points out the difficulty in evaluating groupware: Whereas a system intended to support an individual may fail because an individual fails to learn to use it or the system is difficult to use, complex systems involving cooperation and group interaction require many users to become adept and to buy into the process. As any meeting facilitator can attest, it is relatively easy to torpedo a meeting and thereby taint the process by which future meetings are conducted. This is why facilitators have to work so hard.

When groupware succeeds, it's hard to know just why. Evaluating groupware requires an approach similar to anthropology to understand the complex interaction and social, economic, psychological, and political dynamics and motivations of the participants. Groupware benefits go to specific managers rather than group participants, and this knowledge can easily change the dynamics of interaction and can affect outcome. The potential for failure of GSSs, based on group dynamics, contrasts noticeably with the successes of electronic mail and bulletin boards, which do not require group buy-in, group spirit, or face-to-face group dynamics. E-mail users are free to be as idiosyncratic, inept, or obnoxious as they like (this is also encouraged in a GSS) because the benefits and costs are their own. In the end, the major benefit of groupware may be simply that participants feel free to be themselves in whatever mode they appear.

The Modern Management Imperatives

Reach: Global Competition	Global competition means global alliances. Organizations that are spread around the world, either physically or through business links, require cooperative tools. Distances and time zones make such cooperation formal and difficult. GSSs and e-mail bridge these gaps.
Reaction: Quick Customer Feedback on Products and Services	Traditional market research brought customers together as focus groups to discuss products and services. New technologies can put together e-mail panels, GSS sessions, bulletin boards, and other electronic communities to discuss the same products and services.
Responsiveness: Shortened Concept-to-Customer Cycle Time	Customers can be brought into the design and development cycle directly through bulletin boards and other electronic forums. Setting up user groups or design panels is relatively simple. Within a firm, electronic communication can break down walls that divide organizations because of tradition or job responsibilities and thus speed up product/service development. Managers can manage the process more effectively with electronic tools.
Refinement: Greater Customer Sophistication and Specificity	Customers are becoming smarter—what they know (and you don't) can help you if you can get this information. Electronic highways make it easier to get this information from customers and may, in the future, make it easier for you to get your messages to them. Sophisticated analysis tools available in GSSs make it easier to use customers' increased knowledge in positive ways.
Reconfiguration: Reengineering of Work Patterns and Structures	Working electronically is becoming more widespread as people engage in at-home work or distributed work (sometimes called work flow). Some organizations exist on paper only, using information media to coordinate their virtual work force.
Redeployment: Reorganization and Redesign of Resources	Computer-based project management is moving from analogs of paper used to track progress to more cooperative tools that use tickler files, schedulers, and analytical modeling and simulation to make suggestions to workers.
Reputation: Quality and Reliability of Product and Process	Because quality is a function of expectation as well as performance, cooperation plays two roles in producing quality. First, it makes coordination of work easier, especially when comparing it with plans, while cutting down on unnecessary travel or data seeking. Second, GSSs and e-mail can be used to incorporate customer expectations into design and development, thereby reducing that gap.

■ SUPPORTING GROUPS AT THE CARMART

Trish is keen to use technology to uncover ideas on how to beat the competition. She has read that it is possible to bring people together in a room or in a number of places to discuss electronically an idea or problem simultaneously or over time. A group could trigger ideas from each other—Trish knows this from her experiences with brainstorming—and then the ideas could be more closely considered and the best ones chosen. One thing Trish is concerned about is whether the 20 or so salespeople she is considering consulting will really be able to work together. They're so individualistic—it's the commission nature of car sales, she thinks. Paul, who was very helpful with technology before, says he can arrange a trial session at the local university, where a friend of his works in a group support systems facility. However, another fear that Trish has is whether the results will be any better than a suggestion box. What exactly will this option buy her for her $2,500-per-day meeting? What are the risks and the benefits? ■

1. What are the risks and benefits involved in using this sort of group system? How would using a same-time/same-place system stack up against a different-time/different-place system, a suggestion box, or a facilitated brainstorming session?

2. Assume that Trish and Paul arrange a day-long meeting. What agenda would you advise them to put together, given the sorts of tools you know are available?

3. How should Trish measure the effectiveness of using a GSS (in whatever mode and using whatever agenda they decide) to meet the competition?

Summary

Teamwork and group interaction are becoming increasingly important as business challenges become more complex and require the skills of many individuals working together. Groups can also be supported in their management activities. Several kinds of products (loosely termed *groupware*) are available to provide support at various levels. A group support system helps groups reach conclusions, often in meetings. Groupware-aided meetings are different from face-to-face meetings in that they allow for anonymity, parallel participation, rapid feedback of results, increased meeting structure, and the ability to handle information on-line during a meeting. These characteristics can increase participation, lower barriers to innovation, and make meetings run more quickly, while providing for enhanced capture of ideas and potential solutions. With groupware, meetings can be held at a single site or many sites as well at a given time or across a span of time. Brainstorming, idea structuring, group outlining and writing, and voting can be done on-line. Tools such as electronic mail and bulletin boards allow for mailing lists and discussion groups. Some of the facilities of the Internet can support businesses, too. Work group–oriented groupware is intended to support small teams and their managers, typically within a department or firm. Groupware research consistently shows that such systems provide effective support to existing managerial activities. However, the research raises questions about the kinds of support that should be provided as well as the tasks that are best supported through such technology.

Discussion Questions

9.1 In what way(s) is group support different from the support of individuals? What kinds of tasks are inherently group-oriented and what kind are not? Isn't supporting a group the same as supporting the individuals in the group?

9.2 Most meeting support software is used with the hope that the solutions to the group's problems already exist within the group's numbers and can be elicited, somehow, from them. Do you agree with this assumption? If not, what kinds of tools could be used in a group to create, rather than elicit, solutions?

9.3 In what ways do formal meetings, the users of bulletin boards, and work groups differ with regard to the tasks they typically perform? Does information play a different role for each type of group? What kinds of advice would these three kinds of groups seek? Which would be most effective?

Key Terms

anonymity	electronic meeting	Internet
chauffeured system	facilitator	keypad system
computer conferencing	file transfer	level of group support
computer-supported cooperative work (CSCW)	flaming	list server
	group support system (GSS)	meeting structure
divergent/convergent tool	groupware	participant feedback
electronic bulletin board	hyperdatabase	participation parallelism
electronic mail (e-mail)	information-handling tool	

References

Alavi, Maryam. "Group Decision Support Systems: A Key to Business Team Productivity." *Journal of Information Systems Management* (Summer 1991): 36–41.

Appleton, E. "Recruiting on the Internet." *Datamation* 41, 14 (August 1, 1995): 39–41.

Bales, R. *Interaction Process Analysis.* Reading, MA: Addison-Wesley, 1951.

Baum, David. "Groupware: Is It Notes or Nothing?" *Datamation* 41, 8 (May 1, 1995): 45–48.

Branham Consulting Group, Inc. *Things Change, Economies Evolve: Are You Prepared.* Mississauga, ONT: The Information Technology Association of Canada, December 1992.

Dennis, A., J. George, L. Jessup, J. Nunamaker, and D. Vogel. "Information Technology to Support Electronic Meetings." *MIS Quarterly* 12, 4 (1988) 491–624.

Dennis, A., J. Nunamaker, and D. Vogel. "A Comparison of Laboratory and Field Research in the Study of Electronic Meeting Systems." *Journal of Management Information Systems* 7, 3 (Winter 1990–1991): 107–135.

DeSanctis, G., and B. Gallupe. "A Foundation for the Study of Group Decision Support Systems." *Management Science* 33 (1987): 589–609.

———. "Group Decision Support Systems: A New Frontier." *Data Base* (Winter 1985): 3–10.

Fischer, D. "Electronic Mail," in R. Drummond, ed., *Data Communications for the Office.* New York: Bantam, 1993, 57–104.

Gray, P. "Group Decision Support Systems." *Decision Support Systems* 3 (1987): 233–242.

Grudin, J. "Why Groupware Applications Fail." *Office: Technology & People* 4, 3 (1989): 245–264.

Hiltz, S., and M. Turoff. *The Network Nation: Human Communication Via Computer.* Reading, MA: Addison-Wesley, 1979.

Holsapple, C. "Decision Support in Multiparticipant Decision Makers." *The Journal of Computer Information Systems* (Summer 1991): 37–45.

Huber, G. "Issues in the Design of Group Decision Support Systems." *MIS Quarterly* 8, 2 (September 1984): 195–204.

Jessup, L., T. Connolly, and J. Galegher. "The Effects of Anonymity on GDSS Group Process with an Idea-Generating Task." *MIS Quarterly* 14, 3 (September 1990): 313–321.

Johansen, R., J. Vailee, and K. Spangler. *Electronic Meetings*. Reading, MA: Addison-Wesley, 1979.

Marion, Larry. "Who's Guarding the Till at the CyberMall?" *Datamation* 41, 3 (February 15, 1995): 38–41.

Rollins, C. "The Impact of Teleconferencing on the Leadership of Small Decision-Making Groups." *Journal of Organizational Behavior Management* 10, 2 (1990): 37–52.

Semich, J. William. "The World Wide Web: Internet Boomtown?" *Datamation* 41, 1 (January 15, 1995): 37–41.

Short, J., E. Williams, and B. Christie. *The Social Psychology of Telecommunications*. New York: John Wiley and Sons, 1976.

Siegel, J., V. Dubrovsky, S. Kiesler, and T. McGuire. "Group Processes in Computer-Mediated Communication." *Organizational Behavior and Human Decision Processes* 37 (1986): 157–187.

The, Lee. "Need Groupware? Think Function, Not Products." *Datamation* 41, 11 (July 15, 1995): 67–74.

Vogel, D., J. Nunamaker, W. Martz, W. Grohowski, and C. McGoff. "Electronic Meeting System Experience at IBM." *Journal of Management Information Systems* 6, 3 (Winter 1989–1990): 25–43.

Zigurs, I., M. Scott Poole, and G. DeSanctis. "A Study of Influence in Computer-Mediated Group Decision Making." *MIS Quarterly* 12 (December 1988): 625–644.

CASE

EVERGREEN LANDSCAPING AND MAINTENANCE: PRODUCING THE CRISIS MANAGEMENT PLAN

President Lily Doucette's crisis management system may be valuable to her, but she is worried that without immediate access to a lot of people and data, crisis management may be too much for Evergreen. She is especially concerned that a physical crisis, such as a fire or a flood, may endanger the records she needs or make the people she has to contact inaccessible. And the final concern is resources—is a crisis management system actually worth the cost to her and Evergreen in time and money? Because the MEC has approved Lily's plans for expansion to a second retail site, enhancement of the research program, and negotiations with Pindar Gopal to act as a broker for Evergreen, Lily's concerns are complicated by the distances involved in maintaining these planned relationships.

(In Chapter 6, you answered a number of questions about the telecommunications architecture of Evergreen's information processing, including how plans for expansion might influence this architecture. Please review that case before continuing with this one.)

While the crisis management subcommittee of the MEC has met several times to create a crisis management plan, not much progress has been made. Not only are the members of the committee very busy during this high season, they don't feel they have a good idea of what physical and supplier crises would do to the firm—that is, what the various possibilities and probabilities for crises are and appropriate responses. They would like to find out from front-line workers and supervisors, such as Connie Somerset, Bill Porter, Byron Todd, and Candice Robbins, what they think and what their plans are. In addition, Lily's concerns about the expansion mean getting not only information systems specialists Terry Bonner and Dierdre Tilton involved with the information systems aspects but also calling in Boris Pomfrit, a consultant who has been guiding Lily on telecommunications matters connected with the expansion.

Of some distress to Lily is the fact that while the MEC subcommittee is working to please George & Son (to keep insurance rates reasonable) and the banks (to keep loan rates reasonable), those who would have to respond in a crisis are really focused on day-to-day problems. In addition, there are hundreds of part-time workers who have no long-term commitment to Evergreen. Managers at Connie's level (sales manager) at Evergreen bear the brunt of making things happen. However, from conversations with Connie, Lily knows that Connie thinks that she is *always* fending off crises and that people such as Sven and Sid (retail sales manager and control manager, respectively) would have nothing to do with creating such a plan if they thought that they were going to get all of the responsibility without any authority—and little say about what goes into the crisis management plan.

Lily has compiled her concerns into this list:

■ Maintaining current data on the state of the company, its customers, employees, and suppliers and the state of its resources (products, physical plant, contracts)

■ Maintaining contact with key decision makers during crises

■ Creating a valid crisis management plan that wins approval of George & Son and its creditors

■ Keeping that plan current

■ Getting key staff to buy into the crisis management plan and its implementation as a crisis management system

■ Building a crisis management system and keeping it up-to-date

■ Testing the plan and the system

These concerns will be discussed at the next MEC meeting. Lily wonders what her options are.

Questions

1. What advantages would a GSS session or series of sessions be to Lily in deriving and maintaining a crisis management plan? What aspects of a GSS would be of special advantage here?

2. Suggest a three-session series of GSS meetings that would assist Lily in creating an effective crisis management plan. The first session is concerned with defining crisis management and Evergreen's values in responding to whatever the crisis causes. The second session details risks and options. The third session designs a first draft of the plan, deciding on the content of the plan and assigning responsibilities for improving the plan. Who would attend these sessions? What sort of computer-based tools would be valuable to use? What might the positive and negative effects be of using an electronic meeting system? What kinds of follow-up would prove valuable?

3. What role could electronic mail and bulletin boards play in helping Lily create and maintain a crisis management plan?

4. What kinds of interorganizational systems would you recommend be included in the crisis management system? (Refer to Chapter 6.)

CHAPTER TEN

EVALUATING MANAGEMENT SUPPORT SYSTEMS AND USABILITY

After you have read and studied this chapter, you should be able to:

■ Discuss why it's important to evaluate management support systems.

■ Describe five ways in which the quality of a management support system matters to firms and managers.

■ Discuss why usability is important and describe ways of judging the usability of management support systems.

■ Understand the role, function, and types of standards that operate in the area of management support systems.

Question 1: How is the support that management systems provide evaluated? What are the benefits of such evaluation and what are the hurdles?

"Our prices speak volumes!" "A pleased customer is our only customer!" "If you can get it for less, you'll have to buy less!" These and other similarly enthusiastic slogans poster the staff lounge at Dollar Company, a discount wholesaler to the public. June Chen is the general manager of the Bank Street store, where several thousand customers shop daily, snapping up bargains. June is not much amazed at the sloppy slogans the company's board turns out, but she is concerned about the information systems that have been installed in the past three years. Not only have the cashiers, purchasing agents, and warehouse staff been computerized (who would argue about that?), but almost everything else, too, has been computerized. From member registration to servicing of the cars Dollar now sells, everything goes into the computer. Buyers get advice, customers get entertaining newsletters and personalized buying lists, and employees get reminded about high-turnover items. June uses some of these systems in her own work, as do most of the managers at Dollar Company. But June wonders if anyone really knows whether these systems are worth it.

Answer: Systems are evaluated in terms of economics (will they return money?), personal factors (will users like them?), social factors (will they fit in with how people work and interact?), physical constraints (can they be used in any event?), and organizational factors (will they fit into organizational culture?). In each case, it is difficult to find exact measures, but firms using information systems should be constantly aware of the importance of these factors.

Q u e s t i o n 2 : What makes an information system usable? What design principles are at work? What processes or activities do users engage in that managers ought to know about?

Angrily, Ken O'Callahan stabs away at the Esc key, hoping that something might happen. Of course, nothing does. Then Ken presses the F1, F2, F3, and F4 keys in sequence. A beep. So the little freak inside the screen doesn't like F4! Well, take another one! And another, and another, and . . . "OK, Ken, get hold of yourself, it's only a machine. But I hate this machine!" It's impossible to know what to do because there are no manuals, nobody has been trained, and the system has been changed many times. And it's so illogical; screens with important information disappear before you can write it down or other screens appear with information repeated from previous work. You can't stop it anywhere and get a summary or get things prioritized in date, cost, or any other order. As a manager, Ken knows that responsibility should not exceed authority, but the system seems to want you to know everything to get anything. How are his employees going to create and produce the reports Ken needs with this system?

A n s w e r : It will not be easy. First, Ken has to understand why he is frustrated with this system that violates seven important design principles. Because employees have to use the system, it should be designed with five interfaces (cultural, social, cognitive, perceptual, and physical) in mind. Ken should understand that some of his problems stem from the fact that the system is really inhuman, it is not designed for real people with real cognitive limitations, and it does not involve standard procedures and shared standards.

INTRODUCTION

Previous chapters have defined management support and applications that support managers. The natural challenge that arises, therefore, is how to evaluate a management support system. What criteria should be used? How do we measure these criteria? Do we apply different criteria in different circumstances and, if so, how? How do we make choices among systems? Are these choices made the same way all the time? These questions are related to the general problem of evaluation. **Evaluation** *is* a problem in management support because managers are usually dealing with very complex systems of procedures, software, data, and hardware. Also, these systems change over time. Managers frequently participate in some way in the design, specification, or purchase of these systems, but their involvement is often peripheral before the systems appear yet essential thereafter.

Evaluation is important to managers at three different times. First, they may be asked to participate in a design exercise (Chapters 12 through 14) for a management support system they require. Evaluation of systems at this time poses a problem because the system doesn't yet exist. On the other hand, mistakes at this time can lead to costly reworking, rebuilding, or junking of systems later. A system may not be feasible or even advisable. If systems are purchased off-the-shelf from a store or consulting firm, managers have to arrive at the demonstration with a robust evaluation scheme in hand in order to resist the blandishments of salespeople and do a valid evaluation.

A second time to evaluate a management support system occurs when a system is being created. Managers may be called on to judge whether a management support system meets their needs, capabilities, and expectations. Because others may be potential users, these evaluations are often done by an individual manager on behalf of others. This poses additional dilemmas for managers who represent work groups. When managers are parts of teams that build systems or are even project managers, evaluation becomes an integral part of managing the system creation.

Finally, managers may evaluate systems after they are installed. This may mean investigating organizational, social, and economic impacts as well as more personal and physical effects, both positive and negative.

Three important topics comprise this chapter. First, we look at the problem of evaluation generally. Next, we turn our attention to one of the most obvious factors in the evaluation of management support systems: usability. Following close behind functionality (whether the MSS actually does the job), usability is key—what can't be used won't be used. Finally, we examine the concept of information system standards. Standards make it easier to evaluate and select management support systems by reducing the number of choices and by preselecting evaluation criteria.

Our model of system evaluation is portrayed in Figure 10–1. For each given user or organization, characteristics of that system, along with some contribution from expectations, determine the perceived performance of the system. This **performance** may be thought of in terms of how useful or usable a system is, how much benefit is obtained from using it, what its costs or drawbacks are, and so forth. If **expectations** are met or exceeded, the manager or organization will be satisfied with the MSS. Users judge or rate the system according to their own idiosyncratic measures. One manager may value appearance while another may value cost. In the context of standards by which such systems are made and marketed, these judgments yield an evaluation. A series of evaluations may alter expectations, and these expectations may actually change how a manager uses an MSS, thus subtly or not so subtly altering performance later. This cyclical model of evaluation gives us the structure of this chapter.

Chapter 18 presents a more elaborate view of technology innovation and adoption than does this model. However, even this simple scheme motivates two discussions: What is quality and how do perceptions of quality rise? and What dictates what managers need or perceive themselves to need? The first discussion is the focus of this chapter while the second is the core issue of Module 3, "Managing Risk in the Application Life Cycle."

QUALITY EVALUATION

Quality has been defined in many ways, but inevitably it comes down to a comparison of customer expectations (or needs) with perceived performance. Where expectations are related to customer needs and where performance exceeds expectations, customers judge the product to be of high quality. Where these expectations are not met, customers generally judge the product to be of low quality. If expectations are unrelated to needs, quality evaluations are often unclear or unreliable. The higher the expectations that are met, the higher the judgment of quality.

Of course, there are instances when this definition may fall short. For example, if a customer has low standards, the product being evaluated may actually be faulty but still be judged to be of high quality. In other cases, customers may judge the quality of a product to be low if they have higher standards. For purposes of our discussion, let us assume that managers who are making quality judgments have standards dictated by their work

Figure 10–1 MSS EXPECTATIONS, STANDARDS, USABILITY, AND EVALUATION

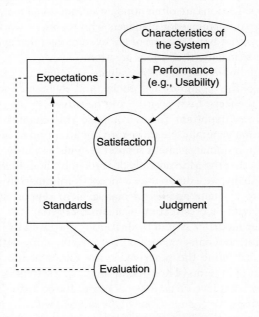

environments. In later chapters, especially those in Module 4, we will speak more about organizations and work groups. In these cases, standards that dictate quality judgment are shared standards developed by a group.

If we are to evaluate management support systems using a quality evaluation umbrella, we have to understand managers' needs (the topic of Modules 1 and 2 and Chapter 13), the performance of the management support systems, and how managers form expectations of systems. Managers work in many environments simultaneously and have complex needs; thus, evaluating management support means asking questions in five distinct areas (see Figure 10–2):

- *Organizational:* Can the organization use and profit from this system?
- *Social:* Will this system fit into the society and culture of the organization?
- *Economic:* Can we afford this system? Is it a good investment?
- *Physical:* Can the system be used? Will it fit into the space and procedures set aside for it?
- *Personal:* Will the system be liked; will employees see value in using it? Will it be used as intended? Can it be used creatively or improved on by users?

These **levels of evaluation** move progressively closer to the individual. The further removed from a manager an evaluation measure is, the more objective it is. As evaluation moves closer to individuals, it becomes more difficult to suggest specific measures because the value of management support becomes more idiosyncratic and more sensitive to individual differences, moods, and values.

| Figure 10–2 | FIVE WAYS TO EVALUATE MSS |

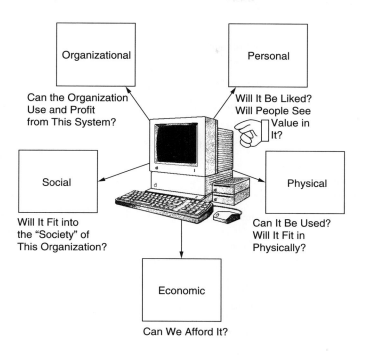

Organizational Factors

At the organizational level (Table 10–1), we are concerned with how well a system provides the needed support to meet organizational goals. Does the system augment or assist the bottom line? Is it aligned with strategic goals? In other words, does it fit with the type of business the organization is engaged in? Hence, evaluation of a system amounts to weighing its contribution to goals. This evaluation is often the goal of a system audit and more specifically with systems analysis, the first phase of the application life cycle (see Chapter 12). Many techniques are used at this level, including a detailed feasibility analysis and a variety of diagrammatic techniques, yet the primary method used is to compare organizational goals with system outputs (sometimes called goal analysis). Additional methods include critical success factors analysis and related techniques. The primary investigative method is interviewing stakeholders and prospective users about their goals and methods.

Information systems are hard to evaluate at all levels, but special difficulties unique to the organizational level include the following:

- There is no established IS tradition as there is in, say, engineering or office management in which it is easy to recognize what fits with goals.

- Information is not a tangible resource like money or materiel, which are easily weighed, located in a fixed site, form, or format, and are easy to

Table 10–1	EVALUATING MANAGEMENT SUPPORT SYSTEMS AT AN ORGANIZATIONAL LEVEL	

Phenomenon at This Level	Risks/Problems	Opportunities
No established IS tradition exists	Difficult to determine what fits or meets established standards	Standard setting, education
Information is not a tangible resource	Difficult to measure information	Becoming aware of the value of information, reengineering
Technology changes	Use styles change; there may be fads, too	Development or awareness of the need for organizational standards
Information effects are not uniform or stable across the whole organization	Evaluation depends on whom you ask and when	Creation of audit procedures; awareness of differences
IS often controlled by individuals not seen as loyalists	Evaluation may not be relevant or politically astute; it may be slanted to technological needs	Integration of IS into firm culture; development of cultural linkages between IS and its clients
Management support systems enable others to be more productive	Difficult to measure effects of MSS directly	Increased awareness of the role and function of management support systems
Systems age and become less strategic	Organizational impact decreases and existing evaluations become less valid	Examination of strategic portfolio; development of measures of strategic impact
Systems interact but evaluations may be narrowly focused	Interaction effect of whole portfolio may be lost	Development of portfolio evaluation; better planning methods; focus on strategic impact
People ignore systems already paid for	Few are interested in evaluating systems that are already running	Life cycle evaluation; merging with quality management procedures
Some firms express their goals poorly	Vague or nonexistent goals are useless in evaluation	Emphasis on goal-driven development of management support systems can spur corporate goal-setting

guard and store; information is easy to copy or steal and its absence may not be noticed.

- **Technological changes** occur and an organization's information uses and styles change rapidly.
- Information affects the whole organization in unpredictable and nonuniform ways, unlike traditional resources whose effects are generally well known and controllable.
- Historically, IS has been in the hands of technicians and not organizational specialists. IS workers are not seen as loyalists, whose political views and backgrounds are in consonance with the organization as a whole. In fact, IS technicians have always been seen—and, in general, are not

uncomfortable being seen—as organizational outsiders whose interests side with the technology, not the organization's goals or work.

- The effects and value of information are neither well known nor measurable. IS audits are related to security checks and performance evaluation. There is no field corresponding to organizational behavior for information. We know little about how information "behaves." A management support system doesn't have an individual return on investment but instead enables others (such as managers) to perform better.

- Today's strategic use of IS will be tomorrow's old hat. As IS uses rapidly evolve, evaluations go out of date very quickly.

- It's unclear how to evaluate individual systems and then combine these evaluations into an evaluation of a portfolio. Hence, it's doubly difficult to evaluate individual systems.

- Another inhibitor is that, having already spent money, managers feel it is better to move on to the next project instead of investing more time and effort on the completed one. This cripples organizational learning and, of course, simply puts off the benefits of evaluation.

- Finally, firms that have poorly expressed goals present an even more difficult evaluation problem.

Thus, when we evaluate management support systems at the organizational level, we must recognize that we are dealing with **nontraditional measurements** of **intangible resources** that change rapidly and affect an organization in unpredictable ways. We should acknowledge that trusting others, especially IS professionals, to make this evaluation involves a leap of faith. It's important to understand that any hard figures put on organizational evaluations are both imprecise and quickly obsolete. It may be easy to create such measures and apply them across the organization; however, we must be aware that they will always remain controversial and at least partly invalid.

Social Factors

Evaluating information systems at the social level (Table 10–2) requires that we first understand the society within which we are working and how its culture functions. This means we have to come to grips with problems and opportunities affecting divisions and departments and the cultural institutions they have set up. This may require studying groups and how they behave (something we don't understand very well in general). Another need is to find out what a group's values are and how these values change. A third approach is to research what people do symbolically and politically as distinct from their behavior as employees working by the book. That is, we have to understand informal culture as opposed to what the textbooks—the procedures manuals—say. Most important, managers have to grasp how technology changes the lives and behaviors of people in groups.

Hence, managers are interested in questions such as how a specific system changes the **reward system** of an organization. Who is rewarded for what accomplishments? Who is punished for failures? What is an accomplishment? How is failure judged? Other important questions are how a management support system affects group communication patterns, leadership within a group, and the metabolism of a group (making it work harder or faster).

Table 10–2	EVALUATING MANAGEMENT SUPPORT SYSTEMS AT A SOCIAL LEVEL

Phenomenon at This Level	Risks/Problems	Opportunities
Technology changes social relationships	New modes or methods of communication are untested or difficult to measure	Understanding of organizational communication; becoming more aware of new channels and their effects
Technology shapes its users	People are affected differently, hence, overall impact or effect is difficult to predict or measure	Understanding how technology changes individuals in a social context.
Users may employ systems faithfully or ironically	Use may not be according to design or intention; problems can result that are unanticipated	Innovation in work processes; development of new systems based on new ways of working
Information technology is essential to organizational communication	Rapid change means unanticipated or uncomfortable changes in communication patterns	Awareness of the role of technology in organizational communication
Computers have become appliances	Individuals may be judged or judge themselves by the systems they use and the products they produce	Awareness of information styles may lead to new corporate standards
Some systems may become status symbols even as computers become appliances	Users may judge information use in terms of status rather than usefulness, effectiveness, or real value related to work	Awareness of the social roles of information systems
Human generations and computer generations don't match	Stratification of the corporate society into older and younger generations, perhaps leading to conflict	Offer of training; sensitivity to needs of different generations of users

Clearly, these are complex questions. Consider a system that supports a manager in organizational communication, making it easy for the manager to disseminate ideas to others for opinions using a consensus system (the lowest and least sophisticated form of management support). Such a system may run counter to established, mandated traditional lines of authority, enabling the manager to circumvent established channels. This can have an enormous effect on higher-level managers accustomed to approving ideas before others in their organization have a chance to comment on them. The system can increase creativity at the price of lowering, at least temporarily, the effectiveness of leadership.

On the other hand, such a system may make it easier for a manager to make rash judgments. E-mail, for example, is known to distort the emotional tone of a message, enabling some people to be far more frank than they might be face-to-face. In the extreme, this is called flaming, and many have been more than contrite when they realize that they have insulted people they don't even know. On the other hand, having a written record of such rash judgments may quickly stifle not only counterproductive flaming but also put a chill on other more productive and less disruptive communication. Such phenomena show clearly that management support systems can have unpredictable or unexpected effects through the social system far out of proportion of the actual support they provide to managers.

Evaluating management support systems at the social level poses peculiar challenges to managers:

- Technology directly changes **social relationships,** as the example points out, by providing new modes of communication.
- People use technology but are in turn shaped by it. Also, different people are shaped differently because everyone has a unique approach to technology and learns how to use it uniquely.
- A technology can be used either faithfully (as its designers or developers intended) or ironically (in some way not intended by designers or developers). The usage style can determine opportunities that can shape or influence the norms of a group the manager works with.
- Much of today's information technology is an essential part of an organizational communication system, and thus already part of organizational culture, yet it changes rapidly, generally leading the culture down unexplored paths.
- Computers have become part of the **social landscape** of our society. One may become known to others not only for personal work and work habits, but also for the kinds of software one uses and the kinds of products created by this software. Word processors, spreadsheets, and presentation managers make it easy to develop personal styles with information that identify an individual to a group.
- Tools that are expensive, as new technology always is, become symbols of **social status.** In today's work culture, the newest technology goes to the computer technicians, but the most expensive off-the-shelf technology may go to managers with status, not need.
- Generational differences still exist and continue to occur as a result of the newness of technology, but the technological generations are becoming short. Thus, users may become stratified into classes unrelated to their actual ages and training, but more responsive to when they acquired or learned to use specific systems.

In evaluating an information system as management support, managers have to consider the cultural and social fallout questions such as who will treat the user with more or less respect, how will social relations be changed, what new cliques will arise and which social groups will die, how will the leader's ability to lead be changed, and how will the garbage left over from the last information system pollute the cultural waters of the firm for those who are left out. As with the organizational level, the social level is easy to talk about, but precise and valid measures are hard to come by. Therefore, most managers are tempted to ignore systematic evaluation at this level. In fact, systems analysis rarely employs tools that are used by sociologists and communications experts to determine potential effects at this level. The social impact of computing remains an unexplored frontier, especially when dealing with the culture and the society of an organization. Techniques from organizational development, training, anthropology, and sociology need to be used.

Managers should thus understand the **social fabric** (the way individuals communicate and relate to others with respect to jobs, tasks, and information) of the workplace they control and contribute to. Social relationships are not all governed by managers' behavior. The technology on desks, in factories, and in fields also creates informal networks. With the convergence of information and communication technologies, managers may see management support systems as additional channels of communication with other managers and employees. Hence, managers must also take the new relationships into account when evaluating management support systems. In determining who gets what systems, managers should stay aware of status and generational considerations, often unvoiced but very much present.

A final social concern is ethical and legal matters. Systems that look good on paper or even perform well after implementation may create a lot of legal or ethical problems. An employee performance monitoring system may seem like a good idea that has a lot of positive points, but on the ethical side there is plenty to ponder. Suppose a system tracks not performance but an employee. This sort of Orwellian nightmare is actually a reality given the availability of radio-based mobile communication within a building. Pocket communicators that continually signal to cell receivers can easily keep track of employees' locations. In some locales, this may be an infringement of their legal rights. Raising ethical and legal issues early in design may avoid legal and ethical quagmires later. Managers should not assume that technical people will catch these problems at any stage of design or development.

Economic Factors

The evaluation of information systems from an economic perspective (Table 10–3) has two aspects. For organizations, traditional cost-benefit analyses have proven almost useless. Derived from engineering project management, these analyses are valuable in a field in which technology is changing slowly, where everyone knows what they want, where market research is possible and clear answers are likely, and where hardware dominates software. Each of these assumptions is false in the field of information systems.

Paradoxically, it is easier to make valid economic evaluations with respect to individuals, yet the results rarely mean anything because systems are rarely costed to individuals. That is to say, it is easy to ask "What's it worth to you?" However, organizations putting systems in place rarely ask these questions of an individual, because actual dollar costs are rarely paid by individuals. Technology for groups is far more difficult to cost. Given that most new applications are not merely labor displacement but are meant to support managers at high levels in the organization where they will not be displaced, these sorts of questions don't have any real meaning. Instead, we have to be aware of the values managers add and the price we put on the benefits of having managers work smarter because they are supported in their work.

Hence, at the economic level, there are the particular challenges in evaluating management support systems:

- Costs are often hidden or **intangible**.
- **Postinstallation** (after acquiring or building a system) **costs** are about the same order of magnitude as **preinstallation costs** (the costs to purchase or construct a system). Postinstallation costs are often in the form of work loss, inefficiency, or morale losses, which are difficult to cost but easy to experience.

Table 10–3   EVALUATING MANAGEMENT SUPPORT SYSTEMS AT AN
ECONOMIC LEVEL

Phenomenon at This Level	Risks/Problems	Opportunities
Costs are hidden or intangible	Putting an accurate price tag on a system is difficult	Chance to think about hidden and intangible costs not only for IS but for other forms of management support
Postinstallation costs compare with development costs but are of different types	True costs are often grossly underestimated, as are drawbacks	Changing the way projects are budgeted and moving emphasis to postinstallation management of use and expectations
Benefits are not achieved through cost-cutting	Cost-benefit ratios are useless	Understanding of where benefits lie; management of expectations
Increased sophistication of management support systems	Costs and benefits are harder to describe accurately	Shift of focus to value added rather than direct benefits
System life span is short; obsolescence is rapid	Traditional decision making based on costs and benefits puts break-even points beyond system life span	Focus on work improvement and other contributors to benefit side; decreasing emphasis on cost-benefit analysis as complete source of decision-making information
Personal benefits and corporate benefits may disagree	Systems evaluated as failures may actually be very useful for managers, and vice versa	Shifting emphasis to value added for managers
Systems are often obsolete by the time they are installed	Perception of "money down the drain"	Development of rapid implementation techniques and reusable software

- Benefits are no longer those achieved traditionally through cost-cutting.
- As systems become more sophisticated, both costs and benefits become even more difficult to evaluate, and this is the obvious trend in the next decade.
- Actual **system life span** (the amount of time we can expect to receive benefits from a management support system before it becomes obsolete) is far shorter than traditional cost-benefit analyses allow for.
- Personal benefits and organizational costs may be in disagreement as noted above.
- Rapid obsolescence and increased speed of innovation make it difficult to apply traditional accounting techniques; systems are often obsolete when they are installed.

So the problem of applying economic analyses to evaluating management support is basically that existing techniques don't work, at least the way they have been applied. Much of the change in how systems are built (such as the move to prototyping) was

| Table 10–4 | NONMONETARY EVALUATION OF ALTERNATIVES |

System or Alternative	Ease of Use	Features	Vendor Reputation	Sum	Cost Index	Cost-Benefit Ratio
Weight	4	4	2			
Alternative 1	5	7	6	60	90	1.5
Alternative 2	6	9	6	72	80	1.1
Alternative 3	6	3	10	56	75	1.3
Alternative 4	8	6	4	64	120	1.9
Status quo	9	2	1	46	100	2.2

spearheaded by the need to get away from traditional costing techniques and move into an evaluation of the product. As the applications move up the management chain from TPS to DSS to ESS (and beyond), questions of economic benefit and costs may become science fiction.

Most economic evaluation schemes are based on **multicriteria evaluation** in which a set of discriminating factors, functions, or features is used to rate a set of competing systems (plus the status quo). The weight of each factor is multiplied by the rating of each system on each factor and is summed across all features for a given system. Then the systems are ranked. Table 10–4 illustrates this calculation. In the diagram, five alternatives are rated on three factors (ease of use, number of features, and the reputation of the vendor). This particular manager rates ease of use and number of features equally important, with vendor reputation about half as important as either of the previous factors. No other factors are considered in this simple example.

Here's how it works. For each alternative, the weight of the factor is multiplied by the perceived value of the factor for that alternative, and these products are summed across the alternative. In the example, Alternative 1 is rated at a 5 (on a scale of 0 to 10, with 0 being worst and 10 being best). The weight of ease of use is 4, giving a contribution of 4×5, or 20. Similarly, number of features contributes 4×7, or 28, and vendor reputation contributes 2×6, or 12. The total is therefore 60. Each of the other alternatives is treated the same and the result is in Column 5, labeled "Sum."

Alternative 2 scores best at 72 while the status quo scores the lowest at 46. Rating the status quo arbitrarily as 100 in terms of cost (effort, time, tears, problems), Alternative 3 is seen as least expensive while Alternative 4 is rated as the most expensive. Note that no real dollar figures are used here. Hence, Alternative 2 is going to be evaluated as best because its cost-benefit ratio is the lowest (at 1.1). At over 2.2, the cost-benefit ratio of the status quo is seen as the worst. In fact, every alternative is better than the status quo.

In using this scheme, we adopt perception as a measure of reality. We assume that ultimately there will be some (perhaps loose) relationship between perceived costs and benefits and dollar costs and benefits. But managers should be wary in making these judgments because of the warnings previously described.

Table 10–5	EVALUATING MANAGEMENT SUPPORT SYSTEMS AT A PHYSICAL LEVEL

Phenomenon at This Level	Risks/Problems	Opportunities
Systems change; software grows and hardware shrinks	Physical characteristics may change as the evaluation is being performed; systems sometimes look and act differently over time	Version management; development of standards
Systems change constantly	Evaluation is focused on period of time when users are learning how to use the system	Control of changes; focus on learnability and procedures for training
System changes may affect the physical form of the system and how it is used	Users have to learn new interfaces, invalidating old evaluations	Control of changes
Systems tax people physically	Often this aspect is ignored, but shows up later in stress, pain, and resistance to use	Emphasis on the design of the human work situation and attention to the physical aspect of using a system, especially aspects such as seating, lighting, work load, privacy, and desks
Changes are made frequently to systems	What looks like adaptation may be the seeds of later revolt	Careful attention to the actual work situation and control of changes
The work force is aging	Systems designed for young people may be uncomfortable for older ones	Careful attention to special needs for lighting, seating, work flow
There is no "average" person	Systems may be designed for a person who doesn't really exist; tall, short, old, physically disabled, or distracted people may find systems uncomfortable	Attention to diversity can create opportunities where before there was only discomfort; systems can be made adaptable with some regard to individual needs

Physical Constraints

Analysis is far easier at the physical level (Table 10–5) because techniques in **human factors engineering** and **ergonomics** are well developed (see the next section). At this level, we are concerned with how an individual manager, employing one or more information styles within an information environment, uses a system that supports various management activities. We can measure how long it takes to perform a task, how many errors occur, how often people use a supporting tool or system, how long it takes them to learn to perform it at a certain level, how fast they read, and how fast they type or use a pointing device such as a mouse. These measures are generally well-verified and valid reflections of use skill.

On the other hand, evaluation at the physical level also imposes a number of challenges:

- Systems tend to grow even as the components in them shrink. Functions that used to be performed by hardware (and hence are easy to describe) are now implemented in software (and are thus more difficult to capture). Examples include character sets, fonts, and keyboards.

■ Technological change means that new components are more desirable, but they almost always have different requirements. New systems often mean entirely new interfaces that have to be learned, and some managers *never* get out of the initial learning phases. A great deal of effort goes into learning how to use a system in the first few days, weeks, or months after it's installed, but if the system is constantly changing, every day can be the first. Evaluation of a system then comes to mean evaluating the *learning* of how to use a system.

■ New software often requires increased hardware capabilities, further increasing the rate of physical change. While additional computer main memory may not cause any noticeable change, other hardware, such as screens, pointing devices, and multimedia, imply a new ball game with every pitch.

■ Users often have unusual and unsupported preconceptions of how a system works physically. They often have expectations that systems will work, if not by thought alone, then by some sort of mystical aura or impulse. Instead, most systems require hard work of a physical nature. Sitting at a computer is tiring and hard on arms, shoulders, backs, and legs for many people and taxing of the mind and senses (especially eyes) of others.

■ Superficially, people adapt to changes very easily. Thus, designers may be eager to make changes, and original plans may not be adequate.

■ The work force is aging. A system designed for one person may be uncomfortable for another. Older workers need lighter, bigger screens and images, better seating, and attention to coordination.

If managers have sophisticated systems built for groups they manage, they can expect all of the above challenges to be important. Failure to be aware of them can spell potential problems later, and it may be difficult to make changes after installing a system.

Because a system's usability is the topic of the next major section, little will be said here except to note that it is relatively easy to measure whether an individual matches a system physically, but very hard to measure in a group.

Personal Factors

Finally, we move to evaluating a system at a personal level (Figure 10–3). It is easy to create measures for an individual but hard to talk about what "personal" means for an organization. Some general principles are known:

■ System perceptions of a personal nature are described in terms of three dimensions: know-how, can, and do. **Know-how** refers to how easy it is to learn a system; this aspect is sensitive to a huge variety of personal characteristics and system features. **Can** refers to how easy a system is to use and its design relative to the task to be performed. This aspect is studied in ergonomics and industrial engineering and is a relatively easy factor to evaluate. **Do** refers to whether the system effectively supports the manager in information tasks. While this may not be easy to measure, it

Figure 10–3 EVALUATING SYSTEMS AT A PERSONAL LEVEL

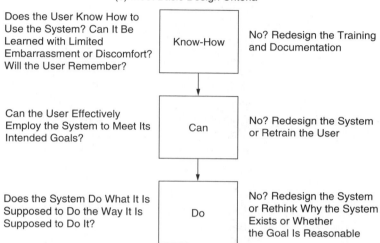

Systems Are Evaluated Highly When They
(1) Are Easy to Learn
(2) Are Effective
(3) Meet Basic Design Criteria

Does the User Know How to Use the System? Can It Be Learned with Limited Embarrassment or Discomfort? Will the User Remember?	Know-How	No? Redesign the Training and Documentation
Can the User Effectively Employ the System to Meet Its Intended Goals?	Can	No? Redesign the System or Retrain the User
Does the System Do What It Is Supposed to Do the Way It Is Supposed to Do It?	Do	No? Redesign the System or Rethink Why the System Exists or Whether the Goal Is Reasonable

certainly is easy to ask managers if this is so after the fact. One characteristic of the technology, called **trialability,** measures how easy it is for people to try out systems before they attempt to integrate them into their working lives.

While many of the basic factors at the personal level are easy to measure, there are still some difficulties:

- Technological change means that most people are always learning new things about systems that are supposed to support them. Sometimes they feel as though they are supporting the systems.

- System capabilities are always being discovered. No one begins using today's complex systems knowing everything about them. In fact, not even the designers can count on knowing what the systems they design and build can actually do. It may take years for non-IS professionals to try out all the features of a word processing package they use every day.

- People adapt and change their work styles rapidly. Actual work style (or folklore, what people tell each other works) soon differs from the work style the system was designed for. Most really good systems take this into account and are evaluated highly because they are flexible and adaptable.

Evaluating a system at the personal level is not always possible or meaningful when it is done by a nonuser. What this means is that individual managers will generally have to perform their own evaluations of know-how, can, and do during trials. The best strategy, of course, is to try out a system before making a commitment to it, if only at the personal level. However, it is increasingly difficult to do evaluations prior to adoption at higher levels (such as social or organizational) and, unfortunately, we have little science to guide us in this pursuit.

USABILITY

Now we turn our attention to the usability of a management support system. **Usable,** according to Webster, means "that can be used; fit to be used." These two meanings are not identical. Not everything that is fit (suitable, compatible) for use actually can be used or will be used. We are concerned here with what computer specialists call the *human-computer interface*, the point at which people interact with computers. This point is not so easy to define, however, because it could involve reading screens and typing text, understanding the content of screens and knowing how to make requests, or even getting the gist of the flow of several screens. Usability can be approached narrowly, event by event (looking at a single screen or typing a single character), or broadly (examining an entire application).

Imagine that you are working with a team to put together a module of a human resource information system that will assist managers in making better performance appraisals (PAs). This system will work from microcomputers networked into a database server on which the HR information will reside. Users will request information, build their own PA interviews and forms, conduct interviews, enter the data, and later examine the data they have collected in a variety of formats.

Why should a manager be concerned with this level of design detail? First, as a user, a manager needs to be able to communicate both criticism and praise to those who provide a system. Knowing what to talk about is important. To say "I don't like it" tells a lot less than "The menus don't make sense to me, they don't have a structure I can understand." Saying "The screens look horrible" is less useful to a designer than "I find the screens cluttered and the use of many different colors that don't systematically represent anything to me makes it even more confusing."

Second, managers evaluate systems prior to, during, and after implementation. The quality of the product owes a lot to expectations about the product. A manager needs to be aware of what shapes expectations, both personal and work group. The following discussion details the dimensions of those expectations. An individual evaluation of a management support system is a personal action, but when group expectations have to be managed at the same time as technical people are working to build, buy, or alter a system, the necessity to understand what makes a system usable becomes critical.

Usability begins with a number of **design principles,** as shown in Table 10–6. These principles work for design in general (e.g., for furniture, houses, procedures, software, speeches), but they are also applicable to management support systems. The first design principle is *parsimony,* which literally means "stinginess." It is used here to imply that smaller is better. A design that contains only a few elements is easier to perceive and thus learn and use than a large design involving many elements. Screens that are designed with only a few choices are usually preferred over those that offer a great many. A display of many types of items (numbers, text, graphics) is harder to understand than a single-type display, unless all the items are merely restatements of one another. Applications

Table 10—6	DESIGN PRINCIPLES

Parsimony

Economy of design; as small as possible, making as few assumptions as possible

Simplicity

Lack of complexity; things go together in obvious, natural ways; elegance

Structure

Divided into coherent parts with limited goals and clear procedures; everything fits together

Black Box

No need to know how insides work; features are available by name or result, not by process specification

Top-Down

Design is goal-based; form follows function; subgoals are available as subsystems

Transportability

No assumptions about operating environment; system will work anywhere with minimal, obvious changes

Transparency

How to use system is apparent from what it looks like; users need not master a new language, clumsy operating procedures, or alien behaviors; systems are convivial

---

that are composed of a few distinct but related activities are probably easier to learn than those composed of many different and mutually unrelatable ones.

Parsimonious designs are also cheaper, which sometimes implies that there is more money available for design. Because these designs are simple, there is less to maintain, repair, or improve, which may imply more attention can be given to maintenance of existing equipment. A large design of a PA module would include different screens to collect information, would collect more information than was absolutely needed, and would require users to generate interviews even if they only wanted to look at data. A simple design would have a few screens, each clearly identified by phase, with the ability to skip phases (such as interview design) if desired, and would collect only the minimum information required to conduct a productive PA.

Simplicity is related to parsimony if only because it's hard for a parsimonious design to be complex. Simplicity also means "uncomplicated, easy to do or understand, without additions, not ornate or luxurious, plain." In a simple design, elements go together in natural and obvious ways. The immediate payoff is that users can understand simple designs much more quickly and thus learn them faster. While they may become bored more quickly, users surely will not fail to learn the design. Be warned, however, that simplicity often comes at a price. Where support is provided at relatively low levels, it may be far harder to design systems that are simple to use because the user has more to do. Making the protocol and navigation of the system ergonomics simple may require miracles of craftsmanship.

The dictionary actually defines "simple" as "lacking in elegance," but most people recognize the concept of "simple elegance." A simple PA module prompts activities that go together in obvious ways. The sequence of activities moves naturally from phase to phase without users having to look things up in a manual. Simple phrases and menus composed of words that everyone understands guard against miscues. Because standard interfaces enable quicker learning and shield users from applying the wrong rules, having the same menu structure for all menus simplifies operating procedures.

The third design principle is *structure,* which means here that a management support system appears divided or partitioned into coherent parts. Each part exists for a limited purpose that is apparent. A structured PA procedure has employees' information clustered in one screen, information about projects or tasks on another, and a third screen may be devoted to reporting relationships. Within these screens, there are clear structures of time (for example, employee history or progress in promotion) or object (all information about a specific project is entered at the same time in close proximity on the screen). Reported information is similarly grouped.

Structure of this sort reduces errors in input or interpretation and promotes proactive thinking because managers can focus on a single topic. Finding information in a structured sequence is easier, too. Natural or easy-to-remember structures are signposts for what is within the structure. Most applications also allow users to create their own structures. For example, it is possible to list directories on floppy or hard disks in order of date, name, extension, or size, which may assist users in locating or comparing files.

In a *black box* design, a function can be used without users having detailed knowledge of how it works. For example, automobile drivers use the steering function by rotating a wheel but don't worry about the details of mechanical linkage. Shutterbugs use point-and-shoot cameras but don't worry about film exposure, film speed, exposure time, or lens aperture. A black box design allows far fewer adjustments, but its benefits are increased ease of use and less potential for errors.

In a good *top-down* design, form follows function. This is most easily seen in menu structures. Each level of the menu is composed of choices that contribute to the function for which the menu exists, and the form or content of the menu reflects the function or purpose of the previous menu choice. In the structured PA example just described, the PA module has a structure of three tasks: interview design, information entry, and information retrieval. These three tasks are coherent and are related to the goal of performance appraisal in a meaningful way. Within the interview design, there are three functions—employee information, task or project information, and relationship information—each of which is created on its own screen. The menus then reflect the structure (see Table 10–7). Structures like this make it easier to organize information and strategies in one's mind, thereby making the work quicker, less prone to error, and ultimately more productive. It's easier for users to remember where they are while they are using it and easier to get back to other areas if they want to correct an error.

Transportability means that few assumptions are made in the design about the operating environment. For a management support system, this means that the use of a system isn't sensitive to the information being entered, who the user is, what kind of equipment is being used, and so forth. One set of operating procedures will do; it is one size fits all in other words. This lessens the number of rules users have to learn and thus lowers frustration. The PA module is nontransportable if it works differently for different job classes or different quarters of the year.

Finally, a system is *transparent* if it is obvious to users how to use it just by looking at it or touching it. By now, most of us are used to pop-up menus, mouses, and windows.

Table 10–7	PERFORMANCE APPRAISAL STRUCTURE IS REFLECTED IN THE MENU STRUCTURE

Interview Design	Information Entry	Information Retrieval
• Employee information	• Employee information	• Employee information
• Task/project information	• Task/project information	• Task/project information
• Relationship information	• Relationship information	• Relationship information

These were designed to take advantage of obvious analogs in the noncomputer world: indexes, pointing, and attending to many things at the same time. For the most part, these features are transparent because knowing how to use them is usually clear without instruction. Other features and systems are not so obvious. An example is using the tab key instead of the cursor key to jump from button to button in windows or using the Ins key in *DrawPerfect* and *WordPerfect* to change scaling for graphics. Many management support tools are severely criticized because they use arcane key combinations to indicate various requests or directions. Ctrl-Y, for example, meant "Delete line" in the original *WordStar* and its descendants. In using *WordPerfect,* the right-hand + and − keys mean "move forward one screen" and "move backward one screen," but the other keys with the same symbols mean hyphen and plus. Standards that are particular to a system or a class of systems help users manage expectations of how the interface is to be handled.

Another view of a system's usability resembles that of Figure 10–2 and uses some of the same dimensions. An interface can be analyzed and evaluated at five levels (Figure 10–4). The **cultural level** is concerned with shared values and relates to aesthetics, conviviality (joy in use, fun), the appropriateness of the interface to users' status, and various privileges users have such as security clearances and rights to access various data.

The **social level** refers to how users relate to tasks and roles designed by others, how authority and responsibility are treated, and what kind of feedback they get. Social considerations may dictate how a particular management support system generally fits into such systems that support management. Some systems are designed for high-security decisions; others are fun to use. Some systems are designed to be used in conjunction with others (for example, Microsoft's OLE architecture allows the free movement of data from spreadsheets to graphics to documents) while others are intended to be batch oriented with little immediate knowledge of results.

The **cognitive level** (see Figure 10–5 for a model of cognitive processing of information) involves individuals' mental processing capabilities. At this level, we are concerned with how understandable a screen is, how interest can be maintained so that errors don't occur, how consistent the interface is from screen to screen or application to application, what kinds of immediate feedback are available in order to verify data and correct errors, and how coherent the tasks are that the system supports. Is the screen too "busy," too full of words or commands? Are error messages displayed where they will be seen? Is information from one screen available in the next if needed or will it have to be written down and transcribed by hand?

Figure 10—4   FIVE LEVELS OF DESIGN INTERFACE

Cultural	Aesthetics Conviviality Status Appropriateness	Privilege
Social	Contribution Task Fit Role Fit	Responsibility/Authority Knowledge of (Value of) Results
Cognitive	Understandability Interest Consistency	Feedback Task Coherence
Perceptual	Mode Appropriateness Discriminability Resolution	Errors
Physical	Access Danger/Care Freedom of Movement	Comfort Practicality Facilitation

The Basic Concerns at Each Level Are:
- Fit (with Status, Social Mechanisms, Task)
- Ease, Cost, Comfort
- Access, Workability
- Feedback, Information about Performance

And at Each Level There Are Peculiar Concerns:
- The "Way" Things Are Done; What Symbols Mean
- How Groups Function
- How Things Are Understood
- What Experience Is Like
- The Way the World Is Actually Constructed

The **perceptual level** is concerned with whether the stimuli needed to carry out a task can be seen or heard accurately and with minimal effort. Concerns at this level include whether the stimuli are in the appropriate mode (graphics, text, colors, sound) and whether images can be seen or read quickly or picked out among many other stimuli. The most common concern is informing users about unusual circumstances, such as input that is out of range or in the wrong format. Colors, for example, are often used to cue various activities. One color may be reserved for text to be entered, another for text that cannot be changed, a third for error messages, a fourth for status information, and so on. Beeps and other sounds alert users to errors they have made or to inform them when a lengthy computation is complete. Information may flash to call attention to itself. Bolding, underscoring, large print, and graphics may also call attention to or distinguish information that has to be retained or copied. These concerns fall under the heading of ergonomics and pertain to human sensory abilities.

Finally, the **physical level** of the design interface is concerned not with the contents of screens but with the design of the work area and procedures. Body motion and articulation, rather than sensory inputs and outputs, are the major considerations. Whether or not physical dangers are present is not a common concern about microcomputers in offices, but it is in factories. Crowded desks may create an unsafe environment, especially if food is anywhere near a keyboard. Freedom of movement, physical comfort, and the practicality of

| Figure 10–5 | COGNITIVE PROCESSING OF INFORMATION |

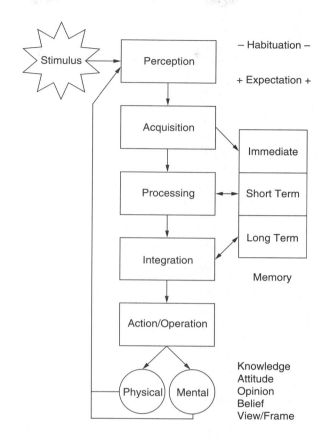

using various devices are concerns for everyone, but especially for the physically disabled. A well-engineered working environment is comfortable to the body, because eye, arm, neck, shoulder, and back pain can result from poorly designed seating and bad lighting. Another problem is "real estate." A computer terminal used to be a single piece of equipment containing a CRT display device with a built-in keyboard. Today's microcomputers, in contrast, do a lot more but may consist of up to six pieces of equipment (display, keyboard, CPU, printer with stand, CD ROM reader, and two speakers for multimedia sound), all occupying one crowded desk. Desk space is hard enough to come by in an office without the added pressure of having to house computers. Where does the printed material go? Internal CD ROM and speakers and CPUs that fit under a desk are part of the solution.

STANDARDS

The evaluation of a management support system depends not only on its intrinsic quality but also on the **standards** by which it is judged relative to the alternatives available. Quality management support systems not only meet existing standards, but also set new ones for users. Standards also increase usability because even before users employ the system, they already expect a number of things that the standards demand.

Standards may be thought of in two ways. First, they can be considered as thresholds of performance. In this sense, a standard is what can reasonably be expected at a minimum from a product. If better performance comes at a high price, these standards may also become descriptions of the exact performance, or at least descriptions of a certain class or level of performance. Standards of this sort are found in system specifications in this language: "The precision of figures will be to at least two decimal places" or "The spreadsheet will be capable of holding information on at least the last six years' production." What is commonly called standard equipment implies that at least those features will be included in the product.

Second, standard can sometimes be a description of the way things are or ought to be either exactly or within a range. In this sense, a standard isn't directly comparable on a scale to other measurements. An RS232C modem interface has to have certain characteristics; otherwise, it won't work. A spreadsheet is practically defined by the way its cells relate to one another. A mouse has two or three buttons. Keyboards follow the QWERTY standard; keys aren't randomly scattered about. A firm may institute a standard look and feel for computer applications with regard to what pressing certain keys will do or what colors are used for certain kinds of messages. Standards in this sense don't mean that more or less of something is better; they mean things *must* be this way or the application isn't valid.

We create standards because software is very fluid and easily changed. Systems, however, are relatively unique, and manufacturers and software houses try to distinguish their software in a variety of ways. Sometimes they make their products incompatible with their competitors' and sometimes they build ways of incorporating input and output from their competitors' products. Software operating environments are easier to build than refrigerators and thus easier to build in many different forms than refrigerators. For some products, the competitive edge may exist only in the interface, because the type of product dictates most of its functionality. Hence, most of the major word processors on the market differ mostly in how they look. In general, they all perform, or can be made to perform, the same functions using different combinations of keystrokes. Many firms struggle valiantly in the courts against competitors that imitate the **interface look and feel** of their products. Many of the major software suppliers have had to defend themselves in this way at some time. It is in this communication medium that the need for standards arises.

Standards are useful in five situations:

- Hardware and software installation procedures
- Database interfaces, sharing of information across database managers
- Networking interfaces so that hardware can be attached to various networks. Interface with users should be standardized, and the International Standards Organization (ISO) has established a number of standards for telecommunications, ranging from how modems communicate with computers to how electronic mail interfaces should function
- Families of software manufactured by the same vendor often exhibit common standards. Microsoft's OLE is one example. Borland's products are able to communicate with each other similarly. Lotus Development Corp. has introduced a series of products that interfaces with its 1-2-3

spreadsheets. Mainframe software has similar standards, and many manufacturers are getting together to develop their own families of standards.

- Operating systems and GUIs (such as Microsoft Windows) create de facto standards for software. In fact, the success of DOS may be due almost entirely to the fact that for the first time a single operating system was available across many different computers. This allowed the possibility for software to communicate regardless of what computer it ran on, in a standard way.

Examples of existing standards are the aforementioned networking hardware interfaces and the GUIs of Windows, OS/2, and the Apple Macintosh. Microsoft's OLE (Object Linking and Embedding) enables different productivity-enhancing tools to share data without having to copy the information laboriously from file to file by hand. Various operating systems such as DOSx, UNIX, and its variants provide standards for operating environments. The UNIX operating system is available in a variety of formats for all kinds of computers ranging from micros to minis to mainframes and even to supercomputers. The hardware of a PC is more or less standard now, although different chips may be used. Most DOS microcomputers use a variety of BIOS (Basic Input/Output System) software, all of which provides roughly the same functions.

Standards are especially important today because buyers purchase separate components and put them together to get the best fit to their needs rather than buying an all-in-one console that is inflexibly wired. Now, to an extent, standards are programmed into software, enabling interconnection if the appropriate data are fed to the software. For a while, very few printers were compatible with any specific microcomputer. Manufacturers now produce standard interfaces and leave it up to software developers to create drivers, small programs that ensure compatibility. Upward compatibility is a big concern because most people note that their systems rapidly become obsolete and need to be upgraded. Having standard hardware and software components means unplugging a piece of hardware or deinstalling a piece of software and plugging the new one in.

A dynamic exists between standards and innovation. For a while, there may be a real or implicit standard that makes servicing and orderly progress possible. However, when the risk of losing business by accepting low-cost standards exceeds the risk of innovating by ignoring standards, new products start to appear that are competitive. These products are adopted and may establish new standards. For many years, *WordStar* was the standard word processor, then along came *WordPerfect* with more features (and a higher cost). These new features were seen as more valuable and worth the risk, so a new standard was established. *WordPerfect* is now being challenged by a host of new word processors, most notably *Microsoft Word*, with its ability to include spreadsheets, graphics, sounds, and even videos dynamically through a linking ability to other Microsoft products.

When standards are adopted in the marketplace, there is generally a tradeoff between guarantees and performance. The IBM PC revolutionized only how computers were marketed. Technically, it represented a compromise between salability and technical capability. It was certainly not as powerful or as flexible as many of its competitors, but it was easy to build and sell. Similar trends have occurred in database packages, accounting software, project management software, spreadsheets, and other commercial products. Even within an organization that develops its own software, there is clearly a period of standardization followed by a period of new innovation. Strategic advantage implies risk, and when the advantage is high, people take the risk.

WORKING WITH TECHNICAL PROFESSIONALS

This chapter has focused on the evaluation challenges and responsibilities of managers who use management support systems. In many cases, managers make these evaluations in isolation of professional, technical assistance. In large organizations, there is often an information systems group (ISG) to help make these evaluations. This group is often available to do all evaluation work and, in fact, they are mandated to do precisely that in many firms.

Even when ISGs are used, it's important for managers to know what they are getting into and how their advisors are making decisions for them. Recall that the mere act of complaining is an evaluation. Complaints that are expressed vaguely and unreliably will be ignored by technical staff. As will be discussed in Chapter 15, there are many risks involved in procuring management support systems, some of which arise from working

The Modern Management Imperatives

Reach: Global Competition	Selection of management support systems has become more complex as the variety of sources expands with global competition. International, rather than national or regional, de facto and legal standards arise, putting pressure on organizations while simultaneously rationalizing the process of evaluation.
Reaction: Quick Customer Feedback on Products and Services	Usability is key to designing systems for management support. Most vendors recognize this and rapidly accommodate users' needs. However, many users are either unaware of their needs and capabilities or are too willing to forgo them because the marketplace is complex and difficult to evaluate. Standards help, even when they are created by the marketplace.
Responsiveness: Shortened Concept-to-Customer Cycle Time	Products tend to be updated rapidly, and obsolescence is a major problem. Not only is an obsolete system a depreciated asset, but the need to track technological advances means that almost every consumer is either a pioneer on the bleeding edge or is using an out-of-date system. Inevitably, management support systems are not working to their full capacity. Managers may be afraid to innovate for fear of buying the wrong technology or technology that is too expensive.
Refinement: Greater Customer Sophistication and Specificity	Managers are becoming more sophisticated, and this means that their information needs are also becoming more sophisticated. An evaluation scheme should take information style, tasks, and skills into account. Usability and learnability are the keys to first-sight evaluation, but functionality has to be explored, too.
Reconfiguration: Reengineering of Work Patterns and Structures	Most software is extremely flexible. In acquiring or building systems for management support, the ability to use the software in a variety of ways is important. This depends on two things: an inherent flexibility in the software and the ability of the user to understand and master the use of the software.
Redeployment: Reorganization and Redesign of Resources	Integrated software (such as spreadsheets or most large word processors) is a great resource user. Reconfiguring computers is not the job that most managers interviewed for before they were hired, but, in fact, managing a network of resources that are computerized (memory, software), informational (manuals), and human (consultants, trainers) is an important skill.
Reputation: Quality and Reliability of Product and Process	Quality software is built consistent with the seven design principles in addition to the requirements of the individual application. Knowing what level of support is required is an important component of systems evaluation. Systems cannot manufacture knowledge; they can store information and produce reports, but if a problem is complex and relatively formless, users can't expect a spreadsheet to produce a number that tells what the answer is. Quality perceptions depend on the manager's expectations of what should be delivered.

with technical professionals. Knowledgeable managers will know what they want from a system and be able to tell when their concerns are being addressed.

▣ EVALUATING COMPUTERS AT DOLLAR COMPANY

One of the first things that June did when she took over as general manager on Bank Street two years ago was to institute an audit of all systems. At that time, Dollar Company was going gangbusters, and everyone assumed that the systems were contributing to success. But June knew from previous jobs in middle management that what people assume is often not connected to reality. What if Dollar Company were just coasting on its initial success? What if the systems really weren't any good and success was just temporary? What if users (clerks, cashiers, stockers, customers, managers) only tolerated the systems they were given and were ready to rebel at the first sign of a blunder on Dollar's part? Merchants in town already were retaliating for DC's retail aggressiveness with better shopping conditions, personalized service, and lower prices. The recession, which enhanced DC's sales through a need for lower prices, was easing, and customers wanted variety now, not case lots that took too long to sort through. June decided to be proactive, and her initial audit showed that there were some weaknesses in the information systems. However, the board of directors vetoed any further action. "We have invested a lot of money in building the best systems. The fact that you don't trust computers is no reason for us to waste valuable DC dollars on a useless evaluation." June knows the board has the wrong idea. ▣

1. Using the five factors of evaluation, name five components to the audit that June wants to have performed.

2. Provide some suggestions to June about how to handle the board to convince them that the evaluation should proceed.

▣ DESIGNING A SYSTEM FOR KEN

Ken is a rates manager for the telephone company. Since recent court rulings and various economic events, the phone company has started operating competitively. Every customer is given a menu of choices through a computer. Rates vary depending on line quality, length, features, duration of the lease, termination characteristics (i.e., customer equipment), and so forth, and may even vary between peak hours (10 A.M. to 2 P.M.) and off-peak hours. It's important that Ken's analysts create and provide up-to-date information on the government-regulated rates charged to customers and also keep track of what the phone company is actually selling in order to create more responsive packages. Ken is really frustrated because all of this information is stored on computer, but it's neither useful nor usable. In particular, he's concerned with the fact that screens are packed with information, but it's hard to get this information printed out, so he ends up doing it by hand. To get to other screens of information (to go from, say, one kind of rate to another), he needs to back (pressing Esc a lot) out of the screen and come back in again with another key number that he's probably forgotten. The system makes Ken feel stupid and clumsy and he knows he doesn't need this in an already stressful job. He really wants to talk to an ergonomics expert who will listen to him and change the design so that work is more natural, easier to handle in chunks, and thus understandable. ■

1. Role play the part of Ken and have someone interview you to determine what frustrates you about computer systems. Then characterize these frustrations in terms of the five design interfaces (cultural, social, cognitive, perceptual, and physical).

2. Which of the role-played frustrations stem from human limitations and which from design limitations in the system? What should be done to correct these problems? What standards could exist?

Summary

Evaluation is a management support challenge because information systems tend to be complex, involve a number of different components, and are dynamic. Managers don't generally strongly participate in their development or procurement. However, they must evaluate the applications, either during their design, development, or use. Evaluation depends on standards (organizational or general) and managerial judgment, which is affected by satisfaction, expectation, and performance at five levels. These levels are organizational, social, economic, physical, and personal. At the organizational level, evaluation relates to organizational goals and the role of information as an organizational resource. Evaluation at the social level depends on the formal and informal social structure of the users, including the network of social relationships, reward systems in place, codes of ethics and legal concerns, and the mode of appropriation of the application by users. Evaluation of the cost effectiveness of an application is influenced by the perception and measurement of benefits and costs and the life span of an application. Physical constraints relate to the fit between the system and physical parameters of use. Finally, personal factors depend on how well users know how to use the application, whether or not users can effectively employ the application to meet their own goals, and whether or not the system does what it is supposed to do. Personal factors relate to usability, which should adhere to the design principles of parsimony, simplicity, structure, black box use, top-down design, transportability, and transparency. Usability can be discussed at cultural, social, cognitive, perceptual, and physical levels. Evaluation depends, ultimately, on standards, which are both thresholds of performance as well as descriptions of how applications should work.

Discussion Questions

10.1 The text asserts that evaluation of an application is influenced by users' judgments, which are influenced by perceived satisfaction, performance expectations, and actual performance. What does this model tell us about *managers'* roles in influencing how employees evaluate management support systems?

10.2 Of all the factors (organizational, social, economic, physical, and personal), which are most important to *you* in evaluating management support systems? Why do you think this is so? Is it possible for an application to be evaluated poorly on all but still be perceived as highly valued? What does this tell us about applications and the use of technology in general?

10.3 What is there about technology and information technology, more specifically, that makes evaluation problematic on all five levels? What is the implication for nontechnical managers who must evaluate their own or their workers' management support systems?

10.4 Think about an object, application, or system you think is well designed. Evaluate it in terms of parsimony, simplicity, structure, black box use, top-down design, transportability, and transparency. Which of these principles is most important? Think about a similar object, application, or system you think is unusable. Why does it fail?

10.5 The text states that standards make progress possible for a while, but eventually competition leads to breaking the standards and developing new ones. Consider how this might happen in a department that has installed a management support system. What forces are at work that allow for the creation and implementation of standards and then lead to the violation and creation of new standards?

Key Terms

can
cognitive level
cultural level
design principles (parsimony, simplicity, structure, black box, top-down, transportability, transparency)
do
ergonomics
evaluation
expectations
human factors engineering
intangible cost

intangible resource
interface look and feel
know-how
levels of evaluation (organizational, social, economic, physical, personal)
multicriteria evaluation
nontraditional measurement
perceptual level
performance
physical level
pre- and postinstallation costs

quality
reward system
social fabric
social landscape
social level
social relationships
social status
standards
system life span
technological change
trialability
usable

References

Gatian, Amy. "Is User Satisfaction a Valid Measure of System Effectiveness?" *Information and Management* 26 (1994): 119–131.

Nielsen, Jakob, and J. Levy. "Measuring Usability: Preference vs. Performance." *Communications of the ACM* 37, 4 (April 1994): 67–75.

CASE

EVERGREEN LANDSCAPING AND MAINTENANCE: CRISIS MANAGEMENT SYSTEM EVALUATION AND STANDARDS

Evergreen's busy season is in full bloom, and Lily, Frances, Heather, and Tom are quickly looking over the results of their GSS sessions with the staff. Let's eavesdrop on their conversation:

LILY: I like what I see. Most of the managers really put some hard work into these meetings. I like some of these suggestions. Did you see the one about CRIMAN, the package that handles all of crisis management?

TOM: Yes, but did anyone follow up on that?

FRANCES: Uh-huh. I had Kim call up Risk Managers, Inc. to get the particulars, and they're sending me the microcomputer version; in fact, it should arrive today or tomorrow. We'll take a look at it. Kim also found three other packages, two of which run on micros, and the other one runs on our mini. We'll test them all. Want to be involved?

TOM: Well, yes, but what are we looking for?

FRANCES: I think the results of the meeting were pretty clear: current data, sales and such, customers, employees . . .

Том: Yes, but how will you know whether or not the package is any good and which one is the best? I mean, I'm sure *all* of them keep a lot of data and meet the general requirements, but how will we know what's good for Evergreen? Wasn't there some stuff in the meeting about usability?

HEATHER: And cost, too. If I remember, these packages range in cost from a few hundred dollars to several thousand, with add-ons and training and upgrades. And do we know whether the expansion is going to be compatible? Do we have to add more costs to the expansion for this software's hardware?

Lily is growing increasingly uneasy. The GSS sessions had gone especially well, a crisis management plan was designed, and the data needs were clear. But when the rubber hits the road, Evergreen will either have to buy or create a crisis management system, and it's clear that no one in the MEC subcommittee has even begun to think about how to select a system. How to create an evaluation scheme is the pressing chore now, but the MEC is really going to be occupied with busy season crises for the next few weeks.

Questions

1. Review the model in Figure 10–1. What expectations will be important based on what you know about the key players? What are the components of satisfaction for this group? For others at Evergreen?

2. Based on your answer to the previous question, create an evaluation plan based on the five dimensions of evaluation (organizational, social, economic, personal, and physical).

3. Role play the parts of Lily, Heather, Tom, and Frances as you discuss each element of this plan. How do the dimensions interrelate? What dimensions are apt to be the most critical for a company like Evergreen? Which dimensions are likely to be unimportant?

4. Imagine that you, rather than Lily Doucette, are the CEO of Evergreen. Describe how you would like to work with a computer-based management support system. What is important to you in terms of each of the five levels of interface design? Check out a number of pieces of software that work on microcomputers. Were your intuitions about your desires correct? How well do you think your needs generalize to everyone? To people like Lily, Tom, and Heather? How important do you think the interface design will be in affecting usability and perceptions about the crisis management system?

5. Evergreen hasn't really developed much in the way of software—its two software developers are novices with only two years' experience at Evergreen and most of what Evergreen uses has been bought from consulting firms or it came along with acquisitions. How important do you think standards are to a firm like Evergreen? What would have to change to make a difference to Evergreen?

CHAPTER ELEVEN

THE CHANGING ROLE OF INFORMATION SYSTEMS

OBJECTIVES

After you have read and studied this chapter, you should be able to:

■ Explain how the modern management imperatives affect how managers can be supported through information in the next century.

■ Discuss how organizations will change in light of new information technology capabilities.

■ Discuss how increased "intelligence" will change competition and management support.

■ List the six stages of creativity and discuss how MSS can be used to enhance creativity.

■ Identify the role and function of technological leadership in an organization and explain how information technology can foster the achievement of technological leadership.

■ Describe each feature of a geodesic organization.

Question: What will the role of IS be in the organization of the twenty-first century?

Yolanda Conwy is manager of strategic planning at 21st Century Tool & Die. Yolanda's job is to advise the company's president on planning matters. To do this, she does environmental scanning, engages in some market intelligence—especially with regard to 21C's competitors—and attends conferences ranging from industry trade shows to futurism and technology forecasting. Yolanda sees the industry from the perspective of an outsider; she has almost no experience in heavy manufacturing, which suits the president fine. Yolanda has been right a lot more than she has been wrong and has helped 21C avoid a number of market fiascos that have plagued its competitors in an era of global competition and ornery markets. Now, however, Yolanda is turning her attention to how 21C functions and is meeting with Don Bradley, the director of human resources, to talk about organizational realignment in a technological era. She wonders what 21C will look like when the twenty-first century arrives.

Answer: As the future unfolds, information systems will play an increasingly important role in organizational change. Meeting the modern management challenges will change companies like 21C by blending information into their products. Managers will work more with information, too. The bases of competition will change, and organizational structure will change in sympathy with that shift. Organizations will respond by becoming more flexible and information-based. Intelligence will become critical, and managing through technology will become a critical aspect of all managers' work.

INTRODUCTION: THE FUTURE OF IS

This chapter discusses the future of management support within organizations that will be essentially information-driven and information-seeking. The widespread availability of personal information technology, and the extreme ease of integrating information services of all types with work procedures from a manager's desktop, have resulted in new kinds of organizations. These new organizations come just in time to meet the challenges brought about by intense competition that these and other technologies engender.

It is clear that information technology plays a role in precipitating these challenges. Chapter 1 introduced the idea of modern management imperatives, and this chapter reviews them in some detail. Here we point out that technology in general, and information technology more specifically, will determine the type and degree of change that will take place. After reviewing those trends, we will examine the effect that information technology has on competition. We are especially concerned with what might be called the "fabric of competition," which means the way organizations become competitive and the kinds of relationships they form with each other while they are competing. The fabric we are most familiar with is based on the idea that sustainable competitive advantage depends on natural advantages of geography or supply. Yet modern technologies are making a mockery of natural advantages by giving preference to those organizations that can work smarter and learn more quickly.

The first part of this chapter ends with a summary and prediction of new forms of management that are both influenced by, as well as take advantage of, these new technologies. Examples include work-at-home, computer-mediated marketplaces, and the brokering aspects of an ICE when placed in a network. The latter half of the chapter features an introduction to technological leadership, a topic we will return to in some detail in Module 4 of this book.

CHANGES IN MANAGEMENT

Chapter 1 mentioned seven trends that make it imperative for managers to seek advice. The business world has changed, and the needs for strength, courage, intelligence, and personal charisma have given way to a necessity to acquire, organize, and interpret information. The primary driver for this change is global competition. The real key to increased global competition is information, enabled through modern computer technology. At the same time, customers expect to provide quick feedback and expect businesses to listen to their increasingly sophisticated needs and demands. Customers don't merely expect quick response, they will shop around to find it. This implies that organizations continuously have to reconfigure their skills and factories, their human and financial resources, their products, and their processes. Shortened concept-to-customer cycle times, increased customer specificity and sophistication, individualized products, and extremely narrow niche markets make information the central success factor in rapid reconfiguration and resource redeployment. These trends are both the effects of and the necessity for modern information technology. This technology embraces the ICE, integrated information architectures, interorganizational cooperation and networking, desktop computing power, and informed and sophisticated information users (Table 11–1).

Global competition has been enhanced by transportation technologies, market intelligence, and factory automation. Information technology has played a critical role for each of these. For example, we are all aware of the problems posed by oil spills and

Table 11–1	TECHNOLOGY AND TRENDS IN MANAGEMENT AND MANAGEMENT SUPPORT

Management Trend	Technological Influences	Management Support Required
Global competition	Transportation, market intelligence, and factory automation open the boundaries of competition	Tools for conceptualization, visualization, sharing, and processing large, unstructured, and distributed databases
Increased customer sophistication	Need to select from a large, technologically diverse set of choices	Need to handle large volumes of very sophisticated, very precise information, public and private; ability to surf through data
Shortened concept-to-customer life cycle time	Technology to create and disseminate new products; fragmentation of markets; advertising, customer sophistication in use of communication channels	Management of large, integrated databases, flexibility in navigation across disciplinary data boundaries
Increased customer feedback	Increased number of channels to express customer needs and desires; customer power to travel, trade, select through technology	Attention to a variety of communication and information channels; accumulation and structuring of data; analysis tools for understanding large databases
Reconfiguration of work and processes	Knowledge-intensive technologies compete for attention; just-in-time technology; competition on time	Network models for project and product management; advanced analysis tools; ability to gather and store precise data on critical path operations; forecasting skills
Resource redeployment	Resource-intensive (energy, people, funding) competition is enabled by information technology to direct resources where they are most needed	Resource management technology; ability to use negotiation technologies to obtain resources; precisely appropriate level of detail required
Quality	Communication, transportation technologies empower customers to evaluate and compare products and services	Quality management tools; group support; consensus and team-building technologies; technology leadership

shipping accidents, but it may not be so apparent that complex information systems make it possible for precise amounts of cargo to be loaded, transported, off-loaded, and trans-shipped again through ports. This dramatically reduces lead times on orders and reduces the paperwork that keeps track of cargo. The Port of Singapore's experience in removing red tape through a computer network and EDI has enhanced both the speed and the safety of ocean shipping, once possibly the most risky form of transportation. The same holds true for air, rail, and road cargo shipping. These have all been revolutionized by systems that track goods in transit, reducing transit times, theft, loss, and danger.

Effective market intelligence depends on the collection and processing of very large amounts of data to seek trends and clusters. The rapid increase in the use of scanner-based information systems has flooded the retail industry with data that begs to be processed and analyzed, and factory automation requires the integration of a variety of equipment with databases and managerial controls. Support for managers in an era of global competition consists of tools to conceptualize, visualize, share, and process large, relatively unstructured databases quickly.

Global competition lowers barriers to entry in local markets but also offers businesses the opportunity to expand their own marketing. It increases competition for business among suppliers and accelerates the search for substitutes. In general, the key to success has always been information, but now information must be on a global basis.

Customer sophistication has increased in response to rising levels of education and the need to select from an increasing volume of similar, but different, commercial products. It is not surprising that this sophistication is blended with increased customer feedback through a variety of means, resulting in a profusion of niche markets with perhaps short lifespans. No longer will simple demographics (e.g., age and gender) suffice for knowledge of a marketplace. These small niche markets have specific expectations based on their sophisticated knowledge of who is making and selling what. Hence, extensive information on markets, products, sales conditions, and the future are necessary. Complex psychographic data, intensive test marketing, and a lot of dealing in market information through public networks and private commercial sources are the order of the day. Managing all of this data is extremely complex, as are the supports management needs.

Similarly, the need to create and market many specific products has led to a shortening of the concept-to-customer cycle time. Today's reality is one of managing many products that relate only generally to one another and may compete for resources in development, manufacture, or marketing. This challenge also calls for large, integrated databases and information architectures that can create and manage flexible boundaries between sets of data. It is no longer the case that a product is developed in stages (market research, production design, marketing). Concepts may be created anywhere along the value chain and new products created at any time. For example, small high-tech firms may hire their customers to work with design teams to create more appropriate designs. Consumer products companies may put together multidisciplinary teams. Information systems implementation teams may be headed by users without any technical training to ensure that customer needs are recognized at every stage and to reduce reworking and redesign times. In other words, managing products and managing customers will become the same exercise. Just as we simplified and rationalized our data in the example in Chapter 5 by creating joint relations (e.g., invoice-item), businesses will create new relationships between customers and products that will be reflected in a more flexible management style (from the customer's viewpoint).

There is also competition for resources between and within organizations. Hence, reconfiguration and rapid resource deployment rather than static organization and long-term budgets will become the norm rather than the exception. Just-in-time resource deployment requires detailed information on resource location, availability, condition, and processing style. Here we are not merely referring to parts or raw materials; human and financial resources are also already being examined in exactly this manner. Contract employees, for example, are becoming much more common. Reconfiguration of products, projects, and human resources based on learned and saved scenarios or group-derived crisis plans necessitates information on these scenarios and intensive support for those charged with doing the work. In the past, a simple Gantt chart would have sufficed for record keeping on a project. Today, however, interlocked projects, tight schedules, strong emphasis on quality, and just-in-time resource provision (perhaps through contracts or matrix management) are needed. In this environment, no single manager can retain all of the information in his or her memory, so networked project and resource management tools are essential. Then, the creation and management of the many models needed to forecast and control the resulting network of activities requires rigorous information systems support. In many cases, these models do not yet exist; that is, the level of support offered is very low. Products such as project management software basically offer visualization and some information management facilities, but communication support is also required.

Finally, the movement toward quality and away from quantity is engendering a competitive spirit that stresses economies of style (see below) rather than economies of scale. Advances in communication and transportation technologies make customers more mobile, and these mobile customers are able to evaluate and compare products and services globally both against each other and against standards. Because of this new emphasis on **competing on quality,** managers need tools to manage many small efforts rather than a few large factories or processes. In order to manage quality, corporate culture needs to change, and managers are natural leaders in this change. Group support, consensus, and team-building technologies are important, and it's important for managers to lead others in adopting and adapting technologies that lever their workers' natural abilities and advantages. Leadership means motivating others either through training (formal or informal), by example, through argumentation and other kinds of communication, or by force of will. In any event, managers can no longer afford to shrink into the background while others introduce technologies that provide advantage for at least a short while.

CHANGES IN COMPETITION

The result of these trends is to change the **bases of competition** from traditional cost, quantity/delivery reliability, or differentiation bases (discussed in Chapter 4) to more quality-related aspects. Nuala Beck contrasts this new, information-intensive economy with the older, industrial model (see Figure 11–1). In the old model, competition is based on cost. Economies of scale create lower per-unit costs (hence lower per-unit prices) with larger runs. These larger runs are sold into mass markets, enabled by mass media and efficient transportation that brings people, aided by advertising to inform them about which products are available, to market.

Even where cost/price is not the basis for product selection, consumers worry about the reliability of a product's source, given that there is some cost in locating a given source. Recall the customer product life cycle (Chapter 4) and the value chain (Chapter 7). Even so simple a matter as finding a breakfast cereal is not cost-free, because the cereal must be purchased and tasted. This leads to the locking-in phenomenon mentioned in Chapter 4. Switching sources or suppliers has this cost.

Another basis for competition is delivery time. If a product is available but takes too long to get, the need may have passed before the product arrives. Sometimes long delivery times can be withstood by consumers because their needs do not pass and new substitutes do not arise quickly. Given the high cost of creating a mass production facility, new entrants are not viable threats to reasonable delivery times, either.

The final traditional basis for competition is differentiation. In a mass market, it is hard for products to be differentiated because of the high production cost of the initial item (remember the economy of scale operating here). Similar products have to be differentiated by some characteristic unrelated to production, and this is often service or advertising related.

Hence, the bases of competition (cost, source reliability, delivery time, and differentiation) are based on an economy that depends on production-based values (resource usage,

Figure 11-1   THE EFFECTS OF TECHNOLOGY TRENDS ON COMPETITION

efficiency) and market intelligence to create and sell products because of the high cost involved in making errors in products. There is a strong production push and a correspondingly weaker market pull. Market pull is expensive when a product already exists—the manufacturer or service provider is to some extent locked into the marketplace just as rigidly as the customer is locked into the supplier.

With the new economy, the bases of competition switch to quality, customer service, and information. While the emerging **new economy** is still a highly controversial topic, no one disagrees that information technology will play a major role in the transformation. Quality—that is, the satisfaction of individual customers—is the newest basis for competition. Vendors will compete with each other for individual customers, an **economy of style,** if you will. Customers' styles rather than their ability to pay will become increasingly important as goods and services move away from heavy industry to become information-intensive and information-rich.

An example of economy of style is the burgeoning marketplace of information-rich personal products such as sweatshirts, greeting cards, business cards, photo finishing, and highway directions. Each product is unique, tailored to the customer's exact specifications through a computer-based interface. The result is an expression of the user's need or will: for example, a sweatshirt with a unique, personal message or directions to a specific location, adjusted for a certain time of day, and a hierarchy of customer concerns such as speed versus traffic.

Niche markets will be fluid, incredibly tiny, vocal, and continuously evolving. They will put intense pressure on service and product providers to collect and process increasingly finer sets of data. On the other hand, the older bases of cost and source reliability will become far less important. First, information-rich products are not necessarily costly, and the costs are relatively easy to control with the new media of distribution. Second, the new media are themselves much more reliable than in the past. Third, the business environment and culture are fluid, with corporate takeovers and buyouts commonplace, which make brand images harder to create and maintain. As trade barriers come down, too, it will be harder for consumers to think, for example, that IBM is an American computer manufacturer, that Jaguar is a British car, or that Minolta is a Japanese camera. The majority of parts for these and other products come from around the world.

More important than reliability of source is the ability to assure customers that there will *be* a source. Such assurance is guaranteed not by the quality of the product per se but by the quality of the firm's management. Similarly, delivery time is not so important because advances in communication and transportation technologies almost always ensure rapid delivery time. Instead, the important distinguishing characteristic will be delivery mode: at home, at work, serialized in chunks, packaged with instructions, self-assembling, and so forth. Individuals now travel a lot more, and information-intensive products and services are available through networks that service the entire world. *Where and how* the service or product is delivered could be more important than *when*.

Finally, product differentiation is a given, because information-intensive products and services are extremely fluid and can be tailored to individual needs and requirements by the customers themselves. What is extremely important is the ability of a customer to learn how to assemble, use, and dispose of the product or to acquire, enjoy, and later inform others about the service. It's almost an equation: energy- or resource-intensive products spawn or engender energy or resource use; information-intensive products engender more information.

The effects of competition based on quality, customer service, and information are to build new kinds of organizations, to supply new modes for managers to operate in, to place a different emphasis on specific values, particularly intelligence, and to require technological leadership as competition becomes more technology-based.

CHANGES IN ORGANIZATIONS

Clearly, effective managers in the coming century will be those who can successfully innovate, as the emphasis moves from quantity to quality, from mass to micro markets, and from scale to style. Organizations will need to innovate, too, and managers are critical to that innovation.

In discussing innovative organizations, Edgar Schein composed the following list of assumptions that such organizations make:

- The world can be changed and those changes can be managed.
- People are proactive problem solvers.
- Truth can be discovered through action.
- The near future, as opposed to the past or distant future, is the best time horizon.
- Innovation is geared to the time units employed.

Table 11–2	ERNST & YOUNG RECOMMENDATIONS BASED ON BEST PRACTICES

Organizational Performance	Suggested Actions	Not Recommended Actions
High performance	Make customer-relationship training paramount; have broad participation in quality meetings; do world-class benchmarking; simplify processes; stay close to customers and suppliers; build customer loyalty; empower employees to act autonomously with customers; use technology to select suppliers and identify products; outsource through technology and strategic partnerships; and emphasize innovation, performance, and adaptability	
Medium performance	Promote department-level improvement teams; get closer to suppliers; simplify processes; and inform middle managers about quality improvement	Avoid emphasis on use of technology in cost reduction
Lower performance	Emphasize teams; train for improved customer relationships; emphasize problem solving; get closer to customers; measure customer satisfaction; and use technology to reduce costs	Avoid developing technology internally

- People are at worst neutral and perfectible.
- Humans relate to each other as individuals and value diversity.
- Decision making involves groups of people.
- Cultural diversity is positive, but subcultures shouldn't be isolated.

Information technology assists innovation if organizations take advantage of it. IT connects everyone because costs are now low enough and provides channels of communication or closes them as necessary because bandwidth is becoming less restricted. Through the use of software, information can be filtered on those channels, thus combatting information overload. Today, many channels into and from the environment are provided to decision makers (through information services, for example), and state-of-the-art technology is available and usable as managers and organizations become more familiar with user friendly technologies. Finally, IT should be used appropriately and sensitively as managers become more sophisticated in its use.

Schein points out that technology, and specifically information technology, that is best used in innovative organizations should be (1) accessible, (2) rapid, (3) simultaneously available to everyone, (4) flexible in presentation format, (5) able to represent complex relationships, (6) familiar to users, (7) accountable and mutual (i.e., users are accountable to one another), (8) supportive of teamwork, (9) flexible in terms of authority structures, and (10) self-designing (with the power to change itself rather than relying on outsiders).

In 1992, the consulting company of Ernst & Young brought out a report jointly with the American Quality Foundation entitled *Best Practices Report*. This report was the result of three years' study of management practices and performance (see Table 11–2). The report defined performance as an amalgam of profitability (Return on Assets—ROA), productivity (value added per employee—VAE), and quality (measured by end user/ purchaser perceptions of quality). In the report, lower-performing organizations are urged to emphasize teams, train for improved customer relationships, emphasize problem solving and training in general, get closer to customers, emphasize the cost-reduction aspects of technology, and measure customer satisfaction. Such firms are urged *not* to develop their own technology internally.

Medium-performance companies are urged to promote department-level improvement teams, work more closely with suppliers, simplify processes, keep middle-managers informed about quality improvement, and avoid a strategy that focuses on cost reduction in the use of technology.

Medium-performance companies are, in essence, seen as technology-transparent situations. Enhanced technology will not help them much and will hurt if the emphasis is on cost reduction. The reason for this logic is apparent from examining advice given to high-performance companies. They are urged to make customer-relationship training paramount for new hires, encourage wide participation in quality meetings, do world-class benchmarking and process simplification, stay close to customers and suppliers, and build customer loyalty. They should also emphasize quality, reliability, and responsiveness, and empower employees to act autonomously with customers, use technology in supplier selection and product identification, outsource through technology and strategic partnerships, and emphasize innovation, performance, and adaptability. As will be clear from the discussion later in this section, information technology is uniquely capable of providing the advantages recommended to high-performing firms.

What *will* the organization of the future look like? Thomas Malone and John Rockart offer four suggestions for the kinds of information-intensive, systems-supported organizations that may develop (see Figure 11–2). One organization is called an **answer network,** which is a network of experts who can be called on to answer questions as they come up. In a way, an answer network is a set of "objects" composed of people with their associated databases. As a question is put to the network, it is passed from expert to expert, acquiring value (and it is hoped truth and validity) as it moves from referral to referral and, of course, accruing charges for each such addition of value. Another form illustrated in Figure 11–2 is the **overnight organization,** akin, in the words of Malone and Rockart, to "overnight armies of intellectual mercenaries." This is a generalization of a lean and mean consulting company that employs only a president and a database of consultant contacts—a kind of holding company for expertise. The third alternative is an **internal labor market** (Figure 11–3) in which each worker (and, of course, each manager) is an autonomous entrepreneur whose income depends on his or her personal ability to bid for and carry out contracts put on the net. Finally, a fourth alternative is a **computer-mediated decision network,** a sort of neural net or brain that makes decisions by merging the powers of a network of intelligent nodes and stored, sometimes shared, data.

Henry Lucas and Jack Baroudi speak about three evolving organizational structures that mirror those mentioned above. They call them the "virtual organization," the "negotiated organization" (essentially a brokerage, a commercial decision network), and the "vertically integrated conglomerate" (an interorganizational network in which suppliers are brought into the organization).

It is appropriate at this point for students of management to consider what effects these sorts of changes in organizational structure and function will have on their careers. Traditional management and business educations prepare students to work in traditional organizations, but recent trends in practice (multidisciplinary teams, outsourcing, looser

| Figure 11–2 | INFORMATION-ENABLED ORGANIZATIONS: ANSWER NETWORK AND OVERNIGHT ORGANIZATION |

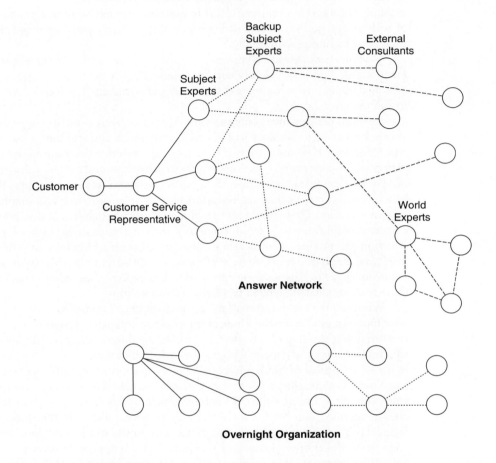

Answer Network

Overnight Organization

organizations, precompetitive cooperation, and interorganizational systems) run counter to much of this training. The capabilities of information systems to facilitate these new structures can only make it more likely that new managers will find themselves in nontraditional organizations.

THE CHANGING MEANING OF INTELLIGENCE

In *The Virtual Corporation*, William Davidow and Michael Malone speak about the organization of the next century as being a **virtual corporation,** that is, producing virtual products that can be made and delivered anytime, anyplace, and in any variety. Virtual products are instantaneous and tailored to customer demands. Examples of virtual products include one-hour eyeglass prescriptions, one-hour photograph developing, camcorders, laser printers, ten-minute oil changes, instant cash from ATMs, overnight

| Figure 11-3 | INFORMATION-ENABLED ORGANIZATIONS: INTERNAL LABOR MARKET AND COMPUTER-MEDIATED DECISION NETWORK |

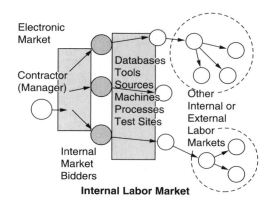

Internal Labor Market

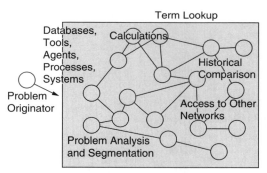

Computer-Mediated Decision Network

couriers, and superfast food that can be delivered in seconds rather than minutes. According to Davidow and Malone, the virtual companies that make these virtual products will be "edgeless, with permeable and continuously changing interfaces between company, supplier, and customers." The only way to produce virtual products will be to create, store, access, and process voluminous and volatile integrated, shared databases on customers, products, distributors, suppliers, and production, and the enabling technology to accomplish this is information technology. Seen this way, just-in-time (JIT) inventory, ICEs, electronic marketplaces, ESSs, and flexible manufacturing appear as different manifestations of the same phenomenon. The organization of the future—and the managers in it—will have to adjust to doing work "virtually." How will this affect managers?

While Davidow and Malone forecast the same reduction in middle management as other pundits do, the most important point they make is the role managers will have in maintaining the organization's intelligence. The key element in tomorrow's organization is not information or information flow but the role that intelligence plays in giving

Figure 11-4 INTELLIGENT AND NONINTELLIGENT INFORMATION SYSTEMS

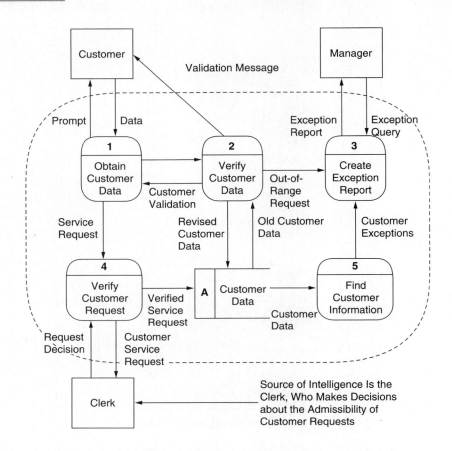

organizations strategic advantage. Because managers will handle this intelligence, they must understand intelligence in this particular sense in order to understand their roles in the new intelligent organization.

Intelligence is related to the ability to *create* information rather than merely to locate it or uncover it from a background of noise. Intelligent people and systems are sources of information for themselves and others. Consider a system that handles customer complaints, as illustrated in Figure 11-4. This data flow diagram demonstrates the difference between intelligent and nonintelligent systems. Processes 1 and 2 verify the customer, the transaction, and that this customer is on file. If a complaint is not in the file, it is called "out of range" and sent to Process 3, where it is kept for an exception report to be handled by the manager. Process 4 verifies the customer request by asking a clerk if the request is reasonable or not. Information on the request is stored temporarily in the data store A, Customer Data. When the manager asks for complaints that cannot be handled routinely, customer data concerning complaints are forwarded. Consider where the intelligence in this system actually lies. It is not in Processes 1 through 5, because they do exactly what they are programmed to do: look up and retrieve data, store, and reformat information. In this example, the clerk is the intelligent agent, providing a ruling (new information not based on programmed procedures) relevant to the customer request. Imagine how this system would work if there were no clerk. In one scenario, the clerk is simply taken out of the loop and, in this case, no service requests can be validated as nonroutine; hence, the manager receives only out-of-range requests from noncustomers. In this case, valuable information is lost. The system is "unintelligent" because it is unable to cope with valid customer complaints of a nonroutine nature. In another scenario, the clerk is replaced by a statistical process that takes historical complaint information into account. Suppose that three-quarters of all complaints are unwarranted—they represent cranky customers with no real reason to complain. One out of 100 complaints is a real disaster and should be attended to immediately. Suppose we replace the clerk with a random number generator and a nonroutine customer request or complaint comes through. A random number between 1 and 100 is generated, and Process 4 now handles the request as follows:

- If the number is less than 75, the request is ignored.
- If the number is between 75 and 99, the request is validated and stored in "Customer Data."
- If the number is 100, the request is stored in "Customer Data" and marked "Urgent—Handle Immediately."

This scenario seems to mimic reality, but the example shows that the clerk's intelligence is being replaced by a process that is actually out of control, run by a random number generator. In fact, the chances are only one in 100 that a truly catastrophic customer complaint will be marked as important and that three out of four such requests will actually be ignored. Although we have an information system, it is not really intelligent—it is profoundly stupid and dangerous!

Most information systems do not "source," or create, information, which results in noisy or buggy systems. An information system can process data into information only in the following ways:

- By *reformatting* (moving data from one column to another)
- By *calculation* (adding or multiplying figures)
- By *reduction* (removing or erasing data)
- By *combining* non-numerical data (concatenation or capitalization)
- By *displaying* (converting a table to a graph)
- By *merging* (putting two or more streams of data together)
- By *sorting* (splitting one stream of data into two or more)

However, no information system actually creates information from nowhere like the random number generator in Figure 11–4. In fact, one of the rules for designing information systems states that "information cannot come from nowhere." Information comes from sources, generally people or machines, who have experiences in the real world and interpret them in terms of numbers or words that are recorded on paper, tape, diskette, film, and so forth. Because information systems do what they are told, they are essentially noncreative. The source of creativity is the user, which presents a dilemma: How can a system that essentially follows orders foster, nurture, or even provoke creativity?

The answer lies partly in the second aspect of information systems, which is their ability to "learn." Unlike other systems that store past experiences in physical changes (e.g., a diamond retains its history in the facets the jeweler has cut in the raw gem and a lump of coal retains some of its history in the fossils embedded within), an information system retains the effects of past activities in the form of information, which is available not only to its users, but to itself. While not all (or even most) information systems are learning systems, many have the potential to accumulate information that can be used later as the basis for self-adjustment to new circumstances.

Another way that creativity is enhanced is by removing roadblocks to creativity. Recall that a management support system provides seven levels of support to managers. Most creativity is blocked because problem solvers seek support at a level that is too high. For example, problem solvers seek a formula or a button to push when, in fact, what is needed is some way to visualize the problem or compare it to a known, solvable problem.

Creativity has two forms. It can be learned as a set of mechanical procedures that massage information into new forms, or it can appear as an artistic or emotional act arising because individuals become dissatisfied with the current state of affairs. Thus, creativity is partly related to information sources and partly to personality and culture. Hence, creativity is both a set of procedures to generate alternatives and emotional and artistic aspects dictating dissatisfaction with existing alternatives.

Alternatives can be mechanically generated by (1) linking—and thus determining patterns among existing information—and (2) sifting—and thus removing distractions that make new ideas difficult to see. This corresponds to a *synthetic* approach (building) and an *analytic* approach (deconstruction and cleaning). Creativity also depends on having a source of information that can be altered, evaluated, and retouched. With regard to the artistic or emotional component, individuals may become dissatisfied with the status quo and therefore seek new alternatives because of personality or culture. Personality may be related to information style while culture may be related to organizational climate and how organizations view and value information. Risk-taking organizations experiment with creativity and foster a climate in which creativity is seen as positive rather than risky.

Creativity Enhancement at Evergreen

Connie has been asked by Shawna Eggert (vice president of sales) to select the exact site for the planned expansion store. Shawna has located many sites that seem equally good from her point of view, based on the criteria the MEC developed. The stages of creativity in this typical management problem are as follows:

- *Mess finding:* Becoming aware of the challenges and opportunities that accompany finding a site
- *Fact finding:* Gathering information to increase understanding of the mess, in particular, potential traffic, demographics, and sales data
- *Problem finding:* Developing and refining the problem. Can the problem be rephrased or approached in a different way?
- *Idea finding:* Generating as many potential solutions or ideas as possible, which includes not just sites (land) but perhaps existing buildings, joint ventures, or shared space
- *Solution finding:* Evaluating potential solutions, judging, and selecting them
- *Acceptance finding:* Overcoming barriers to implementation

Creativity means generating new alternatives for a specific situation. Each of the "finding" stages requires assistance. A management support system can enhance creativity by (1) amplifying the generation process by removing technical barriers, (2) making the generation more effective by motivating better alternatives, (3) increasing confidence in outcomes that already have been obtained, and (4) making solutions already generated more adoptable. Let's now look at each of these four aspects of creativity for Connie's situation.

Removing Barriers to Creativity

Removing technical barriers to creativity means motivating expression, recognition, bringing ideas together, and overcoming fears. James Adams talks about four blocks to creativity:

- *Perceptual*—Stereotyping, difficulty in isolating the true problem, adding artificial constraints, an inability to see a problem from multiple viewpoints, and failure to use all sensory inputs
- *Emotional*—Fear of making mistakes, fear of taking risks, inability to tolerate ambiguity, desire for security and order, preference for judging ideas rather than generating them, inability to relax and put the problem aside for a while, lack of challenge, overmotivation to succeed quickly, lack of imaginative control, excessive zeal, prejudice, and inability to distinguish reality from fantasy
- *Cultural and environmental*—homilies and sayings, taboos, autocratic boss, distractions, lack of time, lack of support in bringing ideas into action
- *Intellectual and expressive*—poor choice of mental tactics, lack of mental ability, using the wrong language or approach, inadequate skills of expression

Connie can use e-mail to discuss the site problem with others and to understand the mess that comes from organizational fear, habit (Evergreen has always used stand-alone facilities), ambiguity (there has never been more than one store), and so forth. Examining maps, for example, is time-consuming and clumsy, but a geographic information system (GIS) could display and pinpoint convenient sites. Such linking of designs into demographic and market data instantly removes many barriers to creativity. These sorts of contextualizing systems enhance creativity by delegating most of the fussy, confusing, and potentially harmful work to systems that are more "patient" and less likely to forget where something is.

Motivating Better Alternatives

Better alternatives come from creative individuals who have these characteristics (those traits that can be supported through information systems appear in italics): *awareness and sensitivity to problems, good memory, fluency, flexibility,* originality, self-discipline, *persistence,* adaptability, intellectual playfulness, humor, nonconformity, tolerance for ambiguity, self-confidence, skepticism, and *intelligence.* Connie can use a GIS with its memory, flexibility, and persistence to assist her intelligence to recall and display data on selected sites and perform analyses on traffic patterns, planned future growth, the pull of near and remote competitors, and opportunities for expansion later on.

Increasing Confidence in Outcomes

Confidence is a major component of feeling supported. Making managers more confident of outcomes is a third way in which creativity is enhanced by information systems. The capability of MSSs to display actual and simulated results in a variety of formats compatible with managers' needs is extremely helpful. Again, the *support* in management support systems comes from the ability to contact others (consensus), find supporting data (management information systems), compare previous outcomes (consulting), and provide a variety of models for asking "what if." While none of these activities constitutes intelligence in the sense of supplying new information, they do motivate the user to attempt more and better solutions to problems. First, it is easier to manage a large number of alternatives if spreadsheets and expert systems handle them. Second, problem solutions are more easily compared by information systems tools such as graphical displays, multiple windows, and multimedia. Because a computer doesn't forget anything unless it's told to, there is no penalty for playing with copies of the data. Finally, the results are easier to share because presentations and reports are more easily produced from computer-based information systems such as word processing, desktop publishing, and presentation managers.

Connie can perform what if analysis by using the GIS to determine the very best site for the expansion store based on existing criteria. She might reason that it would be better to do sensitivity analyses on several important measurements, such as traffic, to see if sales really do depend on existing traffic. If they do, then it may be important to pick out a more store-friendly, visible site. An expert system with appropriate rules could help Connie analyze dozens of parameters including side of street, accessibility to the current store, availability of transportation for the staff, exposure to wind, threat of hail, dust and so forth.

Making Innovations More Adoptable

Finally, we come to the last aspect of creativity, reusing existing innovations or solutions. Information systems can overcome the barriers to generating new or better solutions, but beyond that, they can use old tried-and-true solutions to tailor the innovation to managers' needs. Storing the results of previous attempts at creativity may not seem a very creative act; however, while the world rewards flexible people, it rewards flexible solutions even more, and a solution that was good on Monday may still be passably good by Friday, and it will take far less work to derive it. For Connie, sensitivity analyses and data navigation will be feasible using spreadsheets and EISs. She may actually be able to reconstruct how the current store site was located and repeat the process for the new store site without having to create a new way of thinking about the store. Of course, merely accessing old solutions doesn't guarantee a new solution now, but it does increase the range of solutions available.

Implementing solutions is a major management responsibility, and leading others in the use of technology is a rapidly growing responsibility of managers, as we will explore in the next section.

PREPARING ORGANIZATIONS FOR CHANGE: TECHNOLOGICAL LEADERSHIP

Leadership is a management responsibility that encompasses many efforts. Managers can lead groups, projects, organizations, and causes, but how can a manager be a technological leader? There are two ways in which such leadership can be carried out:

- Leadership *in* technology—Motivating others to use technology to achieve organizational goals, to develop themselves, and to work better
- Leadership *with* technology—Using technology to exercise leadership in other areas

Leadership in technology is the subject of Chapter 18, so only a brief preview will appear here. **Leadership in technology** means understanding how technology is predicted, assessed, developed, diffused, and used and then making that knowledge available and useful to others. A technological leader in this sense can lead by training, example, persuasion, or motivation (i.e., reward and punishment). Managerial technological leaders aren't necessarily technologists themselves; however, a fear of technology would certainly inhibit many managers. Managers who are technological leaders acquire skills that are relevant to specific technologies and then make those skills—and often the corresponding technology—available to others. Skills in specific technologies don't guarantee creativity in the use of those technologies, but not having any skill or understanding will be a recipe for disaster.

Managerial leadership in technology is exercised either as managerial push or pull. Managerial push means overlaying technology atop existing modes or work procedures from the outside, such as happens in automation or process reengineering. In this case, managers bring technology to the work situation. Managerial pull means dragging others along with a trend, motivating workers to acquire technology that they see as advantageous, thereby creating a sort of high-tech bandwagon that others are eager to jump on.

In classical leadership theory, push and pull correspond to **external and internal leadership.** External leaders are essentially motivational because they don't necessarily embody the values of the group or engage in the group's major activities. However, they do have control of rewards and punishments that members of the group either desire or avoid. Group members are willing to work for rewards that accompany the technology because they want the rewards. Consider an organization moving to an integrated customer service information system. The manager who is an external technical leader can demonstrate the benefits of the system through persuasion or by providing rewards (such as reengineered jobs with more responsibility or satisfying interactions).

An internal leader leads by example because he or she is seen not only as powerful and interesting (a legitimate or charismatic authority, in classical terms), but also as typical. The reasoning is this: "X (my manager) uses system S. My manager and I do similar work. X either has some good reason for using S or X really enjoys using S. Because I'm similar to X, I'll have the same good reasons or enjoyment. Thus, I should use S." Where an integrated customer service system is installed, an internal leader will literally demonstrate the value of the system to the users and attempt to build or maintain identity with them. Of course, most employees recognize that managers and supervisors do different work, so this simple analysis is complicated by the necessity to build that identification. Regardless of this difficulty, however, an internal leader in technology must feel comfortable with the technology, because a negative example will have far-reaching consequences.

Leadership with technology is the other way that managers are technological leaders. The trends described in the opening section of this chapter—global competition, increasing power of feedback and specificity of customers, drastically speeded up organizational metabolism, resource reconfiguration and organizational redesign, and an increasing emphasis on quality—spell out a compelling argument for the need for management support that goes beyond traditional sources. Managers who ignore technology because of ignorance or fear are depriving themselves of the benefits of technology to reshape their organizations for strategic gain. Managers who learn to use information technology in their management practice will accrue profits in the following ways:

- More intelligence (more pertinent, better filtered, better processed, more acceptable, and credible)
- Broader span of control (better ability to juggle multiple tasks, finer control over these tasks, more flexibility in views of situations)
- Better network relations (more contacts, quicker access, multiple windows on the organization)
- Increased confidence in the ability to effect change

Students may want to consider their own orientations toward technological leadership. What knowledge, skills, and attitudes will assist them in becoming a leader in or with technology? Which technologies seem more enabling and hence the best to lead with? Which technologies pose the most daunting barriers? How can a course of study help overcome those barriers?

THE GEODESIC ORGANIZATION

In *Reshaping the Organization,* Robert Tomasko describes ways in which a corporation—and the managers in it—can be rethought. He begins his treatise with reference to the pyramids, used, as he ironically notes, "by the ancient Egyptians to entomb their dead leaders." The pyramid is revered not only as a tourist site but also as an extremely stable structure—it can withstand almost anything. Corporations are built along these lines, and we have already referred to both the positive and negative aspects of these lines. However, the imperviousness of the pyramid makes it unmotivated to change either in response to the environment or to the individual manager who is trying to make changes. Tomasko notes that pyramidal organizations are based on these assumptions:

- Bigger is better; bigger pyramids can always be built.
- In-house is best, and another pyramid can be assigned to do a new job.
- The basic building block is the job, held by one individual.
- Standards are crucial; standard jobs are key to the pyramid; changes to standard jobs are threatening; and maintaining standards is best for the organization.
- Middle managers control and coordinate.
- Information needs are determined by where a worker is in the pyramid.
- Career advancement means moving toward the apex of the pyramid.

Tomasko proposes a new architecture for organizations—the dome (pioneered by Buckminster Fuller). Domes differ from pyramids in essential ways. A pyramid is strong only in its upward and downward direction and lateral pressure causes the pyramid to buckle. The only reasons why the Egyptian pyramids have lasted so long are that they are relatively isolated, rock is heavy and difficult to conceal and steal, and it takes a very big battering ram to blast through tons of solid rock. The lateral strength of the pyramids is

Figure 11—5 THE GEODESIC ORGANIZATION

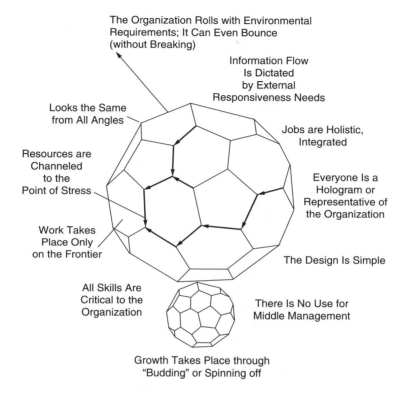

The Organization Rolls with Environmental Requirements; It Can Even Bounce (without Breaking)

Information Flow Is Dictated by External Responsiveness Needs

Looks the Same from All Angles

Jobs are Holistic, Integrated

Resources are Channeled to the Point of Stress

Everyone Is a Hologram or Representative of the Organization

Work Takes Place Only on the Frontier

The Design Is Simple

All Skills Are Critical to the Organization

There Is No Use for Middle Management

Growth Takes Place through "Budding" or Spinning off

found totally in the underlying layers of rock, but as anyone who has ever built a pyramid out of paper knows, there is no lateral strength at all. The geodesic dome, on the other hand, exists entirely on its surface. The strength of the dome is derived from its unique ability to channel all forces to its external supports that go in all directions—up, down, left, right, diagonally—to deflect disturbances by moving the force to a point that can handle it. Hence, domes cover more area than traditional structures for the same cost.

Using this analogy, Tomasko proposes building new organizations that we will call **geodesic organizations.** This kind of company has several qualities that are actually modeled in and reflected by the kind of information architecture we have been discussing in this chapter (see Figure 11–5).

- A geodesic organization looks the same from all angles. Everyone is at the top, everyone has access (within reason) to the same data, and all activities can be initiated at any place in the dome, not just from the apex.

- In a geodesic organization, resources, like the stress along the supporting frame of a dome, are channeled rapidly to that part of the organization which requires them, without disturbing other aspects of the organization. Stress is distributed rather than concentrated. Everyone can drill down, up, and across corporate data, and everyone can access the analysis and processing tools appropriate for the job.

■ The work of a geodesic organization, as with any system, takes place on its surfaces, where it interacts with other systems, not in its interior. We call this surface the **organizational frontier.** It is at the frontier where buying and selling, the business of the firm, take place. In a geodesic organization, everyone is in production, marketing, and information systems simultaneously. Everyone is on the front lines. Support activities are redesigned to be integral, even critical, to operations, be they delivery of service or producing a product. Information systems that support managers at the frontier make it easy to configure services and products into new forms without upper management directive.

■ In a geodesic organization, the skills of all members of the organization are tested continuously by the frontier interaction with the real world rather than in scenarios or plans. Tomasko divides **skills** into four classes: complementary (support), core (the core business of a firm), critical (providing competitive advantage), and cutting edge (sources of tomorrow's critical skills). Geodesic organizations employ only critical skills; as new skills are developed at the frontier, they become critical as the organization offers new services or products in new ways.

■ A geodesic organization grows in two ways. It grows *holistically*, always at the frontier, rather than in parts (internally or at the base or, more harmfully, at the top). The second way it grows is by *budding*. While everyone has the same access to and motivation to move information, some employees will obviously be better at their jobs than others. These employees may form centers of excellence on the frontier, and wise managers will want to bud these off as separate geodesic organizations with strong interorganizational links. Management support systems of an intra- or interorganizational nature assist this sort of growth by maintaining corporate memory, by establishing information-sharing relationships with budded organizations, or by creating the ability to respond to increasingly complex situations engendered by growth.

■ There is no middle management in geodesic organizations. Because all employees are at the frontier, they need not have upper management's directives interpreted for them. They have immediate and full-time access to company values, procedures, and data without needing intermediaries. Corporate communication is enhanced through consensus systems; corporate memory is enhanced through shared databases; and corporate power is enhanced through model-based tools such as expert systems and decision support systems.

■ Geodesic organizations are simple. Because everyone is on the front lines and has access to all pertinent company information, job design is relatively simple, reporting structures don't exist to complicate communication, and political game-playing is minimal.

■ In a geodesic organization, everyone has responsibility, everyone is an entrepreneur, everyone can appear to each customer as the "whole" organization, representing it perfectly. Because of this structure, everyone buys in and is more of a team player.

- Geodesic jobs are more holistic, "reinforced" or enriched, more team-based, and managed by managers who channel the load in the appropriate way, or bear the load themselves when the need arises.

- In geodesic organizations, information flows are dictated by needs that in turn are dictated by responsiveness to the external environment (at the frontier). No one can or would want to hoard information if it means that a neighboring wall on the frontier will be weakened. Instead, everyone has a vested interest in sharing information and moving it as quickly as possible.

One problem that shows up in many real structures built on geodesic principles is a leaking roof. Roofs are specialized structures to keep water out, but geodesic structures are less specialized and hence more prone to being overwhelmed by specific problems. A cure for the leaking roof syndrome is rapid information flow to bring specialized help to the frontier when it is needed.

Another problem that may be encountered in practice is that firms, while shifting primary decision making to the frontier, are also downsizing, doing less training, and hiring more contract personnel. Clearly, the last two trends are counterproductive and put more of a burden on the information system to bring information to the frontier as it is needed. Balancing these conflicting needs is an important aspect of managerial and policy work that needs to be addressed in implementing the geodesic, information-driven organization.

Managing with technology in emerging geodesic organizations means using technology to bear the load at the frontier. The technologically leading manager will be able to command not only workers (this is less important, anyway) but also information technology to support managerial work.

SUMMARY OF MODULE 2

This chapter ends the second module of this text. Module 1 set the stage with a discussion of information technology for strategic advantage in existing organizations. Module 2 evolved from a discussion of managerial support in obtaining and maintaining that advantage in today's organizations to a look at how future organizations will unfold and how managers will function in those organizations using support systems based on three important technologies: integrated databases, client-server applications, and model-creating and manipulating software. This module began with a description of managerial work as that of bringing situations to conclusions that organizations desire. Managers need support in creating those conclusions, and Chapter 7 introduced seven levels of management support. Chapters 8 and 9 presented examples of hybrid management support systems that provide assistance in obtaining advice at more than one level at a time to individuals (Chapter 8) and groups (Chapter 9). Chapter 10 focused on the evaluation of candidate management support systems and this chapter completed the circle, bringing us to the role and function of managers in emerging organizations, supported by information systems that assist, advise, and enable managers.

These support systems do not appear from nowhere. Module 3 examines how these systems are designed and built with an eye toward managing the risks inherent in acquiring them. Chapter 12 introduces the idea of the application life cycle, the life history of a system, while Chapter 13 examines managerial responsibilities during that life span and presents a critical look at how managers research their own and others' needs for support in designing management support systems. Chapter 14 explores the increasingly important managerial responsibility of project supervision in the design and building of management support systems. Finally, Chapter 15 explores the human dimension of risk management, especially the relationships between individuals who are building the systems and those who are using the systems, and what responsibilities managers have to ensure that these relationships are maintained.

▪ REENGINEERING 21ST CENTURY TOOL & DIE

Yolanda is preparing a report to the president about her research into the effects of technological change on heavy-industry organizations. While 21C is a stronger competitor now than it used to be, it works mostly in niche markets, which was its response to global competition. The organization, however, hasn't really changed any—just its marketing. Yolanda is concerned about the following issues:

- ▪ Who is managing the technologies that 21C uses to make its products?
- ▪ How flexible is 21C? Can it respond quickly to any request? How long does it take 21C to develop new products? What influences that effort?
- ▪ Is the organization appropriate to meet the challenges of management in the future?
- ▪ What is or should be the role of information systems in supporting managers at 21C? Are the managers currently well supported by information technology? What is their skill level? Are appropriate mechanisms in place to use this technology well?
- ▪ What issues in technology leadership are being swept under the carpet at this time owing to the focus on marketing and economics? 21C makes technology and uses technology, but is it a leader? ▪

1. How should Yolanda go about answering these questions? Will she be satisfied with the answers she gets?

2. What should she tell the president about the effects of information technology on organizational structure, organizational activities, and management support?

3. What does the word *intelligence* mean to a firm like 21C?

Summary

Changes in the business world have created a need to acquire, organize, and interpret information. The trends (increased global competition, customer sophistication, importance of quality, reconfiguration, resource deployment, and shortened concept-to-customer time) are the effects of as well as the motivators for the need to create advanced information technology. Changes in competition—from cost to quality bases, economies of scale to economies of style, and mass markets to fluid niche markets—point to the increased importance of information-to-business and information-based businesses. The appearance of "virtual organizations," facilitated by the ICE, electronic marketplaces, just-in-time inventory, ESS, and flexible manufacturing, underscores these changes, pointing to more "intelligent" organizations of the future. At an extreme, organizations become geodesic, with all activities taking place along information-system supported surfaces.

**Discussion
Questions**

11.1 Find examples in journals or newspapers of old-to-new competitive shifts such as the following:
- Cost to quality
- Economies of scale to economies of style
- Fixed, mass markets to fluid, niche markets
- Assumption of reliability
- Delivery time to delivery mode
- Differentiation to information

11.2 Assume that you are in charge of creating an information-enabled organization of alumni of your business school. For each of the following organizational structures, explain what roles people and technology would play and describe how the organization would function. What kinds of tasks would best be carried out by the organization in the given structure? For what tasks would the organization fail to function properly?
- Answer network
- Overnight organization
- Internal labor market
- Decision network

11.3 Information systems aren't intelligent in the sense that they merely process information; they don't create it. In what ways are information-enabled organizations more intelligent, however, than those that ignore information opportunities? What is the nature of that intelligence? Is "intelligence" the same as "support," or are there some important differences?

11.4 What would it be like to work for a geodesic organization? What aspects of intelligence are required and what kinds of supports would be necessary for managers working in geodesic organizations? Are such organizations actually feasible? Why or why not?

Key Terms

answer network
bases of competition: price, reliability, differentiation
competing on quality
computer-mediated decision network
economy of style

external/internal leadership
geodesic organization
intelligence
internal labor market
leadership in technology
leadership with technology

new economy
organizational frontier
overnight organization
skills: complementary, core, critical, cutting edge
virtual corporation

References

Adams, James L. *Conceptual Blockbusting: A Guide to Better Ideas*. New York: W. W. Norton, 1974.

Baker, Wayne. "The Network Organization in Theory and Practice." In N. Nohria and R. Eccles, eds., *Networks and Organizations: Structure, Form and Action*. Boston: Harvard Business School Press, 1992, 397–429.

Beck, Nuala. *Shifting Gears: Thriving in the New Economy*. Toronto: Harper Collins, 1992.

Bradley, Stephen, Jerry Hausman, and Richard Nolan. "Global Competition and Technology." In Stephen Bradley, Jerry Hausman, and Richard Nolan, eds., *Globalization, Technology, and Competition: The Fusion of Computers and Telecommunications in the 1990s*. Boston: Harvard Business School, 1993, 3–32.

Crowston, Kevin, and Thomas Malone. "Information Technology and Work Organization." In Thomas Allen and Michael S. Scott Morton, eds., *Information Technology and the Corporation of the 1990s: Research Studies*. New York: Oxford University Press, 1994, 249–275.

Davidow, William, and Michael S. Malone. *The Virtual Corporation: Structuring and Revitalizing the Corporation for the 21st Century*. New York: Harper Collins, 1992.

Eccles, Robert, and Richard Nolan. "A Framework for the Design of the Emerging Global Organizational Structure." In Stephen Bradley, Jerry Hausman, and Richard Nolan, eds., *Globalization, Technology, and Competition: The Fusion of Computers and Telecommunications in the 1990s*. Boston: Harvard Business School, 1993, 57–80.

Ernst & Young. *Best Practices Report: An Analysis of Management Practices That Impact Performance*. New York: American Quality Foundation, 1992.

Hald, Alan, and Benn Konsynski. "Seven Technologies to Watch in Globalization." In Stephen Bradley, Jerry Hausman, and Richard Nolan, eds., *Globalization, Technology, and Competition: The Fusion of Computers and Telecommunications in the 1990s*. Boston: Harvard Business School, 1993, 335–358.

Lucas, Henry, and Jack Baroudi. "The Role of Information Technology in Organizational Design." *Journal of Management Information Systems* 10, 4 (Spring 1994): 9–23.

Malone, Thomas, and John Rockart. "How Will Information Technology Reshape Organizations? Computers as Coordination Technology." In Stephen Bradley, Jerry Hausman, and Richard Nolan, eds., *Globalization, Technology, and Competition: The Fusion of Computers and Telecommunications in the 1990s*. Boston: Harvard Business School, 1993, 37–56.

Malone, Thomas, J. Yates, and R. Benjamin. "Electronic Markets and Electronic Hierarchies." In Thomas Allen and Michael S. Scott Morton, eds., *Information Technology and the Corporation of the 1990s: Research Studies*. New York: Oxford University Press, 1994, 61–83.

Miller, David, Eric Clemons, and Michael Row. "Information Technology and the Global Virtual Corporation." In Stephen Bradley, Jerry Hausman, and Richard Nolan, eds., *Globalization, Technology, and Competition: The Fusion of Computers and Telecommunications in the 1990s*. Boston: Harvard Business School, 1993, 283–308.

Nohria, N., and R. Eccles. "Face-to-Face: Making Network Organizations Work." In N. Nohria and R. Eccles, eds., *Networks and Organizations: Structure, Form and Action*. Boston: Harvard Business School Press, 1992.

Parnas, S. J., R. B. Noller, and A. M. Biodi, eds. *Guide to Creative Action*. New York: Charles Scribner's Sons, 1977.

Popcorn, Faith. *The Popcorn Report*. New York: Doubleday, 1991.

Schein, Edgar. "Innovative Cultures and Organizations." In Thomas Allen and Michael S. Scott Morton, eds., *Information Technology and the Corporation of the 1990s: Research Studies*. New York: Oxford University Press, 1994, 125–145.

Tomasko, Robert M. *Reshaping the Corporation: The Architecture of Change*. New York: American Management Association, 1993.

CASE

EVERGREEN LANDSCAPING AND MAINTENANCE: ORGANIZATIONAL REALIGNMENT

Shawna Eggert and Connie have been looking at alternative sites for the new store and, without knowing it, have been participating in a slow change at Evergreen due to information technology. Although Connie doesn't have a geographic information system available right now, she knows that such applications exist and she has used spreadsheets and databases extensively. She is ready to be supported by information systems that can help her solve problems ranging from very structured ones (like calculating margins) to relatively unstructured ones (like selecting locations for a store).

In other ways, Evergreen is undergoing a transformation. The proposed link with Pindar Gopal, the gardening broker, shows how the global market is making itself available to Evergreen, but competition from "big box" stores and others shows also that the global market isn't exactly a friendly place. Evergreen's customers have become fickle and finicky, but so have the competition's customers. It's becoming very important for Evergreen to turn on a dime, but it's also easy to lose sight of what Evergreen is. Meanwhile, quality has become an important issue, not only because quality has always been Evergreen's hallmark, but because even that natural quality isn't enough any longer. Because life and leisure have become so complex, Evergreen is dealing more in information and training of staff, customers, and suppliers. The effect on the company has been noticeable, too. Managers like Connie are being asked to play multiple roles and to get involved in projects not only in their specialized fields but in the management of Evergreen as a whole. Ten years ago, Shawna wouldn't have asked for Connie's help at all; in fact, ten years ago, Shawna wouldn't have been involved, and only Lily would have made site decisions. However, information and skills that Lily and Shawna need are scattered throughout the organization.

Lily knows that the way Evergreen has operated in the past is not the way it will operate in the future. Already there is strong pressure from technology to change the way Evergreen competes, the way it relates to customers, and the way it operates internally. The hierarchical approach that Lily has perfected over the past 20 years doesn't seem responsive enough. The MEC has not been effective at planning, and plans often seem out-of-date by the time they are put into action. Using a GSS to create a crisis management plan was quite a departure, but Evergreen's younger managers took to this technology very well, while the older managers who are higher up the bureaucratic ladder seem scared and confused by it. Lily knows from her reading that electronic mail has the capacity to change power relationships in companies, and Evergreen seems ripe for this kind of change. What kind of organization Evergreen will become, especially with the expansion, is a mystery to her.

Questions

1. Based on what you know about organizations, what effect will the creation of a second store have on power relationships at Evergreen? Which part of the organization seems to have power now? What, if any, changes would you expect when this organizational change is followed by networking to integrate the other store, the broker, the research projects?

2. What information technology support can be given to managers like Connie, Shawna, and Lily to help them cope with changes in the modern management imperatives (refer to Tables 11–1 and 11–2)?

3. How is technology changing the bases of competition for Evergreen? What information technological supports are available to help Evergreen succeed? Are there ways that Evergreen might succeed, yet fail, at the same time?

4. What point or points in the organization are going to be the most susceptible to organizational change because of new information technology? Why are they susceptible? What change(s) do you think will occur? What will the effects be?

5. In what ways is Evergreen changing into a geodesic organization? How will information technologies—both installed and planned—facilitate these changes? What will result from these changes?

Module 3

MANAGING RISK IN THE APPLICATION LIFE CYCLE

APPLICATION LIFE CYCLE

After you have read and studied this chapter, you should be able to:

■ Define the word *application* in the context of the application life cycle.

■ Describe the four phases of the problem-solving life cycle and explain how they correspond to the four phases of the ALC.

■ Describe the role managers play in each phase of the ALC.

■ Outline the challenges that the ALC presents to managers.

■ Describe the alternatives to the ALC and discuss their advantages and disadvantages.

Question: What is the life cycle of an information system? What are its major phases and what managerial interest and responsibility arises in each?

Lori Cardiff is the reservations manager for The Esplanade, a five-star hotel known for its service, food, and elegance. It is *not,* however, known for its efficiency, especially in reservations. The director of administration wants Lori to observe the computerized reservation system already in place and recommend a course of action. Foremost on her mind are the following concerns:

■ The Esplanade has an atmosphere of comfort and elegance into which speed doesn't fit.

■ Customers are becoming quite demanding about wanting the best rates for the best periods; they want speed *and* accommodation.

■ Increasingly, the best customers come from overseas, where they are used to asking a few questions and getting exactly what they want quickly.

Lori feels that the system needs upgrading and wonders both where to begin and what the most important issues are.

Answer: The place to begin is the problem-solving life cycle that dictates the system development life cycle involving analysis, design, implementation, and installation-use-maintenance. The primary concerns are information requirements analysis, feasibility, and implementation strategy.

INTRODUCTION

This chapter introduces a segment on risk management that examines how applications that provide management support are created and how to manage that process as a user, not as a technical specialist in information systems. This chapter focuses on users' responsibilities in the application life cycle. Chapter 13 discusses how users can manage applications and direct development projects, concentrating on feasibility studies and implementation strategies. That chapter concludes with managers' information requirements. Chapter 14 describes how users can manage application development projects for both small projects for personal use and large, corporatewide projects.

Expanding the relatively narrow focus of the project, Chapter 15 examines human issues in management support systems such as hiring and training of personnel, motivation and reward, ethical issues, and user-oriented and user-driven information systems.

This chapter introduces the application life cycle (ALC) and examines the role managers and users play in the life cycle of applications. An application is not a computer system or a piece of software, nor is it so simple as a task or job. Instead, we use the word **application** to mean the use of a system to meet specific goals over a period of time by an individual or group (generally, a manager, a group of managers, or a team led by a manager).

WHAT IS AN APPLICATION?

The term *application life cycle* replaces the older term **system development life cycle (SDLC).** The latter is a technical term referring to how systems are created by systems professionals. The SDLC has been in use for at least 25 years and concentrates attention on the activities that go along with building systems rather than using or managing them. SDLC emphasizes technical workers and the tasks they perform. Traditionally, this is how the concept of system building has been presented, and in most forms of the system development life cycle there is little role for the user. The application life cycle, on the other hand, focuses on user roles and basically downplays the role of technical specialists.

In this text, we adopt a broad definition of *application* as the employment or use of a software-based information system to support managers in pursuit of a goal that has been accepted by the user. Thus, a given system can appear as many applications, depending on who is using it and what that person is using it for. This is not the general view of application, however. Most technical specialists consider an application a user-transparent system and ignore the actual use of the system or the goals the system is being used to achieve. We use this definition because in Chapter 3 we defined a system as being goal-directed and action-oriented. A system changes its nature depending on the goals it pursues and the methods it employs. Because of this, we are concerned about the people through whose hands an application passes as it is invented, developed, and used.

The SDLC (and our adaptation of it as the ALC) was not invented by computer personnel or even technical people. It was developed in response to a need to systematize how we solve problems with technology that is extremely fluid and expensive to develop and handle. In the earliest days of information systems, computerization was seen as an extremely capital-intensive activity, because computers and their components were expensive, temperamental, and somewhat unreliable. Development of applications and systems was idiosyncratic and unpredictable, with the emphasis on getting as much out of the hardware as possible. There was little concern for users because most of them were

| Figure 12–1 | PROBLEM SOLVING AS A CYCLE OF ACTIVITIES |

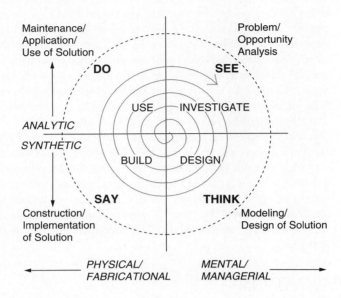

technically adept anyway. The SDLC was an attempt to partition and structure the work of system building in ways that made technical sense and were manageable.

Because the emphasis was on engineering a system from built components rather than on the system's use, coordination of constructed software was ignored. In the past 30 years, the SDLC has become formalized and made part of procedures to manage system development, some of them computerized and many proprietary and sold by consulting companies. As a concept—and a product—the SDLC has worked to manage risk in heavily capitalized system development projects. Most firms honor the SDLC more in its breach than in practice, with many variations and departures from the norm.

However, technology itself has an economic life cycle in which the first products are expensive and hard to use, but within a few years these products become inexpensive and pervasive just before they become obsolete. Accordingly, the SDLC is a bit of a historical dinosaur as labor (for system development) and user time and effort became the expensive components. Our use of the term *application life cycle* moves the emphasis away from the capital-intensive or development-labor-intensive aspects of technology management and places it on users' expense and effort to spread an application around a problem they are attempting to solve.

THE PROBLEM-SOLVING LIFE CYCLE

The problem-solving life cycle (see Figure 12–1) is a more general model of human problem solving related to the model presented in Chapter 1. The **problem-solving life cycle (PSLC)** illustrates the life of a problem as it moves from awareness to solution. The model is derived from the basic notion that people first see a problem, then think about how to solve it, say what they intend to do for a solution, and then act on the solution. The words **see, think, say,** and **do** are concrete forms of the more technical words *investigate, design, build,* and *use.* These words, in fact, are basic terms in an SDLC. A PSLC may also be viewed as four progressive quadrants of an exercise that takes place in two dimensions, one involving physical versus mental distinctions and the other involving the difference between analytic and synthetic activities. This is similar to the distinctions in the cybernetic systems.

The physical/mental distinction applies to the horizontal dimension in Figure 12–1, distinguishing those activities that involve creating and using objects in the real world from those that involve mental models and thought (not that building is without thought, of course, but the emphasis is on production of physical products, that is, solutions). The vertical dimension contrasts analytic activities (taking things apart, understanding what is happening, and why it is happening) and synthetic activities (putting things together or creating new things). These four steps of the PSLC can be described informally then as follows:

- Think about the parts of a problem.
- Think about how the parts together will solve a problem.
- Put the parts together.
- Solve the problem.

To see how this scheme works with a common management support problem, imagine that Connie Somerset (Evergreen Landscaping and Maintenance's sales manager) is faced with the problem of convincing the MEC that the guaranteed green-up plan should not only be continued, it should be beefed up in the coming season. In fact, this isn't the first time Connie has had to convince the MEC and she wonders if her problem isn't actually a class of problems. The essence of that class of problems is to create presentations of data that clearly show the risks and opportunities for spending levels for specific programs. The problem isn't stated very clearly, so her first step is to state it in unambiguous terms:

> I would like to be able to call up sales and forecasting data and convert them quickly into presentations that will show the MEC clearly what the risks and opportunities are for specific levels of expense for aspects of our sales programs.

Connie needs support to create conclusions that convince MEC members. In the PSLC, the first step is to recognize that both a problem and a solution work in the same "space"—the real world of people, meetings, decisions. Ultimately, she will require a support system that works for her with the MEC. To get there, though, she first has to break the problem into conceptual parts. Connie determines there are four parts:

> First, I have to know what data I want to use. There are actual sales and expenditure data and forecasts based on certain scenarios. Second, I need to have the data handy as well as a number of scenarios that I can run the data through. Third, I need to process the data through the models, and finally I need to convert the results into graphs that show break-even points and return on investment outcomes at various times in the future.

Figure 12–2   ANALYZING THE PROBLEM

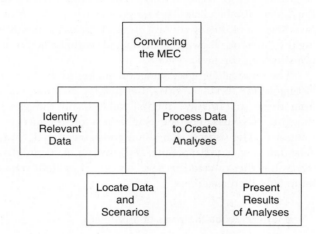

Figure 12–2 illustrates how Connie has broken the problem into four subproblems, each of which may be difficult individually, but certainly none of them is as hard as the overall problem. Each subproblem illustrates a different kind of conceptual challenge. Connie is certain that "identify relevant data" is an intellectual exercise that will involve determining what is important about each sales program at the time and will probably involve talking to others to get their opinions. Of course, it will also mean figuring out which of the many sales figures that Evergreen keeps will be the most relevant. "Locate data and scenarios" will mean asking people where data are kept. Scenarios are difficult to think about, and Connie can always dredge up some nightmarish predictions, but scenarios have to be based on logical thinking about each individual product, so she will have to brainstorm with Sid, Sven, and Shawna (contract manager, retail services manager, and vice president of sales, respectively) about what really could happen. "Process data to create analyses" will be done on the computer, so that will almost certainly require spreadsheets. "Present results of analyses" will mean using graphs, charts, and slides that show numerical results as well as lists of key points that some nonnumerical data will probably turn up. In the case of the guaranteed green-up, Connie thinks that a few interviews with satisfied and not-quite-yet-satisfied customers may spotlight key points that will influence both the scenarios as well as the figures that go into them.

Now Connie gets busy designing solutions based on her problem analysis (Figure 12–3), deciding to design solutions to each part of the problem analysis. While the components of a problem often have strong interactions, Connie is not worried in this case because she has done a lot of work with the MEC and feels that this linear, four-step solution will work fine.

For "identify relevant data," Connie thinks about using only three years' data because older data may be inaccurate, incomplete, or irrelevant. Three years is also sufficient because Connie will use linear projections of past trends by regression analysis. She wants to consult with at least six former customers and find out what drew them to guaranteed green-up (or any program). She also wants to speak with Tulley (purchasing manager)

Figure 12–3   DESIGNING THE SOLUTION

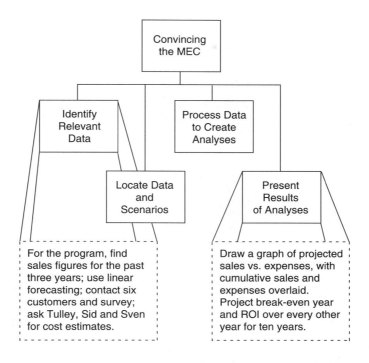

about costs and Sid and Sven (as appropriate) about opportunities and risks. Connie thinks that "present results of analyses" will simply be a graph of projected sales versus expenses (current and cumulative) every other year for the next ten years (+2, +4, +6, +8, +10), noting where the break-even point is and providing annualized ROI for each of these five points. The other two parts of the solution will be designed along similar lines.

Next, Connie actually implements the solution (see Figure 12–4). For example, she creates and checks out a data research procedure to locate and copy the data needed for the analyses. While writing down this procedure, she has checked with her staff, Priscilla Chan, the controller, Shawna, Sid, Sven, and Tulley to see if the procedures are feasible. She discovers that sales figures are kept for the past six years, broken down by line code, although there haven't been special line codes for sales programs until this current year. Some of the figures Connie may need will have to be estimated by hand. Customer lists are hard to find, but they will be available on invoices and, again, this set of data will have to be hand-processed. Sid, Sven, and Tulley have no problem with estimating sales figures for a variety of future sales programs, and Shawna thinks it's certainly possible to call a few customers.

Figure 12–5 illustrates how the data-gathering part of the problem solution is carried out. Only two years' data are available this summer (current and last year), but current customers' identification information will be kept so that feedback can be elicited from them. Because this is the first test of this new kind of marketing procedure, Connie is willing to phone up to 15 current and former customers. She designs a simple form for

---

Figure 12–4   IMPLEMENTING THE SOLUTION

> **DATA RESEARCH PROCEDURE:**
> 1. Look through sales figures for program for past three years; download onto diskette as three files: YR0, YR1 and YR2.
> 2. Find linear forecasting program LINCAST on system.
> 3. Scan customer lists through sales detail figures, create random sample of fifteen customers. Ask assistant to phone until six respond to survey.
> 4. Send Tulley, Sid and Sven the standard sales/expense forecast form.

> For the program, find sales figures for the past three years; use linear forecasting; contact six customers and survey; ask Tulley, Sid and Sven for cost estimates.

Tulley, Sid, and Sven to complete about sales, materials, labor, publicity, training, and administrative costs of programs. Data gathering is complete, and Connie is satisfied that the data are relevant. The next step is to create and run several "what if" scenarios, and she and Shawna have created a best-case, worst-case, and most-likely-case set of scenarios for presentation to the MEC.

Notice that in this example the computer is only part of the solution—a relatively minor part. Developing the data and determining what the most convincing display will be is a more important aspect. In effect, Connie is assuming that the computer, represented by spreadsheets, is an **appliance** that can be applied to whatever aspect of the problem she deems most appropriate. From her point of view, the most pertinent facets of this exercise are designing procedures that can actually be carried out and getting people to buy into them. From Connie's perspective, this is a management exercise that involves developing the best way of going about some task and finding the resources (people, data, computers) to do it.

THE APPLICATION LIFE CYCLE (ALC)

Our discussion now shifts from general problem solving to the specific problem of building an application. It is important to emphasize that the model we present is a normative one. In practice, most firms deviate, often dramatically, from this model. In theory, an **application life cycle (ALC)** follows the same four-step process (Figure 12–6) used in any problem solving. In information systems parlance, "investigate" is called **systems analysis.** For a user, this amounts to finding and defining the problem, contracting for its ultimate solution, and getting approvals in place to create an application to meet a need.

The second step, **system design,** involves users cooperating with designers, evaluating a design as it is completed, testing prototypes as they are created, and managing various versions of prototypes as they are built. A prototype is a model that embodies

| Figure 12–5 | CARRYING OUT THE PROBLEM SOLUTION |

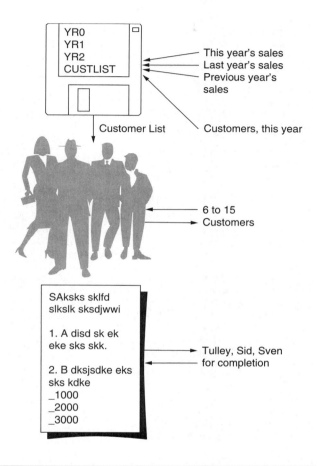

designs but is not the actual final product. Such prototypes can be images or even text, but for information systems they are generally slower, clumsier versions of the final product that users examine to make sure the designers are on the right track. Prototyping is often thought of as the alternative to the ALC because in the past there were no real roles for users except at the final stages when the system was used for production purposes. However, modern life cycle techniques recognize the important central role of user testing of prototypes early in design (or before, in some cases). Prototyping is discussed in detail in a later section.

The third step is **system implementation** in which a system is actually constructed by systems professionals (or sometimes by users). A lot of testing goes on in this phase. Users design and begin training and publicity for system introduction and play a major role in writing procedures for using the system. Again, users were often not involved in this step in the past because intense technical skills were required to program computer systems. However, both technical advances in programming as well as a change in philosophy have led to strong user involvement, especially in testing, procedure writing, and training.

Figure 12-6	THE APPLICATION LIFE CYCLE

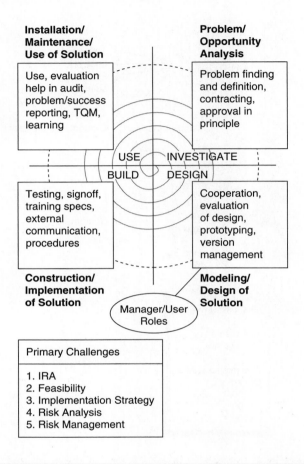

The fourth step is **system installation/use/maintenance.** Users have a role to play in use, evaluation, regular audits of system effectiveness, reporting bugs, learning how to use the system better, and programs of total quality management.

Phase 1 of the ALC: Investigation

The first phase of an ALC (Figure 12–7) includes these steps:

- Determine the business objectives.
- *Audit:* measure existing system performance against objectives or standards.
- *Feasibility:* analyze costs and benefits of proposed or common solutions and determine the risks involved in each solution (sometimes the solution is vague at this stage and feasibility is postponed until the design phase).
- Determine new system objectives from the business objectives.

| Figure 12–7 | APPLICATION LIFE CYCLE: INVESTIGATION PHASE |

Phase: 1. Investigation
Primary Responsibility: Analyst
Goals: Creation of USER Views of the Application
        and Initial Feasibility
Tools: Information Requirements Analysis,
        DFD

Inputs	**Outputs**
Current Performance	Logical or Functional
Description of Current	Specifications
Business	Feasibility Analyses
User Needs	
State of Technology	

Process
Audit System Performance Against Objectives
Analyze Costs and Benefits to Determine the Risks
    Involved
Determine New Business Objectives
Determine System Objectives
Develop Description of System from the Users'
    Viewpoint, Including Functions or Features
    Required

Managerial Responsibilities
Clientship, Stewardship
Resolution of Conflict between System and
    Business Goals

■ Develop a description of the new, required system from users' viewpoint,
  which means creating a list of functions or products for the system.

This phase depends on knowledge of current performance, detailed descriptions of the current business processes, user needs, and an understanding of the current or projected state of technology available as solutions. The result of this phase is a functional description entirely from the users' perspective (sometimes called a **logical design**) of the planned or required system. This is not a time for blueprints and technical drawings. Instead, the emphasis is on understanding the business problem without considering technologies that might be brought forth as solutions. Business analysts may already have some technologies in mind, and sometimes this simplifies, streamlines, or hastens the applications development. Often, pressures to adopt specific technology may force other, better solutions to be filtered out later. Most analysts resist this filtering—managers should do the same, within the bounds of common sense.

A manager has the responsibilities of being a good client and the project steward, if not the project manager (and users often are project managers). Another managerial task is to resolve conflicts between system and business goals based on detailed knowledge of group needs. While slightly different in focus, the trend toward business process reengineering (BPR) shares most of the same goals as an ALC but moves from new or simplified

| Figure 12–8 | APPLICATION LIFE CYCLE: DESIGN PHASE |

Phase: 2. Design
Primary Responsibility: Designers
Goals: Creation of System Views of Application,
　　RFP, RFQ, Blueprints
Tools: Flowcharts, Data Designs, Procedure
　　Analysis, Network Analysis

Inputs	Outputs
Logical Design	Physical Specifications
Current Designs of	RFPs, RFQs, Contracts
Hardware, Software	for Delivery,
Procedures, Network	Timetables,
Data	Agreements
Technical Data on	
Availability	

Process
A. Design Software, Hardware, Network
　Design New Procedures, Job Descriptions,
　　Workflow
　Document and Get Approvals to Build
　　　Or
B. Design Rough Requirements
　Put out RFP, Evaluate Responses
　Select Vendor/Outsourcer/Supplier

Managerial Responsibilities
Understand when Design Is Appropriate, Evaluate
RFP, RFQ, Progress Reports, Prototypes

business objectives (by rethinking how the business is to operate) to new designs. As mentioned in Chapter 3, there is some controversy over whether BPR is really a new way of viewing business or a new way of packaging tried-and-true methods of business repair based on the ALC.

The investigation phase of an ALC includes discovering the experiences of relevant personnel with the current way of doing things and the current business processes. At this phase, user needs, stated and tacit, are on the table, too. A silent but important player is the state of technology. Although it is not yet really important what precise technology will be used, ultimately managers will have to build or buy the system.

Phase 2 of the ALC: Design

The next step is design (Figure 12–8). Two ways to go about design are in-house and outsourced. In-house design means employing IS professionals from one's own business to design software, hardware, communications networks, procedures for work, job descriptions, and work flow. In business process reengineering, these components are *all* new, while traditional systems design makes incremental improvements to existing components. The alternative to in-house design is outsourcing (see also Chapter 16). In this mode, a user designs specifications based on the logical design and submits a **request for proposals (RFP)** to vendors. These vendors then suggest hardware, software, and so forth, that can do the job and submit proposals that the user then evaluates. The user selects the best proposal and detailed design and then proceeds. It is not always the case that the selected supplier for design is also the supplier that builds and installs the system, but of course this is a likely course to follow.

Selecting proposals, in-house or outsourced, is often as political as it is technical and economic and there are always tradeoffs. For example, one vendor may suggest a faster system that has fewer convenient features. Another vendor may suggest a higher-quality, more secure, robust application that takes twice as long to deliver as any other proposal. Different factions (those who use the system output versus those who provide the input versus those who have to maintain it) may favor different proposals. The result is frequently a compromise.

The resulting **physical design** is based on the logical design and the current designs of the components to be replaced, upgraded, or reengineered and includes blueprints for building the system. Blueprints in an IS sense mean file designs and layouts, programming specifications in a variety of technical formats including pseudocode and decision tables, network architectures, and so forth. Design work also culminates in a timetable for development and installation as well as contracts, if necessary, for system development. In the design phase, a manager has the responsibility of understanding when the design is appropriate (which means reading and understanding blueprints), asking for feedback and progress reports frequently enough to catch errors, and handling and approving prototypes.

Phase 3 of the ALC: Build

The building phase (Figure 12–9) involves a number of obvious and not-so-obvious steps. Software is programmed, hardware is bought, leased, or rented, and network capability is located or built. The system is tested in part and in whole at various stages against test materials that managers have the responsibility to create. Examples are an exhaustive set of transactions sampled over a period of time for a transaction-processing system, a challenging set of database searches, or advising situations for more complex systems.

An **installation plan** must be developed, generally by the user and the technical manager. Installation can include not only putting software on a computer but also building new rooms, running cables, and generally disrupting everyone's work life. Hardware and software have to be installed, and often people have to be hired to staff the new system, jobs may have to be redesigned, and new procedures must be created. New procedures have to be documented, and some form of that documentation has to be made available to users who will be trained. While systems professionals may do the training, it is often left to user management to locate and provide detailed training not only in *how* to use the new system, but also *why, when,* and *for what.*

Training often begins in this phase with a prototype system (because it is the **application interface** that people will be trained how to use, not the system proper, it is easy to start training in this phase). Changes need to be publicized and public relations needs to be handled. Public relations is always best handled by user management, not by IS professionals who may be seen as lacking objectivity and credibility. Finally, where there is an existing system, files have to be converted—sometimes a massive undertaking when there are thousands or millions of records.

| Figure 12–9 | APPLICATION LIFE CYCLE: BUILD PHASE |

Phase: 3. Build
Primary Responsibility: Developers
Goals: Creation of Tested, Running, Documented
System and Trained, Informed Users
Tools: Programming, Training, File Conversion,
Testing

Inputs	Outputs
Physical Designs or Contractor's Specs	Running System
	Documentation
Current File and Plant	Procedures
Designs	Trained Users

Process
Program Software
Buy, Lease, or Rent Hardware
Arrange for Network Resources
Test System in Part and Whole
Develop Installation, Publicity Plans
Produce Documentation
Train Staff
Alter Physical Plant or Build New Facility
Convert Files
Publicize Application

Managerial Responsibilities
Project Management, Financing, Staff Training and
(Re)Deployment, Physical Plant Management,
Publicity

Inputs to the build phase are the physical designs. Output is a running, tested system and enough documentation to operate it properly. Managers have project management responsibilities in this phase (even though they cannot manage programmers technically, they are generally responsible for making sure programs are tested to users' satisfaction) as well as **staff training and redeployment** responsibilities. Training often is needed when managers find out that the staff if not going to make the transition successfully. Without a redeployment plan, staff members may end up frustrated and unproductive. Financing also becomes a consideration at this phase because expenses peak just prior to installation and cost pressures can kill many a project because absolutely no benefits have been experienced yet. Finally, managers find themselves embroiled in physical plant management whenever hardware is involved or when new procedures require a change in physical layout.

Phase 4 of the ALC: Installation/Use/Maintenance

Finally, the operational phase—installation, use, and maintenance—occurs (see Figure 12–10). It is always hoped that this will be the longest of the phases, although the half-life (the time it takes for half of the original functionality to disappear or become irrelevant) of most systems may lie between four and five years even for systems that require two years or more to build.

Figure 12–10	APPLICATION LIFE CYCLE: INSTALLATION/USE/MAINTENANCE PHASE

Phase: 4. Installation, Use, Maintenance
Primary Responsibility: User/Operator
Goals: Maintain System, Smooth Operations
Tools: Operations Logging,
        Post-Implementation Audit

Inputs	**Outputs**
Running System	New or Upgraded
Operational	Application
Documentation	Increased Performance
Organizational Goals	New Operational Goals
Previous Performance	
Audits	

Process
Install System or Application
Use System or Application
Fine-Tune Evaluation Program
Fine-Tune Operations through Maintenance
Perform Regular Evaluations, Post-Implementation
    Audits
Rethink and Rework Organizational Goals in Light
    of New Performance of Application and
    Organization

Managerial Responsibilities
Evaluation at All Steps, Technological Leadership,
    Diffusion of Use, Risk Management

Installation is the beginning of this phase, which is followed by a period of use in which users become familiar with the system and fine-tune their evaluation procedure. What is important when a system is first used—learnability—becomes less important as pressure to be productive rises. Operations are fine-tuned, including maintenance involving corrections, enhancements, and regular upgrades from vendors. Upgrades may include new operating systems releases or new products that are seen as enhancements, which must be shoehorned into the existing system to make them useful. Often, new products have unique file formats that require nontransparent interfaces between the existing system and the newly acquired enhanced package. This can happen with new word processors, new GUIs, or even new database management packages.

This phase uses the running system as the intellectual input, along with new or changed organizational goals and previous audits of performance. The result of maintenance and evaluation is a system with increased performance and a number of upgraded features. Managers' responsibilities in this phase include technological leadership of their units, continuous evaluation, and pressure for an improved system and diffusion of its use among those who are supposed to be using it.

Imagine that Connie has asked Terry Bonner, a systems analyst working for Evergreen, to build an application that will allow her to recognize the fastest- and slowest-moving products and produce a report so that she can either run promotions or perhaps look into expanding sales. Here's how an ALC would work in theory. Terry interviews Connie, perhaps several times. Because Connie isn't the only one using the report, Terry may also interview Sven and examine existing sales reports. After a while, Terry puts all the data from the investigation together and comes up with a set of requirements that may satisfy Connie. At this point, Connie either approves or rejects the requirements (called *logical specifications*). Or, she may be so discouraged by what she's been told that she tells Terry to forget it. Most of Terry's efforts are lost in this case, although it may turn out that Connie really doesn't need this report anyway. If Connie likes what Terry tells her, she encourages Terry to design the application.

Because this is a relatively simple application, Terry creates a design quickly. However, the design is a technical document and isn't of much direct use to Connie. Part of the design is a close estimate of the feasibility of the project, including costs and estimated completion dates, which Connie does understand. Presuming Connie will approve the design (again, she might not have much to go on in terms of understanding much of the design terminology), Terry creates the application.

Because the application is essentially a complex database query and display, Terry uses Evergreen's database manager to write the application. While writing the application, Terry also writes a user's manual and some technical notes on the application. The user's manual details how to use the application while the technical notes describe hardware and software requirements. Connie reviews these documents while Terry programs not only to make sure that the application is what she wants but also to learn about the application so that she can use it.

When Terry finishes programming and testing, Connie runs an acceptance test on the application using live data that she can check manually and signs off (i.e., approves) when she is convinced the application runs well. At this point, Connie owns the application. If it runs well, all is fine. If it fails to perform correctly or efficiently, Connie better have bought an extended service warranty.

ALC CHALLENGES FOR MANAGERS

As stated previously, an ALC is at best a conceptualization or a model of how systems are built. It isn't actually a specific plan for action—that depends on what system is being built, who will use it, how it will be used, what the expectations are, and so forth. Nor does attending to everything in the model guarantee success in building systems, because high risks are involved.

Five challenges for managers come along with the ALC model, and they are outlined in Table 12–1. Alternatives to the model (discussed in the next section) may finesse or sidestep some of these challenges while introducing others. These challenges are: determine information requirements; determine the feasibility of various proposed solutions; develop a strategy for implementation, especially when users are doing some of the construction; analyze the risks of implementation; and manage those risks.

Information requirements analysis (IRA) has occupied a central place in the ALC since information systems advanced beyond simple automation of manual processes. IRA originally meant finding out what information managers need to make specific decisions. But in recent years, IRA has expanded to include what procedures and interfaces are needed, what the capabilities of the users are (including what they know as well as what they can do), and what kinds and levels of support are needed. IRA is, of course, the soul of investigation. The result of a good IRA is a good model of the manager-user, and a

Table 12-1	PRIMARY LIFE CYCLE CHALLENGES	

Life Cycle Challenge	Details	Managerial Roles
Information requirements analysis (IRA)	Determine the best method for finding out what information, procedures, and systems are needed for management support	Source of details on information needs, goals of group/department, current procedures and why they exist, history of information, and management support systems
Feasibility	Understand what the possible, affordable, effective solutions may be and evaluate whether they are good enough to proceed with	Budget, time, organizational information
Implementation strategy	Select the best way to acquire a solution: build versus buy; determine who should do the work and in what mode	Management judgment, cost, and time requirements
Risk analysis	Understand economic, scheduling, technological, and organizational risks involved in a project	Familiarity with and judgment of alternatives to the ALC, understanding of organizational policies and politics
Risk management	Manage the risks and cope with the results	Project management

system built with good intelligence from the IRA will have a higher chance of success than without it. But the critical challenge is how to find these information or procedural needs. Who actually knows what they are? Will those persons be able to supply that information reliably and accurately? Is that information volatile, that is, is what we knew about these needs last week still relevant?

Another challenge facing managers is the **feasibility** of system construction. As anyone who has ever had something built or repaired knows, estimates are notoriously inaccurate and sometimes even fictitious. Most governments are aware of huge cost overruns and failure to deliver on contracts involving low-tech projects. High-tech projects involving computers historically have horrendous feasibility records. Most information systems organizations bypass strict feasibility criteria when they build management support systems (although they may insist on lip service to certain engineering methods when they make estimates, knowing that they are going to be up to 100 percent wrong). Because managers are on the receiving end, however, they are going to feel insecure without some sort of feasibility testing.

A related issue is that many management support systems are aimed at limited, even one-time, use. In these cases, full-scale feasibility studies may be unwarranted. Suppose Connie wants to build a spreadsheet to project sales of certain goods using a model she has developed. The model includes the impact of advertising, delivery reliability, and shelf-life considerations. Connie lets Terry know what she wants and tells her she has all the formulas ready but hasn't the time or inclination to build the spreadsheet. Should Terry do a formal feasibility study? No. Instead, Terry and Connie should talk about a *portfolio* of related forecasting applications. The knowledge Terry and Connie will gain from each successive component of the portfolio will significantly lower the perceived costs of each activity.

Similar to the IRS challenge is knowing how to *build* systems. There are a number of implementation choices involving different tools or different procedures. Because many managers don't understand the choices, they often do not adopt valuable and reliable implementation strategies and instead go along with whatever technical advisors tell them. This can sometimes be a disaster. A technically sound system may turn out to be a monster the likes of Frankenstein—easy to build but hard to live with.

Finally, because the buck stops with managers, being able to analyze and manage the risks that come with the ALC is crucial not only to system success but also to managerial success. Understanding the economic, scheduling, technological, and organizational risks is crucial to managing those risks.

ALTERNATIVES TO APPLICATION LIFE CYCLE

In practice, an ALC looks a lot like the way engineers build bridges. In building bridges, engineers apply known technologies to well-researched situations to derive solutions that are demonstrably the best or at least adequate. In adapting this engineering technique, an ALC model makes a number of assumptions, not all of which are true in all cases:

- Each problem is unique; applications are not built on previous solutions.
- Information is not shared from application to application—applications do not "learn" from one another.
- Each of the stages is a unique, separate step in a series of steps.
- These steps cannot or will not be retraced.
- Systems professionals, users, managers, technology providers, and upper management have unique and separate roles.

In practice, applications are not unique. Often, someone, somewhere has already solved the problem and may, in fact, be selling software that accomplishes the solution. And while applications might not "learn," those who work on applications do indeed learn and apply what they know from application to application. However, people sometimes learn bad habits, so learning is not always a blessing.

Theoretically, an ALC is constructed like a **waterfall,** with water flowing from one step to another in strict order. Water, as we all know, does not flow uphill, but the steps or stages of an ALC are more often than not traversed simultaneously or at least with a great deal of overlap. It's quite common for steps to be retraced or repeated. In fact, some commentators speak of a **spiral** or **whirlpool** model rather than a waterfall model. While this repetition can lead to a lot of extra cost, it may also work to enhance the final product through iterated improvement.

Finally, it is only in theory that role players have scripts and directors in an ALC drama. In practice, an ALC resembles freestyle improv theater in which actors trade parts and scripts as the play is performed. Increasingly, users are taking over more technical roles as development technologies, such as CASE and fourth-generation languages (4GLs), merge and user tools become more powerful.

Three alternatives to an ALC violate subsets of these assumptions and include prototyping, end user system development, and package tailoring. Recall the application that Connie asked Terry to create to pinpoint merchandise that is moving exceptionally rapidly or slowly. We will examine the three alternatives to an ALC and how they differ from Connie's viewpoint.

Figure 12–11　HOW PROTOTYPING WORKS

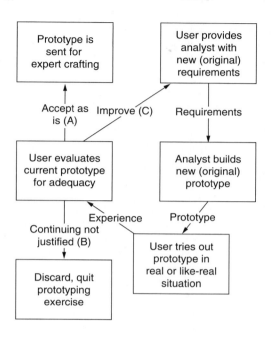

Prototyping

Prototyping (see Figure 12–11) is a class of application-building models that negates the waterfall theory. An ALC proposes strictly linear and separate stages of investigation, design, building, and use. Prototyping, on the other hand, brings one or more users together with a designer in a series of interactions in which investigation, design, building, and use occur almost simultaneously. The goal of this is not to have a working application but to create one or more working prototypes of the application.

Prototyping is both a way to gather requirements and a technique for constructing applications. The process begins with a systems professional, generally a systems analyst, interviewing one or more potential users about their requirements. This interview may be formal or informal and it may take place in a group over one or more sessions. It may even use GSS as a means of gathering information. Regardless of how the original requirements are collected, the analyst then proceeds to build a first prototype of the desired application. The prototype may be constructed using traditional programming techniques, but these are generally far too inflexible to be used in any kind of rapid prototyping technique. Instead, the analyst will probably use either a prototyping tool (spreadsheet programs are useful as are most database managers), a computer-assisted software engineering (CASE) tool, an application generator, or a complex tool such as an EIS (for example, *Commander* or *Lotus Notes*). CASE is really intended to be used by systems professionals in the design stages of complex systems, but it is possible to use CASE for prototyping (see Chapter 14).

There are many application generators, but most are limited as they generate variations on a set theme. These variations are only those foreseen when the generator was designed, so they might not run the gamut of all possible or desired situations. Packages with script-like languages or macro languages are also useful in prototyping. A valuable characteristic of a prototyping tool is its ability to "mock up" screens. Doing so enables managers to practice making queries, building and running models, and interacting with data to get a feel for whether the prototype will be adequate, useful, and painless to use.

After the prototype is built, users look at it, try it out, and stress it in whatever ways are desired. There are three possible outcomes at this stage:

1. *Lucky Guess:* The analyst gets it right the first time and users are pleased with the result.

2. *Total Disaster:* Either the analyst or the users recognize that the application is a nonstarter and that it's not worth any more effort to pursue it.

3. *Work-in-Progress:* The analyst and users agree that there are parts of the prototype that are marvelous while other parts are in need of improvement.

If the prototype proves valuable (1), it may be sent to systems professionals to be made into an efficient management support system. It may also be the case that one of the prototypes actually solves the problem so well that the original problem disappears and the application is not needed. Case 2 is rarely an outcome. When it is, however, at least the analyst and users have learned what the limits are to the technology, the users' patience, or the analyst's skills. Most commonly, the result is Case 3—a bit more improvement is needed. When this occurs, the analyst may modify the prototype, for example, by changing something in the format of the screen or report, altering a formula, adding a new section, deleting unwanted words or calculations, or creating a new format. In any case, the next prototype becomes the subject of another user evaluation and this cycle is repeated until either outcome 1 or outcome 2 occurs.

As prototypes are created and evaluated, the analyst and user build up a fund of knowledge about the application and the user's experience that is incorporated in successive prototypes. The history of the prototype is a kind of cinema of development in which initial user requirements are slowly turned into an application. There are several advantages to prototyping:

- There is cooperation between analyst and user that is not present in the strictly followed ALC. Note, however, that user participation is absolutely essential.
- User requirements may change over time and an ALC has no way to track these rapidly and effectively.
- Creation of an application proceeds rapidly if the prototyping tool is of high quality.
- User approval is based on multiple interactions with the analyst and the prototype, hence it is far more likely to be informed and positive rather than uninformed and begrudging.

There are also a number of drawbacks to prototyping:

- Users who are very particular or who don't really know what they want might drag out the prototyping process forever.

- User requirements may change in response to the prototyping process and ultimately have nothing to do with the user's real desires or initial needs.
- The prototype will, of course, be inefficient because efficiency suffers when the prototype is built rapidly. The effort to turn the sow's ear of a prototype into a silk purse of an application may be too high and the cost prohibitive. A working prototype may turn into an expensive application.
- Prototypes may be insufficiently tested to be used repeatedly without developer intervention. Other technical problems may include lack of documentation, lack of flexibility brought about by a focus on the current problem, and a resulting reinvention of this wheel every time the same requirement arises.
- User participation is essential and may turn out to be very costly both in time and effort. Users should expect to spend a significant amount of time with developers for any critical management support system.

The decision to build a prototype is motivated by a number of factors, and Chapter 13 discusses how to make this choice. In the case of Connie's sales application, the process may be described as follows.

After interviewing Connie, Terry explores the existing database of sales information and, based on initial ideas, produces a prototype using the database manager. Connie explores the data, first paying attention to the information in the mocked-up report. She suggests a number of improvements having to do with ways of selecting "fast-moving" and "slow-moving" and suggests a formula for Terry to use. Terry takes these ideas and makes some quick changes to the first prototype and meets Connie the next day. Connie is pleased with the improvements. But now she wants to examine not just the ten fastest- and slowest-moving products but the fastest and slowest 5 percent of products sorted by department. She wants to isolate not only which items but which *kinds* of items are moving fastest and slowest. Terry makes this change, along with a few formatting changes (colors, column widths, placement on the screen) suggested by Connie, and creates a third prototype. Connie thinks that this prototype is exactly what she wants, except now she's unsure about the 5 percent figure: Can Terry make that percentage variable so that Connie can select the number at will? Terry proceeds to make the change. The fourth prototype is exactly what Connie wants and she accepts it as is. Because Connie is not concerned with speed or finesse, she simply adds the fourth prototype to her microcomputer repertoire.

End User Software Development

Another alternative to an ALC is **end user software development** (Figure 12–12). In this case, end users may use various packages or tools to create applications. Because the number of packages available to users is increasing daily, it would do little good to review specific ones here. However, certain classes of such application-creation tools are important to managers:

- Database managers
- Spreadsheet packages
- Word processors
- Script languages (operating system specific)
- Integrated packages including some or all of the above

Figure 12–12   END USER SOFTWARE

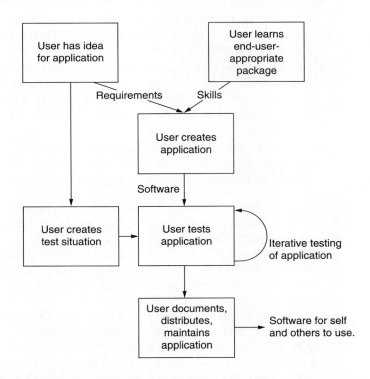

Database managers typically make their facilities available to managers in four different ways. Managers can issue commands from a prompt to access, retrieve, sort, merge, and report on data. A second way to use a database manager is through a GUI or a set of menus that provide access to the same capabilities, but without the necessity of typing the commands. In some cases, managers can create queries by example. A third way of using the capabilities of a database manager is by writing programs. While programming is a highly technical skill, the facilities of a database manager handle much of the detail work including locating data, handling operating system interfaces, formatting, error handling, synchronization, and data conversion. On the other hand, most database managers have a lot of power, which may cause managers who are not familiar with the programming languages to get into a lot of trouble. Complex problem solutions are difficult to implement, if only because there are so many things that could go wrong. The necessity of typing in commands, saving them in a sequence, and testing them later is eased somewhat by a memorization or learning mode. In this mode, a database manager remembers a sequence of commands or keystrokes and makes them available either through a prompt (to memorize and later to recall) or through a GUI. However, this feature cannot disguise the fact that what is happening is programming and not casual usage.

Database managers simply implement many of the features for data management that programmers have always had access to, but spreadsheet packages are and always were programs intended for nonprogrammers. A spreadsheet is essentially a **what you see is**

what you get (WYSIWYG) application, with the results displayed where the formulas lie. However, just as its name implies, a spreadsheet has spread and colonized other areas of management support. Most spreadsheets now provide database management, presentation graphics, advanced numerical calculations, and modeling (including financial and statistical formulas), telecommunications, some word processing, and three-dimensional and linked-sheet models.

Most spreadsheet packages have a way of grouping commands into **macros** that can be recalled with a few simple keystrokes. The macros are defined inside the spreadsheets themselves by users and may be edited like any text in the spreadsheet. It is possible for users to get into a lot of trouble using macros, however. Consider that trained programmers spend a lot of time creating programs that are one-dimensional (i.e., linear). A spreadsheet containing macros and imbedded menus is essentially a two-dimensional program that combines data, commands, and formulas. Remembering where everything is and what labels match what menus and features is an incredibly difficult task for even small spreadsheets. Add to this a very rich macro language and the possibility for problems multiples. The macro language for *Lotus 1-2-3* strongly resembles that of *BASIC* and requires almost as much skill to master. The major saving grace is the relatively limited freedom available in the macro language to manipulate external data. Few users take the time to carefully debug and document their spreadsheets beyond a dump of the formulas in each cell. Debugging a two-dimensional program is at least twice as intricate as debugging a one-dimensional (linear) program. And it is probably as true today as it was for programmers 20 years ago that maintaining spreadsheets is far less attractive than creating new ones. Thus, there is little doubt that users are perpetually reinventing wheels and spreadsheets when sharing templates would probably be a lot more efficient. There are no documented, reliable estimates of the amount of time wasted by users in creating and dressing up relatively minor spreadsheets that are then discarded or reinvented by neighbors, but it must be considerable. Managers have the responsibility of providing for and occasionally checking on the maintenance of the tools their workers use. Workers who create new tools (spreadsheets and database programs) deserve no less attention in this regard.

Word processors also have macro languages that enhance or complicate (depending on your viewpoint) the use of these tools. The appearance of microcomputer-based word processors has had for technology in general a unique social effect on the workplace. Unlike true programming tools and quasiprogramming tools such as database managers and spreadsheets, the migration of typing and formatting skills from the typing pool to the professional and managerial desk has increased support staff capabilities in the organization without an attendant increase in managerial authority. Database skills may give managers access to other people's data or to data that may provide a competitive edge, but word processing skills merely speed up a cycle in which a manager's thoughts are made available to other people. This may work in a manager's favor by increasing span of contact or making contact more quickly with others, but the essential skills (typing, formatting, spelling, and grammar correction) were adequately handled through an efficient system of transcription. In effect, there has been a redistribution of skill in the managerial-secretarial unit quite unlike that anywhere else in the firm. Secretarial skills have been moving to managers (granted, greatly enhanced) and managerial skills have been moving to secretaries, often without an increase in the overall power of the unit. While it may be said with some certainty that knowledge brings power, the word processor has, in the words of some, simply increased the blizzard of paper and thus deflated the value of individual pieces of paper. Or, it may have merely increased the cost of producing words on paper because secretaries and typing pools have been laid off and replaced with expensive managerial typing time. Thus, the managerial use of word processors and presentation managers as end user software development tools may have the strange effect of deskilling and disenfranchising managers by redistributing time and effort in unexpected ways.

Script languages are available as adjuncts to most online interactive packages. Like the macro languages of spreadsheets and the learn modes of word processors, script languages enable users to build an application through a series of learned commands. Script languages are found everywhere, from network managers to operating systems and from telecommunications packages to hypermedia systems. They are very powerful when used by those familiar with programming and the objects of the systems, but they can prove daunting to the casual user. While most script languages are intended for applications setup (such as configuring a network or operating system resources), there is a temptation to turn them into end user programming tools. With the advent of more intelligent GUIs, it is likely that this trend will accelerate. The prudent manager will carefully weigh the resource requirements of learning what might be temporary programming skills that are not necessarily transferable to other aspects of managerial activity against the requirements of the moment for increased access to data and information.

Let's consider again Connie's desire to create software to help her choose the fastest- and slowest-selling items. As an end user, she may approach the task by first learning where the data on sales are to be found. Assume that the data are available through a database management system, but Connie is not familiar with the system. After questioning Terry, Connie discovers that she can use a few canned commands to partition the sales data and recover only the fastest- and slowest-moving 5 percent (i.e., 10 percent of the database). Terry tells Connie that the resulting file can be imported into Connie's spreadsheet processor, so Connie creates headers and formats her spreadsheets so that she can import the data to make two reports, one on fast-moving items and one on slow-moving items. Then Connie creates a set of menus and macros in her spreadsheets to (1) import the data, (2) sort it, (3) calculate totals for different classes of items, (4) create graphics comparing the various classes, and (5) write the data into a file suitable for importing into her word processor. Connie writes a set of macros for her word processor to import both the graphics and text into a boilerplate report she sets up. Her application is now complete.

Of course, Connie could use an integrated package to handle the data management, calculation, graphics, and word processing. Microsoft markets an integrated suite of tools that allows relatively seamless transportation of data, spreadsheets, graphics, and text back and forth across boundaries of the programs doing the processing. However, Evergreen does not yet have a corporate policy on any software purchase, so Connie has purchased these packages herself and developed an end user style that requires a great deal of data importing and exporting. Perhaps next year she will acquire a more integrated package.

Package Tailoring

The third alternative to an ALC is to buy or license existing software (Figure 12–13). This software can often be modified, or tailored, to an organization's needs. **Package tailoring** may simply mean reinstalling software on the buyer's hardware, but it may also mean adding transaction types, data types, databases, or additional screens. Reconfiguring a package for incompatible or enhanced hardware, for networking nonnetworked packages, or for more users than the software can normally handle are also examples of

| **Figure 12—13** | PACKAGE TAILORING |

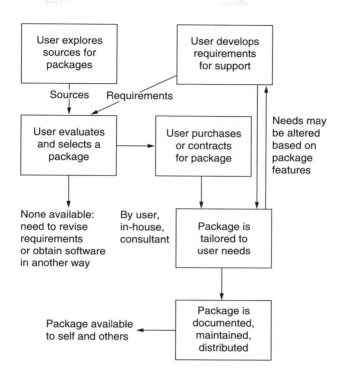

tailoring. Each of these changes may require a unique information systems skill. Buyers should not assume that a given package can be tailored to fit any hardware or accomplish any task just because they think the task is related. Information systems are sometimes remarkably inflexible. The sources of software are multiplying daily, but for most organizations a source list would include the following:

- Consulting companies and accounting firms provide general or customized versions of general-purpose packages that they produce for their clients.
- Relatively inexpensive, off-the-shelf, mass-marketed software for applications ranging from telemarketing to expert systems are available everywhere.
- Professional, trade, and industry associations may contract for and have built for themselves precompetitive software for information handling and sharing that benefit the industry as a whole.
- Shareware is available by downloading from networks or the Internet or in mass-marketed outlets, including supermarkets and hardware stores.
- Fire sales, industrial garage sales, bankruptcy auctions, and commercial disposal sometimes make software available either bundled into hardware or as a separate package.

Consulting companies produce high-quality software that is often tested on client sites first and then later repackaged and offered at a lower price to other clients. Because this is generic software, buyers may also want to purchase the services of the consulting firm to customize the software to their own requirements. As is the case in most of life, you get what you pay for: expensive, reliable software that will probably do precisely what you asked for—and no more.

An alternative is to buy an off-the-shelf package from a specialty or mass-market outlet. By carefully following the installation instructions, it is usually possible for managers to configure or modify the software to suit their special needs. The limit of this flexibility is the imagination of the software designers, and it is further limited by managers' patience and ability to decipher poorly written documentation. As with the software from consulting companies, only multiplied a hundredfold, generic software is only so malleable. Small firms often hire consulting companies just to install complex packages. As microcomputer memory enlarges, so too do software packages' appetites for memory and installation time. Many mass-marketed packages require extensive installation time and resources and they may not be reconfigurable at a later date if the manager decides an additional data source or data format should be added. Of course, many, if not the majority of, packages are relatively easy to install. Managers do not need to be reminded, however, that installation time is not productive or billable.

Purchasing someone else's system may in many cases be a good move. Used software is not a market that many are familiar with, and there are some risks involved. If a company has gone out of business, could its information system have contributed to that failure? A company in disarray may not have complete documentation, solidly installed software, or software without bugs in it. As with buying used cars, managers need to exercise caution, bring along an expert, and test drive the software before signing on the dotted line.

In summary, customizing purchased software is a costly, risky venture for the uninitiated. As an alternative to developing software in-house, it often has the advantage of decreasing development time and capitalizing on the cost advantages of economies of scale. However, for a manager with particular support needs, customizing such systems may prove an expensive hurdle. Consider that purchasing an expert system shell still requires entry of expert rules before it can be productive. An accounting system that handles all but 97 percent of a business may prove to be less than valuable because the missing 3 percent may be the competitive edge the business can never add to the package without expensive redevelopment. Or, suppose an HR system bought from an industry competitor may in fact make it easier for a business to hire and retain people, but its data formats may make the system useless to everyone else in the firm when they want to configure projects, outsource, or move plants to another city.

Connie Somerset may also consider a tailored package that will do the sort of sales analysis she desires. Connie discovers from a marketing trade magazine that a firm in Texas called Special FX has created software called *Sales-1*. This package does an incredible number of sales- and marketing-related analyses, one of which is to produce reports on item movement onto and off of shelves. However, the package is a memory hog (22 megabytes of hard drive and 4 megabytes to run), and it's not clear from the promotional literature whether it will segregate fast- and slow-moving items in the way Connie wants. She phones for a demo copy, which arrives the next day by courier. She discovers that it takes only a few minutes to install the demo, but there is no mention of how long it will take to install the working copy. Still more worrisome is the fact that there is no mention in the demo of customizing the report she wants. However, an attractive range of other sales analysis reports is available including several she has also been thinking about. Two calls to Special FX's sales office reveal that the report she wants isn't available in the format she wants. But Special FX tells her it has been thinking about adding this kind of flexibility and will probably bring it out in the next release, scheduled for next year, as an upgrade for only $250 for current owners. Or, the company volunteers to send Connie an alpha test version (bugs and all) for free (with purchase of the test license) or it can write special software for her to license for only $1,000—delivery sometime this year.

The Modern Management Imperatives

Reach: Global Competition	Competing globally means that organizations can find software and systems worldwide. Some of the best software in the world comes from India. Using homegrown software makes less and less sense if the package has already been harvested elsewhere.
Reaction: Quick Customer Feedback on Products and Services	For management support systems, the customer is the manager, whose involvement in projects means that feedback is immediate and powerful. An ALC historically has meant reduced involvement, but prototyping and end user software development imply intimate participation and commitment.
Responsiveness: Shortened Concept-to-Customer Cycle Time	Rapid prototyping (RAD will be discussed in Chapter 15) and package tailoring significantly decrease delivery times of applications as well as the cost of failure and make it possible to include concepts (needs, ideas) while they are fresh and important to managers.
Refinement: Greater Customer Sophistication and Specificity	As managers become more experienced both with specific management support systems and their creation and maintenance, more of the initial design and fine-tuning of systems can be handled by the managers themselves. Increased involvement can only mean better, more functional systems. The danger is in losing focus (managers aren't system developers). Can managers avoid the problems that technical specialists can't?
Reconfiguration: Reengineering of Work Patterns and Structures	As prototyping and end user software development become more common, managers may find their jobs redefined with more technology management filtering in. This is a mixed blessing because rapid technological change puts pressures on managers to keep up-to-date. Keeping current is a full-time job for technicians; managers may find it daunting at best.
Redeployment: Reorganization and Redesign of Resources	Managers will find their applications define their jobs and that information resources will become, after human resources, the most important class of resources they control. The struggle for information resources is a new challenge for managers, one they may find difficult, especially given political battles.
Reputation: Quality and Reliability of Product and Process	The quality and variety of management support systems can only increase as managers become more involved in their design and development. Quality will become an issue, however, when involvement in technical aspects starts to exceed managers' abilities to program, test, and document their own software. Technical training for nonspecialists is still in its infancy, consisting mostly of computer literacy courses; there is no tradition of this kind of technology management to tap for such training.

■ THE APPLICATION LIFE CYCLE AT THE ESPLANADE

Lori begins by working with the director and the president to understand what they have in mind. Simultaneously, she talks to marketing to get a fix on customer needs. She hopes these two views will be somewhat consistent, but isn't surprised to find out that they are not. Upper management wants to maintain the hotel's stodgy but dependable image. Marketing feels that most of their customers want fast responsiveness to travel plans and changes, packages that suit their own needs, an understanding of what the competition (across several oceans) is offering, and absolutely transparent reservations tied in, if possible, with airline, limousine, and tour schedules. Quite a tall order, thinks Lori. She feels strongly that her first challenge is resolving this conflict—not a new or unexpected one. After all, she was hired by the director, not the president, and she is certainly going to have to carry out project management herself, which requires some boning up on her part. Meanwhile, she feels daunted because she doesn't really understand how to go about creating the new system and what the other priorities are. What she *does* know is that marketing has really scared her and her day-to-day sensitivity to what is happening in the reservations department scares her even more. ∎

1. Outline and then flesh out with role playing the five major challenges Lori faces. What manifestations of these challenges will appear, that is, how will Lori view and handle each challenge as it appears?

2. For each of the four major phases of the ALC, describe what will go on at the hotel and what specific activities Lori will be engaged in and with whom. What critical information will she have to know to get this project done?

3. What happens if Lori fails to carry out her responsibilities?

Summary

An application is the employment or use of a software-based system to support a manager in pursuit of a goal. Applications have a life cycle, beginning with a problem or need. The application life cycle (ALC) is a conceptualization of the development and the use of a set or system of applications based on a more basic, problem-solving life cycle, and an even more primitive notion of problem-solving. (See Chapter 1.) In the problem-solving life cycle, a problem is identified and investigated (see) and a solution designed (think); the solution is then created (say) and finally put into effect (do). The ALC applies this general idea to the creation of applications in four steps: systems analysis, system design, implementation, and use/maintenance. First, a problem requiring information support is thoroughly defined and investigated. Next, one or more solutions (hardware and software together) is designed. Third, the application is built, involving programming and the procurement of hardware. Finally the application is installed and maintained until it is no longer valuable, at which point the cycle may start again. Managers play important roles throughout the ALC, including identifying clients, resolving conflicts, approving and accepting designs and applications, training users, arranging publicity, staff deployment, project management, and evaluation techniques, distributing the application among staff, and managing risk. The ALC is best suited for major projects that involve information systems professionals. Alternatives to the ALC include prototyping, construction of applications by the end users themselves, and tailoring packages to meet users' needs.

Discussion Questions

12.1 The ALC is based on the way we generally solve problems. There are many assumptions built into this process, however. What are they? Are they always true? Can you think of examples in which the problem being solved can't be handled with an ALC?

12.2 One common way of managing application development today is to have an end user manage the entire project. This has advantages and disadvantages. What are they? In what circumstances would you advise not having an end user involved at all in a development project?

12.3 What kinds of applications would best be prototyped? Developed by end users? Tailored?

12.4 In what ways do you think that object-oriented databases might change how the ALC occurs? What kinds of empowerment of users does moving away from data and toward objects make for? Think about a management support system that would be useful to you as a student. Would thinking of the application as a set of interacting objects change your role in the development process?

12.5 System development is often felt to be daunting, and users often back off, even if they aren't excluded. Why do you think this is so? Is this harmful? If so, to whom and in what way? How do you think that it is possible to increase user involvement? Is it possible to have too much user involvement? What harm might be done? How can a balance be struck?

Key Terms

appliance	package tailoring	staff training and redeployment
application	physical design	system design
application interface	problem-solving life cycle	system development life cycle
application life cycle (ALC)	(PSLC)	(SDLC)
end user software development	prototyping	system implementation
feasibility analysis	request for proposal (RFP)	system installation/use/
information requirements	script language	maintenance
analysis	see, think, say, do problem	systems analysis
installation plan	solving	waterfall model of an ALC
logical design	spiral (whirlpool) model of an	what you see is what you get
macros	ALC	(WYSIWYG)

References

Alavi, M. "An Assessment of the Prototyping Approach to Information System Development." *Communications of the ACM* 27, 6 (June 1984).

Cerveny, R., E. Garrity, and G. Sanders. "The Application of Prototyping to Systems Development: A Rationale and Model." *Journal of Management Information Systems* 3, 3 (Fall 1986).

Flaatten, P., D. McCubbrey, P. O'Riordan, and K. Burgess. *Foundations of Business Systems.* 2d ed. Fort Worth, TX: The Dryden Press, 1992.

Hammer, M. "Reengineering Work: Don't Automate, Obliterate." *Harvard Business Review* (July–August 1990).

Huff, S., M. Munro, and B. Martin. "Growth Stages of End User Computing." *Communications of the ACM* 31, 5 (May 1988).

Jenkins, A. "Prototyping: A Methodology for the Design and Development of Application Systems." *Spectrum* 2 (April 1985).

Jones, Caper. *Applied Software Measurement.* New York: McGraw-Hill, 1991.

Kendall, K., and J. Kendall. *Systems Analysis and Design.* 2d ed. Englewood Cliffs, NJ: Prentice-Hall, 1991.

King, W. "Alternative Designs in Information System Development." *MIS Quarterly* (December 1982).

Licker, P. *Fundamentals of Systems Analysis with Application Design.* Boston: Boyd & Fraser, 1987.

Lucas, H., E. Walton, and M. Ginzberg. "Implementing Packaged Software." *MIS Quarterly* 14, 4 (December 1988).

Martin, James. *Application Development without Programmers*. Englewood Cliffs, NJ: Prentice-Hall, 1982.

Rivard, S., and S. Huff. "Factors of Success for End-User Computing." *Cummunications of the ACM* 31, 5 (May 1988).

Rockart, J. "Chief Executives Define Their Own Data Needs." *Harvard Business Review* (March–April 1979).

CASE

EVERGREEN LANDSCAPING AND MAINTENANCE: DEVELOPING APPLICATIONS

Recall Connie's desire to have an application that runs on her microcomputer that will enable her to select the fastest- and slowest-moving items in Evergreen's inventory. In the text portion of this chapter, we have detailed both how this project would move through the four phases of an ALC and how this movement may differ if alternatives to an ALC (such as prototyping) are used. To answer the following questions, refer to this application and the challenges it poses to Connie, Sven, Shawna, and others at Evergreen.

Questions

1. In the investigation phase, Connie has certain responsibilities and Terry has others. What are they? What conflicts could arise and what will happen if they are not resolved? How can Connie work to avoid or resolve these conflicts to Evergreen's advantage? What training, attitudes, skills, or values should Terry have to avoid or resolve these conflicts? Consider ways in which the alternatives to an ALC make these conflicts less likely or less of a problem.

2. Answer the same questions in Question 1 except focus on the design phase.

3. Answer the same questions in Question 1 except focus on the build phase.

4. Answer the same questions in Question 1 except focus on the installation/use/maintenance phase.

5. Consider another application Connie is thinking about that involves long-term analysis of sales data to determine trends. Connie wants to know what natural groupings Evergreen's products (items and contracts) fall into and whether there are any discernible trends. Perform an analysis of this problem in the style of Figure 12–2.

6. Now design a solution to the sales trend problem in the style of Figure 12–3.

7. What would happen next in implementing the sales trend problem solution? Would Connie use prototyping? Package tailoring? End user system development?

APPLICATION MANAGEMENT

After you have read and studied this chapter, you should be able to:

■ Explain the decisions to be made in information requirements analysis and discuss how to make those decisions in specific situations.

■ Describe and evaluate various types of information requirements techniques.

■ Describe the components of feasibility for an application development or procurement project and discuss how those components are evaluated.

■ Explain the decisions to be made in implementation and discuss how to make those decisions in specific situations.

Question 1: How does an organization determine what information it needs to have?

Powerhouse Oil Development Corporation (PODCo) is a young junior oil company with a mission to become one of the majors within ten years. It has aggressively pursued joint ventures and specialty drilling opportunities for the past three years, and its vice president, Nell Blue, is one of the reasons it has been so successful. Nell, who graduated with degrees in geology and business, has spared no effort in developing profitable joint ventures. She has a good nose for oil and gas and has carved out a niche for PODCo, chasing black gold in areas others found either too risky or uninteresting. One of Nell's best qualities is land management; she is able to win contracts others consider too hard, too risky, or too shaky. So PODCo has a number of very good properties, a higher percentage than most other junior oil firms. On the other hand, Nell is not really able to put into words what she's doing right and sometimes worries whether she will be able to train her successor now that she is vice president of exploration. Nell thinks it would be nice to have a computer do it, but how?

Answer: Nell's information requirements can be determined if she uses an appropriate method. Selection of this method depends on the utilizing system (exploration), the users (exploration engineers), the application (land management), and the analyst's skills in analyzing information requirements. Four general strategies are available: ask the users, derive from the existing system, synthesize from the utilizing system, and experiment/prototype. Nell's method choice depends on the overall uncertainty of the information requirements analysis (IRA) process at PODCo.

■ Describe the responsibilities managers have in all phases of application management.

■ Describe a variety of techniques that involve users in the design and implementation of an application and determine their benefits and drawbacks in specific situations.

Question 2: What aspects of information systems applications have to be "managed"? What responsibilities do managers have to do this?

Emanuel (Manny) Roderiguez is director of the regional tourism development policy for the federal government. He is responsible for examining the government's role in tourism for the whole country and specifically for regional balance in an age of global tourism. His staff (clerks, analysts) and constituency (hotel owners, tour operators, airlines, etc.) are awash in data of relatively high quality but poor consistency, so Manny is constantly beset with processing problems, information overload, and missed deadlines for reports. The government is committed to consultation, but without timely reports it's difficult to do it well. Part of the problem is an outdated computer system, but another one, Manny feels, is turf battles and distrust among members of the constituency. They will cooperate in local tourist bureaus, yet they won't engage in national planning unless they are certain their local markets are assured and not under attack regionally or nationally. Meanwhile, Manny wants to replace the information system. What does he need to do? What *can* he do?

Answer: One of the first steps is to evaluate four kinds of feasibility (schedule, economic, technological, and organizational). Next, Manny must decide which implementation strategy to select among four possible ones. In the process, Manny will have to exercise clientship, stewardship, and leadership in a distrustful climate. In addition, he will be responsible for determining training and staffing requirements.

INTRODUCTION

This chapter examines details of the application life cycle that involve managers in critical ways. First we will discuss how to discover information and information processing requirements effectively. Next we discuss feasibility—whether or not an application can be created. Selecting an implementation strategy is examined as we determine how to build (or buy) the appropriate management support system. Finally, we look at managerial responsibilities in the entire ALC, focusing on training, staffing, and installation.

INFORMATION REQUIREMENTS ANALYSIS

What is the best way to determine a manager's requirements for management support? While it may seem obvious just to ask him or her, in fact that tactic is sometimes counterproductive. People are often misled about what they want or need, and it may be more productive to guess or infer needs from other sources. Even sophisticated managers may have wrong ideas for solutions, and in these cases it may be important for an informed and ethical systems professional to help them infer those needs.

Why is analyzing requirements important? The answer is that managers get both too much and too little information. As we discussed in previous chapters, information plays a key and critical role in keeping managers productive. The wrong information may bring catastrophic results with respect to risk and stress. Too much information may result in information overload strategies. Information costs money, and working with the wrong information wastes time, which is also money. As we saw in Chapter 7, most levels of management advice (MIS and above) require a well-formed database complete with data definitions so that appropriate information can be retrieved and used. Those who design management support systems cannot be sure they are providing the proper support if they don't know what the "right" information is.

Hence, it is important for systems designers to be able to pinpoint managers' support needs. Historically, those needs were referred to as *information requirements* and the process of determining those needs was called *information requirements analysis*. Clearly, though, managers have information needs that go beyond simply retrieving data, and higher levels of support include models of varying sophistication. The simple term *information requirements* hides a range of needs that can be divided into the following classes using the basic IS model from Chapter 1:

- Information processing of sources of data
- Information (i.e., results to a manager)
- Information dissemination (i.e., output from a manager)

Processing refers to models and calculations that produce the desired information. The second class includes the specific information needed as well as the channels through which that information travels. Dissemination includes creating presentations and documents as well as accessing a network through which results can be transmitted to bring the situation to a conclusion.

Information requirements analysis (IRA) is the process by which a user's information needs for data, processes, and networks are determined. IRA is an integral part of the first phase of an application life cycle (ALC) and may be a formal, recognized activity in some situations and an informal one in others. When prototyping is used to investigate requirements (rather than as an implementation strategy), the process naturally focuses on a manager's needs for specific information.

It is important to remember that all the techniques described in this chapter are valid ways to understand information requirements; however, some of them are more appropriate or reliable in certain circumstances. It is always possible to ask users what they want or to determine exactly what the components of an accounts receivable application ought to be by looking it up in a textbook. But when there are no current users, when proposed users haven't been hired yet, or when an application deals with nonroutine, perhaps even not-yet-occurring, advising events, neither tactic will bear much fruit. Instead, valuable time will be wasted. In a worst case, false leads may perhaps result in a system that misleads rather than advises.

Five factors (see Figure 13–2) are important in determining information requirements. They are the following:

- *Users and their knowledge and experience:* What they know about their jobs and their needs, often tempered by what they fear, hope for, and expect
- *Existing management support system:* How it functions, what it does, how well it does it, and its basic components (hardware, software, data, procedures, and roles for users)
- *Department or work group:* Its procedures and goals, what it does
- *Systems analysts:* Their skills and experiences
- *Application:* The task being attempted, its products and procedures

Figure 13–1 EVERGREEN'S APPLICATION FORM

> *Return to:*
> HR Department
> Evergreen Landscaping
> and Maintenance, Inc.
> 2010 Forest Road
>
> EMPLOYMENT
> APPLICATION
>
> # EVERGREEN
>
> Landscaping and Maintenance, Inc.
>
> -
>
> Name: _____
> Address: _____
> _____
>
> Phone: _____
> Position Desired: _____
> (Check one) Full Time _____ Part Time _____
> If Part time, indicate days, times:
>
>
>
> Prior landscaping experience/training
>
>
>
> Prior retail experience/training
>
>
>
> How did you hear about this position?
>
>
>
> Signature _____ Date _____

Assume that when managers use an existing system they are doing so to meet departmental or work group goals. Consistent with our definition in Chapter 12, an application is the use of any system to meet those goals. Analysts investigate activities to find out what the information requirements are. In a very real sense, an application isn't visible—it's implicit in what managers do to meet goals.

At Evergreen Landscaping and Maintenance, Connie is having a conversation with her boss, Shawna Eggert:

> CONNIE: Shawna, I think that Sid's going to have a lot of trouble this year managing his staff. He told me most of the best kids he hired last year aren't coming back, so he's got a lot of training to do. And I think that's going to cut into quality in a big way.
>
> SHAWNA: I agree, Connie. He's going to have his hands full. On the other hand, there are a lot of good people looking for work out there; we offer better wages here than fast-food restaurants do.
>
> CONNIE: Sure. But I'm not comfortable with Sid's seat-of-the-pants judgment. We have all those application forms [Figure 13–1] and the performance appraisals we do every fall for continuing employees, so why can't we put them together

| Figure 13–2 | IRA TECHNIQUES |

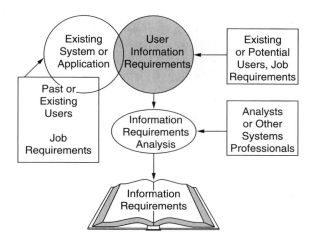

somehow and find out if Sid's right? Then we can design the best training program. Maybe these kids aren't blank slates coming in. Do we really know what we should be teaching them, anyway?

Here we note the following:

- The users of the application will be Connie, Sid, and maybe Shawna.
- The existing system consists of Sid's way of judging how much new summer hires know, the application form, the performance appraisal method, and Connie's and Sid's intuition.
- The department is contract sales, which Sid supervises.
- The systems analyst will be either Terry Bonner or Dierdre Tilton.
- The application may be called "training needs analysis" and it relates to the skills gap between incoming new temporary hires and experienced temporary workers who may or may not return next year.

Determining which IRA technique to use is a complex process that depends on what is known about the department, the existing, potential, or planned users, the application itself, and the skills of the analyst performing or assisting with the IRA. This determination is made on the basis of risk; where there is risk that a particular technique will uncover unreliable or misleading information, that technique is rejected. Finding a technique that produces the most reliable information at the lowest cost is the goal of IRA.

The most common IRA techniques include the following:

- Asking users what they need
- Deriving information needs from the characteristics of the existing management support system

- Synthesizing information needs from what is known about the utilizing system (the department or group and its formal needs)
- Experimenting with a prototype or in a laboratory

Some of the terms just mentioned are quite technical and will require some explanation. A **utilizing system** is not the same as users. Consider an expert system intended to help a bank's loan officers determine whether a specific customer is creditworthy. The users are loan officers, but the utilizing system is the loan-approval system. The latter includes not only the loan officers, but also the rest of the loans department, the procedures used in the loans department, and its history. It may also infringe a bit on other departments that interact with the loans department. A utilizing system is most easily thought of as a work group, greater than the sum of its parts (i.e., the workers). In extreme cases, a utilizing system includes an entire department or company. In Connie's case, the utilizing system is Sid's department. The department is a system because it has elements that are interrelated for a purpose—in fact, the name of the department is the purpose of the department: contract sales.

Three **user classes** interest us here. Existing users are those employees or managers who use whatever management support system currently exists. However, the current system may not exist at all or there may not necessarily be such users. Hence, another important class is potential users who would use the MSS if they had the chance. Any system that has current users has potential users, because there is always some change in staffing over a period of time. Also, people are always learning how to use a management support system better. In that sense, everyone is a potential (better) user. When a new system is being planned, planned users are important. Some of them now may be doing other tasks and some of them will be hired or trained later.

The major challenge with these classes of users is that existing users have a wealth of knowledge—some of it tainted—about the current system. Their opinions are valuable and probably hard to change. Potential users are similar to existing users, but they just don't have access to the system. However, totally new systems do not have existing users, and no users have any experience with anything vaguely resembling the new system. An IRA in this case requires extrapolation, imagination, and visualization on the part of individuals who might be quizzed about their information requirements, all of which are difficult to obtain. In Evergreen's case, Sid is a current user and Connie is a potential user. The system already exists, but in pieces and in unreliable processes such as Sid's intuition. Because no one will be hired to use this system, there are no planned users.

We know a lot about some applications (such as A/R and other accounting functions) because they have been concerns of businesspeople for a long time, refined theories have been developed about them, and support is available at implicational or computational levels. Other applications are still vague, even some that have been used a long time, such as those used for many inventory and production problems. They require advanced mathematics that still may not be completely thought through. Some applications, such as strategic planning, performance appraisal, and product pricing, are even more difficult to conceptualize and automate. Support for these applications may lie only at the MIS level or below. Finally, applications such as product design and hiring admit little in the way of theory (or at least generally accepted theory) and lie in the realm of management or engineering "art." In these cases, there may be a lot of disagreement about what constitutes a good design or a felicitous hiring decision, and we could say that we know a lot, none of it particularly useful.

The application that Connie is dreaming about doesn't have a name yet, but because she and Sid will use it to determine training needs, they will call it a "training needs

| Figure 13–3 | CHOOSING IRA TECHNIQUES |

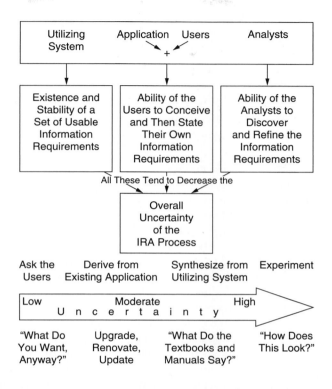

analysis" application. It's possible, too, that the resulting management support system may also be used to select new hires next summer and the application may blossom into a "human resources skills management" package.

Finally, IRA methods require work from those who use them. Sometimes analysts are good interviewers so asking users might be a good thing to do. But if analysts do not have the necessary skills to ask the right questions, even if users know their information requirements, there is a good chance the analysts will ask the wrong questions. Prototyping is relatively costly for users because they have to make precise decisions that they will have to live with. Prototyping also requires a great deal of skill on the part of systems analysts. Hence, an IRA method choice may hinge ultimately on how well and broadly trained investigators are. On the other hand, analysts and users can work on application portfolios and improve over time as each becomes more familiar with the others' needs and working styles.

Determining an IRA Technique

The way to determine an IRA technique (see Figure 13–3) is to assess the overall **uncertainty** of the process by which an IRA is performed. The following conditions contribute to the overall uncertainty of this process:

- There is no stable set of work or task requirements. This may happen because the business environment is changing rapidly, because the utilizing system is undergoing change or hasn't been created yet (as in new ventures), or because there is a lot of disagreement among people in the utilizing system about how things should be done.
- The application is poorly understood, especially by the users.
- The users are in no position to describe their needs because they don't know their jobs, because they are new in their jobs, because their jobs are changing rapidly, or the jobs themselves are recent innovations.
- The analysts lack some skills in interviewing, prototyping, or understanding the utilizing system or they do not have access to the existing system.

If several of these conditions appear, the situation is relatively uncertain. If none of them appears, the situation is certain or low in uncertainty. Where uncertainty is low, users can be consulted as informal and inexpensive sources for information. Users may be considered informal because it requires no professional training to be a user, nothing has to be set up, and people can be simply talked with. On the other hand, where uncertainty is higher, more expensive and more rigorous techniques that resemble laboratory experiments must be used to determine information requirements.

As Figure 13–3 illustrates, where uncertainty is low, users are asked about their requirements. This is possible because users know a lot about their jobs, they work in stable utilizing systems (so their observations will continue to be valid for a while), and the analysts know how to interview them. In more uncertain situations, observing how people work the existing system can be used. Of course, if there is no existing system, this is not possible.

As uncertainty increases, characteristics of the utilizing system may have to be discovered. This can involve looking at procedures manuals or textbooks on how such utilizing systems actually function. For example, if no one knows how a purchasing department is supposed to function because no purchasing department exists (hence, no users and no procedures manuals), we can read a book on purchasing and design and build a purchasing system based on textbook theory. That this method may not be appropriate for the new purchasing department is a risk, and improvement may have to be made to it later. The same could be said for any number of hard management problems. The less sophisticated the state of theory or the lower the awareness (or existence) of users, the greater the chance that we will have to consult outside sources, even textbooks, and the greater the implied chance that we will get it wrong.

Finally, where uncertainty is extremely high, experiments must be done either in a laboratory or with an evolving set of prototypes. This is, of course, extremely risky because inexperienced users have unpredictable expectations prior to using a system and they have less to compare the prototype against. However, although the risk is much higher, the costs are impossibly high if we ask (nonexistent or inexperienced) users directly or attempt to derive from a (nonexistent) existing system.

For Connie's application, she needs to determine how clear it is, how it is to be used, how much the potential users know, and how competent the analysts are.

- The application is fairly vague. Connie has some idea about what it is or could be. Sid trains employees every year in an intuitive way but probably can't spell out exactly how he decides who needs what training. Contribution to uncertainty is significant here.

| Figure 13–4 | INFORMATION-GATHERING TECHNIQUES |

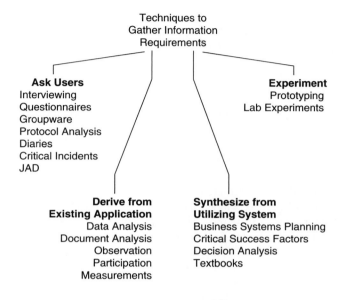

- The users, Sid and Connie, are well-informed, articulate, and skilled managers. It is easy to ask them about this application and they can speak well about it, but not in a very well-informed way. Contribution to uncertainty is moderate.

- The department is stable and well run, goals are well stated, and it has many continuing programs. However, training analysis hasn't been a priority or something that Sid has put much thought into, except for a few days each spring. Contribution to uncertainty is small.

- Finally, the analysts, Terry and Dierdre, are both relatively inexperienced. Terry has worked for Evergreen for only two years. She has a business degree in information systems, however. Dierdre is a technical whiz but knows little about the techniques for determining information requirements and is a bit short on people skills. Contribution to uncertainty is significant.

Because there is no ready formula for computing uncertainty, mentally average the four evaluations: significant, moderate, small, and significant. The general trend is toward the significant side of moderate. IRA techniques are reviewed next. The best choices are those in the "synthesize from characteristics of the utilizing system" group.

IRA Techniques

The range of techniques is quite broad (see Figure 13–4). Asking users includes not just interviews, but may also involve questionnaires, focus groups, and protocol analysis.

Protocol analysis is a combination of interviewing and work analysis—people are interviewed as they perform their jobs. This technique is invasive and may be distracting, especially for detailed work, but it may also be appropriate where management work is concerned. Managers may not be used to talking about their information usage (at least systematically—they are always wondering where needed information is and why junk mail keeps coming across their desks). They may welcome a chance to speak about their information needs with a professional much as people get a lot out of talking with professional counselors.

Managers should be aware that while almost anyone can begin an interview, it is actually not the same as just talking, however therapeutic that may be. A poor interview at best almost certainly results in useless information and at worst may provoke the manager into anger and disappointment. While most systems analysts have at least some interviewing experience, managers may not be skilled interviewees. Being interviewed takes as much effort as interviewing and probably as much skill.

Group interviews are also important means of eliciting requirements. The determination of user requirements was, in fact, the impetus behind one of the first GSSs, a system called Plexsys developed at the University of Arizona. Plexsys has grown into Group-Systems, one of the most widely used keyboard-based GSSs. In recent years, others have used group-based requirements collection using the more sophisticated tools of the 1990s, including joint application development (JAD). A section at the end of this chapter reviews JAD as well as interviewing pointers for managers.

Interviewing may sometimes require a little creativity-enhancing help. Several techniques are available, but the one that shows the most promise is called **cognitive mapping.** A cognitive map is a diagram that begins with a concept which is then graphically linked to others, each of which is in turn linked to more until a web of ideas is generated. Each link describes a relationship that may be of a positive (contributing) or negative (inhibiting) relationship. The links may be thought of as "causes," "contributes to," "is part of," or "consists of." While it is possible to take individuals' cognitive maps and simplify them graphically or even use them as the basis for expert systems (see Chapter 7), when working with groups such maps may become difficult to reconcile. The use of mathematical techniques to merge maps may become feasible in the future, and existing GSSs are starting to have such analysis routines built in. However, building such a web in a group may be an ideal place to begin requirements analysis that leads to a set of data requirements for the group. Individuals may, nonetheless, depart significantly from group averages in this regard.

Deriving from an existing system may include protocol analysis, analysis of the existing system's files and documents, observation of people using systems through direct viewing or videotape, and participant observation. In this last technique, the analyst uses the existing system for a while, observing his or her own behavior systematically. Alternatively, it is possible to train users to observe themselves.

Synthesizing from the utilizing system may involve a number of widely differing techniques. Certainly, there is no systematic way to move from descriptions and theories about systems to their designs (at least designs of the needed information). Business system planning (BSP) is one of a class of techniques including joint application design (JAD) and rapid application design (RAD) that works from users' group impressions of information needs and technical documents such as procedures manuals and hired consultants.

Critical success factors (CSF) analysis begins with a list of the factors that are critical to the success (rather than merely the survival) of an organization (such as "sufficient market penetration" for a sales organization). These factors are then analyzed for their contribution of information to decision making to attain these critical success factors. Then the list of information is considered to be the information required. CSF is a good technique to use in industries where such factors are easy to derive. However, a great deal of relatively unsystematic group work and research has to be performed before CSFs can be considered reliable.

Decision analysis analyzes decisions that are made or need to be made by the utilizing system. Readers who are familiar with modern linguistic theory know decision analysis looks at the "deep structure" of a utilizing system while observation looks at "surface structure"—manifest behavior of actors that is constrained or influenced by the environment rather than the critical work that goes on. Of course, this analogy is true only to the extent that businesses run on decisions. Decisions are only one subset of the conclusions that managers are asked to produce. The most common tool used for decision analysis is the decision table. Such tables resemble the cybernetic programs mentioned in Chapter 3. To date, few techniques exist to uncover the deep structure of business relating to other forms of conclusions.

Finally, textbooks may have appropriate theories. Skills analysis is not an unknown field in human resource management and there are several texts on this topic (in fact, there are several microcomputer-based packages available on the open market, but Connie doesn't know this yet!). Connie and Sid could find these books at the library or they could even surf the Internet for information on packages. Ultimately, Connie is searching for wisdom, formally documented or otherwise, that will give her guidance to understand the problem she wants her application to solve.

The last techniques include prototyping, already discussed, and laboratory experiments. These experiments may involve simply asking people to simulate working or making decisions and using computers to gather data on what they need to make decisions or produce conclusions. Alternatively, pencil-and-paper simulations may work just as well. Research in a laboratory is far removed from business, which results in a great deal of risk—and not a little bit of expense—to uncover information requirements. Often, using the prototype method in IRA will lead to the prototype option in the implementation phase (see Figure 13–5).

There is a moderately high degree of uncertainty in Connie's training needs analysis system. Interviewing Sid isn't advised because he doesn't know how he does what he does. Although Sid can try to explain his training needs to Terry and Dierdre, this probably will not be very successful. Because there are few documents and very little data other than the performance appraisals and application forms, and because these forms were not designed systematically with training needs in mind, there isn't much sense in deriving the new system from the existing one. Besides, here is a chance for BPR in its full philosophical sense. We have proposed hitting the books to find out how training works at Evergreen, how training needs arise from the kinds of jobs Sid has people do, and the kinds of decisions he has to make in assigning people to jobs and motivating them. Because this problem is so ill-formed, it isn't suitable for laboratory experiments or prototypes. Therefore, Connie and Sid must brainstorm to determine what skills various positions require and how skills can and should be matched to applicants and workers in order to redesign Evergreen's forms and procedures around worker skills. In doing this, Evergreen will move from an ad hoc approach to skill management to a systematic skill management system, with training needs analysis as one of the core processes.

FEASIBILITY

It is worth doing a project only if we can determine whether there is at least one practical solution. **Feasibility** has four components (see Figure 13–6):

Figure 13-5 PROTOTYPING IN IRA

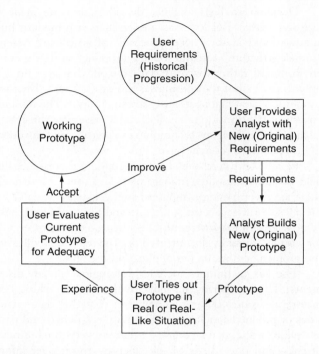

- Schedule: Is there enough time to get the things done that have to be done?
- Economics: Is there money to do this project? Is the expected payback worth the effort?
- Technology: Is the needed technology in place or will it be in place when it's needed? Can the system be built or can suppliers create it? Are the needed skills in place?
- Organization: Does the organization have the will to carry this project through to completion? Are the solutions compatible with the culture?

While there may be more than one feasible solution, in practice, feasibility is met even if only one of the proposed solutions seems feasible. Historically, feasibility analysis was the first step in system development. This was easier when most systems merely automated the work of existing manual systems. However, today's management support is quite complex and may involve processes that are poorly understood (such as meetings, decision making, policy formulation, organizational development, culture, and so forth), so it is almost impossible to know at the start of a project what the possible solutions are because the nature of the problem may not even be known. In these cases, feasibility is delayed, often well into the design phase. Other reasons for delay include the following:

Figure 13–6 FEASIBILITY COMPONENTS

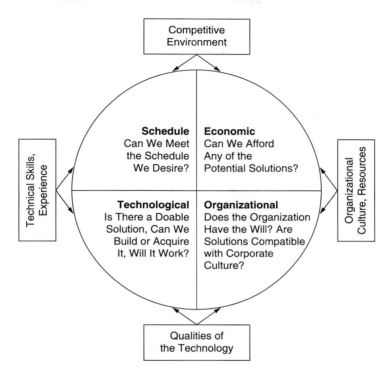

- The manager may not actually need support (for example, there's no reason to build a DSS for decisions that are predetermined); the manager's need for support can be satisfied in other ways (there isn't much need for complex electronic mail to foster consensus in an open office of individuals who work 9 to 5 and see each other all day); or simply asking the question "What support is needed?" actually solves the problem because it gets people thinking about what they do.

- The desired technology will not be available in final form for a while.

- Money isn't spent in the earlier stages of analysis. In later phases, such as implementation, redesigns are expensive, but in the early stages prototypes and words are often used. These are relatively inexpensive and easy to change without major dislocation or political problems. The reason for doing feasibility analysis early used to be because a project was immediately put into construction (e.g., programming and hardware procurement) and this created a heavy draw on funds very early. Now that projects are developed more slowly, managers aren't pushed so much to control expenses early, although generally half of all system development expenses occur before any benefit is obtained (see Chapter 14).

INCREASING FEASIBILITY

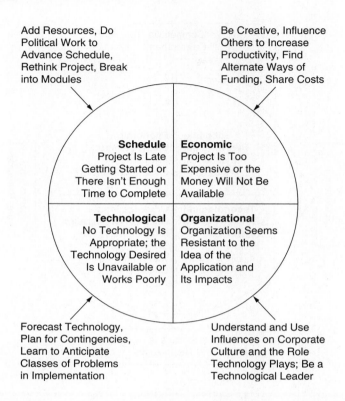

What can a manager do to increase the feasibility of a project or plan? Each of the four components is sensitive to different management activities (see Figure 13–7):

- Schedule feasibility can be increased by "throwing resources" at the project (i.e., more people, more money), although increasing the staff generally increases communication overhead and therefore may be counterproductive. Money resources may not always be available. Managers may do some political or public relations work to adjust others' expectations. Project control techniques such as milestones and lists of deliverables may increase the availability of resources by more efficient use of what is available.

- Economic feasibility requires more efficient work and some creativity. This is generally a motivational problem for managers. Creativity is important because many organizations fall into a rut of always making in-house products and never considering outsourcing as an alternative. Some never realize that existing systems can actually accomplish what is desired with minimal change. Costs might be shared with other departments or firms.

| **Figure 13–8** | INTEGRATED SKILLS MANAGEMENT SYSTEM |

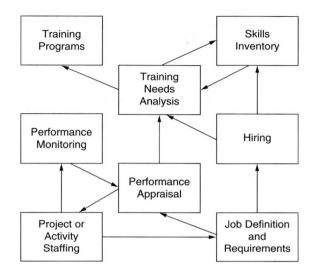

- Technological feasibility is not generally responsive to anything a manager can do directly, but research may help locate suitable technology. Consultants and others with technical knowledge can point the manager in the right direction. Most organizations that have MIS groups on staff also have a future planning or environmental scanning department. Sometimes this is found in the organization's R&D function.

- Organizational feasibility is related to organizational expectations and cultural practices. Every project is a political player—each project has winners, losers, and an image that has to be managed. Leadership helps here. Managers who are also project leaders have an enormous influence on the progress of organizational feasibility, which is changeable. In traditional organizations, rewards are often given to individuals or departments for doing a job well. One department may pay for an application that also benefits another department. The reward system should be ready to reward both, especially the department bearing the costs.

Consider Connie's training needs analysis system. We have already suggested that she find out the needs for the system by using some synthesizing techniques, examining theories and training models to obtain a list of needs. The project has grown in scope. Training needs analysis is now only one process in a network of skills management processes. The system begins to resemble that in Figure 13–8. Training needs analysis uses information from hiring (new hires need training), performance appraisals, and a to-be-created skills inventory system. Hiring is based on job definition and requirements (determined through project or activity staffing), reflecting Sid's needs for each year's temporary and permanent staff. The performance appraisal system to be overhauled accepts job definitions and performance measures, providing both developmental information (for training needs) and job-relevant information to Sid about who should be rehired for the following year. Based on the training needs analysis, training programs are designed and carried out as needed.

Is this system feasible? In terms of schedule and economic feasibility, Connie and Shawna will have to talk with Heather (vice president of finance) to work up some numbers. Because Terry and Dierdre are relatively new and work directly for Frances Harmon (vice president of administration), their input is not crucial at this moment in terms of schedules. If Frances thinks the system is important, it will be given priority. Technically, this looks like an integrated database problem, but much of the data referred to aren't currently collected systematically, or, in the case of a skills inventory, at all. However, Heather and Frances agree with Connie that Connie's PC is sufficiently powerful to add this extra system. Moving to a network will greatly enhance the value of the skills management system, allowing it to grow into an integrated human resource information system (HRIS). Organizational feasibility is a bit risky, because the MEC is unfamiliar with information technology, but with Frances's backing and the increased control Sid and Connie will have over the large temporary sales and maintenance staff, there shouldn't be much of a problem. Now the task is to build the system.

SELECTING IMPLEMENTATION STRATEGIES

Another area in which managers can have a large influence is in the selection of implementation strategies (see Table 13–1). An implementation strategy is the way in which a management support system will be constructed. There are a number of techniques that fall into four classes, as mentioned in Chapter 12:

- ALC (SDLC) is the traditional four-phase approach involving systems professionals or outsourced labor with sign-offs after each phase.
- Prototyping, previously mentioned in Chapter 12, is an iterative technique. A user/manager and a systems professional work together to produce an initial prototype that looks like what the user wants. The prototype is altered in stages until the user is satisfied with it, and the prototype is then ready for optimization. Because the prototype isn't subjected to real operating conditions that may, for example, require speed and the ability to manipulate large files, an optimized, speeded-up, and strengthened version should be constructed by professionals who know how to make the technology dance.
- **Package tailoring.** Many large consulting firms have off-the-shelf software that can be purchased and engineered to an organization's specific requirements. Accounting packages are the most common in this classification, but there are also human resource information systems, factory automation, CAD/CAM, strategic planning, and so forth, which are created for the general customer. Many of these packages come with tailoring software so that an unsophisticated user can create a personal version of the generic software. Vendors often install and modify the software for a fee.

Table 13.1   COMPARISON OF IMPLEMENTATION STRATEGIES

Strategy	Description	Managerial Responsibilities	Advantages, Indicators	Disadvantages, Counterindicators
ALC/SDLC	Long-term project with plans, checkpoints, sign-offs, division of responsibilities; linear network of activities; professionals do the work	Information requirements sign-off; sign-off on unit tests and system tests; some training and publicity; staffing and audit are shared with technical specialists	Logical, linear, good for projects already experienced or well known or if users are nontechnical; technical workers can take responsibility; clear division of responsibilities; good for projects with broad organizational impact	Poor for projects in which user needs are unknown or changing; if resources cannot be guaranteed, if payback period must be short, or if system must be running very quickly, then this is a poor choice
Prototyping	Cyclical, iterative, cooperative work between analyst(s) and user(s); multiple versions are made until a satisfactory one is completed	Shared responsibility with analysts; some documentation	System is developed rapidly with high user involvement; usually suited for a small, well-organized group or one individual who understands the requirements well; analysts must be trained in these techniques; prototyping tools must be available	Unsuitable for users who will not cooperate or accept responsibility or who actually do not know the requirements; poorly trained and inexperienced analysts; poor prototyping tools; large or unruly user group
Package tailoring	Purchase and subsequent modification of a package from a consulting company, software vendor, or equipment supplier; modifications can be made in-house or contracted out	User, analyst, or team reviews existing systems, creates an evaluation scheme, and makes selection; modifications are performed and system is turned over to users	Economies of scale, purchase of technical skills from outside, often much quicker and cleaner; valuable if there are clear candidates, if the application is well defined and familiar to users, or if resources are available for tailoring	Heterogeneous user group that can't agree on modifications; poor systems available; unclear criteria for system purchase; vendors cannot or will not make modifications at reasonable cost or time
End user development	End user handles all aspects of design, development, testing installation, documentation	End user does analysis, design, development, and installation of system	Users learn new skills; expensive resources aren't wasted on small systems; good for low-impact, idiosyncratic systems; requires highly skilled and conscientious user	Users could probably spend the time better doing what they're trained to do; users make lots of errors and don't document well; system may be of very poor quality

■ **End user development.** End users can create a large proportion of their own support systems today using tools such as integrated spreadsheets, powerful GUIs, and database managers.

The strategy choice depends on the size of the system, the impact of the system across the organization, the uniqueness of the system with respect to other organizations, the structure of the problem, and end user abilities. Large systems need to be divided so that tighter control can be exercised, and some of the parts may be amendable to different strategies. Systems with strong impact across the organization may be strategic in nature, requiring careful attention to who is responsible because many people and departments are affected. Systems that aren't unique are probably available somewhere else, perhaps as off-the-shelf packages that can be tailored.

Highly structured problems are far easier to manage in development than "fuzzy" problems—after all, easily understood problems (such as A/R or A/P) can be checked against textbook examples to see if the solutions are working; poorly understood problems (such as staffing or strategic planning) don't have textbook solutions, hence a good solution may be hard to recognize.

Choosing an implementation strategy is presented as a decision tree in Figure 13–9. Large projects are divided. High-impact projects need IS professionals to manage the technology and to span organizational boundaries so that responsibility can be managed well. Low-impact projects can have a high degree of user involvement because if things get out of hand and the project fails to deliver, only the user will be harmed. Unique systems must be constructed as one-offs (at high cost and risk), and nonunique systems can be purchased outside and tailored. Highly structured problems are less risky using the ALC because it is easier to anticipate where things could go wrong. Poorly structured problems require a dialog between the user and the analyst/designer in order to reach some understanding. Finally, low-impact, unique problems can be handled by skilled end users, but if the end users (managers) lack important skills, the job should be turned over to a systems professional.

Because prototyping is the implementation strategy of choice these days and because it is built into RAD and accompanies many CASE tools (see Chapter 14), we will look more closely at the pros and cons of prototyping. A paper by Hardgrave and Wilson describes guidelines for selecting prototyping strategies. First, the authors distinguish two types of **prototyping**: expendable and evolutionary. The former produces software that is thrown away after the prototype is complete. The latter produces an intermediate product that is used later to create a final, presumably higher-quality, application. They point out that there are a number of disadvantages to prototyping, some of which have already been mentioned. Through a survey of 88 organizations involved with 118 information systems projects, they discovered that in these organizations prototyping

■ Is used where there is a need for experimentation and learning

■ Is used where noncritical systems are involved

■ Is *not* used when users are unwilling or unable to participate

■ Is *not* used when users lack experience with prototyping

■ Is *not* used when the developer has extensive experience with the applications under development

■ Is *not* used when developers lack experience or expertise with prototyping

■ Is *not* used for evolutionary prototyping if support tools are not available

Figure 13–9 SELECTING AN IMPLEMENTATION STRATEGY

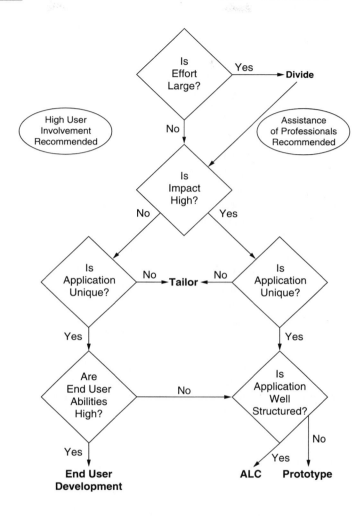

Hardgrave and Wilson see no difference in these guidelines between evolutionary and expendable prototyping, except for the last one listed. They suggest the following relationships exist between prototyping and implementation success:

- Longer projects (in calendar time) profit from prototyping. Shorter projects suffer from too much prototyping, probably because they are extremely simple projects that do not warrant the added overhead of interaction and iteration. In very short projects, especially for one-off or single-use applications, prototyping is useful because it short-circuits all development when the prototype becomes the final product by default. In longer projects, prototyping can be used repeatedly for requirements determination and later in formal development.

- Where innovation is important, prototyping contributes to success because of the increased exposure to different business cultures and user involvement.
- Project success using prototyping is inversely proportional to the size of the module being attempted—large projects need to be broken up for prototyping.
- Where stringent performance requirements are in effect, evolutionary prototyping can actually harm a project. There is little emphasis on performance (gross speed, for example) during prototyping and a strong focus on user requirements (formats, understanding, appearance).
- User and analyst experience helps. Success in prototyping is proportional to the amount of user experience with information systems in general and to analyst experience with prototyping.
- The smaller the number of users, the better. Prototyping can be disastrous when many people are involved because of the large variety of opinions and the potential for conflict.

These guidelines are consistent not only with our selection flowchart in Figure 13–9 but also with the project risk analysis to be discussed in Chapter 14.

A similar analysis could be attempted for end user-developed applications. Quite a lot of thought has gone into evaluating the potential for problems, many of which mirror the problems of systems practitioner-developed applications. Concerns about the quality of such software prompted Edward Cale to seek a framework for establishing good practices for end user application developers. In a survey of Boston, Massachusetts, area managers, he discovered as recently as 1993 that fewer than 10 percent of these managers' firms had any written policies on end user-developed applications. They see the potential for serious problems because managers, who are after all novice technicians, are far less likely to document than systems professionals. If they do document, they are unlikely to use any documentation standards. Most end user-developed applications are intended to be run and used exclusively by the developer-managers themselves. Thus, the potential for problems even in this case is high. Managers who develop their own software, especially spreadsheets, should pay careful attention to debugging and documentation, two time-consuming activities they are not likely to be motivated to engage in. Given the fragmentation of managerial workdays, this sort of careful attention to detail is less attractive to managers, especially if they see themselves as the only person who will ever use the application.

At Evergreen, Connie has progressed to the point of working with Terry and Dierdre to find out what implementation strategy would be best (see Figure 13–10). They conclude that the project is large enough to be divided into five subprojects corresponding to the processes in Figure 13–8.

- Skills inventory, a database of employees and their skills, updated annually, with entries created when employees are hired or leave Evergreen
- Performance appraisal, a database of performance appraisal information, updated annually
- Performance monitoring, a set of forms for monitoring employee performance, used to train managers and supervisors; eventually intended as input to the performance appraisal process

| Figure 13–10 | SELECTING AN IMPLEMENTATION STRATEGY AT EVERGREEN |

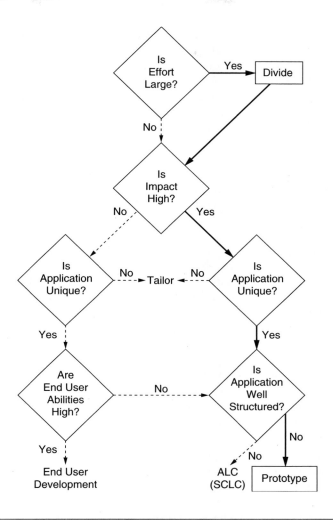

- Job definition and requirements, a database of job descriptions that systematically details what skills are required
- Project/activity staffing, a set of forms that describe positions in projects (i.e., contracts) or activities (for example, office work not directly related to contracts but perhaps needed on a temporary basis)

Connie has had some discussions with Shawna and Frances about using this system throughout Evergreen to replace the existing informal performance appraisal system and create a more formal HRIS over time. Frances and Shawna agree that this is an ambitious project that will impact the whole company and that involvement of information systems professionals is certainly advised. Shawna has hinted that Terry and Dierdre will need additional help and that there are high risks in doing this project totally in-house.

Connie is delaying this decision and for now is concentrating on whether *anyone* should build the system. She, Sid, and Terry, along with Frances's administrative assistant Kim Backer, call a number of sources including the local chapter of the professional training and development society, the local university, several trade journals in marketing and human resource management, and a few software catalogs. They learn that although there are a number of human resource packages available, none seems especially tailored for the kind of high-turnover hiring Evergreen does. The available packages are expensive and tailoring them would be difficult. A call to one vendor indicates that while the purchase price is only about $1,800, to get the specific modules working the way Sid and Connie want them to may cost another $4,000 to $6,000 over a year. Besides, the evolutionary approach they want to take means that they can go slow in the beginning. Most of the other processes are already there, but in a cumbersome format. The system, in other words, seems unique.

Finally, there is a question whether the problem itself is well structured enough to turn it over to a team of professionals. While Sid thinks this is a relatively straightforward challenge of matching skills to recruits, Connie thinks differently. She worries about the problem of high turnover and the fact that the system is still so fuzzy and vague. If it were really straightforward, everything would run like clockwork, but Sid has a lot of problems every spring. Since Sid is not particularly sophisticated in using computers and information, Connie is sure that there would be a problem with *any* system Terry and Dierdre created, which points to using prototyping as the system development method. Now the question is whether Terry and Dierdre should do all the work or whether some should be contracted out. Connie will face this problem in later chapters. Meanwhile, she has some major managerial responsibilities.

MANAGERIAL RESPONSIBILITIES

Managers have three kinds of responsibilities in application management (see Figure 13–11). As clients, they must be concerned with **clientship,** being responsible, capable clients. This may include overall project management (at least of nontechnical work), keeping end users informed about the progress of the project, channeling concerns back to those who are building the systems, ensuring that the system is being built correctly by withholding signatures and payments, and resisting the temptation to settle for an inadequate system. Because clients need to be informed buyers, managers must keep themselves informed.

Managers also have **stewardship** over the application after it is received. They have to make sure all of the applications are being used properly (this is relatively easy for a one-user system strictly intended to support a single manager, but very complex when a whole department is concerned). Users have to be trained, and system performance has to be audited on a regular basis as users' needs, abilities, and job pressures and assumptions change. Finally, as a steward, a manager has the responsibility of paying in money, time, effort, stress, and labor to make sure the application is always available to those who need it. Again, this is far easier for a one-user application, but many are intended for large groups, which complicates stewardship. Stewardship responsibilities are reviewed at the end of this chapter.

Finally, to be successful in these roles, managers should exercise **technical leadership.** First, a manager represents the system's users and those who provide services such as debugging, improvements, and file conversion. There is always the pressure of the *next* system, because as soon as a system is installed it is somewhat obsolete. As stewards, managers need to understand resistance, fear, and demotivation that may make a system less

Figure 13–11 MANAGERIAL RESPONSIBILITIES IN APPLICATION MANAGEMENT

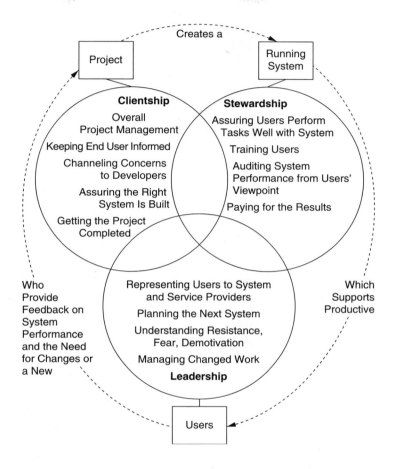

useful. As technology becomes more prevalent, the success of a manager's group (team, department, or division) will depend increasingly on successful planning and organization for implementing and controlling technologies. Finally, all technology changes the social systems in which it is employed. Thus, managers have to cope with changes and mediate these changes to others who work with and for them. Change management in the face of technology is perhaps the most challenging of a manager's leadership responsibilities.

One of the responsibilities that goes across all three facets is training and staffing. Unless users of a system actually know how to use it, no work gets done. Users learn in a variety of ways. They may take formal courses in-house or supplied by vendors (including colleges and universities). Personal experience they have acquired through exploration is important although generally hard for managers to control or know about. Mentors play an important role as do technical leaders within the IS group or technical opinion leaders in the user group. This latter group is composed of people who love the technology (or hate it) and can influence others either because they can show the others what to do or can convince others to keep trying (or give up). Managers can teach by example, too.

Learning takes place in stages. First, users may have preconceptions that may or may not be helpful, or they may simply know nothing about the system. Preconceptions and lack of knowledge are considered barriers to entry for users. Isolated ideas appear with initial exposure (sometimes called first impressions), and these first impressions may shape how additional experience is understood and integrated into patterns that give users the "aha!" experience. With increased integration, users become increasingly capable until they reach fluency or maximum productivity and can then act as mentors to others.

Users learn what is useful, but often they must have the usefulness demonstrated before they will learn. That which is mandated and sanctioned actually may be hard to learn. Technology is attractive to certain people and repulsive to others. Because techno- and cyberphobia are real phenomena, some people are not trainable because they are too afraid. If a manager relies on on-the-job training, a number of surprising phenomena might occur, including unsanctioned and undocumented procedures, performance levels that respond to personalities rather than skill, and ultimately a dilution of responsibility.

Determining an Installation Strategy

Another managerial responsibility is to determine an **installation strategy** (see Table 13–2). Installation means putting the system in place and may require installing software, knocking down walls, and other less dramatic measures. There are five alternative installation strategies, most of which are suitable only in specific circumstances; none works best in all cases.

Parallel installation is running the new system alongside the old one. This is a high-cost solution, but risk is decreased because if anything goes wrong with the new system, the old system continues to function. Of course, if the old system is really horrible, running it may do more harm than good. Even if the old system is usable, there is the question of when to cut over to the new one. There is also serious duplication of effort, data, and responsibility as well as an additional workload placed on employees who may demand additional resources such as time or salary.

Plunge installation is the standard way of installing systems—we simply roll out the old and roll in the new. This is like getting a new stove or refrigerator, and if management support systems were like appliances, most people would plunge all the time. However, new systems don't always work, users aren't always maximally trained, and errors aren't always minor.

Pilot installation means trying out the system on a small scale by making it available to a fraction of the staff. This could be one person, one working group, or a set of volunteers. When all the bugs are ironed out, it is made available to the rest of the staff.

Piecemeal installation is done one function at a time. The advantages are basically smallness and working on coherent activities, but, unfortunately, in many organizations functions are highly interrelated. If only part of a job is handled on a computer, one faces all the problems of integrating data and information from at least two sources and, of course, everyone still needs training.

Phasing-in installation means that new transactions and problems are handled by the new system and past transactions remain with the old system until everything is checked out and all the conversions done. Phase-in costs are relatively high, but the risks are relatively low. Phase-in installation is relatively painless, although it means pursuing two projects simultaneously—current operations with the new system and slow conversion of past operations to the new system. This works especially well with transaction-oriented systems.

The tradeoffs among these alternatives raise some managerial issues:

| Table 13–2 | COMPARISON OF INSTALLATION STRATEGIES | | |

Strategy	Description	Advantages, Indicators	Disadvantages, Counterindicators
Parallel	Operate both the new application and the existing one side-by-side until satisfied the new one works at desired level	Greatly reduces risk; needed for online systems that can't be tested offline	Delays full-scale introduction until full application is ready; slower because every transaction or operation must be done twice
Plunge	Put the new application in while simultaneously removing the one it replaces	Quick, inexpensive at first; if users are adept, they may have few problems, especially with standardized software interfaces	Could be a disaster, especially with untrained users; operational errors must be anticipated and backup must be complete and easy
Pilot	Try out the application on one group rather than on all users	If not completely sure of the validity of the application, piloting will gather data on the experience; use when trying out a new interface, new training methods, new procedures	Delays full-scale introduction of the new application; pilot group may not be representative of the whole user population
Piecemeal	Try out the application one function at a time	If money is not available for developing all functions, this is useful; if users can be productive with only some of the functions, application is used sooner	Users still have to be trained in the functions and may have to be retrained later when new functions are added; if functions are interrelated, a lot of unlearning may have to take place
Phase-in	Try out the application only for new customer, product, or other data while retaining the old one for existing data	If new transactions are frequent, this is a good way to build up a new database without converting data; old transactions or activity remain as backup	Those who are wedded to the old system may not receive the benefits of the new, which is why it was built in the first place; data may still have to be converted; has all the costs of parallel without all the benefits; archives of two types may be a problem

- *Time versus functionality:* Parallel installation delays any new capabilities until the new application is completely ready and field tested. Yet having those capabilities is the major reason for the improvements. Phasing-in at least makes those new capabilities available for new transactions. Plunging makes everything available, but at high risk. If some of the new features or capabilities are critical, organizations won't want to wait for them and will be willing to risk the plunge.

- *Cost versus risk:* Some installation techniques are very costly in reducing risk. Parallel and pilot installations cut risks by retaining the older application for a longer time, thus delaying the benefits of having the improvements. Phasing-in, pilot, and piecemeal installations spread the risk among functions, departments, or transactions. Plunging into the new application before extensive field testing cuts immediate costs, but at very high risk. Where cost, but not time or performance, is critical, pilot installations provide the desired compromise.

■ *Performance versus politics:* Sometimes installation is a political act. Consider a situation in which critical management decision making is hampered by access to high-quality, reliable information. Extensive testing of an application may be politically inadvisable because executives need the information now. Performance is less of an issue than who gets the application and when. Often, just having a system or application improves work quality by raising awareness of quality or accessibility. In these cases, a plunge may be the only politically astute method of installation. Where no existing functionality exists, plunge may be the only alternative.

Stewardship

As a steward, a manager is responsible for ensuring proper usage of the management support system. Think of this as the fine print on the warranty: "Void if the machine has been operated in an unsafe or unsuitable way." If a warranty is like an insurance policy, then stewardship is like risk management. For a system that is used by a community in which there are many usage styles, expectations of rewards, and capabilities, there are a number of ways to prevent voiding the warranty (see Figure 13–12). These include training, system audit, rewards, environmental scanning, and economic conditions.

Existing users need to be trained, and as new users arrive, they need to receive training. This means that manuals and other documentation must be kept up-to-date because all systems change over time. In turn, this means that training programs have to be created. For a one-user system that a manager has built using an end user tool, this kind of training may be nothing more than a few notes or help screens created along with the program. For more extensive systems, especially systems intended to be used by volatile teams, documentation and training programs are essential. Because some users may not stay in their positions, retraining programs may prove a necessary cost.

A **system audit** has two components: ensuring the system continues to function technically as delivered and ensuring that users continue to use it in the most appropriate way. These components imply the need for performance measures for the system (independent of users) and users. How users function with a system depends on a number of factors, though. They include the following: motivation to use the system as expected; conditions under which the system is used and resources given to users; and job responsibilities and task definition. Each of these factors puts special obligations on a manager as steward. While technical system audits are generally the responsibility of a trained technical group, when end user techniques are used or when a package is modified without an agreement to maintain the system, the burden for technical measurement may be shouldered by a manager. Any system that is delivered without **technical performance specifications** is a potential problem.

A reward system plays a large part in motivating system users. Rewards can change subtly over time as workers age or as job definitions slowly change. Most systems age, too. As users (including managers) become accustomed to a system or see alternatives, they may become disenchanted. Alternatively, users and managers may become wedded to a system as it was or is and may be highly resistant to any changes, even necessary changes. Even those who go along with changes may find them hard to learn and even harder to adjust to. These changes include increased pressure for productivity (through a downsized

Figure 13—12 VALIDATING THE "WARRANTY" ON AN MSS

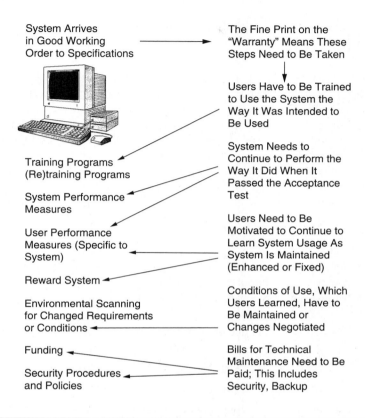

staff, for example), increased need to respond to customers (more speed, fewer errors), new kinds of transactions or conclusions, fewer resources, and different adjacent systems feeding input to the new. The environment within which the management support system functions has to be scanned continuously for challenges, threats, and opportunities. Managers generally have this responsibility.

While a system may be paid for on delivery (as with a package) or over time (as with the ALC or prototyping), there are continuing costs for technical maintenance as well as for systems operation. However costs are incurred, they must be paid, and system stewards must keep their funding sources well lubricated.

Among these costs are those of operating a secure system, including regular backups of data and software, security checks, password changes, and integrity audits of the data to make sure nothing has changed. Just as retail stores have to plan for theft and damage, system stewards must assume that data will be damaged, programs altered, documentation modified in error, and unauthorized access to or use of data granted. The warning, "This warranty is void if the machine is subjected to unusual use or if the owner fails to maintain it," points directly to security procedures. An auditor is often part of a development team, especially where security is critical to the success of the system. This also assures that security concerns are not left until the end of the project when it may be difficult to change designs and operational plans.

INTERVIEWING, JOINT APPLICATION DESIGN, AND USER PARTICIPATION

This chapter would not be complete without a detailed discussion of user participation in application management. While a list of managerial responsibilities for the various phases of an ALC states explicitly what is expected of individual managers, many of the tasks in an ALC involve managers and users as members of groups who also play a role, either as information providers or as directors. In this section, we look at the role of managers as interviewees during requirements definition, as members of teams using a technique called joint application design that is widely used in many phases of an ALC, and as members of steering committees that direct overall project or corporate information systems activities.

Interviewing

During requirements definition, asking users is sometimes recommended, always easy, but not always foolproof. Analysts who ask users for their information requirements are aware of just how difficult it is to get valid information, for these reasons:

- Users may not know what information is important or valuable.
- Users may not know how to describe the information.
- Users may know how to describe the information but not want to.
- Users may want to tell, but the analyst might not understand the answer.
- The analyst may understand but get conflicting answers from people who probably should be providing the same answers.
- The analyst may get clear, concise answers but fail to record the answers properly.
- The analyst may record the answers properly but be told by the project director or the CEO that the real answer is something else because of political or practical reasons.

For these and other reasons, an **interview** and related data-gathering procedures are fraught with the possibility for error. Analysts have perfected about a dozen different techniques to derive information needs, but interviewing forms the bulk of how this procedure is carried out. Disguised as prototyping or as protocol analysis, multiplied in a group interview or sandwiched into a joint application design (JAD) session, interviewing is the weakest link in any information requirements analysis. Interviews are also expensive and sometimes very emotional. In addition, interviewing is not a one-way street; sometimes managers are subjected to bad interviews and ask for them to be canceled or may even complain about them.

Managers should be aware of their responsibilities and rights in interviews, be they face-to-face, informal interviews or as part of other techniques that involve asking questions. Managers' responsibilities include the following:

- Honestly answering questions to the best of their ability
- Asking for clarification if the questions are unclear
- Being courteous and helpful to the analyst
- Providing follow-up information if required
- Honoring the systems analyst's request that the interviews remain confidential so that the interviewing can remain valid

On the other hand, managers, especially managers who are neither client, steward, or project leaders, have rights such as the following:

- The right to ask for justification for any question posed to them
- The right to terminate an interview they feel is inappropriate
- The right to clarification on any question
- The right to complain to the project manager if they feel they are being demeaned, lied to, or treated with disrespect or if the interviewer is behaving unethically
- The right not to answer questions that violate a trust, including trade secrets if speaking with an outsider, or that probe for personal information not connected with job activities or performance
- The right to schedule an interview at their convenience, unless directed otherwise by their managers

In other words, attending an interview is like any other cooperative effort in an organization. Managers should be aware that as members of an organization or team, they have responsibilities to carry out ethical actions that the firm sanctions for the firm's benefit. Managers must remain aware of the professional status of the interviewer, who is acting as an agent for the firm (or in the case of outsourcing, as an agent of an agent of the firm). Clearly, situations will sometimes occur in which one or more of the boundaries listed above are stepped over. In these cases, managers can and should exercise their right to terminate the interview or to indicate that they have nothing else to say. It is also the responsibility of managers to complain to the project director if they feel that the interview has been conducted in an inept, unethical, or unprofessional manner. Information that is collected under duress or by humiliating or uncomfortable means is probably not going to be valid, and the resulting application will probably have serious flaws in it. Managers who have been subjected to poor interviews should take steps to make certain others are not subjected to these procedures.

Joint Application Design

An alternative to an individual interview is the class of **group interviews.** Perhaps the most ubiquitous format for group interviews is a procedure called **joint application design (JAD)** (sometimes called joint application development). A product of IBM process innovation, JAD is based on a prior IBM system development methodology called business systems planning. A truly international creation, JAD began at IBM in Raleigh, North Carolina, and was perfected at IBM Canada before returning to the United States in the early 1980s. The primary characteristics of JAD that make it appropriate for requirements definition are that users participate far more and they do so in a structured way that guarantees involvement. IBM's contribution, among others, was to integrate JAD with the ALC. JAD forms the basis for several methodologies of system development including rapid application development (RAD).

Several studies have shown that JAD is a collection of meeting techniques that saves time, avoids costs, finds errors, and has relatively good user acceptance. JAD is a way of structuring meetings between users and systems professionals based on four principles:

1. Facilitation by a leader to increase control and assist conflict resolution
2. Agenda or meeting structure to provide focus
3. Documentation performed by appointed scribes to record everything
4. A variety of group facilitation techniques such as brainstorming, conflict resolution, and turn-taking to promote creativity and full participation

JAD is used with the ALC so that meetings at different phases of the ALC are conducted differently. For example, during investigation the agenda focuses on high-level issues and definitions, lists of assumptions, constraints and issues, roles, and timeliness. Flip-charts are essential in this phase and the meetings last for one or two days. In later design stage sessions, meetings last three to five days and focus on detailed design.

Six classes of role players are important in JAD. Direct users—end users and their managers—are key role players because it is their requirements that are being defined. The **executive sponsor,** ultimately the client, may or may not be present. The **facilitator** leads the meetings, but is neither a user nor a member of the IS team. The facilitator is responsible for all aspects of the meetings. **Scribes** write down everything for later use, including charts, diagrams, and lists; they manage the group's "memory." The IS team participates, too, although traditionally their role is as interested observers. Recently, more cooperative formats have been used. For example, scribes are being replaced or augmented by Computer-Assisted Software Engineering (CASE) tools and other computer support for graphics or group activities. In this regard, GSSs seem like an apt adjunct to JAD, especially because they further increase participation through parallelism and anonymity and can only assist in enhancing group memory.

Whereas JAD was originally aimed at transaction-oriented systems, it is now being successfully applied to all levels of management support systems. Of interest is that much of what is attributed to JAD's effectiveness is shared with GSSs: structure, group memory, positive effect, strong facilitation, and emphasis on creativity. However, these qualities characterize all good meetings. Clearly, managers who know how to run meetings, regardless of the technological setting, will be more successful in reaching valuable conclusions and obtaining participants' buy-in. Liou and Chen have proposed a model in which JAD, CASE, discussed in Chapter 14, and GSS come together to support groups rather than analysis (see Figure 13–13).

This model is a good summary of how teamwork can be supported by three different **technology types.** JAD is a process technology that enables the facilitator to supply the JAD team with the structure of a set of meetings and the motivators that make their participation voluntary and valuable. As a product technology, CASE is a tool for creating aids that gives the IS staff the ability to visualize quickly production concepts related to the target system through prototyping tools and a repository for all the intermediate software fragments. As a hybrid technology, GSS provides process technical improvement for JAD (through parallelism, anonymity, and automatic documentation) to allow in-

Figure 13–13	COMBINING JAD, GSS, AND CASE

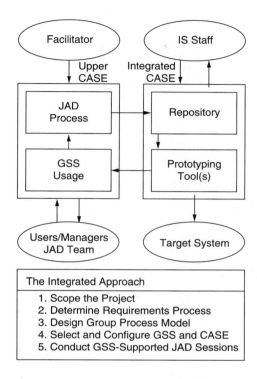

The Integrated Approach
1. Scope the Project
2. Determine Requirements Process
3. Design Group Process Model
4. Select and Configure GSS and CASE
5. Conduct GSS-Supported JAD Sessions

creased focus on interpersonal and group interaction. A GSS also furnishes products such as specifications, evidence, agreement, and arguments supporting the products that result from prototyping. Although this combination has not yet found widespread use, managers should pay attention to it and other convergences of group processes with technology.

Steering Committees

A final group role for managers is found in **steering committees.** Steering committees deal with the risks inherent in large or lengthy projects. Generally, only projects that have a cross-organizational impact will have a steering committee. Projects for single managers, work groups, or departments rarely have them. While the steering committee concept is certainly not limited to application management, it is especially appropriate because of the challenges involved in application development projects. These challenges include high front-end loading of costs, lack of tangible benefits until the entire application or system is up and running, the threat of technological obsolescence, and the high mobility of IS staff. Steering committees are composed of users and managers in positions of authority (i.e., the authority to spend money) who

- Provide overall direction to a project much as a board of directors might to a company

The Modern Management Imperatives

Reach: Global Competition	Global competition enlarges the number of competitors and their general creativity. Building a system with the right requirements and building it the right way become even more crucial. The global software marketplace means that there is a good chance that needed software has already been developed and is for sale or license.
Reaction: Quick Customer Feedback on Products and Services	Customer information is important as many systems are now meant to be used directly by customers or involve some customer input, perhaps indirectly. Prototyping and JAD can include customer suggestions that will improve the strategic value of management support systems.
Responsiveness: Shortened Concept-to-Customer Cycle Time	Rapid application development (RAD) is essential today. Prototyping and CASE tools assist in this by creating systems faster and more exactly to specifications, thereby eliminating rework and errors. Building high-quality applications requires attention to detail and much customer/consumer/managerial input.
Refinement: Greater Customer Sophistication and Specificity	Customers know more about what they want and asking them is increasingly a valid way to find out their desires. The same applies to managers as IS customers. As managers become more sophisticated, however, the problem of balancing IS and managerial needs becomes more acute.
Reconfiguration: Reengineering of Work Patterns and Structures	Prototyping, JAD, GSS, CASE, and reengineering are how applications are designed and built. How users react to systems is subject to similar reengineering as they become increasingly involved and responsible for applications they want. Managers are becoming application managers with different duties and responsibilities, such as stewardships.
Redeployment: Reorganization and Redesign of Resources	In the past, applications were created at arm's length; users could take them or leave them. Participative methodologies make applications as well as data an organizational resource that has to be accounted for and taken into account in managers' working lives.
Reputation: Quality and Reliability of Product and Process	Techniques for increasing managerial involvement in the design and production of their applications can only increase quality and satisfaction. Both JAD and prototyping make applications more visible, testable, and ownable than in the past. Quality counts more than ever and is attainable.

- Act as an interface to the organization as a whole in terms of goals, policy, and strategic planning
- May operate in a technical sense as a review committee by examining progress reports and making or approving major spending, staffing, or scheduling decisions

A steering committee is a high-level, action-oriented group that has the authority to intervene in a project and even replace the project manager. Often, members are divisional managers and have a lot of political and economic clout. Just as important, they can resolve conflicts both among themselves through a political process and among project members by fiat through legitimate authority. Not directly involved in the day-to-day workings of the project, a steering committee exists to make sure that risky projects don't threaten the organization as a whole and that they stay consistent with organizational goals as laid out in strategic plans. In small and medium-sized firms that may not have a formal information systems group, such steering committees may function, if only briefly, as a shell or "holding company" for IS policy-in-the-making. In this case, one of the major goals of the steering committee is to create IS policies and procedures and hire IS personnel, who later will be given day-to-day responsibilities. Steering committees may also receive regular progress reports and have the authority to initiate or approve spending, staffing, or scheduling changes as they arise. The potential for conflict over authority between a project manager and a steering committee may be a problem unless boundaries are formalized.

CONCLUSION

This chapter examined managerial challenges and responsibilities in building or buying management information systems. These challenges include determining users' requirements for information or processes, increasing the feasibility of projects, deciding on implementation strategies, training and staffing, selecting an installation strategy, and providing general stewardship and clientship obligations. Because managers are often involved in groups charged with various application management responsibilities and duties, this chapter also reviewed several group participation formats including interviewing, JAD, and steering committees.

The next chapters further examine the concept of risk management in management support system development by discussing project management (Chapter 14) and human resource management and ethical issues (Chapter 15).

■ ANALYZING PODCO'S INFORMATION REQUIREMENTS

Nell has four exploration engineers working with her. While she used to handle all the land management work herself, the engineers have done most of the work for the past two months, but they are inexperienced. There are a lot of components in land management. Some are specific, such as government paperwork, while others depend on the land itself or the owners, some of whom are sophisticated and drive hard bargains and some of whom don't know very much at all but get angry when they feel they have been taken to the cleaners. Land management and exploration are intricately linked, too. The land under management has to be carefully documented so that money isn't wasted. There are no signs saying "Drill here" that Nell knows about, but there are plenty of signs that say "Wait a minute, this land may not be a good risk, but how about over there?" Nell is thinking about hiring a local consulting firm that has a great deal of experience in the oil patch, and it should be able to ask the right questions and get the right answers. Of course, it's possible that PODCo could buy some off-the-shelf system, but Nell is not at all sure that she would recognize the correct system if she saw it, at least not now. In addition, while she has some fears that hiring outsiders may result in the loss of some confidentiality and intrusion, she hopes that they have some idea of what they're doing and will do it with the least impact on the engineers and her. ■

1. Define the four IRA methods that Nell can select from and describe how they might actually take place at PODCo.

2. How would you rate the uncertainty of the IRA process at PODCo? Why?

3. What IRA process would you recommend for PODCo? What impacts do you think will occur during the IRA process? What can be done to lessen this impact?

■ APPLICATION MANAGEMENT IN A GOVERNMENT TOURISM OFFICE

Manny has determined the following:

- The money for a system is in place, but it is not a lot of money.
- Most new computer systems are based on a database management system that requires a great deal of time to create or convert the old data.
- A lot of new data arrive weekly in formats determined more than 15 years ago and are not of much use in today's competitive environment.
- Any new system should be functional within six months before the peak summer tourism "balloon."
- Manny and his staff have almost no experience developing systems—the current system was installed 15 years ago.
- The system will impact the entire Tourism Directorate and probably tourism nationally.
- While the processing (boiling down) of data is relatively straightforward, the fact that it's tourism and not, say, accounting, data makes the application unique.
- While processing is straightforward, it's not clear right now just what reports need to be produced because of the conflict in the industry and lack of trust.
- Clerks know the existing system too well and may resist a new one.
- The continuous arrival of information may make it impossible to phase out the old system immediately. ■

1. Is the new system feasible? If not, in what ways isn't it feasible?

2. What implementation strategy do you recommend that Manny will be able to carry out? Why?

3. What installation strategy do you recommend and why?

Summary

Managing applications presents several specific challenges for nontechnical managers. First, it is critical to determine the information requirements for applications. Five factors are involved in determining these requirements: the degree of knowledge and sophistication of users, the existing management support system, the department or work group, the systems analysts performing the investigation, and the application itself. Four classes of techniques are generally used in this analysis: asking users, analyzing the characteristics of the existing management support systems, finding out what is known about the user department, and experimentation or prototyping. The second challenge is determining the feasibility of an application development project. There are four aspects of feasibility: schedule (time), economics (money), technology (knowledge), and organization (will). Third, after feasibility has been assessed, managers can influence the choice of implementation either by using the ALC, prototyping, end-user application development, or package tailoring. Generally, strategic applications are developed by professionals because organizational impact is high. Nonunique applications, which are, for the most part, also nonstrategic, can involve tailoring purchased applications or packages. Nonstrategic but unique applications can be developed by users if they have the skill. Poorly structured applications will profit from at least some prototyping. Fourth, managerial responsibilities include clientship (managing the project), stewardship (managing the users and the use of the application), and leadership (managing relationships among people and technologies). An important clientship responsibility is determining installation strategies, selecting from parallel, plunge, pilot, piecemeal, and phase-in strategies.

Discussion Questions

13.1 The term *information requirements* seems to cover only data and report needs (input and output). What else should be included in this list of requirements? Are there specific means of investigation that are better suited to this group of requirements than to data requirements? Is the list of techniques complete, or are more techniques needed?

13.2 Distinguish among the kinds of knowledge that each of these classes of users is likely to have: current users, prospective users, past users, end users, hands-on users, and management.

13.3 Could it be said that prototyping is the best all-around technique for doing everything from IRA to implementation to overall project management? In what ways does prototyping reduce the risks of failure at all stages? What are the costs of prototyping?

13.4 The chapter supplies no arithmetic to determine overall feasibility. What priorities do you think exist among the four feasibility factors? Which, in general, are most important? Is it possible for a project to be infeasible in terms of one or more factors but still be feasible overall? Describe situations in which each of the factors turns out to be a limitation (that is, situations in which three factors are positive but one factor is so strongly negative that it makes for infeasibility).

13.5 End user application development seems "politically correct" in the sense that it empowers users. However, all the other alternatives empower users without the risks of end user application development. To what extent do you agree with the previous two statements? How will a manager go about assessing the true risks and opportunities involved in developing their own applications?

13.6 Implicit in much of Chapter 13 is the notion that user involvement is good, and more involvement is better. Is this true? What are the advantages and disadvantages for managers of increasing levels of involvement in clientship, stewardship, and leadership?

Key Terms

clientship
cognitive mapping
critical success factors (CSF)
decision analysis
deriving from existing system
end user development
executive sponsor
facilitator
feasibility: schedule, economics, technology, organization
group interview
information requirements analysis (IRA)

installation strategy: plunge, parallel, pilot, piecemeal, phase-in
interview
joint application design (JAD)
package tailoring
prototyping: expendable, evolutionary
scribe
steering committee
stewardship
synthesizing from utilizing system

system audit
technical leadership
technical performance specifications
technology type: process, product, hybrid
uncertainty of IRA process
user class: existing, potential, planned
utilizing system

References

Alavi, Maryam. "An Assessment of the Prototyping Approach to Information Systems Development." *Communications of the ACM* 27, 6 (June 1984): 556–563.

Andrews, Dorine. "JAD: A Crucial Dimension for Rapid Applications Development." *Journal of Systems Management* 42, 3 (March 1991): 23–27, 31.

Cale, Edward. "Quality Issues for End-User Developed Software." *Journal of Systems Management* 45, 1 (January 1994): 36–39.

Carmel, Erran, Randall Whitaker, and Joey George. "PD and Joint Application Design: A Transatlantic Comparison." *Communications of the ACM* 36, 6 (June 1993): 40–48.

Cooper, J. D., and E. B. Swanson. "Management Information Requirements Assessment: The State of the Art." *Data Base* 11, 2 (Fall 1979): 5–16.

Couger, J. Daniel, Scott McIntyre, Lexis Higging, and Terry Snow. "Using a Bottom-Up Approach to Creativity Improvement in IS Development." *Journal of Systems Management* 42, 9 (September 1991): 23–27, 36.

Gane, C., and T. Sarson. *Systems Analysis, Tools and Technique.* Englewood Cliffs, NJ: Prentice-Hall, 1979.

Hardgrave, Bill, and Rick Wilson. "An Investigation of Guidelines for Selecting a Prototyping Strategy." *Journal of Systems Management* 45, 4 (April 1994): 28–35.

Jones, Sue, and David Sims. "Mapping As an Aid to Creativity." *Journal of Management Development* 4, 1 (1985): 47–60.

Kendall, Kenneth, and Julie Kendall. *Systems Analysis and Design.* Englewood Cliffs, NJ: Prentice-Hall, 1992.

King, W. R., and D. I. Cleland. "The Design of Management Information Systems: An Information Analysis Approach." *Management Science* 22, 3 (November 1975): 286–297.

Licker, P. *Fundamentals of Systems Analysis with Application Design.* Boston: Boyd & Fraser, 1987.

Liou, Y., and M. Chen. "Using Group Support Systems and Joint Application Development for Requirements Specification." *Journal of Management Information Systems* 10, 3 (Winter 1993/1994): 25–41.

Martin, J. *Rapid Application Development.* New York: Macmillan, 1991.

Montazemi, A. R., and D. W. Conrath. "The Use of Cognitive Mapping for Information Requirements Analysis." *MIS Quarterly* 10, 1 (March 1986): 45–58.

Munro, M. C. "Determining the Manager's Information Needs." *Journal of Systems Management* 29, 6 (June 1978): 34–39.

Munro, M. C., and G. B. Davis. "Determining Management Information Needs: A Comparison of Methods." *MIS Quarterly* 1, 2 (June 1977): 55–67.

Rockart, John F. "Chief Executives Define Their Own Data Needs." *Harvard Business Review* 57, 2 (March–April 1979).

CASE

EVERGREEN LANDSCAPING AND MAINTENANCE: DEVELOPING A SKILLS MANAGEMENT APPLICATION

Recall Connie's training needs analysis application that evolved into a skills management system. Let's review some of the results of the analyses:

- There is a moderately high degree of uncertainty about requirements definition.

- Based on this, synthesizing from the characteristics of the utilizing system seems most appropriate.
- The utilizing system is Sid's department.
- On all four fronts (schedule, economics, technology, organization), the system looks feasible, but growth into an integrated HRIS may pose some problems without a network.
- The system will be composed of five modules, loosely integrated through a common database.
- There are no appropriate packages available on the market at a price Connie is willing to pay. The vagueness that Connie perceives in the problem structure points to prototyping.

Connie has progressed to the point of detailed planning for this project. IRA will include a study of how Sid's department functions (with respect to human resource deployment). Implementation will use prototyping heavily. It is not clear who will do this work.

Questions

1. Prototyping seems like a default recommendation in this case. What pitfalls can Connie expect in using prototyping for this sort of system? What are the advantages?

2. Suppose Connie decides that she can build the system herself. What potential problems should she expect? What benefits may be gained from end user development? Would some other end user be a better choice?

3. Connie is obviously the client for this project, but both she and Sid have clientship responsibilities. What are they? What challenges will both experience in meeting these responsibilities? How can they plan for them?

4. Whom would you recommend as the project steward and why? What will the project steward(s) do? How do you recommend Frances evaluate how well such stewardship is working?

5. The SMS will be used primarily by four people: Connie, Kim, Sid, and his administrative assistant Kayla Dowd. Kim is a trained administrator, but Kayla is basically a typist whose experience has been mostly contracts transcription. What are the training responsibilities, who should be responsible for them, and how should these responsibilities be carried out?

6. The current system is basically manual, based on paper application forms, some notes that individual managers use, and the performance appraisal forms in personnel files. Kim and Frances have computerized the procedure a bit by creating some spreadsheets with performance information that they use with the MEC to talk through the annual performance review. Assuming that it's now March and Evergreen is entering its busiest season, what installation strategy do you recommend? What are the advantages and disadvantages of each to Evergreen?

7. What will a system audit of the SMS produce? Do you recommend such a process to Frances? What role will Terry and Dierdre play in a system audit?

8. Is JAD an appropriate management technology for this project? Why or why not? What benefits will a group-based intervention have for Evergreen? What drawbacks will it have? How would you work prototyping in with the JAD sessions?

9. The IS group at Evergreen is really only Terry Bonner and Dierdre Tilton (see Figure 13–14). Kim Backer, administrative assistant to Frances Harmon, has some experience using computer systems in administration, and much of the routine human resources work (recordkeeping, notifications) is left to her. Parnell Tulley (Tulley Fox's cousin) has

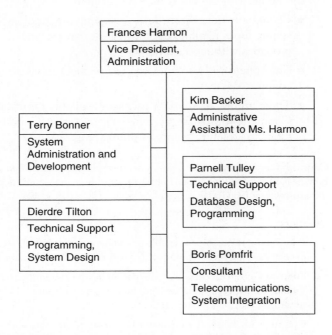

Figure 13–14   INFORMATION SYSTEMS GROUP AT EVERGREEN

recently been hired to do technical support, particularly in designing databases in the networked system anticipated for the expansion. Whom would you recommend lead the prototyping that Connie has determined should be done? Terry? Dierdre? An outside firm? Someone else?

10. Do you recommend to Lily that she create a steering committee for this project? For all IS work at Evergreen? What arguments would convince her? Who would be on such a committee?

CHAPTER 13 APPENDIX   JOB DESCRIPTIONS FOR IS EMPLOYEES AT EVERGREEN

System Administration and Development—Employee: Terry Bonner

Responsibilities: Performs regular audits on all operational systems; determines information requirements; administers all requests for new applications or maintenance of existing applications; creates and monitors IS projects; IS planning (in conjunction with the vice president of administration); environmental scanning for technological opportunities; user training (in conjunction with user management); supervision of all IS employees; contracts for outsourced IS efforts or IS consulting; regular reporting on IS performance and needs to the vice president of administration; hires and evaluates IS staff.

Technical Support—Employees: Dierdre Tilton, Parnell Tulley

Responsibilities: Design and develop new IS applications and maintain existing applications; database design and administration; programming assistance in all phases of the application life cycle as required; consult with users on problems with existing applications; technical training of users as required; regular reporting on project progress to the manager of system administration and development.

Telecommunications—Consultant: Boris Pomfrit

Responsibilities: Design, implement, and install telecommunications technology including networks, applications, and system interfaces; integrate existing systems into planned upgrades of Evergreen's telecommunications networks.

PROJECT MANAGEMENT

Question: When non-IS employees have to manage IS projects, what challenges will they face? How can they cope with project management? What are the economics of such projects?

At Concertina Chips, Don Crowchild is putting his career on the line. "Nope, no way, never, *nein, nyet,* and no! I will not manage the project. You can throw me out on the street and tell me I'll never see another potato chip again and I'll still say no." Don is saying, in his own diplomatic and indirect way, that he doesn't want to have anything to do with the production management system project at Concertina. As factory manager, he is a natural to head the project but, as he complained to the company president, "I know a lot about oil and potatoes; I know beans about computers." And besides, Don thinks, everyone knows how badly the last project turned out. Project management is hard and unrewarding, especially when the resulting system is a chip off the last bad block. Is Don being flaky or is he a smart chip?

Answer: Systems projects are different from other projects for a variety of reasons, and these differences drive many project managers, especially nontechnical ones, into dysfunctional coping strategies that in turn lead to useless systems, poor user morale, and unnecessary expenses and delays. A number of tactics can be used—most of them simply smart business practice and others particular to technology-driven projects—not only to cope, but to prosper. These tactics include rapid training, built-in quality, shared development costs, and sound management techniques. Knowledge of the economic cycle in information system development can lead the prudent and clever project manager to success.

INTRODUCTION

This chapter discusses projects intended to create or purchase management support systems. In the past, these projects were almost always managed and staffed by technical specialists who built arcane, complex systems for perplexed users who were often disappointed. This is changing with client-server architectures, advanced and powerful personal computers, integrated databases, CASE tools, and a more enlightened attitude toward user involvement. Indeed, as Chapter 13 stresses, turning an entire project over to its users is often the solution to a human resource crunch and often profitable for everyone concerned.

In this chapter, we examine several aspects of project management. First, we discuss how systems projects differ from other projects, especially engineering ones. This discussion will carry over to the next chapter because these projects entail human resource concerns that also make them different. Because these projects are different, user-managers who are waiting for applications sometimes engage in counterproductive, dysfunctional strategies to get their applications built. The economics of developing and using such systems is also different from others. Because of this, systems projects have different risks, and we will examine what the concept of risk means and how managers can manage these risks. One beacon on the technological horizon is computer-assisted software engineering. We end the chapter with an examination of how this approach—and the tools it generates—are changing project risk management.

WHY SYSTEMS PROJECTS ARE DIFFERENT

Systems projects are not completely different from other projects except in a few important ways. They involve people, equipment, deadlines, budgets, and so on, as do other projects, but six important differences (Table 14–1) have major impacts on project decision making:

- **Front-end cost loading:** There are a lot of up-front costs for project planning and analysis before any real construction begins. Because high technology is volatile and the newest technology that gives strategic advantage is expensive, planning is very important.
- **Delayed benefits:** An incomplete system cannot be used. All the parts have to be in place and the system working before anyone receives any benefits. A working system includes training, documentation, procedures, job descriptions, and the technology. This implies that testing is extremely important because reworking, redesign, and rebuilding are extremely expensive. Systems have almost no salvage value; badly running software cannot be sold for scrap. Half-converted data are useless—in fact, totally converted data may be even more useless if the system they are supposed to be used with never works correctly.
- **Intangible products:** Unless hardware is being built and major physical plant construction has been undertaken, the products of a software-centered project are intangible and therefore hard to evaluate. It is difficult to see data, and as files are being built they remain intangible and relatively valueless. Software development is an incredibly detailed and

Table 14–1	WHY SYSTEMS PROJECTS ARE DIFFERENT	
Difference	**Why This Difference Occurs**	**What This Means to Managers**
High front-end cost loading	Design work is highly technical and expensive. Technology costs are high, so a great deal of effort goes into making sure the wrong technology is not acquired.	Design mistakes are costly to fix. Planning is essential. Risks should be managed incrementally. Early attempts at cost control should be gentle, otherwise the project will die. Some development costs can be shared with others. Quality must be built in for flexibility.
Delayed benefits	Generally, the parts cannot be used until all the parts work. Hierarchically constructed systems require complex interactions of the parts. Functionality is the desired outcome, and often a functionally partitioned system cannot deliver much value until all functions are working.	Pressure for early release of the system should be resisted. Users must be trained *before* the system is released. Sound project management techniques can reduce the risks.
Intangible products at all stages of development	Software is intangible. Data are difficult to see, and the value of incomplete data is very low, and often negative.	Public relations is important. Visible aspects of the system can be promoted through prototyping. Training users early on prototypes can decrease apprehension (if done right). Keep communication paths open.
Rapidly changing technology	The half-life of computer technologies is three or four years, and sometimes months. New ways of accomplishing a task are invented daily. The field is faddish, with new terminologies and technologies being developed continuously.	The temptation to buy unproven technology should be resisted. Ill-suited, off-the-shelf systems must also be avoided. An evaluation plan is critical to ensure acquired technologies meet standards set by users. User steering committees can help.
High risk of obsolescence	As a system is being developed, newer technologies are also being developed to make the system less than optimal.	There is a great risk that competitors will acquire better, cheaper technology. Obsolescence is more a state of mind than a reality in many cases. Avoid technology stampede.
Rapid turnover of systems professionals	System skills are in demand. Technical people are often more loyal to the technology than to the organization. As technology ages, existing jobs look less attractive. Many, if not most, technical professionals are young and mobile. Lifestyle, not salary, is important.	Users should be involved at all stages. Documentation is essential. Outsourcing makes this the supplier's problem.

precise process. One syntax error, a missing comma, or a misspelled word can dramatically alter performance of the application. Given these requirements, managers often must trust technologists' judgments about processes that are difficult to visualize.

- **Technological change:** The **system half-life** is very short, usually three or four years or less. This field is also faddish, with new terminology describing the technologies appearing daily. Acronyms and technical terms can make technologies appear daunting even when the actual technical advance is quite small. Even nonobsolete technological components change rapidly. A project design may have to be updated monthly as new components come on the market.

- **Technological obsolescence:** When a new technology appears, early adopters may experience strategic advantage and grave risks. Older technology has less advantage, but also fewer risks, because users are familiar with it. Competitors can always acquire new technology, and some of these pioneers survive life on the frontier, making life difficult for you. There is little salvage value to obsolete technology, which can sometimes reduce in value by 90 percent in as little as five years.

- **Mobility of systems professionals:** Despite economic downturns and its chilling effect on mobility, systems professionals remain the most mobile of all professionals. Imagine the effect of an annual 20 percent turnover—a two-year project ends up with only 64 percent of the original technical staff. A five-year project will have few people with any experience (only one in three of the original staff will be around, and most of them will have been promoted into management positions). It is expensive to hire talent and just as expensive to train newcomers. In addition, it is extremely difficult to measure the productivity of these workers and the broad range of tools they use. Because an extraordinary amount of management expertise is required to direct and control application development projects, the temptation to give up is strong.

DYSFUNCTIONAL COPING STRATEGIES

Five factors come together (Figure 14–1) to create a situation in which managers find it difficult to cope. These factors are high front-end costs, delayed benefits, intangible products, obsolescence, and mobile staff. Managers react in various ways, some of which are counterproductive. One **dysfunctional coping strategy** is to push for more rapid development in order to obtain the benefits the project promises before the technology becomes obsolete. Obviously, people can work only so fast. In an attempt to improve delivery dates (or forestall delays), managers may hire additional staff or allocate more money for computer resources. Neither technique is particularly effective. Staff increases only make managing more difficult, and because the work is sequential, putting more people to work only creates more possibilities for people to get in each other's way. Technology becomes obsolete at the same rate; more technology will only become obsolete at more cost. Some early efforts at researching technologies may pay off. Although better technology may become obsolete as fast as ordinary technology, but it generally pays off more quickly and is easier to work with.

Figure 14–1 COMMON STRATEGIES FOR COPING WITH SYSTEMS PROJECTS

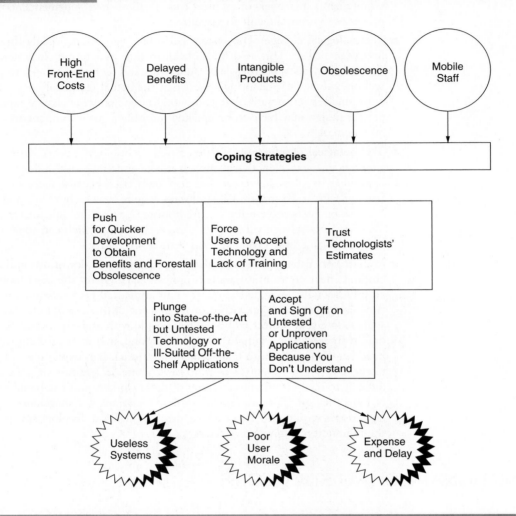

Another coping strategy is to impose the delivery date by fiat and force users to accept technologies when they are unwilling or uneducated. Because education and public relations take time, managers may be tempted to forgo them altogether. They may hope that either the system will be so good that everyone will see its benefits or that users will learn as they earn—that on-the-job training or experience will take the place of education. This strategy rarely works.

Managers may buy state-of-the-art but unproven systems off-the-shelf or they may forgo testing of in-house-developed systems to save time and money. Coupled with plunge installation strategies, this is a formula for total disaster. Few managers actually go to this extreme, but close approximations (such as a one-week trial of an untested system before everyone uses it) abound.

Managers often trust technologists' estimates out of ignorance or fear. Even managers who are actually paying for systems may be tempted to trust any estimate. After all, it is hard work to dig for the facts, and the intangible nature of systems makes it difficult for managers to have an intuitive feel for how "done" the work is. The **two-cultures gap** that exists is dangerous but it is bridgeable. Managers must bridge the gap by becoming familiar enough with the technology so that they feel comfortable challenging estimates.

Finally, out of ignorance, managers may sign off on software or systems that are essentially untested. These managers haven't been trained in clientship and may not have any stewardship responsibilities. It is not a good idea to have clients who have no operational responsibilities because they may be tempted to sign off too quickly.

Better Coping Strategies

Better coping strategies include training, flexibility, cost sharing, and the application of sound management techniques to systems projects. While most of these strategies are obvious or intuitive, the history of information systems development clearly points to a lack of awareness of the importance of these factors. Because of the unusual expenditure curve (see Figure 14–2) of computer-based projects, each of these coping strategies lowers costs or creates additional benefit.

Advance training increases up-front costs but pays off in the end with a shorter learning time after installation. Benefits rise much more rapidly with a trained staff. Hence, training prior to installation dramatically increases payoffs while only redistributing costs in time. Training can also be used to locate flaws and bugs before installation.

Building in quality and flexibility raises development costs significantly. Quality management techniques are expensive, but they have the benefit of making redevelopment less likely because the system is more flexible. The **system brittleness** is less (i.e., less subject to failing or crashing) when users try to use systems in ways they weren't meant to be used or try to get around known bugs or roadblocks. For example, Shawna at Evergreen Landscaping uses a spreadsheet to forecast profit based on net margins for a variety of products. Using the spreadsheet, Shawna discovers that the formulas used in the forecast create errors when she tries to apply negative margins to any product. Because she is concerned about forecasting for the worst as well as the best case, she uses the spreadsheet to produce results for negative margins based on a straight-line extrapolation from 10 percent, 5 percent, and 0 percent. She realizes later that profit isn't a linear function of margin and that she can't trust these extrapolations. Connie uses another application to create a report on average net margins for a variety of products. She discovers that this database application can't handle more than 100 products at a time, so she has the averages computed in batches and then averages the averages. Of course, unless the batches are all the same size, this average of averages is invalid.

In an information system, flexibility means increased functionality that users desire. Redevelopment costs are very high, requiring **retrofitting** (reworking an old system to new requirements) of a system whose original designers may be gone. By building in flexibility and additional functionality early, the necessity for later retrofitting is reduced. A system with more (and well-documented) functionality is also likely to be adopted more quickly.

Some systems can actually be shared or sold. Many organizations are discovering that they can sell systems they have developed to competitors. For example, Baxter Travenol did this with its *ASAP Express* system, creating a money-making service that competitors had to buy in to. Systems can also be sold to suppliers and customers (which was the

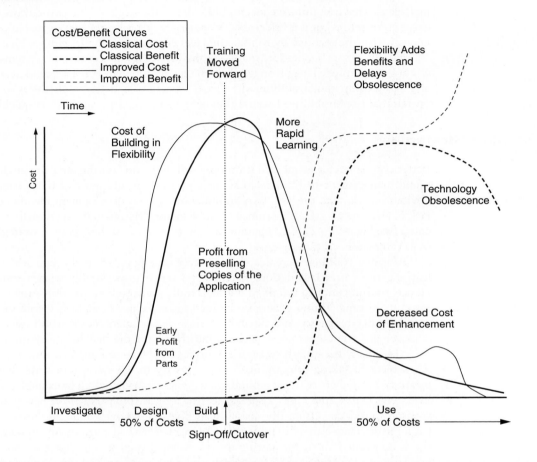

Figure 14–2 APPLICATION LIFE CYCLE PROJECT ECONOMICS

origin of *ASAP Express*) or to others in a joint venture. Managers should consider **precompetitive joint ventures** with competitors to develop software unconnected to their major arena of competition. Accounting systems, for example, rarely have a competitive focus. Sales, on the other hand, have a strong competitive impact. Organizations can also presell copies of software to earn some income before the software is ready. With the experience gathered from creating a particularly difficult system, an IS professional staff can gain important knowledge that may be sellable on a consulting basis to others. Sharing costs, building friends and allies for strategic alliances, and making a few bucks cut the risks involved.

Finally, it is possible simply to apply sound management techniques to motivate staff to stay, to encourage innovation and a spirit of inventiveness, to keep the channels of communication open, and to create a climate in which evaluation is important. Although technology changes a lot and rapidly, there is no reason why technologists shouldn't be evaluated on how they manage to use the technology. While IS professionals are mobile, it is important to make them feel they are part of a team by using appropriate management techniques to personalize their work and motivate buy-in.

The results of these strategies are to move some of the costs forward (training); to add additional costs of building in flexibility very early in design; to presell copies or modules of major systems while increasing the payback from more rapid learning; to avoid total reworks of the system due to obsolescence; to add additional benefits through more flexible functionality; and to forestall technological obsolescence for a while because the system works so well.

ANALYZING PROJECT RISK

We define the word *project* to mean the set of activities surrounding the creation of a management support system. Such systems can be quite small, single-person, single-function systems such as a spreadsheet to calculate rates of return for various investments, or they can be very large, multiperson, multifunction systems such as huge database management systems to handle corporate disaster planning and crisis management. Regardless of the project size or type, we call the entire set of activities from inception to installation (and beyond) a project.

Projects are undertaken for their benefits and used despite their costs, but they involve risks at all times. Quoting Bob Zeibig, an organizational consultant with Norton, Nolan & Co., Deborah Asbrand writes that at any moment in time a third of all companies (this estimate has been traced to a report done by KPMG–Pete Marwick, a consulting firm) will have **runaway projects.** Asbrand cites the example of a client-server project at a Midwestern insurance claims company whose two-year, $5 million project ran away with $15 million within 9 months. Poor management, poor planning, and inexperience were the contributing factors. Large organizations, the use of novel and complex technologies (such as client-server), lack of documentation, and inattention to basic management principles are the common threads in such major cost and time overruns. Although everyone else can see that things are out of control, information systems professionals often go through a process of denial, finding a dozen things to blame for lack of documentation, lack of controls, and lack of leadership. In fact, these tendencies are only human, but there are aspects of management support system projects that tend to set them apart from others and turn these human failings into recipes for disaster.

A model of application development risk factors was created by Barki, Talbot, and Rivard according to their study of 120 such projects. They named five factors as critical in determining project risk, which they defined as the uncertainty of a project (i.e., the probability of it failing to produce the desired application) times the magnitude of loss such failure would engender. These factors are *technological newness* (the novelty of the technology to the implementation team), *application size, lack of expertise* (which is related, of course, to technological newness), **application complexity** (internal complexity of the application and how thoroughly and critically it links to others), and *organizational environment* (e.g., conflicts over resources and how system changes affect the organization). DuWayne J. Peterson, who served in systems management capacities with companies such as Ford, Citibank, RCA, Security Pacific Bank, and Merrill Lynch, implicates four factors that can impede the creation of strategic information systems: *lack of knowledge of business concepts, failure to match technology and need, lack of mutual respect between business leaders and system developers,* and *lack of upper management support.* Several other such lists have been developed by MIS researchers (see references), but the simple three-factor view of McFarlan seems common to all of the lists. Our model of project risk is an

| Figure 14–3 | A MODEL OF IS PROJECT RISK |

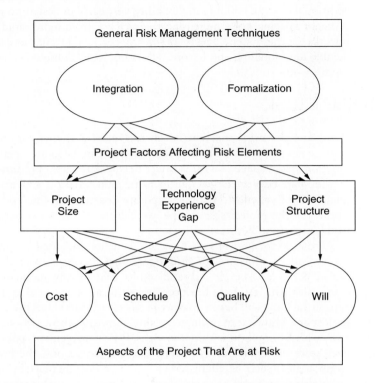

extension of McFarlan's and crafted to be consistent with the previous model of feasibility. The **project risks** include cost, schedule, quality (i.e., the technology), and organizational will. Quality risks are the dangers that the technology will not meet user expectations of reliability.

How these risks arise is illustrated in Figure 14–3. Several factors influence the probability of these risks:

- **Project size:** Large projects obviously cost more, take more time, are more complex, and involve more people.
- **Technology experience gap:** Developers who are unfamiliar with the hardware, software, application, databases, languages, and so forth, are not going to be very good at what they do. The larger the gap in their experience or knowledge, the greater the risk to the project.
- **Project structure:** The product (output, result, deliverable) should be well defined. If it isn't or if changes are occurring frequently, the project is at risk.

Our model stresses that these are *relative* risks, without absolutes. The larger and longer the project is, the more that can go wrong. Users and their needs change, and if these changes are allowed to influence the actual design, the project structure suffers. As project

Figure 14–4	CALCULATING PROJECT RISK

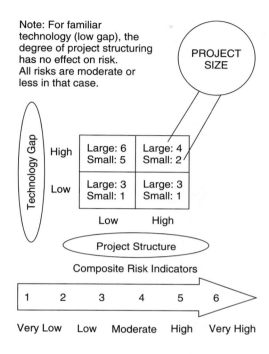

Note: For familiar technology (low gap), the degree of project structuring has no effect on risk. All risks are moderate or less in that case.

time increases, the technology may become obsolete, key personnel may leave or become disinterested or obsolete, and the project may become more complex. Or, company priorities may change, leaving the project an "orphan."

Project risk can be calculated conceptually (Figure 14–4). Again, remember that these are relative risks. It is possible to compare two projects or alternatives without attaching specific monetary values to the risk. Those values depend on the organization's resources and its environment. Here we stress that calculations are beneficial when comparing projects with others *in the same environment for the same firm.*

Where the technology is familiar, project structure has little influence (partly because the technology either defines the deliverable or the project staff feels so confident that they can stay with this technology that they resist temptations to overdesign or overreact). The riskiest projects are large, poorly defined projects using unfamiliar technology. The least risky ones are small projects involving familiar technology. In general, the technology experience gap increases risk more than project size, and size, in turn, increases risk more than project structure.

MANAGING PROJECT RISK

Writing about an unnamed U.S. health insurance company, David Dickson noted that a $200 million group insurance system took 18 months to build and incorrectly paid out $60 million in insurance benefits the first year, causing so much confusion that 35,000 clients were lost at enormous additional cost. Dickson says that up to 90 percent of project

Figure 14–5   THE RISK MANAGEMENT PROCESS

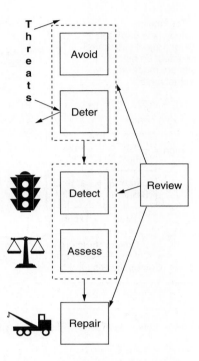

problems result from project management errors. He notes that recommendations to reduce project risks often include appointing an experienced project manager, involving end users, appointing a systems integrator to take over the project, conducting regular reviews and audits, and implementing quality management programs. But he cautions that trouble may still arise. His firm, KPMG, has created practices to curb runaway projects, called "Runaway Systems Management." Three principles underlie these practices:

- *Use objective performance measures:* What does the system actually do *now*, not how much time have you put in? KPMG stresses formal control systems and organizational learning through error analysis.
- *Encourage candid communication:* Projects are too complex for infrequent and irrelevant meetings. Dickson uses the example of an insurance company that spent $2 million not agreeing on the objectives for a policy issuance and claims processing system. A month before the project was killed, sponsors were still being told the project was "just about complete."
- *Detect and manage risk:* KPMG has developed risk assessment tools specific to its projects. The actual tool used to manage risk is less important than being aware of and managing risk.

Risk management lies on a foundation of avoidance, deterrence, detection, assessment, repair, and review (see Figure 14–5). We seek to avoid risks by understanding that they do occur. The previous section discussed what the risks are and what factors control them. Managers can deter these risks by taking steps to ensure that they do not occur or to lessen their impact if they do occur. The impact of risks can be detected by designing measures that are appropriate to the risk and will trigger alarms. For example, measuring the amount of work already done will indeed trigger an alarm when the project is over budget, but managers need measures that precede the actual damage.

Having detected the effects of the risk, managers have to assess how bad the damage is. Because software-based projects have intangible and somewhat unsalvageable products, it is hard to measure the product, so managers turn to the project and measure aspects such as funds spent, project morale, functions delivered by the software, and so forth. For managers used to supervising small projects with deliverables such as reports, this can be very frustrating. Many organizations go through denial, like the insurance company did, but in fact if there is harm, it is better to know about it.

Repairing damage requires reworking the project. This is often attempted with a leadership change or a restructuring of the work. It's hard to say in advance that one technique is better than another, but the framework presented next spells out which of four possible techniques is appropriate in which circumstances. It is also important to remember that projects mature and change, so what is appropriate in the early stages of a project may be harmful later on, and vice versa.

Finally, risk management stresses refinement of risk management processes by asking such questions as "Was the previous project over budget?" "Did the technology fail to work as advertised?" or "Was the problem a gullible technical staff or were the vendors dishonest or overly optimistic?" Documenting and reviewing lessons learned is an important organizational exercise.

The following discussion addresses avoidance, deterrence, detection, assessment, and repair. Applying specific techniques from the classes of general techniques *at the appropriate times in the project life cycle* will avoid some problems, deter others, increase the ability to detect threats, assess their damages, and make appropriate repairs. Most techniques should be used *proactively* to avoid or deter problems. There are four general techniques for managing project risk (Figure 14–6): internal integration, external integration, planning, and control.

- **Internal integration** means having the work team work more closely, which makes communication easier and increases learning. It entails putting experienced, professional leadership in place, having frequent team meetings, taking measures to ensure low turnover and mutual familiarity of staff, and providing outside assistance, perhaps in the form of consultants. **External integration** means linking users more closely with the IS project team. This could require appointing users as project leaders, creating a user steering committee, informing users through frequent meetings or by being members of the project team, consulting users on or including them in major decisions, and giving them major responsibilities.

- **Formalization** makes it easier to know what to do because there are rules and procedures to follow. The phases of an application life cycle are a method of formalizing projects, as are prototyping techniques. Formalization regularizes actions so that they are easier to learn and monitor, leading to greater accuracy and fewer mistakes. Formalization can be applied both to planning before a project begins and control while a project is operating. Formal planning may include planning methods such as program evaluation

Figure 14–6   PROJECT RISK MANAGEMENT TECHNIQUES

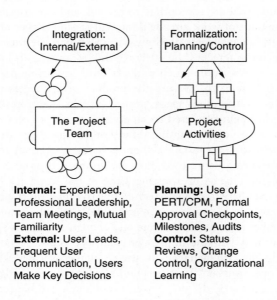

Internal: Experienced, Professional Leadership, Team Meetings, Mutual Familiarity
External: User Leads, Frequent User Communication, Users Make Key Decisions

Planning: Use of PERT/CPM, Formal Approval Checkpoints, Milestones, Audits
Control: Status Reviews, Change Control, Organizational Learning

and review technique (PERT) or critical path method (CPM), milestones, specification standards, formal reviews and approvals from users, and postimplementation audits. Formal control can increase through formal status reviews, formalized change control procedures, milestone meetings, and various organizational learning mechanisms which, while aimed at learning, also serve to remind people and hence serve as a kind of implicit control.

Internal integration is recommended for narrowing technology gaps that may occur with unfamiliar, new, or innovative hardware or software (Table 14–2). Such measures increase the possibility that members of a project team can share whatever knowledge they have with others, and this obviously decreases learning time. Hiring consultants to perform intellectual technology transfer also helps.

When a poorly structured project has unclear objectives or the likelihood of many changes is high, external integration serves well by keeping the project team close to the source of those changes. Formal planning provides the greatest benefits with large, complex projects by making actions more predictable and tractable. Formal control is most valuable in situations where the technology gap is small. In fact, formal project control is problematic where the technology gap is large. In this case, there is the danger of overcontrolling a team that literally doesn't know what it is doing. Instead, rapid learning (i.e., less control) is important.

One controversy in the IS field that has not been authoritatively answered by academics is whether users should manage IS projects. Increasingly, however, users are taking strong control of projects, or at least project planning and expenditures. It is not always easy, however, for users to apply basic management principles to IS projects. One possible reason may be the dearth of computer-based support for project management.

Table 14-2	MANAGING PROJECT RISK	
Risk Management Technique	**How It Works**	**When It Does and Does Not Work**
Integration: Internal	Experienced, professional leadership brings the team together, creating team spirit and mutual familiarity and support. Information passes more quickly among team members. Outside assistance is more quickly accepted if it is directed by leaders. Turnover decreases because of team loyalty.	Can help reduce large technology gap (unfamiliar, new, innovative hardware, software, or architectures). Users on team multiply technical learning by training each other. Leaders can bring in external advice and expertise to teach the team and transfer technologies to the organization.
Integration: External	Users lead the project or a steering committee of users directs the projects. Users are kept informed, if not involved, and may officially join the team. Users have key responsibilities and make key decisions. Customer service ethic increases if users do their jobs well. Could be a disaster if users are cynical, mistrusting, or inept.	Poorly structured project with unclear objectives and the likelihood of many changes of the life cycle of the project. As project structure increases, users may become less involved. Watch out for too much user involvement that may stifle technical creativity or put too many demands on technical people. Very poor for well-structured projects with familiar technology.
Formal planning	Use of formalized planning tools such as PERT or CPM, milestones, standard specifications, formal approvals, and postimplementation audits. Plan must be preapproved by managers and leaders, and team members must buy into the plan.	Large, complex projects require formal planning. Breaking projects into parts will also help. Large, poorly structured projects are extremely high-risk because formal planning is almost impossible, and no amount of formal planning can overcome lack of user definition of goals and desires.
Formal control	Use of formalized control mechanisms such as formal status reviews, change controls, milestone meetings, and mechanisms for organizational learning such as "lessons learned" sessions.	Formal control is useful only for relatively low-risk projects with small technology experience gaps. Where the gap is large, formal control will squelch project creativity and put too much stress on project members. Avoid too much formality while technology gap remains large, but keep project small in these stages.

Writing in *Industrial Engineering,* Tom Rogers points out that it is only recently that project management software with GUIs has lowered what he calls the "threshold to implementation." Corporations now see such software as essential not only to large, high-profile projects of the past, but to newer, user-driven projects of this decade and the future. Point-and-click navigation through data, dragging and shrinking windows, and instant recalculation—these are the hallmarks of today's project management software, which is significantly lower priced than the packages of the previous decade.

Several features characterize the improvements in modern project management packages:

■ Client-server architectures bring more data to bear on more sophisticated software.

- Enterprisewide access enabled by LANs helps project management across departments or divisions, which is especially important for projects with high (and broad) strategic impact.
- GUIs make it possible for more people, especially the computer-averse, to use project management screens in ways that are intuitive to them.
- Real-time processing means that all data are current, correct, and available for validation.

With these interfaces, task networks, timetables, and architectures, project control can now be shared effectively across an entire organization. This can only increase project involvement among workers, empowering them with regard to most, if not all, project decisions, and enhancing productivity. Time-sensitive operations are now integrated as they happen; changes to projects are noted as they occur; critical paths are updated; and workers are informed about schedule changes.

One important computer-based tool that helps build applications is called *computer-aided software engineering* (CASE). Originally, CASE tools were almost exclusively intended for computer professionals' use, but their appearance has brought together prototyping, CAD, and CAM to application development. Managers are being involved in this process and, in some cases, the tools are good enough to be used, at least in part, by managers or teams led by managers.

COMPUTER-AIDED SOFTWARE ENGINEERING

Computer-aided software engineering (CASE) is a term that describes the use of computer applications by information systems professionals and others to simplify and automate the application development process. By this point in the text, even readers unfamiliar with the term *CASE* can probably describe the major aspects of CASE tools. Because much of CASE is intended for users and exploiting computer-based tools has the effect of lowering labor costs and speeding up production (thereby either lowering managerial budgets or enhancing product quality), managers should be familiar with the major components of CASE.

CASE tools assist in three aspects of application development (see Figure 14–7):

- **Upper CASE** (sometimes called *front-end CASE*) has tools for interaction with users to collect information, processing, and output requirements. In addition, graphical tools for creating diagrams (such as DFDs, structure charts, or specialized diagrams that would be of use to specific users for specific systems, such as document flow diagrams) are available. Upper CASE also includes prototyping tools for creating screens, reports, menus, and dialogs with users. Upper CASE is intended for user interaction, so many organizations confine their use of CASE strictly to information requirements gathering and diagraming. In many instances, Upper CASE tools can be used to translate user requirements into physical designs and to produce valuable data dictionaries that assist in later stages of design.
- **Lower CASE** (sometimes called *back-end CASE*) has tools intended for systems professionals to generate software that will be run later. The components of lower CASE include diagraming tools similar to or in addition to those of upper CASE. Also available is an information warehouse or repository of screen layouts, report layouts, previously generated

Figure 14-7 ANATOMY OF A CASE TOOL

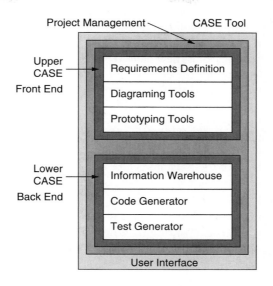

code, and other bits and pieces (called **software fragments**) of CASE-created software that can be standardized and reused. A second additional component is a code generator that takes output from diagraming tools and data dictionaries and actually generates code in appropriate languages (originally COBOL, but lately C and C++), thus greatly simplifying the creation of program language statements. The final component is a systematic way of testing the generated code. Compilers, assemblers, debuggers, editors, and linkers are available in some form or format through the code generator, reducing significantly the amount of labor needed to create a line of code.

■ Project management tools are often available in CASE, too. Because software fragments are related to specific projects and goals, it is natural that management of these fragments be organized through the CASE tool itself. Project planning, security (e.g., passwords to retrieve data on specific projects), documentation, scheduling, and disposition are generally available.

Not every CASE tool offers all these functions. Some are intended only for Upper-CASE situations, while many older systems contain only lower-CASE functions. Where all three functions are present, the tool is sometimes referred to as **integrated CASE (I-CASE).** The ultimate CASE tool would translate raw user specifications into running systems. Skillful use of I-CASE approaches this ideal, but most sophisticated management support applications are too complex for this ideal to be reached today.

The major benefits of CASE to managers are the following:

■ CASE keeps track of software fragments for software developers and project mangers so that no information is lost. In fact, the reuse and recycling of project-related information is encouraged, which can only enhance productivity.

- CASE automatically links many fragments in ways that require little creative thought but a lot of careful attention. For example, data definitions and data flow diagrams and structure charts have natural relationships with one another. As designers and developers change data flow diagrams, new data items appear that require definition, and CASE can prompt the designer for those definitions. Items may disappear, in which case definitions can be removed. Incompatible definitions (e.g., two items with the same definition), processes that have no inputs, and data that magically appear from nowhere are easily detected by CASE tools, prompting IS specialists to correct inconsistencies, redundancies, and weaknesses in the design. In some cases, the tool can actually check the logic of the program before it is tested by examining diagrams or databases, perhaps using expert systems techniques.

- Many CASE tools interface with elements of the manager's information workbench (such as spreadsheets, databases, word processors, and project management software). When made available through a network in a client-server manner, CASE tools can become powerful equipment for successfully supervising and steering application development projects.

- Company standards are easier to create and enforce if every technical person uses the same tools. Users can expect more uniformity and reliability (assuming the CASE tool actually works), perhaps even more civility and politeness.

- Multiproject environments are easier to manage. Technical professionals can leave much of the dirty work to the CASE tool and focus on meeting managers' expectations. Managers can expect more consistency, better spelling (spell checkers seem to be inherent in CASE tools), more timely and useful documentation, better prototyping, better trained staff, and more uniformity in how they are treated.

- The resource drain is lowered for paper and people, although, of course, a computer takes up a lot of space, uses some electricity, and requires training.

CASE also presents all the potential drawbacks of automation, including the following:

- If CASE tools make it easier to produce a good system quickly, just imagine how rapidly a bad system can be produced.

- The more computers there are in the pipeline, the greater the chance that a human error will be blamed on the computer.

- Saving information in a single computer or a network without backup on a regular basis creates the same danger as not saving it in the first place.

- The uniformity that managers like is not universally admired by technical professionals, many of whom like their jobs because they can be creative. It is likely that an imposed uniformity will inhibit creativity.

- There is some evidence that older technical people don't like the automated techniques.

- CASE technology is still in its infancy and it is often not as good as advertised. As with any technology, high initial expectations inevitably lead to some disappointment and failure to use later, improved versions.

- As with any commercial product, shopping around is important, but CASE costs at the moment are very high, with packages running thousands of dollars. Many firms are shy about investing large amounts of money in technologies that, like all other computer-based technologies, become obsolete rather rapidly.

At Global Petroleum, a firm that has $3 billion in annual sales, the IS staff numbers four: a manager, two programmers, and a data administrator. Part of Global's secret is contracting out work, but its use of CASE has also significantly cut down on costs and human resource requirements. Using an integrated CASE tool called *Linc* and an application generator, the small staff can quickly create prototypes for users' screens and reports. A report writer named *EZSpec* generates software in five minutes that might have taken a good programmer up to three hours to create—a 36-to-1 improvement in productivity. The increase in speed means that Global's staff can focus on delivering satisfaction to its customers.

One of the greatest drawbacks to any CASE tool is that using it requires standards, training, common approaches, an emphasis on projects as opposed to handling crises, and a strongly rational, proactive philosophy. Well-organized firms do well with CASE for these reasons, and poorly organized ones do not. That said, there is great hope that CASE tools will actually become end user development aids in the near future. For this to happen, CASE tools that use GUIs, employ prototyping, standard user interfaces, and expert systems will have to be developed. Of course, there is no sin in developing these tools for systems professionals to use, too.

Recently, a convergence of GUIs and CASE with more user-oriented development techniques (such as JAD, RAD, and prototyping) has become available through client-server architectures (see Figure 14–8). This development has bred a stable of new CASE products useful for designing and producing GUI-based systems. Some of these tools are simple and friendly enough for users to build their own systems. Such tools may contribute to shortening half-lives for software, because it is easier to revamp or completely redo each application. Guidelines for acquiring and using these tools include the following:

- Don't forget that existing applications have a reason for existing; make sure that they also get converted to GUIs.

- Don't become dependent on a specific GUI in case a decision is made to use a different one.

- Look for tools that support movement to client-server, multiplatform systems.

- Tools should always generate prototypes; user involvement is important.

- Tools that facilitate end user access to databases will reduce the later need to reengineer and redevelop.

- The focus of JAD sessions and, in fact, any requirements analysis technique is on business needs, not on what screens look like. While JAD sessions may change with the addition of graphics-based tools, do not shift the focus to the technology.

The last bit of advice concerns the need to manage projects *across* the organization. Managing a project as though it affects the entire firm guarantees external integration.

| Figure 14–8 | THE CONVERGENCE OF REQUIREMENTS ANALYSIS AND DEVELOPMENT TOOLS |

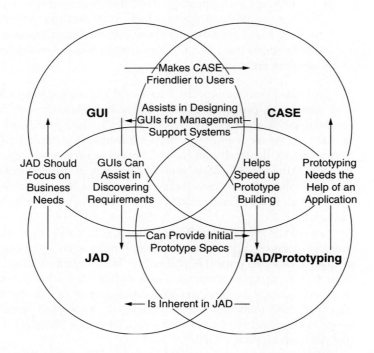

Computer-based project management tools and CASE go a long way toward making application development project information available not only to direct users but also to indirect users and others who may use the application's output or provide its inputs.

■ CHIPPING AWAY AT DON'S RESISTANCE

Basically, Don is worried about looking like a fool. He knows that with his stock options with Concertina and 20 years' experience making chips and snack foods, he will do all right if he keeps his nose clean and avoids failures. And failure is the name of the inadequate system they have now. It's a miracle, he thinks, that the company is doing so well given its paperwork burden and the difficulty involved in finding out how production is doing. Yes, they need a new system, but Don is not the person to head the project. Creating a system based on a chip is different from one that manages the making of chips. Don can't quite describe why this is so, but it seems so intangible to him and he is not comfortable with it. The last project was handled by a consulting company and the president, Tina Tucker, doesn't want to go that route this time. Too many company secrets are involved in the production process, and a really bad system was put into place last time, probably because

Tina trusted the consultants too much. So now she wants an insider to manage the project, and who is more inside than Don? But Don knows, or at least is afraid, that he can't handle the stress without some understanding about what a systems project is and what freedoms he has. ■

1. What do you know about systems projects that would justify Don's fears?

2. Discuss four general strategies that may help Don increase his chances of success as a project manager. What are these strategies and how would they work at Concertina?

3. Describe the economic profile of a project such as the production IS at Concertina in terms that Don can understand. What are the pressure points where decisions have to be made by the project manager?

The Modern Management Imperatives

Reach: Global Competition	IS departments now find competition in four corners of an application development globe that wasn't always so small and threatening. Truly global software firms make software available from everywhere. Users can build their own applications now. CASE and fourth-generation languages along with GUIs make everyone a potential application builder. The life of existing software can be extended if the system is built flexibly using one of these tools. Application development tools can also be used by competitors' IS departments to create higher-quality software faster.
Reaction: Quick Customer Feedback on Products and Services	Managers' needs change with business changes. These are occurring far more rapidly now, and managers need to provide quick feedback, using e-mail, bulletin boards, fax, and voice mail among other technologies.
Responsiveness: Shortened Concept-to-Customer Cycle Time	Prototyping shortens concept-to-customer time practically to zero by creating working prototypes immediately without a long development wait. CASE and GUI generators make screens and reports available quickly rather than after many months of negotiation, which may have to be redone later.
Refinement: Greater Customer Sophistication and Specificity	Managers and other users are becoming more familiar with information systems' capabilities, especially microcomputers and especially because of client-server architectures. Internet access brings new market-oriented information to managers on a daily basis.
Reconfiguration: Reengineering of Work Patterns and Structures	Because managers lead through and with technology, they can reconfigure their own work rapidly and accurately. Information systems now take care of much of the boring, repetitive, memory-based work of supervision, thereby freeing managers for more creative efforts.
Redeployment: Reorganization and Redesign of Resources	Project management software, either enCASEd or not, is increasing resource awareness and control, enabling managers to stay on top of more responsibilities at any one moment.
Reputation: Quality and Reliability of Project and Process	CASE, prototyping, and information requirements tools shift the emphasis from the technology to the users, creating a more effective atmosphere of customer awareness and service. Higher-quality products are the result of using higher-quality tools.

This table illustrates the way in which CASE and other prototyping and end user or client-oriented application development systems meet the imperatives. The customer in this table is a manager who needs a management support system.

Summary

There are major costs to information systems application development, of which managers should be aware. Early stages of development are costly, and benefits are usually delayed until development is complete. The products of development are software, which is difficult to envision for use until development is completed. Technology change during development is also an obstacle, as is obsolescence. Staff turnover during the process can be high, too. Managers may be tempted to cope by hiring additional staff, spending more money on computer resources, accepting untested products, and skipping user relations efforts like education. Relying on overly optimistic promises by technical people can lead to additional problems. Better strategies include advanced training, spending money to build in quality and flexibility, attempting to share costs and risks with others, and applying sound management techniques to encourage innovation, team spirit, and a climate in which evaluation is important.

Project risk increases with project size and the gap between the developer's familiarity with technology and the requirements. Where project products are poorly defined or where the identification of the requirements may change, risk is high. Project risk may be reduced through a program of avoidance, deterrence, detection, assessment, repair, and review. Four techniques for directly addressing project risk include internal and external integration (improving team communication and user involvement, respectively), formal planning, and control methods. Computer-aided software engineering (CASE) tools help reduce risk by lowering costs, speeding production, and increasing the quality. CASE makes it easier to create, manage, and link different versions of software fragments into systems, to create and enforce standards, and to facilitate interproject communication.

Discussion Questions

14.1 What is there about technology, as you think of it, that increases project development risk? What steps can a manager take to reduce these risks in advance of project development?

14.2 Project risk reduction depends on avoidance, deterrence, detection, assessment, repair, and review. What are a manager's responsibilities in these areas? How does a manager go about avoiding project risks, deterring problems, detecting project threats, and so on? What makes technology development projects and, more specifically, management support system development projects more difficult with regard to risk reduction?

14.3 In what ways does CASE assist integration (internal as well as external)? How does CASE make it easier to link and manage difficult versions of software fragments? What aspects of CASE make it peculiar to software development, and what aspects lie strictly in the realm of project management?

Key Terms

advance training
application complexity
computer-aided software
    engineering (CASE)
delayed benefit
dysfunctional coping strategies
external integration
formalization: planning, control
front-end cost loading
intangible product
integrated CASE (I-CASE)
internal integration

lower CASE
mobility of systems professionals
precompetitive joint ventures
project risks: cost, schedule,
    will, quality
project size
project structure
retrofitting
risk management: avoidance,
    detection, deterrence,
    assessment, repair, review

runaway projects
software fragments
system brittleness
system half-life
technological change
technological obsolescence
technology experience gap
two-cultures gap
upper CASE

References

Asbrand, Deborah. "Uncharted Waters Pose Risk of Runaway Project." *InfoWorld* 15, 26 (June 28, 1993): 67.

Barki, Henri, Jean Talbot, and Suzanne Rivard. "Toward an Assessment of Software Development Risk." *Journal of Management Information Systems* 10, 2 (1993): 203–225.

Cash, James I., Jr., F. Warren McFarlan, James L. McKenney, and Lynda M. Applegate. *Corporate Information Systems Management*. 3d ed. Homewood, IL: Irwin, 1992.

Dickson, David A. "Reining in Runaways." *Canadian Insurance* (September 1993): 16–17, 27–28.

Gane, T., and T. Sarson. *Structured Systems Analysis: Tools and Techniques*. Englewood Cliffs, NJ: Prentice-Hall, 1979.

Gill, Phillip. "RAD Tools, Techniques Take Graphic Direction." *Software Magazine* 12, 5 (April 1992): 41–46.

Gillin, Paul. "Petroleum Firm Relies on CASE." *Computerworld* 26, 47 (November 24, 1992): 63–64.

Laudon, Kenneth, and Jane Price Laudon. *Management Information Systems: Organization and Technology*. 3d ed. New York: Macmillan, 1993.

Lin, C., and C. Chung. "End-User Computing in a CASE Environment." *Journal of Information Systems Management* (Spring 1991): 17–21.

McComb, Mary. "CASE Tools Implementation at Amtrak—Lessons Almost Learned." *Journal of Systems Management* 45 (March 1994): 16–20.

McFarlan, F. W. "The Portfolio Approach to Information Systems." *Harvard Business Review* 59, 5 (September–October 1981): 142–150.

Norman, R., and J. Nunamaker, Jr. "CASE Productivity Perceptions of Software Engineering Professionals." *Communications of the ACM* 32, 9 (September 1989).

Rogers, Tom. "Project Management: Emerging As a Requisite for Success." *Industrial Engineering* (June 1993): 42–43.

Umbaugh, Robert E., and DuWayne J. Peterson. "On the Strategic Value of Information Systems." *Information Systems Management* (Summer 1992): 85–87.

CASE

EVERGREEN LANDSCAPING AND MAINTENANCE:
MANAGING THE SKILLS MANAGEMENT SYSTEM PROJECT

Connie has decided to move ahead with the skills management system, with an eye toward using it as the basis for the human resource information system discussed in previous chapters. Connie, Sid, and Sid's administrative assistant, Kayla Dowd, have met with Terry (system administration and development) and Dierdre and Parnell (technical support). One of the major conclusions of these early meetings is that part of the new system should be contracted out to consultants while other parts should be done in-house. Connie and Sid are convinced that this is the biggest project of its sort ever undertaken at Evergreen. Terry and Parnell are just as convinced that the project will be a success, but they admit they haven't had much experience with distributed designs and telecommunications. Connie and Terry meet with Frances (vice president of administration) to talk about the project:

> CONNIE: Frances, we've decided to recommend going ahead with the SMS. Because it's a complex project, we want you to think about using this as the kernel of the human resource information system we talked about several months ago to replace our paper personnel records.

FRANCES: I hear you telling me that since it's going to be risky, we may as well go for broke?

CONNIE: Well, I never would phrase it that way, but there are some risks involved.

FRANCES: Tell me about them. How long is this project going to take and what is it going to cost?

TERRY: We estimate that it will take about three months to complete the system, but we'll have prototypes for you, Connie, and Sid to look at within three weeks,. Your costs will be only our salaries plus whatever fee Boris charges us for the telcoms consulting.

FRANCES: What's that? I thought we've just been using Boris for planning.

TERRY: So far, but we think Boris, Parnell, and Dierdre can put together a neat system on a LAN as the basis for expansion into an integrated HRIS. Otherwise, we'd have to do some serious reworking of the code later.

FRANCES: So there's going to be a lot of up-front cost?

CONNIE: It's inevitable . . .

TERRY: It's unavoidable . . .

FRANCES: How much?

The three of them continue talking money. Frances shows little emotion but Connie has seen this before—she's worrying about money.

FRANCES: Say, can't we just buy a system?

CONNIE: No, we've looked at a lot of packages and they just won't do. However, there are some project management packages and a few performance appraisal schemes that we could purchase or license. Fitting them into the integrated SMS might require some doing, though.

TERRY: We're going to a client-server architecture that will make those incompatibilities less of a problem, though, remember?

CONNIE: And I've recommended a mixed approach—tailor some packages, outsource to Boris, and develop the rest in-house. Or we may approach Business Experts again [the firm that installed Evergreen's retail system on the minicomputer] for a quote.

The meeting ended with everyone agreeing that the project goals were well defined, but apt to change, that this was indeed a large project for Evergreen's small IS group, and that their experience with the various technologies was at best moderate. Connie's training needs analysis application has grown into an integrated HRIS at a company that still uses paper and a few spreadsheets on isolated microcomputers. Connie is also very much aware that she hasn't coordinated her activities very well with Shawna, her boss, and with Heather (vice president of finance), who will make even stronger money arguments. Terry wonders who's going to be the project manager. She has worked only on very small projects and while she gets along with Dierdre, she knows that Parnell, a recent graduate and a hotshot technician, will be hard to direct. And who's the client here? Connie? Sid? The project has grown much bigger than a small training needs assessment application and now it has cross-company implications. It looks like Frances is taking it over. And Business Experts? They were in long before Terry joined, even before Evergreen ever thought to employ a programmer. Terry feels intimidated by this possibility. Meanwhile, a project that involved only Connie and Terry now involves at least seven people, an outsider, and a consulting company. And Connie asked Terry to promise everything in three months!

Questions

1. The text lists six ways systems projects differ from other projects. Which of these six differences will be important in the HRIS project? Who will feel the most stress and how? What specific suggestions should Connie, Shawna, and Frances avoid making? What promises should they have avoided already?

2. Estimate the risk that the HRIS project is going to run. Which of the four aspects shown in Figure 14–3 will be the riskiest? Why?

3. Four general techniques to handle economic risk are discussed in this chapter. How could Frances work to implement each of these techniques? Who should carry out these suggestions?

4. Which of the four general techniques to handle project risk would you recommend to Frances? What will happen if your recommendations are ignored? If they are followed? What are the costs of accepting your recommendations?

5. CASE tools may also work to lower project risk. How would you recommend CASE and any other techniques be integrated to benefit Evergreen in the HRIS project?

CHAPTER FIFTEEN

HUMAN ISSUES IN MANAGEMENT SUPPORT SYSTEMS

OBJECTIVES

■ Describe four roles that people play in an information environment.

■ Discuss the roles and risks of each role player.

■ Describe the knowledge managers need to have to manage people in an information environment.

■ Identify the existing and emerging ethical challenges information technology poses to managers.

Question: What are the risks in managing people for whom information systems tasks play a major role? How can these risks be handled?

Personnel Plus (P+) is a temp agency with a difference. Unlike its competitors, Personnel Plus deals only with executives and high-level professional employees who are looking for temporary assignments in exotic places for up to a year. Warren Wygant is the director of placement and his job is to keep files on prospective employees, matching executive talent with positions. The key to the success of P+ is market intelligence. P+ approaches organizations considering downsizing (through consulting firms that Warren is acquainted with) and gathers data on executives who have requested outplacement assistance as part of termination or early retirement packages. Warren works with a special high-security application that can comb almost any corporate human resources file (with permission, of course) to speed up registration. Sixteen people in three national offices work for him on this application, and two programmer analysts work to maintain the application. Warren recently had a request from a customer to download a portion of Warren's files directly to the customer's minicomputer, and Warren is wondering if this could be a new business opportunity for his firm. In fact, he wonders if any of his employees have thought of this yet on their own. Is this a risky business?

Answer: A number of risks arise from the application roles users, clients, stakeholders, and developers play. These risks also stem from the fact that Warren has to manage people in an information-intensive environment. Warren is also facing a number of ethical issues.

INTRODUCTION: THE HUMAN SPHERE

Chapter 15 moves the focus of risk management from an application or system to people and organizations they work in. Much of the risk involved in developing or buying management support systems comes from technology and the way it is created or bought, but substantial risk stems from people who are involved with these applications and the way organizations perceive and relate to applications in general. In a real sense, we are coming full circle to Chapter 4, paying due respect to the role these applications play in the competitive life of a firm.

Specific topics covered in this chapter include the roles played by individuals in the information environment, human resource management in that environment, and the ethical concerns raised by information technology. The information environment has some unique characteristics that create unique challenges for managers. While previous chapters have stressed the role information plays in management, this chapter stresses the roles management plays in information-centered environments. Working in this sort of environment creates some ethical challenges that, while not really new, are exacerbated by the speed and volume of information now available.

Because this chapter is about people and how their relationships are altered by information, we use many examples from the Evergreen case as illustrations. A brief review of the cast of characters follows:

- Lily Doucette is president and CEO of Evergreen Landscaping and Maintenance, Inc., a company she founded more than ten years ago. She makes major decisions in running the company and relies on a council of vice presidents and selected middle managers, called the Management Executive Committee (MEC), for advice.
- Shawna Eggert is vice president of sales, a longtime associate of Lily, and a member of the MEC.
- Connie Somerset is sales manager, reporting to Shawna. She is in charge of all operational activities in the major sales areas: retail gardening, contract landscaping, and lawn maintenance. Connie is the youngest and newest member of the MEC. She has two assistant managers, Sid Cavenaugh and Sven Haroldson.
- Sid Cavenaugh is assistant manager of contract services. He has day-to-day responsibilities for contract landscaping and lawn maintenance.
- Kayla Dowd is Sid's administrative assistant.
- Sven Haroldson is assistant manager of retail. In this position, he is in charge of the retail gardening store.
- Frances Harmon is vice president of administration. Her responsibilities include human resources, communication, and information systems. Kim Backer is her administrative assistant.
- Terry Bonner is in charge of system administration and development. She manages three other people: Dierdre Tilton is a programmer/analyst, Parnell Tulley is a programmer and database administrator, and Boris Pomfrit is a contract network consultant.
- Heather Cariad is vice president of finance. Her responsibilities include accounting, finance, and risk management. She is a member of the MEC.

- Priscilla Chan is the controller and handles most of the money matters at Evergreen. Priscilla is often at MEC meetings.
- Thomas Davidoff is vice president of operations and has also been with Lily for a long time. He serves on the MEC and is in charge of all logistics, security, transportation, and out-of-store inventory.

ROLES PEOPLE PLAY IN AN INFORMATION ENVIRONMENT

Until now, our emphasis has been on relationships among business processes, organizations, and databases. Databases represent events that organizations experience while they undergo processes. This model was very useful for discussing information architecture in Chapter 5. Now our emphasis shifts to the people involved in those processes as they use applications. What we called a "user" or "user-manager" in previous chapters will mean a person playing multiple roles in this chapter. We refer to these roles as well as to people who play these roles at certain times.

Figures 15–1 through 15–9 depict an application as a region of activity. Within this region, we find a number of role players whose contributions are detailed next. Each role player also has a sphere of activity, within which may be other applications and others who play roles in them. Personal spheres are indicated by solid circles; application spheres are indicated by dashed circles.

An application exists to maintain one or more organizational processes. Applications support organizational goals, and such goals are held by those for whom the success of the firm is critical. We refer to this class of individuals as **stakeholders.** This group includes boards of directors, shareholders, unions, communities, and suppliers. Not all stakeholders have equal stakes, of course, and many of them have little real control over goal setting or how goals are met. Stakeholders are concerned with applications to the extent that applications help set or meet goals an organization creates. Note that with the exception of technology vendors, stakeholders do not generally have goals that include the creation of applications. Such applications are only a means to the end of tangible goals. When a firm's goal is to increase market share, be the first into a market with a specific product, increase profitability, or be a good corporate citizen, an information application is a way to meet the goal.

In any event, managers translate goals into specific activities that need to be carried out. These goals represent desirable conclusions for certain people, called **clients.** The word *clientship*, introduced in Chapter 13, is a special form relating only to the *construction* of applications. Here we focus on the *use* of applications once they are constructed or purchased. Clients may be within an organization (such as managers of departments) or they may be outside the organization (customers). There is an implied hierarchy of clientship. An individual who is a client of an application may have more clients awaiting results that the individual produces. Clients await the outcomes that applications bring, but they may not have much interaction with the application.

The class of individuals who have this interaction are called **direct users.** In this definition, we make a distinction between those who use the application directly and those for whom only the results are important. In our definition here, a user has no stake in the outcome (i.e., a user is not a client) other than for the rewards inherent in carrying out the process (i.e., using the application). Some users also do not care about the ultimate goals for which an application is used (i.e., user is not a stakeholder) other than knowing that the application is in fact used. For example, if an organization markets a

| Figure 15–1 | ROLES AND ACTIVITY SPHERES |

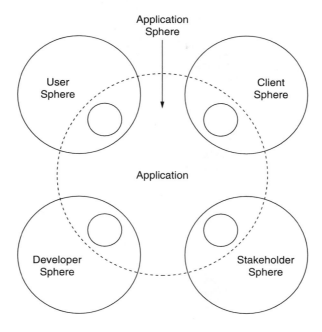

product, sales managers are charged with meeting sales goals—they are the clients. Sales managers guide their departments to meet sales goals and instruct salespeople to use the applications to meet these goals. A second example concerns a manager who uses an expert system to determine the best location in a store to display certain goods. The manager may be both client and user in this case. Finally, consider the case of a financial manager who uses the Internet to locate information about mergers and buyouts among a community of potential lenders. This manager is using a set of applications to navigate through the wide variety of formats and databases to meet his client's needs and at the same time meet his own organization's goals.

Assisting these role players are **developers.** Developers may work for an organization, a client, or a user. They may be direct employees or contracted specialists. In some cases (such as end user software development), a user and a developer may be the same person or team.

Illustrated in Figure 15–1, these four **application roles** (user, client, stakeholder, developer) arise around each application. Although there are clear specialties (particularly in the role of developer), the roles are theoretically distinct from individual personalities. Any person may function in any or all of the four roles at different times. However, there has not been much movement from developer into the other roles. In this chapter, we discuss the interplay of these roles and the risks that the distinctions and movements across the boundaries bring to the creation and use of software-based applications.

Events are happening at Evergreen. Connie has moved forward in building the SMS and some parts of it are already available. The way the SMS works is that Sid gives the

Figure 15–2   THE APPLICATION USER ROLE

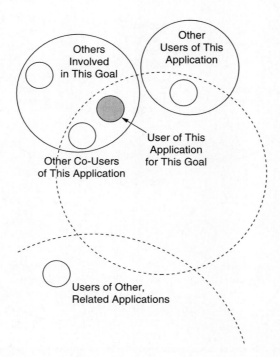

application forms to Kayla Dowd, his assistant, for entry into the system. He is prepared to enter the information from the performance reviews himself. Connie and Sid will work with Terry over the next several months to design a series of dialogs and screens for navigation through this data. They will prepare it for sorting and retrieval and ultimately export it to a spreadsheet for analysis to determine what skills are needed and who has them. Over the winter, Sid, Connie, and Shawna will work with the data to develop a series of profiles for hiring and a database of existing employees who can be approached for rehire. Based on the results of the analyses, Connie and Frances will work on advertisements for positions for the coming year. Kayla will enter all this data and check it for accuracy. Meanwhile, Sven will use it to store his group's applications and performance reviews as a test. If it works out that the system is really general, Frances and Shawna will work out a plan to show it to all the other managers in the company and expand it to a complete HRIS in the coming months.

User Roles and Risks

An **application user role** involves use of the application (see Figure 15–2). This may range from data entry to data navigation to trend analysis and advanced mathematical modeling. Users interact directly with software, typing commands or moving and clicking mouses or myriad input devices to indicate what services are desired. A user may work alone or with a work group. Members of the work group are called **co-users,** and these work groups have all the attributes of groups mentioned in Chapter 9. That is, co-users may work at the same time or at different times and at the same place or at different places.

There may be other users of the same application who are using the application for other goals or other clients. There will probably be minimal interaction with these other users, and whatever interaction there is may appear sporadic, uncoordinated, or it may be highly stylized. For example, it is common for organizations to deal with multiple clients whose needs are not coordinated. Consider a financial services company whose clients range from high rollers to one-bond-a-month purchasers. The use of a portfolio management application may differ from client to client, but ultimately all users have to adhere to certain standards that they may have a role in setting. In some firms, usage may be highly regulated, so that all direct use of the application is done by a select group of individuals. This may be done for security, because the application is hard to use, or simply because most of the users are too new to have learned the application well enough. During training, users may work in pairs, one showing the other how to use the application.

There may be other users who do not use the application but may be involved in the same goal. Secretaries, clerks, receptionists, analysts, marketing reps, and managers all may be involved with an application without using it by preparing forms or memos, checking results, passing results on to others, collating or summarizing results, and so forth. Finally, there may be users of other, related applications.

In the Evergreen SMS, Kayla is the direct user, but Sid, Sven, and Connie will also be users. For Sid's use of the application, Connie is co-user for the same goal (development of a profile for seasonal hiring), while Shawna is also involved with this goal but doesn't use the application. Sven is another user of the application, with only a loose relationship to Sid in this regard, because he is meeting a similar, but different, goal (seasonal contract hiring). Other applications, most not computerized, are related to the SMS. They include the entire hiring scheme and the performance appraisal method. Ultimately, when these applications are more automated, they will be blended into the consolidated HRIS and treated as a single application.

What risks do these role players present? As shown in Figure 15–3, a model of risks involves the following factors:

1. The technical capabilities of the application are not sufficient.

2. The application works but the users fail to use it correctly either because they are not trained correctly or because the application is inherently unusable by this group.

3. The users use it correctly but they fail to appreciate or use the results in a productive manner.

4. The users are productive with the application but the clients or other stakeholders have objections to the results or the manner of use.

The first risk is **inadequate technology,** which represents a failure of communication between users and developers. This happens because the application should not have been attempted in the first place (the technology is inherently inadequate), the wrong application has been built or acquired (the developers have made an error in determining requirements), the application has been built or acquired incorrectly (the developers have made an error in construction or purchase), or the technology has been installed incorrectly (not to the users' requirements).

Figure 15–3 USER RISKS

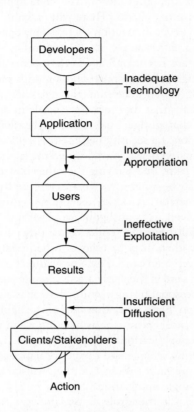

The second risk is **incorrect appropriation,** which also represents a communication failure between developers and users, because users haven't received the correct instructions on how to use the application (or such instructions don't exist because the application is unusable). Some factors of incorrect appropriation include:

- The users fail to set up the initial conditions correctly (asking for the wrong functions or files, for example).
- The users don't know how to move from step to step (for example, how to go from one screen to another or how to get back to previous screens).
- The users don't know how to request reports or results and so produce incorrect or unreadable results or no results at all.
- The users don't know how to terminate usage "cleanly" (i.e., put everything back the way it is supposed to be).

Users who appropriate a technology incorrectly may resort to several tactics, among which are these:

- Ask someone who appears to be using the application correctly or is at least (temporarily) satisfied with the results
- Guess, perhaps based on work with apparently similar applications or based on a learned logic about how such applications should work
- Muddle along, trying everything until something works
- Ask someone else to use the application

The first tactic is generally profitable, assuming anyone at all can use the application appropriately. However, this may in fact limit creativity and establish practices that are not very effective. In the case of Connie's SMS, Sid may observe how Kayla works and copy her work style, but Kayla may be an expert typist who has developed a series of shortcuts that Sid can use but not understand. At some point, Sid will realize that he hasn't entered any data at all, because he has learned only part of how Kayla works. Her style doesn't fit his style, and he has learned a number of inappropriate procedures.

The next two tactics are potentially disastrous. It is true that some people can quickly get the look and feel of many relatively simple applications, but many other applications are not particularly consistent, either from function to function or with other applications. While it may be obvious to every untrained user how an application *should* work, in fact the application may be constructed along an entirely different pattern, making everyone's work habits counterproductive. For example, Kayla checks every page after entering all the data when she types it onto forms, but that doesn't mean that the computer-based application checks forms a screen at a time. By today's standards, good applications check for format and reasonableness at every field. Touch typists cannot assume that just because they have entered a field it has been accepted (that's why beeping is so important in designing interfaces for touch typists). This is the problem with muddling along.

Asking someone else to use an application means giving up on it. The more complex the application, the more likely it is that untrained users will develop counterproductive techniques for using it that kill productivity. Sid uses a microcomputer package to schedule lawn-maintenance crews. Never having read the application's scanty documentation, he learned how to use the package by trial-and-error. The functions are basically menu-driven. Because he likes working from labor requirements (so many people, so many hours), he enters that information first. Then he enters details of the job and requests the schedule. Not knowing he can enter patterns for jobs (in a submenu called "Job Type"), he has to enter the requirements every time. This costs him in terms of time and error. Because the patterns do exist, Sid has lost the chance to think of his crews as teams running plays and thus he really can't see the big picture. Therefore, he thinks the application is difficult to deal with when in fact it could revolutionize how he sees work crew scheduling.

The third user-based risk is **ineffective exploitation.** This risk is created by poor communication among users, clients, and stakeholders. While using an application is one matter, using the results of an application effectively really depends on how well users and their clients communicate the clients' needs. Sid and Kayla may find the SMS very easy to use and generate voluminous reports Connie finds horrible to review, either because there is too much information (i.e., not well summarized) or it's poorly presented (hence the real information is lost in the noise).

Ineffective exploitation of regular reports can be corrected quickly because clients are usually very vocal about what they want. If applications are meant for quick response to environmental changes and are based on client-server architectures to produce on-demand reports, such communication problems may never be worked out. One cause of ineffective exploitation is incorrect appropriation, because users who don't understand how to get results will hesitate to promise those results and in fact may be quite resistant.

Suppose Connie and Shawna want skills profiles broken down by job category, but Sid hasn't figured out how to get the SMS to do this breakdown. This may be because he hasn't received proper training or because the interface hides most of the functions in a haze of computer terminology. Sid may say, "I'm sorry, Connie, but the SMS doesn't produce those kinds of reports and Kayla and I haven't got time to do this by hand." Connie may insist on the report, perhaps based on her recollection that during prototyping she saw such a screen. In this case, she may argue with Sid about his attitude or his skills as a manager. However, Sid may actually be saying that he suspects he doesn't know and doesn't want to spend the time fooling around with the application trying to get this report. So Connie doesn't get her report, Sid gets a reprimand, and Kayla probably gets glowered at.

The fourth risk is **insufficient diffusion** of technology from a laboratory or marketplace into an organization. This represents a failure of the political system that binds stakeholders, clients, and users together. Because top-down innovation is generally driven by management directive, more often than not developers are given responsibility for diffusion of technological innovation to prospective and potential users. This may be because top management is often technologically illiterate and the developers are often the most convenient and knowledgeable group to do this sort of publicity. However, this is often risky because developers have little political credibility with organizational clients (both internal and external) and stakeholders. Innovation initiated at the grass roots or the frontier is generally not supported by a management-driven publicity campaign and may suffer from "a voice crying in the wilderness" syndrome. Such voices are rarely heard by the majority of clients and stakeholders. In general, informed and committed upper-level management **champions** are the best bets for sufficient diffusion of technology—and its results—to clients and stakeholders. Champions can influence policy and procedures and generally have access to the most effective organizational communication channels. Political work is often just as important as technology and training work that is far more visible. Steering committees really do their job when they provide a forum for working out these political dramas, because these committees involve stakeholders in tangible ways.

A project like Evergreen's SMS probably doesn't need a steering committee because it is confined to marketing (for now) and because Shawna has given her support to the application. Before the SMS can evolve into the integrated HRIS that Frances envisages, the political ramifications must be worked out among people at high decision-making levels, that is, by people capable of bringing about major conclusions.

Client Roles and Risks

Because client goals are far more diverse than user goals, it is more difficult to make generalizations about **application client roles** and risks (see Figure 15–4). Applications are intended to meet client goals, and a given application has associated with it a set of clients that is dynamically changing. Clients have a stake in the results of application use. Connie and Sid are clients for the SMS and applicants for positions are also clients. However, these clients are generally not users or stakeholders. A client may be a client for only a short period of time (as are job applicants) or continually (as is Sid).

| Figure 15–4 | THE APPLICATION CLIENT ROLE |

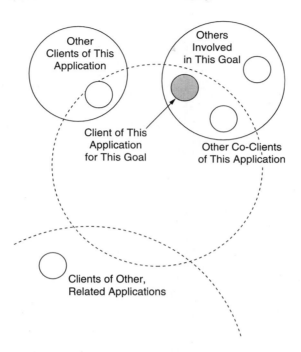

Clients may appear singly or in groups. For example, applicants for a specific position that Evergreen advertises would constitute a set of co-clients, and the outcome of the job competition affects them all. Hence, use of the SMS application to record and compare their applications with skills profiles of the job in question makes their fates interrelated. Only one person or a limited number of persons will get the job. Other clients, such as Connie, are also concerned with the SMS, but for different reasons. Connie is not a co-client of the job applicants.

Client risks (see Figure 15–5) are less clear than user risks because of the indirect relationship between clients and applications (through users). One valuable model of client risks can be derived by extending the Yale three-step model of persuasion: **attention, comprehension, and yielding.** Think about using the results of an application effectively in a situation that requires persuasion. Just because the computer has produced a piece of paper or a set of screens doesn't make these particular results valuable. Instead, clients have to "acquire," or believe in, the results so that they can act. Ultimately, action depends on the following factors:

- Have the results available in a usable format (attend or perceive)
- Understand the results (comprehend)
- Trust the results (yield)
- Implement the results (act)

| Figure 15–5 | CLIENT RISKS |

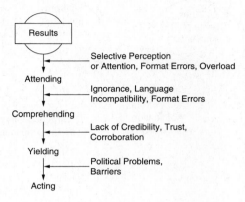

Clients may work with an application in any of several different modes. **Client modes** vary along three major dimensions. They may receive reports (1) on a regular basis versus on an ad hoc basis, (2) through different channels (memo, e-mail, phone), and (3) in real time (with the user acting as chauffeur) versus delayed. Regardless of how the application is worked, results have to be perceived before clients can begin to understand them. Attention problems are often caused by format errors such as the level of summarization or where columns are placed or what appears in column or row headers. Having too much output may simply kill clients' desire to look at all. Many voice-mail applications suffer from too many choices that are spoken too quickly for patrons to hear.

Results may be incomprehensible, and again this is often due to formatting errors, but it can also be caused by an incompatibility in language. What is appropriate for a user may drive a client crazy, or vice versa. Consider the last time you required service at a bank and were given several choices, none of which was understandable because you didn't know what the terms meant. Or think about a voice-mail situation in which you had no idea how to choose between: "Press 1 if you want rate information" and "Press 2 if you would like price and availability."

Even understanding choices, column headings, and the meaning of particular figures in a spreadsheet may not lead to valuable results that clients can act on if they do not trust the results. Lack of trust may stem from a number of causes:

- The figures or results appear incredible—for example, they are out of the normal range but appear with other normal figures in the same typeface (i.e., the application doesn't see them as unusual).
- There is no corroborating evidence, either in the application itself or from another source, to make the results believable.
- The application has produced untrustworthy results in the past.
- The client has had poor results with similar applications in the past.

Credibility problems can be eased by careful attention to **boundary conditions.** These are potential results that, while possible, may appear out of range or out of the ordinary. Typically, these are discovered during design or in prototyping.

The perception of risk is proportional not only to the sheer economic cost of failure, but also to the probability of that failure, and the less time given to cross-check, the greater the perception of that probability. When clients have a learned distrust of computer-based applications, pilot installation and client training may be ways to increase credibility. Most client training is, unfortunately, very informal and may consist of only a few spoken words of reassurance or, in the case of customer-oriented applications, a brochure or advertisement. Clever wording can, of course, convince a lot of people, but memories of bad experiences die hard for most, especially where there is tangible risk. For example, the SMS that Connie is building may have to contend with Sid's poor image of computers' ability to produce valuable results. Connie, on the other hand, has no problem believing results because her skeptical attitude led her to build boundary conditions into the application at the design stage of the ALC.

Finally, perceived, understood, and believed results may simply be unworkable because of political problems. "Political" problems include entrenched values ("We don't work with computers"), vested interests ("We've got three loyal people who work in personnel and I'm not letting them go"), and fear ("What if the thing fails?") that work against putting results into action. Of course, believing results can work the opposite way, too. Those who are gung-ho for computer-based applications may be willing to act on anything a computer produces because of values ("We love technology here"), vested interests ("We've got to keep those computer people and the computer busy"), or fear ("But what about the competition? They use computers"). Finally, no matter how well designed and credible an application is, if results are inconsistent with the way the world works, they can't be acted on. Connie's SMS may be used to make hiring decisions, but it could conceivably say that there are two qualified candidates whereas only one can be hired.

Stakeholder Roles and Risks

An **application stakeholder role** is similar to a client role, but much further removed from the application (Figure 15–6). A stakeholder attends to organizational, not personal, goals. Familiar stakeholders on the corporate scene include stockholders, members of boards of directors or advisors, employees, customers, suppliers, and managers. As mentioned, stakeholders rarely have goals related to application construction or acquisition except as a means to an end.

At Evergreen, the MEC may decide to advise Lily that Evergreen should go ahead with the proposed expansion even more quickly than planned in order to increase market share to counter increased competition from "big-box," warehouse-style stores. Their goal is increased market share and their strategy is expansion. Abetting this expansion will be the creation of a corporate network to link the stores. When certain personnel changes are added to the mix, the corporate network may change again, but nothing about the technology is expressed in corporate goals. Instead, technology is seen—and used—as a tool for meeting these goals. While information technology can be used for strategic advantage (Chapters 4 through 6), the application of technology into corporate practice is only a means of achieving strategic goals.

As with clients and users, stakeholders may work together on an application or they may work on a goal without being involved in the application itself. Frances Harmon, for example, is involved in new hiring to meet corporate profit goals, but she has little direct

Figure 15–6	THE APPLICATION STAKEHOLDER ROLE

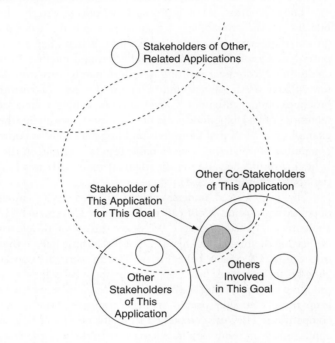

use for the SMS. On the other hand, Shawna, who as vice president of sales is a stakeholder, actually hires the people. Other stakeholders, such as equipment vendors, are involved with the application but don't appreciate the application the way Shawna does. Finally, Heather Cariad is a stakeholder in various financial applications. These applications are distantly related in the sense that the entered data support hiring or performance appraisal to the SMS, but Heather has no real interaction with the other stakeholders with regard to the SMS. However, political problems can arise at the stakeholder level and should be worked out.

Stakeholder risks are related to the stakes, which are represented by the classical threefold classification of organizational resources. To this we add information as the fourth classification and organizational integrity as the fifth (see Figure 15–7). The most direct threats perceived by stakeholders are to informational resources; the security and integrity of data, software, and applications must be preserved through all applications. Information systems employees are stakeholders who are vested with authority to ensure this security, so they are directly involved.

To the extent that physical resources are either dedicated to construction or installation of applications, stakeholders have a concern. With increasing automation, many resources are secured and monitored, stored, and dispensed using computer-based applications. JIT inventory, for example, depends acutely on the correct functioning of information systems. Evergreen's proposed link with Pindar Gopal, the plant broker, may actually increase the perception of risks in terms of materials until the connection has been proven to be effective.

| Figure 15–7 | STAKEHOLDER RISKS |

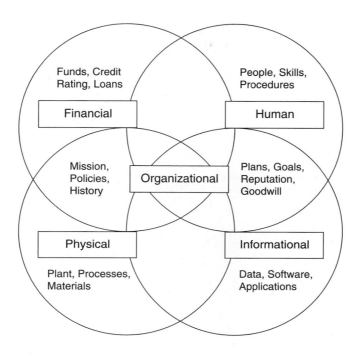

Management support applications are also related to financial and human resources, which may give stakeholders some concern. Finally, organizations have nontangible resources that are often at risk, especially with strategic applications (which the HRIS will evolve into as competition heats up around the planned expansion). In particular, technological solutions to organizational problems are often untried, without much history, or with bad history. Companies like Evergreen that have a reputation for good customer service and a recent happy history of growth based on customer service-compliant policies may find it difficult to trust new technologies, especially when they are handled by either relatively small and untested IS groups or outsiders. These risks often end up being played out as political dramas at high levels or in relations between IS groups and their clients.

Stakeholder risks may be more diffuse than user or client risks; however, the risks are borne by decision makers or influential political elements in the corporate culture. Thus, the cost of failure is heightened by the intensity of powers involved. Projects that promise good return on investment but are politically unpopular are often terminated at the first crisis of confidence. Stakeholders are held together and to applications by the promise of tangible benefits (jobs, dividends, interest, products) rather than by the procedures that hold clients and users together. Because these tangible benefits are limited, the potential for conflict is very high. User or client conflict doesn't pose much of a threat to an application's success. However, conflicts among the stakeholders can result in significant

Figure 15–8   THE APPLICATION DEVELOPER ROLE

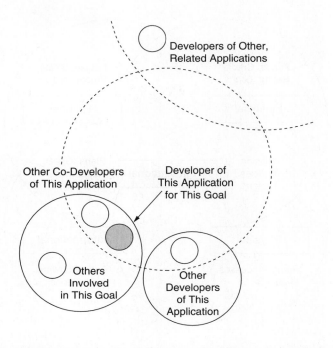

loss of project resources, championing activities, or credibility. Again, guarding against the effects of this sort of conflict is a role that steering committees can fulfill.

Developer Roles and Risks

Application developer roles fall into groups similar to those of the other role players (see Figure 15–8). Multiple co-developers work on a single application as a team or separately. Involved with the goal of producing an application may be others who have no direct involvement with the application (funders, for example, or prospective users who do not take part in the prototyping), and there may be individuals who are developing other, related applications. Terry and Dierdre work as co-developers of the SMS. Kayla Dowd is involved with the goal of producing the SMS, but she is not developing the application. Later, when the SMS is expanded to include additional functions and becomes Evergreen's HRIS, Boris Pomfrit will be hired to work on the application's telecommunications to make it available in a client-server environment. Because the HRIS will have to interact with payroll and accounting applications, Parnell Tulley will develop these financial interfaces in the future.

Because of the unique history of information systems, the following discussion may appear unnecessarily adversarial. That is, there have been, and sometimes continue to be, very poor relations between application developers and their clients, users, and stakeholders. These relations may be due to the relative youth of the technology and the technologists, but the bulk is due to a natural development of "two cultures." One culture is

Figure 15–9	DEVELOPER RISKS

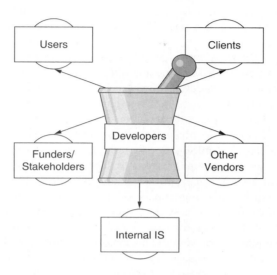

dependent on rapidly changing technology and the other is trying to harness that technology or avoid the risks of change. The next section will explore some of that unhappy history and then discuss ways in which the risks can be countered to mutual benefit.

There are many developer risks. The history of the information systems field is littered with the casualties, IS professionals and otherwise (Figure 15–9). Other than actually damaging a firm's competitive capability by producing poor applications, five other developer risks include:

- Risk of alienating users or giving them bad experiences, either with the technology or with technical specialists
- Risk of alienating clients, especially the risk that systems may malfunction and produce bad results for clients
- Risk of alienating stakeholders
- Risk of damaging how the information systems group works internally
- Risk of engaging or disengaging other vendors whose cooperation or competition is counted on or accounted for

Users who have bad experiences or whose expectations aren't met are not going to be cooperative the next time around. The most apparent risk is that of alienating users through a loss of goodwill. The same risks apply to clients who have to put up with the results of poorly built systems. However, there is an important difference: Users drive applications to produce results whereas clients are generally the driving forces behind implementation of applications—they are the ones who need the applications. In some cases, especially for small management support systems, the users are the clients, but it is clients rather than users who have nontechnical experiences with developers.

Those nontechnical experiences are the cause of unsatisfactory relations between clients and developers. While users can complain about the usability of an application (colors, layouts, procedures, dialogs, etc.), these complaints tend to be discussions about technical, demonstrable matters. Managerial clients, on the other hand, have budgets, timetables, functional specifications, promises, politics, and structures to argue about.

At the root of this conflict is an **opaque technology,** one that is difficult for users to use without understanding and difficult to understand. Most of the technology we use is the product of decades, or even centuries, of evolution and much of it is highly stable. Despite rapid changes in the internal technology of automobiles, most of the visible technology drivers interact with makes the cars easier to use: power steering, power brakes, automatic transmission, variable-speed wipers, antilock braking, and so forth. Computers and information systems, however, do not fall into this category.

There are two reasons for this. First, rapidly changing technology ensures that almost no user becomes an expert before the technology changes. This lack of a stable, educated, and experienced user population makes mentoring difficult for new users and makes crafting difficult because there aren't enough experienced users. Second, computer technology today is like the early days of cars or typewriters. It is important to know *how* the technology works in order to master and apply it. The major source of this need to understand technology comes from the fact that, until recently, applications were crafted not to users but to the technology underlying the application.

We can learn lessons from the history of technology. When autos were simpler and mechanics were few, it was common for drivers to fix their own vehicles. They not only understood what a car could do but also how it worked. As cars became more complex, the tasks an untrained individual could do became fewer, and a reliance on trained specialists increased. The same has occurred with information systems, but much more rapidly. When computer mechanics were rare, users were far more likely to get under the hood and work on computers themselves. As interfaces become more standardized and information system maintenance becomes increasingly complex, users have come to rely on simple "driving" skills, leaving repair to the professionals.

This separation of simply driving an application and knowing how it runs doesn't eliminate the problem of poor relations between clients and users on the one hand and developers on the other. Such difficulties continue to materialize in a variety of ways:

- A **culture gap** is engendered by training and experience; technical specialists are far more motivated by technology and technological challenge than they are by other people and the challenges they present.
- A **language gap** is due to jargon or specialized language.
- **Information systems specialists'** training has historically been the job of university or junior college computer science or technology departments, which select students who are interested in technology rather than people. More recently, the IS discipline has developed in North American and European business schools, and the most recent trend has been for larger organizations to hire liberal arts graduates with strong logical skills and train them specifically for their organization's technology. In general, this trend encourages IS specialists to have a broader view more consistent with the organization, but the pressures to perform as a specialist once employed may not actually allow this broader view to be of much value.

- *Job pressures* create a situation in which sharing of organizational values between technical specialists and their clients is not rewarded. Cross-training and job rotation is by far more the exception than the rule. Without this mutual understanding of organizational values, the possibility for unresolved conflict remains high.

- The pressure that comes from *tracking a rapidly changing technology* means that many technologists are not keeping up with increasingly opaque technologies. This job-skills gap may also become an age gap. This will make IS a unique field in which the more experience an individual has, the less valuable the individual becomes for future projects. In an extreme case, a technical specialist who has worked on a single-technology project for three years may be unemployable because the project's technology is now obsolete.

- With *increased user sophistication* in both information systems and other business systems comes increased tension between expectation and delivery. Manager-clients who think they know the technology, but actually don't, are harder for IS specialists to deal with than completely technology-ignorant manager-clients who at least defer to the specialists. In neither case will the product be acceptable. However, user education in general can lead to a better appreciation of technologists' work, and increased sophistication of end user (client-oriented) tools may reinforce those views in some cases or leave a wrong impression that IS work isn't too difficult in other cases.

The remaining risk involves other vendors of IS services. While many large organizations retain relatively large IS groups, most of them, and the majority of medium- and small-sized organizations, outsource at least a portion of their information systems work. This trend means that IS groups experience competition in new ways.

Paradoxically, IS also have to cooperate with outside vendors in ways other industries do not. Some organizations outsource completely, privatizing their IS groups by spinning them off and then contracting out all IS work for competitive bidding. Other organizations form strategic alliances with equipment and software vendors for their applications. Most organizations in this era of PC-based client-server applications buy off-the-shelf software and tailor it to their needs. Thus, most IS groups need to maintain good relations with a host of vendors, some of whom may be former employees. This sort of relationship is not as difficult to maintain as others, but the risks are just as high. While all developers are, to an extent, enchanted with the technology they employ, the trend is toward very narrow specialties. The days of the IS generalist are numbered, which means that an IS group may become a supercontractor for a set of IS trades, few of which are actually understood.

In summary, interaction among developers, clients, users, and stakeholders poses risks to managers and their organizations. Managing these risks depends on the political, technical, and social skills of the manager, who plays at least one of the roles discussed and directly experiences risk-creating pressures. Rapidly changing technology, an evolving social system, a maturing profession, and volatile expectations from clients and stakeholders all influence these risks and make contending with them serious work for managers. Just as demanding are the challenges of managing people in an information environment, to which we now turn our attention.

MANAGING PEOPLE IN AN INFORMATION ENVIRONMENT

In the first section of this chapter we scrutinized the roles people play in building and using applications and the risks that arise from those roles. A second major source of risk in the information environment arises from attempts to manage it; that is, management practice is somewhat different in an information-centered environment than in a different milieu. This section explores those differences.

Management adjusts to an information-centered environment in two ways: Managers must lead individuals whose jobs have become more information-centered and managers must lead individuals whose jobs are creation and maintenance of that environment.

Leading Employees in Changed Jobs

Consider how Sid's and Connie's jobs are changing under the influence of the SMS (and the nascent HRIS). Prior to this system, neither spent much time thinking about the complex problem of analyzing staff skills in relation to the existing staff or temporary seasonal hires. With the availability of the job skills profiles, Sid feels more pressure to hire more rationally by profiles rather than by intuition. Of course, this will create some dissonance when he interviews a candidate who doesn't fit the profile.

Meanwhile, Kayla also finds her job changed. She is doing a lot more data entry and wonders why she can't handle some of the analyses that Sid obviously feels uncomfortable with. Connie now feels able to ask Sid complex questions about staffing, staffing levels, turnover, and the labor component of not only Sid's products but also Sven's (the retail side). Shawna can now safely request analyses of sales versus skills in classes of contracts, and Frances and Heather can now legitimately voice their concerns that certain workers are being paid too much and others too little.

As an additional consideration, Tom Davidoff is wondering if he should go with the same sort of system, which is influencing how he is hiring this year. The continuing interaction between Connie's staff and Terry, Dierdre, and Parnell has changed both perceptions of management support systems as well as perceptions of the technology and the people supporting it.

These considerations lead to changes in management. Consider the following questions that Connie and Sid must answer in the coming months:

- How should Sid and Kayla be rewarded for their effective use of the SMS?
- What should be done when conflict arises between Sid and Terry over a desired enhancement to the SMS?
- What kind of hand-holding will need to be done when the SMS fails, as it does every week in the early days of operation?
- Is use of the SMS or other microcomputer applications going to be a permanent part of Kayla's job description and how will training be provided?
- Should requests for enhancements or repairs to the SMS go through Connie, who is the client, or directly to Terry?
- Should excuses from Sid that "the system was down" be accepted as a reason why a profitability report was a week late?
- What part will computer literacy play in performance appraisals for those who have to use systems like the SMS in their daily work?
- Who is responsible for keeping information up-to-date and accurate and who has responsibility for decisions made in error based on bad data?

These questions become more complex as an application or system becomes more complex, strategic, and companywide. When the HRIS is fully implemented, all human resources management activities (including project and contract work) will have to have at least some interface with this and related applications. Relationships that have evolved over the years at Evergreen based on interpersonal perceptions, liking, and trust will now be affected by individual access to applications like the HRIS.

Consider Sid's decision to place a certain worker on a certain contract. In the past, Sid may have phoned one of his team supervisors to find out who might be available and appropriate, if he couldn't remember himself. The team supervisors are usually returning university students, although a few are long-term employees or even landscape architects. Sid placed a lot of faith in his supervisors' ability to evaluate and recommend people for contracts, which made Sid confident that he could bid accurately for contracts that Evergreen could complete with high quality. With the HRIS, he will be tempted to find out for himself who is both available and skilled before calling the supervisors, if he calls them at all. This will certainly have an effect on his relationships with the supervisors, all of whom had come to recognize that obtaining Sid's trust in this kind of decision was critical to advancement at Evergreen.

While this sort of socio-political posturing is not necessarily a good management practice, it is often the way managers and their employees build trust. Because supervisor turnover is rather high, Sid is psychologically ready to trust an application that has some permanence rather than individuals whose loyalty and competence may be flawed. In other words, a social system that, for better or for worse, works well for the employees is being replaced by an information system whose major evaluation criterion is economic—the placement of the right people in the right projects. In time, the long-term employees and the landscape architects may begin to feel that the computer system has usurped some of their rights. It is likely that Sid may never notice this change unless the HRIS lets him down and someone remarks that "things were better before the HRIS was operating."

Managers like Connie and Sid have to be aware of how information systems change informal relationships. The design of social systems is an intrinsic aspect of BPR today, but most IS technical specialists are not trained in management disciplines. Thus, it's necessary for managers to understand what these changes might be and prepare themselves and their staff for the changes through informative or persuasive communication, job redesign, training, and leadership by example.

Both direct and indirect users of an application and those who feel the influence of a new application should be notified of its pending arrival and given sufficient information to ease the transition. An employee information campaign may be necessary for large, strategic systems. These campaigns may be led by corporate communication specialists in large firms, but in small companies managers may have to handle this personally. These campaigns may cover the following:

- Nature of the application
- Planned changes to work and work relationships
- Benefits and costs to the company, the department, and individuals in the department
- Management expectations of user and employee behavior
- Rewards and punishment for specific behaviors that go along with using the new application or its results
- Potential problems and their remedies, including problems with the information system

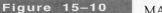

Figure 15–10   MANAGING TECHNICAL EMPLOYEES

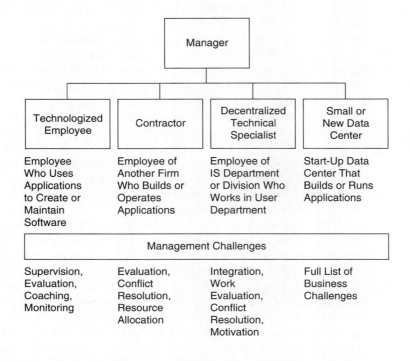

- Potential ethical concerns employees may have and how to resolve them
- Trust- and credibility-building messages

While it may seem manipulative to include trust- and credibility-building messages, consider that a manager has every right to want employees to use the tools the company provides at high cost. While an employee's opinions are private and inalienable, how an employee reacts on the job to job tools and changes is a manager's responsibility. If a manager is not trusted or seems incredible as a source of information about projected changes, it will be difficult for employees to accept any of the campaign.

Leading Technical Employees

The other major change that many managers face in an information-centered environment is supervising technical employees or those who may be called **technologized employees** (see Figure 15–10). The latter are employees whose work involves creating or maintaining applications. The term *technical employee* has in the past included programmers, systems analysts, network analysts, data administrators, and operations personnel (such as data center operators and supervisors). Supervision of these employees is no longer a clear-cut responsibility of an IS department. Rather, as firms begin to move technology out to the frontier of the organization, technical employees have moved with it. Fully decentralized technical groups are becoming more the norm. However, centralized IS groups remain near headquarters personnel to do long-range planning and coordinate what often are massive hardware and software budgets.

With the arrival of end user tools, more nontechnical employees are creating and managing their own applications, building spreadsheets, creating word processing macros, enjoying the benefits of "canning" database queries, and building protocols and scripts to ease repetitive work. In short, the boundary between technical specialists and business specialists is blurring. Managers increasingly find their employees are building and maintaining software. While there are no accurate figures available, the flood of microcomputers that hit North American businesses in the past decade practically guarantees that many workers and most managers spend a significant portion of each day creating and maintaining software. This may represent increased productivity or it may indicate lost time that could be spent doing other work, and managers have to make this determination for each employee. A series of concerns arise that managers must deal with. They include:

- Strains on budgets for software training
- Use of the microcomputer as a crutch or alternative to good business practices
- Blaming the computer, a network, or technical specialists for errors or delays
- Overreliance on computerized data to the detriment of direct experience; atrophy of intuition based on personal contact or responsibility
- Poor time management with excess time spent beautifying spreadsheets and documents at the expense of productive work
- Unacknowledged errors, unrecognized lack of skill, and deceptive work practices (such as cover-ups)
- Resentment for (1) having to work with computers without proper training or (2) lack of rewards for having mastered applications in favor of rewards for more traditional production

In these situations, technologized employees may be difficult to deal with, especially if a manager insists on using traditional rewards and punishments. Understanding how information systems integrate with work and tying rewards and punishments to appropriate performance objectives are the best antidotes to these problems.

In addition, some managers, especially those in small businesses, may find that they are saddled with supervision of more traditional technical employees. This may range from supervising an outsourcing contract to direct, day-to-day responsibilities of managing programmers and analysts to running a data center.

In the past, information systems applications entered firms through accounting and finance departments. Accounting managers have often been the first data processing managers, and much of the IS evolution has been shaped by the kinds of work and policy accounting and finance departments are characterized by. The most recent trend has been to outsource all or most of the IS work, perhaps retaining a skeleton staff to maintain a set of applications that are either too old or too strategic to outsource.

In small firms like Evergreen, an executive like Frances Harmon may be given the responsibility of managing a nascent IS staff and then "riding the tail of the tiger" through a period of rapid growth. Because there is much expertise available for sale today from consulting companies, most firms find that this sort of operation setup is rather easy but time-consuming.

Another trend that brings interaction between technical specialists and business managers is the decentralization if IS. The way this works is that a centralized IS group organized around traditional IS disciplines of system operation, construction, maintenance, and planning is split into subject-matter groups. For example, two programmers and an analyst may go to marketing; a programmer, a database analyst, and a network analyst may go to finance; or two system operators, a trainer, and a PC administrator may move into operations. Technicians may be moved around on an irregular basis, creating a kind of skill chowder whose nourishment value may be questionable.

Any manager who must supervise technical employees can take comfort in the following:

- IS people are people; they respond to rewards and praise like others.
- IS people are also individuals; it is unfair to stereotype them except to say that they probably all like information systems technology.
- Technically inclined people usually want to work on the best, most advanced technology (hardware and software) available.
- Managers who have no knowledge of information systems and who especially lack programming knowledge will find it hard to be respected during technical discussions with technical experts.
- In any group, the more individuals can overlap skills, the stronger the group. IS specialists can profit from a bit of job rotation and so can their colleagues.
- There are paradoxical trends in employment in the technical ranks that may present opportunities for learning for everyone. Nontechnical employees may have some technical components created for them. Technical specialists who are not needed may be good additions for groups that anticipate contracting out.
- The two-cultures syndrome is always a threat. Managers who encourage free interchange of discipline-based ideas will be ahead of the game in the end.

ETHICAL CONCERNS

In addition to the challenges that surround applications and the pressures those applications create to change human resource management, several unique challenges arise in the sphere of ethics. These challenges are generally presented in the form of decisions that managers have to make. Sometimes these decisions are made easily and without conscious thought, sometimes they require a lot of painful deliberation, and sometimes they cannot be made at all. The development of a **code of ethics,** a list of principles that guide decision making, is helpful. Most professions have codes of ethics, but as for any set of standards, the trick is in their application.

Ethical behavior (Figure 15–11) is neither characteristic of nor foreign to information-centered environments; there is nothing about information per se that creates ethical problems. Some information-centered situations have always posed ethical dilemmas for people. They include the following:

- What information about a person belongs to that person and what belongs to everyone else (the privacy dilemma)?

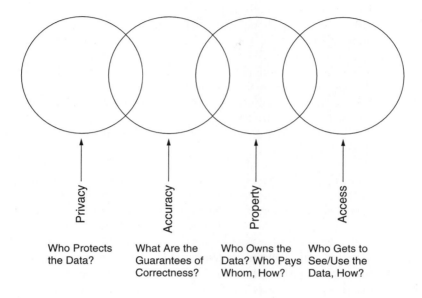

Figure 15–11 ETHICAL ARENAS

Privacy — Who Protects the Data?

Accuracy — What Are the Guarantees of Correctness?

Property — Who Owns the Data? Who Pays Whom, How?

Access — Who Gets to See/Use the Data, How?

- How do we handle rumor, slander, and libel in our relations with others (the accuracy dilemma)?
- Whose property are ideas (the property dilemma)?
- What do we do if we discover information that we are not supposed to have (the access dilemma)?

These four major areas of concern (privacy, accuracy, property, and access) have been put together by Richard Mason under the acronym, PAPA. They refer to problems that people and groups may experience when making decisions about information acquisition, use, and distribution.

Before examining the specific ethical issues that affect managers in an information-intensive environment, let's examine three general issues about ethics and information:

- Can we expect ethical behavior as a norm? What makes people behave unethically?
- What cues do people seek out to guide their behavior in ethical ways?
- What about information systems might foster unethical behavior?

For the answer to the first question, we turn to Stanley Milgram, whose work explored these questions: How ethical are people? Are some people more ethical than others? What would cause good people to behave badly? He examined the ways in which people transfer responsibility for their own behavior to others, a concept he labeled *agentic shift*. Why this is of interest here should be clear: If a computer is always right, why bother thinking differently? If it's right in the sense of being error-free, then isn't it also right in the ethical sense?

In Milgram's experiments, conducted in the 1960s, hundreds of people answered newspaper ads that asked for participants in an experiment on learning and promised a payment of a few dollars. As each participant arrived, he or she was met by a "scientist" in a white coat (an actor, not actually a researcher). The "scientist" paired each participant with another person, actually briefed on how to behave. Then both were given instructions on an experiment. One of the pair was a teacher (the selection, apparently random, was actually rigged so that the participant was the teacher) and the other was the learner. In most experimental conditions, the learner and teacher were taken to a separate chamber where the teacher watched as the learner was strapped into a chair in front of a console that communicated with the teacher in the other room. Then the teacher and the "scientist" returned to the other room.

There were two phases to each session. First, the teacher conducted a teaching session in which the learner learned word pairs. The goal was for the learner to memorize the pairs so that, given one word of a pair, he or she could respond with the correct corresponding word. The second phase was testing. The teacher read words from a prepared list, expecting the learner to respond with the correct word. If the learner did so, the teacher went to the next word on the list. If the learner responded incorrectly or failed to respond, the teacher shocked the learner by pressing a buzzer on an intimidating control panel of lights and dials, one of which was marked in volts from 0 to 360 with labels reading "Mild," "Strong," "Severe," and "Warning, potentially lethal" placed at equal points around the dial. Each failure was punished with a shock and instructions to the teacher to advance the dial a notch to the next level, marked in 30-volt increments. Teachers were given a test jolt with a mild shock to experience the punishment they were about to mete out.

Of course, there were no real shocks. Once the teacher and "scientist" left the chamber, the learner undid the straps and hooked up a tape recorder (to be used in the second phase) to the console. After the first phase, the learner said nothing, but instead manipulated the tape recorder so that the responses were sometimes right and sometimes wrong. As each mistake was made, the "scientist" instructed the teacher to issue a shock and advance the dial one notch. Because the tape was created to simulate a lot of errors, all teachers eventually found themselves up in the painful range and beyond. If teachers hesitated, the fake scientist exhorted them to continue, saying that the rules of the experiment were to do so and that the teacher had agreed to these rules.

Milgram wanted to know how far people would go toward inflicting pain (and potential death) in return for a few dollars and the promise of advancement of science. How far do you think people would go? A team of psychiatrists was asked this question before the experiments began. Their estimate was that fewer than 1 percent would issue the highest shock, marked "Danger." In fact, across a wide variety of conditions (including some in which the teacher held the learner's hand—in this condition, the tape recorder wasn't used and actor had to feign pain), well over a majority of all participants went up to 360 volts. Even when the learner failed to respond at all after complaining about a heart condition at lower voltage levels, most participants continued giving shocks and raising the voltage.

How is this behavior explained? Were all the participants inhumane murderers? Probably not, since they represented a wide cross-section of humanity from New Haven, Connecticut, in the 1960s. Perhaps they didn't believe they were really shocking the learner. That, too, is unfortunately false. In postexperiment interviews, a majority of participants claimed they thought the learner was being shocked and most expressed remorse. Even after meeting the learner and being told about the deception, many participants still believed that they had severely injured or even killed someone.

Instead of these explanations, Milgram offered one that is germane here. The "scientist" represented an authority figure to whom the participants transferred responsibility. Instead of being autonomous decision makers, participants became agents of the "scientist" or even science, shifting their own decision making out of the picture. Milgram postulated that the role science plays in society (always right, precise, moral) allows or even encourages this responsibility, or "agentic," shift, much as members of a military group transfer decision-making rights to sergeants, lieutenants, captains, and generals. Because information systems are also always right and precise and because we consider them to be at worst morally neutral, the temptation to shift from authority into agency is always present. Managers should be ready to counter this trend not only in their personal judgment but in the judgment of those they supervise.

The cues that guide ethical behavior come from our personalities, the groups we identify with, our experiences with others, and environmental sanctions against unethical behavior. In a series of experiments that also began in the 1960s, Phil Zimbardo looked at a process he called *deindividuation* in an attempt to explain why people sometimes behave badly in groups. It is a kind of generalization of the agentic shift, but instead of shifting responsibility to a specific authority figure, deindividuated persons lose their ability to differentiate their behavior from that of the crowd they are in. High stress, high arousal, and the cloak of anonymity can trigger deindividuation, according to Zimbardo. In a deindividuated crowd, no one has authority, so behavior is dictated by random events. Many researchers also say that deindividuation is responsible for the heightened creativity found in GSS brainstorming sessions where constraints that force people to toe an organizational line and thus be less creative are relaxed. However, many experiments have demonstrated that ethical behavior, at least institutionally sanctioned ethical behavior, is thrown out in the deindividualized bathwater. Because information systems divorce people from the actual subject (i.e., they deal with data rather than people, descriptions rather than events) and because many technologized jobs are stressful, deindividuation may result and unethical behavior may ensue. Researchers have shown that anonymity releases most people from a feeling of responsibility. Irresponsible people, acting on what they deem to be nonreal objects without feeling, through scientifically validated tools may feel that normal ethics need not apply.

Anecdotal evidence that people will, indeed, respond to nonreal objects is provided by Joseph Weizenbaum in his book, *Computer Power and Human Reasoning*. Weizenbaum was an early experimenter in artificial intelligence. He created a simple program called "Eliza" (which is still available today) more than 30 years ago. The program was created to see if people would have conversations with a computer. Eliza actually possessed no intelligence whatsoever. Instead, the program was alerted to key words (such as "mother," "love," or "money") and chose at random a response that seemed to address that key word or a general response chosen also at random. Thus, this conversation could take place:

PERSON: I think that no one loves me.

ELIZA: Oh? Tell me more about love.

PERSON: Love is really important to me.

ELIZA: Is that true?

PERSON: Yes.

ELIZA: You don't seem to have much to say about this.

Weizenbaum was amazed at the response to Eliza. People actually believed they were having conversations with a person. One day, Weizenbaum returned early from lunch to discover that his secretary, who had skipped lunch that day to use the terminal in his office, asked him to leave because she was having a "private conversation with Eliza."

Actually, there is some attractiveness to that analysis, since Weizenbaum consciously chose phrases and dialogs that mimicked what is called "nondirective therapy," a kind of psychological interviewing technique pioneered by psychiatrist Carl Rogers. To the extent that Eliza met the expectations of a caring and involved conversationalist, users believed in what Eliza was saying.

Does this mean that people will follow anything that seems vaguely intelligent? Possibly so, says Paul Watzlawick. He reported on experiments in which college students were given the task of observing a sequence of numbered lights flashing around a circle and predicting where the next light would flash. Some sequences (1, 2, 3, 4, 5, 6 . . .) led to stereotypical responses (almost always 7), while others produced random responses. In fact, the majority of sequences were random, generated by a computer. But *all* the participants in the experiment insisted that there were patterns and that if they were given enough time, they would be able to figure them out. In other words, the human mind looks for order, even where there isn't any. Much of our perceptual apparatus, and a great deal of our ability to understand the world, is based on filling in missing data with extrapolations based on theories we concoct about how things go together.

Computers shape behavior because of their power, the authoritative way they treat people, their simulation of human authority-responsibility structures, and our desire to see order in the universe. Ethical behavior is taught to us on these bases in the first place, as well as on the basis that there is inherent goodness in us all. This goodness can be neutralized by fear, stress, or time pressure, resulting in an agentic shift, perhaps in deindividuation and perhaps in anthropomorphization of the computer along with a depersonalization of the individuals about whom the computer has stored data. These are the dangers to ethics in an information-intensive environment.

Consider the promises that Frances Harmon made to employees in a memo concerning the HRIS:

> All the data we collect will be confidential. [Followed by a discussion of how difficult it would be to gain unsanctioned access.] Under no circumstance will we share information with former or future employers or government officials unless we legally have to (as in the case of a lawsuit). [Followed by assurances of this.] We've also put into place a process by which any employee can peruse *all* personal and job-related information we have on file at any time, either on the PC or in a printed report. We never have released, nor do we contemplate releasing, HR information to any outside agency except as directed by employees or required by law. [Followed by technical reassurance.] Our policies here have been modeled on the ethical standards of the professional organizations senior management belongs to [a list is included]. We already have extensive computerized files for accounting and retail operations, and the HRIS has afforded us the opportunity to update our ethical standards because we understand how sensitive HR information is to individuals we consider part of our team. If you feel you are being treated unethically or are asked to use the HRIS in an unethical fashion, do not hesitate to contact me to discuss the matter.

This memo illustrates a heads-up approach to dealing with ethical concerns: Bring them to the surface and show how they will be handled. The HRIS establishes the possibility for ethical problems with privacy (because of the large amount of personal data that has use outside Evergreen), accuracy (because it will be collected on forms by imperfect people), property (because employees have to cede rights to the data as a condition of employment), and access (because people other than authorized managers may want to have or see the data). Most databases pose these sorts of dilemmas. Even a parts list may be valuable to an industrial spy. Evergreen's competitors would very much like to know where the new store will be located and how Sid prices contract bids. Human resource databases contain information about people, who, unlike parts or bids, have a stake in keeping information about themselves private.

The four concerns become managerial responsibilities when databases and data communication move out of the data center into line departments. There, questions of access and ownership come up against departmental or company policies that are often drafted to handle the responsibilities of technical personnel for system quality without concern for the **quality of usage.** Stated another way, it is relatively easy to create policies when dealing with technical specialists. Firms can ask them to post a bond, for example, or require them to submit to close supervision and frequent technical testing. When a firm deals with the use of an application by nontechnical employees, however, these policies are of little use because they have no information system-relevant technical skills. Instead, a firm must build psychological motivation and practical sanctions for ethical behavior. Perhaps the easiest way to motivate ethical behavior is by example. Successful managers who don't copy software, who respect employees' privacy, and who don't try to access files they don't need for their job demonstrate that one doesn't have to cheat to get ahead.

It is also far easier to train employees in ethical work activity than it is to impose an ethical framework on individuals. "Ethical work is effective work" is one phrase that is helpful in building ethical behavior. Management support systems that follow these principles encourage ethical behavior, not only because they limit the potential for damage but also because they reinforce ethical practice:

- Information about individuals should be available only to those individuals and a prespecified list of recipients based on written company policy.
- Access to information should be keyed to identification even down to the level of a field in a record.
- All information should be checked for accuracy at least once upon entry, preferably by the person whose information has been entered.
- Notice of ownership can be prominently displayed on screens and printouts. Corporate policy on the privacy (or lack thereof) of e-mail messages should be displayed noticeably to senders and receivers.
- All reports should be dated to prevent out-of-date information from harming individuals.
- All training in how to use a system should stress PAPA and ethical use of information.

Some aspects of ethical information behavior are relatively straightforward because they are dictated by legislation. For example, it is an offense to copy software and databases that others have paid for or developed. Some intellectual property may not be quite so clearly owned—an example from a previous chapter is rules a domain expert may create in an expert system. Some concerns are relatively easy to handle because information is becoming increasingly an object. Copying commercial software without paying the licensing fee resembles theft. Distributing free copies of someone else's software seems like depriving the developer of potential sales. Destroying your employer's databases because you are angry looks like malicious mischief. The differences between these behaviors and their analogs may have to be fought out in court, but for managers seeking ethical behavior, the models serve well as a starting point.

Discouraging and, if necessary, punishing illegal behavior should *not* pose an ethical dilemma to managers. Data theft, copying commercial software, introducing viruses, selling trade or commercial secrets (including company-created software), wilfully destroying employer's property, altering audited or legal reports, and other attempts at fraud are clearly illegal. The fact that they involve information should not cloud the obvious illegality of these acts. While the manager-as-cop idea is not particularly savory to most of us, it is conspicuously a managerial responsibility to protect the employer's interests. Disgruntled employees who walk off with company files or who plant trojan horses (alterations to computer programs that cause them to fail to operate after a specific date or in a specific way) are breaking the law. While recent history demonstrates that not all laws are just or ethical, the trust that employers place in their employees isn't more manipulable in an information-intensive environment. It's just sometimes harder to notice the damage when the trust is breached.

In summary, ethical behavior with regard to information can be treated in several ways through traditional managerial roles:

- *Training*: Ethical activities are effective activities.
- *Work/application design*: Ethical systems are effective systems.
- *Example*: Ethical managers are successful managers.
- *Analog to legislation*: Legal activity is ethical activity.

■ PEOPLE COME FIRST AT PERSONNEL PLUS

At P+, Warren used to do all the initial placement screening, but owing to an increase in the number of downsized and reengineered organizations, he can't attend to every placement. His staff of 16 does the screening using microcomputers and writes up reports on the progress of placements. His assistant prepares summaries on a weekly and monthly basis and keeps a list of prospective companies. P+'s business changes in concert with business cycles and the economy and because outplacement really depends on finding positions for executives and maintaining contact. So Warren's assistant works continuously with the programmer analysts to improve P+'s suite of applications. This suite currently consists of prospect management, outplacement contact, customer data acquisition, placement profitability analysis, skills inventory, e-mail, customer contact boilerplate (word processing), a multimedia business clipping service, and a few EDI applications for billing and placement reporting. Not only are the programmer analysts (whom Warren supervises) constantly creating new reports and applications, but Warren's assistant is getting adept at using spreadsheeting and the database manager to tweak new knowledge out of the data. Remembering that he is an employee, not a partner, Warren keeps the partners up-to-date on the business and relies on the partners' consulting contacts to bring in customers. Advertising helps, too, but direct mail is Warren's best tool, and several of his computer applications are used to keep that process running smoothly. In fact, everything runs so smoothly that Warren wonders if he isn't missing some risks. ■

1. What role-related risks is Warren facing with respect to users, clients, stakeholders, and developers of his applications?

2. What does Warren have to know about managing employees in an information-intensive environment that will affect how he operates? What risks are involved here?

3. Warren faces a number of ethical dilemmas that he has ignored. What are they? How should he handle them?

The Modern Management Imperatives

Reach: Global Competition	Competitive forces motivate organizations to rethink their human resource deployment in information systems. Outsourcing is a distinct possibility, and outsourcers are available worldwide for almost all aspects of information system development, including programming and operations.
Reaction: Quick Customer Feedback on Products and Services	Quick feedback from customers and businesses' more sympathetic orientation toward customers lead to more awareness of ethical conduct. Stewardship of customer and employee databases, the possibility of industrial espionage, and increasingly tighter interorganizational linkages based on strategic information systems pose ethical challenges to managers as customers, clients, and partners become more aware of their rights.
Responsiveness: Shortened Concept-to-Customer Cycle Time	Building, acquiring, or changing an information system or management support system on short notice to respond to customer needs creates pressures on managers to have their requests satisfied quickly. Managers often find themselves supervising IS personnel or rapidly technologized employees when they themselves haven't been trained for this responsibility.
Refinement: Greater Customer Sophistication and Specificity	Customers are beginning to understand the information systems that affect them. Not only is there a movement toward more ethical behavior in all aspects of information systems management, but users are discovering technical glitches and demanding accurate responses to these problems.
Reconfiguration: Reengineering of Work Patterns and Structures	The boundary of apportioning IS skills to a specific group is becoming fuzzy. Much of managerial work is now computer mediated, and the ICE is becoming a reality in many firms. Client and stakeholder risks are multiplying as MSSs are infused into the daily life of managers and workers. As users become developers, they run the whole gamut of developer risks, few of which they are trained to cope with.
Redeployment: Reorganization and Redesign of Resources	Corporate IS resources (data, people, machinery) are now up for grabs. Culture gaps make it harder to manage these resources and assign them rapidly and effectively.
Reputation: Quality and Reliability of Product and Process	Customer satisfaction with applications is increased by user involvement, attention to customers' needs, stakeholder support, provision of the appropriate tools to application developers, and ethical behavior.

Summary

People can play roles in four computer application spheres: roles as users, clients, developers, and stakeholders. Users interact with applications either directly or through intermediaries. Users should make sure to procure adequate technology from developers, to employ the application correctly, to exploit the results of using an application effectively, and to diffuse the application's results to clients and stakeholders sufficiently. Clients are concerned with whether an application meets their goals. They should insist that applications present results in perceivable, understandable, convincing, and useful ways. Stakeholders are concerned with organizational as opposed to personal goals. Stakeholders are concerned with maintaining and expanding organizational resources that are financial, human, physical, or informational. Finally, developers have roles in the creation and maintenance of applications. Developers are concerned with their relationships with users, clients, stakeholders, vendors, and other IS personnel as modified by the very technologies they work with. These relationships are affected by cultural gaps, language gaps, job pressures, the pressures of rapidly changing technology, and increased job sophistication. Managers are frequently called on to manage individuals whose jobs are information centered and individuals who are developers. Technology-savvy employees and contractors and decentralized technical specialists present specific management challenges to nontechnical managers. Managers also face ethical challenges or dilemmas in terms of privacy, accuracy, property, and access.

Discussion Questions

15.1 Do you see the four human spheres presenting role conflicts for managers with regard to information systems technologies? Imagine some situations in which a manager might play more than one role and experience conflict. What might a manager do to handle these conflicts?

15.2 Managing "technologized" employees presents unique challenges to nontechnical managers, as does managing highly technical employees. Several of the challenges include handling employee fears and standing up to technical employees who may look down their "technological noses" at nontechnical managers. What strengths does a good manager bring to these two situations that might mitigate these problems?

15.3 What do you think about Milgram's experiments? Were they ethical? Are you surprised at his findings? Do you think the findings would be the same today? Do you think that computers and information systems are ethically neutral or are active ethical agents? Does a manager who manages information applications ever face difficult ethical situations? How can managers cope with these ethical challenges?

Key Terms

application client role	client	ineffective exploitation
application developer role	client mode	information systems specialist
application role	code of ethics	insufficient diffusion
application stakeholder role	co-user	language gap
application user role	culture gap	opaque technology
attention-comprehension-	developer	quality of usage
yielding model	direct user	stakeholder
boundary conditions	inadequate technology	technologized employees
champion	incorrect appropriation	

References

Brod, C. *TechnoStress—The Human Cost of the Computer Revolution*. Reading, MA: Addison-Wesley, 1982.

Brooks, F. *The Mythical Man-Month: Essays in Software Engineering*. Reading, MA: Addison-Wesley, 1975.

Cougar, J. D., and R. Zawacki. *Motivating and Managing Computer Personnel*. New York: Wiley, 1980.

DeJoie, R., G. Fowler, and D. Paradice. *Ethical Issues in Information Systems*. Boston: Boyd & Fraser, 1991.

Janz, T., and P. Licker. "Transporting a Measure of Corporate Culture to the Information Services Area." *Journal of Systems Management* 38, 9 (1987).

Kraft, P. *Programmers and Managers: The Routinization of Computer Programming in the United States*. New York: Springer Verlag, 1977.

Licker, P. *The Art of Managing Software Development People*. New York: Wiley, 1985.

Mason, R. "Four Ethical Issues of the Information Age." *MIS Quarterly* 10, 1 (March 1986).

Milgram, Stanley. *Obedience to Authority: An Experimental View*. New York: Harper & Row, 1974.

Miller, Marc. "Problem Avoidance in the User/Analyst Relationship." Parts I and II. *Journal of Systems Management* 32, 5 and 6 (1981): 14–18, 34–39.

Senn, J. "A Management View of Systems Analysts: Failures and Shortcomings." *MIS Quarterly* 2, 4 (1978): 25–42.

Straub, D., and R. Collins. "Key Information Liability Issues Facing Managers: Software Piracy, Proprietary Databases and Individual Rights to Privacy." *MIS Quarterly* 14, 2 (1990).

Watzlawick, P. *The Language of Change: Elements of Therapeutic Communication*. New York: Basic Books, 1977.

Weinberg, G. *The Psychology of Computer Programming*. New York: Van Nostrand Reinhold, 1971.

Weizenbaum, J. *Computer Power and Human Reasoning*. Cambridge, MA: MIT Press, 1976.

Zimbardo, P., E. Ebbesen, and C. Maslach. *Influencing Attitudes and Changing Behavior*. New York: McGraw-Hill, 1977.

CASE

EVERGREEN LANDSCAPING AND MAINTENANCE: PERSONNEL SHAKE-UPS

After almost three decades with Evergreen and Petty's Garden Supply, Tulley Fox (purchasing manager) is retiring. Tulley's cheerful personality and ready wit will be missed, especially by Shawna, whom Tulley mentored for ten years. But Lily sees this as an opportunity to reorganize the firm to be more aggressive in its marketing. After a heart-to-heart with Shawna, Lily also realizes that Shawna wants less demanding work and intends to retire shortly after Tulley does, as soon as Lily can find a replacement. Because Lily has decided to go ahead with the expansion, she has asked Terry Bonner how soon the new store, as well as the link with Pindar Gopal, the broker, can be put into action. Terry and Lily have this conversation:

> TERRY: I think we can put the store online just as soon as the building's complete.
>
> LILY: Well, I didn't think there would be any problem with that.
>
> TERRY: No problem, it's just that I'm a little worried because there are only the three of us, plus Boris, to do the work, and we're really backed up now as it is.
>
> LILY: Terry, I didn't hire you all to hear that the work can't get done. Is there something here I need to know about?

TERRY: This HRIS has us completely occupied. Because Frances wanted it so badly, we gave it top priority and we can't just drop it now.

LILY: Uh-huh, I see. I haven't heard much about this project; give me a quick look at it.

Lily finds out that the HRIS has grown out of the SMS and she is more than a little dismayed to discover how much of Evergreen's IS resources are being put behind this project. Lily brings this up at the next MEC:

LILY: OK, next is the HRIS. Frances, is it true that the IS team is totally devoted to this project for the next six months?

FRANCES: Sure, and maybe longer. It's a really crucial . . .

LILY (INTERRUPTING): And that means that we can't do anything else, right?

FRANCES: Well, we've got Boris, of course, and we could always bring in a consultant, but I don't see . . .

LILY (INTERRUPTING AGAIN): Why is this important? The crucial thing, we agreed, is going ahead with the expansion, but that can't work without the right systems. Even if we completely outsource the job, we've got to have people inside riding herd on the project and that means somebody technical, doesn't it? Who's the HRIS important for?

SHAWNA: Originally, this was a project that Connie asked for so that Sid could do better-quality hiring of temporary staff, but I guess the project's grown. Because it's really a general problem and because of the competition, we wanted to make sure that we could use it across the company, not just in sales. So now everyone has a stake in it and it's really critical.

LILY: But not strategic. If we can't expand, it isn't going to matter how well we hire; we won't have any jobs to hire for!

TOM: Lily, if I may butt in here, we all agreed on doing this at the last meeting. Have you moved up the timetable for the expansion?

LILY: No, but I think we need to start reengineering this firm as quickly as possible, and I don't want a very specialized project like the HRIS holding us up. Expansion is the best opportunity to redo all the systems here.

After the meeting, Lily calls Connie into her office. Connie has always taken an interest in information systems applications, and Lily thinks that Connie may be the ideal person to head the HRIS project. And if she does well, thinks Lily, there's room at the top when Shawna retires.

Questions

1. Who are the stakeholders in the HRIS project? What risks do they run? Are the stakeholders in the retail expansion the same?

2. Who are the clients for the HRIS project? How do they relate to clients for other IS projects? What risks do they perceive? How are they managing the human resource aspects of these risks? Are some of these clients also stakeholders? Do they experience any conflict in these two roles?

3. Who are the users for the HRIS project? How do they relate to the clients for this project? What are the risks for them? What ways do they have to manage their risks?

4. Who are the developers for the HRIS project? What relationships do they have with the users? The clients? The stakeholders? How might the personnel changes affect them? Would

these changes be specific to the HRIS or would they experience these changes regardless of the purpose of the application?

5. Who are the project champions? What powers or skills do they have that prepare them for this role? What extra risks do they run, especially at Evergreen?

6. Given the changes that might occur at Evergreen owing to increased use of information systems applications, how might the management and leadership styles of Connie, Sid, and Frances have to change with regard to managing their newly technologized employees?

7. What are Lily's options with regard to staffing the expansion project and the future of her small IS group? How would selecting different options affect the leadership responsibilities of people like Connie, Sid, and Frances?

Module 4

INFORMATION SYSTEMS AND TECHNOLOGICAL LEADERSHIP

CHAPTER SIXTEEN

THE SOFTWARE MARKETPLACE AND OUTSOURCING

OBJECTIVES

After you have read and studied this chapter, you should be able to:

■ Describe the characteristics of software that pose challenges for managers who require management support systems.

■ Discuss the tradeoffs between buying and building software-based systems.

■ Identify the advantages and disadvantages of outsourcing classes of applications.

■ Determine the risks involved in working within the software marketplace.

Question: What are the characteristics of the marketplace in which software is sold commercially? What does the software buyer need to know? What does the seller need to be aware of?

Phyllis Franklin is the program director for Cable 10. The bulk of her job is concerned with community programming, which means running a channel that can be universally accessed by anyone meeting a set of professional standards. Her major goal is to sift through dozens of proposals in a fair manner while keeping standards high. In general, the informal system she uses works, but she has to rely a lot on memory and scribbled notes, and some community groups are quick to yell "discrimination" if their program gets turned down for someone else's. Sometimes programs are rerun if they're especially good or popular. Phyllis knows she can use a computer to help her—Cable 10 has modern equipment and even a computer programmer—but thinks that maybe there are packages she can buy. If she can't buy a package, perhaps she can have one developed and sell it to other community channels. How should she handle this decision?

Answer: Software is different from other products because of its intangible qualities, changeability, portability, and esoteric image. When purchasing software, buyers should look for ease of use, compatibility with industry standards, documentation, reputation of the vendor, and cost. The build-or-buy decision is especially complicated, with long-term implications. Outsourcing is a possible alternative that requires great management attention. Finally, organizations developing specialty software can attempt to sell it to others but must keep an eye on the competition, work continuously with customers, pay attention to legalities, avoid technical entanglement, and remember that there is some price sensitivity involved.

MODULE 4: LEADERSHIP

Chapter 16 introduces the fourth module of this text, which discusses leadership in an information-centered environment. Leadership implies bringing together all the concepts covered in the three previous modules on strategic advantage, management support, and risk management. Understanding these concepts should enhance a manager's ability to lead in an environment that will soon differ in important ways from today's. The most important difference is that the technology that is an important business driver today—software that programs the microchip—is already being turned over to users in major ways. Users are now designing their own systems, participating in building new applications, managing major development projects, and sharing software and data with each other. This trend will continue.

In Chapter 11, we discussed technological leadership in the context of Tomasco's proposed geodesic organization, in which technological leaders exercise their authority from the organization's frontier. Such leaders relate to technology in two ways:

- Leadership *in* technology: Motivating others to use technology to achieve organizational goals, to develop themselves, to work better by using technology, and to redefine organizational goals to include technology in a meaningful way.
- Leadership *with* technology: Using technology to enhance a manager's ability to exercise leadership.

In Modules 1 and 2, we discussed how information technology brings competitive advantage. Managers can gain advantage in four ways:

- More intelligence (more pertinent, better filtered, well-processed, acceptable, and credible information)
- Broader span of control (better ability to juggle multiple tasks, finer control over these tasks, more flexibility)
- Richer network of relations (more contacts, quicker access, multiple windows on the organization)
- Increased confidence in and ability to effect change

Leadership *in* technology is the focus of Module 4. As mentioned briefly in Chapter 11, **technological leadership** means understanding how technology is predicted, assessed, developed, diffused, and used and then making that knowledge available and useful to others. Technological leaders lead through training, example, vision, persuasion, or motivation (i.e., reward and punishment). Managerial technological leaders aren't necessarily technologists themselves, but they obtain skills relevant to specific technologies and then make those skills—and often the corresponding technology—available to others. These skills come from the knowledge of what various technologies can accomplish, what is necessary to acquire and use those technologies, and how to evaluate them.

Because managerial leadership in technology is exercised either as **managerial push** or **business environment pull,** managers learn how to push or harness the pull (see Figure 16–1). Managerial push arises from managers' needs. Work pressures dictate a need for information technology support, and managers often have their own ideas that they think

Figure 16–1   MANAGERIAL TECHNOLOGICAL LEADERSHIP

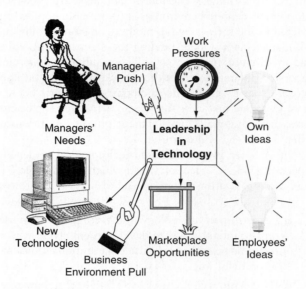

others should appreciate. The pull on managerial leadership systems comes from the continuous obsolescence of old technologies and the appearance of new technologies, changes in the marketplace for information technology, and ideas from employees. In Module 4, we examine this push and pull and what managers need to know to exercise technological leadership in an information-intensive environment.

In previous chapters, we discussed the risks involved in developing (and in some cases purchasing) applications. Chapter 16 examines the information systems marketplace, with an emphasis on buying, building, leasing, and outsourcing applications and application development. There is also some discussion about how to sell software. While there is a market for data, the emphasis of this chapter is the robust and unregulated software applications and systems market.

The software marketplace is among the most volatile because of the nature of software and the relative youth of the marketplace. Because there are both internal as well as external markets for software, the phenomenon of outsourcing—organizations seeking IS services outside their firms—presents challenges both in terms of management as well as marketing. Chapter 16 is essentially about managing the market pull on leadership in technology.

In Chapter 17, we see how managers can profitably and appropriately lead in technology through managerial push. Managers are not the only innovators in their organizations, but they need to understand the innovation process and actively participate in it. Managing innovation is an important aspect of working in a technological environment, and information technology places unique demands on managers, users, and clients.

Chapter 18, the final chapter of the book, discusses specific topics in technological leadership. The prediction, evaluation, acquisition, and management of information technology in an organizational context is a nascent science that managers are expected to understand. Chapter 18 focuses on techniques for managing information technology that are practical and valuable to managers.

INTRODUCTION

This chapter discusses the value of software in an open market, the decision to build versus buy software, and vendors' perspective on software. Here we aim to answer this question: What is the value of software? Because software is a relatively new product in historical terms, its value can be seriously distorted by vendors, fads, trends, buyers, or other players. The chapter begins with a discussion of the essential characteristics of software and ends with a guide for those who want to market their own.

There are several reasons why a manager should understand the marketplace for software and the characteristics of software that create that unique marketplace. First, the "user revolution" indicates that many managers are purchasing software, and the software they are purchasing is not merely single-user, single application packages, or productivity enhancement tools (of the sort that make up the manager's information workbench). Instead, managers are being asked to purchase **off-the-shelf systems** or **applications** with complexity levels that IS managers used to puzzle over. These applications are available through outlets that bear only a superficial resemblance to the kinds of outlets managers are familiar with. Second, managers are being asked to intervene in situations in which software is an important work mediator or tool. Workers who cannot use software that has been purchased for them will naturally ask for help, and managers need to supply that help. Third, managers are finding that in an increasingly interconnected business environment, the small suite of applications that pertain only to their own areas of responsibility is being encroached upon by other areas' applications. For example, at Evergreen, sales and accounting, production, and marketing are becoming more interconnected, and managers are being asked by their colleagues to help select software. They are also becoming aware that they *should* have a say in these purchases.

Changes in development methodologies, upper management's stronger control of technology expenses, and the sheer volume and complexity of the software marketplace are also important reasons for managers to pay attention to and learn how to cope with that marketplace.

However, software is a product few managers are familiar with, which could be said of most products any business purchases. In addition, it is sold in a new marketplace in which good advice is hard to find. Software has characteristics in common with other business products, but it also has some unique traits. The next section explores the contribution that software's unique qualities make to the challenge of buying and selling.

ESSENTIAL CHARACTERISTICS OF SOFTWARE

One of the most important things about modern information systems is the distinction between hardware and software. In what we now call "manual" information systems—filing cabinets and typewriters included—information was difficult to treat separately from the media in which the information was recorded. Procedures for handling information were cumbersome, generally involving reading, copying, transcribing, and moving folders, and these procedures were heavily dependent on the media being handled. For example, adding numbers from five records in five different folders may have meant keeping intermediate totals at every step.

The advance represented by computers has only a little bit to do with the equipment that did the arithmetic. Computers were faster and more reliable, but so were mechanical adding machines. The real advantage of computers was the flexibility afforded by the stored program concept. The idea was that procedures ("programs" in modern terminology) would be coded and stored along with the data. During computation, all the data were stored in the same electronic medium in a consistent way. Each program instructed the computer to treat the data in a certain way based on the codes that represented each sequence of simple operations (such as addition, copying, output, and multiplication). Changing the procedure now meant changing only a few characters of the program. This meant that a set of programs could be created to do different computations based on a model or template that could be easily changed.

Of course, remembering all the codes and enciphering a long sequence of numbers was a difficult, demanding, and tedious task. Programmers quickly responded by building other programs (called autocoders or assemblers) that could accept sequences of words that represented the operations and assemble the required codes. These were in the form of alphabetic or mnemonic names. Because programs were merely sequences of codes (i.e., data), creating automated tools to generate code became relatively simple. The history of software engineering began with autocoders and became a succession of increasingly sophisticated tools to translate programmers' ideas into code that commands computers. The CASE tools mentioned in Chapter 15 are simply the latest in this succession. Autocoders, compilers, and all the applications we have referred to as "management support systems" are examples of software. That such products could become consumer products was, however, far from the minds of those who developed applications almost half a century ago.

Software is different from the consumer products we are familiar with. It's only within the last 25 years that software has been available, divorced from the hardware that it ran on. Until IBM "unbundled" its software from its hardware in the late 1960s, it was rarely possible to buy software without a hardware and service contract. We characterize this early era as a captive **software market,** in which almost no one could really purchase software separately. In the next 15 years or so, the marketplace was exclusively *technical*—software was bought almost exclusively by individuals in organizational information systems groups (ISGs). This software was intended for use on mainframes and minicomputers, usually in a centralized environment.

With the arrival of the microcomputer, the nature of the software marketplace changed. IBM's decision to market a nonproprietary operating system (DOS) created by a small, non-IBM company (Microsoft) and its simultaneous release of design details of some (but not all) of its PC hardware architecture guaranteed that inventive, creative people would start to create software for the hardware that IBM hoped to (and did) sell. Apple, too, pursued a similar, though ultimately quite different, path in encouraging thousands of software writers to produce a critical mass of applications and tools. The result was a consumer market for software rather than either a *captive* or technical marketplace.

The market is drastically different now. That small software vendor, Microsoft, is one of the wealthiest and most successful companies in history. IBM, as of this date, is only just now making a profit again after record losses in recent years. Software seems to be "where it's at" in the computer field, at least in the PC market. Why has software overtaken computer hardware as a good to be bought? Software is a new kind of product. We are used to thinking of the distinction between goods and services, things and activities, but software has aspects of both. It is a thing in the sense that it has a physical component (on diskettes or CDs, for example) and can often be found inside packages that one purchases at a variety of stores. It is a service in the sense that the software itself has no value apart from what it can do for the buyer. It has aspects of being a tool because it is not an end in itself, but a means to an end (except for games, whose "ends" may be considered mere playing).

Apart from these semantic distinctions, however, software has other important dissimilarities from hard goods. **Software properties** include the following:

- Software is malleable and changeable. It can be produced in many forms and it is easy to copy and change into something else. Very small changes to software may make it inoperable or appear to be something entirely different.

- Software is evanescent (tending to fade from sight), hard to see and conceive of, and hard to hold on to. One knows the software is right only by using it on appropriate hardware. This is unlike a hammer whose value as a tool can be appreciated with a simple swing. Think of software as the most complicated tool you can imagine, a tool that can be used only in very special circumstances.

- Software is controlling in that it can make hardware and systems do things. While it is possible to erase software or damage it so that it doesn't work right, software is really in charge, not the other way around.

- Software provides leverage. Small changes in software create great changes in results. It is not normally possible to change hardware like this. Two objects that differ in very small, physical ways normally serve the same function (unless, of course, one is broken and serves no function at all). Two programs that differ even in just one line of code may well serve different or incompatible functions.

- In the animal kingdom of products, software is the chameleon. It changes form easily and without great expense. Sometimes these changes are bugs, but other changes are marketed as advances consumers are willing to pay for; these are called new releases of software. Still other changes may be unannounced, that is, they were there all along as what is sometimes called undocumented features.

- Software is the soul and emotion of the machine. It gives computers their character or takes it away. Software, especially operating system software and GUIs, comprises the bulk of what users think of as the window into the computer, the commands or movements that the user makes to get the computer to perform. Software determines the entire nature of the ICE to a user.

- Software is both a plan for action as well as the execution of that action. It describes in a language what is going to happen and then causes those events to take place. This results in two kinds of products, usually referred to in software engineering jargon as **source code** and **object code** (the latter is sometimes called executable code). Source code contains the original statements in a programming language that describe what is going to happen. Object code is the translation of those statements into a form that, when interpreted by a computer, results in computation. Purchasers may buy software in either format, depending on what the vendor feels like parting with. Source code is more generic and needs to be compiled or translated into object code for a specific computer. Because of this, and because source code is easily read by people, especially programmers, it is more valuable and hence more expensive. Object code is very difficult to debug and maintain without the use of special tools. Source code, for example, contains comments and documentation on why certain design decisions were taken, but object code has only an arcane series of numbers. Buyers who want to tailor an application themselves generally will need either source code or a program that contains a set of screens that allow them to input information to cause changes in how the source code works. Vendors are reluctant to sell source code. Not only does this effectively give away many other versions of the program—those that will run on other computers, for example—but it also makes it difficult for vendors to guarantee performance. Purchasers who make changes to source code are likely to introduce new bugs into the software that the vendor will not cover under a warranty.

- Software is portable and transportable. Most software, especially that available on the open market, is not intended so much for a specific computer as for a specific operating system or environment. Software is written for DOS, for the Mac, for *Windows,* for the *Motif* environment, and so forth. It used to be that buying a new computer meant users had to throw out their software investment, but now they can transport all of that software to their new computer. But, of course, users won't want to, because the new computer has so much exciting software created for its own environment.

- Software is arcane. Its qualities are esoteric, hidden, and cabalistic. The people who create it speak strange languages. Those who tend software are the high priests of cybernetics, and being able to experience their mystical moments depends on having taken specific language courses.

- Finally, it's not even clear what constitutes "software." Many would define software as any program that runs on any computer, but some of these programs are really script files (such as AUTOEXEC.BAT in DOS). Others are called drivers and are little subroutines that link hardware or software with an operating system and application programs. On the other hand, the file allocation table that makes it possible for DOS to know where files are located is rarely thought of as software. This is primarily so because it contains records of file creations and erasures—it doesn't do anything directly.

In addition, software is sold in ways quite different from most consumer products.

- Software is sold in stores, by mail order, through TV, and on the Internet. Because it is so easy to create new software and there is not much desire on the part of regulators to license software creators, the marketplace is a wide-open bazaar. Given the regularity with which the major software vendors announce and withdraw vaporware (software that is supposed to be released on a certain date, but actually doesn't exist and that is announced as a trial balloon or to counter a real or suspected competitor's real or suspected new release), an active market in software futures should emerge soon.

- Software is generally licensed rather than sold. Because it has performance aspects (like an audio recording), vendors license the use of software rather than sell it outright. A **software license** tends to restrict how the product can be used in terms of copying or distributing. In many ways, software is like a book that is covered under copyright laws in many countries. Curiously, software is licensed by machine (i.e., a license gives users the privilege of using the software on one machine, although they can make a backup of the original recorded software—something you *cannot* do with audio cassettes, by the way), not by user. This method of licensing fails to recognize the mobility of individuals today and the reality of the client-server environment, which is rapidly revolutionizing the marketing of site licenses. **Site licenses** are agreements that allow a certain number of copies of a given application or system to be used at a single site, as opposed to at a single machine. So far, no one has implemented a charge-by-the-use license. While this concept may not make much sense for a product that can't wear out, purchasers, not vendors, may be interested in frequency or time-limited licenses because software obsoletes so quickly.

- Software is an ordinary consumer product, available at any corner store. Some vendors actually give it away and hope recipients will mail them $5, $25, or $100 if they like it. This software is called **shareware.** Users who purchase the diskette on which the shareware resides temporarily are urged by the creator or vendor to pay for their acquisition of the software, generally in return for continued upgrades at preferential prices. No other marketplace works this way.

Software shares qualities of video and audio recordings, published books and articles, procedures, and ideas. These particular characteristics make software an interesting product to develop and sell. Many have learned to rebundle software with hardware and services. One software vendor sells its product, which is similar to that of its competitors, for less than half the competitors' price in order to get lucrative consulting and teaching contracts with customers. In 1983, this writer created software for physicians to bill the Alberta, Canada, provincial health-care agency. The product was second on the marketplace and the first microcomputer-based physician billing system available locally. Within six months, however, there were 24 other vendors. The original product sold for $4,000 (including computer and setup), or $2,000 for the software. After another year, a competitor licensed an American product, made some minor output and interface changes, and sold its "new" product for $200. The original product was wiped out quickly when yet another competitor brought out an integrated medical office management package for $500. None of this software had any inherent value at all, so pricing was arbitrary and competition soon had no real price/cost basis.

The open **software marketplace** (see Figure 16–2) is really four markets. The *commercial public mass market* is dominated today by microcomputer products for two platforms, the IBM PC and its many clones (based on an Intel 486 or Pentium chip) and the Apple Macintosh and related PCs (no clones, thanks to vigorous legal action). Other platforms, however, are appearing. This marketplace is the one most students are familiar with. It is oriented toward the unspecialized user. The resilience and perseverance of this

| Figure 16–2 | THE FOUR SOFTWARE MARKETS |

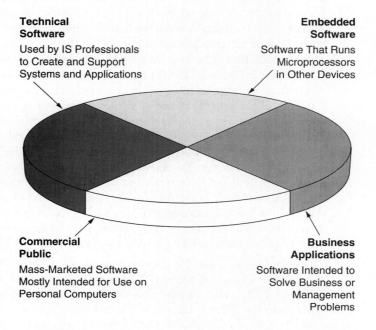

**Technical
Software**

Used by IS Professionals
to Create and Support
Systems and Applications

**Embedded
Software**

Software That Runs
Microprocessors
in Other Devices

**Commercial
Public**

Mass-Marketed Software
Mostly Intended for Use on
Personal Computers

**Business
Applications**

Software Intended to
Solve Business or
Management
Problems

marketplace over the past 15 years are remarkable, given the changes in the basic hardware, the names and natures of the major players, and the revolutionary role played by microcomputers in education.

The second marketplace is for commercial software for minicomputers, mainframes and supercomputers, networks, and associated programmable, intelligent devices. This marketplace is served by small software houses, consulting firms, garage hobbyists, and those who sell their own and others' products. We call this market the *business applications market* because most of the software written for it is intended to be applied to some business problem. Some of the vendors are companies that have created software for their own use and have realized that others may be willing to pay for it.

The third market is highly technical and is aimed at professionals who support information systems and users at arm's length (i.e., they don't create applications but instead build the infrastructure for the applications). This software includes operating systems, protocol converters, telecommunications software, computer language compilers and interpreters, and CASE tools, among others. We call this the *technical software marketplace*. While most of the software in this class is intended only for those with an in-depth knowledge of computer fundamentals (and beyond), managers often have to create an infrastructure for their applications.

The fourth marketplace is for software that is **embedded** in other products such as microwaves, cars, arcade games, and automated equipment. Because the software is intimately connected to the chips that do the computing rather than to general-purpose computers, we won't concern ourselves with this segment but, instead, focus on the first two.

The variety of software available now is bewildering. A partial list might include operating systems, games, networks, GUIs, a plethora of application software, and the whole gamut of productivity-enhancing tools including word processing, database management, spreadsheets, expert system shells, telecommunications packages, and so forth. This variety can be quite daunting to consumers. How does one buy software? What does one look for?

Important software attributes include **ease of use,** which also implies **learnability.** Next is the **capacity** of the software. Capacity is measured in many ways, including, for example, transactions per unit time processed; maximum file, spreadsheet, or record size; record types; and number of fonts. Large capacity and flexibility signal forward thinking on the part of designers and a relatively longer useful life span for buyers. A third attribute to look for is a regular series of meaningful **software updates** or **versions** brought out on time. *WordPerfect* is in its sixth version, and each new version brings increased capability as well as problems with existing versions. However, new versions should not be incompatible with previous ones and should not require massive file reformatting or learning entirely new interfaces. The look and feel of the new version should remain consistent with the existing version unless, of course, the existing package is really horrible.

Upgrading to new versions is also something of a trap. Users who come to depend on a relatively simple application may not need the new, improved, more sophisticated version. However, they may have to purchase every new version that comes out in order to retain support from vendors who, after all, don't want to have to maintain older, perhaps buggier, versions of their software. Riding the version whirlwind is a tiring and costly avocation for many users who are actually satisfied with what they have.

Software packages should be compatible with industry standards, even if the standards are those of competitors. As pointed out in Chapter 10, standards are useful for shortening learning time and increasing or facilitating communication among systems. If you have just spent two years creating a series of valuable files or applications in one format, it doesn't pay to have to convert them all, perhaps losing some information in the process, to another format.

Many of the ways we work now have been handed down from previous successful packages. Vendors would dearly love to differentiate their products with new interfaces and procedures, but buyers balk at having to learn new ways of working. The typewriter is a good example. The QWERTY keyboard used today was developed at the end of the nineteenth century to slow typists down because mechanical keys of earlier machines were jamming under the onslaught of high-speed typists. So now typists are stuck with a keyboard that slows them down, induces errors, and is hard to learn. But also now typists are used to this keyboard. Similarly, the "/"-initiated menu of VisiCalc shows up in Quattro Pro. The [ALT]-initiated menus of many of the Microsoft products for the PC (e.g., *Windows, DOSSHELL,* and *QBASIC*) use drop-down menus pioneered by others, while ProComm's pop-out menus are hardly unique. These standards make it easy to use new software because we have come to expect various keys to mean specific things. This is part of what is commonly called computer literacy, the expectation that certain conventions will be carried through regardless of the product.

Another feature that enhances learning is good documentation and a built-in tutorial, perhaps separate from the main application or perhaps connected with online, context-sensitive help that guides users. Help that can be turned off is valuable for sophisticated, experienced users, too. A toll-free number certainly helps, especially if the person at the other end can answer users' questions. A further guide to quality is the vendor's reputation (and certainly the reputation of the package itself) and its history.

Companies that are built through acquisitions of incompatible products may not have the consistency to maintain and release successively better versions of the acquired software. For example, we may wonder what will happen with WordPerfect as it moves from vendor to vendor. It may seem easier to buy the commercial rights to a package than to build new ones, especially if a strong market already exists, but then the new vendors have to learn the packages, too, because they have to support them.

Finally, there is the consideration of cost in terms of cash, time, and hardware. Some software really eats up storage space. *Windows* chews up more than 7 megabytes of hard disk at a minimum. Some innocuous-looking games may spread out over 10 to 20 megabytes and use every available bit of RAM, too. While hard disk space is increasing rapidly (and disk doublers such as DBLSPACE packaged with DOS 6.x and STACKER can provide up to twice the space), it is annoying to have to keep adding memory. For commercial systems that use very large disk memories, the incremental cost of drives is quite high, and small additions that require an additional disk drive are budget busters.

The best estimate of software's worth is the same as for any other product or service: what the market will bear. As users become more used to software and as various niches are established, they find the $500 database manager to be acceptable while the $500 word processor is not, despite the fact that they really can't say that one regularly does $500 worth of work while the other does not. The only sure things are that prices seem steady as functionality is rising.

BUILDING VERSUS BUYING

Before continuing with the question of what to pay for software, let's examine the more important question of whether to pay at all. Firms often face the decision of building versus buying software (see Table 16–1). Building generally implies following some version of the ALC (see Chapter 12). Buying involves contracting or outsourcing to a service bureau, consulting firm, or software house through a **request for proposal (RFP)** or **request for quotation (RFQ)** process. Building is advantageous, especially for strategic applications, because it involves familiar faces that are generally trustworthy and friendly. Building capitalizes on and keeps the products of organizational learning. Buying frequently means taking advantage of someone else's economies of scale. There are no developer training costs, generally lower user costs, and, in fact, it is now possible to shop around for the lowest prices.

On the down side, building is costly after the software is built because a permanent staff has to be paid for and kept up-to-date for the next project. Also, having a staff means handling staff problems. IS professionals are not always completely aligned with company objectives (this is improving dramatically, however, because IS is becoming more crucial to most firms, and executives and managers are becoming more attuned to computer possibilities). Buying is disadvantageous at times because outsiders can be unfriendly, unfamiliar, and unconcerned. There is also no chance to learn new skills and distribute them around the organization if outsiders do all the work. Building is indicated when strategic applications are concerned—when company secrets must be kept in-house. Buying is indicated when there is no ISG staff or when the ISG staff lacks the necessary skills and there isn't enough time for them to acquire them.

Of course, there may be other overriding considerations in the build versus buy decision. For example, if an ISG development staff is already available and being paid, why not have them develop the system? On the other hand, if there is no organized ISG, buying is the only alternative.

Table 16–1	**THE BUILD VERSUS BUY DECISION**	
	Build	**Buy**
What This Entails	ALC/end user construction/prototyping; requires a trained and available staff and information infrastructure (development tools, computers)	Request for proposal (RFP) or request for quotation (RFQ); dealing with a service bureau, consulting company, consultant, or software house
Advantages	Strategic applications stay in-house and under wraps ("house arrest"); the process becomes familiar and is sometimes friendly; the organization learns continuously	Purchaser takes advantage of economies of scale; no training costs; the opportunity to shop around; prices are set by the market and can seem fair; there is no continued expense for staff; capital equipment can be expensed
Disadvantages	Costly to retain staff and keep them up-to-date; political fights can be divisive; firms may be constantly reinventing wheels others are already rolling along on	Not necessarily friendly or private; little chance to learn new technological skills; firms may go out of business and fail to support the applications already purchased; economies of scale may be misleading, lowering quality as the lowest common denominator is appealed to
When Most Appropriate	When company secrets require inside workers	When there is no IS staff, staff lacks skills, or time is very short and the application already exists

When buying applications, especially for a client-server environment in which interoperability and smooth transitions between applications are needed, users must consider the following:

- Note which database formats the application works with. You may be tying yourself to a database that is unique for this application and that will make later expansion difficult. The application may be more efficient, but you are stuck with this application unless you want to buy a new database.
- Examine how each function of the application is performed. No matter how many functions this application provides, another will provide more next week. However, it is quality, not quantity, that counts.
- Pay attention to multinational, multilingual, and multicultural aspects. Global competition means that you have to operate across language, tax, currency, and legal differences, and some packages may be inflexible in this regard.
- Vendor reliability is important. Not only must vendors be accessible to you via a toll-free number, for example, they must be able to provide on-site help.
- If you're going to be a good customer of an expensive package, make suggestions for subsequent versions—become a partner, not just a customer.

The build versus buy decision is often not very clear-cut. Most bought software, especially complex client-server applications, needs significant in-house tailoring to make it productive, and most systems built from scratch require packaged systems or modules to become effective. Existing interfaces have to be tailored, either into the new application (i.e., the existing applications need changing) or into the **legacy systems** already in place (i.e., the package needs customizing). These considerations complicate and fractionate the decision. Some software needs to be built while other applications need to be purchased. Training and staffing need to be distributed between in-house and contracted agents.

An important concern for managers is handling the RFP or RFQ. Managers who request proposals or quotations for management support systems need to evaluate both tangible and intangible costs when making decisions. In fact, they need to think about this when they write the requests. Evaluating the proposals or quotations requires an evaluation scheme as well as a good idea of requirements. On the other hand, deciding to build does not excuse a manager from having a solid scheme to evaluate proposals or quotations or from having some idea of information requirements. In fact, from a manager's point of view, contracting out, either through outright purchase of an existing product or through outsourcing application development, helps only in application development. Even those who let the state-of-the-market dictate requirements have to understand at least the minimum needed for satisfactory performance.

In many firms, though, there is no choice—all systems must be built or at least heavily tailored in-house, that is, there is effectively no free market for software development labor. Most firms have found this difficult in terms of productivity and quality of the product. The recent trend has been to put the ISG on an equal footing with outside suppliers and to outsource the construction, and sometimes the operation, of new software applications. Technically, outsourcing also encompasses the purchase of software packages as well as operations (such as data entry or routine data processing). However, in this chapter, we are mostly concerned with contracting out software development services.

OUTSOURCING

Outsourcing (see Figure 16–3) is a process of acquiring products or services from outside the organization. Loh and Venkatraman define outsourcing as "the significant contribution by external vendors in the physical and/or human resources associated with the entire or specific components of the IT infrastructure in the user organization." This definition, or some form of it, seems to lie at the heart of outsourcing. Unlike a simple build or buy decision, in which software is considered a commodity, outsourcing involves the transfer of significant energies between a firm and its outsourcing supplier. In its simplest form, this process can be characterized as a **technology transfer** (discussed more in Chapter 18) from a knowledgeable organization (the outsourcer) to a learning organization. Purchased software doesn't provide for this transfer. In many cases, purchasers of an application are not allowed to take it apart or use any part of it except in very limited ways. While outsourcers may also specify a similar hands-off approach to their products, most firms hope to acquire the knowledge without the continuing risks involved in retaining human resources or owning computing resources. Outsourcing can therefore be seen as a risk management technique. Later we will examine a simple risk management model in outsourcing that is appropriate for most managers.

In the not-too-distant past, most large organizations developed applications in-house, but this strategy is becoming expensive and risky. The more recent trend is to outsource. Outsourcing is defined by Grover and Teng as "the practice of turning all or part of an

| **Figure 16-3** | THE OUTSOURCING PROCESS |

Outsourcing:
Contracting All or Part of an Organization's IS Development,
Operations, or Management to an Outside Firm

Requirements:
Firm Specifications or User Requirements
Nerves of Steel
A Firm Hand on the Purse
Bright, Energetic, Skeptical Users

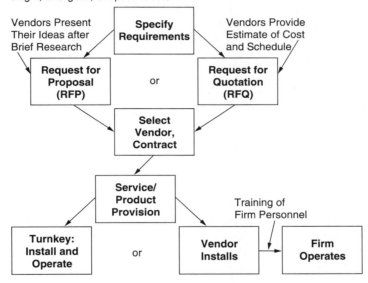

organization's IS functions to one or more external service providers." The functions could include both application development and operations and may extend so far as outsourcing human resource management (i.e., outplacement of all ISG employees), selling or spinning off the entire technical infrastructure (hardware, software, and even offices), or simply buying software outside.

According to Grover and Teng, outsourcing is not a new phenomenon—this writer remembers the early 1960s when the term *service bureau* was coined. In those days, users stayed home, data were gathered in-house and shipped out, and reports came back. Today, users are moving around the world, data are gathered from around the world and sent to multiple points around the world, application design and development are contracted to experts around the world, computer facilities around the world process the data—sometimes in pieces—and reports are sent back to the mobile managers around the world.

Grover and Teng propose that the decision to outsource should be made in two stages. The first stage is a decision tree resulting in four possibilities: Yes (outsource), Marginal Yes, Marginal No, and No (don't outsource). Their model is based on three independent dimensions of the outsourcing problem (see Figure 16–4). The first two of these dimensions correspond loosely to two of the three dimensions involved in the

| Figure 16–4 | OUTSOURCING MODEL: STAGE 1 |

System Maturity	Competitive Role	ISG Capability
Initiation	Low	Weak
Growth	High	Average
Mature	Sustainably High	Superior
What Stage the Application or System Is in; Early Stages Are Riskier in General for Outsourcing.	A Strategic System Is Not a Good Bet for Outsourcing.	You're in the Skills Market When You Outsource. If Your ISG Is Very Skilled, the Advantage of Outsourcing Is Lessened.

project risk analysis model: project structure and technology gap. The third dimension relates more to presence, or strategic impact, as opposed to mere project size. Analogous to the project risk model, then, Grover and Teng's measures can be considered to be the following outsourcing risk factors:

- The system or **application maturity**: initiation (early stages of maturity), growth (where everyone who can is trying it), or mature (where learning is complete). Grover and Teng advise that maturity in this sense doesn't merely apply to one firm. Rather, in the case of a set of applications involving new technology, maturity may be viewed across an industry. For example, client-server architecture is relatively new everywhere, while database management is relatively mature everywhere.
- Significance to competitive advantage: low (little competitive advantage), high, or sustainably high (expected to remain high for the long haul)
- ISG technical capability relative to competitors: weak, average, or superior

Immature applications should be considered for outsourcing only if they are unimportant to the competition or can't be produced otherwise because the ISG is not technically competent (see Figure 16–5). Applications irrelevant to a firm's competitive stance are good candidates for outsourcing because of cost savings. Mature applications that have sustainably high competitive advantage may be candidates for outsourcing if an appropriate outside supplier can be trusted with a long-term relationship.

Grover and Teng don't recommend using only the single-stage evaluation, which is a general indicator of the desirability of outsourcing in general. Where choices are marginal or where additional arguments are needed one way or the other to evaluate a specific

| Figure 16–5 | THE OUTSOURCING DECISION: STAGE 1 |

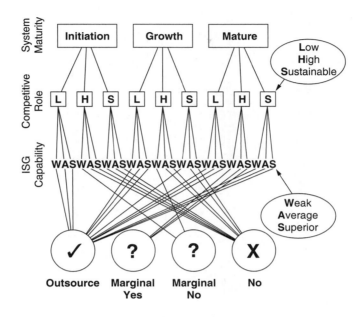

outsourcing maneuver, Grover and Teng propose a second stage of decision making involving a risk or impact analysis of outsourcing (see Figure 16–6). Positive evaluations of the following considerations move toward outsourcing; negative ones, away. The first set is derived from the benefits of outsourcing (score + if these benefits can be realized by a specific outsourcing strategy):

- *Business*: Allowing the business to focus on core business competencies
- *Competitiveness*: Redirecting IS activities to those that are strategic
- *Competence*: Capitalizing on others' reputations, specializations, or abilities with leading-edge technologies
- *Personnel*: Not having to employ long-term employees
- *Economies*: Capitalizing on economies of scale; Grover and Teng estimate that by 1997 U.S. companies will be spending $27 billion on outsourcing, mostly to receive these kinds of savings
- *Cost control*: Allowing more predictable costs
- *Technologies*: Facilitating access to technologies that might not otherwise be used

But Grover and Teng point out a number of risks involved with outsourcing (score – if each risk applies):

- *Risk of obsolescence*: The outsourcer—not the firm paying the bills—may have control over just how obsolete an application or system is

| Figure 16–6 | THE OUTSOURCING DECISION: STAGE 2 |

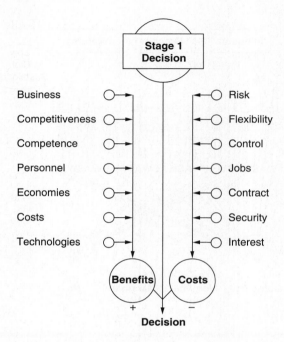

- *Lack of flexibility*: Loss of flexibility resulting from lack of control over the infrastructure or having to bend to the needs of the outsourcer
- *Loss of control*: The importance of maintaining control over quality and schedule
- *Jobs*: Anger from IS professionals who will be laid off and insecurity of those who remain
- *Contracts*: The need to negotiate contracts and legal costs
- *Security*: Mentioned in the build versus buy decision
- *Interest*: The outsourcer is not necessarily working in the company's best interests and may in fact be working for, or even owned by, a competitor

For a specific outsourcing contract, it is possible to look at these last 14 evaluations to determine an index of desirability. If none of the vendors or their contracts scores positive, even a high indicator of the desirability of outsourcing in Stage 1 will not suffice. On the other hand, an extremely beneficial Stage 2 outsourcing evaluation may overcome a relatively low Stage 1 outsourcing indicator and make outsourcing desirable.

Mary Lacity and Rudy Hirschheim look through the other end of the outsourcing telescope and caution managers against jumping on the outsourcing bandwagon. They note the increasing popularity of outsourcing IS functionality and quote several IS managers who view IS as a commodity rather than as an artistic function. But they claim that the industry press presents an overly optimistic view of outsourcing, and the failures aren't being reported. They question the belief that outsourcing is the universal panacea by exposing, through their research, several outsourcing myths found in the business press.

Lacity and Hirschheim surveyed 14 Fortune 500 companies, interviewing executives involved in outsourcing in a variety of industries, mostly in the chemicals and petroleum manufacturing sector. Most companies considered outsourcing all IS functions, although several outsourced only the data center (operations of routine data processing). Of the 14, 5 decided against outsourcing, and of the 9 that decided to outsource, 2 terminated their contracts prematurely. Their research exposes, in their opinion, these myths:

- *Myth 1*: Outsourcing vendors are strategic partners.
- *Fact 1*: Vendors are in it for the money. A strategic partner shares strategic goals, but outsourcers are in the business to maximize profit from each customer.

- *Myth 2*: Outsourcing vendors are more efficient than ISGs.
- *Fact 2*: ISGs can become cost competitive. Economies of scale are only theoretical and apply best to data processing. Vendors' hardware discounts (presumably passed on to customers) may actually be negligible. Vendors' advantage in contracting is changing, and simple economies of scale may not apply to licensing. Customers are often supported in outsourcing by their own staff, rehired through the outsourcer, at more expensive rates. Access to talented staff is limited through competition. A low bid may only mean potential disaster.

- *Myth 3*: Savings can be from 10 percent to 50 percent.
- *Fact 3*: ISGs, too, can save this amount. Some of this advantage comes from financing packages offered by outsourcers. Many cost efficiencies can be achieved internally, too, perhaps by integrating data centers, by getting rid of old, expensive hardware, and by instituting chargeback and other free market economy measures internally.

Lacity and Hirschheim advise companies to pay careful attention to contract procedures. For example, they shouldn't use a vendor's standard contract, shouldn't sign incomplete contracts, should develop service level measures and reports along with escalation procedures, should incorporate cash penalties for nonperformance, should include termination clauses, and should watch out for clauses that escalate costs if processing requirements change even slightly. Companies should also use legal help that is expert in outsourcing contracts, measure performance during a baseline period so that the outsourcer has something to live up to, watch out for growth rates, and take care of the remaining IS employees. Outsourcing is risky business, and attending to contracts is a way to control the risk.

In fact, the ISG at Amoco successfully outbid its competitors to build its Engineering and Facilities Services Unit's Service Tracking and Request System (STARS). The $25 million contract was too attractive for the ISG at Amoco's research center in Naperville, Illinois, to pass up. Despite the fact that the RFP called for a fixed-price bid—most ISGs typically charge on a time plus materials basis—Amoco's ISG bid and won, with a chance to make a profit and retain the distribution rights to the important client-server application.

This latter aspect is no small plum because of the generic nature of the software (see the next section of this chapter). Curiously, the ISG was not the low bidder, but won on service (proximity makes response more likely), ability to interface with existing systems, and experience with the designated technology. These three characteristics, along with a hard look at efficiency, make qualified ISGs formidable opponents of outsourcers.

Applying information systems to outsourcing, Clemons, Reddi, and Row adopted a modified view of outsourcing, called the "move to the middle hypothesis." They contend that information technology lowers the coordination costs inherent in an internal market without increasing transaction risk. It is these risks that Lacity and Hirschheim object to. Lowering these risks should result in more outsourcing and a less vertically integrated firm. This also means that interorganizational relationships (outsourcing in general) without ownership are less risky because coordination is better. Ultimately, this results in more outsourcing, but with fewer organizations. Although they use the word *outsourcing* as a generalization of interorganizational relationships, it can also apply to the ISG itself. Information technology can significantly decrease outsourcing risks while increasing coordination. Outsourcing risks include the cost of communicating with the outsourcer, the cost of agreeing to be supplied by an unreliable supplier, and the risk that suppliers will jump ship and supply others. EDI, for example, drastically lowers information technology costs, and communication advances make the technology less costly and risky. Ultimately, the benefits of shoeing the shoemaker's children point to increased outsourcing in IS, but with closer relationships to a smaller number of suppliers, one of whom can be the firm's former ISG.

There are a variety of ways to outsource. Many firms contract outside through an RFP or RFQ, which result in contracts of two different natures. Some firms supply just the product (say, the software) and may assist with installation and training. Other firms provide **turnkey service,** which includes development, installation, training, and operation; that is, the contractor does everything. Another way to outsource is for a firm to spin off its ISG and **contract back** for that firm to operate all the company's IS operations.

Whatever variety of outsourcing that is attempted, managers are responsible for expressing their needs through specifications that end up as RFPs or RFQs and riding herd on the contractor at all stages. This requires nerves of steel: it's hard enough to manage projects inside, and working with outsiders makes it even more difficult. A firm hand on the purse strings may also be required, as economies of scale are generally in the vendor's favor. The best defense against bad software and poor vendor performance is a staff of bright, skeptical users who ask embarrassing questions and whose needs are thoroughly documented in the initial specifications.

SELLING YOUR OWN SOFTWARE

There will be times when you or your organization will want to approach the free market for software and make some money (see Table 16–2). Many attempt it, but few get rich. There are a number of key points to learn. First, the competition is fierce. Everybody knows that programming is easier than building factories, and any idea you have, someone else already has.

Whatever the competition is now, you should always have the next product ready, because others will, too, and you will need to leapfrog them in the marketplace. Asking customers to help designers ensures that designs will always be relevant and that there will be no major glitches, such as interfaces that can't be used or file formats that are incompatible with work styles.

Table 16—2	CONCERNS FOR SELLING YOUR OWN SOFTWARE

Marketing Concerns	Business Concerns	Technical Concerns
Competition is fierce	Don't lose control of your company	Remember compatibility
Always have the next product ready	Hire users to work with your developers	Have the next version ready or in the research and development pipeline
Work with customers	Development costs come far in advance of the first revenues	Try not to be on the "bleeding edge"
Get to know market segments and avoid some	Remember that the technology will change as you market your applications	Ease of use is the most important technical and marketing consideration
Worry about legalities and contracts; prepare legal work in advance	Alpha testing: in-house; beta testing: friendly, tame users; never beta test on your market	Create good training and user manuals in language users can understand
Marketing really counts		
There is some price sensitivity	Form alliances for marketing and later development, perhaps with your best customers	
Prices drop significantly when second and third competitors enter the market	Software is no get-rich-quick scheme; you can lose your shirt, though	
The box counts; packaging counts; promotions count		

Certain markets should be avoided. Specialty markets are very tricky for application software—the only customers may be you! Just because the product is software doesn't mean it will sell itself. Worry a lot about legalities because your software is going to be easy to copy, and there is absolutely no protection for your copyrights overseas. Even if you do have legal protection, you won't be able to afford the fight that will probably not be settled in your favor ten years after the software is obsolete anyway.

All the general principles of marketing apply to software. Marketing really counts, appearance is almost everything, and it pays to advertise. It's worth saying again: The product will not sell itself. Success stories like *Lotus* and *Word* are few and far between. Remember compatibility with industry standards, real and defacto, and remember that different countries may require your software to do things you never dreamt of to comply with local practice, even if the laws might never be enforced for domestic software. (An example is compliance to audits concerning data privacy in DBMS software.)

Try not to be on the "bleeding edge," running potentially lethal risks by being too far ahead of the marketplace. The real pioneers, such as *VisiCalc* and *WordStar*, are now only distant memories. Be the second into the marketplace. Don't lose control of your company to people who want you to sell only software or to someone who wants to take you over.

Following are four more points to think about in terms of marketing:

■ Be innovative, but remember that the way the box looks also counts. You can be too innovative, years ahead of your time. *Incremental* is the watchword.

- Ease of use is important.
- Training manuals, operations manuals, and repair manuals have to exist, have to be written in language users understand, and have to be correct. If one of these is deficient, your product will only anger your frustrated users, who will tell everyone else they know.
- There is some price sensitivity to software that you will have to discover through market research.

The Modern Management Imperatives

Reach: Global Competition	Outsourcing is an excellent way to build in global linkages. Not only can firms establish relationships with organizations that have global reach, but they can profit from the knowledge that the outsourcers accumulate from all of their other customers. Of course, outsourcers learn from firms, too, and share that knowledge with other customers.
Reaction: Quick Customer Feedback on Products and Services	Outsourcers and software vendors *must* respond to their markets, which are increasingly vocal and powerful. By tapping into these merchants' resources, a firm can at least simulate responsiveness to customers by using existing applications. Those who want to be on the "bleeding edge" with ultrastrategic applications will continue to run the risks of doing so.
Responsiveness: Shortened Concept-to-Customer Cycle Time	While outsourcing or purchasing applications isn't inherently quicker than in-house development, it does increase the likelihood of a quick response—no wheels need to be reinvented if they already exist. The most successful outsourcers develop products quickly because *their* markets are in turmoil. Check outsourcers' references, though, and look at their balance sheets to make sure they can provide service in the future.
Refinement: Greater Customer Sophistication and Specificity	Good outsourcers are excellent at incorporating customer knowledge into their products and services. As customers become more sophisticated, so, too, do the outsourcers who survive. You lower your risk by tapping into this survival instinct.
Reconfiguration: Reengineering of Work Patterns and Structures	Formerly, in-house development was seen as private and protected, like an economy protected by trade barriers. This froze work patterns and styles. Having a variety of applications to choose from allows either fitting the application to the organization or creating new work models as desired. Learning is the key. What sells (i.e., what is available) is what works. The more kinds of applications there are for sale, the more ways there are of working.
Redeployment: Reorganization and Redesign of Resources	Again, intellectual tariff barriers also prevented organizations from redeploying their resources in novel ways. While there is a possibility for conflict with outsourcers over resource usage (see Lacity and Hirschheim), this burgeoning marketplace is full of ideas, and the movement to client-server architectures is freeing up funds for information resources rather than machinery.
Reputation: Quality and Reliability of Product and Process	The larger the choice, the greater the chance for quality, and the greater the expense in locating quality. Benchmarking (locating the best software and comparing your needs and designs to it) is a must for intelligent outsourcing of critical applications. Developing benchmarking procedures is assisted by attention to consumer periodicals that run regular reviews of software and systems. Selecting outsourcing firms is, however, a real research project. Don't assume that bigger is better or that high-priced help is the best; do the research.

■ CABLE 10'S FABULOUS SOFTWARE "HOOK"

After conversations with Eleanor Wright, Cable 10's systems professional (one-stop shopping for programming and operations), Phyllis has determined the following facts:

- She really doesn't understand computers very well (or maybe Eleanor doesn't explain them very well).
- Almost nobody in town has written software for any broadcaster other than accounting packages (most of which were tailored commercial packages).
- Phyllis's needs aren't particularly sensitive, although the data will be of strategic importance when the system is running, because it directly affects Cable 10's image in the community (not many people watch the community channel, but it has high visibility among those who care about and evaluate Cable 10's service to the community).
- Dozens of highly capable computer consultants are available.
- Cable 10 is used to contracting out technical services, has a good legal department, and has many people on staff who have bought technical equipment and services (although not much in the way of computers).
- There is at least one community channel in every major market in the country, but nobody is selling software to them. ■

1. Evaluate the value of software for Phyllis. Are there some problems in how Phyllis might handle software as a commercial product?

2. What should Phyllis look for in commercial software, assuming it is available? How will this affect her build or buy decision?

3. If Phyllis wants to outsource and then resell the software, what advice would you give her?

Summary

Software is an unusual product. Originally bundled with hardware and then sold only to technical specialists, software has become an item requiring intelligent purchasing by relatively untechnical purchasers. Software has a number of characteristics that distinguish it from hard goods. It is easy to change and copy but hard to understand and describe. It controls hardware and other systems and gives computers their "personalities." It is portable and transportable and comes in so many forms that it's difficult to decide what really falls into the class of "software." Software can be sold, licensed, and embedded in hardware. In whatever manner it is distributed, desirable software traits include ease of use and learnability, capacity, history of updates, compatibility, availability of documentation, reputation of the vendor, and a price that is reasonable.

An important market decision is whether to build or buy software. Building is recommended when an application is strategic and keeping knowledge in-house is important. Buying is necessary when technical staff are untrained or unavailable or when a trusted, reliable, and inexpensive vendor can be located. Building may entail outsourcing, that is, having an application or system constructed by an outside firm. When outsourcing, an organization should specify system requirements, invite bids for proposals or quotations, select a vendor, and pay for the services, which may include only development of the application or may extend to operating the application. Mature, nonstrategic applications and weak information systems groups are best outsourced, although there are major risks involving control, obsolescence, inflexibility, contracts, and security. Organizations that develop or outsource software development can also market the software to others, but they should pay attention to marketing, innovativeness, training, and ease of use.

Discussion Questions

16.1 The term *software* includes information systems applications and tools. But in other fields, software also includes videos, databases, radio and television broadcasts, audio recordings, and film. What characteristics do these types of software share with the kinds of software we have focused on in the text? Do you consider them software? Compare and contrast the development of these other kinds of software with management support systems.

16.2 Consider your own buying habits with regard to software. Is buying software different from buying hard goods and services? What criteria do you consider important in making purchasing (or licensing) decisions? What do you like and dislike about the way software is marketed? Are nontechnical, business-software purchasers at any disadvantage in this marketplace?

16.3 The build-vs.-buy decision clearly favors the building of strategic information systems. However, there are exceptions, especially if no one in-house has the skills to build the system needed. In cases such as these, what must a buyer do to manage the risks threatening the strategic advantage? (Hint: Consider the section on outsourcing for ideas.)

16.4 The trend toward outsourcing has been seen recently as unstoppable and ultimately leading to the demise of in-house information systems groups. While the trend remains strong, in fact, many in-house ISGs still exist and are growing. Speak with organizations that are not outsourcing, have cut back on outsourcing, or have discontinued outsourcing to find out what accounts for the continued robustness of in-house development and management of information systems.

16.5 Imagine that you have developed a software package you think would be of interest to others in your college or university. What steps might you take to market this software to others? What specifically would you have to do, and whom would you do this with? What costs will you incur? Do you have a way to estimate those costs? What risks would you run? Do you have a way to estimate those risks? What factors seem most influential in determining costs and risks and how they can be controlled?

Key Terms

application maturity	off-the-shelf system/application	software properties: malleable,
capacity	outsourcing	evanescent, controlling,
contract back	request for proposal (RFP)	levering, changeable,
ease of use	request for quotation (RFQ)	portable, transportable,
embedded software	shareware	arcane
learnability	site license	software updates/versions
legacy systems	software license	source code
managerial push/business	software market: captive,	technological leadership
environment pull	technical, consumer	technology transfer
object code	software marketplace	turnkey service

References

Booker, Ellis. "How IS Beat the Outsourcers at Amoco." *Computerworld*, January 10, 1994, 77.

Clemons, Eric, Sashidhar Reddi, and Michael Row. "The Impact of Information Technology on the Organization of Economic Activity: The 'Move to the Middle' Hypothesis." *Journal of Management Information Systems* 10, 2 (Fall 1993): 9–35.

Garner, Rochelle. "The Search for Financial Security: Accounting Programs Are the First Target for Many Users Who Are Ready to Downsize." *Information Week,* December 20–27, 1993, 46–47.

Greenbaum, J. "Build or Buy?" *Information Week,* December 20–27, 1993, 37–38, 40, 42–43.

Grover, V., and J. Teng. "The Decision to Outsource Information Systems Functions." *Journal of Systems Management* 44, 11 (November 1993): 34–38.

Huff, S. "Outsourcing of Information Services." *Business Quarterly* 55 (1991): 62–65.

Lacity, M., and R. Hirschheim. "The Information Systems Outsourcing Bandwagon." *Sloan Management Review* (Fall 1993): 73–86.

————. *Information Systems Outsourcing: Myths, Metaphors and Realities.* New York: Wiley, 1993.

Lederer, A., and A. Mendelow. "Coordination of Information Systems Plans with Business Plans." *Journal of Management Information Systems* 6, 2 (Fall 1989): 5–19.

Loh, L., and N. Venkatraman. "Determinants of Information Technology Outsourcing: A Cross-Sectional Analysis." *Journal of Management Information Systems* 9, 1 (Summer 1992): 7–24.

Shank, M., A. Boynton, and R. Zmud. "Critical Success Factor Analysis As a Methodology for MIS Planning." *MIS Quarterly* 2 (June 1985).

Sherman, Stratford. "How I Bought My Computer." *Fortune,* January 10, 1994, 76–79, 82.

CASE

EVERGREEN LANDSCAPING AND MAINTENANCE: EVALUATING AN INVENTORY SYSTEM

Given Connie's inquisitiveness and energy, it didn't surprise Sven Haroldson (retail services manager) to see her pounding away at a microcomputer and looking very proud of herself. Connie has had the microcomputer for about a year and has been relentlessly creating graphics for MEC presentations. Like everyone else, Sven can recognize a "Connie slide" in seconds. But she had rarely poked the keyboard with such gusto. Here's part of their conversation:

SVEN: Hi, Connie. You look pretty excited. Another great slide?

CONNIE: Better than that. Come around here and look.

SVEN: Hey, that's not a slide, it looks like some sort of listing of products.

CONNIE: That's right, but see what kinds they are.

SVEN: Hmmm. "Juniper, 2 gallon pot, 2314563, 6, 14, 4.92, 12.95." Hey, that's like our inventory . . .

CONNIE (INTERRUPTING WITH A SMILE): Not! It only looks like our inventory. This is different. It's about live material.

SVEN: Oh, I see, yes, we don't have any inventory on plants, but it looks like our hard goods inventory listing.

CONNIE: Yep. This kind of inventory listing will give us an idea of what's selling, what's going to spoil, what we should start marking down, and maybe even some idea of the shelf life of the products we get shipped or we grow ourselves. Right now, all I get is an eyeful whenever I go out to the nursery. Nobody ever really seems to know what we've got in stock and what shape it's in. Customers call up to ask, and we always have to go out and count. Having a system like this could eliminate the wear on our shoes. What do you think about *that*?

SVEN: Great. Let's get this going.

CONNIE: Well, not so fast. It looks like we've got one problem solved and several others started, doesn't it?

SVEN: What do you mean?

CONNIE: Well, you know the story. We can inventory hard goods because they have SKUs and don't really age on the shelves, but the live materials are a real problem because they don't have real SKUs and they can go from great to garbage in a day or two. This little piece of software is just a bunch of macros on a spreadsheet and it runs on this microcomputer. I think it could be tied into our POS terminals [cash registers] so we can keep track of how the plants and trees are moving. Won't that be a help?

SVEN: And the problem it creates?

CONNIE: Not only do we have to enter all this data, but we have to keep it current, and you know what a pain *that* will be. Every time a tree loses a leaf, it becomes a different product. And you know how often we transplant or get plants in the wrong-sized pots. The SKU for a 2-gallon juniper is 2314563, but what about a 1-gallon juniper that is shipped to us in a 2-gallon pot by mistake? How are we going to know it's really a 1-gallon juniper? And suppose someone forgets to water it for a week and it dries out and looks ugly—it's not a 2314563 any longer, is it?

SVEN: Well, we can handle damaged goods the way we always do, with special SKU for marked-down goods.

CONNIE: Yes, but the really hard part is constantly doing that as the products age, especially toward the end of the season. And it's not a system, Sven, it's just something I whipped up. I've read in some of the retailing mags that there are lots of these systems available, but each is a little different. We've got to evaluate them. Mine's only a little prototype. Really, this is only a partial solution, but think about the possibilities.

SVEN: OK, yeah, I see. We can keep track of inventory . . .

CONNIE: Uh-huh, and look at this. I've entered some sample data here just to see how long it would take to come up with estimates of turnover, and it looks like we could use this scheme to track inventory. Say it takes a few seconds to tag an item and a few more seconds to retag it each day. With 2,000 items out there, we'd be employing someone full-time, just like we do now, to update the inventory. I think you know how accurate we are—not! [Sven nods agreement here.] But think of what we'd get for it. We would know what is out on the floor, what is being moved, what plants are in what shape, how fast the items are moving—so we'd know what we have to mark down—and what our peak inventory is. From the retailing mags, I have an idea what this kind of package should cost, so it's not going to be hard to work up some figures on what we should pay. Meanwhile, we'll save by not having to throw dead inventory out, we won't sell dead trees to our customers, and we can tell our suppliers and shippers when they're sending us sick or dying material. What do you think?

Questions

1. What characteristics of software give Connie trouble in evaluating the live inventory application? What troubles do they give her? How can she counter these difficulties?

2. Explore the open marketplace for software in your business community. What characteristics make it a vigorous one? A difficult one for purchasers? Expensive and risky?

3. If Connie is going to buy a system from a vendor, what characteristics would you recommend she put high on her list to distinguish one from the other? What should definitely be avoided?

4. Suggest to Connie criteria by which she would judge RFPs for the sort of inventory system she is considering.

5. Connie doesn't have to buy the software; Terry and Dierdre could build her an application and handle the installation, along with the necessary hardware purchases. What considerations should go into Connie's build versus buy decision? How will Connie sell her decision to Shawna (vice president of sales)? Who else should be involved in this decision?

6. Using the Grover and Teng model in Figures 16–4 through 16–6, determine whether the inventory system should be outsourced.

7. If Connie is convinced by Dierdre and others that Evergreen should develop its own application, what advice would you give them about trying to sell it to recoup their costs? Given the competitive situation, do you think there are any risks involved? What are they and how strong are they? What policies do you think Evergreen should have in place concerning buying, building, and selling software-based applications?

CHAPTER SEVENTEEN

MANAGING TECHNOLOGICAL INNOVATION

OBJECTIVES

After you have read and studied this chapter, you should be able to:

■ Explain the basic concepts of technological innovation in the workplace.

■ Describe a model of adopting technological innovations.

■ Describe the four phases of growth in the contagion model and identify the various roles users adopt during these four phases.

■ Discuss the characteristics that influence the adoption of an innovation.

Question: What has to happen for a technological idea to be accepted by a group of workers? What can managers do to take advantage of this knowledge?

City Symphony has been in existence for more than 50 years, but this year is going to be the most difficult, thought Renata Cameron, director of development and public relations. But she has an idea! In the past, Renata divided her attentions between three different, but connected, responsibilities: fund-raising, internal communications, and public relations. For each responsibility, she built an extensive, if somewhat informal, database. For example, the fund-raising Rolodex contains cards for more than 300 contacts of current and past donors, and the public relations card file contains more than 200 cards for additional contacts. Renata resisted computerizing these files for years, intending to do it when she had the time, but, in fact, someone in her position never has the time. Her staff, consisting of two clerks, one secretary, and three part-time volunteers, uses computers for word processing and simple spreadsheets for tracking donations, but they are unsophisticated about computers. Renata would like to build an integrated database on a computer and then use it for all aspects of her work. The major problem she sees is getting her staff and the board to agree to the project and use the product. Technology, while a mystery, just seems to happen, but changing people's attitudes is difficult, as Renata, a professional fund-raiser, knows.

Answer: Diffusion of technological innovations is a complex responsibility of managers of new or improved applications, and includes managing introduction, motivating proper use, and using communication channels to maintain the innovation in use. Managers can influence workers' impressions and attitudes and control the management environment, thus influencing workers' inclination or potential for adoption. Knowledge of adoption patterns and the forces influencing adoption can help managers produce the desired level of innovation and level of adoption.

INTRODUCTION

This chapter discusses the role that management plays in the diffusion of technological innovations as represented by information systems applications. This is the "soft" side of system development. If systems face risks while they are being developed, these risks merely become preliminary hurdles if the systems are never used. The technological leadership that managers can exercise is improved when managers understand their roles in diffusing technological innovations to those who can use them to their advantage. Of course, this chapter focuses on information systems applications and systems. While it is not entirely fair to say that this chapter is about getting people to use applications, it does explore, in some detail, the factors that lead either to adoption and use or rejection of an application or system.

We begin with a look at the term **diffusion of innovation** and investigate its meanings and then interpret a general model of innovation. Then, we examine a specific model of diffusion of technological innovation, pointing out where managers have responsibility and some influence over eventual adoption of an innovation or system.

BASIC TERMINOLOGY

In the following discussion, we examine how individuals adopt a **technological innovation.** Most of the discussion will be general, referring to all technologies, but where information technologies differ will be made explicit. The term *technological innovation* is more complex than it may seem at first blush. An innovation is a new way of working or a new tool used in working (we are not speaking of an innovation such as a new product or service that a company may offer). Sometimes an innovation has been in existence for a while and is new only to those who are being asked to adopt it. Regardless of its actual age, an innovation is perceived as different and new. Because innovations are new, they are compared with the old, called a **precursor.** A precursor is whatever currently occupies the same niche as the innovation. For example, a typewriter replaced its precursor, pen and ink; electronic mail is pushing aside its precursors, the post office and memos. Pencil-and-paper computations were the precursor to spreadsheets. Each innovation may displace many precursors, and those precursors provide a context in which potential adopters make comparisons.

In a general sense, adoption means to choose, select, or take as one's own. In the context of management support systems, adoption of a system means to use it in work processes. There is an element of choice here, too; adoption means that a person more or less voluntarily elects to make a selection from a number of alternatives (although we will examine only one actual alternative—the status quo—in any detail). Adoption has several dimensions, and we will be more specific about which aspects we are concerned with later in this chapter.

The innovations of interest here are, of course, management support systems. These systems share many characteristics, but the major ones are the following:

- The innovations are *technological*; they won't work without using high technology, specifically, computer technology.
- They are *opaque,* not immediately understandable by everyone. They involve understanding electronics, physics, or mathematics—some field that

potential adopters actually don't want to understand, and really should not have to.

■ They are *tool-providing*; the innovation is actually a tool used to do work. The innovation is not appreciated for itself, as art might be. It is appreciated only if it functions well in performing some other work.

All technological innovations share characteristics of short life span, high initial expense, low initial knowledge, and dependence on technologists to keep them working right. At one time, all of the following were technological innovations and all have gone through myriad changes in the marketplace: automobiles, railroads, electric power, typewriters, clocks, assembly lines, and printing presses. While the innovations in this list are still with us, most are **mature technologies** in which changes, while often important and positive, do not alter the nature of the innovation and in which these same changes don't instantly render all previous versions of the innovation totally obsolete. High technologies are merely relatively new technologies that, because of the newness of the general technology itself, share a short life span, high initial cost, and low initial knowledge as well as the need for technology "chauffeurs" to keep them running.

Information systems applications are considered high technological innovations because they have the characteristics mentioned above. Of course, some are "higher" than others, some are more technological than others, and some are more innovative than others. These differences may be important in specific cases, but in this chapter we won't make much of the actual technical characteristics of the applications. We are far more concerned with the perceptions of people who have to use them than how complex the programming is or how many connections have to be juggled at once by the software.

The following sections describe in great detail adoption models developed by Moore and by Hamer based on work by Leonard-Barton, Leonard-Barton and Deschamps, Johnson and Rice, Davis, Rogers, and Ajzen and Fishbein. These models make little reference to software or applications, so we will point out where qualities of software may make a difference in the model. The basis of these models is common sense, which is the basis of most managerial work. People use what is comfortable and profitable to use and avoid what seems uncomfortable and punishing. The models also show how managers can be technological leaders.

For example, let's return to Evergreen and refer to the innovation mentioned in Chapter 16, the use of SKUs for live plant materials to track inventory in a computer-based application. As you will recall, Connie is considering purchasing or developing software to track live materials in the greenhouse and on the retail floor. Connie wants to raise margins by pricing this material better as it gets older. Sven and Sid are interested in this software, too, although Sven's interest is more as a customer, because he doesn't sell trees and shrubs directly but uses them in contract work. Suppose Connie purchases a package, called *LIVELY,* and integrates it with the POS system. Each plant, tree, and shrub has a tag that is scanned by Tulley's assistants as it arrives and scanned again when it is sold. Because trees and shrubs are dated, the application dates and flags different materials as they approach different stages in estimated attractiveness to customers, so that the price can be adjusted correctly. Floor workers in the store and in the greenhouses use the application each day to watch the growing plants. Connie and her staff also use the application to keep track of inventory levels, make projections, and decide on pricing and stock. We will look at the concept of adoption of technological innovation as we explore how managers, also, might adopt *LIVELY* at Evergreen.

| Figure 17–1 | WHY MANAGERS ARE CONCERNED WITH DIFFUSION OF INNOVATIONS |

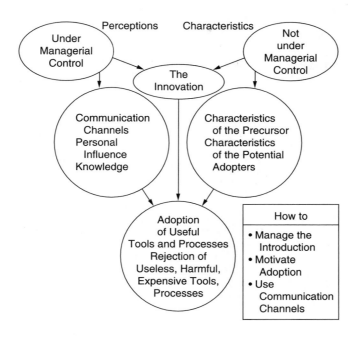

A MODEL OF ADOPTION

Managers naturally want their employees to adopt and employ useful and advantageous tools and processes and to avoid or drop useless, expensive, or harmful ones (see Figure 17–1). Managers have at their disposal the objective, positive qualities of the innovation. They also have access to and control of communication channels to deliver messages to change perceptions of these qualities, that is, to create **subjective impressions.**

However, managers have little control over the objective characteristics of the precursor. At Evergreen, *LIVELY* has no tangible precursor. The previous inventory system was entirely manual, based on visual checking. If Connie wants to influence greenhouse staff, she may try to present *LIVELY* in a good light by communicating with the staff. She can also let people know that she recognizes the shortcomings of the existing method of handling inventory.

Most noncomputerized organizational communication channels (such as memos) have been around for a long time. How people use and trust these channels is very much tied to how they perceive the organization and its culture. Managers can do little to change these perceptions, and they can also do little to change the traits of the perceivers, the potential adopters. While managers can sometimes provide training, counseling, or mentoring, in reality these do not change the individual so much as enhance the individual's knowledge of self and others. Most communication efforts are and should be directed toward behavior. Thus, managers face the task of managing the introduction of a new

Figure 17-2 | MANAGING ADOPTION OF INNOVATIONS

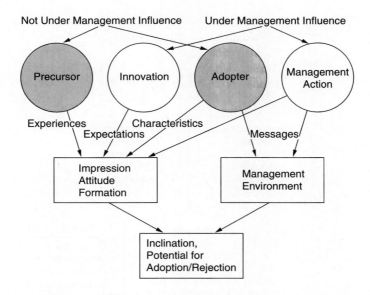

innovation given the (objective) qualities of the technology and its precursor and the perceived (subjective) qualities of the innovation by using communication opportunities to motivate employees to change their minds about the innovation.

A general model of innovation and adoption (see Figure 17–2) iterates four factors (two factors are under management control—communication channels and the innovation—while the precursor and the adopter are not under management control) and their influence on both employee attitudes and the management environment of employees. This in turn influences employees' inclination to **adopt** or **reject** the innovation. This model is derived from a general model of adoption pioneered by Zaltman, Duncan, and Holbeck (abbreviated here as ZDH) based, in turn, on a well-understood, noncontroversial model of attitude change created at Yale University in the early 1960s. This basic model posits that for an innovation to be adopted on a continuous basis, a number of steps have to occur. These steps include in order the following (see Figure 17–3):

- Attention or awareness
- Comprehension or knowledge
- Yielding or attitude change
- Use or adoption
- Reinvention and continued use (this last concept credited to E. Rogers)

Attention or awareness means knowing that there is an alternative to the status quo. It is immediately connected with advertising and public awareness campaigns through newsletters, memos, and word of mouth. Managers influence and commonly control formal channels of managerial communication, and to an extent they dictate what the

| Figure 17–3 | A MODEL OF ATTITUDE CHANGE |

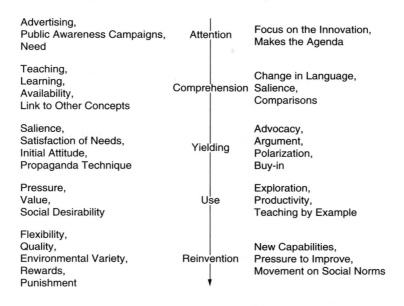

Advertising, Public Awareness Campaigns, Need	Attention	Focus on the Innovation, Makes the Agenda
Teaching, Learning, Availability, Link to Other Concepts	Comprehension	Change in Language, Salience, Comparisons
Salience, Satisfaction of Needs, Initial Attitude, Propaganda Technique	Yielding	Advocacy, Argument, Polarization, Buy-in
Pressure, Value, Social Desirability	Use	Exploration, Productivity, Teaching by Example
Flexibility, Quality, Environmental Variety, Rewards, Punishment	Reinvention	New Capabilities, Pressure to Improve, Movement on Social Norms

technological agenda of their team, department, or division is—the technology that people talk about and think about. Connie is in a position to shape the technological agenda of her department and bring up the topic of the live material inventory. She can use memos, the company newsletter, or informal conversation. She began that process by demonstrating a simple spreadsheet approach to Sid (Chapter 16).

Comprehension or knowledge arises from information about the innovation that is found in books, manuals, advertising literature, and courses. Managers provide information and motivation to learn. By talking about a new application, managers influence the very words that people use to express themselves. Each new application has its own special jargon, its series of screens, its input formats—all of these are unique to the application and make their way into conversation. Workers compare application concepts with job concepts. If they match, workers learn about the application. If they don't learn about it—and are not using it—there is little chance that they will be able to evaluate it honestly or at all. Connie's demonstration to Sid showed him what a computerized live material inventory application could do. It also gave him something tangible to talk about and a kernel of experience to work later information into. Later, when Connie received information on *LIVELY*, Sid already knew something about what such an application should do.

The next step, yielding, means that a potential adopter decides to try out or use the innovation. This implies a change of attitude, and normally happens only after the knowledge stage. Propaganda techniques, however, appeal to people's emotions, and there is no doubt that techniques such as fearmongering, guilt by association (and its opposite, the halo effect), and the bandwagon effect can influence yielding, too, without any real factual knowledge. On the other hand, these same techniques may predate the innovation and may have to be countered. Managers increase yielding by advocacy and argument. They make the new application salient through promises of rewards and punishment. The result of this, however, may be polarization, with some workers buying-in early while others resist. Connie doesn't have this problem, because she tries arguing by example. She shows that she is willing to use *LIVELY* and that it helps her in her work. This tactic will not work with everyone, but she recognizes that a leader who won't use what she urges others to use is hardly credible.

Yielding is not enough for adoption, however. Many of us would like to adopt the lifestyles of the rich and famous but we don't have the opportunity. Creating that opportunity can assist in passage to the next step, which is use. In this step, many of the objective qualities of the innovation become important. Applications that are hard to use won't be used. Management support systems that frustrate or embarrass people will be rejected, despite good intentions (yielding) on the part of potential users. Some applications and systems are used only because there is pressure to do so, because managers, rather than users, value their use, or because managers let workers know it is desirable to use the application. As applications become used, new usage is spawned. Workers show others by example, and productivity may increase, making the application more desirable.

Another important factor in convincing others to adopt an innovation is their involvement in the design, procurement, and deployment of the innovation. In this case, individuals may be predisposed to yielding because they have a vested interest in the innovation itself. In addition, involvement at one stage implies a greater chance for involvement during use to help improve the applications.

Applications that aren't improved (or fail to perform or get worse) will be dropped later on, so that there will be no continued use and further innovation. This is what Everett Rogers calls *reinvention*. Reinvention means to continue to find ways to push the innovation into other aspects of work to get the maximum benefit out of it. An application is reinvented when it is used for a new job function or task, perhaps one not intended by the designers, but, in any event, one not yet attempted by the user. When the greenhouse staff at Evergreen adopted the live inventory application (*LIVELY*), they initially used it only for reminders to change tags. However, some of them learned to anticipate this and used the application to rearrange the material so that the oldest material would be handled first. They reinvented an application intended for pricing to assist in warehousing. Reinvented applications introduce new capabilities and increase pressure to improve the application. Improved performance may affect social norms in the workplace, too, by helping some more than others and disturbing the social balance created by the reward structure already in place.

Hence, a manager will exert influence at all of these stages by making employees aware of the innovation, providing them with information about the innovation to shape their attitudes, and then making it available to them in working form.

Note the similarity between the ZDH model of innovation adoption and our models of decision making, problem solving, or the cybernetic system (see Table 17–1). All are reflections of how we, as individuals, make changes in our or others' behavior. We could view decision making as "self-convincing" à la ZDH, see innovation adoption as assisting others in making decisions, or view both as a kind of problem solving, but the four stages are still there: becoming aware of the possibility of change or decision, gathering information about the change or decision, making the change mentally, and then following through in the real world. It is not surprising that much of human behavior follows this pattern as we live in both a physical world of actions and a mental world of ideas and models that can be independently analyzed and manipulated.

Table 17–1	PHASES OF INNOVATION ADOPTION	

Phase	**Results**	**Managerial Actions**
Attention/awareness	Potential adopter (PA) is aware of the availability of the innovation	Manager makes others aware of the innovation
Comprehension/ knowledge	PA comes to understand the features and value of the innovation and how it is used	Manager shows the innovation to PA and informs the PA about innovation's features
Yielding/attitude change	PA decides to use the innovation or selects it from a set of alternatives	Manager demonstrates the advantages of the innovation and acts as its champion
Use/adoption	PA uses the innovation	Manager provides the innovation and makes training available
Reinvention/ continued use	PA uses the innovation for more job functions	Manager motivates continued exploration of the innovation through rewards

A MODEL OF CONTAGION

When we shift our focus from the individual adopter and look at all potential adopters, we can chart the course of an innovation's use over time (see Figure 17–4). In this view, some innovations are accepted rather quickly. In a technology stampede, individuals may accept a particular new way of working very quickly, reaching saturation within a short period of time. Other innovations may be adopted rather quirkily, gaining adopters now and losing some of them later, perhaps at some point losing all adopters and becoming a failure. Some innovations never really become widely popular. Despite the fact that all innovations are eventually replaced by other innovations, most are considered failures only if a significant proportion of potential adopters fail to adopt.

There is also an ideal profile, the standard S curve, which we will use as an example in the following discussion. This curve is also sometimes called a learning curve or a **contagion curve** because it is characteristic of the way people acquire knowledge or catch diseases. These processes begin with a small amount and grow slowly. When a critical mass is reached, growth starts to take off. However, after a while, one has learned almost everything one can or almost everyone who isn't naturally resistant or immune to the disease has caught it. At this point, the law of diminishing returns takes over and growth falls dramatically, reaching a characteristic **saturation point** (which may be less than 100 percent, depending on the knowledge, disease, or innovation).

This curve illustrates four **phases of growth** (Figure 17–5) across time or effort. This model is derived from observations by Nolan in the 1970s concerning the diffusion of information systems services throughout individual organizations. This model has come under attack by academics in recent years as having limited validity with respect to when various phases actually begin; however, its value for discussion has never been doubted.

Connie wants others, especially managers, in the organization to recognize the value of *LIVELY*. In the early stages of diffusion of this innovation, Connie read about some applications in her retail marketing journals. The systems perhaps ran on microcomputers

Figure 17–4 CONTAGION MODEL: SAMPLE PROFILES

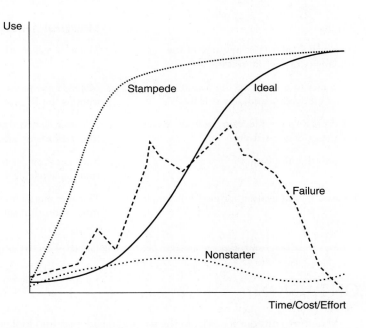

Figure 17–5 CONTAGION MODEL: PHASES

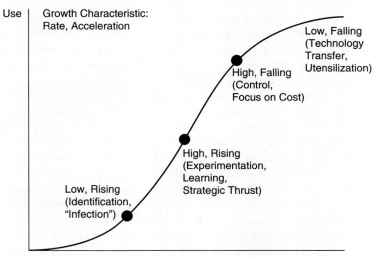

and Connie, who uses a microcomputer to perform spreadsheeting, wondered if she could try out this innovation to find out if it's really advantageous. This growth stage is called the identification phase.

After acquiring *LIVELY*, she tried it out and showed it to others who work with her. She had already convinced Lily that *LIVELY* was an important addition to the sales function, and *LIVELY* was integrated with the POS system. Then Connie developed a few spreadsheet applications for forecasting and pricing based on the newly available data. During this experimentation phase, some other managers may appreciate the advantage that such a system will give them. During this phase, managers learn how to use the system and extend its use into other areas of work, different from marketing, perhaps in purchasing. This phase uncovers strategic uses for inventory related to just-in-time ordering, and stretches the *LIVELY* application to the limit of the software's original ability. As more people begin to use the whole system, the attention of upper management is attracted again because the larger number of users is starting to make a significant impact on IS resources (such as computers, consulting time of IS professionals, and additional related software).

At this point, the rate of growth of new users or uses is still high, but starts falling as upper management regularizes the use, perhaps making it generally available to everyone, but limiting the amount of consulting the IS group will do for new users. In this control phase, there are fewer potential new users as everyone who might want to use it already knows about it—only the diehard nonusers remain to be converted. This last phase (which Nolan calls technology transfer—we will use a different definition of this term in Chapter 18 to apply more generally to transfer of any technology from an inventor or developer to a user) is characterized by few new users or uses. The technology has been transferred completely to the set of potential adopters and has become a "utensil," a tool that is so thoroughly integrated into work procedures that, like pencils and telephones, it's almost unnoticed unless it doesn't work at all. Six months after introducing *LIVELY*, for example, almost everyone who can possibly use it in sales, warehousing, or transportation is doing so. Within a year, there is nothing more to be done with the package, although pioneers like Connie are already thinking about new applications to work on the data that *LIVELY* originally made valuable.

During these four phases, users adopt several different **innovation roles** (see Figure 17–6). Early adopters like Connie are called *pioneers*. They bear all the risks of initial implementation, but there are fewer pressures to achieve any specific outcomes. Pioneers demonstrate the innovation to others and may serve as role models, although their inherent inventiveness and risk taking make them unusual and perhaps, in the extreme, not role models at all. The word *demonstrator* may be more apt here. Those who adopt the innovation at the end, when most potential adopters have adopted, are called *laggards*. Their inherent conservatism and risk aversion have led them to avoid the innovation, clinging to existing work methods. Bill Porter, Evergreen's transportation supervisor, thought he might have some use for *LIVELY*, but in fact never made much effort to do so because he has other ways to get the information he needs about the few trees that occasionally die. He is a laggard with regard to *LIVELY*.

The ratio of pioneers to laggards is not one-to-one. Where a stampede exists, many people are pioneers. Where an innovation is a nonstarter, almost everyone is a laggard. Corporate culture has a strong influence on this ratio, because how an organization rewards risk taking dictates, to a great extent, how risky the innovation really appears. Laggards may be thought of as stick-in-the-muds in organizations that reward risk taking and inventiveness, but they are considered heroes in firms that frown on threats to tradition and punish those who disturb unbroken processes that some may say need to be fixed.

Figure 17–6 ADOPTER ROLES IN THE CONTAGION MODEL

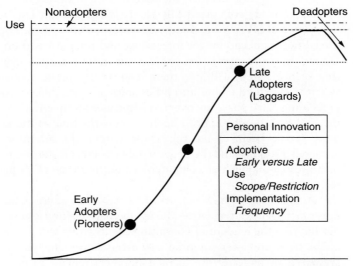

There are three types of **personal innovation.** Adoptive innovation refers to how early or late an individual adopts an innovation, as mentioned previously. Use innovation refers to how widely an adopter integrates the innovation into work. Connie, for example, is not only a pioneer, but she has thought of many different ways to use *LIVELY* and the data it generates. Greenhouse workers use it for far fewer tasks. Restricted use innovation means to apply the innovation only to its original, intended use with little inventiveness. The alternative is to apply the innovation to as many areas of work as possible. Finally, implementation innovation (later referred to as frequency) is defined as how often an adopter uses the innovation, regardless of the kind of use. Connie uses *LIVELY* only once or twice a week, while greenhouse workers may use it daily.

In our previous discussion, we attempted to refer to all three kinds of innovation at the same time, but there are obvious differences. One company may acquire software that everyone uses, but for only a narrow range of applications. The firm is obviously experiencing a different kind of innovation from that experienced by a firm in which adoption is limited to a third of potential adopters who press the innovation to the limit of its design, using it for everything they can and asking the ISG to make it even more functional. Are 100 half-hearted users the same as 50 who go whole hog? That depends on corporate culture, the pressure for strategic applications, and the IS budget but, in general, strategic applications arise not from pioneers but from later early-phase adopters who have the ability to translate the innovation into competitive terms. A system could have many strategic applications developed by pioneers, but they will not normally be accepted by others unless the pioneers also have the corporate ear and are capable of proving to upper management that there are strategic benefits. Normally, they will have to do better than proving this—they will have to turn upper managers into adherents,

| Figure 17–7 | MANAGING TECHNOLOGICAL INNOVATION |

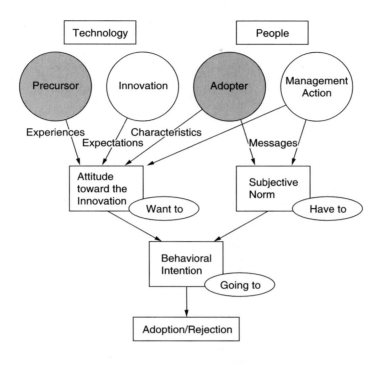

even champions. Strategic applications are expensive because they require the best technology, strong technical support, and secrecy. Now is the time to return to individual adoption and illustrate how to turn a curiosity into a trend.

INFLUENCES ON ADOPTION

Characteristics of Innovation

The diffusion of innovation model introduced in Figure 17–2 can be elaborated in Figure 17–7. The givens are the qualities of the precursor and the innovation, characteristics of the adopter, and communication channels, some of which are under the control or influence of a manager. They affect both individual attitude toward the innovation ("Want to") and the necessity or force to adopt ("Have to," also referred to as subjective norm).

The attitude toward the innovation is influenced by all four classes of givens, including personality factors of the potential adopter and the characteristics of the messages they are given about the innovation. That attitude is influenced by six characteristics (see Figure 17–8). Refer again to Connie's *LIVELY* innovation:

- **Result demonstrability**: How easily the potential adopter can see, understand, and communicate the results of using the innovation to others.

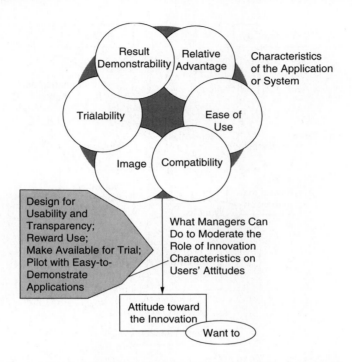

Figure 17–8 INNOVATION CHARACTERISTICS INFLUENCING ATTITUDE

If results cannot be seen, then it is unlikely that positive benefits can be appreciated. *LIVELY* has attractive displays that immediately show how fast material is moving and data navigation tools that make it evident that this is a powerful tool.

- **Relative advantage**: How much better the innovation is seen than its precursors. This, of course, depends on the objective qualities of the precursor as well as how much benefit the innovation seems to provide. This is considered a subjective quality, influenced by perceptions that in turn are influenced by education and promoted by champions. Connie can easily show that *LIVELY* has many advantages over the old method of eyeballing stock—she only has to refer to the shrubs and plants that are tossed out when they die or become unattractive.

- **Ease of use**: Almost all innovations will be rejected if they are hard to use. This is a hygiene factor, meaning that above some level of ease of use, additional ease will not be noticed, but below some level, everyone will probably complain. Because *LIVELY* is complex, its ease of use could be improved; Connie considers this one of its weak points. A fair amount of training is required, as is some sophistication with data navigation.

- **Compatibility**: This is the transparency and transportability factors mentioned in Chapter 10. The greater the amount of mental and physical work one has to do to transfer the innovation to the workplace in unnatural or unfamiliar ways, the less likely the innovation is to be adopted. Because the adoption hasn't occurred yet, this transfer tends to go on in the minds of potential adopters, and this mental imagery is sensitive to management influence and role models as well as to the truth about the innovation. *LIVELY* assists in performing a familiar process—inventory tracking. However, management has not used it much, so Connie will have to show other managers, especially those who work for her, that they *would* work this way if they could.

- **Image**: Some people refuse to learn how to type and think it's beneath them. Others feel that it's an honor to have the latest software installed on their machines first. Image depends a lot on the messages adopters get about the innovation and its role and importance in the firm. "No problem," thinks Connie. Evergreen's managers are not at all computer-averse, but they have little experience.

- **Trialability**: Because the innovation hasn't been adopted yet, potential adopters will have to try it out. Innovations that admit trials without much risk and organizations that can set up relatively risk-free trials will experience more complete and more rapid adoption. People do not accept everything on faith. Connie worked in stages to demonstrate trialability. First she integrated the live material inventory SKU scheme with the POS terminal system. Only later did she show other managers how easy it was to download the data and use them with spreadsheets she had already built for forecasting.

These same six characteristics are in operation after initial adoption, too. Relative advantage increases as the bugs are worked out or decreases as more bugs appear. Ease of use increases in normal applications. Compatibility increases as users become more familiar with the software; the new software may, in fact, become the new standard against which new innovations will have to measure up. Image is unpredictable. As more people adopt, certainly there is less feeling that the adopter is divergent, but also less feeling that the adopter is elite. Trialability is less important, although reinvention may require adopters to try out *new* uses without penalty. Result demonstrability may be enhanced with a reward system that positively values the results of use.

Characteristics of Users

A number of user factors influence attitudes. In Figure 17–9 are six that have been shown to have an influence on users' attitudes toward technological innovations:

- Demographic characteristics such as age, educational level, job tenure, and gender have been shown at various times to affect attitudes, although it is unclear whether these factors are stable or merely an artifact of particular times. Because demographic factors are not under management control or influence, they do not enter into the equation here.

- Existing attitudes about technology, computers, and the precursor strongly influence attitudes about innovations. Not only are people relatively consistent, or at least desire consistency in themselves and others, but they also base attitudes on expectations of reward and punishment, pleasure and pain.

Figure 17–9	USER CHARACTERISTICS THAT INFLUENCE ADOPTION

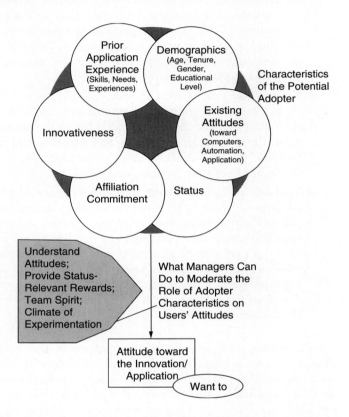

- The user's status in the organization may influence attitudes toward the innovation. High-status individuals (those with high organizational rank or prestige) may view some applications as "beneath them." Shawna, for instance, might see LIVELY as clerical and avoid using it, whereas operational managers might view *LIVELY* as a chance to get higher-quality information or more responsibility, that is, more status.

- Affiliation with a group and commitment to the group's goals influence attitudes. If a group commands an individual's loyalty and, at the same time, expresses strongly positive attitudes toward an application, it is likely that the individual will go along with the group, and vice versa.

- Personal innovativeness is an individual's tendency to try out new things and welcome change. People differ on this scale, just as they do with other personality traits.

- Prior experiences and skills with an application and needs that arise from this or related applications can create strong expectations of what the innovation will be like. Sometimes expectations are so strong that reality is not allowed to intrude.

| Figure 17-10 | PRECURSOR CHARACTERISTICS THAT INFLUENCE ATTITUDE |

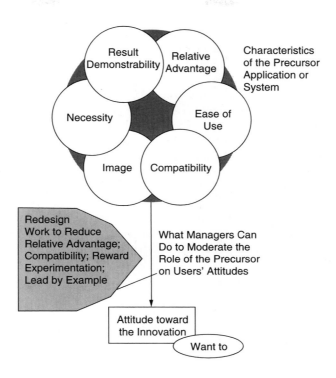

Managers should understand where user attitudes come from in order to shape them. By providing status-relevant rewards and creating a team spirit and a climate of invention and experimentation, managers can influence attitudes. Of course, in our discussion we assume that ethical issues are being considered, too. It is not the intention of researchers to develop methods to get people to do things that they don't wish to do or that are harmful to them.

In the case of *LIVELY*, Connie counted on, and was rewarded by, the personal innovativeness of her own staff, especially Sid and Sven. In addition, she found out that Byron Todd is comfortable with computers and data, and his example spurred quick adoption by the warehouse employees he manages. Although many managers were a bit computer shy, Kim Backer's ability to show them what to do was a real plus in the training that Connie delegated to Frances's assistant.

Characteristics of Precursors

Managers, of course, can't influence characteristics of the precursor, but they can influence prospective users' *perception* of them. As an application, the precursor has the same six salient characteristics as the innovation, except that trialability is not a concern (Figure 17–10). Trialability is replaced by necessity, the need to use the application to get work done. As they mature, applications may fail to meet workers' new needs, and they will then find other ways to work. They may then perceive the application as a non-necessity and no longer use it.

Managers can make attitudes toward the innovation more positive by redesigning work to reduce the relative advantage of the precursor or to make the precursor less compatible with work. This does not mean making the software fail or putting burdens on workers to use manual procedures. It does mean improving work processes and then showing workers that the new application will help them in the improved work situation. Workers who experiment with the precursor will discover its lower flexibility. Managers can also lead by example, showing workers that the innovation is more of a necessity and has a more positive image.

LIVELY's precursor was visual checks of inventory. There were some advantages to this method: greenhouse staff became adept at judging when plants were in distress and needed additional care; they had a good mental image of where plants were located; and they could alert Byron or others if they thought that plants had contagious infections. This work was time-consuming and risky, and it took a long time for this detailed knowledge to benefit Evergreen's sales programs. Managers almost never discovered opportunities until too late. Connie, in particular, felt that Evergreen's goals were to sell plants, not nurse them. There was no particular strategic benefit in these skills, as valuable as they might prove themselves to be occasionally. In terms of relative advantage, Connie and Sid saw very few advantages in the manual system, and many drawbacks. However, the greenhouse workers obviously felt comfortable working the way they did.

Characteristics of Communication Channels

Managers can also use communication channels at their disposal to shape attitudes (Figure 17–11). The term *communication channels* is used also to encompass the messages that managers use to persuade others, including other managers. There are six important characteristics:

- *Availability of the channel*: Do the intended users get a chance to see or hear the messages?

- *Formality*: Formal channels include memos, training sessions, and formal meetings. Informal channels include conversations, e-mail, and casual meetings.

- *Demonstrability*: Messages that relate to the application should say something tangible about its advantage or use. Simple "motherhood" statements like "We have looked around for the best packages available and have chosen *LIVELY*" are simply ignored.

- *Accessibility*: Channels of communication may be available but not accessible. While they may provide interesting or valuable information, they may not be accessible when users are working. Formal meetings may be available, but unless an application is available during a training session, what managers have to say about it is not accessible when workers actually use the application.

- *Salience*: Messages should be about the work situation, not about workers' lifestyles, habits, or beliefs. People ignore messages they feel intrude or violate boundaries.

- *Credibility*: Managers are not technical people, and a pronouncement in the computer realm will immediately be seen as bogus. On the other hand, technical people aren't seen as credible managers or the organization's

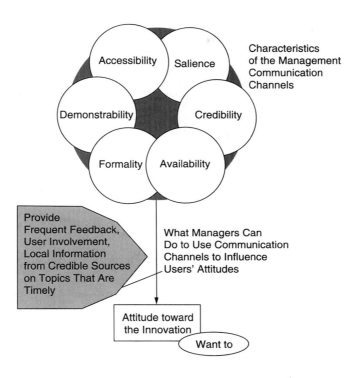

Figure 17-11 COMMUNICATION CHANNELS CHARACTERISTICS THAT INFLUENCE ATTITUDES

representatives. If a programmer says that an application increases accountability, will a worker believe it? Generally, **out-of-role statements** are seen as more credible. For example, if a manager says, "I'm really impressed by these IS people" when the manager's role traditionally has been to blast them, this may be seen as a more credible statement.

Managers can provide frequent feedback, increase user involvement in design and installation, and provide information locally (from within the group rather than from management or the ISG) from credible people on timely and pertinent topics to influence attitudes.

There is no doubt that Connie and Sid have good access to corporate communication channels and can deliver salient and credible messages about computerized systems to workers. However, because warehouse employees report to Byron Todd and ultimately to Thomas Davidoff, Sid's ability to access these workers is limited. He has to go through more formal channels. Connie's position on the MEC and her sales talents make it easy for her to convince other managers that *LIVELY* and the data it made available should be used by others. In this effort she has the support of Heather Cariad, vice president of finance. Heather saw immediate advantage to the bottom line. Tom Davidoff, vice president of operations, was already convinced about computers, but he was worried that

---

Figure 17–12 THE ROLE OF SUBJECTIVE NORM IN INFLUENCING ATTITUDES TOWARD APPLICATIONS

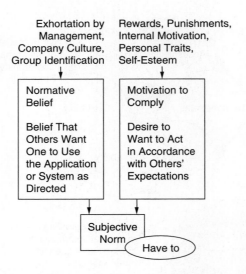

---

his workers wouldn't see the advantage to them in doing more work so that others could manage more easily. Connie, Heather, and Sid eventually put together a two-hour demo with Dierdre's help that allayed Tom's fears about the amount of work his staff would have to perform. They gave Tom materials salient to his workers that he could show them. Motivating Tom's workers to keep the data current and convincing other managers to look at product data were the two major hurdles in promoting *LIVELY* as an innovation.

INFLUENCES ON SUBJECTIVE NORM

Another major factor in the diffusion model is **subjective norm** (see Figure 17–12), the pressure on a potential user to adopt an innovation. This pressure arises in two ways. First, **normative belief (NB)** is the belief that one is expected to adopt the innovation. This pressure can arise from management, co-workers, customers, or subordinates and is influenced by messages from these people as well as implicit messages from the corporate culture. An organization with a lot of team spirit may well experience groupthink, with high pressure to conform. Or the team spirit may be manifested in a climate encouraging free thinking, with very little pressure on people to behave like others.

Second, **motivation to comply (MC)** is the degree to which a potential adopter is motivated to act in accordance with those pressures, regardless of personal belief about the innovation. People can and do resist pressures to conform or comply for a variety of reasons. The organization's reward system has a strong influence on this, as does, of course, individual personality.

The subjective norm is the conceptual product of these two influences:

$$SN = NB \times MC$$

| Figure 17–13 | BEHAVIORAL INTENTION AND USE |

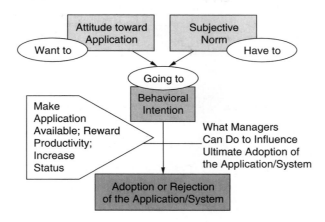

In order for subjective norm to be high, there has to be some perception of outside pressure to adopt as well as an internal motivation to comply with that pressure. Obviously, managers have a strong potential for influence here.

As in most organizations that use a lot of part-time assistance, normative belief at Evergreen, particularly at the workers' level, is not particularly high. Evergreen, however, rehires workers who demonstrate aptitude and loyalty, and this keeps motivation to comply rather high among workers. The managerial cadre, on the other hand, shares a strong positive orientation toward Lily and her way of working. Evergreen's slow but steady growth has built an expectation that they are doing the right thing in the right way.

THE COMPLETED MODEL: BEHAVIORAL INTENTION

Our model is completed by showing that both attitude toward the innovation (the new application) and subjective norm influence **behavioral intention** (see Figure 17–13). A worker is "going to" use an application if the worker either "wants to" use it or feels he or she "has to" use it. These two factors work independently to influence behavioral intention. The former users are called "voluntary" and the latter are called "involuntary" or "forced." Because forced use does not lead to buy-in, most managers are not content with forcing workers to use applications or systems.

Behavioral intention is, of course, not actually sufficient to adopt or reject an application. As noted previously, if an application is unavailable or there are no rewards for using it, workers will avoid it. That is why missed development deadlines are lethal to application adoption. Behavioral intention fades quickly. "Want to" becomes "wanted to," and then expectations fail to be met, which creates a poor climate for adoption.

Technological innovation (see Figure 17–14) has some peculiar characteristics because the innovation involves technology. There are three **levels of adoption,** and a manager must adopt three different strategies depending on which level is being considered. When a company or firm decides to pursue an innovation, it is a top-down, executive-driven innovation. This may also come about because of a grass-roots

Figure 17–14 THREE LEVELS OF TECHNOLOGICAL INNOVATION

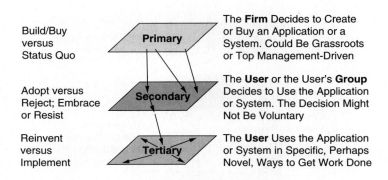

Build/Buy versus Status Quo

Primary

The **Firm** Decides to Create or Buy an Application or a System. Could Be Grassroots or Top Management-Driven

Adopt versus Reject; Embrace or Resist

Secondary

The **User** or the User's **Group** Decides to Use the Application or System. The Decision Might Not Be Voluntary

Reinvent versus Implement

Tertiary

The **User** Uses the Application or System in Specific, Perhaps Novel, Ways to Get Work Done

movement to innovate that percolates to upper management. This is called primary adoption and represents a corporate policy. Obviously, technological leaders who work at this level of adoption are concerned with policy rather than individual behavior.

At the next level of individual or secondary adoption, a person decides to use the innovation in work and begins integrating it into work procedures. At this level, workers or groups of workers act to adopt or reject a new technology, to actively embrace it or to resist it. Most of our discussion so far has been concerned with secondary innovation.

The bottom level, tertiary adoption, is the actual use or integration of the technological tool into the work. It is at this level that individuals innovate by inventing (reinventing) ways of using the tool and applying it to the job. It's an unusual tool, of course, because it keeps changing over time and is eventually replaced by yet another tool. Tertiary adoption occurs within an individual's work sphere, where workers have control over their own tasks. Perceived characteristics of the innovation and the managerial climate with respect to innovativeness and exploration are important in encouraging tertiary innovation. Active organizational learning is enhanced by this sort of innovation. It's not clear, however, that extensive tertiary adoption is always advantageous. The use of a graphics package may prompt a lot of experimentation, but that might not be desirable. The payroll department may have a lot of fun with the package but have little real reason to be trying out all of its features.

Our final distinction concerns five ways of thinking about innovation. We can measure innovation by (1) the number of times someone uses an innovation, (2) how frequently that innovation is returned to, (3) how eager (or early) the user is to adopt the application, (4) how long the user has been employing the innovation, and (5) the variety of uses to which the application has been put. Each of these measures some aspect of the extent of innovation and many of them are related. Managers want to know if a particular innovation is successful or not. Sometimes they have this desire only from curiosity but, clearly, organizations need to have reassurances that applications and systems built at significant cost are actually being used productively.

What strategies a manager resorts to will depend on the measures employed to gauge innovation through use. Using something often doesn't necessarily mean a stable or loyal adoption. An application may simply have a lot of bugs in it, requiring multiple uses to get it working correctly. Similarly, frequent use over a fixed period of time doesn't necessarily signify pleasure or productivity. Using an application over a long period of time may mean using it once in 1987 and once in 1994, indicating early adoption, too, but very little productive use. Tertiary adoption—variety and reinvention—is a healthy measure of innovation, but it may depend as much on a user's vigor and desire for challenge as on anything having to do with the innovation itself. Selecting the appropriate measure or measures for use is an important step in managing technological leadership.

A few thumbnail histories will show a variety of ways in which adopters relate to innovations. Levels of innovation and types of use are indicated in parentheses. Consider a firm whose CEO decides to put in a network of microcomputers (primary innovation) so that managers can access sales and production data at their desks using a set of applications. They are not, of course, supposed to *change* this data. Manager A may decide to experiment with the applications as part of a pilot trial (secondary innovation, early adopter) and uses the network a few times to test out its ease of use and learnability (small number of times used). After a while, Manager A is using it many times a day (frequency of use) and starts integrating it into the way she works. For example, the system can help the manager track down lost purchases or make decisions about product lines or product availability (variety of uses). Because of this novelty, the way Manager A works has been changed (tertiary innovation). This is an example of a long-term user. B, another manager, may adopt the application as a secondary innovation, but only do so after seeing many others using it (late adopter). Manager B learns to use it for only one job function— monitoring sales—and uses it infrequently for a short period of time. Manager C, another early adopter, may find that the application doesn't really provide much advantage even when he uses it frequently, perhaps because he uses it only to check on production. Once Manager C is satisfied production is humming along, interest wanes and he deadopts, or ceases to use, the innovation.

■ CITY SYMPHONY BECOMES TECHNOLOGICAL

Renata realizes that there is a cost involved in upgrading and integrating disparate systems. At the moment, the board and the president are concerned with cost, not strategic advantage, but they will be worried if they imagine that Renata will have problems getting her staff to use the system properly. Because Renata knows that this is a relatively straight-forward database application with a relatively low cost, she is willing to invest some effort into assuring the board that adoption will also be straightforward. She has gathered some information that she would like to present in a memo to the board:

- While none of her staff are computer fanatics, they all have good keyboarding abilities and recognize the value of rapid information search and reporting.
- The Symphony has just gone through a major computer development of its bookkeeping activities.
- As director, Renata is in a position of influence (by example or through authority) over her employees and volunteers. They look up to her, and she is known as an expert in her field.
- The volunteers are elderly Symphony fans with little exposure to or training in computers. Renata thinks, maybe incorrectly, that they will probably not want to learn to use the computer system.

■ All have, however, indicated that it's difficult to get work done now, constantly looking things up in paper files. What they want is to work the same way, only more effectively and with greater conviviality. No one really hates computers; in fact, they see them as the wave of the future. ■

1. Write a one-page memo reassuring the board that a new public relations information system can be adopted with relative ease.

2. As notes for an upcoming board meeting, list in detail for Renata what uses (amount, frequency, earliness, length, and variety) and adoption levels (primary, secondary, tertiary) can be expected with the new system.

The Modern Management Imperatives

Reach: Global Competition	Organizations that can effectively and quickly diffuse innovations internally are more competitive because they can react more quickly and effectively to competitive forces. Organizational learning is enhanced and may build in the means to diffuse the innovation more quickly.
Reaction: Quick Customer Feedback on Products and Services	Users need to provide feedback during the diffusion process. Most firms are aware of the need to provide "help desks" to facilitate complaints and problems. Users are eager to spot bugs and can help improve the application.
Responsiveness: Shortened Concept-to-Customer Cycle Time	There are three possible outcomes of innovation diffusion. Users may reject it, they may adopt it, or they may reinvent it. The second outcome may not be sufficient in today's competitive environment—users of applications are a major source of innovative uses of the application.
Refinement: Greater Customer Sophistication and Specificity	Sophisticated users can reinvent applications quickly and effectively. Studies have shown that users are the major source of their own training—they learn from each other and are the most credible source of information about the application. Their needs often can be satisfied within the group. Managers, on the other hand, are often ineffective at convincing users to employ systems with little apparent benefit, especially if they are hard to use.
Reconfiguration: Reengineering of Work Patterns and Structures	Because applications generally change work patterns, compatibility and transparency are important criteria. Incompatible ways of working may still be accepted if they are seen as remarkably better than before. However, a good system is hard to replace, especially if prior experience with information systems applications has been poor.
Redeployment: Reorganization and Redesign of Resources	Applications are corporate resources. Characteristics of these applications affect acceptance. While image is no longer the major stumbling block to executive acceptance it once was, users still balk when they feel their jobs are being de-skilled or they are becoming less able to manage their own work environments.
Reputation: Quality and Reliability of Product and Process	Customer satisfaction is the ultimate measure of diffusion, although forces of legitimate authority in the workplace do not make it necessary that workers be happy with applications. However, studies show that while satisfaction, usage, and performance are only loosely related, multiple experiences with low-quality applications can only build an attitude that all IS products are poor, leading to poor relations with the ISG and later problems.

Note: In this analysis, the customers are the prospective users of an application; the firm is the manager who leads the users and diffuses the application.

Summary

For managers, managing the adoption of technological innovations means encouraging others to learn to use new, technology-based tools in their work while dropping or avoiding others that are useless, expensive, or harmful. The perceived qualities of the innovation and its precursor, the attributes of the workers, who will use it, and the channels of communication that managers have access to determine how successful a manager might be. Managers attempt to influence their employees by changing attitudes towards innovations and by motivating employees to adopt innovations. A five-step process of attitude change includes becoming aware of the innovation, understanding it, yielding to it, adopting and using it, and reinventing or improving it. Innovation is dynamic in two ways. First, innovation involves identification, experimentation, control, and utensilization. Second, people differ in their receptivity to innovations. Some people, called pioneers, adopt innovations early, while others may adopt them at a later time or not at all. One's intention to use an innovation (going to) is influenced by attitudes toward the innovation (want to) and motivation to adopt (have to). Important characteristics of innovations that influence attitudes are demonstrability, relative advantage over the precursor, ease of use, compatibility with established work practices, perceived social image of using the innovation, and the ability to try out the innovation without risk. The pressure on potential adopters to accept the innovation (subjective norm) is due in part to a belief that the innovation should be used (normative belief) and the motivation to comply with that belief. Attitude and subjective norm determine the behavioral intention of the individual. Adoption can be viewed at three levels: organizational (primary), individual (secondary), and task-related (tertiary).

Discussion Questions

17.1 Because managers have a responsibility for diffusing innovations, it is likely that they will be responsible for what we've called the "precursor" to the innovation. What ethical dilemmas might managers face when trying to encourage employees to discard past innovations?

17.2 What is there about technology and information technology that poses particular challenges for managers as innovations? Which characteristics of the innovation may most strongly influence attitudes as technology becomes more complex, more information intensive, more knowledge-based?

17.3 Think of some examples of tools that are utensils and others that are not. Can you see how utensilization takes place? What happens as tools become utensils in terms of your perception of them, ease of use, differentiation from other tools, how they are marketed, and how their use is taught? What would make a given information system a utensil?

17.4 Consider any technological innovation you are familiar with or use. Describe it in terms of level of technological innovation (primary, secondary, tertiary). What measures of innovation seem appropriate or valuable in this case? Characterize it in terms of "want to," "have to," and "going to." What is the contagion profile of this particular innovation? Is it a stampede, a nonstarter, or a failure? What adopter role did you play? What influenced you in this role?

17.5 Does innovation have limits? Are all innovations good? Can innovating become so continuous that it is counterproductive? What prevents continuous innovation? What is a manager's role in managing innovation progress?

Key Terms

adoption/rejection
behavioral intention
compatibility
contagion curve
diffusion of innovation
ease of use
image
innovation roles: pioneer, laggard
levels of adoption: primary, secondary, tertiary

mature technology
motivation to comply (MC)
normative belief (NB)
out-of-role statements
personal innovation: adoptive, use, implementation
phases of growth: identification, experimentation, control, technology transfer

precursor
relative advantage
result demonstrability
saturation point
subjective impression
subjective norm
technological agenda
technological innovation
trialability

References

Ajzen, Icek, and M. Fishbein. *Understanding Attitudes and Predicting Behavior*. Englewood Cliffs, NJ: Prentice-Hall, 1980.

Davis, F. D. "User Acceptance of Computer Technology: A Comparison of Two Theoretical Models." *Management Science* 35, 8 (August 1989).

Hamer, S. "The Role of Communication in the Implementation of Technological Innovation: An Empirical Case Study." Unpublished manuscript, Faculty of Graduate Studies, University of Calgary, March 1990.

Huff, S., and M. Munro. "Information Technology Assessment and Adoption: A Field Study." *MIS Quarterly* 9, 4 (1985): 327–340.

Johnson, B. D., and R. Rice. *Managing Organizational Innovation: The Evolution from Word Processing to Office Automation Systems*. New York: Columbia University Press, 1987.

Leonard-Barton, D. "Experts As Negative Opinion Leaders in the Diffusion of Technological Innovation." *The Journal of Consumer Research* 11 (1985): 914–926.

Leonard-Barton, D., and I. Deschamps. "Managerial Influence in the Implementation of New Technology." *Management Science* 34, 10 (October 1988): 1252–1265.

Moore, G. "End User Computing and Office Automation: A Diffusion of Innovations Perspective." *INFOR* 25, 3 (1987).

Nolan, R. "Managing the Computer Resource: A Stage Hypothesis." *Communications of the ACM* 16, 7 (1973): 399–405.

Rogers, E. *Diffusion of Innovations*. New York: The Free Press, 1983.

Zaltman, G., R. Duncan, and G. Holbek. *Innovations and Organizations*. New York: John Wiley, 1973.

Zimbardo, P., E. Ebbesen, and C. Maslach. *Influencing Attitudes and Changing Behavior*. New York: McGraw-Hill, 1977.

CASE EVERGREEN LANDSCAPING AND MAINTENANCE: DIFFUSING THE INVENTORY SYSTEM

A few months after ordering and successfully installing *LIVELY*, Connie and Shawna decide to have the entire inventory system redone by outsourcing. Their goal is to construct an EIS that brings together most production and marketing functions. They perform a build versus buy analysis first and decide that, although there are several systems available, some even by mail order, their situation is unique enough to build their own. For one thing, they want to completely integrate the functions of *LIVELY* and treat live inventory specially without losing the integration and data exploration facilities. Frances and Heather join them in thinking that with the retail expansion on the horizon and the involved networking, an outsourcing exercise is good preparation for the expensive and risky efforts they will have to put forth later. Perhaps the short list of bidders will provide a good start for the longer list they need for the expansion work.

Terry and Dierdre work with Connie to produce the RFP for a project they call *EVERY*, which Heather and Shawna approve. This is sent to 18 potential bidders located in town and regionally. Of the 18 bidders, 11 respond and 5 are considered reasonably good proposals. Three bidders clearly indicate that they are available to do further work for the retail system expansion, which pleases Heather and Frances. When the outsourcing team, consisting of Terry, Connie, and Heather, finishes deliberations, it decides to go with Business Experts (BE) again. This is looking like a partnership. Not only had BE installed the original POS system, but their work with the HRIS was top-notch and their proposal for the small, but important, *EVERY* seems to give them the edge for the later retail expansion.

Important, too, is BE's emphasis on training. While *EVERY* is a very limited application relative to all of Evergreen's various businesses, in fact, live material is the unifying element in Evergreen's mission. The initial number of direct users will be small—including some retail clerks and stockers, some greenhouse assistants, and a few managers—but their cooperation is going to be critical. So training is very important. Also, BE always produces clear technical documentation because their technical writer, Susan Yan, spends a long time getting to know the clerks and assistants and their skills. The POS system, installed several years ago, is working extremely well, no doubt due to the fact that the clerical and sales staff have access to documentation that doesn't require three reads and a computer science degree.

The application is now ready and installation is set for three weeks from today. Connie is a bit concerned about the acceptability of the application, but BE has assured her that their training and documentation will do the trick. Connie has a nagging fear that something could go wrong. Yes, the clerks and assistants have to use the application—it's been integrated into the POS system and they can't avoid it—but they could surely sabotage its use. On the other hand, Connie thinks *EVERY* has absolutely irresistible characteristics that make it easy to use and far more advantageous to Evergreen than the old manual system used for plants and shrubs. Managers can now call up production, sales, marketing, inventory, and transportation information at will. Can anything go wrong?

Questions

1. Connie's concerns can be translated according to the model in Chapter 17. Looking first at attitudes, what about the situation will affect the users' attitudes? What control does Connie have over the situation?

2. Use of the system isn't voluntary, but how well the software is applied is certainly under control of the users. Describe how the concept of subjective norm works in this case and what influences there are on subjective norm. Are any of these influences under Connie's control? What can she do to ensure a high level of quality use?

3. Behavioral intention is controlled by two factors. What are they? How do they relate to ultimate use of the application? What external factors should Connie be concerned about?

4. What are the different dimensions of use that are important in the diffusion of innovation model? How will these dimensions appear to Connie? What plans should she have for rewarding the kinds and degrees of usage she thinks are valuable to Evergreen? How should she react to usage that she feels may be counterproductive?

5. What is the worst that can happen here? What are Connie's risks? Should she plan for the possibility of the worst scenario? What should she do? What *can* she do?

6. What is the best that can happen? How much credit could Connie actually take for the success of the implementation of *EVERY*? As a client, what kinds of rewards can she expect to receive?

CHAPTER EIGHTEEN

TECHNOLOGICAL LEADERSHIP

OBJECTIVES

After you have read and studied this chapter, you should be able to:

■ Discuss these technological leadership components: assessment, forecasting, and management.

■ Apply the technology life cycle to management support systems.

■ Describe the process of innovation and commercialization of technological products.

■ Demonstrate how corporate and technological strategies are related.

■ Describe how technological revolutions work and identify the technologies managers should know, watch, and respect.

Question: What does it take for a nontechnologist to become a technological leader?

Everyone always assumed that Sonny Glissman, former accountant and now financial manager for Eastwick Nursing Home, was a kind of gray figure, presiding over numbers but definitely not a charismatic leader. But Sonny has a trick or two up his not-yet-middle-aged sleeve and it involves becoming a technological leader. About ten years ago, Sonny computerized the home's accounting system. Since then, the dining room, maintenance, stores, and the pharmacy have been computerized, with personnel and other administrative functions soon to follow. Sonny's noticed, though, that while eight functions in all will have been computerized in ten years, no one in the organization is taking the lead in shepherding these changes through. Preston Bestwick is president of Health Enterprises, Inc., an umbrella firm owning Eastwick and six other nursing homes. Health Enterprises is about to acquire a chain of nursing homes, making it a major player. It would surely impress Bestwick if Sonny could somehow show that he was the technological leader who integrated all of the information systems. Even better would be for Sonny to exercise leadership for the upcoming multihome integration, based on his experience at Eastwick. Maybe there would be a better position for him in headquarters. Sonny is perplexed about where to start.

Answer: Sonny should realize that technological leadership requires three components: technology assessment, forecasting, and management. He should learn techniques of assessing technology to become more confident about systems. Technology forecasting is difficult because the future is hard to predict, but essential. Technology management requires a plan, research, development of procurement processes, continuous improvement, and understanding of obsolescence factors.

| **Figure 18–1** | COMPONENTS OF TECHNOLOGY MANAGEMENT |

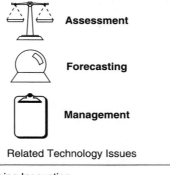

Assessment

Forecasting

Management

Related Technology Issues

Managing Innovation
Technology Life Cycle
Commercialization and Marketing
Linking Business and Technology Strategy
Managing R&D
Technology Revolutions

INTRODUCTION

This chapter discusses how to attain leadership in technological management. Technological leadership has three major components: technology assessment, technology forecasting, and technology management. The chapter also looks at some new technologies and concepts. As technologies become more commercialized, they increasingly influence our working lives and provide both competitive pressures as well as the opportunities to meet them.

This final chapter in the text brings together its major topics: strategic advantage, management support, risk management, and technological leadership. While the chapter presents technology theory in general, it provides examples from information technology to illustrate the theory. Much of this text has focused on technology transfer, the exchange or movement of technological ideas from organization to organization. A clear technology leadership goal of any manager is the transfer of technologies into an organization. The old model of business manager as a reactive recipient of technology's largesse (and trials and tribulations) is no longer valuable now that information systems technology is so widely available. As mentioned in previous chapters, leadership also implies leadership with technology while helping one's organization lead in technology.

Technological leadership also requires concern for the following issues (see Figure 18–1):

- Riding the bucking bronco of technology transfer into, within, and out of the company
- Managing (encouraging, channeling, and capitalizing on) innovation
- Understanding the technology life cycle

- Initiating and steering commercialization and marketing of technological advances both outside the firm and within it
- Linking business strategy—and the bottom line—with technology strategy
- Managing research and development (R&D) efforts
- Understanding technological revolutions and their effect on business

These issues are covered throughout the chapter. In this chapter, we use the following example from Evergreen.

It is now two years later (than it was in Chapter 17). Connie and Frances have been experiencing the expansion program that Lily pushed forward. The second retail store has been open for three months, and the systems that were installed to support retail store and contract operations have been working well. The network tying all the aspects of the retail operation together has worked fine, too. There is now talk of bringing the other aspects of the business—landscaping contracts and lawn maintenance—onto the network as quickly as possible. Connie thinks this would be a good idea, but Sid is balking at the idea. He isn't convinced that the existing way of working is actually effective. Some members of the MEC, most notably Heather Cariad, are also raising some questions. The information system works OK, but what about the business processes?

The newly organized Management Support Department (MSD), headed by Terry Bonner, seems content, if somewhat out of breath, with their work. Not only have the networking and retail systems been installed without major blowups or turnoffs, but the HRIS has been completed, too. Working with outsourcers was a learning experience for Terry and Dierdre (who has since resigned and gone to work on her own as a consultant). Good relations with Business Experts have helped to keep the network going, because they trained Boris well. Boris joined the staff full-time six months ago, and Terry thinks the group is working well together. They have even programmed some extensions to the networking package that Business Experts used as the kernel. BE has offered Evergreen a deal whereby they market the extensions as part of their service to other companies.

Meanwhile, Frances has hired a part-time trainer from a local company to teach courses in spreadsheeting and database management use for clerks and managers. While she is not 100 percent sure that it is the retail system that accounts for increased productivity, she certainly doesn't want to lose the momentum. Connie and Shawna assure her that customer service values have increased almost 30 percent according to a survey of customer opinions and employee attitudes have improved by more than 45 percent. Having information evidently makes employees feel more competent and able to handle customer queries and complaints, or so Connie reasons from her data.

Finally, Lily and the MEC are considering putting information systems on their agenda on a permanent basis. Lily suspects that IS and the increased professionalism of the MSD have something to do with how smoothly the new store opening went, but she realizes now that she has never considered *any* technology to be crucial to her business. She thinks that a long-range technology plan would be useful to have and wants to bring in some consultants to talk to an expanded MEC about this. Some of the managers at Evergreen are becoming vocal about specific technologies, many of them information-based. For instance, Candice Robbins is talking about computerized video-based security. Byron Todd has been exploring "smart" greenhouses. Peter Nunn and Nancy McNabb spoke with her at length recently about using EDI to do billing and ordering with institutional customers. Meanwhile, Shawna has evidently been besieged over the Internet with advice and products, thanks to connections set up by Pindar Gopal. She wonders what the priorities here are.

Many of the ideas in this chapter are adapted from three books. Frederick Betz's book, *Managing Technology: Competing through New Ventures, Innovation, and Corporate Research,* is a handbook for technology managers, but it also has a strong, optimistic message for technology users, like most IS end users who become stewards of the technology they request. *Reorganizing MIS: The Evolution of Business Computing in the 1990s* by Don Thompson is a strongly worded cautionary tome, filled with common sense and portent both for CIOs and users. Cyrus Gibson and Barbara Bund Jackson's book, *The Information Imperative,* focuses on how to manage the impact of IS on businesses and people. This book is a call to integrate IS (and its technology) with business. All three books take a protechnology-integration stance without necessarily striking a protechnology (of the "golly-gee-whiz" variety) pose.

We begin our discussion of technological leadership with a technology transfer.

TECHNOLOGY TRANSFER

Sometimes **technology transfer** is associated with sales, foreign aid, or teaching. The term is used loosely to encompass all of those processes by which one organization acquires technologies for its own use from another. It is also applied to campaigns to move modern technologies to third-world countries or regions from other countries. On a national scale, the goal is to raise living standards, the quality of products, literacy, productivity, and education. A hidden agenda is to use lower technology as a lever to build markets for those who produce even higher technology. Within organizations, the goal is to learn additional tactics for coping with competition. In our discussion of outsourcing, we used the term *technology transfer* to mean the acquisition of advanced information systems technologies by companies through interfirm relationships. One of the goals of outsourcing is for the receiving organization to obtain, in addition to services or software, the knowledge that goes along with the development and operation of the application or system.

Technology transfer can take a number of different routes. From the viewpoint of an organization's ISG—and the ISG is by no means the only source of information technology—there are six technology transfer routes, referred to here as types of technology transfer (Figure 18–2):

- **Technology innovation** puts new technology directly into the hands of user-managers and other end users through the process described in Chapter 17. The HRIS now brings information directly to managers like Connie and Sid whereas before they had to make requests to clerks and secretaries. Sid and Kayla like the new innovation and have helped infuse it by showing others the skills management system that came before.

- **Technology infusion** brings new technologies to users through training, information centers, and experiences from prototyping, end user development, and, less directly, through the ALC itself. Terry and Dierdre have infused technology through their efforts with the HRIS and the new

Figure 18–2 TYPES OF TECHNOLOGY TRANSFER

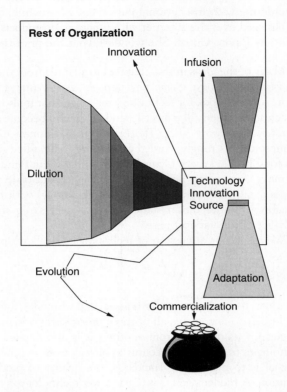

multistore retail system. Users' participation in JAD sessions and prototyping of screens have helped.

- **Technology dilution** makes technology more palatable, that is, easier to digest and use and in a more understandable form. This process makes arcane specialist tools available to all users. For example, programming is available in another guise as spreadsheets that use macros or formulas in a way that real programming would not. Database managers, network interface software, and statistics packages similarly bring the power of programming to the user's desk without the need to program. The cost of this dilution is sometimes speed and sometimes functionality. Courses in spreadsheeting and database management have helped Evergreen's managers understand some of the computer capabilities without them actually having to program computers. Instead, they just download the data using a GUI to their spreadsheet program and build their own models.

- **Technology adaptation** takes technical jobs, like programming and systems analysis, and changes their content and format so that they can be performed by nontechnical individuals (perhaps through technology dilution). Data administration, office automation administration, and user analyst positions are examples of such responsibilities. Sometimes the technology does the job directly, sometimes indirectly. Typewriters created jobs for secretaries when before only a few who had perfect handwriting could do the tasks involved. There hasn't been much technology adaptation at Evergreen. However, having data available in distributed databases has enriched the jobs of some clerks. Before, they had to find the same data over and over, but now they are considered experts at finding, retaining, and processing needed clerical and administrative information, especially through the retail system.

- **Technology evolution** is the means by which members of an ISG make a contribution to their own disciplines through academic and professional journals, conferences, and tutorials. Much of their experience becomes grist for the case study mills of business schools, and this experience, when shared, increases overall industry learning. Terry and Dierdre aren't hot-shot academic computer scientists yet, but they did host a business school team that built a case study for their information systems course on Evergreen's conversion to client-server systems during the retail expansion. This experience was an enriching one for Terry and Dierdre. It started them thinking systematically about their own activities, especially those that brought them into contact with users like Connie and Kim.

- Finally, **technology commercialization** is a means by which technologies developed in or through an ISG (or in conjunction with outsourcers) become commercial products that can be sold to others. The MSD is actually going to be bringing money into Evergreen through their arrangement with Business Experts. It's not a lot of money, but it certainly makes Heather take notice of the possibilities.

Technology transfer, even where a product is concerned, involves the movement not only of a product or system or application but also the knowledge necessary to apply the technology at the right time for the right ends and in the right way. Selecting the technologies to acquire often involves judgments on the knowledge as well as the product. Technology assessment is a complex process, as the next section points out.

TECHNOLOGY ASSESSMENT

We live in an age of rapid technological innovation and obsolescence, but we feel the pressure of users' increased sophistication and need to provide feedback that will be responded to. Thus, it is important that managers not directly charged with developing technology become aware of the need to assess new technologies as they are developed. **Technology assessment** is important for these reasons:

- To make wise investments for experimenting with technologies that have a limited life span
- To understand why and how technologies have specific effects or benefits
- To develop an understanding of the true costs of technological innovations
- To improve existing technologies and make them more appropriate, efficient, or effective for their intended tasks
- To develop new, more effective ways of working with new or existing technologies

| Table 18–1 | TECHNOLOGY ASSESSMENT METHODS |

Evaluation Research	Benchmarking
Goals	**Goals**
Measure the effectiveness of particular technologies on particular desired outcomes Rule out other causes as the source of the outcomes	Compare your product or system with the best in the marketplace Determine what you must do to have the equivalent of the best
Techniques	**Techniques**
Determine desired outcomes and measures Take baseline measurements, perhaps based on critical success factors Take measurements at appropriate points in time (0, 3 months, 6 months) and places	Determine your desired outcomes Determine the class of technology to be benchmarked Locate the best and study them Compare Note how to move the quality horizon
The differences over *time* that technology makes	**The differences between the best technology and the current one**

Even when economic investments are already sunk into a specific technology, an organization that wants to avoid the same mistakes needs to understand what specific role technology played in bringing about the noticeable conclusions.

There are several reasons why technology assessment is challenging, however:

- Nontechnical managers don't have the technology base that engineers, scientists, and computer people have.

- Prior experience may overcome current perceptions. Strong halo or guilt by association effects may have serious, and flawed, effects on current judgment regardless of what we now see.

- Many nontechnical managers actually fear technology and don't like thinking about it or dealing with it, especially if they feel they will not be able to use it without embarrassment or error.

- There are major personality differences between those who develop and market technology and those who have to use it. These differences may make it even more difficult for nontechnical managers to get the assistance they need and it certainly will not help bridge the language gap that almost always arises over new technologies.

Despite these difficulties, managers in nontechnical areas can still attempt to assess new technologies by forming strategic alliances with technical people, so long as assessment proceeds in a systematic fashion. There are two general techniques for performing technology assessment: evaluation research and benchmarking (see Table 18–1).

Evaluation research focuses on the measurement of technological effectiveness over a period of time. It attempts to answer these questions: Did (does) this technology produce those effects? Did the technology avoid producing undesired outcomes? What else aided in producing the desired effects—was the result exclusively the product of the technology or were some other conditions necessary? While evaluation research is undeniably aimed at improvement rather than blame, it is important to find out if, when undesired effects occur, the technology played some role in bringing them about.

The technique is related to many in TQM, especially benchmarking. Most total quality management efforts have to begin with what is known before improvement is attempted. Thus, as a first task, we need to determine the desired outcomes and how to measure them. Next, **baseline measures** are taken, perhaps based on critical success factors. Then, after appropriate introduction of the technology, measurements are taken at suitable intervals. Often these are three months, six months, and one or more years later. Obviously, evaluation research is neither quick nor sure. We can't actually control everything and this is not exactly like a laboratory research effort. Additionally, because evaluation occurs after installation, we have to run pilots to gather this data or obtain it from others who have used the technology before. In the absence of longitudinal, systematic evaluation research, many firms adopt a task force approach to evaluating new or emerging technologies by drawing up a list of goal-based criteria that technologies have to meet.

The goal of longitudinal research is to be able to conclude that a particular application or system did or did not have the desired effects. There are two sources for this conclusion: the application or another enabling cause. Consider Evergreen's situation. Sid and Heather aren't sure that technology really helps them. A well-designed evaluation research study could have dispelled some of the doubt. The case study conducted after the fact wasn't adequate. Impressions of *now* can easily cloud impressions of *before*. Instead, the assessment process should have begun with critical business success factors and moved to baseline measurement of those business factors. Sales, returns, employee turnover, revenue from all sources, customer confidence, and employee confidence are possible measures. They relate to the role of information in Evergreen's business and could have been measured every three months starting six months before installation of the retail system. In social systems analysis, it is often possible to remove the treatment and make measurements of how badly things fare afterwards, but few businesses can afford two losing quarters to prove that business was better with a specific suite of applications.

In a sense, this book is aimed at motivating students with the desire—and supplying them with some of the material—to create such static evaluation lists. The key always is that criteria should be related (1) to company goals and (2) to appropriate theory (see Chapters 2, 3, 10, and 17 for guidelines).

Benchmarking is a kind of technology assessment derived from total quality management (TQM) techniques. In benchmarking, an organization assesses its own operations by comparing them to another organization's. This would be an organization that excels above all others in performance in that area, generally a competitor, but not always. This is a static evaluation technique. Most firms, especially competitors, will not allow outsiders to conduct longitudinal studies of them. The differences considered here are those between systems or applications. Locating the best in class means understanding what that means—what criteria are important to the organization. In Evergreen's case, benchmarking would have meant examining a number of retail sales systems, finding the best in class, and then using the characteristics of that best one to create one that is as good or better.

These two techniques, evaluation research and benchmarking, with different origins, provide a two-dimensional assessment technique to weigh the effectiveness of information systems applications across users or organizations and across time.

Table 18–2		TECHNOLOGY FORECASTING
Limitations	Knowledge and experience with specific technologies are limited	
	Technology is discovery-driven	
	Modern technologies require team effort	
	Modern technologies require knowledge that is not accessible to nonspecialists (chemistry, physics, mathematics)	
Assumptions	Hunger for technology is huge	
	Technology implies change	
	A generation of technology is about four years	
	Software half-life is about four years	
	Technology responds to societal influences, but in unknown ways	
	Different cultures assimilate technologies differently	
Philosophical Basis	All predictions are wrong	
	Technology will not solve all problems or create all opportunities	
	There are always unintended side effects	
	Technology is X-neutral	
	Technology is good (for X)	
Problems	There is a gap between technical and nontechnical cultures	
	Technology is packaged	
	The media present distorted views of technology	
	Advertising presents distorted views of technology	
	There are true technophobes	
	We all have incomplete information on technology and forecasting	
Methods	Market-driven	
	Focus groups, GSS	
	Delphi	
	Trend analysis	
	Cultural analysis	
	Political analysis	
	Technology-driven	
	Life cycle (S curve)	
	Historical analysis	

TECHNOLOGY FORECASTING

Technology forecasting may seem like a fool's errand, given the rapid changes that always seem to take place in the technological arena (see Table 18–2). Certainly, there are limitations. Most managers don't have enough of the appropriate knowledge or experience in chemistry, physics, or mathematics. Technology forecasting is discovery-driven in that it depends on discovering technological principles that already exist and are being discovered every day. Many of these are proprietary or trade secrets. Much of the advancement we observe in technology comes from physics, chemistry, and biology labs that most managers have little access to or little desire to penetrate. While these are important barriers, they are not totally insurmountable.

In addition to these barriers are the effects of the **two-cultures gap,** first pointed out by Sir Charles Percy Snow. In his famous 1958 Reed Lecture at Cambridge, he used the example of nuclear technology. His assessment was that those who have to make regulatory decisions (in his case, parliamentarians) had almost no worthwhile knowledge of that particular technology. Those charged with creating (and, in the case of nuclear weapons, deploying) them were rather ignorant of cultural and political considerations involved in making these sorts of decisions. At the time, Snow felt this was a dangerous situation. Now, half a century later, the same kinds of things may be said of information systems and the kind of power they bring. Generally, those who create information technologies seem to care very little about the effects of this technology on society, and those who regulate (legislators, civic leaders) seem to know almost nothing about information technology. The media also seem to present one-sided views of technology. Often the news and magazine-format TV and radio programs show us the computer monster in the basement, but the accompanying advertisements want us to believe that information systems will bring a Shangri-la of entertainment and ease to our lives.

In addition, there are the usual problems that arise when marketing takes over. Packaging may hide or enhance certain characteristics. The media create and jump on technological or antitechnological bandwagons. Advertising may educate or mislead in a society in which there is always an undercurrent of **technophobia.** In general, everyone suffers from lack of information, especially about proprietary products.

In forecasting technologies, we make a number of assumptions, many of which are culturally specific and could be wrong over the long haul. For one, we assume that the hunger for technology of all sorts is huge and probably unsatiable. We also assume that technology is both a force for change as well as one of the beneficiaries of various paradigm shifts that are going on about us. A rule of thumb is that a technology lasts about four years until it is supplanted by another. As has already been mentioned, software tends to become less useful as it matures; half the benefit from using an application typically disappears after four years. Technology responds to societal changes, but we are not sure at all how this takes place—certainly, the attitude a society has toward engineering and science has something to do with it. Different cultures assimilate technologies at different rates. While we have assumed in the years since the Industrial Revolution that western European and descendant societies assimilated technologies the most rapidly, it is apparent that the societies of southeast Asia do as thorough and rapid a job.

The methods used to forecast technology examine either market-driven or technology-driven (pull versus push) forces. Techniques for uncovering market-driven forces include (1) focus groups (or GSS sessions) with users, (2) analysis of trends, (3) Delphi groups, (4) analysis of culture, and even (5) political analysis. Technology-driven trends show up in focus groups of technologists and scientists, historical analysis of technological eras and revolutions (discussed in a later section), and some theories of technology growth that are illustrated through the technology S curve (see the "Technology Life Cycle" section later).

What is known is that all predictions about technology have generally been wrong— technological pundits rank down there with economists in terms of accuracy. However, the hunger for technology everywhere is huge, and our society seems to be able to absorb high technology without a whimper, the Unabomber notwithstanding.

In addition, we need to understand that many of the problems in the world are created by and nurtured by people. Technology will never solve all the world's problems or even a major portion of them. Each technology will, in fact, bring with it a host of new "people" problems. Consider reproductive technology, the most highly visible on the political stage, as well as atomic energy, air pollution from internal combustion engines, noise pollution from airplanes, high expectations created from the "green revolution" in agriculture, the ethical battles over euthanasia and life-support systems, and, of course, the specter of job losses due to automation. Most high technologies, even the clean ones, are dirty in some stages of their manufacture and most probably support widening economic disparities in some way. No one's hands are clean when we consume the world's resources, and there are always unintended side effects, some appreciated and others not.

Another major issue, particularly of importance to environmentalists, is the idea that technology is generally neutral, whatever the scale. Some may claim that technology is *economically neutral* (a force toward neither unemployment nor employment), *ethically neutral* (a force neither toward ethical behavior nor away from it), or *socially neutral* (a force toward neither social change nor social institution), but, in fact, we know very little about these forces. Experience with cars, planes, telephones, railroads, pharmaceuticals, and atomic energy shows that statements about neutrality are probably wrong, but which way they are wrong is difficult to guess even momentarily. This leads to statements, generally unsupportable, that "Technology is good for X," where X can be anything such as the economy, business, society, or even the poor. In fact, it is not known whether these statements are true or even really testable. And it is just as clear that how society in general views these two issues dictates to some extent how much research and development goes on in universities and businesses. And this, in turn, affects forecasts of technology. The current arguments on genetic engineering, advanced-age parenting, and the technologies of abortion and life-support systems invoke the entire galaxy of ethical and economic quandaries and perplexities that our public and private political universes are filled with.

At Evergreen, most players in the upgrading have forecast little immediate change in technology and have implemented a system based on today's star performers: client-server, distributed databases, microcomputer servers, and broadband LANs. By using outsourcers, whose business depends on being able to predict, or at least keep up with, technology, Evergreen has bought, at some price, an insurance policy. As technology changes, Evergreen can return to Business Experts for updating its applications.

TECHNOLOGY MANAGEMENT

One response to technology is to plan and regularize. **Technology management** (see Figure 18–3) is one of several management-appropriate responses. Technology management incorporates technology assessment and forecasting as well as a technology plan that is an integral part of a firm's strategic plan (remember that strategic advantage is easy to gain technologically but relatively hard to sustain). The cycle runs as follows:

- *Plan:* Develop the technology plan in conjunction with strategic planners.
- *Research:* Find out what is needed through technology forecasting and assessment.
- *Procure/Develop:* Find out what's available or buildable, determine the techniques for acquiring the technology, and lay the groundwork for financing (remember technology's short half-life).
- *Improve:* Develop techniques for continuous monitoring and improvement of technologically driven processes. The technology needs to be improved in consonance with the technology plan. (Few firms do this, by the way.)
- *Control:* Plan for obsolescence of the technology, keep training as an integral part of the plan, and watch out for culture clashes.

| Figure 18–3 | THE TECHNOLOGY MANAGEMENT PROCESS |

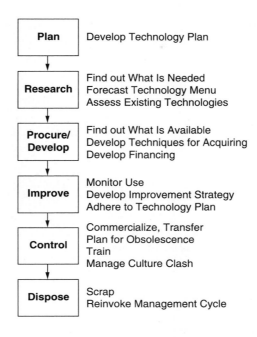

> **Plan** — Develop Technology Plan
>
> **Research** — Find out What Is Needed / Forecast Technology Menu / Assess Existing Technologies
>
> **Procure/ Develop** — Find out What Is Available / Develop Techniques for Acquiring / Develop Financing
>
> **Improve** — Monitor Use / Develop Improvement Strategy / Adhere to Technology Plan
>
> **Control** — Commercialize, Transfer / Plan for Obsolescence / Train / Manage Culture Clash
>
> **Dispose** — Scrap / Reinvoke Management Cycle

- *Dispose/Renew:* Scrapping, salvaging, and rebuilding high-tech systems is a way of life. Those who procure may also be those who discard.

General advice for managing technology includes a continuous reading or environmental scanning process to stay alert (as all businesses are learning systems). Firms should develop standardized demonstration procedures that vendors and potential suppliers of technological innovations have to pass before being considered. Finally, managers will find it profitable to invest time and effort in refining the RFP/RFQ/outsourcing process to make sure that technologies acquired or built are the best.

For example, Lily's initiative to bring information systems technology to the MEC is a first step in technology management. Requests and musing by Candice, Byron, Peter, and Nancy tell her that the amount of technology that Evergreen will have to contend with is growing. Having mostly stumbled through the procurement of the retail system and having been lucky in selecting Business Experts as outsourcers for their network services, Lily doesn't want to chance fate again. The systems will get old quickly and technologies for which she doesn't have a technical group to tend (such as "smart" greenhouses) are going to plague her purse later on without a plan.

THE TECHNOLOGY LIFE CYCLE

The concept of the **technology life cycle** (Figure 18–4) according to Ford and Ryan is important in technology management. As with all the life cycles discussed in this book,

| Figure 18–4 | THE TECHNOLOGY LIFE CYCLE |

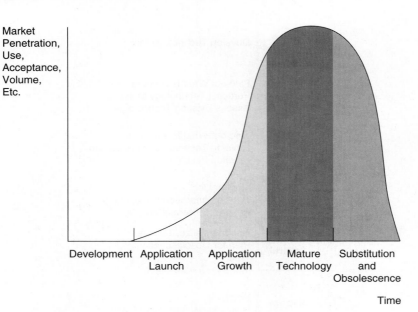

the technology life cycle demonstrates the familiar S curve as technology is developed and applications of it are launched. We saw this in Chapter 12 with the ALC, but now we are looking beyond development to acceptance and use. After applications are launched, their use usually increases over time. This use can be likened to market penetration, even when the market doesn't buy systems. A mature technology is thoroughly diffused—transferred to those willing or forced to use it. Ways of working with the application are developed and taught to each wave of new workers, and perhaps some folklore is created about the application. Some major applications may develop newsletters or user groups and may become minor industries in their own right. For example, some major products such as word processors and database managers obviously meet this criterion. Even in small organizations, applications can become institutions, especially if the firm depends on them or has had a traumatic time creating and installing them.

Regardless of the application used, after a while other newer, and presumably better, technologies are substituted for this one and it becomes obsolete. Usage drops, withers, or disappears completely.

While Ford and Ryan used this model to refer to entire industries (such as the automobile), our use of a single application or suite of applications is appropriate here. In fact, a related concept is called the product life cycle. Each application is an industry itself, providing a unique service to a set of consumers. This set of consumers may be permanent and voluntary or pressed into service momentarily. An ISG may have to resell the application continually either to the same set of users, a rotating group, or a different set with a different identity.

Managers, especially clients and stewards of applications, need to recognize the characteristic signs of technology/product life cycle stages. Few managers can ignore a

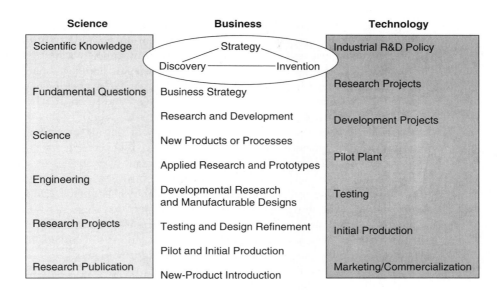

Figure 18–5 MANAGING INNOVATION

rising tide of complaints that an application is too slow, makes errors, doesn't handle new codes, or is incompatible with data coming from newer, related applications. In fact, *managers need to plan for obsolescence* because one certainty of life cycles is their end. Few applications last for more than a decade. The marketplace for software is a stern master requiring new versions every other year and new releases every year. Internally, ISGs could probably get away with an install-and-forget attitude if the technology didn't change so rapidly. Trends such as BPR or new architectures such as client-server almost guarantee obsolescence of even the most well-engineered applications. With obsolescence comes a replacement, an innovation. Managing innovations is a crucial part of technological leadership, because not all innovations come from the ISG—in fact, a significant proportion originate with users, a generally unheralded source of new ideas.

MANAGING INNOVATION

Betz makes a strong case that science, business, and technology are interrelated, and that understanding this interrelationship is one of the keys to business success. That triangle— represented by research, management, and engineering (Figure 18–5)—is crucial to the firm's competitive posture in order to reduce the risk of innovating for management support.

Science, through research, discovers principles and increases scientific knowledge. Technology, in the form, but not exclusive, of engineering (including computer engineering and information systems groups), applies that knowledge tempered by industrial research and development policies in application research and development projects to harness the principles. Each component runs through a parallel path toward culminating experiences. While scientific publication may not seem of much interest to businesses, this is the marketplace for scientific ideas, as close to commercialization as science ever becomes. Applied science always aims for practical ends, one of which—commercialization—is of interest to us in the next section. Businesses are interested both in new processes (which software represents) that help deliver existing products as well as in new products (which may have a strong technology component).

One of the major advantages of information technology is that users can make a major contribution to application through reinvention. By finding out that the published procedures manual really doesn't work, users can invent new ways to apply software to their jobs. Because users now participate in prototyping and developing manufacturable designs in software, their ideas are essential and profitable in creating new applications. In fact, the "Business" column in Figure 18–5 is often handled entirely by users. They may discover that their new ways of working are not only superior to the old ways but are so much better that the firm could sell the software outside or provide outsourcing to competitors or partners. Firms such as Sears have discovered that their credit card payment system could also be used as the basis of a financial management system that others could use. It also enabled Sears to run leasing companies (especially cars) more easily.

Managing the innovation process requires the skills discussed in Chapter 17. The reason for repeating them here is to remind readers that there needs to be cooperation among the three major disciplines: business, science, and technology. Business contributes strategic ideas, science discovers principles, and the technological experts, represented by the ISG, contribute their inventions (applications).

Evergreen isn't a research lab, but its relationships with the agricultural college, the university, and the biotech firm bring Lily and her management team into direct contact with scientists who want to understand basic phenomena and engineers who want to commercialize processes based on them. Lily's original interest was purely self-serving: weed control and disease resistance for greater profit. Now she sees that there are some commercial possibilities as well, and managing this sort of innovation will be one kind of challenge. Noting that Byron is interested in state-of-the-art "smart" greenhouses and that Peter and Nancy are interested in applying EDI to billing reminds her of how innovative her own employees are. Surely Evergreen will learn a lot from them that will be valuable. Can Lily do something to harness this creativity?

COMMERCIALIZATION AND MARKETING OF TECHNOLOGY AND IDEAS

Figure 18–6 illustrates the by-now-familiar, cost-versus-benefit curve that all products experience, only here it is expressed in terms of profits or sales. We could also label the vertical axis as "Use" or "Diffusion." Notice that all products experience R&D costs up front. High technology is characterized by the amount of knowledge necessary to get an idea into production. This knowledge costs money because it is commonly based on research and development. The higher the technology, the greater the proportion of up-front R&D costs and the longer the break-even time. Because of these factors, the number of "hits" is probably a lot smaller the higher the technology, because once the capital is gone, there are no funds left for commercialization. Sales growth falls before sales decline. In many IS outsourcing firms, high-tech products have life spans of six months or less. Some telecommunications products (particularly chips) often aren't even patented because the patenting process takes longer than the life cycle.

Most companies do not commercialize every, or even a tiny proportion, of ISG-developed or outsourced application. On the contrary, the tradition has been that *every-*

| Figure 18–6 | COMMERCIALIZATION AND MARKETING OF TECHNOLOGY |

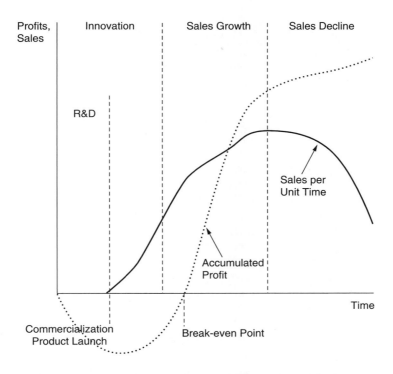

thing is a loss leader. That is, all products are free to users in order to convince them to adopt more software. Obviously, this trend cannot continue in an era of cost consciousness, but the marketing metaphor is quite apt here. Products, such as applications, need to be commercialized internally and treated as part of the value-added costs of business.

The commercialization of the networking extensions to retail situations by Business Experts was a small step toward general commercialization of technological innovations at Evergreen. Terry and Shawna aren't really set up to do this on a large scale, but since Evergreen has professionalized its MSD, Shawna finds that Connie is not the only person with marketing prowess. When Shawna retires, Lily is going to find that Evergreen is a much different kind of company when it comes to technology.

LINKING CORPORATE AND TECHNOLOGY STRATEGIES

Another aspect of technological leadership is linking corporate and technology strategies. In the best of all possible worlds, these two would automatically be linked—the technology strategy would derive naturally from the corporate strategic plan. However, because the role of technology in corporate strategy is murky at best, there is no natural niche for technological planning in the corporate strategy.

Part of the reason for this is general lack of knowledge about technology at the highest levels of organizations. Attempts to fit technology into a strategic plan by adding

| Figure 18–7 | LINKING CORPORATE AND TECHNOLOGY STRATEGIES |

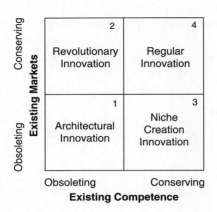

Source: W. Abernathy and K. Clark, "Mapping the Winds of Creative Destruction," *Research Policy* 14, 1 (1985): 2–22.

technology as another line item are, however, doomed to failure precisely because technology should not be forced to fit in. Instead, firms should note that technologies play two roles for firms:

- As *processes:* Process technologies improve an organization's functioning by making production, support, or administration more effective or efficient.
- As *products:* Product technology provides customers with increased value for their money or with a special product they want or need.

Both roles are covered in a general model from Abernathy and Clark (cited in Betz). Although they speak of innovations, we are concerned only with information technological innovations. In the model shown in Figure 18–7, two dimensions are key. First, innovations can either make obsolete or reinforce existing competences (i.e., processes) in a firm. Second, they may either make obsolete or reinforce existing market relationships (i.e., customers and products, channels of distribution). Abernathy and Clark derive four types of innovations:

Those that obsolete competence by creating new and better processes:

1. Obsoleting markets (new relationships): architectural innovations

2. Conserving markets (same relationships): revolutionary innovations

Those that conserve competence by improving existing processes:

3. Obsoleting markets (new relationships): niche creation innovation

4. Conserving markets (same relationships): regular innovation

Clearly, only those innovations in Class 4 support the status quo with improvements. Technology in this class cannot be considered strategic and will not be found in a strategic plan. Firms that use technology to cut costs or make quantum improvements in production quality will not find that technology planning has any impact on strategic planning except indirectly through the additional availability of funding.

Technology in Classes 2 and 3 is less conservative. In Class 2, processes are dramatically changed, but the customer relationships remain untransformed. In this case, revolutionary innovations may come under scrutiny at the time of strategic planning because of large expenses on process technology. For example, moving from a rolling to a floating technology for plate glass creation was a revolutionary step for Pittsburgh Plate Glass that required massive retooling.

Those that can be used as new relationships with customers (Class 3) created by existing processes are seen as niche creators. This is a common strategy in organizations. Those following this plan will need to include technology plans only to the extent that marketing needs to be informed. Nothing in production and service will change. It is likely that the product is similar to an existing technologically based product but sold to different customers or in a different way. Consider what repackaging an existing product to sell to another market may require in the way of technology. The packaging process may have to be changed a small degree, but the major change will involve only salespeople. A good example is the need to create packaging in different languages for different markets. The technological change is minor, and the real effort is in having to sell to the new market in a different language.

Finally, sometimes old processes are changed at the same time as new products are created or new relationships with customers begin. In these cases, the strategic plan *must* include technology because of the great expense, large change in production mode and management style, and potentially great change in corporate culture. Changing to computer-aided design/computer-aided manufacturing (CAD/CAM) or computer-integrated manufacturing (CIM) from manual production systems in order to produce a new product line is a major adjustment for most organizations—a radical transformation in the organization's architecture.

By understanding both product and process technologies, managers can gain useful knowledge for planning their own competitive strategies. Because nothing in the previous discussion depends on a corporation, it can apply equally to a division, a department, a work group, or even person work space.

Evergreen's marketing department, now led by Connie, is going to be in several new businesses, some of them very short lived, and many linked intimately with information systems technologies as well as others. Lily is certain that Evergreen's products and processes are going to change under the influences of Evergreen's new competitive position as market leader in landscaping and gardening research and development. The changes from a store to a source and from a service center to a server are going to mean major changes for Lily's business in the next few years. Most of these changes are technology-driven in response to customer and competitive pressures as well as changing personnel. The only word for this is *revolution*.

TECHNOLOGICAL REVOLUTION

Betz points out that the models we use to describe the relationship between business, science, and technology are often couched in terms of a few **technological revolutions.** Biotechnology is one example; the transistor and the industries it spawned form another. Most technologies do not turn out to be revolutionary in that grand sense, but all technologies transform and all technologies are products of similar, revolutionary processes that may not appear all that revolutionary while they are undergoing the revolution.

Technological leaders recognize that technology is the product of a lengthy and risky process that begins when scientists pose basic universal questions. The desire to answer these questions—such as "What makes life work chemically?" or "How do atoms change electrical state?"—requires instrumentation to observe and measure. Science is risky and expensive, but eventually the holes in the theories are filled in by rigorous and replicable experiments. Eventually a theory is created with enough credence and supporters to convince businesspeople to put money behind technologists' inventions. The science then supports the bright ideas which are often developed into systems to support managers. These applications of scientific knowledge (applied science) are then turned into business opportunities or expansion of existing businesses.

The history of computing is a good example of this process. The mechanics of computation were established in the nineteenth century, based on simple tools such as the abacus and adding machine. There is even a precedent for programming in the Jacquard loom of the eighteenth century, in which coded cards and tape directed the loom to weave specific threads in specific ways. But modern computing has its origins in higher mathematics of the early twentieth century and computing theories developed by Kurt Gödel and Alan Turing, among others. They attempted to solve arcane mathematical problems, with little thought about management applications. With the mathematics firmly in place, it was only a question of time before the burgeoning field of electronics engineering was married to the theory of computation. By the late 1930s, spurred by wartime pressures, several universities and defense agencies in the United States, Canada, and Great Britain developed prototype electrical and electronic computers. Bit by bit, pieces of the puzzle were filled in. John von Neumann contributed the idea of the stored program computer, and from telephone technology, the relay was imported to be used as a data storage device, and later the vacuum tube. As early as the first decade of the twentieth century, television technology had already been integrated into computation, but, curiously, as a storage device rather than as a display. Stored program computers appeared in research labs by the mid-1940s and commercialization began, on a very small scale, immediately thereafter, led by a company called Sperry Rand, later known as Univac (after the machine it manufactured), and now known as Unisys. But it took ten years until computers moved from the laboratory, where they were used for scientific applications, to business. The key was the development of programming as a job using a programming language (COBOL—COmmon Business Oriented Language) to create a cadre of people who could create software for a living. Until then, most "programmers" were the engineers who used the computer. Ultimately, a firm better known for marketing than for research—International Business Machines Corporation—took the lead.

To this date, new technological ideas come from research laboratories in industry and academia. The transistor came from Bell Labs in the late 1940s, but wasn't used in computers until the late 1950s. Many new ideas in information technology come from computer scientists who work on abstract problems. Structured programming, for example, revolutionized the way programmers work and, according to most software managers, increased productivity. The techniques involved are based on a little recognized paper published in the 1960s on software theory that was totally unrelated to the activity of programming. Similarly, techniques of object-oriented programming and database management all arose from the pursuit of abstract research questions. Applied research takes these principles and creates applications.

With this in mind, let's turn our attention now to the frontier that individual managers have to face, the frontier of their own knowledge.

NEW TECHNOLOGIES TO KNOW, WATCH, AND RESPECT

Readers of this text are not among the first generation of newly trained managers to have their lives changed by technology. This has been going on for 30 years with computers and 5,000 years in general. However, they will find their working lives influenced by information technology in ways undreamt of by the previous generation of management trainees. The kinds of technologies that are appearing in retail shops today were developed in the past five to ten years and commercialized only in the most recent three or four. What we know about multimedia, client-server architecture, executive-level information systems, group support systems, and office information systems has come about through a very narrow window of experience. Most of these technologies will hardly have been stressed when they are replaced by yet others.

Consider database management systems. They were first developed in the 1960s in rudimentary form and have been available as commercial products since the late 1960s. Yet it is only in the past ten years that massive, integrated databases have been accessible to managers. Only in the past five years have nontechnological managers used these systems extensively, 20 years after so-called "management information systems" were supposed to have revolutionized management! We are not speaking here of the clerks who access large databases for transaction purposes, such as airlines reservations systems, but of managers who use information to make business decisions unrelated to specific transactions.

Technological leaders, such as today's newly appointed managers, should be aware of three kinds of technologies that are going to play a major part in their working lives over the next 10 or 20 years (see Table 18–3):

- Technologies to *know:* These are technologies (mostly hybrid classes of management support systems or the technologies that make them possible) that managers should become familiar with as users. It would also help to understand the bases on which they function. What is a client? A server? How do relational databases work? What is an index? A relation? What forms of multimedia are compatible with today's computers? What is drill-down? How do GUIs work? What are the forms of GSS that are available on microcomputers? How are the various technologies of the office coming together? Managers need to know these technologies because they will be buying or renting them and using them every day to support their work.

- Technologies to *watch:* These will be technologies to know in five or ten years. As today's business students graduate, these systems, standards, and methods will reach the marketplace. While most of them (except open systems) are not yet available to business users at reasonable prices, choices to go with applications built around them will become strategic decisions. Pen-based computing creates real opportunities, along with radio-based LANs, for mobile computing and very small handheld or pocket devices. EDI is only one of an exploding world of interorganizational systems that our economy of fiercely competitive alliances will be spawning before the next century. Hypermedia, currently limited by hardware and input barriers, will become the preferred way to navigate through a real-time integrated communications network of data and services that today's merger mania in telecoms is creating. Virtual presence, already available in laboratories, blends TV and sound to create realistic meeting settings in which everyone feels a sense of place. Voice input, now just emerging from the laboratory,

Table 18–3	INFORMATION TECHNOLOGIES TO KNOW, WATCH, AND RESPECT

Technologies to Know	Technologies to Watch	Technologies to Respect
Client-Server Linking places, distributing services, increasing knowledge	**Pen-Based Computing** Creates opportunities for real portable computing with handwriting input	**UNIX** The unifying force in computer science that brings systems together
Database Linking disciplines, enhancing creativity, raising awareness and knowledge	**Open Systems** Creates new networks and markets for products, ISDN, EDI	**Object Orientation** The latest, most efficient way to create applications and systems
Multimedia Increasing range of knowledge, lowering concept-to-customer time, imaging, visualization	**Hypermedia** Allows new modes of data search and diffusion, especially for teaching	**Internet** The emerging information and business marketplace
Executive Support Systems Linking organizations, increasing executive productivity and presence	**Real-Time Telecoms** Blends computers, TV, telephone, new kinds of markets, mobility	**Intelligent Agents** The way that business will be conducted in coming years
Group Support Systems Linking people, enhancing creativity, testing new organizations	**Virtual Presence** Creates new kinds of interaction and involvement, new markets, new opportunities for sales/alignments	**End-User CASE Tools for the ALC** The emerging and preferred way to create and manage in the information-centered environment
Office Information Systems Enhancing office productivity, linking functions together	**Voice Input** Provides truly mobile, potentially highly secure, easy computing	**Parallel Processing** Thousands of tasks running simultaneously, massive model processing, multiple servers

will remove the typing restriction from the input and control side of applications, making GUIs seem old-fashioned by the year 2005.

■ Technologies to *respect:* A number of technologies are available in laboratories and in ISGs that will remain opaque to nontechnical managers but that will create the new world of computing in the closing years of this century. Managers cannot be expected to understand them without a great deal of training, but they can cast a caring eye toward them and respect technicians' appreciation of them. UNIX is the unifying agent in operating systems. Moving toward client-server architectures means abandoning proprietary mainframe operating systems and adopting a shared, common way of expressing control over information resources. Although UNIX is at least four generations old, it is also the most modern of the operating systems and its latest incarnations will run most of the computer systems available to managers. Managers will see GUIs and talk to them, but UNIX sits behind and runs things. Object orientation is the way applications will soon be built by technicians and users, unless something better comes along. BASIC and COBOL will be around for a long time, but building with objects is better for everyone. In fact, object-oriented COBOL is now a reality. The Internet, now a pastiche of processors and programs, will mature, and even if you don't understand how World Wide Web and FTP work, you'll be using them, although through a GUI like *Mosaic*, which launches intelligent agents to do your bidding as they swim through the Internet. Meanwhile, CASE tools for users, already starting to appear, will be the preferred way of gathering requirements and constructing prototypes for managers. One reason why this will occur will be the massive increase in computing power available through parallel processing, the harnessing of hundreds or thousands of microprocessors into megacomputers.

The barriers to management support systems, the real risk factors, remain personal and political. Our available, useful knowledge of how managers use the information they want is severely limited and will continue to be so. Revolution after revolution in technology makes technologies obsolete before academics can study them. They are often obsolete even before the managers themselves can decide how they can use the technologies. Only this remains certain: The future will belong to those who can learn, harness, and ride these technological waves (including, but not limited to, information technology).

◼ EASTWICK NURSING HOME MOVES TO THE FOREFRONT

Sonny has done some homework. It seems that the changes to accounting were somewhat proactive (he had moved to Eastwick from a medical supply firm that was already computerized and wanted to work in a similar environment). However, other technological moves were responses to problems. The dining room was computerized when it was discovered that food was spoiling and residents complained about lack of response to menu change requests. Other moves were forced on Eastwick. The computerization of the pharmacy came about because of the way the home's pharmacist, who operates the pharmacy remotely from her store, decided to change operations. The home seems to follow trends, but can't anticipate them, and when technology arrives it's a hodge-podge of machines, most of which can't talk to one another. Most systems are obsolete and none have been demonstrated to be essential or productive. No one on staff seems to understand the machines (except Sonny, of course) and not a few seem scared of them. Sonny phoned Health Enterprises and learned that Bestwick is content to have all of his acquisitions run independently. Bestwick is making enough money and so has no plans to integrate anything. Sonny thinks integration would be a money saver, and that there has *got* to be a lot of waste in duplication and poor decision making. This should impress Bestwick. The key will be to convince Bestwick that his integration plan in a framework of technological leadership would be a winner. ◼

1. What is the evidence of lack of technological leadership at Eastwick? At Health Enterprises? What are the costs of this lack of leadership?

2. What process would you recommend to Sonny *before* he tries to convince Bestwick to integrate? How can Sonny demonstrate technological leadership *now*?

3. What program of technology management would you recommend Sonny pursue at Eastwick? What should follow at Health Enterprises? Can Sonny succeed?

The Modern Management Imperatives

Reach: Global Competition	Technological leadership is important because the latest technology is available worldwide. Assessing technologies from around the world and acquiring them from diverse sources will require skills that managers are not normally trained to have. A technology plan is essential, even if predicting specific technologies and their impacts is difficult.
Reaction: Quick Customer Feedback on Products and Services	Pressures from customers will motivate organizations to acquire technologies that competitors have as well as develop their own. Some of these technologies will be commercially viable. This will lead to significant interorganizational cooperation and new alliances based on technology marketing and use.
Responsiveness: Shortened Concept-to-Customer Cycle Time	Most technologies have long development times relative to their commercial life spans. While IS applications have half-lives of four years or more, the underlying technologies may have even shorter useful life spans, requiring frequent reworking and updating. Outsourcers will be breathless trying to keep up and technology managers will be nervously eyeing the research labs. Recognizing the phases of the technology life cycle will be important in staying on top of trends.
Refinement: Greater Customer Sophistication and Specificity	Keeping innovation levels high both in ISGs and among users is a key challenge to managers who want to be technological leaders. Leaders of the pack will encounter tough customer requirements that employees should be able to counter with ideas.
Reconfiguration: Reengineering of Work Patterns and Structures	Corporate and technology strategies must take into account the immense effects that technology has on processes and products. Architectural technological innovations can transform an organization. Even regular innovations, coupled with business process reengineering, can change a firm's metabolism.
Redeployment: Reorganization and Redesign of Resources	Technological resources are becoming a major agenda item in companies' strategic plans, and the position of technology manager is increasingly a strategic one. Information systems technology is a major component of every firm's technology strategy.
Reputation: Quality and Reliability of Product and Process	Techniques from TQM (such as benchmarking) play an important role in technology management. Quality (customer satisfaction) is the outcome of improved processes and products. Managers who are technological leaders strive to meet quality goals.

Summary

Becoming a technological leader involves two things: using technology to lead and leading an organization that is developing new technology or new uses for existing technology. Managers are responsible for transferring technologies into their areas of authority. Technology transfer includes infusion, innovation, dilution, adaptation, evolution, and commercialization. Technological leadership has three components: assessment, forecasting, and management. Assessment involves evaluating research over time, as well as benchmarking, a technique borrowed from total quality management. Technology forecasting is either market driven (based on consumer needs and desires) or technology driven (based on technology life cycles and historical trends). Technology management involves planning, research, procurement and development, improvement, administration, disposal, and renewal. Key to technology management is the technology life cycle of development, launch, maturity, and obsolescence.

An important relationship exists among science, technology, and businesses in which technologies move out of the lab and into commercialization. As innovations, technologies may affect both organizational competence (by improving or replacing processes) and markets (by improving or creating new relationships). Sometimes technological innovations radically change how business is conducted. Technologies that are relatively mature but important to businesses include client-server, database, multimedia, executive support systems, group support systems and office information systems. Technologies that may someday become viewed as revolutionary include pen-based computing, open systems, hypermedia, real-time telecommunications, virtual presence, and voice input. Finally, technologies that presently are emerging include UNIX, object-orientation, the Internet, intelligent agents, end user CASE tools, and parallel processing.

Discussion Questions

18.1 If technology forecasting is so hard, why bother doing it? What makes it imperative that managers at least make intelligent guesses about future (information) technologies? Have you been accurate in forecasting technologies, including information technologies? What makes your intuition right or wrong?

18.2 What aspects of the process of technology management are hardest for nontechnical managers?

18.3 Identify technologies in each of the phases of Betz's technology life cycle (development, launch, growth, maturation, substitution/obsolescence). What forces drive technologies through these phases? Do technologies compete? If so, how? Who or what causes this competition?

18.4 As a nontechnical manager, how would you best come to understand and take advantage of the relationship among science, technology, and business?

Key Terms

baseline measurement	technology commercialization	technology life cycle
benchmarking	technology dilution	technology management
evaluation research	technology evolution	technology transfer
technological revolution	technology forecasting	technophobia
technology adaptation	technology infusion	two-cultures gap
technology assessment	technology innovation	

References

Abernathy, W. *The Productivity Dilemma*. Baltimore: Johns Hopkins University Press, 1978.

Abernathy, W., and K. Clark. "Mapping the Winds of Creative Destruction." *Research Policy* 14, 1 (1985): 2–22.

Betz, F. *Managing Technology: Competing through New Ventures, Innovation, and Corporate Research*. Englewood Cliffs, NJ: Prentice-Hall, 1987.

Ford, D., and C. Ryan. "Taking Technology to Market." *Harvard Business Review* (March–April 1981): 117–126.

Gibson, C., and B. Bund Jackson. *The Information Imperative*. New York: Free Press, 1987.

Haeffner, E. "Critical Activities of the Innovation Process." In B. A. Vedin, ed., *Current Innovation*, 129–144. Stockholm: Almqvist & Wiksell, 1980.

Licker, P. *Fundamentals of Systems Analysis with Application Design*. Boston: Boyd & Fraser, 1987.

———. *The Management of Technology and Innovation*. Calgary: The University of Calgary, 1989.

———. *Technology Transfer: Global, National, Corporate*. Calgary: The University of Calgary, 1990.

Thompson, D. *Reorganizing MIS: The Evolution of Business Computing in the 1990s*. Carmel, IN: SAMS, 1992.

EVERGREEN LANDSCAPING AND MAINTENANCE: CONNIE SOMERSET, TECHNOLOGICAL LEADER

In the past year, Connie has moved from sales manager to vice president of marketing at Evergreen with Shawna's retirement. Tulley Fox's position has been eliminated, as purchasing has been completely outsourced. A strategic alliance has been struck with a biotech firm. Other such alliances include Business Experts and a truck leasing firm. The leasing firm has been operating the transportation pool after Bill Porter's sudden departure following an argument with Heather over control of expenses at the second retail store. Connie has been handling the diffusion of many new applications in the retail sector. Terry's recent promotion to director of MSD and the expansion of the group to handle all high technology seem to have brought Evergreen into a new era in its orientation toward technology. A third of a century after Lucien Doucette left the woods to go into the tree business, Evergreen has been reengineered into a firm that runs on information.

Leading this movement has been Connie Somerset. Unafraid of technology, Connie has always experimented with her own systems and has maintained very good relations with the small, but growing, MSD. Despite the professionalization and the intense and close IS planning, Connie still can phone Terry and get an answer to a question quickly. She also continues to read about the use of information technology in the businesses that Evergreen pursues: retail gardening, landscaping, and lawn care. Connie now has heavy responsibilities running an organization that is so diversified, but she continues to push the MEC toward reexamination of existing technology and business systems (not all of them involved with computers). Connie considers herself a manager who is a technical leader.

Questions

1. What kinds of technology transfer have occurred at Evergreen over the course of the 18 minicases in this text? What has Connie's role been in them? Lily's? Terry's?

2. Where has technology assessment played a key role in Evergreen's recent history? Is this role likely to diminish? Who needs to know what in order for Evergreen to continue to purchase, develop, and use appropriate technology in the future?

3. What should Connie know about technology forecasting that will be of help to a firm like Evergreen, heavily invested in what is surely yesterday's (i.e., what today will look like tomorrow) technology?

4. What kinds of cultural gaps will Connie have to bridge with regard to technology at Evergreen? How has she managed to succeed so far? Will those tactics and skills suffice for the future in her new position?

5. As technology makes its way to a permanent place on Evergreen's MEC agenda, how can the IS plan be expanded into a technology plan? What components should be whose responsibilities?

6. What advice can you give Lily, Connie, and Frances about managing innovation at Evergreen? What characteristics of this firm will make this a difficult task? What will make it easy? Why is managing innovation important for Evergreen in its competitive environment?

7. What kinds of technologies is Evergreen sensitive to? Would revolutions in these technologies make a great immediate difference to Evergreen? A great long-term difference? Is it possible for a small firm like Evergreen to lose its way in the face of these revolutions?

8. Examine the list of technologies to know, watch, and respect. Which of these will be important to Evergreen? How would you propose to Terry and Lily that Evergreen know, watch, and respect them? Are there risks? Are there strategic benefits? Are there opportunities for others at Evergreen to become technological leaders?

*[Page numbers indicate the first appearance of the term in the textbook in **bold** type]*

Abstracting: Merging information in a way that shows the underlying unifying concepts or ideas. *See* information overload (p. 179).

Action loop: The interaction (action/reaction) of a simple system with its environment (p. 51).

Administrative processes: Organizational processes that manage or account for the resources that the basic processes require (p. 57).

Adoption/rejection: Accepting a technological innovation or refusing to accept it into one's work methods and environment (p. 464).

Advance training: An improvement over dysfunctional coping strategies that trains users on systems before they are actually installed by focusing on the user interface (p. 379).

Alliance: Attaining strategic advantage by joining with competitors, suppliers or buyers to gain efficiencies through nonduplication or to create effective or secure business relationships (p. 81).

Allocational management model: A model of management that sees managers as controllers or owners of organizational resources (money, people, and physical objects) (p. 30).

Alternatives: A component of being informed; the number of different ways in which a situation can be described accurately (p. 35).

Anonymity: A feature of some groupware that allows an individual to feel unidentified and, hence, free from fear of repercussions, thus allowing the person to be more creative (p. 228).

Answer network: A network of experts who can be called on to answer questions as they come up (p. 287).

Appliance: An item of technology that can be applied to whatever aspect of a problem deemed appropriate by the user (p. 312).

Application: The use of a system to meet specific goals over a period of time by an individual or a group. Often extended to mean the particular system itself (including the procedures for using the system) (p. 307); or a business process which is heavily information-driven (and, consequently, requires an information system) (p. 103).

Application client role: Those roles that pertain specifically to the clients of an application (p. 406).

Application complexity: Internal complexity of an application and how thoroughly and critically it links to other applications (p. 381).

Application developer role: Those roles that pertain specifically to the developers of an application (p. 412).

Application interface: That aspect of an application the user sees and interacts with (p. 317).

Application Life Cycle (ALC): A four-step process, based on the problem-solving life cycle, for creating information system applications; this includes systems analysis, system design, system implementation, and system installation/user/ maintenance (p. 312).

Application maturity: The stage of use of an application (initiation, growth, or full maturity) generally related to how well an organization is familiar with and competent in the use of an application (p. 448).

Application role: Roles played by people with respect to applications. *See* client, developer, stakeholder, and user (p. 401).

Application stakeholder role: Those roles that pertain specifically to stakeholders of an application (p. 409).

Application user role: Those roles that pertain specifically to those who interact directly with software applications. *See also* direct user (p. 402).

Attention-comprehension-yielding model: A three-step model of persuasion that describes how individuals are moved to action by first becoming aware of the possibility of new action, understanding the value of the action, and then accepting the value of the action; specifically used here when the action refers to the results of using an application (p. 407).

Attenuation: The gradual disappearance of a signal over time and distance (p. 126).

Attribute: A characteristic of an event or object that serves to distinguish it from others in the same class of events or objects (p. 107).

Authority: The value that management adds by creating new information or procedures to handle crises and commanding others to carry out nonstandard procedures (p. 160).

Avoidance: An information overload coping technique involving making sure that some amount of information is not encountered (p. 179).

Bandwidth: Roughly equivalent to bits per second (p. 128).

Bargaining power of buyers: The ability of buyers to secure a firm as a supplier, keep product quality high, and prices low (p. 85).

Bargaining power of suppliers: The ability of suppliers to secure a firm's business, lower quality, and keep prices high (p. 85).

Barriers to entry: The ability to keep new entrants and substitutes out of the competitive marketplace. *See also* competitive forces model (p. 86).

Baseline measurement: An aspect of evaluation research in which base measurements are made before research begins with an intervention or program to be compared with measurements taken later (p. 493).

Bases of competition: The qualities of a product or service that an organization emphasizes to attract and retain customers. Traditional ones are price, reliability, and differentiation; more modern ones include quality, customer service, and information (p. 283).

Basic processes: Those processes of an organization that convert inputs into its products and services (p. 57).

Baud: A measure of communication volume, one signal per second; each signal may contain one or more bits. *See also* bits per second (p. 128).

Behavioral intention: Whether or not a potential adopter actually intends to use the technological innovation (p. 479).

Benchmarking: The assessment of a firm's operations by comparison with an organization that excels above all others in performance in the firm's area of competition (p. 493).

Bits per second (BPS): A measure of the information (not signalling—*see* baud) rate of a telecommunication device or network. BPS equals bauds if each signal is only one bit but may be far

larger if each signal can carry more than one bit (p. 128).

Breadth of knowledge: The range of subject matter that is understood and available to support managers (p. 36).

Bus configuration: A network topology in which all communicators are attached to a single link (or bus) for which they contend for the right to send a message. *See* contention (p. 135).

Business Process Reengineering (BPR): The improvement of organizations through rebuilding organizational processes from their basic assumptions upward (p. 68).

Buyer value chain: A value chain from the buyer's viewpoint (p. 158).

Can: How easy a system is to use and how effective its design is relative to the task it is meant to perform or assist in (p. 264).

Capacity: The "volume" of an application, measured in many ways including, for example, transactions processed per unit time, maximum file size, and number of fonts (p. 443).

Certainty: The value that management adds to ensure that the product gets out or the service is provided (p. 159).

Champion: One who can influence policy and procedures to see that technology is diffused sufficiently (p. 406).

Characteristics of information: timeliness, precision, relevance, usefulness, specificity, validity (p. 37).

Chauffeured system: A form of groupware that allows input only from the facilitator, who elicits verbal responses from meeting participants and performs the input alone (p. 232).

Circuit switching: A coordination technique in which two communicators on a point-to-point network have exclusive use of the electrical circuit between them for their entire session (p. 132).

Classificatory theory: An understanding of an event or object based on how it resembles other, already understood objects or events in the same class (p. 164).

Client: An individual for whom specific organizational goals represent desirable personal conclusions (p. 400).

Client mode: How clients work with an application. Modes vary according to the basis of receiving reports (regular or ad hoc), the nature of the medium of the report, and in real time or delayed (p. 408).

Client-server architecture: An architecture of machines and software in which part of an application is run in one machine (the client) that is asking for service, and the rest is run in another machine (the server) that provides data, network access, or processing (p. 139).

Clientship: Being responsible for keeping a development project going as an informed buyer rather than a technical manager (compare with stewardship and technical leadership) (p. 356).

Co-users: Members of a work group who use a specific application (p. 402).

Coaxial cable: A signal-carrying technology with greater capacity than a twisted pair in which a single signal-carrying wire goes through the center of a plastic coating which is, in turn, wrapped in a static-resisting metallic sheath (p. 126).

Code of ethics: A list of principles that guide decision making in a professional field (p. 420).

Cognitive level: How understandable reports and screens are, how interest can be maintained, how coherent tasks appear, how consistent an interface is, and how valuable performance feedback is when using a system (p. 269).

Cognitive mapping: A creativity-enhancing technique using diagrams that graphically link concepts (p. 344).

Common carrier: An organization (often a phone company) that is required by law or custom to carry signals from anyone willing to pay the price (p. 133).

Common events: Events in business processes that are common to two or more divisions or departments, affecting both and generating common data (p. 102).

Communication systems: Applications to enable communication among a set of cooperating individuals; a component of the Manager's Information Workbench (p. 183).

Compatibility: How compatible (transparent and transportable) the use of an innovation is with current work habits and styles (p. 472).

Competing on quality: Responding to customers' mobility, increased ability to evaluate and compare products, and purchase globally to achieve satisfaction (p. 283).

Competitive advantage: Another term for strategic advantage (pp. 77, 78).

Competitive forces model: A model that illustrates where organizations compete and the bases of competition. Involves resisting the bargaining powers of suppliers and buyers and locking out substitutes and new entrants (p. 84).

Competitive interaction: Interaction aimed at increasing or maximizing individual gain (p. 24).

Competitive motivation: The desire to compete arising from a limited supply of resources (p. 6).

Computational (causal) theory: An understanding of an event or object based on what causes the event or creates the object (p. 164).

Computer conferencing: A form of group communication in which messages are sorted by topic and perhaps according to work group and from which users may access messages at their leisure (p. 240).

Computer-Aided Software Engineering (CASE): The use of computer applications by information systems professionals and others to simplify and automate the application development process. *See also* upper CASE, lower CASE, and integrated CASE (p. 388).

Computer-mediated decision network: A network that makes decisions by merging the powers of a network on intelligent nodes and stored and shared data (p. 287).

Computer-Supported Cooperative Work (CSCW): A system that supports a work team, focusing on design and implementation groups needing shared graphics and work spaces (p. 227).

Concept-to-customer cycle time: The time it takes to move an organization from having an idea that is of competitive advantage to having a product or service available to the customer (p. 12).

Configuration: The structure of the physical connections of a network (p. 134).

Conflict: A struggle in the real world over resources. *See also* irresolution and dynamism (p. 175).

Consulting: The activities involved in providing advice to others on one problem or a set of problems (p. 10).

Contagion curve: Also called a "learning curve" or "S curve." Profiles in a graphical manner the way people acquire knowledge or catch diseases (p. 467).

Contention: A situation in which two or more nodes in a network topology desire to use the network to send a message at the same time (p. 134).

Contextualizing: The use of a set of tools for information capture, formatting, and display. A component of the Manager's Information Workbench (p. 184).

Contract back: To spin off an information system group from an organization and then retain the services of the group on a competitive basis (p. 452).

Control loop: An iterative set of processes in a cybernetic system that enables it to sense its environment's actions and select an appropriate response (p. 52).

Cooperative interaction: Interaction aimed at increasing or maximizing a group's gain (p. 24).

Coordination: A telecommunication challenge to have remote equipment interact on a regular and predictable basis, generally through protocols (p. 132).

Corporate model base: A set of models relating to common applications, often formulae and algorithms, distinct from the programs and applications themselves and different from the corporate database (p. 103).

Cost: A major telecommunication challenge that increases with distance, rate, volume, lack of noise, and reliability (p. 129).

Critical Success Factors (CSF) technique: Determination of a set of factors that spell the difference between successful and unsuccessful organizations within an industry and subsequent analysis of the information necessary to make that determination (p. 344).

Cultural level: The shared values, aesthetics, conviviality, appropriateness, and various privileges that users enjoy when employing systems (p. 269).

Culture gap: Differences between developers and other roles that come about because of specific training and experience. Technical specialists tend to be much more concerned with and motivated by technology and technological challenges than they are by other people (p. 414).

Customer Product Life Cycle (CPLC) model: The process of engaging a customer to purchase a product or use a service (p. 82).

Cybernetic system: A system that responds to changes in its environment in order to meet or maintain a set of predetermined conditions (p. 52).

Data: Facts about an object or event, input to an information process. Compare with information (p. 10).

Data-based knowledge: Knowledge that is derived from empirical (experience) data (p. 6).

Data communication device: An electrical device that converts electrical signals from a source device into signals that can be transmitted over some distance. *See* modem (p. 127).

Data compression: The capability of removing redundant data prior to transmission and its replacement after reception (p. 128).

Data flow: An input-output relationship between two processes or (sub)systems (p. 62).

Data Flow Diagram (DFD): A diagram depicting information flows among processes. Includes symbols for processes, data flows, and data stores (p. 62).

Data relationship: The relationship that two or more systems have when their primary vehicle of interaction involves sharing of data (p. 61).

Database: The data involved in a single application (or a set of related or common applications, p. 103) or a collection of information with an internal structure. A component of the Manager's Information Workbench (p. 182).

Decision analysis: The study of the decisions that a class of users make or need to make within the utilizing system (p. 345).

Decision model: A model that is useful in making a decision (p. 10).

Decision Support System (DSS): A hybrid system that supports managers' decision making (p. 201); also, a set of tools to assist in decision making involving problem formulation and description, modeling, evaluation, and selection. A component of the Manager's Information Workbench (p. 185).

Delay: An information overload coping technique that involves putting off information in order to deal with it later (p. 179).

Delayed benefit: The fact that the benefits of most application development projects are delayed until all or most of the technology is developed, tested, installed and released. *See also* front-end cost loading (p. 375).

Depictional theory: An understanding of an event or object based on what it looks like (p. 164).

Depth of knowledge: The amount of knowledge or number of facts available that relates to problems managers have to solve (p. 36).

Deriving from Existing System: A class of techniques for determining information requirements that is based on observation or analysis of an existing system or application (p. 344).

Descriptive theory: An understanding of an event or object based on a description according to a fixed set of dimensions (p. 164).

Design principles (parsimony, simplicity, structure, top-down, transportablity, transparency): General principles on which any system should be designed (p. 266).

Developer: An individual who assists in the creation of an application (p. 400).

Differentiation strategy: Attaining strategic advantage by making a firm's products or services noticeably different from those of competitors (p. 79).

Diffusion of innovation: The movement of an idea or new product through a group of adopters (p. 461).

Direct user: An individual who has an interaction directly with an application (p. 400).

Distance: A telecommunication challenge created by signal attenuation and, hence, the loss of a message over distance (p. 126).

Divergent/convergent tool: Groupware tools to generate/amalgamate ideas and to diverge "off topic" or "converge" to a solution (p. 232).

Do: Whether or not a system effectively supports a manager in information tasks (p. 265).

Drill-down: A capability of an executive information system to move from one level of detail to more detail or more summarized data in a database (p. 210).

DSS shell/generator: A tool for creating decision support systems (p. 205).

DSS toolsmith: An individual who assists managers in creating decision support systems (p. 207).

Dynamic architecture: An information architecture that enables us to see where structures come from and how they influence managers' behavior, arising from the interaction of business processes and the organization (p. 103).

Dynamism: The result of conflict and irresolution that induces change in the business environment (p. 175).

Dysfunctional coping strategies: Ways in which managers react to the major factors influencing project success (pushing for quicker development, forcing users to accept technology, skipping testing, trusting technologists' estimates, and accepting technology on faith alone) (p. 277).

Ease of use: How little difficulty a prospective user experiences in harnessing the power of a technological innovation (p. 472). The most important characteristic of software from a user's viewpoint. *See also* learnability, capacity, and software updates/version (p. 443).

Economy of style: A competition for individual customers (with their own styles and quality requirements) as opposed to competition based on a need to keep prices low through large lots (p. 284).

Electronic bulletin board: An electronic analog of a bulletin board or a conference (p. 240).

Electronic Data Interchange (EDI): The use of interorganizational systems to facilitate the electronic equivalents of forms in order to eliminate paper and speed up interorganizational business relationships (p. 81).

Electronic mail (e-mail): An electronic analog of mail (p. 236).

Electronic meeting: The use of information systems to plan, run, and analyze meetings of groups either in the same or multiple places and either at the same or multiple times (p. 323).

Embedded software: Software that is bundled with hardware that does a fixed task that needs to be controlled by a program (p. 442).

Encapsulation: A characteristic of the object-oriented approach to database modeling in which objects "present" themselves as data plus methods to process the data making it unnecessary to understand how the object is internally structured or how it functions internally (p. 115).

End user application development: The creation of applications by those who require the results of the application, generally without professional assistance (p. 174).

End user development: The creation of a large portion or all of an application by the users themselves. (p. 352).

End user software development: An alternative to the application life cycle in which end users do the bulk of the work in determining user requirements, designing, and implementing applications (p. 325).

Environment: A set of systems within which a given system interacts. Environments may be placid, disturbed, or turbulent; the higher the degree of turbulence the more sophisticated the system architecture has to be (p. 48).

Equilibrium: A condition of a set of systems in which long-term exchange of resources is balanced (p. 49).

Ergonomics: The science of studying the interaction of people and systems (similar to human factors engineering) (p. 263).

Error: A telecommunication challenge brought about by the fact that equipment and networks fail to operate perfectly. Errors are frequently expressed in terms of unwanted changes in bits from 1 to 0 or 0 to 1 (p. 130).

Error-correction technique: Adding additional information to a message (redundancy) in order to be able to reconstruct the correct message in the event of an error (p. 130).

Error-detection technique: Adding additional information to a message (redundancy) to be able to detect when it has been transmitted or received in error (often through a parity technique) (p. 130).

Evaluation: The process of determining the value and usability of a management support system, putting a figure on some aspect of a system's performance (p. 252).

Evaluation research: The process of measurement of technological effectiveness over a period of time (p. 492).

Executive Information System (EIS): An information exploration system that focuses on information important to executives (p. 209).

Executive sponsor: The client or a representative of the organization ultimately paying for the development of a system or application. Present during Joint Application Design sessions (p. 364).

Executive Support System (ESS): A hybrid system that includes the capabilities of an executive information system augmented by communication capabilities, text, and graphics processing and perhaps simulation (p. 209).

Expectations: What a user feels a system ought to do and how the system ought to perform (p. 253).

External integration: A project risk coping strategy that means linking users more closely with the IS project team (p. 385).

External/internal leadership: Leaders whose abilities to lead come from either motivational prowess (from appearing powerful or interesting) or appearing typical (p. 295).

Facilitator: A person trained in meeting process who runs meetings (p. 226) or the leader of Joint Application Design meetings (p. 364).

Factory quadrant: Part of the Strategic grid in which only existing IS applications are heavily strategic in nature (p. 91).

Feasibility (schedule, economics, technology, organization): Determining whether there is at least one practical solution based on timing, fund availability, the capabilities of existing or foreseeable technology, and organizational will and culture. *See also* feasibility analysis (p. 345).

Feasibility analysis: Determining whether an application is a practical solution to information requirements. Part of systems analysis (p. 321).

Feedback: Information routed back to a source of data in an information process (p. 10) or a process in which the results of a system's actions are "fed back" to a mechanism that programmatically compares the results to the desired outcomes in order to take corrective action; characteristic of a cybernetic system (p. 52).

File transfer protocol (ftp): An Internet capability allowing users to move files directly from host to host (p. 238).

Filtering: An information overload coping technique that means avoiding information from specific sources at specific times or on specific topics (p. 179).

Firm value chain: A linked set of processes within a company or organization that provides the added values buyers are willing to pay for (p. 158).

Flaming: Rude behavior on the part of groupware users (often some form of electronic mail or bulletin board) (p. 238).

Formalization (planning, control): Making projects more effective because there are rules and procedures of planning or control to follow (p. 385).

Frame: A view of data that users can read or use in a hypermedium (p. 215).

Frequency Shift Keying (FSK): A method used by a modem to convert between analog and digital signals in which a given tone or frequency represents a digital "1" and another a "0" (for a single bit; larger numbers of tones are used to represent multiple bits—four tones are required for two bits, eight tones for three, and so forth) (p. 128).

Front-end cost loading: The costs of most application development projects are incurred heavily at the project start (p. 375).

Full duplex: A coordination technique in which two communicators on a point-to-point network may both speak to each other at the same time (p. 132).

Gateway: A node in a network that has the responsibility of handling communication between the network and the rest of the world (p. 136).

General Systems Theory (GST): A unified and orderly way of thinking and talking about systems (p. 47).

Geodesic organization: A hypothetical organization in which all members of the organization work on the organizational frontier supported by information systems to handle resources, requests for expertise, and coordination (p. 296).

Goal-centered management model: A view of management that concentrates on management's role in moving organizations towards goals (p. 32).

Group interview: An interview of two or more people simultaneously. Takes advantage of group dynamics, that is, the interaction among those interviewed (p. 363).

Group Support System (GSS): A set of hardware, software, and procedures that supports a group of people engaged in activities intended to produce a conclusion (p. 226).

Groupware: Hybrid systems that support human communication in groups (p. 224).

Half duplex: A coordination technique for point-to-point networks involving alternating one-way communication between a pair of communicators; first A "speaks" to B, then B speaks to A (p. 132).

Hierarchical management model: A model of management that stresses responsibility and authority (p. 29).

Hierarchy configuration: A network topology in which communication for a given set of nodes is coordinated by a single node; these coordinating nodes are in turn coordinated by higher-level nodes, and so forth, mimicking a bureaucracy (p. 134).

Human factors engineering: The fashioning of artifacts to conform to human attributes, skills, and limitations (p. 263).

Hybrid: A network that may be a WAN of LANs or involve a variety of network topologies (p. 136).

Hybrid system: A management support system that spans a variety of support formats at several levels (p. 201).

Hyperdatabase: A set of databases organized so that the content of some items contains links to other items, allowing direct access from database to database. An integral part of World Wide Web (p. 241).

Hypermedium: A nonlinear medium for presentation or storage of information (p. 214).

Hypertext: A hypermedium optimized for the management and use of textual information (p. 215).

Image: How consistent the use of a technological innovation is with an individual's (or others') view of him or herself (p. 473).

Inadequate technology: A risk to direct users in which the technical capabilities of an application are insufficient (p. 403).

Incorrect appropriation: A risk to direct users in which the application works but the users fail to use it correctly as required (p. 404).

Ineffective exploitation: A risk to direct users in which the users use the application correctly but fail to appreciate or use the results in a productive manner (p. 405).

Indexing: Using key words or a search facility to allow filtering of information that has been collected. *See* information overload (p. 179).

Information: The output of an information process. More highly refined data, more pertinent to a manager or decision maker's task (p. 10).

Information acquisition: Locating sources of information, obtaining and formatting the information, and building an information supply (p. 37).

Information architecture: How corporate information is broken into manageable pieces and distributed across disciplines (p. 99).

Information Centered Enterprise/Environment (ICE): An information system that represents the entirety of a manager's business environment and enables the manager to access and control events in that environment through an information interface (p. 191).

Information-handling tool: An application that runs in conjunction with groupware to keep track of meeting process and enhance output. This may involve voting, comment-organizing, statistical analysis of results, and graphics (p. 230).

Information overload: A mental state resulting from having to process too much information in a limited amount of time (p. 178).

Information presentation: The display of information in tables, graphs, text, sound, and so forth. (p. 37).

Information processing: Manipulating information according to a manager's needs (p. 37).

Information Requirements Analysis (IRA): The process by which a user's information needs for data, processes, and networks are determined (p. 337); finding out what information managers need as well as the procedures and interfaces required, what user capabilities are, and what kinds of supports are needed. Equivalent to a "model of the user" and an essential part of systems analysis (p. 320).

Information shadow (or data shadow): Information or data generated by real-world events (p. 175).

Information style: The way that one works with information in terms of perception and use in terms of ten dimensions (pp. 37–41).

Information systems specialist: An individual possibly playing a developer role who is trained in information systems specialties (p. 414).

Information workbenching: The way managers work with information physically (p. 38).

Inheritance: The ability of objects to have the same attributes and methods of those of its superclasses (p. 115).

Innovation roles (pioneer, laggard): Those who are early adopters of a technological innovation and those who are late adopters or fail to adopt at all (p. 469).

Installation plan: A plan for how a new system or application will be made available for initial use, it may include job design, hiring, procedure writing, and the modification of physical locations (p. 317).

Installation strategy (plunge, parallel, pilot, piecemeal, phase-in): Putting a system or application into place capable of being used either all at one time, for some period of time in conjunction with an existing system or application, on a small scale as a pilot project, function by function, or with regard to new transactions only (p. 358).

Insufficient diffusion: A risk to direct users in which the users are productive with the application, but the clients or other stakeholders have objections to the results or the manner of use (p. 406).

Intangible products: The results of application development work that tend to be relatively intangible software applications rather than hard goods (*see also* delayed benefit) (p. 375).

Intangible resource: A resource such as information, which has little physical presence, is difficult to price, can change rapidly, and can affect an organization in unpredictable ways (p. 257).

Integrated CASE (I-CASE): A Computer-Aided Software Engineering application that combines the features of upper CASE and lower CASE with project management software (p. 389).

Integrated Services Digital Network (ISDN): One set of standards for providing a wide range of digital services through public networks or common carriers at high speed with little error (p. 139).

Integrated spreadsheet program: A spreadsheet package/ processor that includes other kinds of management support, such as communications, database creation and access, graphing, text creation and display, and advanced graphics (p. 206).

Intelligence: The characteristic of a system to create information (p. 290).

Interface look and feel: The appearance of screens and the dialogues, keystrokes, mouse motions, and sequences of codes that users employ with an application (p. 272).

Internal integration: A project-risk coping strategy that means having the team assigned to the project work more closely together (p. 385).

Internal labor market: An organization in which each worker is an autonomous entrepreneur whose income depends on his or her personal ability to bid for and carry out contracts put on a network (p. 287).

International Standards Organization (ISO): A multinational body charged with creating and enforcing a variety of standards, including telecommunication standards (p. 138).

Internet: An amorphous collection of networks, nodes, participants, list servers, mailing lists, discussion groups, files, programs, Websites, and over 25,000,000 users worldwide (p. 240).

Interorganizational system: A system that spans organizational boundaries (p. 81).

Interview: A formal conversation aimed at acquiring individual information from an individual or a group through questioning (p. 366).

Irresolution: The result of conflict among players over resources, a "dance for advantage" that entails planning and strategy (*see also* conflict and dynamism) (p. 175).

IS model: Three stages in the informing process: input of data, processing of the data to refine it, and output of the information (p. 10).

Joint Application Design (JAD): A form of group interview useful in defining information requirements (p. 363).

Key: A unique identifier or attribute that by itself can distinguish any event or object from all others in the same class of events or objects (p. 107).

Keypad system: A type of group support system that allows participant input only from a keypad, generally limiting responses to single digits or simple choices (p. 233).

Know-how: How easy it is to learn to use a system (p. 264).

Knowledge: An understanding about a phenomenon or some aspect of the real world (based on systematic acquisition and processing of data in the case of data-based knowledge) (p. 6).

Knowledge management: A set of tools to enable managers to organize knowledge into groups related to the work being done and to manage rules, data, rules of thumb, and complex interactions of these; a component of the Manager's Information Workbench (p. 186).

Knowledge-oriented management model: A model of management that emphasizes the role that development and diffusion of knowledge plays in an organization; managers are seen as teachers, coaches, or mentors (p. 32).

Language gap: A gap in terminology and language between developers and other role players (p. 414).

Leadership in technology: Understanding how technology is predicted, assessed, developed, diffused, and used and then making that knowledge available and useful to others (p. 295).

Leadership with technology: The employment of technology (primarily information technology) to support and ultimately improve management practice (p. 295).

Learnability: How easy it is to master usage of a particular item of software—an important distinguishing characteristic of software from a user's viewpoint. *See also* ease of use, capacity, and software updates/versions (p. 443).

Learning system: A more-than-cybernetic system that can change its program or habitual way of reacting to its environment (p. 54).

Legacy systems: Systems that have been in use in an organization for some time and that generally do not require new functions (p. 446).

Level of adoption (primary, secondary, tertiary): The adoption of a technological innovation either by the organization as a whole, by individuals within the organization, or by the user for a specific task; also called *reinvention* (p. 479).

Level of evaluation (organizational, social, economic, physical, personal): Evaluation of a system in terms of what it does for the organization, how it fits into the social and cultural aspects of the work environment, how costs compare to benefits, how it is used physically, and whether or not it meets personal criteria for usability (pp. 254).

Level of group support: (1) communication aids only—a consensual system; (2) group decision-making aids—a contextual system; (3) comprehensive modeling and simulation tools—an implicative or computational system (pp. 321–323).

List server: An electronic mail facility that automatically remails incoming messages to a list of subscribers (p. 238).

Local Area Network (LAN): A network often found within a single building or campus (p. 136).

Logical design: The outcome of systems analysis, a functional description of what the new system or application should perform from the user's perspective (p. 315).

Logical theory: An understanding of an event or object based on related or implied objects or events (p. 164).

Low-cost strategy: Attaining strategic advantage by making a product or service available at a cost that is lower than that of all or most of a firm's competitors (p. 79).

Lower CASE: A Computer-Aided Software Engineering application intended for systems professionals to generate software that will be run later (p. 388).

Lumping: An information overload coping technique involving creating summaries, averages, trends, indices, graphs, and other forms of aggregation (p. 179).

Macros: Spreadsheet or word processor commands that can be stored and given a name in order to perform useful functions. Falls into the category of script languages (p. 327).

Management Information System (MIS): An integrated user machine system that provides information to support organizational functions (p. 5).

Management Support System (MSS): A system designed to support managers in pursuit of their goals (p. 34).

Manager's Information Workbench (MIW): A hypothetical managerial environment which combines a number of information tools that are valuable: databases, communication systems, text and graphics processing, decision support systems, knowledge management packages, simulation and statistics packages, and operational (real-time or process-control) systems (p. 181).

Managerial push/business environment pull: The sources of technological leadership arising either from the needs that managers experience or from forces in the business environment (p. 435).

Mature technology: A technology in which changes, while often important and positive, do not alter the nature of the innovation and in which these same changes don't instantly render all previous versions of the innovation totally obsolete (p. 462).

Meeting structure: The result of a computer-generated and facilitator-controlled agenda in an electronic meeting (p. 230).

Menu-managed data entry and display: A feature of a spreadsheet package/processor that allows users easy entry and display of data, often built using a spreadsheet macro language (p. 205).

Message: The way objects interact is through sending each other messages (p. 115).

Message switching: A technique of sending an entire message from one point to another as a whole (p. 132).

Method: A description of what an object can do or what can be done with the object (p. 115).

Mobility: A telecommunication challenge brought about because communicators may move physically from one location to another between or even during sessions (p. 137).

Mobility of systems professionals: The movement of systems workers (programmers, analysts, and managers) from employer to employer (p. 377).

Model: A simplification of a process, activity, or set of events (p. 8).

Model base: A set of rules for manipulating data in order to provide advice (p. 166).

Modem: A data communication device that converts signals from analog to digital formats and back (p. 128).

Motivation to Comply (MC): The degree to which a potential adopter is motivated to act in accordance with the normative belief (p. 478).

Multicriteria evaluation: An evaluation technique in which a set of discriminating factors, functions, or features is used to rate a set of competing possible solutions against the status quo (p. 262).

Multimedia system: A hybrid system that incorporates a variety of frames in formats that include image, moving image, sound, and text (p. 215).

Multipoint-to-multipoint transmission: A network configuration in which multiple communicators have access to one another during a given session. Equivalent to a conference call (p. 134).

Multipoint-to-point transmission: A network configuration in which a single communicator collects messages from many communicators during a single session. Equivalent to polling (p. 134).

Navigation: Moving from database to database, picking up relevant information along the way, and building sets of data that will be further processed later (p. 99).

New business: Attaining strategic advantage over competitors by defining a new business (p. 80).

New economy: A term describing an information-intensive economy with new bases of competition (p. 284).

New entrant: A potential competitor entering an existing marketplace (p. 86).

Niche marketing: Attaining strategic advantage by selling a product or service into a small, relatively homogeneous market that is interested in one type of product or service (p. 80).

Noise: An unwanted message (p. 129).

Nontraditional measurement: Evaluation of an intangible resource (such as information or its use) according to criteria that are not equivalent to monetary costs and benefits (p. 257).

Normative Belief (NB): The belief that one is expected (by others) to adopt a technological innovation (p. 478).

Object code: The translation of source code into a form that computers can directly use ("execute" or "run") without further translation (p. 439).

Object-oriented approach: A way of modeling databases in which each object is modeled in terms of its attributes and the methods that are used to process the data describing the object (p. 114).

Off-the-shelf systems or applications: Prebuilt software available through commercial outlets (p. 437).

Opaque technology: A technology that is difficult for users to use without understanding and also difficult to understand (p. 414).

Operational management: Handling the day-to-day activities of producing services or products and working directly with customers and suppliers (p. 25).

Operational System: A system that functions to change things in the real world through commands that the operational system interprets and carries out. A component of the Manager's Information Workbench (p. 188).

Organization: The particular set of interactions or mutual constraints among a system's elements that enable the system to carry out its activities (p. 49).

Organizational frontier: The "surface" of an organization in which it interacts with other systems (customers, competitors, suppliers, for example); sometimes called the *front line* (p. 298).

Out-of-role statements: A statement made that seems to conflict with one's apparent role (p. 477).

Outsourcing: The process of acquiring products or services from outside the organization (p. 446).

Overnight organization: A generalization of a consulting company that employs a database of consultant contacts (p. 287).

Package tailoring: The modification of purchased or licensed software to fit an organization's specific needs. An alternative to the application life cycle (p. 328).

Packet switching: A technique of breaking a message into a set of uniformly sized packets of bits that are sent independently across a network and reassembled in the correct order at the recipient's side (p. 133).

Parity technique: The addition of redundant information to a message to indicate whether there are an even (or, alternatively, an odd) number of bits for purposes of error-detection. Usually applied to each character (six to eight bits) but can be applied to an entire message (p. 131).

Participant feedback: A characteristic of some groupware that provides for rapid printed output of results of meetings for participants (p. 230).

Participation parallelism: That characteristic of some groupware that allows all participants in an electronic meeting to provide input simultaneously, if desired (p. 229).

Perceptual level: Whether the stimuli needed to carry out a task using a system can be seen or heard accurately with minimal effort (p. 270).

Performance: The usefulness and usability of a system, the benefit obtained from using it, and its costs and drawbacks (p. 253).

Personal innovation (adoption, use, implementation): How early or late one adopts, how widely an adopter integrates the innovation into work, and how often an adopter uses the technological innovation (p. 470).

Phases of growth (identification, experimentation, control, technology transfer): A set of roughly distinguished phases in the rise of degree of adoption of a technological innovation by prospective users (p. 467).

Physical design: The output of system design, a "blueprint" for a system, including file designs and layouts, programming specifications, network architectures, and so forth (p. 317).

Physical level: The suitability of the design of a work area and the procedures of employing an information system (p. 270).

Physical theory: An understanding of an event or object based on what embodies the event or object physically and what commands make the event happen or create the object (p. 164).

Point of sale (POS): A terminal in a network that originates transactions and collects data on the transaction for later transmission to the elements in the network that actually process the data (p. 136).

Point-to-multipoint transmission: A network configuration in which a single point can broadcast a message to many receivers simultaneously (p. 134).

Point-to-point transmission: A network configuration in which each session involves only two communicators (p. 132).

Policy loop: An iterative set of processes in a learning system that enables it to determine whether or not its set of responses to its environment remains appropriate and then to change the programmed responses (p. 54).

Precompetitive consortium: Associations of competitors who agree that some aspect of their business should not be the basis of competition (p. 81).

Precompetitive joint ventures: Working with competitors in a precompetitive consortium to build systems that are unconnected to their major areas of mutual competition (p. 380).

Pre/postinstallation costs: Costs (tangible and otherwise) that precede and follow the beginning of use of an item of technology. Postinstallation costs tend to be ignored, but they are considerable and often match preinstallation costs, although many of the costs are in terms of intangible resources (p. 260).

Precursor: The old way of working or old tool for work that precedes a technological innovation (p. 461).

Presentation (view) manager: An application or system that presents a picture or representation of a situation (p. 166).

Problem-Solving Life Cycle (PSLC): The life of a problem as it moves from awareness to solution (*see, think, say, do* problem solving) (p. 308).

Problem-solving paradigm: A set of steps or a pattern of thought involved in solving a problem consisting of investigation of the facts, representation of the problem and facts in one or more models, and an interpretation of the results of using a model to draw conclusions (p. 7).

Process model: A model that describes a process in a simplified way (p. 10).

Project risks (cost, schedule, will, quality): Those characteristics of a project that measure potential loss in terms of money, time, organizational culture, and quality (p. 382).

Project size: The economic or physical size of a project affecting project risk (p. 382).

Project structure: How well-defined and stable over time the outputs, results, and deliverables of a project are. This affects project risks (p. 382).

Protocol: A set of codes or rules of turn taking that have been developed to govern how telecommunication interchanges are to take place under certain circumstances (p. 130).

Prototyping: An alternative to the application life cycle in which physical prototypes are created during the initial stages of application development and then tested and refined over time resulting in the best possible design (p. 323).

Prototyping (expendable, evolutionary): Two forms of prototyping, either disposable after initial use (expendable) or used to create a final, high-quality application (p. 352).

Quality: The evaluation of a system's performance as meeting or exceeding customer/user expectations or needs (p. 253).

Reconfiguration: Changing the pattern of usage of organizational resources (p. 13).

Redeployment: Changing the type of use of organizational resources (p. 13).

Redirecting: An information-overload coping technique that sends information to other people for handling and almost always creates delays (p. 179).

Redundancy [communication]: The addition of information to a message that is of no value to the recipient but that merely repeats information in the message (often for error-detection or error-correction purposes). Redundancy may be relative as when a pattern of bits is replaced by a code in order to perform data compression (p. 131).

Redundancy [database]: A characteristic of databases in which information on a single event or object appears more than once in the database. The relational database model allows for little or no redundancy (p. 107).

Regularity: The value that management adds by responding to crises in standard ways (even as they act with authority to interpret those standards) (p. 160).

Related events: Events in business processes that affect two or more divisions or departments indirectly (particularly relevant to administrative processes related to basic processes) (p. 102).

Relational Database Management System (RDBMS): A system that provides access to data in a standardized way (p. 140).

Relational database model: A way of viewing a database as describing a set of objects or events in terms of a fixed set of characteristics or attributes that distinguish events from one another within a class of events or objects (p. 107).

Relational theory: *See* logical theory.

Relative advantage: The extent to which technological innovation seems better than its precursors (p. 472).

Request for Proposal (RFP): An announcement to potential vendors who wish to contract to design and build a system or application asking for proposals for hardware, software, and so forth (not to be confused with *Request for Quotation*) (p. 317).

Request for Quotation (RFQ): A request to potential vendors to submit a bid for constructing a defined system or application (pp. 317, 444).

Result demonstrability: How easily a potential adopter can see, understand, and communicate the results of using a technological innovation to others (p. 471).

Retrofitting: Reworking an old system to new requirements (p. 379).

Reuse: The movement of objects from application to application without detailed knowledge of how the object actually functions or is structured (p. 115).

Reward system: The way an organization rewards desired activities and punishes undesirable ones. Often changed by technology (p. 257).

Ring configuration: A network topology in which all communicators are hooked in a circular way, passing messages among themselves in a fixed order (p. 135).

Risk: The probability that a process will not produce the intended results (p. 6); or, the danger of loss resulting from uncertainty in the business environment (p. 178).

Risk management (avoidance, detection, deterrence, assessment, repair, review): Anticipating and coping with project risks; a six-step framework ranging from avoiding risks to reviewing the results after a loss (p. 384).

Routing: Sending information to the appropriate people for handling. This technique is a more positive way of redirecting to handle information overload (p. 179).

Runaway projects: A project whose costs increase dramatically beyond those budgeted (p. 381).

Saturation point: The point on a contagion curve beyond which there are few additional cases of adoption (p. 467).

Scalability: The ability of a system or architecture, particularly a client-server architecture, to expand in function or scope without a major increase in hardware requirements (p. 141).

Scribe: A role in Joint Application Design with the function to record meeting content (p. 364).

Script language: A set of codes that can be stored to direct an application to perform a set of activities over time—really a program that makes applications into appliances (p. 328).

See, think, say, do **problem solving:** The four stages of the problem-solving life cycle: See a problem, think about how to solve it, say what is (or involve) one

or more possible solution(s), and then act on the solution(s). The basis for the application life cycle (p. 309).

Semi-structured decision: A decision which is neither fully structured nor completely unstructured (p. 201).

Session: The time between the commencement and the termination of a conversation (p. 130).

Shared architecture: An information architecture that allows the sharing of data across related applications through navigation and/or information processing (p. 106).

Shared database: Data generated by a set of common events and related events (p. 102).

Shareware: Software that is given away for trial or sold for a very low price through mass distribution; users are free to copy the shareware and are urged to license it to receive further benefits such as updates, manuals, and user information (p. 441).

Simple system: A system whose interaction with its environment does not respond to environmental influences (p. 51).

Simulation: An application that creates a model of a situation and runs it to predict the results of the situation in the real world. A component of the Manager's Information Workbench (p. 187).

Site license: A software license that allows use of an application within a specific geographic or organizational site with limited copying rights (p. 441).

Skills: Abilities of members of a geodesic organization that are constantly tested by the frontier interaction with the real world. They are divided into four types (complementary, core, critical, cutting edge) corresponding to support, core business, competitive advantage, and tomorrow's skills (p. 298).

Social fabric: The way individuals communicate and relate to others with respect to jobs, tasks, and information (p. 260).

Social landscape: The set of objects that one surrounds oneself with and uses on the job and that make it easy to develop personal information styles that identify an individual to a group (p. 259).

Social level: How users relate to tasks and roles assigned to them by others; how authority and responsibility are treated and what kinds of feedback they get (p. 269).

Social relationships: Specific parts of the social fabric; the kinds of dependencies individuals have on one another (p. 259).

Social status: The esteem that one is held in by others; responsive to the kinds of technology one uses (p. 259).

Software fragments: Screen layouts, report layouts, and previously generated code from Computer-Aided Software Engineering tools (used in lower CASE applications) (p. 389).

Software license: Permission to use an application "purchased" from a commercial source. The license is generally restricted to a specific user and/or machine. Not equivalent to ownership (p. 441).

Software market (captive, technical, consumer): The nature of the presentation of software to potential buyers, either bundled with hardware, sold only to technical experts or presented as a consumer good (p. 438).

Software marketplace: A set of types of software distinguished by the kind of buyer (p. 441).

Software properties (malleable, evanescent, controlling, levering, changeable, portable, transportable, arcane): Those properties that distinguish software from hard goods (pp. 439–440).

Software updates/versions: The availability of future improved versions of a given item of software. An important characteristic from the user viewpoint. See also ease of use, capacity, and learnability (p. 443).

Source code: The original programming language statements an application is written in. Must be changed to object code to be useful (except for script languages) (p. 439).

Source device: Any input device that accepts mechanical input from a user and converts it to electrical signals (p. 127).

Specific DSS: A decision support system to support managers in one particular area, often related to a single business process (p. 205).

Spiral (whirlpool) model of an ALC: The successor to the waterfall model of the ALC, the view that steps in the application life cycle can be repeated and even retraced in reverse order (p. 322).

Spreadsheet macro language: A simplified language that assists users in creating spreadsheets for a spreadsheet package/processor (p. 205).

Spreadsheet package/processor: An application that creates and runs spreadsheets, often in conjunction with other kinds of applications (*see also* integrated spreadsheet program) (p. 205).

Staff training and redeployment: A managerial responsibility in the implementation phase of the application life cycle (p. 318).

Stakeholder: One who seeks goals that are tied up with the success of an organization (as opposed to an individual; *see* client) (p. 400).

Standards (conventions): Agreement on how telecommunication devices, networks, nodes, protocols, etc., ought to work either within a specific network or across an administrative region, such as a country or even the world (p. 138).

Standards (personal or organizational preferences): Preexisting criteria which either set the minimum expectations for performance or usability or a description of the way in which systems ought to function (p. 272).

Star network: A network topology in which all message communication is initiated by and handled by a single central hub node (p. 134).

Steering committee: A committee with responsibility to provide overall project direction; act as an interface to the organization in terms of goals, policy and strategic planning; and also act as a technical review committee for a project (p. 366).

Stewardship: Making sure an application is being used properly after development (p. 356).

Strategic advantage: An advantage over other competitors (p. 78).

Strategic grid: The basis for distinguishing firms based on whether or not existing IS applications are strategic and whether or not there are new strategic IS applications under development (*see* Strategic IS Cycle) (p. 91).

Strategic IS Cycle: The movement of firms through development of new and maintenance of existing strategic IS applications over time. (p. 91).

Strategic management: Working in an integrative fashion to create plans for an organization that spans internal organizational boundaries (p. 25).

Strategic quadrant: Part of the strategic grid in which both existing and in-development IS applications are heavily strategic in nature (p. 91).

Strength of knowledge: The degree to which individual facts are easy to relate to one another to support management functions and activities (p. 36).

Structured decision: A decision which is implicit in the facts of the case and for which no discretion is required (*see also* semistructured and unstructured decisions) (p. 201).

Structured Query Language (SQL): A standardized form of requesting information (p. 140).

Subclass: A class of objects that fits within another class (p. 115).

Subjective impression: The perceptions that users have of the qualities of a potential technological innovation (p. 463).

Subjective norm: The pressure on a potential user to adopt a technological innovation (p. 478).

Substitute: An available alternative to an existing product or service within an already defined marketplace. Technological products and services are often themselves substitutes and may be easily substituted (p. 86).

Summarizing: Creating summaries of information to reduce it and to cope with information overload (p. 179).

Summary/detail information: A level of information that an executive information system can navigate by using a drill-down capability (p. 212).

Superclass: A class of objects that encompasses another class (p. 115).

Supplier value chain: A value chain from the supplier's viewpoint (p. 158).

Support process: Organizational processes that contribute to or make possible the organization's basic processes, often dealing with managing, scheduling, or controlling the basic processes through information (p. 57).

Support quadrant: Part of the strategic grid in which neither existing nor in-development IS applications are heavily strategic in nature (p. 91).

Sustainable competitive advantage: A competitive advantage that remains over time; not a strong characteristic of technology (p. 88).

Switching cost: The cost to a buyer of finding a new supplier or, alternatively, the cost to a supplier of finding a new buyer (*see also* competitive forces model) (p. 84).

Switching system: An electrical or electronic device that disperses telecommunication signals throughout a network (p. 127).

Synthesizing from utilizing system: A class of techniques for determining information requirements that is based on knowledge of theories concerning what the utilizing system is attempting to accomplish (p. 344).

System: A collection of elements (things, procedures, people) that interact in order to meet a goal. A business system is composed of business processes (*see* basic, support, and administrative processes) (p. 48).

System architecture: The internal design and construction of a system that pertains to its interaction with other systems in the environment (*see* simple, cybernetic, and learning system architectures) (p. 51).

System audit: Steps taken to ensure that a system continues to function technically as delivered and ensuring that users continue to use it in the most appropriate way (p. 360).

System boundary: Elements of a system that deal with elements in the system's environment (p. 49).

System brittleness: The quality of a system for crashing or failing (p. 379).

System design: The second phase of the application life cycle, in which a new system or application is designed and prototypes are tested (p. 312).

System Development Life Cycle (SDLC): A traditional, and technical, view of the stages of the process of creating an application by systems professionals (p. 307).

System half-life: The period of time between system installation or release and the point at which the system provides half of its original benefit (p. 377).

System implementation: The third phase of the application life cycle, in which a system or application is constructed by systems professionals or by users (p. 313).

System installation/use/maintenance: The fourth and final phase of the application life cycle, in which a new system or application is made ready for use, used, and kept in working order (p. 314).

System life span: The calendar time that one can expect to receive any benefit from a management support system, that is, before it becomes obsolete or a net expense (p. 261).

System view: An orientation to seeing businesses as sets of interlocking and mutually interacting processes that enables us to pinpoint where and how information and information systems support managers in competitive and cooperative situations (p. 47).

Systems analysis: The first phase of the application life cycle, in which the user's needs are discovered and application development goals are formulated (p. 312).

Tactical management: Creating coping mechanisms that ensure operations will continue despite what happens in the firm's environment (p. 26).

Task-oriented management model: A model of management that views managers as performing the tasks of planning, staffing, organizing, directing, and controlling, roughly in that order (p. 29).

Team effort management model: A model of management that sees an organization's management group as a complex set of interlocking teams in which some players are coordinators and the primary goal of the team is cooperation (p. 31).

Technical leadership: Representing the system's users and those who provide technical services, planning for the next system, understanding and managing resistance, fear and demotivation, and change management (p. 356).

Technical performance specifications: A statement of the literal performance standards a system or application must meet (p. 360).

Technological agenda: The technology that a specific group of people talk and think about (p. 465).

Technological change: The advance of technology over even short periods of time (*see also* technological obsolescence) (p. 377).

Technological innovation: A new way of working or a new tool for work that is technological in nature (p. 461).

Technological leadership: Understanding how technology is predicted, assessed, developed, diffused, and used and then making that knowledge available and useful to others (p. 435).

Technological obsolescence: The loss of value of existing technologies over time due to technological change (p. 377).

Technological revolution: The societal process in which one or more technologies fairly rapidly and pervasively arise to replace an existing set of technologies (p. 503).

Technology adaptation: Changing the content and format of technical jobs so that they can be performed by nontechnical individuals (p. 490).

Technology assessment: The evaluation of new technologies. May involve evaluation research or benchmarking (p. 491).

Technology commercialization: The process by which technologies developed in or through an information systems group, perhaps in conjunction with outsourcers, become commercial products that can be sold to others (p. 491).

Technology dilution: Making technology more palatable, easier to use and digest, and available in a more understandable form; making specialist tools available to all users (p. 490).

Technology evolution: The means by which members of an information systems group contribute to their own disciplines (p. 491).

Technology experience gap: The difference between developer experience or knowledge and that needed to produce project results effectively (p. 382).

Technology forecasting: The process of predicting technologies in the future (p. 494).

Technology infusion: Bringing new technologies to users through training, information centers and experiences from prototyping, end user development and the ALC (p. 489).

Technology innovation: Putting new technology directly into the hands of user-managers and others (p. 489).

Technology life cycle: A five-stage process in which technology is developed, launched, promoted, used, and substituted or retired (p. 497).

Technology management: A cycle of management processes aimed at harnessing the power of a particular technology. (p. 496).

Technology transfer: Moving technology from its sources (which could be an outsourcing company or consultant) to another organization (often a client firm) (p. 446).

Technology type (process, product, hybrid): Technology that creates or modifies a process, technology that is a tool to be used in conjunction with a process or technology that improves the functioning of tool technologies in the process. Applicable to Joint Application Design (p. 365).

Technologized employees: Employees whose work involves creating or maintaining applications but who are not information system specialists (p. 418).

Technophobia: A fear of technology (p. 495).

Telecommunication: Communication across a distance (p. 124).

Theory: A set of statements that relate events in the real world to one another or an explanation of how some process or activity works in the real world (p. 8).

Topology: The geometry of a network configuration. *See* star network, hierarchy, ring, and bus (p. 134).

Transactional management model: A view of management that stresses the role that management has in adding value to the raw resources an organization uses to produce its products or services (p. 30).

Transparency/opacity: The ability (or lack thereof) of an information centered enterprise to present data shadows to the user in a way that makes them easily understandable and usable (p. 192).

Trialability: How easy it is for people to try out a system (without penalty or real risk) before they attempt to integrate it into their working lives (p. 265).

Turbulence: Unpredictability in the data comprising the data shadow (*see also* uncertainty and risk) (p. 177).

Turnaround quadrant: Part of the strategic grid in which only in-development IS applications are heavily strategic in nature (p. 91).

Turnkey service: Development, installation, training and operation of an application or system by the contractor (p. 452).

Twisted pair: A pair of wires that are twisted to reduce static. An early technology common to telegraphy and telephony, it is limited in its signal-carrying capacity (p. 126).

Two-cultures gap: A gap that arises between two segments of society at large. One segment understands a particular kind of technology (IS in our case) but might not understand the larger cultural and societal implications, while the other segment has opposite qualities (p. 495).

Uncertainty: A mental state brought about through lack of knowledge resulting from conflict, irresolution, and dynamism (p. 177).

Uncertainty of IRA process: The fuzziness or risk or degree of guesswork in determining the information requirements of a set of users (p. 342).

Uniformity: A value that management adds in ensuring that the basic and support activities work the same way all of the time to produce the same product or deliver the same service (p. 159).

Unstructured decision: A decision that is made solely on the basis of intuition without reference to facts or standard procedures (*see also* semistructured and structured decisions) (p. 201).

Upper CASE: A Computer-Aided Software Engineering application with tools for interaction with users to collect information, processing, and output requirements as well as graphical tools for design work, screen and report prototyping, and dialogues (p. 388).

Usability: The extent to which a system is both fit to be used and actually employable in a task (p. 266).

User class (existing, potential, planned): The current users of an application, those who might use an application if they had a chance, and those who will be using a new application or system (p. 340).

Utilizing system: A work group, department, division, or some other organization that is a subsystem of a larger system and which depends on the results of an application or system (p. 340).

Value chain: A chain of business processes that adds value to raw materials by creating finished products or providing services (*see also* firm, buyer, supplier and value chain) (p. 158).

Value-added network (VAN): A network that in addition to carrying signals may also provide additional services such as electronic mail, remote sensing, specialized data processing, or other facilities (p. 134).

Vertical integration: Joining together of buyer-supplier relationships so that all aspects of manufacturing and marketing are connected efficiently (p. 81).

View base: A set of prestored images, charts, sounds, texts and representing a situation (*see* contextualizing) (p. 166).

Virtual corporation: A hypothetical organization that produces instantaneously designed products tailored to customer demands, deliverable anywhere, anytime, and in any variety (p. 288).

Visualization: The ability of a user of a hybrid system to locate where in a database the current access resides. *See also* drill-down (p. 214).

Volume: The rate of information or messages being communicated; measured in bauds (p. 128).

Waterfall model of an ALC: The idea that the steps of the ALC must be followed strictly in order, each attempted only after the previous has been successfully completed. Mostly superseded by the spiral model of the ALC (p. 322).

What You See Is What You Get (WYSIWYG): An application attribute in which the output of an application appears on the screen exactly as it would appear printed out. More generally this refers to output that is in exactly the format ultimately desired at every stage in which the output is developed. Most relevant for word processing and spreadsheeting (p. 327).

Wide Area Network (WAN): A network that may extend over very long distances—across cities, states, or countries (p. 136).

INDEX

Abstracting, 179
Access, 421
Accuracy, 37, 421
Action (primary) loop, 51
Administrative business process, 57–59, 61
Adopter, potential (PA), 467, 473–475
Adoption
  innovation, 461, 463–467, 464
  levels of, 479–480
Adoptive innovation, 470
Ad hoc query facility, 210–211
Advising, 165–174
Affiliation, group, 474
Agentic shift, 423
Alliance-formation competitive strategy, 80–82
Analog communication, 128
Anonymity, 227–230, 364, 423
Answer network, 287–288
Anthony's triangle, 99–100
Anthropology, 259
Appliance, 258, 312
Application, 99–103, 272, 307, 324–325, 337, 341, 352, 400
  analyst, 338
  appropriation of, incorrect, 404
  diffusion of, insufficient, 404, 406
  exploitation of, ineffective, 404–405
  feasibility of, 314–315
  interface to, 317
  management, 365
  maturity of, 448
  off-the-shelf, 437
  server, 140
  strategic, 90–91, 106, 444, 470–471
  technology, inadequate, 403–404
Application Life Cycle (ALC), 307–322, 331, 337, 350–351, 445, 489, 498
Architecture
  client-server, 82, 92
  object-oriented information, 114–117
  shared information, 112–114
  system, 51–57
Artificial Intelligence (AI), 182, 215
Attention, 464, 467
Attenuation, 126–127
Attitude, 271
  change, 464, 467

Attribute, 115–116
Audit, 314–315, 319
Authentication, 243
Authority, 159–160
Avoidance, information, 179

Back-end CASE, 388–389
Backup, 106
Bandwidth, 128, 286
Barriers to entry, 86–87
Basic business process, 57–60
Baud, 128
Behavioral intention, 471, 479
Belief, 271
Benchmarking, 453, 492–493
Bits per second (BPS), 128
Bottleneck, 70
Boundary, system, 49
Boundary-spanning, 26
Brainstorming, 231, 234–235
Briefing book, 210–211
Brittleness, system, 379
Broadcasting, 134
Bug, software, 439–440, 473, 480
Building
  application, 317–318
  Build-vs-buy decision, 444–446
Bureaucracy, 99–100
Business analyst, 315
Business application market, software, 442
Business environment pull, 435–436
Business objective, 314–315
Business process, 56–60, 82, 100, 134
  administrative, 57–59, 61
  basic, 57–60, 144
  core, 70
  redesign of, 144
  support, 57–60, 70
Business Process Reengineering (BPR), 47–48, 66–70, 145, 295, 315–316
Business strategy, 488
Business System Planning (BSP), 68
Business transformation, 144–145
Bus network, 134–136
Buyers, bargaining power of, 84
Buyer value chain, 158, 161

Capacity, Information, 40
Causality, 172
Causal theory, 164
Certainty, 159–160
Certification, 243
Champion, application, 406
Change
  control, 263, 385
  management of, 357
  resistance to, 360–361
Channel Richness, Information, 40
Chief Information Officer (CIO), 90
Chunking, Information, 40
Circuit switching, 132–133
Classificatory theory, 164
Client
  application, 401, 404, 406–409
  clientship, 315, 356–357, 379, 400
  project, 315
Client-server architecture, 124, 135, 139–142, 218, 387, 391, 415, 441, 445, 505–506
Coaxial cable, 126
Code
  digital, 130
  object, 439–440
  source, 439–440
Cognitive mapping, 344
Comfort, 270
Commercialization of technology, 488, 499–501
Commercial public mass market, software, 441–442
Commitment, maintaining, 34
Common carrier, 133
Communication
  channel, 281, 463–464, 476–477
  organizational, 258
  software, 181
  technology, 260
Compatibility, 472–473
Competition, 24–25
  bases of, 283–285
  fabric of, 280
  generic strategies, 79–82
  global, 11, 138, 224, 280–282, 295, 445

Competitive advantage, 77–93, 138, 448
  information-intensive, 89
  sustainable, 78, 88–89, 142, 146, 280
  technology-intensive, 89
Competitive forces model (Porter),
  84–87
Competitiveness, 449
Complexity, 69, 381
Comprehension, 464, 467
Computational management support
  level, 163–164
Computational system, 171–172,
  174–175, 207, 340
Computational theory, 164
Computer-Assisted Software Engineering
  (CASE), 322, 323, 364–365, 388–392
Computer-based meeting support,
  226–236
Computer conferencing, 134, 183, 217,
  224, 232–233, 240
Computerization, 307
Computer-mediated decision network,
  287, 289
Computer-Supported Cooperative Work
  (CCSW), 227
Compute server, 140
Concept-to-customer life cycle, 12, 224
Confirmation, 243
Conflict, 175–177
Connect time, 129
Consensual (consensus) system, 165–166,
  213, 227–228, 232, 258, 294, 298
Consensual management support level,
  162
Consistency, 202, 211
Consortium, precompetitive, 81
Consultative management support level,
  163
Consulting, 10–12
  firm, 329–330
  system, 168–171, 294
Contagion curve, 467
Contention, 134–136
Contextualizing, 183–185, 207, 293
Contextual management support level,
  162
Contextual system, 166–168, 207, 232
Contracting back, 452
Control
  business process, 69
  formal project, 384–387
  (secondary) loop, 52
Convergent tool, groupware, 233–234
Conviviality, 269
Cooperation, 24
Coordination, telecommunication, 127,
  132–134
Core business process, 68
Corporate model base, 103

Corporate strategy, 501–503
Cost, 283–284, 325, 380
  control of, 376
  intangible, 260–261
  postinstallation, 260–261
  preinstallation, 260–261
  reduction of, 287
Cost-benefit analysis, 261
Co-user, 402
Creativity, 202, 230, 258, 291–294, 364,
  405
Critical incident, 214
Critical Path Method (CPM), 385
Critical Success Factor (CSF), 214, 344,
  493
Culture, 292
Customer expectation, 218
  focus on, 70
  Product Life Cycle, 82–84
  service, 387
Customization, software, 330
Cybernetic system, 52–54, 177, 180, 202
Cyberphobia, 358

Data
  communication, 124, 127–128, 205,
    425
  compression, 128
  Description Language (DDL), 181–182
  dictionary, 167, 173, 182, 388, 390
  entry, 205
  flow, 62–65, 70
  Flow Diagram (DFD), 62–66, 388, 390
  Manipulation Language (DML),
    181–182
  relationship, 61
  shadow. *See under* Information
  store, 62–65
  terminal equipment (DTE), 128
Data Access Language (DAL), 181–182
Database, 100–110, 139, 173, 181–183,
  190–191, 273, 281, 391, 400, 425
  integrated, 144, 282, 289
  management system (DBMS), 103,
    505
  manager, 167, 272, 325–327
  personal, 182
  relational, 82, 107–114, 182
  shared, 102, 104–107
Debugging, 327, 354
Decision
  analysis, 345
  making, 33–34, 160–161, 185, 228,
    261, 286
  Support System (DSS), 82, 181,
    185–186, 201–209, 212, 218, 231,
    262, 298
  table, 201, 345

Deindividuation, 423
Delay, information, 179
Delivery, information, 283–284
Delphi, 495
Depictional theory, 164
Descriptive theory, 164
Design
  black box, 267–268
  in-house, 316
  logical, 315, 317
  manufacturable, 500
  physical, 317
  principles of, 266–268
  top-down, 267–268
Desktop publishing, 217
Developer, application, 401, 404, 406,
  412–415
Development, application, 347
Differentiation competitive strategy,
  79–80, 283–284
Diffusion of innovation, 406, 461, 471
Digital network, 128
Directing, 29
Disaster recovery, 106
Display, data, 184
Distance, 126
Divergent tool, groupware, 233–234
Diversity, 263
Documentation, application, 317–318,
  354, 360–361, 375, 389, 443
Domain, 182
Drill-down, 111, 210–216
Driver, software, 273
Dynamism, 175–177

Ease of use, application, 443, 472–473
Economy of scale, 145, 284, 351
Economy of style, 284
Effectiveness, 203
Efficiency, 144–145, 202
Electronic bulletin board, 240, 246
Electronic Data Interchange (EDI), 81,
  143, 145, 218, 243, 505–506
Electronic mail (E-mail), 132, 139, 183,
  217, 224, 236–240, 245–246, 258, 272,
  293
Electronic marketplace, 289
Electronic meeting, 232
Electronic vote, 225
Element, system, 49
ELIZA, 423
Embedded software, 442
Employee
  technical, 418–420
  technologized, 418
Encapsulation, 115
Encryption, 243

End-user
  application development, 174, 322, 325–328, 331, 351–352, 354, 489
  CASE tool, 506–507
Engineering, 499
Envelope services, 236
Environment
  competitive, 347
  system, 48
  turbulent, 56
Equilibrium, 49–50
Ergonomics, 263–264, 267, 270
Error
  correction of, 130–131
  detection of, 130–131
  in design, 376
  telecommunication, 127, 130–132, 134, 136
  user-created, 268–269
Ethics, 5, 260, 363, 420–426, 475, 496
Evaluation
  Management Support System, 251–275
  of application, 314, 319
  plan, application, 376
  research, 492–493
Executive Information System (EIS), 106, 209–214, 218, 294, 323
Executive Support System (ESS), 209–214, 218, 262, 289
Expectations, user, 261, 266, 415
Experimentation, IRA, 342, 345
Expert system, 170–171, 173, 182, 187, 231, 294, 298, 329, 344, 391

Facilitation, JAD, 364
Facilitator, 225, 226, 231, 235, 245, 364–365
Facsimile, 245
Factory automation, 281
Factory quadrant, 90–91
Fault-tolerant system, 130
Feasibility, 321, 345–350
  economic, 346–348
  organizational, 346–349
  schedule, 346–348
  technological, 346–349
Feature, undocumented software, 439
Feedback, 10, 32, 52–53, 229–233, 269, 317, 477
File
  conversion, 317–318
  design, 317
  layout, 317
  server, 137, 139–140
  transfer, 238
  transfer protocol (FTP), 240
Filtering, information, 179–180

Firm value chain, 158, 161
Flaming, 238, 258
Flexibility, 202, 380
Flexible manufacturing, 289
Focus group, 343
Folklore, user, 265
Forecasting, 281
Fourth-Generation Language (4GL), 322
Fragmentation, 107
Frame, 215, 271
Frequency shift keying (FSK), 128
Front-end CASE, 388–389
Full-duplex communication, 132

Gateway, 136–137, 245
General Systems Theory, 47
Geodesic organization, 296–299
Geographic Information System (GIS), 293
Global competition, 6, 281–282, 295
Goal
  analysis of, 255
  organizational, 255, 319, 366
  settting of, 256
  strategic, 255
  system, 48
Gopher, 241
Graphics, 207
  processor, 181
Graphic User Interface (GUI), 188, 240, 242, 273, 294, 326, 328, 387, 391–392, 439, 505–507
Group, 31, 224–246
  autonomy in, 228
  cohesion of, 226
  commitment, 226
  decision making by, 228
  dominance in, 227
  life cycle, 31
  support, level of, 231–232
  Support System (GSS), 226–236, 246, 364, 495, 505–506
Groupthink, 230, 478
Groupware, 225
Growth phase, adoption, 467

Half-duplex communication, 132
Hardware, 106–107, 271
Hierarchy, 29, 32
  network, 134–136
High technology, 375, 461–462, 496, 500
History of information systems, 419, 438, 504
Human factors engineering, 263
Hybrid
  network, 136–137
  system, 201, 208
  technology, 364

Hygiene factor, 472
Hyperdatabase, 241
Hypermedia, 214–218, 505–506
Hyperspace, 190–191
Hypertext Markup Language (HTML), 242

Icon, 190–191
Idea consolidation, 234
Image, 472–473
Implementation
  innovation, 470
  strategy, 321–322, 347, 350–356
Implicative (implicational) system, 169–173, 340
Implicative management support level, 163
Indexing, 179
Industrial engineering, 264
Inefficiency, 260
Information, 10, 24–25, 37, 52, 77
  acquisition of, 37
  architecture, 99–107, 112–114, 280, 282, 297
  creation of, 183–185
  flow, 33
  hoarding of, 180
  overload, 178–180, 286, 336
  processing, 37
  role in management, 26
  shadow, 175–177
  style, 37–41, 256, 258, 274, 292
  system, 10, 58, 62, 86, 101
  system professional, 11
  value of, 256–257, 292
Information-Centered Enterprise/Environment (ICE), 191–195, 213, 280, 289, 435
Information Requirements Analysis (IRA), 320–321, 336–345, 362, 388
Information Systems Group (ISG), 274, 439, 444, 446–448, 451, 470, 491, 498, 506
Information Technology (IT), 83, 88, 143–145, 225, 258, 286, 435, 500
Inheritance, 115
Innovation, 258, 273, 285, 354, 380, 406, 461, 463, 471–473
  management of, 436, 487, 499–500
  measures of, 480–481
  personal, 470
Innovativeness, personal, 474, 480
Input, 10–11, 61
Input mode, Information, 39
Installation, 317, 319, 330, 358–360, 379, 381
Integrated, CASE (I-CASE), 389
Integration, project, 385–387

Integration, vertical, 81
Intelligence, 288–291, 293, 296
  market, 280–281
Intelligent agent, 506–507
Interface, 320
  application, 254, 317
  design of, 269–271
  human-computer, 266
  look and feel of, 272
Internal labor market, 287, 289
International Standards Organization
(ISO), 138, 272
Internet, 240–244, 506
  security on, 243
Interorganizational System (IOS), 81, 92,
124, 142, 144, 288, 505–506
Interview, 344, 362–363
  group, 344, 363
Investigation (ALC), 314–316
Irresolution, 175–177

Job redesign, 317
Joint Application Design (JAD),
362–365, 391–392
Joint venture, 228
  precompetitive, 380
Junk mail, electronic, 238, 243
Just-in-time (JIT), 289, 410

Keyboarding, 231
Keypad system, 233
Knowledge, 6, 178, 229–230, 271, 340
  acquisition, 143
  management, 186–187

Labor displacement, 81, 260
Language, programming, 439
Leadership, 31, 160–162, 185, 258, 417,
435–437
  and technology, 295–296
  external/internal, 295
  technical, 356–357, 418–420
  technological, 319, 348–349, 486–507
Learnability, application, 263, 274, 319,
443
Learning
  curve, 85
  organization, 32, 446
  organizational, 444
  system, 54–55, 292, 497
License, software/site, 441
Life cycle
  evaluation during, 256
  technology, 487, 497–499
Lighting, 263
List server, 224, 238, 241

Local Area Network (LAN), 136, 218,
388, 505–506
Locking-in, 84–85, 283
Logical design, 315, 317
Logical model, 186–187
Logical theory, 164
Look and feel, application, 443
Loop
  action (primary), 51
  control (secondary), 52
  policy (tertiary), 54–55
Low-cost competitive strategy, 79–881
Lower CASE, 388–389
Lumping, information, 179

Macro language, 324, 328
Mainframe, 134, 136–137, 141–142
Maintenance, software (application), 443
Management
  activities in, 33–35
  allocational model of, 30
  changes in, 280–283
  goal-centered model of, 29
  hierarchical model of, 29
  models of, 27–33
  of technology, 90
  style, 282
  support, 29–30, 34–37, 162–174, 201,
  252, 274, 280, 295, 307, 326, 346
Management Information System (MIS),
5, 167, 212, 231, 294
Management support system (MSS),
34–35, 37, 82, 89, 157, 179, 251–275,
292–293, 298–299, 324, 331,
337, 364, 399, 461
Manager, role of in organizations, 25–27
Managerial push, 435–436
Manager's Information Workbench
(MIW), 180–189, 191
Managing innovation, 499–500
Manual, user's, 320
Marketplace, information system
(software), 436, 438
Maturity, application, 448
Measurement in BPR, 69
Measures, baseline, 493
Meeting
  computer-based, 231
  structure of, 229–230
Memory, 61
Merging, 64
Message, 133
  object-oriented, 115
  folder, 238
  switching, 132–133
Method, 115–116
Microcomputer, 139, 142
Microwave, 126

Minicomputer, 135–137, 140
MIS management support level, 163
Mobility
  network, 137–138
  of system professional, 377
Modality, data, 184
Mode, Information, 40
Model, 8–10, 47, 69–70, 103
  base, 166
  decision/process, 10
  logical, 186–187
  management, 207
Modeling software, 327
Modem, 127
Modern management imperatives, 10–14
Morale, 260, 378
Motivation to comply (MC), 478
Multicriteria evaluation, 262
Multimedia, 214–218, 242, 294
Multipoint-to-multipoint transmission,
134
Multipoint-to-point transmission, 134
Music, 217

Navigation, database, 99, 205, 267, 281,
294
Necessity, 476
Network, 127, 180, 272
  configuration of, 134–137
  management of, 132–133
  operator, 134
  point-to-point, 132
  server, 139–140
  topology of, 134–137
New business competitive strategy, 80, 82
New entrants, 86
Niche marketing competitive strategy,
80, 82, 284–285
Node, network, 131
Noise, 207, 289
  telecommunication, 126–130, 134
Nominal group technique (NGT), 231
Nonrepudiation, 243
Normative belief (NB), 478

Object-oriented information architecture,
114–117, 157, 506–507
Obsolescence, 261, 274, 377–378, 380,
436, 449, 498–499
Online processing, 182
Operating system, 188–189, 242, 273,
439–440, 442
Operational management support level,
164
Operational system, 172–173, 176,
188–189, 213
Opinion, 271

leader, technical, 357
Organization, 56, 68
  geodesic, 296–299
  nonprofit, 5
  public sector, 5
Organizational climate, 160–161, 292
Organizational communication, 258–259
Organizational/corporate culture, 346–347, 463, 478, 503
Organizational development (OD), 68, 259, 346
Organizational frontier, 297–298, 418
Organizational integrity, 410
Organizational learning, 143, 385
Organizational redesign, 68
Organizing, 29
Orientation, Information, 39
Output, 10–11, 61
Outsourcing, 286–287, 316, 348, 376, 446–452
  contracting for, 451
  myths about, 450–451
  risk factors in, 448–449
Overnight organization, 287–288

Package tailoring, software, 322, 328–331, 350–351, 415, 446
Packet switching, 133
Paradigm, problem-solving, 6–8
Parallel application installation, 358–360
Parallel processing, 506–507
Parameter, in operational system, 173
Pareto's Law, 87
Parity, 131
Parsimony, 266–267
Participant observation, 344
Participation
  group, 229
  of user (in ALC), 325
Pen-based computing, 505–506
Perception, 271
Performance, 253–254
  of system, 356–357
Personality, 292
Persuasion, 407
Phase-in application installation, 358–360
Physical design, 317
Physical plant, 318
Physical theory, 164
Piecemeal application installation, 358–360
Pilot application installation, 358–360, 409
Plan, strategic, 366
Planning, 29
Plunge application installation, 358–360

Point-of-sale terminal (POS), 136–137, 202
Point-to-multipoint transmission, 134
Point-to-point transmission, 134
Policy (tertiary) loop, 54–55
Policy analyst, 54
Politics, 408–409, 414
Portfolio, application, 341
Precision, 37
Precursor, 461, 463–464, 471, 475–476
Prescreening, E-mail, 237
Presentation graphics, 327
Presentation manager, 166
Primary adoption, 479–481
Primary loop, 51
Print server, 139–140
Privacy, 263, 420–421
Problem solving, 6, 226, 308
Problem-Solving Life Cycle (PSLC), 308–312
Procedure, 190–191, 320
Process (Data), 62–65
Processing, 11
Processing style, Information, 38–39
Process model, 58–59
Process technology, 364
Productivity, 405
Program Evaluation and Review Technique (PERT), 385
Programming, 11, 347, 438–439
Project
  life cycle, 385
  management of, 245, 282–283, 318, 374–392
  manager, 315, 366–367
  runaway, 381, 384
Propaganda, 465
Property, 421
Protocol
  analysis technique, 343–344, 362
  telecommunication, 130, 144
Prototype, 312–313, 317, 340, 347, 499
Prototyping, 261, 322–325, 331, 337, 341–342, 345–346, 350–353, 362, 376, 388, 390–392, 445, 489, 500
Public relations, 317–318
Public switched network, 133

Quality, 253, 282, 287, 295, 376
  management, 256, 271, 281, 379
Query, 64
Questionnaire, 343

Rapid Application Development (RAD), 364, 391–392
Reach, 13
Reaction, 13

Reconfiguration, 13
Redeployment, 13
  staff, 318
Redirection, information, 179
Redundancy, 131
  business process, 68–69
  data, 107–108
  hardware, 70
Refinement, 13
Regularity, 159–160
Reinvention, 464–467, 473, 500
Relational Database Management System (RDMS), 140
Relationships, social, 259
Relative advantage, 472–473
Reliability, application vendor, 445
Repository, CASE, 365, 388
Reputation, 13
Request for Proposal (RFP), 316–317, 444–447, 452, 497
Request for Quotation (RFQ), 316–317, 444–447, 452, 497
Research and Development (R&D), 349, 499–501
Resource, 30, 255–256, 281–282, 297
  information, 331, 410
  measurement of intangible, 257
  server, 140
Response time, 107
Responsiveness, 13
Result demonstrability, 471–473
Retrofitting, 379
Reverse engineering, 70
Reward system, 257
Ring network, 134–136
Risk, 177–178, 273, 308, 321–322, 336, 342, 359–360
  management of, 307, 319, 321–322, 446
  project, 381–388
Role
  application, 400–415
  in innovation, 469
Routing, 179

Satellite communication, 126
Scalability, 136–137, 141
Scanner, 217, 281
Scenario testing, 202
Science, 499
Scribe, JAD, 364
Script language, 324–325, 328
Seating, 263
Secondary adoption, 480–481
Secondary loop, 52
Security, 106, 361–362, 389, 410
Selective attention, 408
Selective perception, 408

Index | 559

Virtual presence, 505-508
Regulation, 106, 187, 284-289
Vocabulary control, 184
Voice
  recognition, 317
  mail, 317
  mail, 505-508
Volume, Information, 152, 156, 161-163

Wendell, Andre (AUE), 92
What You See Is What You Get
  (WYSIWYG), 326-327
Wide Area Network (WAN), 134-135
Word processor, 325, 325-326
Work analysis, 344
Work group management, 244-245
Workstation, 135, 136, 512
World wide web (WWW), 240-243

Yearbook, 182

direct application, 400, 402, 403
expression, 253-254, 315
involvement, 183, 301-302, 319-380,
  432
management, 317
installation of, 254
training of, 205, 265
types of, 340
Utilizing system, 340-342

Value (added) chain, 36-37, 47-50
Value-added network (VAN), 134-135,
  243-244
Values, organizational, 413
Vaporware, 440
Vendor management, 194, 261, 514
Vertical integration, 81, 184
Video, 221
  base, 166, 215
  information, 38-40
Virtual corporation, 288
Virtual meeting room, 272-273

Thinking, 265, 412-413
Tool, 512
Bottleneck, environmental, 172, 178
Turnkey, 442
Tutorial, student, 163
Testbed, pilot, 139
Teleconference, 316, 412, 415-417

Document library, 91-92
Upper CASE, 360-380
Usability, 294-295, 295-296
Usage, style, 412
Guidelines, 91
Use, information, 92
Data, 145, 147, 151, 152